An Introduction to Substr

"Restall has written a masterful book that is well motivated by persuasive examples, a book that is marvellously lucid, and chock full of a distinctive combination of conceptual insight, good taste and mathematical elegance. This book is a perfect authoritative introduction to a burgeoning topic, eminently suitable to graduate students. Everything is explained from the ground up in a style that makes difficult mathematical ideas readily accessible. It is the first book in a long time that has made me want to teach from it straight away."

Nuel Belnap, University of Pittsburgh

"Restall's book represents the first systematic collection of new results in our approach to and understanding of logics flowing from cognate movements in mathematical and philosophical study, producing a new area of study, substructural logics. The book is outstandingly well-informed, rich and full of great insight and comprehension. I learned a great deal from reading it. It is very well presented, both in organisation and style."

Stephen Read, University of St Andrews

"Restall's introduction to substructural logics is a tour de force. He has a remarkable ability to focus on the essence of an issue, and explain it simply and lucidly — whilst still doing justice to its complexities. I think that the book is likely to become a standard, and remain so for many years to come."

Graham Priest, University of Queensland

Greg Restall is Senior Lecturer in Philosophy at Macquarie University in Sydney, Australia.

*To the memory of Minke Restall
for teaching me how to think,
and for so much more.*

An Introduction to
Substructural Logics

Greg Restall

Routledge
Taylor & Francis Group
New York   London

First published 2000
by Routledge
11 New Fetter Lane, London EC4P 4EE

Simultaneously published in the USA and Canada
by Routledge
29 West 35th Street, New York, NY 10001

Routledge is an imprint of the Taylor & Francis Group

British Library Cataloguing in Publication Data
A catalogue record for this book is available from the British Library

Library of Congress Cataloging in Publication Data

Restall, Greg, 1969–

An introduction to substructural logics / Greg Restall. p.   cm.
Includes bibliographical references and index.

1. Logic, Symbolic and Mathematical. I. Title.

BC135.R47 1999

160–dc21   99-15946 CIP

ISBN 978-0-415-21534-3

Reprinted 2008

Contents

List of Figures

List of Tables

Acknowledgements

Without friends no one would choose to live,
despite having all other goods.
— Aristotle

Books tend not to be written in isolation, and this one is no exception. It is my pleasure to acknowledge those who have contributed to its formation.

My education in logic took shape under the encouragement of Graham Priest. His example and his enthusiasm have taught me much about how to do logic. The Philosophy Department at the University of Queensland was a welcoming place for a mathematics undergraduate to make the transition into philosophy. In this fertile environment I grew up loving logic and philosophy.

The this book took form when I was a Postdoctoral Research Fellow at the Automated Reasoning Project in the Australian National University. Thanks to the Australian Research Council for the research fellowship, and many thanks to my colleagues and friends at the ARP: Rajeev Goré, Pragati Jain, Bob Meyer, John Slaney and Tim Surendonk. Their company, and their ideas and thoughts have influenced me greatly. While in Canberra I valued time with Richard Sylvan whose critical sense helped me think about the philosophical issues behind relevant logic. Bob Meyer's ready wit and sharp grasp of how to *do* things has taught me more than I can readily acknowledge.

This book was completed in the Philosophy Department at Macquarie University. Thanks to my colleagues for being friends and for giving me the space to finish writing.

Friends and colleagues around the world provided insight and answered many questions. I thank especially Nuel Belnap, Ross Brady, Max Cresswell, Mike Dunn, André Fuhrmann, Rod Girle, Chrysafis Hartonas, Philip Kremer, Ed Mares, Chris Mortensen, Daniel Nolan, Uwe Petersen, Stephen Read and Heinrich Wansing.

Immeasurable help was provided by Nicolette Bonnette, Piero Pagliani, Graham Priest, Stephen Read, Koji Tanaka and Luca Viganó, who each gave me detailed comments on a draft of the book. The manuscript is much better because of their attention to detail.

Andrew Trevorrow's OzTeX and Paul Taylor's TeX macros enabled me to concentrate on the content instead of worrying about how to produce strange symbols or diagrams.

Friends, especially Fernando Gros and Leanne Cutts, and many at Dickson Baptist Church in Canberra and Trinity Chapel Macquarie in Sydney, helped me stay human. Finally, my thanks and affection belong to Christine Parker not only for the coffee grinder, but also for much needed love and support along the way.

Greg Restall
Sydney
January 1999

Chapter 1

Introduction

... foundational pretensions have been removed.
This allows us to make good use of an idea
which may have spectacular applications
in the future.
— *Jean-Yves Girard*, Proofs and Types [99], *1989*

1.1   *Introducing the Topic*

Logic is about *consequences*. Take a body of propositions. The job of a *logic* is to tell you what follows from that body of propositions. Sometimes we are interested in consequence relations on propositions "in general." That is, we pay no attention to the *subject matter* of the propositions, we pay attention only to the logical relationships between them. This is the traditional scope of philosophical logic. But logic is pursued in other ways too. Sometimes we are interested in particular sorts of propositions — those which have to do with particular structures. We might be reasoning about *times* or *places* or *processes* or some other kind of structure. Logic can be *particular*. This multiplicity of interests affects the state of logic as a discipline. Logic has a home in philosophy because it studies reasoning with propositions in their generality. But the techniques used in philosophical logic can be fruitfully brought to bear on particular problems, for reasoning about particular structures. This is what makes formal logic useful in computer science (we can reason about processes, functions or actions), theoretical linguistics (we can reason about grammatical structures), mathematics (we can reason about mathematical structures), and other fields.

Substructural logics arise in each of these different fields of study. They apply in both the general and the particular applications of formal logic. As a result, this book should appeal to philosophers, mathematicians, theoretical linguists and theoretical computer scientists. The techniques we will use will draw from each area. Sometimes we will consider abstract accounts of what might follow from what. At others we will reason about (relatively) concrete structures.

Substructural logics focus on the behaviour and presence — or more suggestively, the *absence* — of *structural rules*.[1] These are particular rules in a logic

---

[1]   The name is due to Schröder-Heister and Došen, who write, in the introduction of their edited

1

which govern the behaviour of collections of information. To see why this is
important, consider this example. For a wide range of formal systems we have
something like this:

$$X; A \vdash B \text{ if and only if } X \vdash A \to B$$

which states that I can validly deduce B from X taken together with A, if
and only if I can validly deduce the conditional $A \to B$ from X alone. This
ties together three important notions. First, *validity*, which is encoded by the
turnstile '$\vdash$.' Second, the *conditional*, written as '$\to$.' Finally, there is the mode
of *premise combination*, encoded here by the semicolon. *Structural rules* dictate
the properties of premise combination. Because of the deduction theorem, as
premise combination varies, the conditional varies as well. Conversely, if I am
interested in different sorts of deduction, then correspondingly I will examine
different sorts of premise combination and different conditionals too.

This general scheme has arisen in a number of different areas in logic, motivated by different ideas. I will introduce just three here, leaving more until
later.

EXAMPLE 1.1 (RELEVANCE)
Many people have wanted to give an account of logical validity which pays some
attention to conditions of *relevance*. If $X \vdash A$ holds, then X must somehow be
relevant to A. Premise combination is restricted in the following way. We may
have $X \vdash A$ without also having $X; Y \vdash A$. The new material Y might not be
relevant to the deduction.

In the 1950s, Moh [245], Church [46] and Ackermann [2] all gave accounts of what a "relevant" logic could be. The ideas have been developed
by a stream of workers centred around Anderson and Belnap, their students
Dunn and Meyer, and many others. The canonical references for the area are
Anderson, Belnap and Dunn's two-volume *Entailment* [6, 7]. Other introductions can be found in Read's *Relevant Logic* [206] and Dunn's "Relevance Logic
and Entailment" [75]. A more polemical introduction and defence of relevant
logics can be found in Routley, Plumwood, Meyer and Brady's *Relevant Logics and Their Rivals* [231]. (Recent historical investigation by Došen [64] has
shown that a basic relevant logic was discussed by I. E. Orlov in the 1920s.
However, Orlov's work was not known to Anderson and Belnap, unlike each
of Moh, Church and Ackermann, whose work was explicitly taken up in the
Anderson–Belnap tradition.)

---

collection *Substructural Logics*: "Our proposal is to call logics that can be obtained in this manner,
by restricting structural rules, *substructural logics*." [238, page 6]

EXAMPLE 1.2 (RESOURCE CONSCIOUSNESS)
This is not the only way to restrict premise combination. Girard [96] introduced *linear logic* as a model for processes and resource use. The idea in this account of deduction is that resources must be used (so premise combination satisfies the relevance criterion) and they do not extend indefinitely. Premises cannot be *re*-used. So, I might have $X; X \vdash A$, which says that I need to use X twice to get A. I might not have $X \vdash A$, which says that I can use X once alone to get A. A helpful introduction to linear logic is given in Troelstra's *Lectures on Linear Logic* [261].

There are other formal logics in which the *contraction rule* (from $X; X \vdash A$ to $X \vdash A$) is absent. Most famous among these are Łukasiewicz's many-valued logics. There has been a sustained interest in logics without this rule [54, 91, 139, 212].

EXAMPLE 1.3 (ORDER)
Independently of either of these traditions, Joachim Lambek considered mathematical models of language and syntax [133, 134]. The idea here is that premise combination corresponds to composition of strings or other linguistic units. Here $X; X$ differs from X, but in addition, $X; Y$ differs from $Y; X$. Not only does the number of premises used count but so does their *order*. Good introductions to the Lambek calculus (also called *categorial grammar*) can be found in books by Moortgat and Morrill [177, 179].

These are three different concerns which motivate different families of *substructural logics*. In Chapter 2 and in the rest of the book we will see these examples in more detail, and introduce others. One theme of this book is the multiplicity of potential applications of substructural logics. Insights from many different areas will be brought to bear on the topic.

1.2 Introducing the Book

This book is an introduction to substructural logics. It is intended to serve as both an introduction and a reference work to a growing field of logic. It presumes no *special* knowledge on the part of the reader other than what might be gained from an introductory course in logic. However, further experience in any of mathematics, computing or philosophy will, of course, be helpful.

Each chapter contains exercises, suitable for anyone from a beginner to a doctoral student or researcher in the field. The exercises are designed to draw the reader deeper into the material. *Practice questions* reinforce concepts introduced in the chapter, *problem questions* fill in gaps in proofs, extend ideas to analogous contexts and apply results to areas not explicitly covered in the text, and *project questions* are research projects in their own right. Some of these are problems for which solutions exist in the published literature. Others are, as of the time of writing, open problems. A growing collection of solutions to the problems is available at the *Introduction to Substructural Logics* website:

http://www.phil.mq.edu.au/isl/

This website also contains the errata, and up-to-date bibliographical information, together with links to other resources on substructural logics to be found on the Internet.

The book is divided into five parts. After the introduction, Part I covers *Proof Theory*, the theory of proofs and deductions, how to put them together and pull them apart. Part II covers *Propositional Structures*, which are one kind of *model* for logics, and Part III covers *Frames*, which are another kind of model. Part IV examines *Decision Procedures*, the complexity or simplicity of the consequence relations in these logics. Part V, the *Coda*, considers some philosophical issues arising from the study and interpretation of substructural logics.

Later chapters depend on earlier ones, but in general, not on *all* earlier ones. So, there are more ways to use this book fruitfully than the traditional path from start to finish. Figure 1.1 depicts dependencies between chapters. An arrow from n to m means that Chapter m depends on Chapter n.

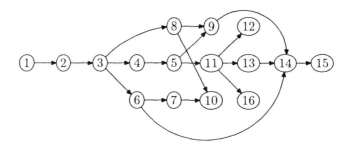

Figure 1.1: Chapter Dependencies

Most chapters contain Definitions, Examples, Lemmas, Theorems and Corollaries. These are numbered sequentially: Theorem 2.6 is the sixth Definition, Example, Lemma or Theorem (in this case, it is a Theorem) in Chapter 2. So, Theorem 2.6 comes after Definition 2.4 and Lemma 2.5 and before Corollary 2.7. Lemmas, Theorems and Corollaries typically come with Proofs. A proof starts with the word PROOF and ends with a box at the right, like this. □

If a statement of a Lemma, Theorem or Corollary ends with a box, that means its proof has been omitted. This is because either the proof is given in the discussion leading up to the claim or it is a straightforward matter, or it is left as an exercise.

Bibliographical references are given by bracketed numerals such as this: [1]. The numeral refers to the itemised entry in the Bibliography, which starts on page 349.

In the text, I use "I" to refer to me, the author. I use "we" to refer to you and me together.

Of course, there is a great deal of fruitful work in substructural logics which is absent from this book. I could not help but be selective. The first boundary is an obvious one: The logics in view are *propositional*. We do not cover quantification of any kind. Useful work has been done on individual quantification, propositional quantification and full second-order quantification in substructural logics. However, the problem of giving a suitable semantic treatment for individual quantification in substructural logics is not well understood. The groundbreaking work of Fine [85] is formally astounding but philosophically opaque.

Second, even restricting our attention to work in propositional logic much had to be left out. I have had no space to discuss Girard's work on *proof nets* [96] as it is unclear how they are to be generalised to the wider setting of other substructural logics. Urquhart's work on the *complexity* of decidable propositional logics has also, regrettably, been left out [269, 272].

Be that as it may, collecting together the work which remains has helped it become clear (at least to me, and hopefully to you) that the study of *substructural logics* has a coherence, a depth and a family resemblance all of its own. Methods, insights and proofs from disparate fields belong together in what becomes a pleasing whole.

Part I

Proof Theory

Chapter 2

Ifs, Ands and Ors

> *A syllogism is a form of words*
> *in which when certain assumptions are made,*
> *something other than what has been assumed*
> *necessarily follows*
> *from the fact that the assumptions are such*
>
> — *Aristotle, Prior Analytics 24b18*

2.1   Consequences

Given that logic is a discipline concerned with consequence, we will focus our attention on claims of the form

$$X \vdash A$$

where X is a body of premises, each one expressed in some language, and A is a conclusion also expressed in that language. The claim '$X \vdash A$' states that A is a consequence of X, or that given X, A follows as a matter of logic. We will call claims like this *consecutions*[1]; they will feature heavily in the rest of this book.

Our interest is in languages which allow us to encode information about the consequence relation in the language of propositions. Formal logic is most interesting when the language we *reason about* is expressive enough to make claims pertaining to consequence. This is typically achieved using conditionals. If our language contains a conditional-forming operator (usually written '$\rightarrow$'), then there is scope for what is known as the *deduction theorem*.

$$\frac{X; A \vdash B}{X \vdash A \rightarrow B}$$

This is a *two-way rule*, and you read it like this: from top to bottom it states that if X *taken together* with A entails B (written as '$X; A \vdash B$'), then X entails the

---

[1]   I follow Anderson and Belnap [6] in using 'consecution' in place of the more prevalent 'sequent.' Their reasons for doing so (given in *Entailment*) still hold, even if no-one else has taken up the usage. Further to their reasons I will add another. 'Sequent' carries the idea of premises or conclusions being listed. In 'consecution' the idea is muted. In our setting premises can be bunched together in a more structured way than simply listing them. We co-opt 'consecution' to do duty for this kind of structured representation of premises and conclusions.

conditional $A \to B$ (which can be read as any of 'if A then B,' 'that A entails that B,' 'A implies B' or just 'A arrow B,' depending on the context).[2] Then from bottom to top we have the converse: If X entails $A \to B$, then we can deduce B from X taken together with A. This is commonly known as the 'deduction theorem.' This is important, because it provides a way of talking about the relation of entailment inside the language of the formulae themselves. The work is done by the notion of "taking together," here encoded by the semicolon. Traditionally, the "taking together" has been thought to behave just like set union. That is, it has been traditional to read the result of taking A together with B as no different from that given by taking B together with A, that taking A together with itself is no different from only one occurrence of A, and so on. However, "taking together" need not have these properties. As the properties of this "taking together" vary, so will the properties of the conditional.

Before examining the formal properties of consequence relations, we will consider a number of different fields of application of the ideas of substructural logics. These different areas of application will be very important throughout the book. They are just some of the topics which can be studied using the techniques in this book. Study them carefully and keep them in mind. The abstract definitions of the next few sections will make more sense if you have examples at hand with which to compare them.

EXAMPLE 2.1 (PROPOSITIONS AND CONSEQUENCE)
The first problem field of application considers propositions in their generality. Consider bodies of information. It makes sense to think of the *application* of one body of information (say X) to another (say Y). X may give us some *conditional information*, which may be expressed as propositions of the form $A \to B$. For example, X might be a scientific theory, which licenses inferences from causes to effects, or from earlier physical states to later physical states. Or X might be a theory of cooking, which licenses inferences from desired ends (say, a particular dish) to means towards those ends (particular processes). These bodies of information are the sort of things which can be *applied*. By applying all of these pieces of information to the data in Y, you get a new body of information, $X;Y$.

Now suppose that $X;A$ warrants B. That is, when we apply X to A, we can legitimately deduce B. Then it follows that X licenses the inference from A to B. We can record this by saying that $A \to B$ is a consequence of X. So,

---

[2] Purists about use and mention will realise that in some of these readings the propositions 'A' and 'B' are used, for example 'if A then B' or 'that A entails that B,' and in others they are mentioned, for example 'A implies B' or 'A arrow B.' Quine and Scott, among others, have held that logics such as these essentially confuse use and mention [203, 239]. This appears wrong to me, for reasons outlined in the *Grammatical Propaedeutic* in Anderson and Belnap's *Entailment* [6].

$X \vdash A \rightarrow B$ follows from $X; A \vdash B$. Conversely, if $X \vdash A \rightarrow B$, then if we apply X to A, then B is a consequence, for $A \rightarrow B$ is a "conditional fact" given by X. So, in reasoning about bodies of information in general, the deduction theorem makes sense.

If we read the semicolon, the conditional and the turnstile in this way, what properties does application have? Is X applied to Y the same as Y applied to X? Is application associative? (That is, is $X; (Y; Z)$ the same body of information as $(X; Y); Z$?) Can we infer $X; Y \vdash A$ from $X \vdash A$? Different choices for these questions will give you different systems of consequence, with varying behaviour of the conditional.

The relevant logic R was motivated by allowing application to be commutative and associative, so $X; Y$ and $Y; X$ are the same bodies of information, and so are $X; (Y; Z)$ and $(X; Y); Z$. Furthermore, premise application is *idempotent*. Anything you can get from $X; X$ you can get from X alone. However, in R you cannot infer $X; Y \vdash A$ from $X \vdash A$. The idea in reading $X; Y \vdash A$ is that *both X and Y are used in the deduction of A*. If you like, both X and Y are *relevant* to the conclusion. So, if X gives A, it need not follow that $X; Y \vdash A$ (or that $Y; X \vdash A$), as Y might not have been used to get the conclusion A.

The notion of *use* in consequence is very important. However, there is no widespread consensus that conditions on use of premises yields us exactly these conditions for premise combination. These ideas motivate a family of related logics. We will study R and other logics like it in much more detail in the rest of these pages.

EXAMPLE 2.2 (SYNTACTIC TYPES)
The next example comes from the world of linguistics. Suppose we have a language, which for our purposes can simply be a collection of syntactic units closed under concatenation. So, if runs, Mary and Joe are syntactic units, then so are Mary runs, runs Joe, Joe Mary runs, and so on. Concatenation is associative, so the result of concatenating Mary runs with Joe is the same as if you had concatenated Mary with runs Joe. (The result is Mary runs Joe in either case.)

Now we can classify syntactic units and reason about them as well. Specifically, a piece of syntax x is of type $A \rightarrow B$ just in case whenever you concatenate it with any string y of type A, the resulting string xy is of type B. You can see the deduction theorem again, where '$X \vdash A \rightarrow B$' means 'any string of type X is also of type $A \rightarrow B$,' and '$X; A \vdash B$' means 'any string given by concatenating a string of type X with one of type A is also of type B. These are equivalent, as you can check.

In our case, Mary runs is of type S — it is a sentence. And runs is of type IV — it is an intransitive verb. Note that according to our analysis, Mary is of type $IV \rightarrow S$. For the result of concatenating Mary with any intransitive verb (for example, runs) is a sentence. In this case, it is Mary runs. But Mary dances, Mary solves Fermat's Last Theorem and any other result of choosing a different intransitive verb is still a sentence. Joe also has type $IV \rightarrow S$ for the same reason.

Note that here, $(X;Y);Z$ is the same type as $X;(Y;Z)$, as any string of the former type must also be of the latter type. Concatenation of strings is associative. However, concatenation of strings does not allow "contraction." A string of two intransitive verbs is not the same thing as an intransitive verb: $IV;IV \neq IV$. A string of two sentences is not itself a sentence: $S;S \neq S$.

EXAMPLE 2.3 (ACTIONS)
Something similar can be said about actions. (By 'actions' we mean action-types, not action-tokens — we assume actions are repeatable.) We can reason about actions in the following way: we can define an action x to be of type $A \rightarrow B$ just when for every action y of type A, the conjoined action xy of performing x and then y is of type B. Take x to be the action of giving away 10 dollars. Let an action be of type F_n just when after performing that action, I have n dollars. Now not many actions will be of type F_n for *any* n at all, but there are some. In particular, x is not of type F_n for any n. However, x is of type $F_n \rightarrow F_{n-10}$, for whenever I compose x with an action of type F_n the result will see me having 10 fewer dollars than when I started.

Action application is associative — performing an action of type $A;B$ and then one of type C is the same as performing an action of type A and then one of type $B;C$. Application of actions is not commutative. Having an argument and then making up is not the same sort of action as making up and then having an argument. So far, this makes reasoning about action much like syntactic strings. However, the similarity is not complete. Syntactic strings can always be concatenated. If you have a string of type A and one of type B, there must be a string of type $A;B$. The same need not be true for actions. There is no action given by combining giving all of my money away and then (immediately) giving you 10 dollars. I cannot perform the next action, because it has been ruled out by the first one. Some actions are so drastic (e. g. suicide) that they rule out *any* subsequent actions. We will see later how this difference in the behaviour of structures makes a difference in the underlying logics of these systems.

EXAMPLE 2.4 (NUMBERS AND FUNCTIONS)
The next area of application is the world of functions. I will give a concrete example of a particular class of functions, and this will generalise simply to other cases. Take a set S of functions from the set $\omega = \{0, 1, 2, \ldots\}$ of natural

numbers to themselves. So any $f \in S$ is a function which, when given a number x, returns a number $f(x)$. The function $f : x \mapsto 3x + 1$, when given 5, returns 16, for example.

We will assume that the set S is *countable*. That means that every function f in S has a unique natural number n_f associated with it. So we can talk about functions applying not only to numbers but also to other functions. We define $f(g)$ to be $f(n_g)$.

Now functions and numbers have various *types*. We can classify them in many different ways. In particular, even numbers have type *Even*, odd numbers have type *Odd*, and so on. The functions in our set have various types too. (Not only by virtue of their "coding" in terms of numbers.) The function $f : x \mapsto 3x + 1$ has the type *Odd* $\rightarrow$ *Even*, by which we mean that whenever it is given an odd number, the function returns an even number. This function f is *also* of type *Even* $\rightarrow$ *Odd*, as you can check.

This interpretation of the arrow in terms of functions also supports the deduction theorem. We can define $X \vdash A \rightarrow B$ to mean that any function of type X is also of type $A \rightarrow B$. That means, whenever we have a function of type X, and we apply it to an argument of type A, the result has type B. Now if we symbolise 'a function of type X applied to an argument of type A' as '$X; A$,' then the conclusion is '$X; A \vdash B$.' For this can be read as saying that anything of type $X; A$ is of type B. That is, anything which is something of type X applied to something of type A is also of type B.

The deduction theorem follows as a matter of course. Whenever $X; A \vdash B$ we have $X \vdash A \rightarrow B$, and vice versa. It is straightforwardly true, as that is the way we defined things.

Things get more complex when you notice that we can apply functions to themselves. This is why in our example we "coded" the function f with its number n_f. Then $f(g)$ is defined as $f(n_g)$. Then in this domain of functions we do not necessarily have $X; X = X$ (as $f(n_f)$ need not equal n_f). Neither will we have $X; Y = Y; X$ (as $f(n_g)$ need not equal $g(n_f)$), or $X; (Y; Z) = (X; Y); Z$, and so on.

This class of functions is a simple example. There are other, more interesting examples of where functions can operate on other functions, in terms of models of the λ-*calculus*. We will see these models in Chapter 8. There is an extensive literature on the λ-calculus, including a number of comprehensive introductions to the area [10, 106, 116].

EXAMPLE 2.5 (POSSIBILITIES AND TIMES)
Traditional work in modal and temporal logic also fits this framework. In the case of temporal logics we are classifying *moments*, which are ordered in time.

We can say a moment m is of type $A \to B$ (or more naturally, we say 'at m, $A \to B$ is true') if at every moment m' later than m, if A is true at m' then B is also true at m'. So $A \to B$ is 'from now, if A then B.' Now take $X \vdash C$ to mean that any moment of type X is also of type C. As a result, if $X \vdash A \to B$ is true, then any moment making X true also makes $A \to B$ true. Now define the $X; A$ by taking a moment m' to make $X; A$ true just when m' makes A true, and at some moment m prior to m', X is true. Then if $X \vdash A \to B$ we can show that $X; A \vdash B$ too. For if m' makes $X; A$ true, it follows that A is true at m', and X is true at some earlier time m. But $X \vdash A \to B$ tells us that $A \to B$ must be true at m too, and since m' is after m, and A is true there, B must be true there too. We can deduce $X \vdash A \to B$ from $X; A \vdash B$ too, as you can check.

That should be enough possible applications to prime your imagination. Keep them in mind as we work through the formal techniques used to study structures like these. It is also a good idea to try to find other ways in which the ideas of substructural logics can be applied.

2.2   *Languages and Structures, Consecutions and Proofs*

To study phenomena like these, we need a *language* (for the claims like A, B and $A \to B$), a concept of *structure* (the structured collections of premises X), a definition of a *consecution* (the claims of the form $X \vdash A$) and the notion of a *proof* (for demonstrations that consecutions are valid). In this section we will work through these definitions. To start, we need to establish just a few properties of strings, as our languages will be made up of strings of symbols.[3]

DEFINITION 2.6 (THE STRING ALGEBRA ON A SET)
The *string algebra generated by a set* X is a set $\text{String}(X)$ together with a binary operation $\frown$ (concatenation) on $\text{String}(X)$ satisfying the following conditions:

$\diamond$ $X \subseteq \text{String}(X)$.

$\diamond$ Concatenation is associative. That is, $a\frown(b\frown c) = (a\frown b)\frown c$ for each $a, b, c \in \text{String}(X)$.

$\diamond$ The elements of X are atomic. That is, for each $a \in X$, there are no $b, c \in \text{String}(X)$ where $a = b\frown c$.

$\diamond$ Elements are finitely generated. That is, for each $a \in \text{String}(X)$, there are $b_1, \ldots, b_n \in X$ where $b_1\frown b_2\frown \cdots \frown b_n = a$.

$\diamond$ Strings uniquely decompose. That is, if $a = x\frown b$ and $a = y\frown c$ where $x, y \in X$, then $x = y$ and $b = c$.

---

[3]   This section is rather detailed and somewhat pedantic. If you are familiar with the notion of a formal language, and if you are comfortable with proofs by mathematical induction, feel free to skip to Definition 2.13 on page 19.

We have defined string algebras to be any sort of thing which satisfies these criteria. However, merely *listing* a set of criteria does not ensure that there *is* something which satisfies them. After all, our requirements could be inconsistent. In this case they are not. There are many ways to construct string algebras. Here is just one — for any set X, we can define a string of length n to be a function from $\{1, \ldots, n\}$ to X. The concatenation of a and b, where a is of length m and b is of length n, is the string $a^\frown b$ of length $m + n$, defined by setting

$$a^\frown b(l) = \begin{cases} a(l) & \text{if } l \leqslant m \\ b(m - l) & \text{if } l > m \end{cases}$$

This construction of strings and concatenation of strings satisfies the conditions for a string algebra. We will not stop to go through the details. They are left for Exercise 2.8.

Our languages are made up of atomic formulae on the one hand, and *connectives* on the other, which are used to put them together.

DEFINITION 2.7 (CONNECTIVES)
A *connective* c is an object together with a number $a(c) \in \omega$, its *arity*.

The arity of a connective is the number of input propositions it expects. Negation has arity 1, the conditional has arity 2. Note that connectives can have arity *zero*. These connectives take no formulae as arguments. They are, in effect, special formulae. The connectives you will see regularly in this book are found in Table 2.1.[4]

Together with each connective and its arity is an explanation of (roughly) how it will behave. This gives you some idea of how to interpret formulae containing that connective.

Given atomic formulae and connectives, the language is simple to define.

DEFINITION 2.8 (A LANGUAGE)
Given a well-ordered[5] set AForm of *atomic formulae*, and a finite set Conn of *connectives*, disjoint from AForm, the *language* Lang(AForm; Conn) is the smallest subset of String(AForm ∪ Conn) satisfying the following conditions:

---

[4]   Note that we use '$\frown$' as a negation connective and the slightly smaller and slightly raised '$^\frown$' to symbolise the function of concatenation. The context will suffice to determine which notion is at use at any point in the text.

[5] X is well-ordered by the relation $<$ if and only if every subset Y of X has a least member according to $<$. For example, written words of English have a well-ordered by the dictionary ordering. Well-ordering of a set X is an issue only when the set X *cannot* be placed in one-to-one correspondence with some set of ordinal numbers. Languages are almost invariably assumed to be well-ordered. In this book we use it explicitly only in the Pair Extension Theorem, on page 94, and its corollaries. Chief among them are the admissibility of disjunctive syllogism (Theorem 5.33) and the completeness theorem for the frame semantics of Chapter 11.

Connective	Arity	Behaviour
$\rightarrow, \leftarrow, \supset$	2	Conditional; if . . . then . . .
$\wedge, \circ$	2	Conjunction; . . . and . . .
$\vee, +$	2	Disjunction; . . . or . . .
$\sim, \neg, \frown, \smile$	1	Negation; not . . .
$\square, \boxminus, !$	1	Necessity
$\lozenge, \Diamond, ?$	1	Possibility
$*$	1	Iteration
$t, \top$	0	Truth
$f, \perp$	0	Falsehood

Table 2.1: Common Connectives and their Readings

◇ AForm ⊆ Lang(AForm; Conn). This means that every atomic formula is a part of the language Lang(AForm; Conn).

◇ If $c \in$ Conn and $a(c) = n$, then for every $A_1, \ldots, A_n \in$ Lang(AForm; Conn) the string $c \frown A_1 \frown \cdots \frown A_n$ is also in Lang(AForm; Conn).

In other words, any atomic formula is a formula, and the other formulae are things you can build up from "already existing" formulae using the connectives. This means that the language satisfies the *unique decomposition condition*.

LEMMA 2.9 (UNIQUE DECOMPOSITION)
If $A \in$ Lang(AForm; Conn) and $A = c \frown A_1 \cdots \frown A_n = d \frown B_1 \cdots \frown B_m$, then $c = d$, $m = n$ and for each $i = 1, \ldots, n$, $A_i = B_i$.

PROOF The condition follows from the properties of strings. We will not give a detailed proof. That is left for the exercises. □

Our definition treats connectives in Polish notation. We will actually *write* binary connectives in infix notation instead. That is, $\rightarrow$ applied to A and B will be written $A \rightarrow B$, instead of $\rightarrow AB$. We will drop parentheses whenever the formula is defined unambiguously. For example, we need to write $(A \rightarrow B) \rightarrow C$ or $A \rightarrow (B \rightarrow C)$ instead of $A \rightarrow B \rightarrow C$, so you know which arrow is the main connective.

Our original notation uses no parentheses at all. If you write the conditional as $\rightarrow AB$ then you can live "parenthesis free." But then, there are precious few who can read $\rightarrow \rightarrow A \rightarrow BC \rightarrow \rightarrow AB \rightarrow AC$ and understand it without translating it back into infix notation, so Polish is not a viable option for use throughout the rest of this text, despite its attractive formal properties.

When we are talking about a language Lang(AForm; Conn) and we do not particularly care about AForm or Conn, we will simply refer to it as 'Lang.' We use 'A,' 'B' and other capitals from the beginning of the alphabet to refer to formulae in a language.

DEFINITION 2.10 (SUBFORMULAE)
We define the *subformulae* of a formula as the smallest set of formulae satisfying these conditions:

⋄ Any formula A is a subformula of itself.

⋄ If A is $c \frown A_1 \frown \cdots \frown A_{a(c)}$, then every subformula of any of the formulae A_i is also a subformula of A.

The following result is an important fact about languages

THEOREM 2.11 (INDUCTION OVER A LANGUAGE)
Take any language Lang(AForm; Conn). *Suppose the property* Φ *holds of every element of* AForm, *and suppose that for each connective* $c \in$ Conn, *whenever* Φ *holds of each* $A_1, \ldots, A_{a(c)}$ *then* Φ *holds of* $c \frown A_1 \frown \ldots \frown A_{a(c)}$ *too. Then it follows that* Φ *holds of each formula in* Lang(AForm; Conn).

PROOF   Consider the class P of all the strings satisfying Φ. P satisfies the two conditions in the definition of Lang(AForm; Conn). As Lang(AForm; Conn) is the smallest such collection, we must have Lang(AForm; Conn) $\subseteq P$, so every formula in Lang(AForm; Conn) satisfies Φ, as desired.   □

This means that to show that something holds of every formula in a language, you need only show that it holds of the atomic formulae, and if it holds of a collection of formulae, then it also holds of the formulae you can make out of those formulae using the connectives. This is a powerful method of proof, and you will see it repeatedly.

   To give you a feeling for how these proofs go, we will establish a trivial fact about languages, using induction.

THEOREM 2.12 (COUNTING ATOMIC FORMULAE)
For any formula $A \in$ Lang(AForm; Conn), *if* A *contains* n_m *connectives of arity* m, *for each* $m \in \omega$, *then* A *contains exactly*

$$1 + \sum_{m \in \omega} (m - 1)n_m$$

atomic formulae.

This theorem uses "sigma" notation for sums.   Read '$\sum_{m \in \omega}(m - 1)n_m$' as 'the sum over each m in ω of each $(m - 1)n_m$.' In other words, $\sum_{m \in \omega}(m - 1)n_m$ is the sum

$$(0 - 1)n_0 + 0n_1 + n_2 + 2n_3 + 3n_4 + \cdots$$

This sum is not infinite, because each formula has a finite length (strings as we have defined them have finite lengths), so for some m, n_m, n_{m+1}, n_{m+2}, ... are all zero. Similarly, '$\sum_{i=1}^{l} b_i$' is shorthand for the finite sum '$b_1 + b_2 + \cdots + b_n$.' With that notation in hand, we can prove the theorem by induction.

PROOF   The induction hypothesis Φ is the statement that the formula A contains exactly $1 + \sum_{m \in \omega}(m-1)n_m$ atomic formulae, given that it contains n_m connectives of arity m. Does Φ hold of the atomic formulae? Well, these have *no* connectives of each arity, and they contain exactly one atomic formula. In this case the sum gets the number right, as $1 + \sum_{m \in \omega}(m-1)n_m = 1$ when $n_m = 0$ for each m. That completes the first step of the inductive argument.

Now suppose $A = c^\frown A_1^\frown \cdots ^\frown A_l$, where $l = a(c)$, and that furthermore, each A_i contains $1 + \sum_{m \in \omega}(m-1)n_m^i$ atomic formulae, given that it contains n_m^i connectives of arity i. Then A must contain

$$\sum_{i=1}^{l}\left(1 + \sum_{m \in \omega}(m-1)n_m^i\right)$$

atomic propositions, adding them all up. But we can shuffle this sum around as follows:[6]

$$\sum_{i=1}^{l}\left(1 + \sum_{m \in \omega}(m-1)n_m^i\right) = l + \sum_{i=1}^{l}\sum_{m \in \omega}(m-1)n_m^i$$

$$= l + \sum_{m \in \omega}\sum_{i=1}^{l}(m-1)n_m^i$$

$$= l + \sum_{m \in \omega}(m-1)\sum_{i=1}^{l}n_m^i$$

How many connectives of arity m does A have? Given that each A_i contains n_m^i, A as a whole must have $\sum_{i=1}^{l} n_m^i$ connectives of arity i, *except for the case* $m = l$. Then A contains one extra connective, its main operator. So,

$$n_m = \begin{cases} \sum_{i=1}^{l} n_m^i & \text{if } m \neq l \\ 1 + \sum_{i=1}^{l} n_m^i & \text{if } m = l \end{cases}$$

This means that our sum collapses to

$$1 + \sum_{m \in \omega}(m-1)n_m$$

---

6   If you are not familiar with Σ notation, it is very instructive to verify each step in this "shuffle."

as we "eat up" $l - 1$ of the l in the front of the sum to beef up the l-numbered value of the sum in the interior to n_m. This means that the hypothesis Φ holds of A too, given that it holds of the subformulae of A. By induction, then, Φ holds of every formula in Lang(AForm; Conn).   □

The proofs by induction we will see later all have this form. We prove the hypothesis for the base case, then we use an *inductive step* to extend the hypothesis to the whole language. Proving new things by induction is a balancing act — you must choose the inductive hypothesis Φ to be weak enough to be provable at each stage but strong enough to support the inductive hypothesis.

To define consecutions we need a way of collecting formulae together to form a structured collection. Structures are defined analogously to languages. They combine propositions not with connectives but with *punctuation marks*

DEFINITION 2.13 (PUNCTUATION MARKS)
A *punctuation mark* p is an object together with a number $a(p) \in \omega$, its *arity*.

Punctuation marks stand to structures in the same way that connectives stand to formulae.

DEFINITION 2.14 (STRUCTURES)
A collection Struct of *structures* is made up of a *language* Lang, and a set Punct of *punctuation marks*, disjoint from Lang. The set Struct(Lang; Punct) of structures on Lang and Punct is the smallest subset of String(Lang ∪ Punct) satisfying these conditions:

◇ Lang ⊆ Struct(Lang; Punct). That is, every formula in Lang is a structure.

◇ If $p \in$ Punct, and $a(p) = n$, then for any $X_1, \ldots, X_n \in$ Struct(Lang; Punct), the string $p^\frown A_1 {}^\frown \cdots {}^\frown A_n \in$ Struct(Lang; Punct).

Structural induction holds for structures, just as we can use structural induction on formulae. Exercise 2.11 asks you to state and prove such a theorem.

We will use letters like 'X,' 'Y' and 'Z' to stand for structures. The punctuation we will see will mainly be the semicolon, the comma (both binary and written infix, in the usual way), a zero-place punctuation mark 0, and a one-place punctuation mark •. We may see others as well, and I will warn you of them before the time comes.

Structures may have substructures in the same way that formulae have subformulae.

DEFINITION 2.15 (SUBSTRUCTURES)
We define the *substructures* of a structure as the smallest set of structures satisfying these conditions:

◇ Any structure X is a substructure of itself.

⋄ If X is $p(X_1, \ldots, X_{a(p)})$, then every substructure of any of the structures X_i is also a substructure of X.

Note that the substructures of a structure go down only to the formulae out of which the structure is made — not to the subformulae of those formulae. The formulae are indivisible atoms as far as structure goes. For example, the substructures of $(A \rightarrow B; A); C$ are the structures

$$A \rightarrow B \qquad A \qquad C \qquad (A \rightarrow B; A) \qquad (A \rightarrow B; A); C$$

The formula B is not a substructure of $(A \rightarrow B; A); C$, but it is a *subformula* of a substructure of $(A \rightarrow B; A); C$.

We will write '$X(Y)$' to indicate a structure with Y as a substructure. The structure $X(Z)$ is given by replacing that occurrence of Y in $X(Y)$ by Z. For example, $X(Y)$ might be $A; (B, \bullet Y)$ and then $X(Z)$ would be $A; (B, \bullet Z)$.

Once we have structures and formulae, consecutions are easy to define.

DEFINITION 2.16 (CONSECUTIONS, ANTECEDENTS AND CONSEQUENTS)
Given a set Struct of structures over a language Lang, a *consecution* on Struct is of the form $X \vdash A$, where $X \in$ Struct is the *antecedent* of the consecution and $A \in$ Lang is the *consequent* of the consecution.

A proof of a consecution is a demonstration that the consecution is valid. There are many different ways to define proofs. In this section we will see just one. Before we launch into the definition of a proof we need some background ideas.

To demonstrate that a consecution is valid, we can start from consecutions we know to be valid (by some means or other) and apply to them rules which preserve validity until we get to the consecution we are trying to prove. Looking at this backwards, we have the consecution we are trying to prove, and this is either an axiom (something we know to be valid independently) or it follows from other consecutions by a rule. These too are either valid or they follow from other consecutions by a rule. These sorts of structures are so "tree-like" that we call them *trees*. Trees are made up of *nodes*, connected by *arcs*. The bottom node in a tree is called its *root*, and for any nodes, the nodes immediately above are its *parents*. (Think of a family tree, except that in our trees a node can have any number of parents.) A node without any parents at all is said to be a *leaf*. A maximal path upwards from the root in a tree is called a *branch*. (Note that in a tree a branch need not end in a leaf, since the branch may be infinite. However, if a branch contains a leaf, it has only one leaf. This makes *these* branches rather different from branches in everyday trees.) In a tree, we will call the pair consisting of a node and its parents an *inference*, for we have *inferred* that node from its parents. We will make these claims more formal.

DEFINITION 2.17 (INFERENCES AND RULES)
An *inference* is a pair consisting of a set of consecutions (the *premises* of the inference) and a single consecution (the *conclusion* of the inference). The premises may be an empty set, and in that case we call the inference an *axiom*. A *rule* is a set of inferences. A member of a rule is said to be an *instance* of that rule.

Recall that we are interested in many different logics, as we are interested in applying these methods in different ways. As a result, we will need many different notions of proof to deal with different domains, and that is why our notions of languages and structures have been completely general. We will therefore define a general notion of a proof, and only after that will we look at some specific examples. First, to a definition of a system in which we might construct proofs. To construct proofs we need a language (we have that) and consecutions built on a language (we have that), and a conception of which inferences are good ones to make (we do not yet have that). That is our next definition.

DEFINITION 2.18 (PROOF SYSTEMS)
A *proof system* is a language Lang with a set Struct of structures made up from that language, and a family of rules, made up from consecutions over those structures.

Once we have a *proof system* we can determine which are the proofs in that system.

DEFINITION 2.19 (PROOFS)
A *proof* of a consecution $X \vdash A$ in some proof system is a tree, with root $X \vdash A$, and in which every node is a consecution in the language of the proof system, and for which every inference in the tree is an instance of some rule of the proof system. In addition, every branch of the tree is finite. (Note that, according to this definition, a proof may still be infinite, provided that some inference has infinitely many premises. It is possible to consider proofs of this form, but we will not see any examples in this book.)

Sometimes we are interested in *proofs from assumptions*. That is, we grant that the consecutions in some set Σ are valid, and we wish to proceed to form proofs on that basis. We define a *proof of $X \vdash A$ from assumptions Σ* in some proof system to be a tree with root $X \vdash A$, and in which every node is a consecution in the language of the proof system, and for which every inference in the tree is an instance of some rule in the proof system, *or* it is an element of the assumption set Σ, and in that case, the node is a leaf in the tree. (Or equivalently, it is a proof in the expanded system in which the elements of Σ are added as new axioms.)

That has been quite a long list of definitions. Now that we have the definitions, we can examine different proof systems which contain different rules.

The basic rule in any of our proof systems is the *identity* rule:

$$A \vdash A \quad (Id)$$

This rule is an *axiom*. It has no premises. And the conclusion is any consecution in which the antecedent is the consequent formula. We say that any *instance* of the scheme written above is an instance of the rule. That is, A is perfectly general. The rule of identity is the family of all inferences from no premises to a conclusion of the form $A \vdash A$.

2.3 Ifs and Ands

In natural deduction proof systems it is traditional to have two rules for each connective. One rule tells you how you can *get* the connective. For the conditional, for example, it is a rule which tells you how you can prove $A \to B$ (from assumptions). It is called the *introduction rule* for the conditional. And we have already seen how you can prove $A \to B$ from X. You prove B from $X; A$. So this will be our arrow introduction rule. We label the rule $(\to I)$.

$$\frac{X; A \vdash B}{X \vdash A \to B} \, (\to I)$$

This rule has one premise, as you can see. The other rule to do with a connective is to *get rid of it*. This is the corresponding *elimination* rule.

$$\frac{X \vdash A \to B \quad Y \vdash A}{X; Y \vdash B} \, (\to E)$$

Note that this rule is slightly different from the formulation in the deduction theorem. We have two premises. This is important, for we want our proofs to have a particular property. That is, we would like every formula which occurs in the antecedent of some consecution of a proof to also appear in the antecedent of one of the premises of that consecution (if it actually has any premises). This makes proof construction easier, for you know that if you have to prove $X \vdash A$, then you need to assume the content of X in the axioms.

So, instead of inferring $X; A \vdash B$ from $X \vdash A \to B$, we used $X \vdash A \to B$ and $Y \vdash A$ to deduce $X; Y \vdash B$. The antecedent assumption of Y will be preserved upwards in a proof of $X; Y \vdash B$. This rule clearly makes sense, however you interpret the logic, as its validity follows from that of the deduction theorem. If $Y \vdash A$, then anything of type Y is of type A, and so anything of type $X; Y$ is also of type $X; A$, and hence, it must be of type B as we wanted.

Note that these rules assume that we are in a language with a conditional, and a system of structures with at least the semicolon. These rules make sense in *any* language with at least these resources. We have a formal definition of a connective:

DEFINITION 2.20 (RULES FOR THE LEFT-TO-RIGHT CONDITIONAL)
The connective $\rightarrow$ is a *left-to-right conditional* for the punctuation mark ';' if and only if it satisfies the two rules $(\rightarrow I)$ and $(\rightarrow E)$.

This definition picks out a unique connective, as the next lemma shows us.

DEFINITION 2.21 (EQUIVALENCE IN A PROOF SYSTEM)
The formulae A and B are equivalent in a proof system if and only if the system proves both $A \vdash B$ and $B \vdash A$. We write this as '$A \dashv\vdash B$.'

LEMMA 2.22 (UNIQUENESS OF CONDITIONALS)
If $\rightarrow_1$ and $\rightarrow_2$ are both left-to-right conditionals for the one punctuation mark, then $A \rightarrow_1 B$ and $A \rightarrow_2 B$ are equivalent for all A and B.

PROOF   We prove $A \rightarrow_1 B \vdash A \rightarrow_2 B$.

$$\frac{\dfrac{A \rightarrow_1 B \vdash A \rightarrow_1 B \quad A \vdash A}{A \rightarrow_1 B; A \vdash B} (\rightarrow_1 E)}{A \rightarrow_1 B \vdash A \rightarrow_2 B} (\rightarrow_2 I)$$

Interchanging '1' and '2' proves $A \rightarrow_2 B \vdash A \rightarrow_1 B$ and hence the equivalence holds.   □

In a system with these few rules, very few things are provable. However, we can do some interesting proofs from assumptions. For example, we can prove $B \rightarrow C \vdash A \rightarrow C$ from the assumption $A \vdash B$. Here is the proof.

$$\frac{\dfrac{A \vdash B \quad B \rightarrow C \vdash B \rightarrow C}{(B \rightarrow C); A \vdash C} (\rightarrow E)}{B \rightarrow C \vdash A \rightarrow C} (\rightarrow I)$$

We have written this proof as a simple tree. We write it as a string of inferences pasted together, end to end. It has only two branches. One leaf is our assumption — that $A \vdash B$ holds. The other is the axiom $B \rightarrow C \vdash B \rightarrow C$.

Proofs presented in this way are easy to read, as you can see at a glance what depends on what. However, proofs are not so easy to construct in tree form — often it is easier to construct proofs writing the consecutions in a *list*.

As an example, here is how I first wrote out the proof I have shown above. I listed on two lines (lines 1 and 2 below) the assumption $A \vdash B$, and the axiom $B \rightarrow C \vdash B \rightarrow C$. I knew to do that because I knew that $B \rightarrow C$ is the antecedent in what I am trying to prove. (Note that I labelled both of these lines indicating where they came from.) Then I could apply $(\rightarrow E)$ to these two lines to get line 3 (see the label), and then I could apply $(\rightarrow I)$ to line 3 to get line 4.

$$
\begin{array}{llll}
1. & A \vdash B & \text{Assumption} \\
2. & B \rightarrow C \vdash B \rightarrow C & (Id) \\
3. & (B \rightarrow C); A \vdash C & 1, 2\,(\rightarrow E) \\
4. & B \rightarrow C \vdash A \rightarrow C & 3\,(\rightarrow I)
\end{array}
$$

From now on, I will write proofs in tree form, unless they are too large to fit across the page. In that case, they will appear in linear form to make them fit.

To apply our methods to different areas, we need different ways to rearrange structures. For example, when reasoning about syntactic strings, and when the semicolon is interpreted as concatenation of strings, the semicolon ought to be associative. That is, if we have $X; (Y; Z) \vdash A$, then we ought to be able to infer $(X; Y); Z \vdash A$, and vice versa. There is no way of doing this using the rules we have so far, there is no way to rearrange assumptions. Order and bracketing of assumptions all count in the system at present. To make moves like that from $X; (Y; Z) \vdash A$ to $(X; Y); Z \vdash A$ we need a rule which licenses such a move. A rule like this is said to be a *structural rule*. Structural rules take the form

$$\frac{X \vdash A}{X' \vdash A}$$

where X' is obtained from X by rearranging structures. This is an imprecise notion. We will tighten it by introducing a formal definition.

DEFINITION 2.23 (STRUCTURAL RULES)
A rule

$$\frac{X \vdash A}{X' \vdash A}$$

is a *structural rule* if it is closed under substitution for formulae. That is, given any instance of the rule, and any formula B appearing in either X or X' (or both), and given any structure Y you like, then the result of replacing every instance of B in X and X' by Y is still an inference of the rule. Similarly, the A in the consequent can be replaced by any formula you like, resulting in another instance of the rule.

For example, the collection of all inferences of the from

$$\frac{X;(Y;Z) \vdash A}{(X;(Y;W));Z \vdash A}$$

is a structural rule. For the A in the consequent position is arbitrary, and so are the formulae which appear in the antecedent. On the other hand, the rule made up of all inferences of the form

$$\frac{X;(A;Z) \vdash B \to C}{Z;(A;X) \vdash B \to C}$$

is *not* a structural rule, for two reasons. First, you cannot replace the $B \to C$ with any formula you like — the formula must have an arrow as the main connective. Second, the formula A in the antecedent cannot be replaced by an arbitrary structure. It can only be replaced by another formula. (For instance, $X;((Y_1;Y_2);Z)$ does not have the required form to be an antecedent in the rule.)

We will write structural rules of this form as $X \hookleftarrow X'$. This means that from $X \vdash A$ we can deduce $X' \vdash A$ — the X gets replaced by the X'. This notation is meant to convey that the X' is "plugged in" where the X used to be, and the arrow indicates that X' in some sense *entails* X.

This form of displaying structural rules is a start, but it is not the best way of describing them. Consider a rule of the form $X;(Y;Z) \hookleftarrow (X;Y);Z$. Suppose we have $W(X;(Y;Z)) \vdash A$. The structural rule as given does *not* license the conclusion $W((X;Y);Z) \vdash A$, as the rule guarantees only that entire antecedent structures may be reassociated, not that they may be reassociated *inside* other structures. However, in many applications of our logics, if you can do something to the entire antecedent, you can do it to any substructure of the antecedent. For example, if action composition is associative, then composition of *sub-actions* of an action must also be associative, as these are just more actions. The same goes for syntactic strings, pieces of information, times or possibilities or other things. This motivates the notation $X \Leftarrow X'$ to stand for the structural rule of the form

$$\frac{Y(X) \vdash A}{Y(X') \vdash A}$$

where Y is an arbitrary context in which structures may appear. Given this notation, Table 2.2 lists standard structural rules. Clearly the list is not exhaustive, but it is a good indication of the kind of structural rules you will see quite often. The list groups together the rule, together with the labels we will use for them,[7] and their names, which describe their behaviour.

---

[7] You may wonder what the labels have to do with the structural rules. The labels for all except

Name	Label	Rule		
Associativity	B	$X;(Y;Z)$	$\Leftarrow$	$(X;Y);Z$
Twisted Associativity	B′	$X;(Y;Z)$	$\Leftarrow$	$(Y;X);Z$
Converse Associativity	B^c	$(X;Y);Z$	$\Leftarrow$	$X;(Y;Z)$
Strong Commutativity	C	$(X;Y);Z$	$\Leftarrow$	$(X;Z);Y$
Weak Commutativity	CI	$X;Y$	$\Leftarrow$	$Y;X$
Strong Contraction	W	$(X;Y);Y$	$\Leftarrow$	$X;Y$
Weak Contraction	WI	$X;X$	$\Leftarrow$	X
Mingle	M	X	$\Leftarrow$	$X;X$
Weakening	K	X	$\Leftarrow$	$X;Y$
Commuted Weakening	K′	X	$\Leftarrow$	$Y;X$

Table 2.2: Structural Rules

The structural rules influence what we can prove. The more structural rules you have, the more you will be able to prove. For example, if we allow ourselves K, the weakening rule, then the following proof is valid.

$$\frac{\dfrac{A \vdash A}{A;B \vdash A}\,[\text{K}]}{A \vdash B \to A}\,(\to I)$$

Using K we can "weaken in" irrelevant premises (hence the name — we get a "weaker claim," that $X;Y \vdash A$ from the stronger claim that $X \vdash A$). The absence of K and its sister rule K′ is a characteristic feature of *relevant logics*. For relevant logics the conditional $A \to B$ encodes the fact that we used A in a deduction of B. If we allow ourselves weakening, then we lose all sight of what was actually *used* in a deduction. Note that in the proof above there is a label indicating the step at which K is invoked. We will continue this practice whenever we wish to call attention to the application of a rule.

---

the mingle rule M originate with combinatory logic [56, 167]. There is scope for confusion here, as some authors use 'C' for *contraction* and 'W' for *weakening*. I have decided to follow the more established tradition here, at variance with English spelling, in order to emphasise the historical connection with combinatory logic.

Here is another proof, using C.

$$\cfrac{\cfrac{\cfrac{\cfrac{\cfrac{A \to (B \to C) \vdash A \to (B \to C) \quad A \vdash A}{A \to (B \to C); A \vdash B \to C}(\to E) \quad B \vdash B}{(A \to (B \to C); A); B \vdash C}(\to E)}{(A \to (B \to C); B); A \vdash C}[\text{C}]}{A \to (B \to C); B \vdash A \to C}(\to I)}{A \to (B \to C) \vdash B \to (A \to C)}(\to I)$$

The structural rule C gives us strong commutativity, it allows us to swap two places. Note that the consecution it lets us prove also involves commutativity — the consequent $B \to (A \to C)$ is a commuted form of the antecedent $A \to (B \to C)$. The two antecedents in $A \to (B \to C)$ are swapped to give $B \to (A \to C)$.

A weaker form of commutativity is provided by CI.

$$\cfrac{\cfrac{\cfrac{A \vdash A \quad A \to B \vdash A \to B}{A \to B; A \vdash B}(\to E)}{A; A \to B \vdash B}[\text{CI}]}{A \vdash (A \to B) \to B}(\to I)$$

Not only do some structural rules allow us to commute structures — other rules allow us to reassociate them. Here is a proof using B.

$$\cfrac{\cfrac{\cfrac{\cfrac{A \to B \vdash A \to B \quad \cfrac{C \to A \vdash C \to A \quad C \vdash C}{C \to A; C \vdash A}(\to E)}{A \to B; (C \to A; C) \vdash B}(\to E)}{(A \to B; C \to A); C \vdash B}[\text{B}]}{A \to B; C \to A \vdash C \to B}(\to I)}{A \to B \vdash (C \to A) \to (C \to B)}(\to I)$$

Another kind of structural rule allows the contraction of proof resources. This is W, the rule of *contraction*.

$$\cfrac{\cfrac{\cfrac{A \to (A \to B) \vdash A \to (A \to B) \quad A \vdash A}{A \to (A \to B); A \vdash A \to B}(\to E) \quad A \vdash A}{\cfrac{(A \to (A \to B); A); A \vdash B}{A \to (A \to B); A \vdash B}[W]}(\to E)}{A \to (A \to B) \vdash A \to B}(\to I)$$

Note that the consecution proved also allows the contraction of two uses of A to give B in the antecedent into one use of A to get B in the consequent.

So far our language uses only arrows. We can extend things further by allowing another binary connective 'o,' called *fusion* in the literature on relevant logic and *multiplicative conjunction* in linear logic. We follow the earlier usage and call it fusion. Fusion mirrors in the language of formulae the behaviour of the semicolon on structures. It has these introduction and elimination rules.

$$\cfrac{X \vdash A \quad Y \vdash B}{X; Y \vdash A \circ B}(\circ I) \qquad \cfrac{X \vdash A \circ B \quad Y(A; B) \vdash C}{Y(X) \vdash C}(\circ E)$$

These rules follow from the interpretation of fusion. If X is of type A and Y is of type B, then the concatenation of X and Y is of type $A \circ B$. If X is enough for $A \circ B$, and given that $Y(A; B)$ gives me C, then I can replace that reference to $A; B$ in Y by a claim to X (which, after all, is sufficient for $A \circ B$). So, $A \circ B$ is the formula equivalent to the structure $A; B$.

DEFINITION 2.24 (RULES FOR FUSION)
The connective $\circ$ is a *fusion* for the punctuation mark ';' if and only if it satisfies the two rules $(\circ I)$ and $(\circ E)$.

The next lemma follows immediately from the definition. Its proof is deferred to Exercise 2.13.

LEMMA 2.25 (UNIQUENESS OF FUSION)
If $\circ_1$ and $\circ_2$ are both fusion connectives for the one punctuation mark, then $A \circ_1 B$ is equivalent to $A \circ_2 B$.

Note that the rules for fusion make sense however you interpret the logic. In the world of function typing, an object is of type $A \circ B$ just when it can be obtained by applying something of type A to something of type B. A string is of type $A \circ B$ just when it is made up of a string of type A concatenated with a string of type B. I leave it to you to consider how you should read fusion in other applications.

Whatever the *interpretation* of fusion, we have a number of important behaviours. For example, we can prove $A \vdash B \rightarrow A \circ B$ as follows.

$$\dfrac{\dfrac{A \vdash A \quad B \vdash B}{A; B \vdash A \circ B} \, (\circ I)}{A \vdash B \rightarrow A \circ B} \, (\rightarrow I)$$

Properties of fusion are inherited from properties of the semicolon straightforwardly. If the semicolon is associative, so is fusion.

$$\dfrac{B \circ C \vdash B \circ C \quad \dfrac{\dfrac{\dfrac{A \vdash A \quad B \vdash B}{A; B \vdash A \circ B} \, (\circ I) \quad C \vdash C}{(A; B); C \vdash (A \circ B) \circ C} \, (\circ I)}{\dfrac{A; (B; C) \vdash (A \circ B) \circ C}{A; (B \circ C) \vdash (A \circ B) \circ C} \, (\circ E)} \, [B^c]}{A \circ (B \circ C) \vdash A \circ (B \circ C)}$$
$$A \circ (B \circ C) \vdash (A \circ B) \circ C$$

Another possible connective is the *right-to-left conditional* '$\leftarrow$.' It interacts with the semicolon in the converse way to the left-to-right conditional. Its rules are as follows.

$$\dfrac{A; X \vdash B}{X \vdash B \leftarrow A} \, (\leftarrow I) \qquad \dfrac{X \vdash B \leftarrow A \quad Y \vdash A}{Y; X \vdash B} \, (\leftarrow E)$$

DEFINITION 2.26 (RULES FOR THE RIGHT-TO-LEFT CONDITIONAL)
The connective $\leftarrow$ is a *right-to-left conditional* for the punctuation mark ';' if and only if it satisfies the two rules $(\leftarrow I)$ and $(\leftarrow E)$.

As with our other connectives, the rules uniquely characterise the connective $\leftarrow$, in the sense that any two connectives satisfying the rules are equivalent.

This connective is especially useful in the contexts of reasoning about actions or strings. Take strings. Recall that a string x is of type $A \rightarrow B$ whenever for any string y of type A, the concatenation xy is of type B. The backward arrow lets us look at concatenation *on the left* instead of on the right. That is, a string x is of type $B \leftarrow A$ if and only if for every string y of type A, the string yx is of type B. Note that if we have CI as a structural rule, then $\leftarrow$ and $\rightarrow$ are equivalent (see Exercise 2.2).

We need one final piece of convention when describing this set of connectives. We have seen that ∘, → and ← belong together. They are all defined in terms of the semicolon, and their logical behaviour is inherited from the structural rules satisfied by the semicolon. Furthermore, the fusion connective mirrors the behaviour of the semicolon directly. As a result, fusion has a special place in this group of connectives.

DEFINITION 2.27 (THE FUSION/IMPLICATION FAMILY)
The connectives ∘, → and ← form a *family*, with ∘ as the *parent*. Furthermore, we will say that → is *left residuates* ∘, and ← *right residuates* ∘. The connectives → and ← are said to be *residuals* of fusion.

The way that fusion differs from the implication connectives (as their "parent") will become clearer in later chapters. For now, however, we go on to consider other connectives.

2.4   Truth

So far we have focused on consecutions. We examined how to prove claims of the form $X \vdash A$ in a wide variety of systems. This is an appropriate emphasis, since logic is fundamentally the study of consequence. As a result of this emphasis, we have said nothing about what counts as a *theorem* — that is, we have not defined what it is for a particular *formula* to be proved by a particular logic. Given that we want to record *theoremhood*, we need some way of recording provability in the object language. The traditional way to do this is to take theorems to be those formulae which follow from *nothing at all*. In other words, theorems are the formulae A where we have $\vdash A$. But this is not possible for us, for $X \vdash A$ makes sense only when X is a structure, and "nothing" is not a structure. The way around this is to introduce a new zero-place punctuation mark '0,' which will "label" theorems. We use '$0 \vdash A$' to indicate that A is a theorem.

DEFINITION 2.28 (IDENTITIES)
A zero-place punctuation mark is a *left identity* (with respect to the binary punctuation mark ';') if it satisfies the following two structural rules:

$$
\begin{array}{rcl}
X & \Leftarrow & 0; X \qquad \text{Left Push} \\
0; X & \Leftarrow & X \qquad \text{Left Pop}
\end{array}
$$

The Left Push rule allows us to "push" a 0 on the left structure of premises. And the Left Pop rule allows us to "pop" the 0 off that structure.[8] Similarly, 0 is a

---

[8]   I owe the terms 'Push' and 'Pop' to J. Michael Dunn [77].

right identity (with respect to the binary punctuation mark ';') if it satisfies the following two structural rules:

$$X \quad \Leftarrow \quad X;0 \qquad \text{Right Push}$$
$$X;0 \quad \Leftarrow \quad X \qquad \text{Right Pop}$$

If 0 is a left identity, then applying 0 to X (on the left) yields no more and no less than X itself. The 0 object has different readings in different applications. For functions, 0 is the type of the identity function, for strings it is the type of the empty string, for 'information' it is the logical body of information — that is, it is the body of information which licenses all of the inferences of the form $A \to A$, for actions, it is the type of the empty action, and for times, it is the proposition which is true at all times.

Once we have 0, we have a way of recording consequences inside the language of implication.

THEOREM 2.29 (REGISTERING CONSEQUENCE)
In any system containing the $\to$ *rules, and in which* 0 *is a left identity for the semicolon, there is a proof of* $0 \vdash A \to B$ *if and only if* $A \vdash B$ *is provable.*

PROOF   Add the following reasoning to any proof of $A \vdash B$.

$$\vdots$$
$$\frac{\dfrac{A \vdash B}{0; A \vdash B} \text{ [Left Push]}}{0 \vdash A \to B} (\to I)$$

The result is the proof we want. Conversely, given a proof of $0 \vdash A \to B$, we can find a proof of $A \to B$, by adding the following reasoning:

$$\vdots$$
$$\frac{\dfrac{A \vdash A \qquad 0 \vdash A \to B}{0; A \vdash B} (\to E)}{A \vdash B} \text{ [Left Pop]} \qquad \qquad \Box$$

If a system contains a left identity 0, we can mirror its behaviour in the language by considering a zero-place connective t, which satisfies the following two rules

$$0 \vdash t \ (tI) \qquad \qquad \frac{X \vdash t \quad Y(0) \vdash A}{Y(X) \vdash A} (tE)$$

DEFINITION 2.30 (A TRUTH CONSTANT t)

The zero-place connective t is a truth constant for the punctuation mark 0 if and only if it satisfies the rules (tI) and (tE)

It is left as an exercise to show that if t_1 and t_2 are both truth constants for the one punctuation mark, then they are equivalent.

Once we have Right Pop we can prove $t \to A \vdash A$.

$$\cfrac{\cfrac{t \to A \vdash t \to A \quad 0 \vdash t}{t \to A; 0 \vdash A}\ (tE)}{t \to A \vdash A}\ \text{[Right Pop]}$$

This rule is plausible when reading consequence as applying to information in general. Given that t is the information warranted by *logic*, then $t \to A$ (that t implies A) seems to entail A, since t is true.[9]

This rule also makes sense in terms of actions or strings. If a string (or action) is of type $t \to A$, it means that whenever it is concatenated with a string (or action ...) of type t, then the result is of type A. But the empty string is of type t, so concatenating it with the original string leaves you with the original string — so that string must be of type A as well.

The readings in terms of strings and actions also motivate the Right Push rule since concatenating a string with the empty string results in the same string. Concatenating an action with the empty action gives you the same action. It is trivial to show that this structural rule enables us to prove $A \vdash t \to A$.

It is important not to confuse t with another propositional constant, which we will write as '⊤.'

DEFINITION 2.31 (THE TRIVIAL TRUTH ⊤)

The propositional constant ⊤ is said to be a *trivial truth* if and only if it satisfies the rule

$$X \vdash \top \quad (\top I)$$

The introduction rule is simple. We can infer $X \vdash \top$ whenever we like. The connective has no elimination rule, as you can gain no new information from $X \vdash \top$.

In some applications (such as the temporal one) we might have t and ⊤ having the same interpretation (they are both the proposition which is true at all times). In fact, in systems with K′, we can prove t and ⊤ to be equivalent.

LEMMA 2.32 (t AND ⊤ EQUIVALENCE)

In any system including K, t and ⊤ are equivalent.

---

[9]   This postulate is one of the rules in the logic E of *entailment*, developed by Anderson and Belnap [6], which is designed to model entailment between propositions.

PROOF   In any system with $\top$ we have $t \vdash \top$ as an axiom, and with K we have

$$\dfrac{\dfrac{0 \vdash t}{0; \top \vdash t} \; [\text{K}]}{\top \vdash t} \; [\text{Left Pop}]$$ □

But in some applications of substructural logics, K fails, and t and $\top$ are not equivalent in general. Dual with $\top$ there is $\bot$.

DEFINITION 2.33 (THE TRIVIAL FALSEHOOD $\bot$)
The formula $\bot$ is the *trivial falsehood* if and only if it satisfies

$$\dfrac{X \vdash \bot}{Y(X) \vdash A} \; (\bot E)$$

Clearly any two trivial truths are equivalent, as are any two trivial falsehoods. No string, no action, no function and no piece of information (in any context) has type $\bot$. Dually to $\top$, $\bot$ has no introduction rule. There is nothing you could do to get $X \vdash \bot$ apart from using the identity rule.

2.5   Ands and Ors

Logic is more than merely the behaviour of the connectives $\circ$, $\rightarrow$ and $\leftarrow$ with t, $\top$ and $\bot$. It has been traditional for logic to deal with connectives like conjunction and disjunction (written '$\wedge$' and '$\vee$,' read 'and' and 'or'). In each of our applications, $\wedge$ and $\vee$ have a straightforward meaning. For example, an action is of type $A \wedge B$ just when it is of type A and of type B, and it is of type $A \vee B$ just when it is of type A or of type B. Conjunction and disjunction are binary connectives (as you would expect), and we read them as binding *more tightly* than the implication connectives. That is, we read $A \vee B \rightarrow C \wedge D$ as $(A \vee B) \rightarrow (C \wedge D)$. We have the following rules for conjunction:

$$\dfrac{X \vdash A \quad X \vdash B}{X \vdash A \wedge B} \; (\wedge I) \qquad \dfrac{X \vdash A \wedge B}{X \vdash A} \; (\wedge E_1) \qquad \dfrac{X \vdash A \wedge B}{X \vdash B} \; (\wedge E_2)$$

In any system with these rules and the rules $(\rightarrow I)$ and $(\rightarrow E)$ we have the following proof (written in linear form to save space):

1.	$(A \to B) \wedge (A \to C) \vdash (A \to B) \wedge (A \to C)$	(Id)
2.	$(A \to B) \wedge (A \to C) \vdash A \to B$	$1 (\wedge E_1)$
3.	$(A \to B) \wedge (A \to C) \vdash A \to C$	$1 (\wedge E_2)$
4.	$A \vdash A$	(Id)
5.	$(A \to B) \wedge (A \to C); A \vdash B$	$2, 4 (\to E)$
6.	$(A \to B) \wedge (A \to C); A \vdash C$	$3, 4 (\to E)$
7.	$(A \to B) \wedge (A \to C); A \vdash B \wedge C$	$5, 6 (\wedge I)$
8.	$(A \to B) \wedge (A \to C) \vdash A \to B \wedge C$	$7 (\to I)$

So conjunction behaves quite normally. The disjunction introduction rules are also simple.

$$\frac{X \vdash A}{X \vdash A \vee B} (\vee I_1) \qquad \frac{X \vdash B}{X \vdash A \vee B} (\vee I_2)$$

The elimination rule is not quite as straightforward as the other rules. It reflects the fact that to prove C from a disjunction, it is sufficient to prove it from both disjuncts.

$$\frac{Y(A) \vdash C \quad Y(B) \vdash C \quad X \vdash A \vee B}{Y(X) \vdash C} (\vee E)$$

Once we have disjunction and the other rules, we can perform proofs such as the one in Figure 2.1.

1.	$(A \to C) \wedge (B \to C) \vdash (A \to C) \wedge (B \to C)$	(Id)
2.	$(A \to C) \wedge (B \to C) \vdash A \to C$	$1 (\wedge E_1)$
3.	$A \vdash A$	(Id)
4.	$(A \to C) \wedge (B \to C); A \vdash C$	$2, 3 (\to E)$
5.	$(A \to C) \wedge (B \to C) \vdash B \to C$	$1 (\wedge E_2)$
6.	$B \vdash B$	(Id)
7.	$(A \to C) \wedge (B \to C); B \vdash C$	$5, 6 (\to E)$
8.	$A \vee B \vdash A \vee B$	(Id)
9.	$(A \to C) \wedge (B \to C); A \vee B \vdash C$	$4, 7, 8 (\vee I)$
10.	$(A \to C) \wedge (B \to C) \vdash A \vee B \to C$	$9 (\to I)$

Figure 2.1: Proof of $(A \to C) \wedge (B \to C) \vdash A \vee B \to C$

DEFINITION 2.34 (EXTENSIONAL CONJUNCTION AND DISJUNCTION)
The connectives $\wedge$, *extensional conjunction* and $\vee$, *extensional disjunction* are
defined by the rules $(\wedge I)$, $(\wedge E_1)$, $(\wedge E_2)$ and $(\vee I_1)$, $(\vee I_2)$, $(\vee E)$, respectively.

This way of adding conjunction and disjunction is proof-theoretically very simple. These connectives are the *additive conjunction and disjunction* of linear
logic. Algebraists will recognise that in $\wedge$ and $\vee$ we have the standard *lattice*
operators. The conjunction $\wedge$ is a *greatest lower bound*, in that $A \wedge B$ entails both
A and B, and any C entailing both A and B also entails $A \wedge B$. The disjunction
$\vee$ is a *least upper bound*: either of A and B entail $A \vee B$, and if A entails C and
B also entails C then $A \vee B$ also entails C.

Lattice operators like $\wedge$ and $\vee$ need not be *distributive*. That is, in our context
we need not have a proof of the following consecution.

$$A \wedge (B \vee C) \vdash (A \wedge B) \vee (A \wedge C)$$

Any proof of this consecution (and Figure 2.2 is an example of such a proof)
must appeal to the structural rules WI, K′ and K. There is no way to prove
distribution without appealing to these structural rules. What are we to make
of this? It is obvious that in many of our applications of our logics, none of WI,
K′ and K are valid. Yet it is just as clear that in some of these interpretations,
distribution is valid. Consider function typing. A function f is of type $A \wedge B$ if
and only if it is of type A and of type B, and it is of type $A \vee B$ if and only if
it is either of type A or of type B. Clearly, $A \wedge (B \vee C) \vdash (A \wedge B) \vee (A \wedge C)$
ought to be valid, as anything is of type $A \wedge (B \vee C)$ only if it is of type A and of
type $B \vee C$, but this is only if it is of type B or of type C, so it must be of type
$(A \wedge B) \vee (A \wedge C)$ as desired. The same reasoning goes through with syntax or
in actions. But in none of these interpretations do any of WI, K′ or K come out
as valid.

The way ahead for logics which validate distribution was found independently by J. Michael Dunn [72] and Grigori Mints [172] when they were working on the proof theory of the relevant logic R. They showed that it is possible
to prove distribution of $\wedge$ over $\vee$ without altering the logic of $\rightarrow$, $\circ$ and t (that
is, without changing the behaviour of the semicolon). They did this by adding a
new punctuation mark. In our work we will use the comma for this new notion.
The idea is that X, Y is a new type of structure, and that the comma mirrors the
behaviour of *conjunction* (just as the semicolon mirrors the behaviour of *fusion*).
How do we interpret the comma in our systems? Recall that in the functional
interpretation an object is of type $X; Y$ if and only if it is an object of type X
applied to an object of type Y. Well, the comma is simpler. An object is of type
X, Y if and only if it is an object of type X as well as an object of type Y. A

1.	$A \wedge (B \vee C) \vdash A \wedge (B \vee C)$	(Id)
2.	$A \wedge (B \vee C) \vdash A$	$1\,(\wedge E_1)$
3.	$B; A \wedge (B \vee C) \vdash A$	$2\,[\mathsf{K}']$
4.	$B \vdash B$	(Id)
5.	$B; A \wedge (B \vee C) \vdash B$	$4\,[\mathsf{K}]$
6.	$B; A \wedge (B \vee C) \vdash A \wedge B$	$3, 5\,(\wedge I)$
7.	$B; A \wedge (B \vee C) \vdash (A \wedge B) \vee (A \wedge C)$	$6\,(\vee I_1)$
8.	$C; A \wedge (B \vee C) \vdash A$	$2\,[\mathsf{K}']$
9.	$C \vdash C$	(Id)
10.	$C; A \wedge (B \vee C) \vdash C$	$9\,[\mathsf{K}]$
11.	$C; A \wedge (B \vee C) \vdash A \wedge C$	$8, 10\,(\wedge I)$
12.	$C; A \wedge (B \vee C) \vdash (A \wedge B) \vee (A \wedge C)$	$11\,(\vee I_2)$
13.	$A \wedge (B \vee C) \vdash B \vee C$	$1\,(\wedge E_2)$
14.	$A \wedge (B \vee C); A \wedge (B \vee C) \vdash (A \wedge B) \vee (A \wedge C)$	$7, 12, 13\,(\vee E)$
15.	$A \wedge (B \vee C) \vdash (A \wedge B) \vee (A \wedge C)$	$14\,[\mathsf{WI}]$

Figure 2.2: Proof of Distribution of $\wedge$ over $\vee$

similar story goes through for other readings of our logics, which I leave for you to check. The comma will satisfy the structural rules in Table 2.3.

Name	Label	Rule
Associativity	eB	$X, (Y, Z) \Leftarrow (X, Y), Z$
Commutativity	eCl	$X, Y \Leftarrow Y, X$
Contraction	eWl	$X, X \Leftarrow X$
Weakening	eK	$X \Leftarrow X, Y$

Table 2.3: Extensional Structural Rules

These structural rules are labelled with 'e' because they are the *extensional* versions of their intensional cousins. Given these structural rules, we can run through the proof in Figure 2.2 with the semicolon replaced by the comma. There is one small wrinkle. You must use eCl and eK to simulate the K' rule as follows: $A \wedge (B \vee C) \vdash A$ with eK gives $A \wedge (B \vee C), C \vdash A$, which using eCl gives $C, A \wedge (B \vee C) \vdash A$.

It will be shown in Chapters 9 and 11[10] that adding the comma with these structural rules does not alter the properties of any connectives other than $\wedge$ and $\vee$. This is not *obvious*, because there just might be a consecution involving just the intensional fragment (say, the semicolon, fusion and implication), which can be proved by taking a detour through the extensional language (using comma, $\wedge$ and $\vee$) but which cannot be proved without taking such a detour.

Such things happen in other logical systems. For example, the consecution $(p \supset q) \supset q \vdash p$ is not provable in the standard natural deduction system for classical logic when you remove negation from the system. Any proof of this consecution (called 'Peirce's Law' after the American logician and philosopher Charles Sanders Peirce, working in the late 19th Century) in the natural deduction system requires a detour through negation, even though negation does not appear in the consecution itself. That shows that either the original system without negation was incomplete or that adding classical negation to it is a *mistaken* addition. We will show that this sort of thing does not happen with the addition of extensional structure. At no stage does this addition disrupt any logics given by our natural deduction systems. This indicates that natural deduction systems are "robust" in some sense. There is a healthy separation between the extensional structure, which is tied closely to the entailment relation, and the intensional structure, which sits more loosely.

2.6   Cutting and Pasting Proofs

The *Cut* rule is important in proof theories.

$$\frac{X \vdash A \quad Y(A) \vdash B}{Y(X) \vdash B} \text{ (Cut)}$$

In an inference of this form we "cut out" the middle term A. In our systems the inference is *admissible*, meaning that whenever we have a proof of the premises, there is also a proof of the conclusion. So there is no need to add it as a new rule, for adding it will not increase the stock of provable consecutions. To show that our systems have this property, we need to give a few more definitions.

DEFINITION 2.35 (PARAMETERS AND FAMILIES OF PARAMETERS)
In an inference *Inf* falling under some rule, a collection of instances of a structure X is said to be a *family of parameters* if and only if for all structures Y, the inference $Inf(Y)$, given by replacing all of those instances of X in *Inf* by Y, is also an instance of that rule. A structure X occurring in a family of parameters in an inference is said to be a *parameter*.

---

[10] We give a different proof in each chapter, one using propositional structures and the other using frames.

For example, any inference of the form

$$\frac{X \vdash A \quad Y \vdash B}{X;Y \vdash A \circ B}$$

both occurrences of X and its substructures are parameters, as are both occurrences of Y and its substructures, but $X;Y$ is not a parameter, and neither is A, B or $A \circ B$.

DEFINITION 2.36 (CONGRUENCE OF PARAMETERS)
Two structures in an inference are said to be *congruent* if they are both members of the same family of parameters in that inference.

So, in that rule instance above, both instances of X are congruent, as are both instances of Y. If $X = (\bullet Y; Z)$, then the instances of Y in those instances of X are congruent with each other (and with themselves) but they are not congruent with the other instances of Y in that inference.

DEFINITION 2.37 (ANTECEDENT REGULARITY)
A system is *antecedent regular* if for every inference in the system other than (Id) each formula in the antecedent of the conclusion of that inference is a parameter.

Note that every system made from any of our rules is antecedent regular. For example, in the inference

$$\frac{X \vdash A \vee B \quad Y(A) \vdash C \quad Y(B) \vdash C}{Y(X) \vdash C} (\vee E)$$

each formula appearing in $Y(X)$ is a parameter. Its parametric family consists of the formula instance itself, and the corresponding instances occurring in either X in the first premise or in both $Y(A)$ and $Y(B)$ in the second premise.

THEOREM 2.38 (CUT ADMISSIBILITY FOR NATURAL DEDUCTION)
Cut is admissible in every antecedent regular system.

PROOF Take a proof of $Y(A) \vdash B$. We transform it into a proof of $Y(X) \vdash B$, given that we also have a proof of $X \vdash A$ at hand. An instance of the formula A is said to *match* the A in $Y(A) \vdash B$ if either it is in the parametric family of A or it is in the parametric family of some other instance of A which already matches A. Consider the tree given by replacing every matching A in the proof of $Y(A) \vdash B$ by X. This is almost a proof of $Y(A) \vdash B$. Every arc in the tree is an instance of a rule, as rules are closed under substitution of parametric families. The only place where we do not have this substitution is instances of the axioms. The only leaves which might have changed from the old proof to the new one are those of the form $A \vdash A$. But these change to $X \vdash A$, and we have a proof of this consecution, so we can simply "paste" this proof on to conclude $X \vdash A$, giving us the desired proof.   □

This construction is an important one. We will see more of it in Chapter 7, when we analyse the structure of proofs in more detail.

2.7 Putting Things Together

We have actually seen a whole host of formal systems here, so we need a notation for naming different points on the landscape we have sketched out. There is no standard notation as yet, so I will propose one.

The idea is this. We name a logic by listing its structural rules. So, a logic which uses B, C and W, I will call BCW. For Right Push and Right Pop we will use rPu and rPo as abbreviations, and similarly lPu and lPo for Left Push and Left Pop. rP abbreviates rPu + rPo, lP abbreviates lPu + lPo, and P abbreviates rP + lP.

If in addition we use the comma, we prefix a 'D' to indicate the presence of distribution of conjunction over disjunction. So, DBCW is the logic BCW with the addition of the comma as a punctuation mark to the semicolon.

This leaves out one basic logic: the logic without any structural rules at all. We will call this 'BSub' for 'basic substructural logic', and its distributive sibling is 'DBSub.'

So much for structural rules. We also have a choice of connectives. If the logic has the full complement of connectives we have discussed ($\rightarrow$, $\leftarrow$, $\circ$, t, $\top$, $\bot$, $\wedge$, $\vee$) we will leave the name as it is. If it uses fewer connectives, we will list them in brackets after the name. So, BCW$[\rightarrow, \circ]$ is the logic with rules for only $\rightarrow$ and $\circ$. Table 2.4 lists some popular logics.

The logics L and LI in this table are associated with reasoning about syntactic strings. In these logics we consider fusion and the semicolon to be string concatenation. This is clearly associative, so B and B^c are sensible rules. In the case of LI, we admit an identity for both the left and the right of concatenation, which is the type of the empty string.

The logics TW$^+$, T$^+$, E$^+$ and R$^+$ are all motivated by considerations of the need for relevance in everyday logical consequence. In the logic R$^+$, for example, premise combination by the semicolon reflects the condition that both premises collected together were *used* in the conclusion deduced. However, the order of the premises used or the number of times they are re-used are irrelevant, so C and W are admitted as structural rules. For E$^+$, the condition on use is *tighter*, as the arrow is intended to encode *entailment* and not merely the

Our Label	Common Label	Name
$BB^c[\rightarrow, \leftarrow, \circ]$	L	Lambek Associative Calculus
$BB^cP[\rightarrow, \leftarrow, \circ, t]$	LI	Lambek Associative Calculus with Identity
$DBBlP'[\rightarrow, \circ, \wedge, \vee, t]$	TW$^+$	Positive Ticket Entailment without Contraction
$DBBlP'W[\rightarrow, \circ, \wedge, \vee, t]$	T$^+$	Positive Ticket Entailment
$DBB'lPrPuW[\rightarrow, \circ, \wedge, \vee, t]$	E$^+$	Positive Entailment
DBCW	R$^+$	Positive Relevant Logic
DBCWM	RM$^+$	Positive Relevant Logic with Mingle
BC	MALL$^+$	Positive Multiplicative Additive Linear Logic
BCK	BCK	Positive Affine Logic
BCWK	J	Intuitionistic Logic
$BCWK[\wedge, \vee, \rightarrow]$		Minimal Logic

Table 2.4: Some Popular Logics

conditionality of R$^+$. C and its cousins make no sense on this interpretation, as they make consecutions such as

$$A \vdash (A \rightarrow B) \rightarrow B$$

valid. This is not valid if '$\rightarrow$' is read as entailment, for which a certain amount of *necessity* is required for an entailment to be true. $A \rightarrow B$ means not just that if A happens to be true so does B, but rather that *however things might turn out*, if A is true, B is true too. Given this reading, it is possible to construct counterexamples to our suspect consecution: let A and B be merely contingent, but such that A really entails B. For example, A is 'Greg is a philosophy lecturer' and B is 'Greg is an academic'), B ought not be *entailed* by $A \rightarrow B$, as there are plenty of possibilities in which $A \rightarrow B$ is true, but in which B fails.

In E$^+$ premises cannot be reordered arbitrarily, but a degree of reassociation is allowed. The reassociation in B and B' is enough to give us the rules of prefixing and suffixing,

$$A \rightarrow B \quad \vdash \quad (C \rightarrow A) \rightarrow (C \rightarrow B)$$
$$A \rightarrow B \quad \vdash \quad (B \rightarrow C) \rightarrow (A \rightarrow C)$$

which clearly make sense when reading '$\rightarrow$' as entailment. The logic of E$^+$ has the right push rule rPu, which ensures that t satisfies $t \rightarrow A \vdash A$ but not that $A \vdash t \rightarrow A$. If we read t as 'logic,' then this too makes sense. If A is entailed by logic then it follows that A must be true. However, if A is true, it need not follow that it be entailed by logic. It may be merely contingent.

You can go weaker still than E$^+$ by disregarding any thought of t and by restricting yourself to B, B$'$ and W. This is the logic T$^+$ of "ticket" entailment. The idea behind this logic is to distinguish between true conditionals, which are inference tickets from premises to conclusions, and other formulae. The condition restricting premise combination is that implications cannot be used as information in ways other than as tickets for inference. This brings $t \rightarrow A \vdash A$, and its cousin $(A \rightarrow A) \rightarrow A \vdash A$ into question, as in these, the formula t, or $A \rightarrow A$, is not used as a ticket for inference but rather as an antecedent for further inference. Volume 1 of *Entailment* contains a lengthy discussion of this distinction [6, pages 41–44].

Linear logic was motivated by considerations of resource use. The idea here was that antecedents must be used once and once only in the proof of a consequent. This means that contraction is not allowed, in that this suppresses duplicate uses of the one resource. Similarly, weakening is not allowed as this introduces resources which are not used in generating the conclusion. The stronger logic BCK allows weakening but still bars contraction. Linear logic and BCK have traditionally been studied with extensional conjunction and disjunction, but in the absence of distribution. This has largely been because these logics have been studied in the context of proof theory, in which distribution is hard to deal with. In what follows we will be studying all of our systems in the presence of distribution and in its absence.

If you add contraction to BCK you allow all of the structural rules, and you end up with a well-known logic — intuitionistic logic. Intuitionistic negation is recovered by setting $\sim A$ to be $A \rightarrow \bot$. In the absence of $\bot$, you have no negation, and you have Johansson's minimal logic.

2.8   History

Work on proof theory has a long and noble history. Gerhard Gentzen first formulated systems of natural deduction for intuitionistic and classical logic in the 1930s [93]. See Prawitz's monograph [196] for a good account of the history of the development of natural deduction.

While Gentzen did define natural deduction with consecutions, most of the early work on natural deduction stems from Gentzen's *other* formulation of natural deduction proofs. He also defined proofs as trees of formulae. The introduction rules for conjunction and disjunction have these forms

$$\frac{A \quad B}{A \wedge B} \qquad \frac{A}{A \vee B} \qquad \frac{B}{A \vee B}$$

The elimination rules for conjunction and the conditional are straightforward

$$\frac{A \wedge B}{A} \qquad \frac{A \wedge B}{B} \qquad \frac{A \quad A \to B}{B}$$

But for the other rules, you must do more work to keep track of assumptions. The idea is that some of the leaves above any node in the proof tree are the *open assumptions* at that node. Some of the inferences *close* assumptions. For example, the implication introduction rule is of this form:

$$\frac{\begin{array}{c} [A] \\ \vdots \\ B \end{array}}{A \to B}$$

which indicates that at the node for B there is a collection of open assumptions A, and we can derive $A \to B$, closing those assumptions. Different systems can be given by varying the behaviour of the rules which close assumptions. For example, you may only allow one assumption to be closed at a time — or you may allow assumptions to be closed only in a particular order. It is clear that this is similar to the behaviour of structural rules in the systems we have studied. However, it is not as powerful — you do not have the same control over assumptions as you do in our systems, in which you keep the assumptions explicit at every step. That is enough of the story of natural deduction proof theories.

The particular systems we have considered arose in many different contexts. Concern for the way premises are used perhaps first surfaced in the work of relevant logicians. Došen has shown us that this dates back to 1928 with Orlov's axiomatisation of the implication–negation fragment of the relevant logic R [64]. However, the obvious historical antecedents for work on relevant logic are Moh and Church, who formulated R[∘, →] in the mid-1950s [46, 245] and Ackermann, who formulated E in the late 1950s [2]. Work on relevant logic was established by Anderson and Belnap, along with many others, including their students Dunn and Meyer. See their *Entailment* [6, 7] for much of the work, and for many detailed references. As we have already noted, the proof theory of relevant logics in the style we are using was first given independently by Mints and Dunn, though their work was on Gentzen-style consecution systems (with introduction rules for connectives in the antecedent and consequent, instead of introduction and elimination rules in the consequent).

Lambek worked on his calculus (our $BB^c[\rightarrow, \leftarrow]$) in order to model the behaviour of syntactic types. He used proof-theoretical means like these — as well as techniques from category theory, which we will see later [133, 134]. The systems Lambek studied were in the language $\rightarrow, \leftarrow, \circ$ (he wrote these as $'/, \backslash, \bullet'$). It is clear, however, that other connectives can work well in this interpretation. A string is of type $X; Y$ if and only if it is the concatenation of a string of type X with one of type Y. This motivates the structural rules B and B^c for the semicolon. However, extensional structure is also possible. A string is of type X, Y just when it is *both* of type X and of type Y. This motivates all of the extensional structural rules and gives us a standard logic of conjunction and disjunction when reasoning about syntactic types [213]. We will consider more about the behaviour of this sort of logic in later chapters.

Logics without the contraction rule W and related rules are important in the analysis of the paradoxes of self-reference [54, 91, 170, 246, 209]. Consider the claim

$$\text{If } \langle p \rangle \text{ is true then } q$$

where $\langle p \rangle$ is a name for the displayed proposition. If '$\langle p \rangle$ is true' is true if and only if $\langle p \rangle$ is (which seems reasonable enough) then we have the following valid consecutions.

$$p \vdash p \rightarrow q \qquad p \rightarrow q \vdash p$$

However, given just a little reasoning we can deduce q.

$$
\cfrac{
  \cfrac{
    \cfrac{
      \cfrac{
        \cfrac{p \vdash p \rightarrow q \quad p \vdash p}{p; p \vdash q}(\rightarrow E)
      }{p \vdash q}[\text{WI}]
    }{0 \vdash p \rightarrow q}[\text{Left Push}],(\rightarrow I) \quad p \rightarrow q \vdash p
  }{0 \vdash p}[\text{Cut}]
  \quad
  \cfrac{
    \cfrac{p \vdash p \rightarrow q \quad p \vdash p}{p; p \vdash q}(\rightarrow E)
  }{p \vdash q}[\text{WI}]
}{0 \vdash q}[\text{Cut}]
$$

But q was completely arbitrary, so we ought not be able to prove it by means of logic alone! In the absence of WI this proof breaks down, and this has motivated many to seek an understanding of logics without the contraction rule and rules like it.

Some historical research by Hazen has revealed that in Russell's 1906 paper "The Theory of Implication" his propositional logic (without negation) is free of the rule W [112, 232]. It is only when negation is introduced that contraction can be proved.

Meyer and Routley [167] did a great deal of work showing how a whole host of logics fit together, all with the theme of *residuation* or the connection of fusion with implication. The presentation most accessible and most similar to our own is given by Slaney [250], in which he presents this natural deduction system as a general framework for many different systems.

Finally, Girard, in 1987, introduced *linear logic*, which is a particular system that allows commuting and reassociating of premises, but no contraction or weakening [96]. Perhaps his major innovation is to add particular *modalities* that allow the recovery of these structural rules in a limited, controlled fashion. We will consider how to treat one-place operators like modalities and negations in the next chapter. Girard's notation for the connectives differs from the one we have chosen here. We will end this section with a little translation manual, in Figure 2.3.[11]

Connective	Here	Girard
Implication	$A \to B$	$A \multimap B$
Negation	$\sim A$	$A^\perp$
Fusion	$A \circ B$	$A \otimes B$
t	t	$\mathbf{1}$
Conjunction	$A \wedge B$	$A \& B$
Disjunction	$A \vee B$	$A \oplus B$
Top	$\top$	$\top$
Bottom	$\perp$	$\mathbf{0}$

Figure 2.3: Translation between our notation and that of Linear Logic

2.9 Exercises

Each set of exercises is divided into three sections. *Practice* questions reinforce the ideas and concepts of the chapter. *Problem* questions extend the techniques to other areas and fill in proofs absent from the main text. *Project* questions are research projects in their own right.

---

[11] We have left out two connectives from the multiplicative and additive fragment linear logic which we have not yet seen. The upside-down ampersand is intensional disjunction. We write this as '+' and call it 'fission', dual to fusion. Similarly, the intensional false constant we will write 'f', and confusingly for us, Girard writes this '$\perp$'.

Practice

{2.1} In the table below, match each consecution with the structural rule needed to prove it.

$A \vdash A \to A$	K'
$B \leftarrow A \vdash (B \leftarrow C) \leftarrow (A \leftarrow C)$	M
$A \wedge (A \to B) \vdash B$	B^c
$A \vdash B \to B$	WI
$A \to B \vdash (B \to C) \to (A \to C)$	B'

{2.2} Show that in any system containing CI as a structural rule, $A \to B$ and $B \leftarrow A$ are equivalent.

{2.3} Prove that if $0 \vdash A$ and $0 \vdash A \to B$, then $0 \vdash B$ too. Then show that $0 \vdash A$ if and only if $0 \vdash t \to A$. Finally, show that $0 \vdash A \circ B \to C$ if and only if $0 \vdash A \to (B \to C)$, if and only if $0 \vdash B \to (C \leftarrow A)$. (BONUS: Try doing this without using *Cut*.)

{2.4} Prove the following consecutions in all systems with the appropriate connective rules.

$$A \to B \vdash A \wedge C \to B \qquad A \to B \vdash A \to B \vee C \qquad 0 \vdash A \wedge B \to A$$
$$0 \vdash A \wedge B \to B \qquad 0 \vdash A \to A \vee B \qquad 0 \vdash B \to A \vee B$$

{2.5} Prove the *family connections* between $\leftarrow$ and $\to$: $A \vdash B \leftarrow (A \to B)$ and $A \vdash (B \leftarrow A) \to B$.

{2.6} Verify these important *fusion facts*: $A \circ (B \vee C) \dashv\vdash (A \circ B) \vee (A \circ C)$, $\bot \vdash \bot \circ A$ and $\bot \vdash A \circ \bot$.

{2.7} Verify these important *implication facts*: $\top \vdash A \to \top$, and $\bot \to A \vdash \bot$. Prove corresponding facts for $\leftarrow$ as well.

Problems

{2.8} Show that the construction of string algebras given on page 15 satisfies the string algebra conditions of Definition 2.6.

{2.9} Find an alternative construction of string algebras.

{2.10} Prove the UNIQUE DECOMPOSITION THEOREM for formulae in languages.

{2.11} State and prove a structural induction theorem for structures.

{2.12} Recall that in our definition of 'proof,' a proof cannot have infinite branches. What would happen if we allowed proofs to have infinite branches? Find one undesirable consequence of modifying the definition in this way.

{2.13} Show that each of fusion, right implication and t is uniquely determined by their rules. That is, if $\circ_1$ and $\circ_2$ both satisfy the fusion introduction and implication rules, then $A \circ_1 B$ and $A \circ_2 B$ are equivalent, and similarly for $\leftarrow$ and t.

{2.14} Try proving each of the following consecutions, noting what structural rules you need to employ to prove them. $A \to B \vdash A \wedge C \to B \wedge C$, $(A \to B) \wedge t \vdash A \wedge C \to B \wedge C$,

$A \to (B \to C) \vdash (A \to B) \to (A \to C)$, $A \to (B \to C) \vdash B \to (A \wedge B \to C)$, $(A \to B) \to A \vdash A$, $0 \vdash (A \to B) \vee (B \to A)$, $A \to (B \vee (C \to D)) \vdash A \to (C \to (B \vee D))$.

{2.15} Explore the relationships between conjunction and fusion in substructural logics of varying strength. In which logics do we have $A \circ B \vdash A \wedge B$? In which logics do we have $A \wedge B \vdash A \circ B$? In which logics do neither hold? In which logics do both hold?

{2.16} In which logics is $A \leftarrow \top$ equivalent to $\top$?

{2.17} In which logics is $A \leftarrow t$ equivalent to t?

{2.18} In which logics is $\top \leftarrow A$ equivalent to $\top$? Is it possible for $\top \leftarrow A$ to be equivalent to A? To $\bot$?

{2.19} Give a rigorous proof that anything provable using B' and B^c can be proved using B and C.

{2.20} Show that if A and B are equivalent in a system, then so are $C(A)$ and $C(B)$, where $C(B)$ is found by replacing the indicated occurrence of A in $C(A)$ by B. (HINT: Try structural induction on the construction of $C(A)$ out of A.)

{2.21} Consider the list of structural rules appearing in Table 2.2. Which rules hold in which application of substructural logics? For those that do not hold in a particular application, find concrete counterexamples. (In some applications this is a relatively straightforward matter. However, in the field of information and entailment answers to this question are a matter of some philosophical debate. The idea is for you to consider the options and give reasons for your answers.)

{2.22} Consider commutativity (the structural rule C). Can you find any applications of substructural logics in which C holds? Similarly for W and K.

{2.23} There is (as yet) no negation connective in any of our systems. However, we can do *something* negation-like with what we have. Take any proposition you like, and call it f, for 'false.' Consider the connective $\sim$ given by defining $\sim A$ to be $A \to f$. Explore the behaviour of $\sim$. How many negation-like properties can be proved of $\sim$?

Try proving each of the following consecutions, noting what structural rules you need to employ. $A \to \sim A \vdash \sim A$, $A \vdash \sim\sim A$, $A \wedge \sim A \vdash f$, $\sim A \wedge \sim B \vdash \sim(A \vee B)$, $A \to \sim B \vdash B \to \sim A$, $A \to B \vdash \sim B \to \sim A$, $\sim A \vee \sim B \vdash \sim(A \wedge B)$, $\sim(A \wedge B) \vdash \sim A \vee \sim B$, $0 \vdash A \vee \sim A$, $\sim\sim A \vdash A$, $\sim(A \vee B) \vdash \sim A \wedge \sim B$.

Projects

{2.24} Consider extensional conjunction and disjunction. Can you find any uses of conjunction and disjunction for which it is obvious that distributivity must fail? Examine the literature on linear logic (especially the literature which considers *applications* of linear logic) to find whether their examples motivate the failure of distributivity. (For more on the failure of distribution, see Belnap's "Life in the Undistributed Middle" [25].)

{2.25} Note that if we have more than one semicolon-like punctuation mark, then it may well be appropriate to have more than one "identity object" 0. Explore this. In particular, find a problem domain in which there are multiple notions of application in which different identities are important.

Chapter 3

Modalities

A Modal Proposition
may be stated as a pure one,
by attaching the mode
to one of the Terms.

— *Richard Whateley*, Elements of Logic, 1826

In the previous chapter we examined the proof theory of conditionals, conjunctions and disjunction, along with a few constants. None of these are *unary* (one-place) connectives. Unary connectives have an important role to play in logic. These unary connectives are *modalities* of various sorts. They modify the content of the formula upon which they operate. For example, $\Box A$ might assert that A is not only true but *necessarily* true. Or $\Diamond A$ might assert that A is *possibly* true. These are "positive" modalities. They typically either weaken or strengthen the content of the claim they modify. We can formalise this definition in the following way:

DEFINITION 3.1 (POSITIVE MODALITIES)
A one-place connective m is a *positive modality* if and only if the rule

$$\frac{A \vdash B}{mA \vdash mB}$$

is valid for all formulae A and B.

Clearly, necessity and possibility are both positive modalities. If A entails B, then the possibility of A entails the possibility of B, and the necessity of A entails the necessity of B. However, other interpretations of modalities other than possibility or necessity also give rise to positive modalities. In the logic of time, 'tomorrow' is a positive modality. If $A \vdash B$, then at any time when A is true so is B. But then at any time at which 'tomorrow A' is true is also one at which 'tomorrow B' is true too.

3.1 Positive Modalities

The simplest example of a positive modality comes from relevant logics of entailment such as E. In these logics t is 'logic,' the conjunction of all theorems, and $\to$ is entailment. In these logics, $t \to A$ is a good candidate for 'A holds as a matter of necessity,' since it states that A is entailed by logic alone. Any connective defined in this way is a positive modality.

LEMMA 3.2 (POSITIVE MODALITIES FROM IMPLICATION)
In any logic of implication, and for any formula C

$$\frac{A \vdash B}{C \to A \vdash C \to B}$$

is valid for all A and B.   □

In E, this $\square$, defined by setting $\square A = t \to A$, is very much like a necessity operator. First of all, the properties of implication give us $\square A \wedge \square B \vdash \square(A \wedge B)$ (from $(t \to A) \wedge (t \to B) \vdash t \to (A \wedge B)$) and $\top \vdash \square\top$ (from $\top \vdash t \to \top$), so $\square$ satisfies two of the conditions of a normal modal operator. The 0 rules give us $t \to A \vdash A$ and $t \to A \vdash t \to (t \to A)$. Or more directly, $\square A \vdash A$ (the characteristic rule T) and $\square A \vdash \square\square A$ (the distinctive behaviour of the logic S4, so we call this the 4 rule).

The parallels with necessity extend to other systems. In the Lambek calculus with identity, $t \to A$ is equivalent to A, but $\top \to A$ behaves like a necessity. A string x is of type $\top \to A$ if and only if for every string y you choose, xy is of type A. It is of type $A \leftarrow \top$ if and only if for every string y, yx is of type A. These are positive operators with many of the features of necessity.

A function is of type $\top \to A$ if its output is of type A, no matter its input. For example, the function $x \mapsto 2x$ (of natural numbers) is of type $\top \to Even$.

Implication defines not only a positive modality — in each case the modality defined by implication is very much like a necessity operator, as the next result shows.

LEMMA 3.3 (IMPLICATION GIVES RISE TO NECESSITIES)
In any logic of implication and conjunction, and for any formula C, $(C \to A) \wedge (C \to B) \vdash C \to (A \wedge B)$ holds for all A and B, and $\top \vdash C \to \top$.   □

These conditions (that $\square A \wedge \square B \vdash \square(A \wedge B)$ and that $\top \vdash \square\top$) are characteristic of modalities like necessity. If A and B are necessary (holds in all related states) then their conjunction is necessary (holds in all related states) too. $\top$ must be necessary as it holds everywhere. This intuitive justification will be made formal in Chapter 11.

There are also "possibility"-type positive modalities inside our systems.

LEMMA 3.4 (FUSION AND POSSIBILITY)
If we set $\Diamond A$ to be $A \circ B$ for some particular B, then $\Diamond$ is a positive modality, $\Diamond(A \vee B) \vdash \Diamond A \vee \Diamond B$ and $\Diamond\bot \vdash \bot$.   □

These conditions are characteristic of possibility-style operators. If $A \vee B$ is possible (true in some related state) then one of A and B must be possible too. Similarly, there is no way that $\bot$ can be possible, as it is true nowhere. As with necessities, this reasoning will be developed in Chapter 11.

In the rest of this section we will abstract away from the detail of necessity and possibility, as defined by implication and fusion, to study operators like these in their generality. In this case, our rules involve another kind of punctuation mark. Consider the introduction and elimination rules for the conditional:

$$\frac{X \vdash C \to A \quad Y \vdash C}{X ; Y \vdash A} \qquad \frac{X ; C \vdash A}{X \vdash C \to A}$$

In both cases we modify the structure X by attaching the information in the antecedent of the conditional (either C itself, or Y, where Y gives us C). We can abstract away the details of this and introduce rules for a necessity operator $\Box$ which instead modifies the structure X with a one-place punctuation mark $\bullet$.

DEFINITION 3.5 (RULES FOR NECESSITY)
The introduction and elimination rules for a necessity operator are as follows:

$$\frac{X \vdash \Box A}{\bullet X \vdash A} \; (\Box E) \qquad \frac{\bullet X \vdash A}{X \vdash \Box A} \; (\Box I)$$

Note that these rules are antecedent regular.

LEMMA 3.6 ($\Box$ IS A NECESSITY)
In any antecedent regular proof system, a necessity $\Box$ is a positive modality, and in addition, we have $\Box A \wedge \Box B \vdash \Box(A \wedge B)$ when $\wedge$ is present, and $\top \vdash \Box\top$ when $\top$ is present.

PROOF   The rules for conjunction and $\top$ are quite simple to demonstrate.

$$\frac{\dfrac{\dfrac{\Box A \vdash \Box A}{\Box A \wedge \Box B \vdash \Box A}}{\bullet(\Box A \wedge \Box B) \vdash A} \quad \dfrac{\dfrac{\Box B \vdash \Box B}{\Box A \wedge \Box B \vdash \Box B}}{\bullet(\Box A \wedge \Box B) \vdash B}}{\dfrac{\bullet(\Box A \wedge \Box B) \vdash A \wedge B}{\Box A \wedge \Box B \vdash \Box(A \wedge B)}} \qquad \frac{\dfrac{\bullet\top \vdash \top}{\top \vdash \Box\top}}{}$$

For preservation of order a little more work is needed. There seems to be no simple way to use $A \vdash B$ in a proof of $\Box A \vdash \Box B$. The rules for $\Box$ seem to say that $\Box A \vdash \Box B$ ought to come from $\bullet\Box A \vdash B$. But where can this come from? There is, in general, no proof of $\bullet\Box A \vdash B$ from $A \vdash B$. However, we need not construct our proof in that way. Rather, we can use the Cut Theorem (Theorem 2.38, page 38). As the system is antecedent regular, we can use the proof

$$\frac{\Box A \vdash \Box A}{\bullet\Box A \vdash A}$$

and cut this with our proof of $A \vdash B$ (whatever this proof might be, in our system) to get a proof of $\bullet\Box A \vdash B$, from which we can derive $\Box A \vdash \Box B$. So the proof of $\Box A \vdash \Box B$ may not use $A \vdash B$ as a hypothesis. Rather, it will be found by transforming the proof of $A \vdash B$.   □

Positive modalities might not just be necessitive. We have already seen that fusion gives rise to modalities which are like possibility operators.

DEFINITION 3.7 (RULES FOR POSSIBILITY)
The introduction and elimination rules for a possibility operator are as follows:

$$\frac{X \vdash A}{\bullet X \vdash \Diamond A}\,(\Diamond I) \qquad \frac{X \vdash \Diamond A \quad Y(\bullet A) \vdash B}{Y(X) \vdash B}\,(\Diamond E)$$

These are related to fusion in the same way as the necessity rules are related to implication. We use '$\Diamond$' instead of '$\Diamond$' in this definition because the modality so defined is not related to $\Box$ by a definition as $\sim\Box\sim$, as possibility is often defined, but rather, they are tied together by the following rule:

LEMMA 3.8 ($\Box$ AND $\Diamond$)
If $\Box$ and $\Diamond$ are defined in the one antecedent regular proof system, then $\Diamond A \vdash B$ is provable if and only if $A \vdash \Box B$ is provable.

PROOF   For right to left, we have the proof

$$\frac{\Diamond A \vdash \Diamond A \quad \dfrac{\dfrac{A \vdash \Box B}{\bullet A \vdash B}\,(\Box E)}{}}{\Diamond A \vdash B}\,(\Diamond E)$$

For left to right, we cut on $\bullet A \vdash \Diamond A$ (which is provable) and $\Diamond A \vdash B$ (our assumption) to get $\bullet A \vdash B$ and hence $A \vdash \Box B$.   □

With or without the presence of $\Box$, $\Diamond$ is a possibility-type modality.

LEMMA 3.9 ($\Diamond$ IS A POSSIBILITY)
For any $\Diamond$ defined using the possibility rules, $\Diamond$ is a positive modality, $\Diamond(A \vee B) \vdash \Diamond A \vee \Diamond B$ and $\Diamond\bot \vdash \bot$, in logics with $\vee$ and $\bot$.

PROOF The positive modality and $\bot$ properties are simple to prove:

$$\cfrac{\cfrac{A \vdash B}{\lozenge A \vdash \lozenge A \quad \bullet A \vdash \lozenge B}(\lozenge I)}{\lozenge A \vdash \lozenge B}(\lozenge E) \qquad \cfrac{\cfrac{\bot \vdash \bot}{\lozenge \bot \vdash \lozenge \bot \quad \bullet \bot \vdash \bot}(\bot E)}{\lozenge \bot \vdash \bot}(\lozenge E)$$

For the disjunction property, we have

$$\cfrac{\cfrac{\cfrac{\cfrac{A \vdash A}{\bullet A \vdash \lozenge A}(\lozenge I)}{\bullet A \vdash \lozenge A \vee \lozenge B}(\vee I) \qquad \cfrac{\cfrac{B \vdash B}{\bullet B \vdash \lozenge B}(\lozenge I)}{\bullet B \vdash \lozenge A \vee \lozenge B}(\vee I)}{\bullet (A \vee B) \vdash \lozenge A \vee \lozenge B}(\vee E)}{\lozenge(A \vee B) \vdash \lozenge A \vee \lozenge B}(\lozenge E) \qquad \qquad \square$$

(with $A \vee B \vdash A \vee B$ on the left feeding $(\vee E)$)

As with the intensional family, $\square$ and $\lozenge$ belong together, and as with that family, one connective especially mirrors the structure. In this case $\lozenge$ has the logical properties of $\bullet$.

DEFINITION 3.10 (THE MODAL FAMILY)
$\square$ and $\lozenge$ constitute the *modal family*, and $\lozenge$ is the parent of the family.

Label	Rule		
T	$\bullet X$	$\Leftarrow$	X
4	$\bullet X$	$\Leftarrow$	$\bullet\bullet X$
Kr	0	$\Leftarrow$	$\bullet 0$
Kr^c	$\bullet 0$	$\Leftarrow$	0
mMP	$\bullet X; \bullet Y$	$\Leftarrow$	$\bullet(X; Y)$
mWI	$\bullet X; \bullet X$	$\Leftarrow$	$\bullet X$
mK	X	$\Leftarrow$	$X; \bullet Y$
m2t	$\bullet X$	$\Leftarrow$	$X; 0$
t2m	$X; 0$	$\Leftarrow$	$\bullet X$
m2T	$\bullet X$	$\Leftarrow$	$X; Y$
T2m	$X; \top$	$\Leftarrow$	$\bullet X$

Table 3.1: Modal Structural Rules

Once we have modal operators, defined by the structural operator •, structural rules dictating the behaviour of • are inherited by the logics of $\Box$ and $\diamondsuit$. Table 3.1 lists some possible structural rules involving •. The first two rules are adopted from classical modal logic. The rule T is enough to prove $\Box A \vdash A$.

$$\dfrac{\dfrac{\Box A \vdash \Box A}{\bullet \Box A \vdash A}\ (\Box E)}{\Box A \vdash A}\ [\mathsf{T}]$$

The rule 4 enables a proof of $\Box A \vdash \Box\Box A$ as follows.

$$\dfrac{\dfrac{\dfrac{\dfrac{\Box A \vdash \Box A}{\bullet \Box A \vdash A}\ (\Box E)}{\bullet\bullet \Box A \vdash A}\ [4]}{\bullet \Box A \vdash \Box A}\ (\Box I)}{\Box A \vdash \Box\Box A}\ (\Box I)$$

The other rules in our table give us connections between the modal part of the language and the intensional part. Kr gives you both $t \vdash \Box t$ and $\diamondsuit t \vdash t$, while Kr^c is sufficient for the converses, $\Box t \vdash t$ and $t \vdash \diamondsuit t$ (confirming these is left to the exercises). The rule mMP (modal *modus ponens*) gives us $\Box(A \to B) \vdash \Box A \to \Box B$ as follows

$$\dfrac{\dfrac{\dfrac{\dfrac{\dfrac{\Box(A \to B) \vdash \Box(A \to B)}{\bullet\Box(A \to B) \vdash A \to B}\ (\Box E) \qquad \dfrac{\Box A \vdash \Box A}{\bullet\Box A \vdash A}\ (\Box E)}{\bullet\Box(A \to B);\bullet\Box A \vdash B}\ (\to E)}{\bullet(\Box(A \to B);\Box A) \vdash B}\ [\mathsf{mMP}]}{\Box(A \to B);\Box A \vdash \Box B}\ (\Box I)}{\Box(A \to B) \vdash \Box A \to \Box B}\ (\to I)$$

mWI and mK allow us to contract and weaken (respectively) in modalised premises. With mWI you can prove $\Box A \vdash \Box(A \circ A)$, for example

$$\dfrac{\dfrac{\dfrac{\dfrac{\Box A \vdash \Box A}{\bullet\Box A \vdash A}\ (\Box E) \qquad \dfrac{\Box A \vdash \Box A}{\bullet\Box A \vdash A}\ (\Box E)}{\bullet\Box A;\bullet\Box A \vdash A \circ A}\ (\circ I)}{\bullet\Box A \vdash A \circ A}\ [\mathsf{mWI}]}{\Box A \vdash \Box(A \circ A)}\ (\Box I)$$

With mK, you can prove $A \circ \Diamond B \vdash A$

$$\cfrac{A \circ \Diamond B \vdash A \circ \Diamond B \qquad \cfrac{\Diamond B \vdash \Diamond B \qquad \cfrac{\cfrac{A \vdash A}{A; \bullet B \vdash A} \, [\text{mK}]}{A; \Diamond B \vdash A} \, (\Diamond E)}{A; \Diamond B \vdash A}}{A \circ \Diamond B \vdash A} \, (\circ E)$$

The rules m2t and t2m provide $\Box A \vdash t \to A$ and $t \to A \vdash \Box A$ respectively. For example, we have

$$\cfrac{\cfrac{\cfrac{t \to A \vdash t \to A \quad 0 \vdash t}{(t \to A); 0 \vdash A} \, (\to E)}{\bullet(t \to A) \vdash A} \, [\text{t2m}]}{t \to A \vdash \Box A} \, (\Box I)$$

The rule m2⊤ provides $\Box A \vdash \top \to A$ in a similar way. We have

$$\cfrac{\cfrac{\cfrac{\Box A \vdash \Box A}{\bullet \Box A \vdash A} \, (\Box E)}{\Box A; \top \vdash A} \, [\text{m2t}]}{\Box A \vdash \top \to A} \, (\to I)$$

You might think that the converse of the m2⊤ rule, $X; Y \Leftarrow \bullet X$, would be appropriate to prove converse consecution, $\top \to A \vdash \Box A$. However, that would be wrong, as the structural rule $X; Y \Leftarrow \bullet X$ is *too* strong. With it, you get

$$\cfrac{\Diamond A \vdash \Diamond A \qquad \cfrac{\cfrac{A; \bot \vdash \bot}{\bullet A \vdash \bot} \, (??)}{\Diamond A \vdash \bot}}{\Diamond A \vdash \bot} \, (\Diamond E)$$

which is not a particularly savoury result. In particular, it does not follow from the consecution $\top \to A \vdash \Box A$, so we need a different rule to model this consecution. A suitable rule is

$$\cfrac{X; \top \vdash A}{\bullet X \vdash A} \, [\top 2\text{m}]$$

However, this is not, strictly speaking, a structural rule — the formula $\top$ is not a parameter in the antecedent of the premise.

So these rules go some way towards connecting the modality $\Box$ with implication, as our original examples of necessity defined it. However, with this new machinery, we can allow *some* connection between necessity (or possibility) and implication without defining necessity in terms of implication. One example might be in the logic E. In E, t is best read as 'logic.' We may hold that if A is entailed by logic, then A is indeed necessary, so $t \to A \vdash \Box A$. However, you might think that is not the only way a proposition may be necessarily true. Perhaps there are necessary truths not entailed by logic alone. The truths of mathematics, for the non-logicist, might be an example. In that case, you would allow t2m but reject m2t. Other combinations might be motivated in other interpretations of these formal systems.

This approach is one way to define positive modalities in substructural logics. In later chapters we will study the behaviour of such modalities. Before going on to study negative modalities (negations), we need to consider some modal operators outside this class.

3.2   Non-Normal Modalities

Each modal operator discussed so far has certain "distribution" properties. Connectives with these properties are called *normal* modal operators, for reasons we will come to when we discuss frame semantics in Chapter 11. There are other modalities which arise in substructural logics which do not have these distribution properties. We will look at just two modalities of this form.

Consider the Lambek calculus, used for interpreting syntactic types. If some string has type A, we might be interested in strings which are made up of *iterating* strings of type A. For example, if we have the category of noun, we might be interested in the category list of noun. Something is a list of noun if and only if it is either a noun, or a noun concatenated with another noun, or a string of three nouns, or four nouns, and so on. Writing $A \circ A$ as A^2, $A \circ (A \circ A)$ as A^3, and in general, $A \circ A^n$ as A^{n+1}, we have a natural type A^* defined by setting

$$A^* = A \vee A^2 \vee A^3 \vee \cdots$$

This modality $*$ is called the Kleene star operation for *iteration*. The Kleene star is like neither a possibility nor a necessity. It is easy to see that it is not a possibility, because

$$(A \vee B)^* \vdash A^* \vee B^*$$

ought to fail, since something might be a string of objects which are each either As or Bs, without being either a string of As or a string of Bs. For example, let A be the type of the string a, and let B be the type of the string b. Then the string abab is a string of $A \vee B$s, but it is not a string of As or a string of Bs.

It is a bit harder to show that $*$ is not a necessity by showing that

$$A^* \wedge B^* \vdash (A \wedge B)^*$$

ought to fail, but it does. Consider the same string abab as before, but now let A be the type of two-letter strings and let B be the type of palindromes (strings which are the same backwards as forwards). The string abab is a concatenation of two two-letter strings, ab and ab, so it has type A^*. It is also a concatenation of two palindromes, aba and b, so it has type B^*. Is the string also of type $(A \wedge B)^*$? Unfortunately not. A string is of type $A \wedge B$ if and only if it is a two-letter palindrome — something of the form aa or bb. The string abab is not the concatenation of a list of two-letter palindromes, as you can see. So the Kleene star is not a necessity operator.

This means that there is no hope of modelling the * operator with the rules of the previous section. However, this does not mean that the operator cannot be modelled. First, note that it ought to satisfy at least these two rules:

$$\frac{X \vdash A}{X \vdash A^*} \ (*I) \qquad \frac{X \vdash A^* \quad Y \vdash A^*}{X;Y \vdash A^*} \ (*M)$$

The first tells us that anything of type A is also of type A^*. The second tells us that anything which is a concatenation of two objects of type A^* is also of type A^*. This goes some way to fixing the interpretation of A^*, but it is not far enough. The rules tell us that $A \vdash A^*$ and that $A^*; A^* \vdash A^*$. They do not tell us that A^* is the *least* type with those properties. So far A^* could be equivalent to $\top$ and that would not conflict with anything in the rules. This is bad, as we would like to demonstrate that $\bot^* \vdash \bot$ holds, at least. After all, nothing is a concatenation of objects of type $\bot$, as there are no objects of type $\bot$.

The rule needed to fill out the proof theory for * was discovered by Ng and Tarski [183, 184] and adapted to the setting of dynamic algebras by Vaughan Pratt [194, 195]. It is a formalisation of the induction rule. In our notation it is as follows:

$$\frac{B; B \vdash B \quad A \vdash B \quad X \vdash A^*}{X \vdash B} \ (*E)$$

The motivation for this rule is simple. If B is a type closed under concatenation (that is, if $B; B \vdash B$) and if $A \vdash B$, then A^* must entail B. Take any object of type A^*. It is a concatenation of n objects of type A, for some $n \geq 1$. This means it is a concatenation of n objects of type B. We can show that it is therefore of type B too, as $B; B \vdash B$ gives $(B; B); B \vdash B$, $((B; B); B); B \vdash B$, and so on. So, the rule makes sense under this interpretation. This gives us our rules for the Kleene * operator.

DEFINITION 3.11 (KLEENE * RULES)
The rules for a Kleene * operator are $(*I)$, $(*M)$ and $(*E)$.

LEMMA 3.12 (STAR IS A POSITIVE MODALITY)
A Kleene star operator is a positive modality.

PROOF   Suppose we have $A \vdash B$. We can prove $A^* \vdash B^*$ as follows.

$$\dfrac{\dfrac{B^* \vdash B^* \quad B^* \vdash B^*}{B^*; B^* \vdash B^*}\ (*M) \qquad \dfrac{A \vdash B}{A \vdash B^*}\ (*I) \qquad A^* \vdash A^*}{A^* \vdash B^*}\ (*E) \qquad \qquad \square$$

Similarly, we can show that $\perp^* \vdash \perp$

$$\dfrac{\dfrac{\perp \vdash \perp}{\perp; \perp \vdash \perp}\ (\perp E) \qquad \perp \vdash \perp \quad \perp \vdash \perp^*}{\perp^* \vdash \perp}\ (*E)$$

It is instructive to note that these rules characterise the Kleene $*$ insofar as any two operators satisfying these rules must be equivalent. If $\star$ also satisfies the rules, we can show that A^* and $A^\star$ are equivalent:

$$\dfrac{\dfrac{A^* \vdash A^* \quad A^* \vdash A^*}{A^*; A^* \vdash A^*}\ (*M) \qquad \dfrac{A \vdash A}{A \vdash A^*}\ (*I) \qquad A^\star \vdash A^\star}{A^\star \vdash A^*}\ (*E)$$

Exercises numbered from 3.9 to 3.13 examine more of the behaviour of the Kleene star. Linear logic uses a modality, written '!', and read 'of course', which also fails to be a normal modality. In the interpretation of linear logic as a logic of resource use, $!A$ is as many copies of A as you need for the task at hand. (Recall that linear logic has the structural rules B and C, so fusion is associative and commutative.) It is *suggested* by the equivalence

$$!A \dashv\vdash t \wedge A \wedge A^2 \wedge A^3 \wedge \cdots$$

Under this interpretation, you have $!A \vdash A^n$ for each n. $!A$ gives you n copies of n for *any* n you choose. You can duplicate $!A$ or contract it at will. The modality (read as 'of course' and called an *exponential* to parallel the additive and multiplicative connectives of LL we have already seen) is used in linear logic to provide a modelling of inferences in which resources can be duplicated or ignored at will. In other words, it provides the wherewithal in linear logic to model intuitionistic logic, which is free of constraints on structural rules.

   To give a simple natural deduction system for LL, we will expand our definition of structures just a little. For LL, a structure is either a *formula* or a *bracketed formula* (that is, $[A]$, for some formula A) or a structure of the form $X; Y$, where X and Y are already structures. You can view the bracketing as a limited form of punctuation, which applies only to formulae, and not to any greater depth. For any structure X, we will write '$[X]$' for the structure given by bracketing all the unbracketed formulae in X. Once we have this form of structure, we can define the new rules for '!'.

DEFINITION 3.13 (! NATURAL DEDUCTION RULES)
The rules for bracketing are as follows

$$[A] \vdash A \quad [\text{Bracket-Id}] \qquad X \Leftarrow X; [A] \quad [\text{Bracket-K}]$$

$$[X]; [X] \Leftarrow [X] \quad [\text{Bracket-WI}]$$

The exponential rules are then straightforward:

$$\frac{[X] \vdash A}{[X] \vdash \,!A}\,(!I) \qquad \frac{X \vdash \,!A \quad Y([A]) \vdash B}{Y(X) \vdash B}\,(!E)$$

"Of course" has some interesting properties. First, it is almost immediate that $!A \vdash A$.

$$\frac{!A \vdash \,!A \quad [A] \vdash A}{!A \vdash A}\,(!E)$$

A more interesting result is the way that ! distributes over extensional conjunction.

LEMMA 3.14 (OF COURSE AND CONJUNCTION)
$!A \circ !B$ *is equivalent to* $!(A \wedge B)$.

PROOF First, for left-to-right

$$\frac{!A \vdash \,!A \quad \dfrac{!B \vdash \,!B \quad \dfrac{\dfrac{[A] \vdash A \quad \dfrac{[B] \vdash B}{[B]; [A] \vdash B}}{[A]; [B] \vdash A \quad [A]; [B] \vdash B}}{\dfrac{[A]; [B] \vdash A \wedge B}{\dfrac{[A]; [B] \vdash \,!(A \wedge B)}{[A]; !B \vdash \,!(A \wedge B)}\,(!E)}\,(!I)}\,(\wedge I)}{\dfrac{!A; !B \vdash \,!(A \wedge B)}{!A \circ !B \vdash \,!(A \wedge B)}\,(\circ E)}}{!A \circ !B \vdash !A \vdash !B}$$

And conversely

$$\dfrac{\dfrac{[A \wedge B] \vdash A \wedge B}{[A \wedge B] \vdash A}}{[A \wedge B] \vdash !A} \qquad \dfrac{\dfrac{[A \wedge B] \vdash A \wedge B}{[A \wedge B] \vdash B}}{[A \wedge B] \vdash !B}$$

$$\dfrac{!(A \wedge B) \vdash !(A \wedge B) \qquad \dfrac{\dfrac{[A \wedge B];[A \wedge B] \vdash !A \circ !B}{[A \wedge B] \vdash !A \circ !B} \text{ [Bracket-WI]}}{[A \wedge B] \vdash !A \circ !B} \text{ (!E)}}{!(A \wedge B) \vdash !A \circ !B}$$

$\square$

Again, ! is not a normal modality, as it does not have the right distribution properties. We cannot prove $!A \wedge !B \vdash !(A \wedge B)$. (Try it!)

The exponential allows linear logic, which does not contain the structural rules of contraction and weakening, to recover them in exponential contexts. A translation $^\tau$, defined by Girard as follows, provides the recovery of these structural rules:

$$\begin{aligned}
p^\tau &= p \\
\top^\tau &= \top \\
\bot^\tau &= \bot \\
(\neg A)^\tau &= !A^\tau \to \bot \\
(A \to B)^\tau &= !A^\tau \to B^\tau \\
(A \wedge B)^\tau &= A^\tau \wedge B^\tau \\
(A \vee B)^\tau &= !(A^\tau \vee B^\tau) \\
(X, Y)^\tau &= X^\tau; Y^\tau
\end{aligned}$$

Girard proves the following theorem:

THEOREM 3.15 (INTUITIONISTIC TRANSLATION)
$X \vdash A$ *is provable in intuitionistic logic if and only if* $[X^\tau] \vdash A^\tau$ *is provable in* LL.

PROOF First, we note that if $[X^\tau] \vdash A^\tau$ is provable in LL, then any proof, when you erase all instances of !, and of the bracketing, is a proof of $X \vdash A$ in intuitionistic logic. The only difficulties are involved in the exponential rules. The structural rules become their intuitionistic analogues when the brackets are deleted. In this transformation, [Bracket-Id] becomes standard identity, [Bracket-K] becomes K and [Bracket-WI] becomes WI. So, the result is an intuitionistic proof, as the rules K and WI are available for intuitionistic premise combination.

Conversely, we show that if $X \vdash A$ is provable in intuitionistic logic, then $[X^\tau] \vdash A^\tau$ is provable in LL. We do this by taking the intuitionistic proof and replacing every consecution $Y \vdash B$ by its translation $[Y^\tau] \vdash B^\tau$. We then need to show that this resulting structure can be transformed into a proof. We do this by inspecting each intuitionistic rule, to check that we can pass from the translation of the premises to the translation of the conclusion by valid moves of linear logic. We will just work through two representative cases and leave the rest to the exercises. For conjunction introduction, the intuitionistic rule

$$\frac{X \vdash A \quad X \vdash B}{X \vdash A \wedge B}$$

is straightforwardly mapped to the same rule in LL

$$\frac{[X^\tau] \vdash A^\tau \quad [X^\tau] \vdash B^\tau}{[X^\tau] \vdash A^\tau \wedge B^\tau}$$

For implication elimination, the intuitionistic rule

$$\frac{X \vdash A \supset B \quad Y \vdash A}{X, Y \vdash B}$$

is mapped to the following proof fragment

$$\frac{[X^\tau] \vdash !A^\tau \rightarrow B^\tau \quad \dfrac{[Y^\tau] \vdash A^\tau}{[Y^\tau] \vdash !A^\tau}}{[X^\tau; Y^\tau] \vdash B^\tau}$$

For disjunction introduction, the intuitionistic proof

$$\frac{X \vdash A}{X \vdash A \vee B}$$

becomes

$$\frac{\dfrac{[X^\tau] \vdash A^\tau}{[X^\tau] \vdash A^\tau \vee B^\tau}}{[X^\tau] \vdash !(A^\tau \vee B^\tau)}$$

The rest of the proof is just as straightforward.   □

In Chapter 10, we will see how Girard discovered the exponential. For now, however, we will move on to negative modalities.

3.3 Negative Modalities

Modalities can also be *negative*.

DEFINITION 3.16 (NEGATIVE MODALITIES)
A one-place connective m is a *negative modality* if and only if the rule

$$\frac{A \vdash B}{mB \vdash mA}$$

is valid for all formulae A and B.

Characteristic examples of negative modalities are the connectives we use when we deny something, or when we express the fact that we wish to reject something, or when we contradict someone. If A entails B, then *excluding B* involves *excluding A*. *Ruling out B* entails *ruling out A*. The *possibility of B failing* brings with it the *possibility of A failing*.

One way to deny a claim is to say that from it you can infer a falsehood. So, if we let f be a falsehood, then $A \rightarrow f$ is a good candidate for $\sim A$ — the *negation* of A. For if A is false, then it is plausible that it implies f (a falsehood) and if $A \rightarrow f$ is true, then since f is false, A must be false too. Indeed, in any of our logics of $\rightarrow$, this negation is indeed a negative modality, as you can check.

LEMMA 3.17 (IMPLYING f IS NEGATIVE)
In any logic with implication, we have the rule

$$\frac{A \vdash B}{\sim B \vdash \sim A}$$

PROOF   The proof

$$\frac{A \vdash B \quad B \rightarrow f \vdash B \rightarrow f}{\frac{B \rightarrow f; A \vdash f}{B \rightarrow f \vdash A \rightarrow f}}$$

relies on no special behaviour of implication or the semicolon, so it is valid in all of our proof systems containing implication.   □

Indeed, the proof relies on no properties of the so-called "false proposition" f. It need not even be false for $\sim$ to be a negative modality.

Furthermore, in many of our logics there are two candidates for the conditional to use in defining negation. We may also take $\neg A$, defined as $f \leftarrow A$, to be our candidate negation. There is little to choose between these two alternatives if both implication connectives $\rightarrow$ and $\leftarrow$ are available. Both say that A leads to a falsehood. They simply describe the "following from" in a different way.

Given these definitions of negation, if $A \vdash \sim B$ then we have $A; B \vdash f$, and so, $B \vdash \neg A$, and vice versa. This holds no matter what the behaviour of $\rightarrow$, $\leftarrow$ or f turns out to be.

In some applications, both $\neg$ and $\sim$ are worthwhile connectives and they have different interpretations. To make this more concrete, consider actions as an example, and let f pick out some class of actions. Then $\sim A$, defined as $A \rightarrow f$, and $\neg A$, defined as $f \leftarrow A$, are two different sorts of action. The first, $\sim A$, describes any action such that if composed with any action of type A it results in an action of type f. The second, $\neg A$, describes any action such that any action of type A, composed with it, results in an action of type f. The order of actions is important.

So, if $f = \bot$ (so there are *no* actions of type f), an action is of type $\sim A$ if it *cannot* be followed by an action of type A. If G is the type of any action of Giving all your money away, and if B is the type of any action involving Buying a Ferrari, then clearly $G \vdash \sim B$. Any action of type G is also an action of type $\sim B$, for it is impossible to give all your money away and then to buy a Ferrari (without any intervening actions, like receiving a gift of a large sum of money). However, it is possible to buy a Ferrari, and *then* give all your money away. So, we do not have $G \vdash \neg B$.

These negations make sense for choices of f other than $\bot$. If f is some other class — say the class of actions you wish to avoid — then an action is of type $\sim A$ if following it with an action of type A is a *bad thing*. Conversely, a type is of type $\neg A$ if whenever it *follows* an action of type A you get as a result an action of type f.

The same sort of thing can be given in other domains as well. In the world of functions, an object is of type $A \to \bot$ if it does not take inputs of type A. An object is of type $\bot \leftarrow A$ if it is not an acceptable input of a function of type A.

It turns out, then, that we can say quite a lot about negative operators in the context of our language of implication. However, this might not be the whole story of negative modalities.

For one thing, it is not immediately obvious that negation of a proposition must be equivalent to its implying some particular false proposition.[1] For example, we might consider a logic in which there are no implication connectives, or in which the implication connective necessary to define *our* negation is absent. At any rate, in this section we will abstract away from the particular behaviour of negative operators defined in terms of implication to find a general phenomenon which may be repeated in the absence of implication as well as in its presence.

We will take the following two rules as basic for our treatment of negation. We will at first abstract away from the interaction with the semicolon to leave the two negations interacting with the rules equating $A \vdash \sim B$ with $B \vdash \neg A$. The rules we choose modify the simple equivalence just enough to make the

---

[1] Though there are some good arguments to the effect that this must be the case. Consider the disjunction of all false propositions. This is a good candidate for f. If A is false, then $A \to f$, as A is one of the disjuncts of f. If, on the other hand, $A \to f$, then A must be false, as it implies a false proposition, f. (The proposition f must be false as a disjunction is true only if one of its disjuncts are true, and all of the disjuncts of f are false.) So, $A \to f$ is true if and only if A is false. In other words, $A \to f$ is true if and only if the negation of A is true. This idea has been discussed by Curry [54] and has been taken up in the relevant logic literature by Meyer and Martin among others [163].

rules antecedent regular. We will call our two negation connectives a 'split negation' following Hartonas [80, 111].

DEFINITION 3.18 (SPLIT NEGATION RULES)
The pair $\langle \sim, \neg \rangle$ is a *split negation* if and only if it satisfies

$$\frac{A \vdash \sim B \quad X \vdash B}{X \vdash \neg A} \, (\neg I/\sim E) \qquad \frac{A \vdash \neg B \quad X \vdash B}{X \vdash \sim A} \, (\sim I/\neg E)$$

Note that these rules involve no punctuation marks, and no connectives other than $\sim$ and $\neg$. They define only the interaction between the two negations $\sim$ and $\neg$ and logical consequence.

Split negations are the first connectives we have introduced which are not uniquely characterised by the rules in which they feature. There is no way to prove that if $\langle \sim_1, \neg_1 \rangle$ and $\langle \sim_2, \neg_2 \rangle$ are both split negations then they are, in any way, equivalent.

From these rules we can show that $\sim$ and $\neg$ are, in fact, negative modalities.

LEMMA 3.19 ($\sim$ AND $\neg$ ARE NEGATIVE)
From $A \vdash B$ it follows that both $\sim B \vdash \sim A$ and $\neg B \vdash \neg A$ for any split negation $\langle \sim, \neg \rangle$.

PROOF We prove a more general result

$$\frac{\dfrac{\sim B \vdash \sim B \quad A \vdash B}{A \vdash \neg \sim B} \qquad X \vdash \sim B}{X \vdash \sim A}$$

Now substituting $\sim B$ for X gives us the desired result for $\sim$. Swapping $\sim$ and $\neg$ in this proof gives us the same result for $\neg$. □

Another simple result is a basic form of double negation introduction.

LEMMA 3.20 (DOUBLE NEGATION INTRODUCTION)
In any logic including a split negation, we have

$$\frac{X \vdash A}{X \vdash \neg \sim A} \qquad \frac{X \vdash A}{X \vdash \sim \neg A}$$

PROOF

$$\frac{\sim A \vdash \sim A \quad X \vdash A}{X \vdash \neg \sim A} \qquad \frac{\neg A \vdash \neg A \quad X \vdash A}{X \vdash \sim \neg A}$$

□

We can also relate our negation operators to conjunction and disjunction.

LEMMA 3.21 (ONE DE MORGAN LAW)
For any split negation we have $\sim A \wedge \sim B \vdash \sim(A \vee B)$ in any logic in which $\wedge$ and $\vee$ are present (and similarly for $\neg$ in place of $\sim$).

PROOF Consider the following proof:

$$
\cfrac{
\cfrac{
\cfrac{\sim A \wedge \sim B \vdash \sim A \wedge \sim B}{\sim A \wedge \sim B \vdash \sim A}
}{A \vdash \neg(\sim A \wedge \sim B)}
\quad
\cfrac{
\cfrac{\sim A \wedge \sim B \vdash \sim A \wedge \sim B}{\sim A \wedge \sim B \vdash \sim B}
}{B \vdash \neg(\sim A \wedge \sim B)}
\quad A \vee B \vdash A \vee B
}{
\cfrac{A \vee B \vdash \neg(\sim A \wedge \sim B)}{\sim A \wedge \sim B \vdash \sim(A \vee B)}
}
$$

There are two important things to notice in this proof. First, we use the inference from $A \vee B \vdash \neg(\sim A \wedge \sim B)$ to $\sim A \wedge \sim B \vdash \sim(A \vee B)$, leaving the other premise $\sim A \wedge \sim B \vdash \sim A \wedge \sim B$ *sotto voce*. This is a simple abbreviation of the two-premise negation rules and it helps to cut down the length of proofs. Second, note that we can rewrite the proof swapping $\neg$ and $\sim$ — and the result is still a proof.   □

From now, we will state theorems using only one negation operator, and we leave it to the reader to note that it applies to the other negation.

That last result showed that one of the de Morgan laws (distributing negation over an extensional connective, in this case, disjunction) holds for our negation operators. Two more of the de Morgan laws hold for our negation. In fact, these are the simple de Morgan laws which hold for *any* negative operator at all.

LEMMA 3.22 (DE MORGAN LAWS FOR NEGATIVE OPERATORS)
If $-$ is any negative operator, the two de Morgan laws

$$
\begin{aligned}
-(A \vee B) &\vdash -A \wedge -B \\
-A \vee -B &\vdash -(A \wedge B)
\end{aligned}
$$

hold in any logic containing conjunction and disjunction.

PROOF

$$
\cfrac{
\cfrac{\cfrac{A \vdash A}{A \vdash A \vee B}}{-(A \vee B) \vdash -A}
\quad
\cfrac{\cfrac{B \vdash B}{B \vdash A \vee B}}{-(A \vee B) \vdash -B}
}{-(A \vee B) \vdash -A \wedge -B}
\qquad
\cfrac{
\cfrac{\cfrac{A \wedge B \vdash A \wedge B}{A \wedge B \vdash A}}{-A \vdash -(A \wedge B)}
\quad
\cfrac{\cfrac{A \wedge B \vdash A \wedge B}{A \wedge B \vdash B}}{-B \vdash -(A \wedge B)}
}{-A \vee -B \vdash -(A \wedge B)}
$$

□

This result relied on no particular property of the negative operator other than its being a negative operator.

We have another property of our negations, tied this time to $\top$ and $\bot$

LEMMA 3.23 (TOP AND BOTTOM IN SPLIT NEGATIONS)
For any split negation $\sim$, $\top \vdash \sim\bot$ *in any logics in which* $\top$ *and* $\bot$ *are present.*

PROOF
$$\frac{\bot \vdash \neg\top \quad \top \vdash \top}{\top \vdash \sim\bot} \qquad\qquad \square$$

That will do for properties of our split negation connectives. We can strengthen the logic by considering different possible extensions by way of more rules. One kind of extension looks at strengthening the negation itself, by adding more negation rules. The other kind ties the negation to other operations in the logic.

One way of adding conditions on negation itself is to collapse $\sim$ and $\neg$ into one connective.

DEFINITION 3.24 (SIMPLE NEGATION)
A connective $\sim$ is a *simple negation* if it obeys the single rule

$$\frac{A \vdash \sim B \quad X \vdash B}{X \vdash \sim A} \ (\sim I/\sim E)$$

or equivalently, if $\langle \sim, \sim \rangle$ is a split negation.

LEMMA 3.25 (SIMPLE DOUBLE NEGATION INTRODUCTION)
If $\sim$ *is a simple negation, it satisfies*

$$\frac{X \vdash A}{X \vdash \sim\sim A} \ (\sim\sim I)$$

This is obvious, as split negations satisfy the inference from $X \vdash A$ to $X \vdash \sim\neg A$, and a simple negation identifies $\sim$ with $\neg$.

Other possible rules strengthening a split negation are the elimination rules $(\sim\neg E)$, and $(\neg\sim E)$.

DEFINITION 3.26 (DOUBLE NEGATION ELIMINATION RULES)
The *double negation elimination* rules are

$$\frac{X \vdash \sim\neg A}{X \vdash A} \ (\sim\neg E) \qquad\qquad \frac{X \vdash \neg\sim A}{X \vdash A} \ (\neg\sim E)$$

If we add these rules we have a *converse contraposition* result.

LEMMA 3.27 (CONVERSE CONTRAPOSITION)
In any logic containing both double negation elimination rules, the two-way contraposition rule

$$\frac{\sim A \vdash B}{\neg B \vdash A}$$

holds also.

PROOF

$$\frac{\neg B \vdash \neg B \quad \sim A \vdash B}{\dfrac{\neg B \vdash \neg \sim A}{\neg B \vdash A}} \qquad \frac{\sim A \vdash \sim A \quad \neg B \vdash A}{\dfrac{\sim A \vdash \sim \neg B}{\sim A \vdash B}} \qquad \square$$

Converse contraposition brings with it the remaining de Morgan law.

LEMMA 3.28 (FINAL DE MORGAN NEGATION LAW)
In any split negation with double negation elimination rules, the de Morgan law
$\sim(A \wedge B) \vdash \sim A \vee \sim B$ *holds.*

PROOF

$$\frac{\dfrac{\sim A \vdash \sim A}{\dfrac{\sim A \vdash \sim A \vee \sim B}{\neg(\sim A \vee \sim B) \vdash A}} \qquad \dfrac{\sim B \vdash \sim B}{\dfrac{\sim B \vdash \sim A \vee \sim B}{\neg(\sim A \vee \sim B) \vdash B}}}{\dfrac{\neg(\sim A \vee \sim B) \vdash A \wedge B}{\sim(A \wedge B) \vdash \sim A \vee \sim B}} \qquad \square$$

These definitions combine to give us a connective well known in the literature on relevant logic.

DEFINITION 3.29 (DE MORGAN NEGATION)
A *de Morgan negation* is a simple negation satisfying double negation elimination.

It follows that a de Morgan negation satisfies all four de Morgan laws, and double negation introduction and elimination. This is a lot of what negation is taken to satisfy. The negation of the relevant logics R and E is a de Morgan negation, as is the negation in linear logic.

However, there is still more you could want of a negation connective. For example, you could tie negation to $\bot$ in new ways.

DEFINITION 3.30 (EX CONTRADICTIONE QUODLIBET)
The *ex contradictione quodlibet* rule (ECQ) is

$$\frac{X \vdash A \quad X \vdash {\sim}A}{X \vdash \bot}$$

This rule brings with it $A \wedge {\sim}A \vdash \bot$, and consequently, $A \wedge {\sim}A \vdash B$ for any B you choose. This is rejected in relevant logics and their cousins on grounds of relevance. (What has $A \wedge {\sim}A$ to do with B?)

DEFINITION 3.31 (ORTHO-NEGATION)
An *ortho-negation* is a de Morgan negation with ECQ.

This is almost all there is to add. In fact, given the distribution of conjunction over disjunction, an ortho-negation is very well known indeed.

DEFINITION 3.32 (BOOLEAN NEGATION)
A *Boolean negation* is an ortho-negation in a logic with conjunction distributing over disjunction.

In Chapter 8, we will see that Boolean negation is uniquely defined. That is, if $\sim$ and $\neg$ are two Boolean negations in some logic, then ${\sim}A$ and $\neg A$ are equivalent. This does not hold with any weaker negations we have seen. It is possible to have two distinct ortho-negations in a logic.

Ortho-negations are also tied to $\top$ in addition to $\bot$.

LEMMA 3.33 (EXCLUDED MIDDLE FOR ORTHO-NEGATION)
If $\sim$ is an ortho-negation, then $\top \vdash A \vee {\sim}A$.

PROOF   From ECQ we have ${\sim}A \wedge {\sim}{\sim}A \vdash {\sim}\top$, and hence ${\sim}(A \vee {\sim}A) \vdash {\sim}\top$ by a de Morgan law. Then the order-inverting properties of $\sim$ gives ${\sim}{\sim}\top \vdash {\sim}{\sim}(A \vee {\sim}A)$, and clearing away double negations gives $\top \vdash A \vee {\sim}A$ as desired.
□

This version of excluded middle follows from the ortho-negation laws, but it can stand on its own as an axiom.

DEFINITION 3.34 (STRONG EXCLUDED MIDDLE)
The *strong excluded middle* axiom is $X \vdash A \vee {\sim}A$.

This is called the strong excluded middle, as it holds that instances of excluded middle are as true as can be (they are entailed by anything at all). There are weaker versions of excluded middle that we will see which hold merely that excluded middle is true in some other sense. Strong excluded middle is dual to ECQ, which holds that all instances of contradictions are as false as can be (they entail anything at all).

We have considered axioms which strengthen negation on its own. There are also axioms which relate $\sim$ and $\neg$ to the intensional structure.

DEFINITION 3.35 (SEMICOLON NEGATION RULES)
The standard rules tying together a split negation with intensional structure are
these:

$$\frac{X; A \vdash \neg B \quad Y \vdash B}{X; Y \vdash \sim A} \; (\sim I; \neg E) \qquad \frac{X; A \vdash \sim B \quad Y \vdash B}{X; Y \vdash \neg A} \; (\neg I; \sim E)$$

Note that in these rules, if you substitute 0 for X, you get the original rules
back.

LEMMA 3.36 (NEGATION AND IMPLICATION)
In the presence of $(\sim I; \neg E)$, we can prove $A \to \neg B \vdash B \to \sim A$, and dually, for
$(\neg I; \sim E)$.

PROOF

$$\frac{\dfrac{A \to \neg B \vdash A \to \neg B \quad A \vdash A}{A \to \neg B; A \vdash \neg B} \quad B \vdash B}{\dfrac{A \to \neg B; B \vdash \sim A}{A \to \neg B \vdash B \to \sim A}}$$

$\square$

Other additions can be contemplated. For example, the rule

$$\frac{X; A \vdash \neg B \quad Y \vdash B}{Y; X \vdash \sim A}$$

allows the proof of $(A \to \neg B) \to (\sim A \leftarrow B)$. We need not consider these
extensions in detail here. We now have the wherewithal to define standard
logics like R and LL. The negation of these logics deserves a name.

DEFINITION 3.37 (STRICT DE MORGAN NEGATION)
A de Morgan negation satisfying $(\sim I; \sim E)$ and $(\neg I; \sim E)$ is said to be a *strict de
Morgan negation*.

These rules are enough to capture the negations of R and linear logic. R is R$^+$
together with a strict de Morgan negation. Similarly, LL adds a strict de Morgan
negation to MALL$^+$, together with !.

The first step to understanding this is to show when semicolon negations
become negations defined with implication.

LEMMA 3.38 (WHEN NEGATION IS IMPLYING $\sim t$)
*In any logic with Cl, 0 and a semicolon simple negation (not necessarily de Mor-
gan), $\sim A$ is equivalent to $A \to \sim t$.*

PROOF

$$\dfrac{\dfrac{\sim A \vdash \sim A}{0 \vdash t \quad 0; \sim A \vdash \sim A}}{\dfrac{\dfrac{t; \sim A \vdash \sim A}{\sim A; t \vdash \sim A} \text{ [CI]} \quad A \vdash A}{\dfrac{\sim A; A \vdash \sim t}{\sim A \vdash A \to \sim t}}}$$

$$\dfrac{\dfrac{A \to \sim t \vdash A \to \sim t \quad A \vdash A}{\dfrac{(A \to \sim t); A \vdash \sim t \quad 0 \vdash t}{\dfrac{(A \to \sim t); 0 \vdash \sim A}{\dfrac{0; (A \to \sim t) \vdash \sim A}{A \to \sim t \vdash \sim A}} \text{ [CI]}}}}{} \qquad \square$$

THEOREM 3.39 (WEAK EXCLUDED MIDDLE)
In any logic with CI, and WI, 0 and a strict de Morgan negation, $0 \vdash A \lor \sim A$.

PROOF   First, note that $\sim(A \lor \sim A) \vdash A \lor \sim A$, since we have $\sim(A \lor \sim A) \vdash \sim A$.
But this gives us $\sim(A \lor \sim A) \vdash \sim\sim(A \lor \sim A)$ by double negation introduction.
But for any B where $B \vdash \sim B$, we have (by the previous lemma) $B \vdash B \to \sim t$,
and hence $B; B \vdash \sim t$, giving $B \vdash \sim t$ by WI and hence $0 \vdash B \to \sim t$, and again
by our lemma, $0 \vdash \sim B$.

   In our case of $B = \sim(A \lor \sim A)$, we have $0 \vdash \sim\sim(A \lor \sim A)$, and by de Morgan
negation properties we get the desired $0 \vdash A \lor \sim A$. $\square$

So, in logics with de Morgan negations tied the intensional structure, with 0
and with CI and WI, we have a version of excluded middle which admits that
every formula of the form $A \lor \sim A$ is true, but which does not go so far as to say
that such formulae are entailed by *everything*.

   In these logics you can read t as the conjunction of all truths, as we have
$A \dashv\vdash t \to A$: A holds if and only if it follows from t. The false constant $\sim t$ is
then the disjunction of all falsehoods. For something to be false it must imply
$\sim t$. It will follow (by WI) that $A \land \sim A \vdash \sim t$, so every contradiction entails a
falsehood, and in particfular, every contradiction entails the false constant $\sim t$.
It does not follow that all contradictions entail *anything whatsoever*.

THEOREM 3.40 (FUSION, IMPLICATION AND NEGATION)
*In any logic with C, B, 0 and a strict de Morgan negation, $A \circ B$ is equivalent to
$\sim(A \to \sim B)$.*

PROOF In these proofs we use Lemma 3.38 and double negation elimination liberally, sliding between $\sim A$ and $A \to \sim t$, and between B and $\sim\sim B$ at will.

$$\frac{\displaystyle\frac{\displaystyle\frac{\displaystyle\frac{\displaystyle\frac{A \to \sim B \vdash A \to \sim B}{(A \to \sim B); A \vdash B \to \sim t}}{((A \to \sim B); A); B \vdash \sim t}}{(A; B); (A \to \sim B) \vdash \sim t}\;[\text{B, C}]}{\displaystyle\frac{A; B \vdash (A \to \sim B) \to \sim t}{A \circ B \vdash \sim(A \to \sim B)}}$$

Note that in this proof we did not use double negation elimination. For the other direction, we must use it at the last step.

$$\frac{\displaystyle A \circ B \vdash A \circ B \quad \frac{\displaystyle\frac{A \circ B \to \sim t \vdash A \circ B \to \sim t \quad A \circ B \vdash A \circ B}{(A \circ B \to \sim t); (A \circ B) \vdash \sim t}}{\displaystyle\frac{(A \circ B \to \sim t); (A; B) \vdash \sim t}{\displaystyle\frac{((A \circ B \to \sim t); A); B \vdash \sim t}{\displaystyle\frac{A \circ B \to \sim t \vdash A \to (B \to \sim t)}{\displaystyle\frac{\sim(A \to \sim B) \vdash \sim\sim(A \circ B)}{\sim(A \to \sim B) \vdash A \circ B}}}}}{\ }$$

$\square$

At this point we have gone full circle, back to our original account of negation in terms of implication and falsehood. We will learn more about negations and other negative operators in later chapters when we introduce models for our logics.

3.4 History

Work in one-place modalities in substructural logics is much less developed than the two-place connectives, fusion and implication. The treatment of positive modalities here owes much to Wansing [281], who used a one-place punctuation mark for modal operators in the context of *display logic*.[2] Dunn's "Positive Modal Logic" [79] is the first extensive treatment of modal logic of $\square$ and $\Diamond$ in the absence of negation. We will examine some of its results in Chapter 11. Pratt [194, 195] has studied the behaviour of the Kleene star in the context of substructural logics. Our rules for the star are due to him.

---

[2] For more on display logic, see Chapter 6.

Girard's linear logic is introduced in the paper "Linear Logic" [96]. It was not particularly obvious how to give linear logic a natural deduction system with nice properties (such as antecedent regularity). Our treatment follows Wadler's clear presentation of the issue [278, 279]. This system, with separate treatment of intuitionistic formulae — to which all structural rules apply — and others, is due originally to Girard, who uses it in his *Logic of Unity* [98]. We will see a smoother presentation of linear logic in Chapter 6, where we see a proof system which needs no recourse to bracketing to give the desired behaviours to the exponentials.

The proof theoretical treatment for negations presented here is, to the best of my knowledge, original to this chapter. Split negations are due to Dunn [78, 80], but named by Hartonas [111].

3.5 Exercises

Practice

{3.1} Prove $A \vdash \Diamond A$ directly, using T.

{3.2} Show that $t \vdash \Box t$ and $\Diamond t \vdash t$ hold in the presence of Kr, and that their converses hold in the presence of Kr^c.

{3.3} Show that $A \vdash \Box \Diamond A$ and $\Diamond \Box A \vdash A$ hold in any logics with $\Box$ and $\Diamond$.

{3.4} What negation rules or structural rules are necessary to prove the following consecutions? $A \vdash B \vdash \sim B \vdash \sim A$; $\sim B \vdash \sim A \vdash A \rightarrow B$; $A \rightarrow \sim A \vdash \sim A$; $\sim \top \vdash \bot$; $\sim(A \rightarrow \bot) \vdash \sim A \rightarrow \bot$; $\sim(A \rightarrow A) \vdash \bot$.

Problems

{3.5} Under which circumstances does $\top \vdash \Diamond \top$? When does $\Box \bot \vdash \bot$?

{3.6} Devise a structural rule with which you can prove $\Box \Box A \dashv\vdash A$. Show that under these conditions $\Box$ is possibility-like, as well as necessity-like. (HINT: show that under these circumstances $\Box A \dashv\vdash \Diamond A$.)

{3.7} Define $\heartsuit A$ to be $A \circ A$. Does $\heartsuit A$ act like a possibility operator? Does it satisfy the conditions in Lemma 3.4 for a possibility-style operator? If it does not in an arbitrary substructural logic, are there any structural rules you can impose on fusion to make it a possibility style operator?

{3.8} Consider the connective $\Rightarrow$, defined by setting $A \Rightarrow B$ to be $\Box(A \rightarrow B)$ for some connectives $\Box$ and $\rightarrow$. What connective does it residuate? Similarly for $\Box(B \leftarrow A)$.

{3.9} Show that $t \dashv\vdash t^*$.

{3.10} Show that $A^* \vdash A^* \rightarrow A^*$.

{3.11} Show that if $A \vdash B^*$ is provable then $A^* \vdash B^*$ is provable too.

{3.12} Convince yourself that $(A \circ B)^* \vdash (A \vee B)^*$ ought to be valid using the interpretation of the Kleene star. Then prove it. (HINT: It might help to prove $A \circ B \vdash (A \vee B)^*$ first, and then apply the result of Exercise 3.11.)

{3.13} Is A^* equivalent to A in R? Are they equivalent when you add the structural rule M?

{3.14} Show that $A \circ !B \vdash A$, $!A \vdash A$, $t \vdash !t$ and $!A \vdash !A \circ !A$ in LL.

{3.15} Show that $!A$ is equivalent to $t \wedge A \wedge (!A \circ !A)$.

{3.16} Show that t is equivalent to $!\top$. What is $!\bot$?

{3.17} Show that $!(A \circ B) \vdash !A \circ !B$ and that $!(A \wedge B) \vdash !A \wedge !B$.

{3.18} Show that $!(A \wedge B)$ is equivalent to $!(!A \wedge !B)$.

{3.19} Under what circumstances does $A \circ \sim A \to \sim t$ hold? What about $A \wedge \sim A \to \sim t$?

{3.20} Show that it is possible to have two split negations $\langle \sim_1, \neg_1 \rangle$ and $\langle \sim_2, \neg_2 \rangle$ such that no pair of the four negation connectives are equivalent. (HINT: This will be difficult if you wish to use techniques we have seen so far. Once you get to either Chapter 8 or 11 the problem will become much simpler.)

{3.21} Show that $\sim\neg$ is a positive modality. Is it possibility- or necessity-like?

{3.22} Try proving $\top \vdash \sim\bot$, $\sim(A \vee B) \vdash \sim A \wedge \sim B$. Try proving $\sim A \vee \sim B \vdash \sim(A \wedge B)$ and $\sim\top \vdash \bot$ using $(\sim\neg E)$ and $(\neg\sim E)$.

{3.23} Under what circumstances is $\Diamond A$ equivalent to $\sim\Box\sim A$?

{3.24} Suppose $\sim$ is a de Morgan negation, and consider a system in which C holds. Define $A + B$ to be $\sim A \to B$, and define f to be $\sim t$. Show that every formula is equivalent to one in which the only occurring negations are of the form $\sim p$, where p is an atomic formula.

{3.25} Consider syntactic strings. When is a string of type $A \to \bot$? When is a string of type $\bot \leftarrow A$? Are there any strings of type $A \wedge (A \to \bot)$? (If x was such a string, what type would xx have?) So, are the logics L or LI a good match for the theory of syntactic strings when it comes to admitting types like $\bot$ and operators like $\wedge$? What other structural rules should you add to L or LI to make it a better fit?

Project

{3.26} An alternative way to introduce negation is to treat $\sim p$ as primitive, and to define $\sim A$ in terms of the subformulae of A. So we can say $\sim(A \wedge B)$ is simply $\sim A \vee \sim B$, and $\sim(A \vee B)$ is $\sim A \wedge \sim B$, $\sim\sim A$ is A, and so on. Defining $\sim(A \to B)$ leaves us with options. The most often taken one is $A \wedge \sim B$. Clearly, $\sim\top$ can be $\bot$ and $\sim\bot$ can be $\top$ (these are practically forced by the conjunction and disjunction rules). Defining $\sim(A \circ B)$ and $\sim t$ leaves you more room to move. Then one has rules for negated connectives in much the same way as one has rules for the connectives in a standard system. For example, if we take $\sim(A \to B)$ to be equivalent to $A \wedge \sim B$ then we have the following introduction and elimination rules for a negated conditional:

$$\frac{X \vdash A \quad X \vdash \sim B}{X \vdash \sim(A \to B)}(\sim{\to}I) \qquad \frac{X \vdash \sim(A \to B)}{X \vdash A}(\sim{\to}E_1) \qquad \frac{X \vdash \sim(A \to B)}{X \vdash \sim B}(\sim{\to}E_2)$$

Formulate natural deduction rules for the other connectives. Show in the system that all of the de Morgan laws hold. Show that the negation rules in this chapter need not be satisfied by a negation of this type. Characterise the differences between this approach to negation and the one we have taken.

   This kind of theory of negation is inspired by Nelson's theory of constructible falsity [182] and has been extensively studied in the context of substructural logics by Heinrich Wansing [280]. Related work in relevant logics is in Dunn's semantics for RM [73].

Chapter 4

Hilbert Systems

What is now proved
was once only imagin'd.

— *William Blake*, The Marriage of Heaven and Hell

We have examined natural deduction systems for the last two chapters. These are not the only way to present a logic — another way is what has come to be known as a *Hilbert system*. A Hilbert system for a logic is a way of generating a set of formulae, called the *theorems* in the logic. These are the logical truths. They are generated from a list of *axioms* and a list of *primitive rules*. The set of theorems is the smallest set containing all of the axioms and which is closed under all of the rules. A *Hilbert proof* is a list in which every element is an axiom or follows from earlier elements in the list by way of one of the rules. Here is an example Hilbert system for the logic DMALL[$\circ, \rightarrow, \wedge, \vee, \sim$], the exponential-free fragment of linear logic, with distribution added. (Or equivalently, R without contraction.) The axiomatisation has two rules

$$A, B \Longrightarrow A \wedge B \qquad A, A \rightarrow B \Longrightarrow B$$

These rules are read as follows. If A and B are both theorems of the logic, so is $A \wedge B$. If A and $A \rightarrow B$ are theorems of the logic, so is B. The comma in these rules is not related to the comma as a punctuation mark in structures.

The Hilbert system has many axioms. The first two deal with implication alone

$$(A \rightarrow (B \rightarrow C)) \rightarrow (B \rightarrow (A \rightarrow C)) \quad (A \rightarrow B) \rightarrow ((C \rightarrow A) \rightarrow (C \rightarrow B))$$

Then we have axioms dealing with implication and its interaction with conjunction and disjunction

$$A \wedge B \rightarrow A \quad A \wedge B \rightarrow B \quad (A \rightarrow B) \wedge (A \rightarrow C) \rightarrow (A \rightarrow B \wedge C)$$

$$A \rightarrow A \vee B \quad B \rightarrow A \vee B \quad (A \rightarrow C) \wedge (B \rightarrow C) \rightarrow (A \rightarrow B \vee C)$$

$$A \wedge (B \vee C) \rightarrow (A \wedge B) \vee (A \wedge C)$$

Axioms connect implication to fusion

$$(A \to (B \to C)) \to (A \circ B \to C) \qquad (A \circ B \to C) \to (A \to (B \to C))$$

And finally, for a de Morgan negation to this system, you add the axioms

$$(A \to \sim B) \to (B \to \sim A) \qquad \sim\sim A \to A$$

This Hilbert system is quite elegant, because it has many axioms but few rules. The rules dictate the minimal behaviour of conjunction and implication, and the axioms lay over that the extra behaviour of the connectives. The axioms are nicely separable too. The implication axioms are adequate for the implication part of the logic, the conjunction axioms pin down the behaviour of conjunction, and so on.

In this chapter we will see how to construct Hilbert systems, like this one, for the logics we have constructed with natural deduction systems. The main theorem of this chapter will be the equivalence theorem, which shows that the Hilbert system and the natural deduction system do exactly the same work. In the first section we will "mass produce" Hilbert systems for a large class of natural deduction systems. Then in the second section we will see how to "hand tune" these Hilbert systems to make them more like the elegant system we have just seen.

4.1   Mass-produced Hilbert Systems

To relate our systems of natural deduction to a Hilbert system, we need to understand how a Hilbert system is to be read. What are the axioms and the theorems of a Hilbert system understood to *be*? The simple answer is that they are logical truths. But in our logics, there are choices for the notion of logical truth. Are they the formulae entailed by $\top$? Or by t? If you have more than one t constant, which one do you pick? Our answer here will be simple. You can pick any truth constant you like. Provided that the language of your logic is expressive enough to allow you to build your Hilbert system. For this to occur, a number of requirements need to be met. First, you need a truth constant. Second, you need an implication connective related to that truth constant. If the truth constant models an identity punctuation mark 0, which is the identity for a binary punctuation mark, then you need a conditional modelled with that binary punctuation mark.

Finally, you need a way to interpret all of the structures of the natural deduction system in your Hilbert system. So, if your proof system has a binary punctuation mark, your language needs the corresponding fusion operator. If your proof system has a one-place punctuation mark, your language needs the corresponding possibility operator.

DEFINITION 4.1 (EXPRESSIVITY OF A LANGUAGE)
A language Lang is *expressive* of a set of structures Struct if and only if

⋄ For every identity punctuation mark 0 in Struct, Lang has a corresponding truth constant t.

⋄ For every one-place punctuation mark • in Struct, Lang has the corresponding possibility operator $\Diamond$.

⋄ For every two-place punctuation mark ; in Struct, Lang has the corresponding fusion operator $\circ$.

⋄ For *some* two-place punctuation mark in Struct, Struct contains an identity 0 (either left or right) and Lang contains a corresponding conditional $\rightarrow$, such that if 0 is a left identity, $\rightarrow$ is a left-to-right conditional, and if 0 is a right identity, $\rightarrow$ is a right-to-left conditional.

From now, we will assume we have some natural deduction system in mind, with an expressive language. We will use '0' for the chosen identity, ';' as the chosen two-place punctuation mark and '$\rightarrow$' as the chosen conditional. We will assume that the conditional is a left-to-right conditional. If, instead, you wish to apply our translation to right-to-left conditionals, you will have to make some appropriate adjustments to the translation. These will be straightforward.

Once we have a language expressive in this way, we can translate the consecutions of our natural deduction system into formulae, ready to be used in the Hilbert system.

DEFINITION 4.2 (THE TRANSLATION OF A CONSECUTION)
If X is a structure, the translation $\tau(X)$ of X is given recursively as follows.

$$
\begin{aligned}
\tau(A) &= A \quad \text{(where A is any formula)} \\
\tau(0) &= t \\
\tau([A]) &= !A \\
\tau(X;Y) &= \tau(X) \circ \tau(Y) \\
\tau(X,Y) &= \tau(X) \wedge \tau(Y) \\
\tau(\bullet X) &= \Diamond \tau(X)
\end{aligned}
$$

The translation of a consecution $\tau(X \vdash A)$ is defined to be $\tau(X) \rightarrow A$.

This chapter is devoted to proving the following theorem.

THEOREM 4.3 (HILBERT SOUNDNESS AND COMPLETENESS)
$X \vdash A$ *is provable in a system* $\mathfrak{S}$ *if and only if* $\tau(X \vdash A)$ *is a theorem of the corresponding Hilbert system* $\mathfrak{H}\mathfrak{S}$, *provided that the system* $\mathfrak{S}$ *is expressive.*

To prove this result we need to define the corresponding Hilbert system $\mathfrak{H}\mathfrak{S}$ for any system $\mathfrak{S}$. To do this, we will have a number of *rule sets* which will model the behaviour of different parts of the system $\mathfrak{S}$.

First, the core rule set, which dictates the behaviour of our chosen implication connective and its intensional structure.

DEFINITION 4.4 (CORE RULE SET)
The *core rule set* for a Hilbert system consists of the following axiom (the identity axiom) and rules

$$A \;\to\; A$$
$$A \circ B \to C \iff A \to (B \to C)$$
$$A \to B, C \to D \implies (B \to C) \to (A \to D)$$
$$t \to A \iff A$$
$$A, A \to B \implies B$$

Some of these rules are two-way rules. If $t \to A$ is a theorem, so is A, and conversely. The last rule, from A and $A \to B$ to infer B, is the *modus ponens* rule.

DEFINITION 4.5 (CONJUNCTION RULE SET)
The *conjunction rule set* is made up of the following axioms, together with one rule.

$$A \wedge B \;\to\; A$$
$$A \wedge B \;\to\; B$$
$$(A \to B) \wedge (A \to C) \;\to\; (A \to B \wedge C)$$
$$A, B \implies A \wedge B$$

DEFINITION 4.6 (DISJUNCTION RULE SET)
The *disjunction rule set* is made up of the following axioms.

$$A \to A \vee B$$
$$B \to A \vee B$$
$$(A \to C) \wedge (B \to C) \to (A \vee B \to C)$$

DEFINITION 4.7 (TOP AND BOTTOM AXIOMS)
The constants $\top$ and $\bot$ are governed by these axioms (respectively).

$$A \to \top$$
$$\bot \to A$$

If we have extensional punctuation, you need the distribution rule set, consisting of just one axiom.

DEFINITION 4.8 (DISTRIBUTION AXIOM)
The *distribution axiom* is

$$A \land (B \lor C) \to (A \land B) \lor (A \land C)$$

DEFINITION 4.9 (EXTRA INTENSIONAL RULES)
For any extra conditional or fusion connectives not axiomatised we add the rules

$$A \circ' B \to C \iff A \to (B \to' C)$$
$$A \circ' B \to C \iff B \to (C \leftarrow' A)$$

as relevant. If $\circ'$ is present *without* left-to-right implication, you must add

$$A \to B \implies C \circ' A \to C \circ' B \qquad C \circ' \bot \to \bot \qquad C \circ' (A \lor B) \to (C \circ' A) \lor (C \circ' B)$$

similarly, if $\circ'$ is present *without* a right-to-left implication, you must add

$$A \to B \implies A \circ' C \to B \circ' C \qquad \bot \circ' C \to \bot \qquad (A \lor B) \circ' C \to (A \circ' C) \lor (B \circ' C)$$

In these rules we deal with any extra structural connectives we had not already modelled, and with the remaining conditional other than $\to$ tied to our core punctuation mark.

Then if you have negation connectives, you need to add the corresponding rule sets.

DEFINITION 4.10 (NEGATION RULES)
The negation rules are

$$A \to \sim B \iff B \to \neg A$$
$$A \to \sim B \implies B \to \sim A$$
$$\sim \neg A \to A$$
$$(A \to \sim B) \to (B \to \neg A)$$
$$(B \to \neg A) \to (A \to \sim B)$$
$$A \land \sim A \to B$$
$$A \to B \lor \sim B$$

a split negation, simple negation, double negation elimination, an intensional negation, ECQ and strong excluded middle, respectively.

DEFINITION 4.11 (POSITIVE MODAL RULES)
If a matching $\Box$ and $\Diamond$ are present, then we add the rules

$$A \to \Box B \iff \Diamond A \to B$$

If $\Diamond$ is present alone, without a corresponding $\Box$, we have instead

$$A \to B \implies \Diamond A \to \Diamond B \qquad \Diamond \bot \to \bot \qquad \Diamond (A \lor B) \to \Diamond A \lor \Diamond B$$

DEFINITION 4.12 (KLEENE STAR RULES)
For the Kleene star, we add the rules

$$A \rightarrow A^*$$
$$A^* \circ A^* \rightarrow A^*$$
$$B \circ B \rightarrow B, \; A \rightarrow B \Longrightarrow A^* \rightarrow B$$

DEFINITION 4.13 (OF COURSE RULES)
For the exponential !, we add the rules

$$!A \rightarrow !!A$$
$$A \circ !B \rightarrow A$$
$$!A \rightarrow !A \circ !A$$
$$t \rightarrow !t$$
$$A \rightarrow B \Longrightarrow !A \rightarrow !B$$

DEFINITION 4.14 (TRANSLATIONS OF STRUCTURAL RULES)
For any structural rules of the form $X \Leftarrow X'$, we add the axiom

$$\tau(X') \rightarrow \tau(X)$$

DEFINITION 4.15 (THE HILBERT SYSTEM CORRESPONDING TO $\mathfrak{S}$)
The Hilbert system $\mathfrak{H}\mathfrak{S}$ corresponding to an expressive natural deduction system $\mathfrak{S}$ is the collection of rule sets corresponding to the connectives and rules appearing in $\mathfrak{S}$.

Our result then is made up of two theorems. First, that anything provable by the Hilbert system is also provable in the natural deduction system. And then its converse. We attempt the first theorem first.

THEOREM 4.16 (SOUNDNESS FOR $\mathfrak{H}\mathfrak{S}$)
If there is a proof of A in $\mathfrak{H}\mathfrak{S}$, then in $\mathfrak{S}$, $0 \vdash A$ can be proved.

To prove this we need a small lemma, about τ.

LEMMA 4.17 (τ IS A FITTING TRANSLATION)
In any natural deduction system $\mathfrak{S}$, we can prove $X \vdash \tau(X)$. Furthermore, if $X \vdash A$ is provable, so is $\tau(X) \vdash A$.

PROOF   The first part is a simple induction on the complexity of X. Clearly, if X is a formula or 0, then the proof is an instance of an axiom. Otherwise, note that $Y; Z \vdash \tau(Y) \circ \tau(Z)$ follows from $Y \vdash \tau(Y)$ and $Z \vdash \tau(Z)$ by $(\circ I)$, and $Y, Z \vdash \tau(Y) \wedge \tau(Z)$ follows from $Y \vdash \tau(Y)$ and $Z \vdash \tau(Z)$ by eK and $(\wedge I)$, and finally, $\bullet Y \vdash \Diamond \tau(Y)$ follows from $Y \vdash \tau(Y)$ by $(\Diamond I)$. So each induction step goes through.

The second part is harder. We will prove it by step-by-step replacing the punctuation marks in X by their corresponding connectives. The rule $(\circ E)$ tells us immediately that if $X(B; C) \vdash A$ then $X(B \circ C) \vdash A$, and (tE) tells us that if $X(0) \vdash A$ then $X(t) \vdash A$, and $(\Diamond E)$ that if $X(\bullet B) \vdash A$ then $X(\Diamond B) \vdash A$. For the extensional comma, if $X(B, C) \vdash A$ then since $B \wedge C \vdash B$ and $B \wedge C \vdash C$, two cuts give us a proof of $X(B \wedge C, B \wedge C) \vdash A$, and by eWI, $X(B \wedge C) \vdash A$. Continue this process, step-by-step replacing each punctuation mark by its corresponding connective, and you have the result.   □

Now we can prove the theorem.

PROOF   This proof is a tedious induction on the length of the Hilbert proof of A. We first must show that if A is an axiom of the Hilbert system, then $0 \vdash A$ can be proven in the natural deduction system. Then the inductive step involves going over each rule of the Hilbert system and showing that if you can prove the premises of the rule in the natural deduction system, you can also prove the conclusion.

There are an awful lot of rules and axioms we have seen, and going through every last one of them would make this chapter much more tedious than it need be. I will go through a representative sample of the axioms and rules.

Proofs of many of the axioms have been presented already. For example, on page 34 you have a proof of $(A \to C) \wedge (B \to C) \vdash A \vee B \to C$, and this is easily transformed into a proof of $0 \vdash (A \to C) \wedge (B \to C) \to (A \vee B \to C)$. The same goes for the other conjunction or disjunction axioms. For the fusion distribution laws, we have the following:

$$
\dfrac{
\dfrac{
\dfrac{\dfrac{C \vdash C \quad A \vdash A}{C; A \vdash C \circ A}(\circ I)}{C; A \vdash (C \circ A) \vee (C \circ B)}(\vee I) \qquad
\dfrac{\dfrac{C \vdash C \quad B \vdash B}{C; B \vdash C \circ B}(\circ I)}{C; B \vdash (C \circ A) \vee (C \circ B)}(\vee I)
}{
\dfrac{\dfrac{C; A \vee B \vdash (C \circ A) \vee (C \circ B)}{C \circ (A \vee B) \vdash (C \circ A) \vee (C \circ B)} *(\circ E)}{\dfrac{0; C \circ (A \vee B) \vdash (C \circ A) \vee (C \circ B)}{0 \vdash C \circ (A \vee B) \to (C \circ A) \vee (C \circ B)}(\to I)}[\text{Left Push}]
} *(\vee E)
}{}
$$

(We have suppressed some side formulae in the steps marked with an asterisk.)

Another example is the exponential axiom $A \circ !B \rightarrow A$.

$$
\cfrac{
  \cfrac{
    A \circ !B \vdash A \circ !B \quad
    \cfrac{
      !B \vdash !B \quad
      \cfrac{A \vdash A}{A; [B] \vdash A}
    }{A; !B \vdash A}
  }{
    \cfrac{
      \cfrac{A \circ !B \vdash A}{0; A \circ !B \vdash A} \text{[Left Push]}
    }{0 \vdash A \circ !B \rightarrow A} (\rightarrow I)
  } (\circ E)
}{}
$$

The remaining axioms are also straightforward to prove, except for the axiom $\tau(X) \rightarrow \tau(X')$, corresponding to the structural rule $X' \Leftarrow X$. This requires the lemma. The lemma gives us $X' \vdash \tau(X')$, and the structural rule then gives us $X \vdash \tau(X')$. The second part of the lemma then shows us that $\tau(X) \vdash \tau(X')$ is provable, which is then transformed into $0 \vdash \tau(X) \rightarrow \tau(X')$ by 0 and $\rightarrow$ rules.

We will try a couple of the rules. From $0 \vdash A \circ B \rightarrow C$ we can derive $0 \vdash B \rightarrow (A \rightarrow C)$ like this

$$
\cfrac{
  \cfrac{
    \cfrac{
      \cfrac{A \vdash A \quad B \vdash B}{A; B \vdash A \circ B} (\circ I) \quad 0 \vdash A \circ B \rightarrow C
    }{A; B \vdash C} (\rightarrow E)
  }{A \vdash B \rightarrow C} (\rightarrow I)
}{0 \vdash A \rightarrow (B \rightarrow C)} \text{[Left Push]}, (\rightarrow I)
$$

From $0 \vdash A \rightarrow B, 0 \vdash C \rightarrow D$ you can derive $0 \vdash (B \rightarrow C) \rightarrow (A \rightarrow D)$ like this

$$
\cfrac{
  \cfrac{
    \cfrac{
      B \rightarrow C \vdash B \rightarrow C \quad
      \cfrac{0 \vdash A \rightarrow B}{A \vdash B} (\rightarrow E), \text{[Left Pop]}
    }{(B \rightarrow C); A \vdash C} (\rightarrow E) \quad
    \cfrac{0 \vdash C \rightarrow D}{}
  }{
    \cfrac{(B \rightarrow C); A \vdash D}{B \rightarrow C \vdash A \rightarrow D} (\rightarrow I)
  } (\rightarrow E), \text{[Left Pop]}
}{0 \vdash (B \rightarrow C) \rightarrow (A \rightarrow D)} \text{[Left Push]}, (\rightarrow I)
$$

From $0 \vdash A$ and $0 \vdash A \rightarrow B$ you can derive $0 \vdash B$ trivially by $(\rightarrow E)$, and from $0 \vdash A \rightarrow {\sim}B$ you have $0 \vdash B \rightarrow \neg A$ using the negation rules.

Finally, for the Kleene star rule, suppose $0 \vdash B \circ B \rightarrow B$ and $0 \vdash A \rightarrow B$ are provable. Then we have proofs of $B; B \vdash B$ and $A \vdash B$ by simple manipulation, and hence, (with $A^* \vdash A^*$) the rule $(*E)$ gives $A^* \vdash B$ and hence $0 \vdash A^* \rightarrow B$ as desired.

This inspection of the rules completes our presentation of the proof.   □

COROLLARY 4.18 (PROVING CONSECUTIONS IN 𝔥𝔊)
If $\tau(X \vdash A)$ is provable in the Hilbert system $\mathfrak{H}\mathfrak{G}$, then $X \vdash A$ is provable in $\mathfrak{G}$.

PROOF If $\tau(X \vdash A)$ is provable in the Hilbert system, then our previous theorem shows that there is a proof in $\mathfrak{G}$ of $0 \vdash \tau(X \vdash A)$. That is, there is a proof of $0 \vdash \tau(X) \to A$. However, we have a proof of $X \vdash \tau(X)$, so we can paste these two proofs together like this:

$$\frac{X \vdash \tau(X) \quad 0 \vdash \tau(X) \to A}{X \vdash A}$$

resulting in the proof of $X \vdash A$ we wanted. □

That shows us that the Hilbert system is sound. Anything it can prove is already provable in the natural deduction system. However, this leaves open the possibility that the system is too weak. Maybe there are not Hilbert proofs of *everything* provable in the natural deduction theorem.

The rest of this section is devoted to showing that this cannot be the case. The Hilbert system is also *complete*. It covers all of the ground of the natural deduction system. To prove the completeness theorem, it is helpful to first prove a few more lemmas.

LEMMA 4.19 (TRANSLATION LEMMA)
If there is a Hilbert proof of $A \to B$ then there is also a Hilbert proof of $\tau(X(A)) \to \tau(X(B))$.

PROOF This is a simple induction on the complexity of $X(A)$. The atomic case is simple. For the induction steps we need only that $t \to t$ is provable (simple) and that if $A \to B$ is provable, so are

$$\Diamond A \to \Diamond B$$
$$C \circ' A \to C \circ' B$$
$$A \circ' C \to B \circ' C$$
$$C \wedge A \to C \wedge B$$
$$A \wedge C \to B \wedge C$$

in any Hilbert system in which the rules for $\Diamond$, $\circ'$ and $\wedge$ are included. We will choose the possibility rule, one fusion rule and one conjunction rule, and leave the others for you.

First, possibility. If the necessity operator $\Box$ is available, we can reason as follows. We have $\Diamond B \to \Diamond B$, and so one Hilbert rule gives us $B \to \Box\Diamond B$. The transitivity $A \to B, C \to D \implies (B \to C) \to (A \to D)$ gives us, when $B = C$, with *modus ponens*, simple transitivity. In other words, if $A \to B$, and $B \to C$ are provable, so is $A \to C$. Applying this to our case, where we have

$A \rightarrow B$ and $B \rightarrow \Box \Diamond B$, we get $A \rightarrow \Box \Diamond B$. But the necessity and possibility rule applies again, to give us $\Diamond A \rightarrow \Diamond B$ as desired.

If $\Box$ is not available to give us this trick, then we must rely on the rule $A \rightarrow B \Longrightarrow \Diamond A \rightarrow \Diamond B$ to give us the result.

Now for $C \circ' A \rightarrow C \circ' B$. If the left-to-right conditional $\rightarrow$ for $\circ'$ is available, we can reason like this. We have $C \circ B \rightarrow C \circ' B$ as an axiom, so the fusion rule gives us $C \rightarrow (B \rightarrow' C \circ' B)$. But we have $A \rightarrow B$, so we also have $(B \rightarrow' C \circ' B) \rightarrow (A \rightarrow' C \circ' B)$, so putting these together we have $C \rightarrow (A \rightarrow' C \circ' B)$ and hence $C \circ' A \rightarrow C \circ' B$ as desired.

If the left-to-right conditional is not available, we must rely on the rule $A \rightarrow B \Longrightarrow C \circ' A \rightarrow C \circ' B$, provided for the occasion.

Lastly, $A \wedge C \rightarrow B \wedge C$. Clearly we have $A \wedge C \rightarrow B$ (since $A \rightarrow B$) and $A \wedge C \rightarrow C$. But $(A \wedge C \rightarrow B) \wedge (A \wedge C \rightarrow C) \rightarrow (A \wedge C \rightarrow B \wedge C)$ is an instance of an axiom, so by the *modus ponens* rule, we have $A \wedge C \rightarrow B \wedge C$.

The other two cases are similar. $\Box$

LEMMA 4.20 (DISTRIBUTION OF STRUCTURE)
$\tau(X(A \vee B)) \rightarrow \tau(X(A)) \vee \tau(X(B))$ *is provable in the Hilbert System* $\mathfrak{H}\mathfrak{S}$.

PROOF   This is also an induction on the complexity of X. The base case is trivial. For the induction steps we need to show that if $X(A)$ is of the form $Y(A), Z$ or $Z, Y(A)$ or $Y(A); Z$, $Z; Y(A)$ or $\bullet Y(A)$ then granted that the hypothesis holds of $Y(A)$ then it also holds of $X(A)$. We will do three out of the four steps.

If $X(A) = Y(A), Z$ then we need only show that $(Y(A \vee B)) \wedge Z \rightarrow (Y(A) \wedge (Z)) \vee (Y(B) \wedge (Z))$ (We suppress the each τ for convenience). But we have $Y(A \vee B) \rightarrow Y(A) \vee Y(B)$ by hypothesis, and so, we have $Y(A \vee B) \wedge Z \rightarrow (Y(A) \vee Y(B)) \wedge Z$. But because we have a comma in the system $\mathfrak{S}$, we have distribution in $\mathfrak{H}\mathfrak{S}$. As a result, $(Y(A) \vee Y(B)) \wedge Z \rightarrow (Y(A) \wedge Z) \vee (Y(B) \wedge Z)$, giving us the result.

If $X(A) = Y(A);'Z$, then we need to show that $Y(A \vee B) \circ' Z \rightarrow (Y(A) \circ' Z) \vee (Y(B) \circ' Z)$. If the left-to-right conditional $\rightarrow'$ of $\circ'$ is available, we have $Y(A) \rightarrow (Z \rightarrow' Y(A) \circ' Z)$ and $Y(B) \rightarrow (Z \rightarrow' Y(B) \circ' Z)$, so we have $Y(A) \rightarrow (Z \rightarrow' (Y(A) \circ' Z) \vee (Y(B) \circ' Z))$ and $Y(B) \rightarrow (Z \rightarrow' (Y(A) \circ' Z) \vee (Y(B) \circ' Z))$, which together give us $Y(A) \vee Y(B) \rightarrow (Z \rightarrow' (Y(A) \circ' Z) \vee (Y(B) \circ' Z))$, but the hypothesis that $Y(A \vee B) \rightarrow Y(A) \vee Y(B)$ means that $Y(A \vee B) \rightarrow (Z \rightarrow (Y(A) \circ' Z) \vee (Y(B) \circ' Z))$ is provable, and hence, we have $Y(A \vee B) \circ' Z \rightarrow (Y(A) \circ' Z) \vee (Y(B) \circ' Z)$ as we desired. If the relevant conditional is not available for this argument, then we rely on the axiom $(A \vee B) \circ' C \rightarrow (A \circ' C) \vee (B \circ' C)$.

If $X(A) = \bullet Y(A)$ then we wish to prove $\Diamond(Y(A \vee B)) \rightarrow \Diamond Y(A) \vee \Diamond Y(B)$. If $\Box$ is present, then we have $Y(A) \rightarrow \Box \Diamond Y(A)$, and $Y(B) \rightarrow \Box \Diamond Y(B)$, and hence $Y(A) \rightarrow \Box \Diamond Y(A) \vee \Box \Diamond Y(B)$, and $Y(B) \rightarrow \Box \Diamond Y(A) \vee \Box \Diamond Y(B)$, which together give us $Y(A) \vee Y(B) \rightarrow \Box \Diamond Y(A) \vee \Box \Diamond Y(B)$, and hence $Y(A) \vee Y(B) \rightarrow \Box(\Diamond Y(A) \vee \Diamond Y(B))$, and $\Diamond(Y(A) \vee Y(B)) \rightarrow \Diamond Y(A) \vee \Diamond Y(B)$ as desired. If $\Box$ is not available for this proof, you must rely on the axiom $\Diamond(A \vee B) \rightarrow \Diamond A \vee \Diamond B$ for this result. $\qquad\qquad\square$

Now we can prove our completeness theorem.

THEOREM 4.21 (COMPLETENESS FOR $\mathfrak{H}\mathfrak{S}$)
If $X \vdash A$ is provable in the system $\mathfrak{S}$, then $\tau(X \vdash A)$ is provable in $\mathfrak{H}\mathfrak{S}$.

PROOF   If $X \vdash A$ is an axiom, then $\tau(X \vdash A)$ is provable. The only axioms are $A \vdash A$, $0 \vdash t$, or a special negation axiom. These translate into axioms in $\mathfrak{H}\mathfrak{S}$.

If $X \vdash A$ follows from a collection of consecutions by a rule, then we can assume that the premises in that rule are all provable (under translation) in $\mathfrak{H}\mathfrak{S}$. It remains to show that the translation $\tau(X \vdash A)$ of the conclusion is also provable. To do this you must inspect every rule to show that if the translation of the premises are $\mathfrak{H}\mathfrak{S}$ theorems, then so is the translation of the conclusion. This is a tedious but simple task. We will work through the details of some representative rules and leave the rest as an exercise.

Consider $(\rightarrow E)$, $(\circ E)$, $(\vee E)$, $(\sim I)$, $(\Diamond E)$, and the structural rules.

First, if the premises of $(\rightarrow E)$ are provable, then we have a Hilbert proof of $\tau(X) \rightarrow (A \rightarrow B)$ and $\tau(Y) \rightarrow A$. We need a proof of $\tau(X;Y) \rightarrow B$, that is $\tau(X) \circ \tau(Y) \rightarrow B$. From $\tau(X) \rightarrow A \rightarrow B$ we can derive $\tau(X) \circ A \rightarrow B$. From $\tau(Y) \rightarrow A$ we can derive $\tau(X) \circ \tau(Y) \rightarrow \tau(X) \circ A$, and from these we have $\tau(X) \circ \tau(Y) \rightarrow B$ as desired.

For $(\circ E)$, we want to derive $\tau(Y(X)) \rightarrow C$ from $\tau(X) \rightarrow A \circ B$ and $\tau(Y(A;B)) \rightarrow C$. Now $\tau(Y(A;B)) = \tau(Y(A \circ B))$, and that if we have a proof of $A \rightarrow B$ then we have a proof of $Y(A) \rightarrow Y(B)$.

For $(\vee E)$, we need a proof of $\tau(Y(X)) \rightarrow C$ from $\tau(X) \rightarrow A \vee B$, $\tau(Y(A)) \rightarrow C$, and $\tau(Y(B)) \rightarrow C$. But by Lemma 4.20 $\tau(X) \rightarrow A \vee B$ gives us $\tau(Y(X)) \rightarrow \tau(Y(A)) \vee \tau(Y(B))$, and hence $\tau(Y(X)) \rightarrow C$ as desired.

For $(\sim I)$, suppose we have a proof of $A \rightarrow \neg B$, and of $\tau(X) \rightarrow B$. Then we have $B \rightarrow \sim A$, by the $\neg/\sim$-rule of $\mathfrak{H}\mathfrak{S}$, and hence $\tau(X) \rightarrow \sim A$ as desired.

For $(\Diamond E)$ we need to show that if $\tau(X) \rightarrow \Diamond A$, $\tau(Y(\bullet A)) \rightarrow B$ are provable then so is $\tau(Y(X)) \rightarrow B$. But $\tau(Y(\bullet A)) = \tau(Y(\Diamond A))$, and so we have a proof of $\tau(Y(X)) \rightarrow \tau(Y(\bullet A))$, which with transitivity gives us $\tau(Y(X)) \rightarrow B$ as desired.

For structural rules of the form $X' \Leftarrow X$, we need to show that if $\tau(X') \rightarrow A$ is provable, so is $\tau(X) \rightarrow A$. But we have $\tau(X) \rightarrow \tau(X')$ as an axiom, so simple transitivity suffices.

For ECQ, if $\tau(X) \to A$ and $\tau(X) \to {\sim}A$ are provable, then we have $\tau(X) \to A \wedge {\sim}A$, which with $A \wedge {\sim}A \to \bot$ gives $\tau(X) \to \bot$ as we wished.

For $(*M)$, if $\tau(X) \to A^*$ and $\tau(Y) \to A^*$ then $\tau(X) \circ \tau(Y) \to A^* \circ A^*$ and by the Hilbert axiom $A^* \circ A^* \to A^*$ we get $\tau(X) \circ \tau(Y) \to A^*$, but this is just $\tau(X;Y) \to A^*$ as we desired.

For $(!I)$, we need just a little more work. First, we note that in LL, $\tau([X])$ can be transformed into a proposition of the form $!B$, since $!C \circ !D$ is equivalent to $!(C \wedge D)$. Now, we will show that if $!A \vdash B$ is provable, so is $!A \vdash !B$. This follows from $!!A \vdash !B$, and the axiom $!A \to !!A$.

These examples complete our presentation of the proof. □

4.2　Hand Tuning

The Hilbert system we have seen has been adequate for our logics, though the systems contain redundancy in many cases. It is good for a Hilbert system to have *few* rules. In this section we will see what changes can be made in order to cut down on the number of rules used.

LEMMA 4.22 (PREFIXING AND SUFFIXING)
If the system contains B *and* B′, *the transitivity rule*

$$A \to B, C \to D \Longrightarrow (B \to C) \to (A \to D)$$

can be replaced by the axioms

$$(A \to B) \to \big((C \to A) \to (C \to B)\big)$$
$$(A \to B) \to \big((B \to C) \to (A \to C)\big)$$

which do the same job.

PROOF　The axioms are provable with B and B′, as is simple to check. Once you have these axioms, if $A \to B$ is provable, so is $(B \to C) \to (A \to C)$, by the second axiom, and *modus ponens*. If $C \to D$ is provable, so is $(A \to C) \to (A \to D)$, by the first axiom and *modus ponens*. Applying the second axiom again, with *modus ponens*, we get $(B \to C) \to (A \to D)$ as required. □

We can also eliminate the t rules.

LEMMA 4.23 (t AXIOM)
In the presence of Right Push *and* Right Pop *you can replace the* t *rules with* $A \leftrightarrow (t \to A)$.

PROOF　Straightforward. □

LEMMA 4.24 (FUSION AXIOMS)

In the presence of B *and* B^c *you can replace the fusion rules with* $(A \circ B \to C) \leftrightarrow (A \to (B \to C))$.

PROOF It is sufficient to show that these are provable in the natural deduction system, given B and B^c, as they, with *modus ponens*, give the fusion rules. The following proofs suffice:

$$\cfrac{A \circ B \vdash A \circ B \quad \cfrac{A \circ B \to C \vdash A \circ B \to C}{A \circ B \to C; A \circ B \vdash C}}{\cfrac{(A \circ B \to C); (A; B) \vdash C}{\cfrac{((A \circ B \to C); A); B \vdash C}{A \circ B \to C \vdash A \to (B \to C)} 2 \times (\to I)} [\text{B}]}$$

$$\cfrac{A \circ B \vdash A \circ B \quad \cfrac{\cfrac{A \to (B \to C) \vdash A \to (B \to C)}{(A \to (B \to C); A); B \vdash C} 2 \times (\to E)}{A \to (B \to C); (A; B) \vdash C} [\text{B}^c]}{\cfrac{A \to (B \to C); A \circ B \vdash C}{A \to (B \to C) \vdash A \circ B \to C} (\to I)}$$ □

LEMMA 4.25 (NEGATION RULES)

In the presence of $\sim E; \neg I$, *you can replace the negation rules with* $(A \to \sim B) \to (B \to \neg A)$ *and* $(A \to \neg B) \to (B \to \sim A)$. □

For the other structural rules, we can replace the fusion axiom with the following axioms in Table 4.1.

For each row of the table, you can replace the fusion axiom with the corresponding implication axiom, which does the same job. For example, instead of the WI axiom $A \to A \circ A$, we can use the implication axiom $(A \to B) \land A \to B$. The equivalence holds as follows. If we have $A \to A \circ A$, then we can show that $(A \to B) \land A \to B$, as follows. First, it is straightforward to show that $(A \to B) \circ A \to B$ is provable in the Hilbert system. But $(A \to B) \land A \to ((A \to B) \land A) \circ ((A \to B) \land A)$ is an instance of the WI fusion axiom. Then we have $((A \to B) \land A) \circ ((A \to B) \land A) \to (A \to B) \circ A$, so transitivity of $\to$ gives us $(A \to B) \land A \to B$ as desired.

Conversely, to prove $A \to A \circ A$, we have proofs of $A \to A$ and $A \to (A \to A \circ A)$, so we have $A \to (A \to A \circ A) \land A$. But by our axiom, $(A \to A \circ A) \land A \to A \circ A$, so transitivity gives $A \to A \circ A$ as desired.

Demonstrating the other axioms directly is a good exercise in constructing Hilbert proofs, and they are left for Exercise 4.2.

Label	Axiom
B	$(A \to B) \to ((C \to A) \to (C \to B))$
B'	$(A \to B) \to ((B \to C) \to (A \to C))$
B^c	$((B \leftarrow C) \leftarrow (A \leftarrow C)) \leftarrow (B \leftarrow A)$
C	$(A \to (B \to C)) \to (B \to (A \to C))$
CI	$A \to ((A \to B) \to B)$
W	$(A \to (A \to B)) \to (A \to B)$
WI	$(A \to B) \wedge A \to B$
M	$A \to (A \to A)$
K	$A \to (B \to A)$
K'	$A \to (B \to B)$

Table 4.1: Structural Rules

4.3 *Consequence and Deduction Theorems*

In Hilbert systems, we can define a new notion of consequence, by setting $\Sigma \vdash_H$ A if there is a Hilbert proof of A using additional axioms from among those in the set Σ. In substructural logics in general, $\vdash_H$ differs from $\vdash$. For example, we have $\{B\} \vdash_H A$ whenever A is provable, no matter how irrelevant B is to A. Similarly, we have $\{B\} \vdash_H B \circ B$ even in the absence of contraction, since $\vdash B \to (B \to B \circ B)$ and using *modus ponens* twice, we have $B \circ B$. In this section, we will examine logics with no modal connectives $\square$ and $\diamondsuit$, with one set of intensional connectives from among $\circ, \to, \leftarrow, t$ and with perhaps negation connectives. We will show that $\vdash_H$ is related to implication in a similar way to the standard deduction theorem

$$\frac{X; A \vdash B}{X \vdash A \to B}$$

The Hilbert consequence relation allows contraction and irrelevance. For this, we need a definition

DEFINITION 4.26 (CONFUSION)
A *confusion* of the propositions in the set Σ is defined inductively as follows.

  $\diamond$ t, $\top$ and any element of Σ are confusions of Σ.

  $\diamond$ If C_1 and C_2 are confusions of Σ, so are $C_1 \circ C_2$ and $C_1 \wedge C_2$.

The name is taken from the combination of *conjunction* and *fusion*.

Note the following result.

LEMMA 4.27 (CONFUSION CLOSURE)
In any Hilbert system defined above, $\Sigma \vdash_H B$ whenever B is a confusion of Σ.

PROOF By induction on the complexity of B. For the base case, $\Sigma \vdash_H t \Sigma \vdash_H \top$, and $\Sigma \vdash C$ for any $C \in \Sigma$.

For the induction step, if $\Sigma \vdash_H C_1$ and $\Sigma \vdash_H C_2$ then $\Sigma \vdash_H C_1 \wedge C_2$ by the conjunction rule. And similarly, $\vdash C_1 \rightarrow (C_2 \rightarrow C_1 \circ C_2)$ gives, by two applications of *modus ponens*, $\Sigma \vdash_H C_1 \circ C_2$. □

THEOREM 4.28 (HILBERT DEDUCTION THEOREM)
In any Hilbert system in which the only rules are modus ponens *and conjunction introduction, $\Sigma \cup \{A\} \vdash_H B$ if and only if $\Sigma \vdash_H C \rightarrow B$ where C is some confusion of $\{A\}$.*

PROOF If $\Sigma \vdash_H C \rightarrow B$ then $\Sigma \cup \{A\} \vdash_H C$ (by Lemma 4.27) so $\Sigma \cup \{A\} \vdash B$ by *modus ponens*.

For the converse we assume that $\Sigma \cup \{A\} \vdash_H B$. Assume that the proof is of length m and that the result holds for proofs of smaller length. Now B is either in $\Sigma \cup \{A\}$, or it is an axiom, or it follows from earlier propositions in the proof by means of the rules. In the first cases, if B is in $\Sigma \cup \{A\}$ or is an axiom, we are home, as $\Sigma \vdash t \wedge A \rightarrow B$. Suppose B follows from earlier claims in the proof by way of the rules. If the rule is *modus ponens* we have confusions C_1 and C_2, where $\Sigma \vdash_H C_1 \rightarrow (B' \rightarrow B)$ and $\Sigma \vdash_H C_2 \rightarrow B'$, since $C_1 \rightarrow (B' \rightarrow B), C_2 \rightarrow B' \vdash_H C_1 \circ C_2 \rightarrow B$ gives us $\Sigma \vdash_H C_1 \circ C_2 \rightarrow B$ and $C_1 \circ C_2$ is the desired confusion.

If the rule is conjunction introduction, then we have confusions C_1 and C_2, where $\Sigma \vdash_H C_1 \rightarrow B_1$ and $\Sigma \vdash_H C_2 \rightarrow B_2$, where $B = B_1 \wedge B_2$. Clearly, $C_1 \wedge C_2$ is the confusion, such that $\Sigma \vdash_H C_1 \wedge C_2 \rightarrow B$.

By assumption, these are the only rules and this completes the proof. □

4.4 History

Anderson and Belnap, and Ackermann and others used Hilbert systems extensively in their presentations of substructural logics [2, 6]. They facilitate some formal proofs (such as those for metavaluations, in Chapter 5) in which it is helpful to have many axioms and few rules. However, as the exercises show, they are not simple to use when it comes to actually constructing proofs. Meyer and Routley have given alternative axiomatisations of relevant logics which contain Boolean negation '$-$', and the material conditional $A \supset B =_{df} -A \vee B$, as the primary connective [168, 169].

4.5   *Exercises*

Practice

{4.1} Construct Hilbert proofs of $(A \rightarrow B) \circ A \rightarrow B$, $(A \rightarrow B) \rightarrow (A \rightarrow B \vee C)$, $(A \rightarrow B) \rightarrow (A \wedge C \rightarrow B)$ using only basic Hilbert axioms and rules (no axioms corresponding to structural rules).

{4.2} For each of the rows of Table 4.1, verify that the implicational axiom holds in a Hilbert system if and only if the corresponding fusion axiom can be proved in that system.

Problems

{4.3} Work through the rest of the proof of Lemma 4.17.

{4.4} Compare and contrast the two consequence relations $\vdash$ and $\vdash_H$. In what ways are they related? In what ways do they differ?

Projects

{4.5} If you are familiar with the term assignment systems of Chapter 7, and you are familiar with combinatory logic [55, 56, 57, 116] you may be interested to know that you can give a 'term assignment' system for Hilbert Systems involving $\rightarrow$ formulae. Each axiom has its own combinator. For example, W is $(A \rightarrow (A \rightarrow B)) \rightarrow (A \rightarrow B)$. If X is the term for one axiom, and Y is the term for another, then XY is the term for the result of the application of X to Y using *modus ponens*. Make this definition rigorous, and show how combinators can be related to arbitrary Hilbert proofs using the axioms in Table 4.1 and the rule *modus ponens*. Then, show how the reduction rules for combinators (for example — Kxy reduces to x) correspond to rules for shortening Hilbert proofs.

{4.6} Reformulate the axiomatisation with neither $\leftarrow$ nor $\rightarrow$ as primary. That is, find an axiomatisation of the $\vdash$ relation where you axiomatise the validities of the form $A \vdash B$ where A and B are formulae.

Chapter 5

Theories

Dear friend,
theory is all grey,
And the golden tree of life is green.
— Goethe, Faust

Logic is not merely about individual propositions and consequence relations between them. *Theories* are interesting too. Theories are bodies of propositions with some degree of internal coherence or structure. Real-life theories — such as the theory of general relativity, Frege's theory of naïve set theory, Luther's theory of justification by faith or Marx's theory of dialectical materialism — are very complex entities, with many different kinds of coherence and structure. In our logics we abstract away from almost everything in a real theory to concentrate on just one aspect of theories.

5.1 Defining Theories

DEFINITION 5.1 (THEORIES)
Given a system $\mathfrak{S}$, a *theory* in that system is a set of formulae closed under consequence, and closed under conjunction (if conjunction is present in the language). So, T is a theory if and only if

◇ If $A \in T$, and $A \vdash B$ then $B \in T$.

◇ If the language contains conjunction, if $A, B \in T$ then $A \wedge B \in T$.

In this chapter we will examine theories in logics, partly because they are interesting structures in their own right, partly because we can use them to prove useful theorems, and partly because this will become important in later chapters, when we use theories to give modellings of logics.

EXAMPLE 5.2 (THE THEORY OF A STRUCTURE X)
Given a natural deduction system $\mathfrak{S}$, and given some structure X, the set of all consequences of X is a theory. In other words, the set

$$\{A : X \vdash A\}$$

is a theory. If $X \vdash A$ and $A \vdash B$, then $X \vdash B$ by Cut, and if $X \vdash A$ and $X \vdash B$ (and conjunction is present) then $X \vdash A \wedge B$ by $(\wedge I)$.

EXAMPLE 5.3 (THE SET OF HILBERT THEOREMS IS A THEORY)
Given any Hilbert system $\mathfrak{H}S$, the set of formulae provable in that system is a
theory. This follows from our previous example, as the set of Hilbert-provable
claims is the set of propositions A such that $0 \vdash A$ in the natural deduction
system.

EXAMPLE 5.4 (THE TRUTH IS A THEORY)
The set of true propositions (in some language, or other) is, no doubt, a theory.
If A is true, and B follows from A, then B is also true. If A and B are both true,
then $A \wedge B$ is true. This is a special sort of theory because it has very special
properties, as we shall soon see.

EXAMPLE 5.5 (THEORIES CLASSIFYING STRINGS)
In the world of the Lambek calculus, the set of types of a particular string ought
to be a theory. If $A \vdash B$ and a string is of type A, then it is also of type B. If a
string is both of type A and of type B then it is also of type $A \wedge B$. Similarly,
the set of types of a class of strings is a theory.

Theories can be classified in various ways. One important way to classify theories is to see how close they approximate the set of truths.

DEFINITION 5.6 (CLASSIFYING THEORIES)
A theory T in a system $\mathfrak{S}$ is

 ⋄ *prime* iff $A \vee B \in T$ only if $A \in T$ or $B \in T$.[1]
 ⋄ *∼-consistent* iff for no A is $A \in T$ and $\sim A \notin T$.
 ⋄ *∼-complete* iff for every A either $A \in T$ or $\sim A \in T$.
 ⋄ *t-normal* iff $t \in T$.
 ⋄ *→-detached* iff whenever $A \to B \in T$, then $A \in T$ only if $B \in T$.
 ⋄ *non-empty* iff $\top \in T$.
 ⋄ *non-full* iff $\bot \notin T$.
 ⋄ *non-trivial* iff it is both non-empty and non-full.

Each of these criteria makes the theory T respect the behaviour of the connectives in the language, or equivalently, they make the theory T approximate the
set of truths in some language. Consider primeness first. A theory is prime if
and only if it "gets disjunction right." Read '… $\in T$' as '… is true.' Then the
primeness condition is 'if $A \vee B$ is true then A is true or B is true.' Similarly, the
negation conditions together are '$\sim A$ is true if and only if A is not true.'

---

[1]   Here, and elsewhere, we use 'iff' as shorthand for 'if and only if.'

The t condition is 't is true.' The implication condition is 'if $A \to B$ is true, then if A is true so is B.' The non-triviality conditions mean simply that $\top$ is true and $\bot$ is not.

In traditional, classical logics, many of these conditions stand or fall together. In substructural logics, they are distinct.

LEMMA 5.7 (PRIMENESS IS $\sim$-COMPLETENESS, IF $\top \vdash A \vee \sim A$)
If strong excluded middle holds for $\sim$, then any non-empty prime theory is negation complete.

PROOF   If $\top \vdash A \vee \sim A$, and $\top \in T$, then if T is prime, since $A \vee \sim A \in T$ then either $A \in T$ or $\sim A \in T$, so T is complete.   □

If strong excluded middle fails, then you may have a prime theory which fails to be $\sim$-complete. We will prove this when we get to the next section and we have a technique for constructing prime theories.

LEMMA 5.8 (ECQ AND $\sim$-CONSISTENCY)
If ECQ holds then any $\sim$-inconsistent theory is the full theory.

PROOF   If T is $\sim$-inconsistent, then $A, \sim A \in T$ for some A. It follows then that $A \wedge \sim A \in T$, and by ECQ, $\bot \in T$, and T is full.   □

If ECQ fails, we can construct a $\sim$-inconsistent theory T which is not full. This is a simple construction. Take a proposition A such that $A, \sim A \nvdash \bot$. Consider the set $\{B : A \wedge \sim A \vdash B\}$. This is a $\sim$-inconsistent theory, yet it is not full, as $A \wedge \sim A \nvdash \bot$.

LEMMA 5.9 (t-NORMAL THEORIES WITH K$'$)
In the presence of K$'$, any non-empty theory is t-normal.

PROOF   If we have K$'$ then we can prove $\top \vdash t$, and hence any non-empty theory contains t.   □

If $\top \nvdash t$, then the set $\{A : \top \vdash A\}$ is a non-empty theory which is not t-normal.

LEMMA 5.10 (WI AND DETACHMENT)
If WI holds, then any theory is both $\to$- and $\leftarrow$-detached.

PROOF   If $A, A \to B \in T$ then $A \wedge (A \to B) \in T$, and in the presence of WI we can prove $A \wedge (A \to B) \vdash B$ so $B \in T$, so T is $\to$-detached. Similarly, with WI we can prove $A \wedge (B \leftarrow A) \vdash B$, so all theories are $\leftarrow$-detached.   □

As with our other cases, if $A \wedge (A \to B) \vdash B$ fails, we can construct a theory which fails our condition. Take $\{C : A \wedge (A \to B) \vdash C\}$ to be our theory. It fails to be $\to$-detached, but it remains a theory.

Primeness is an important property of theories, at least when it comes to applications in classifying strings or actions. In each of these applications, the set of all types of an object is a prime theory. This happens *whenever* you interpret formulae as follows: x is of type $A \vee B$ if and only if x is of type A or x is of type B. It will turn out, in Part III, that prime theories will play a very important role in studying models of our logics. The next section is devoted to a very useful technique for constructing prime theories.

5.2 *Constructing Prime Theories*

Suppose T is a theory and $A \notin T$. Is there a prime theory T' which extends T and which still avoids A? This section is devoted to finding conditions under which this is possible.

One way to extend T into a prime theory avoiding A is to keep on adding as many formulae as possible to T, while keeping A out. This will result in a prime theory, for if we could throw $B \vee C$ into the theory, we ought to be able to add in either B or C. This construction is at the heart of the Lindenbaum Lemma of classical logic, and such a construction works in a wide range of logical systems. Our first definition will characterise the logics in which the construction works.

DEFINITION 5.11 (PAIR EXTENSION ACCEPTABILITY)
A consequence relation $\vdash$ is *pair extension acceptable* if and only if for each A, B and C the following conditions hold

⋄ $A \vdash A$.

⋄ $A \wedge B \vdash A$ and $A \wedge B \vdash B$.

⋄ If $A \vdash B$ and $A \vdash C$ then $A \vdash B \wedge C$.

⋄ $A \vdash A \vee B$ and $B \vdash A \vee B$ for each A and B.

⋄ If $A \vdash C$ and $B \vdash C$ then $A \vee B \vdash C$.

⋄ $A \wedge (B \vee C) \vdash (A \wedge B) \vee (A \wedge C)$.

⋄ If $A \vdash B$ and $B \vdash C$ then $A \vdash C$.

These are *extremely* weak conditions. Note that the consequence relations $\vdash$ defined by any of our natural deduction systems are pair extension acceptable if they contain the extensional punctuation mark. (This is needed in order to prove the distribution of conjunction over disjunction.)

The condition of distributivity is necessary, for our proof will fail without it. If $A \wedge (B \vee C) \nvdash (A \wedge B) \vee (A \wedge C)$, then we would like to construct a prime theory containing $A \wedge (B \vee C)$ but not $(A \wedge B) \vee (A \wedge C)$. If there were such a theory, it would contain either $A \wedge B$ or $A \wedge C$. But since the theory contains $A \wedge (B \vee C)$, it must contain A and $B \vee C$, and by primeness, either B or C. This means that the theory contains $A \wedge B$ or $A \wedge C$, and hence $(A \wedge B) \vee (A \wedge C)$, which we wished to avoid. So, no such theory exists.

To prove our theorem, we will need to keep track not only of formulae we wish to add to our theory but also of formulae we wish to avoid.

DEFINITION 5.12 ($\vdash$-PAIRS)
An ordered pair $\langle x, y \rangle$ of sets of formulae is said to be a $\vdash$-*pair* if and only if there are *no* formulae $A_1, \ldots, A_n \in x$ and $B_1, \ldots, B_m \in y$ where $A_1 \wedge \cdots \wedge A_n \vdash B_1 \vee \cdots \vee B_m$.

A helpful shorthand will be to write '$\bigwedge A_i \vdash \bigvee B_j$' for the extended conjunctions.[2]

It will turn out that if $\langle x, y \rangle$ is a $\vdash$-pair, it can be "extended" to a new pair, where the left element of the pair is a prime theory. The set y is the set of formulae we wish to leave out of the prime theory extending x. Here is the definition of extension:

DEFINITION 5.13 (PAIR EXTENSION)
A $\vdash$-pair $\langle v, w \rangle$ *extends* $\langle x, y \rangle$ if and only if $v \supseteq x$ and $w \supseteq x$. We write this as '$\langle x, y \rangle \subseteq \langle v, w \rangle$.'

Now we show how to construct pairs.

LEMMA 5.14 (THEORIES AND $\vdash$-PAIRS)
If T is a theory such that $A \notin T$, then $\langle T, \{A\} \rangle$ is a $\vdash$-pair.
PROOF If $A \notin T$ then there are no formulae $A_1, \ldots, A_n \in T$ such that $\bigwedge_i A_i \vdash A$. It follows that $\langle T, \{A\} \rangle$ is a $\vdash$-pair. $\qquad \square$

DEFINITION 5.15 (FULL $\vdash$-PAIRS)
A $\vdash$-pair $\langle x, y \rangle$ is a *full $\vdash$-pair* if and only if $x \cup y$ is the entire language.

Full $\vdash$-pairs are important, for the following reason.

LEMMA 5.16 (PRIME THEORIES FROM FULL $\vdash$-PAIRS)
If $\langle x, y \rangle$ is a full $\vdash$-pair, x is a prime theory.
PROOF We need to verify that x is closed under consequence and conjunction, and that it is prime. First, consequence. Suppose $A \in x$ and that $A \vdash B$. If $B \notin x$, then since $\langle x, y \rangle$ is full, $B \in y$. But then $A \vdash B$ contradicts the condition that $\langle x, y \rangle$ is a $\vdash$-pair.

---

[2] Note that here we assume that the association of conjunctions and disjunctions does not matter.

Second, conjunction. If $A_1, A_2 \in x$, then since $A_1 \wedge A_2 \vdash A_1 \wedge A_2$, and $\langle x, y \rangle$ is a $\vdash$-pair, we must have $A_1 \wedge A_2 \notin y$, and since $\langle x, y \rangle$ is full, $A_1 \wedge A_2 \in x$ as desired.

Third, primeness. If $A_1 \vee A_2 \in x$, then if A_1 and A_2 are both not in x, by fullness, they are both in y, and since $A_1 \vee A_2 \vdash A_1 \vee A_2$, we have another contradiction to the claim that $\langle x, y \rangle$ is a $\vdash$-pair. Hence, one of A_1 and A_2 is in x, as we wished.   □

THEOREM 5.17 (PAIR EXTENSION THEOREM)
If $\vdash$ is pair extension acceptable, then any $\vdash$-pair $\langle x, y \rangle$ is extended by some full $\vdash$-pair $\langle v, w \rangle$.

To prove this theorem, we will assume that we have enumerated the language so that every formula in the language appears somewhere in the list

$$C_1, C_2, \ldots, C_n, \ldots$$

This way, we will be able to consider each formula one by one, to check to see whether we should throw it in with x or in with y instead. We assume, in doing this, that our language is *countable*. Not all languages are countable. We will not go into the details here, but the proof will still work in the absence of countability, provided that the language is *well ordered*. (The appropriate changes are left to the exercises.) The proof of the Pair Extension Theorem relies on one crucial lemma: the Step Lemma.

LEMMA 5.18 (STEP LEMMA)
If $\vdash$ is pair extension acceptable, then if $\langle x, y \rangle$ is a $\vdash$-pair, then so is at least one of $\langle x \cup \{C\}, y \rangle$ and $\langle x, y \cup \{C\} \rangle$.

PROOF It is sufficient to show that if $\langle x \cup \{C\}, y \rangle$ is not a $\vdash$-pair, then the alternative, $\langle x, y \cup \{C\} \rangle$, is. If this were not a $\vdash$-pair either, then there would be some $A \in \bigwedge x$ (the set of all conjunctions of formulae from x) and $B \in \bigvee y$ (the set of all disjunctions of formulae from y) such that $A \vdash B \vee C$. Since $\langle x \cup \{C\}, y \rangle$ is not a $\vdash$-pair, there are also $A' \in \bigwedge x$ and $B' \in \bigvee y$ such that $A' \wedge C \vdash B'$. But then we can reason as follows. First, $A \wedge A' \vdash B \vee C$. But this means that $A \wedge A' \vdash (B \vee C) \wedge A'$. Now by distributive lattice properties, we then get $A \wedge A' \vdash B \vee (A' \wedge C)$. But $A' \wedge C \vdash B'$, so cut, and disjunction properties give us $A \wedge A' \vdash B \vee B'$, contrary to the fact that $\langle x, y \rangle$ is a $\vdash$-pair. □

With that out of the way, we can prove the Pair Extension Theorem.

PROOF Take an enumeration of formulae in the language as $C_1, C_2, \ldots$ Define the series of $\vdash$-pairs $\langle x_n, y_n \rangle$ as follows. Let $\langle x_0, y_0 \rangle = \langle x, y \rangle$, and given $\langle x_n, y_n \rangle$ define $\langle x_{n+1}, y_{n+1} \rangle$ in this way.

$$\langle x_{n+1}, y_{n+1} \rangle = \begin{cases} \langle x_n \cup \{C_n\}, y_n \rangle & \text{if } \langle x_n \cup \{C_n\}, y_n \rangle \text{ is a } \vdash\text{-pair,} \\ \langle x_n, y_n \cup \{C_n\} \rangle & \text{otherwise.} \end{cases}$$

By the Step Lemma, each $\langle x_{n+1}, y_{n+1} \rangle$ is a $\vdash$-pair if its predecessor $\langle x_n, y_n \rangle$ is, for there is always a choice (*left* or *right*) for placing C_n while keeping the result a $\vdash$-pair. So, by induction on n, each $\langle x_n, y_n \rangle$ is a $\vdash$-pair. It follows then then $\langle \bigcup_{n \in \omega} x_n, \bigcup_{n \in \omega} y_n \rangle$, the limit of this process, is also a $\vdash$-pair, and it covers the whole language. It must cover the whole language as we have thrown in every formula in either the left or the right. And if $\langle \bigcup_{n \in \omega} x_n, \bigcup_{n \in \omega} y_n \rangle$ is not a $\vdash$-pair, then we have some $A_i \in \bigcup x_n$ and some $B_j \in \bigcup y_n$ such that $A_1 \wedge \cdots \wedge A_l \vdash B_1 \vee \cdots \vee B_m$, but if this is the case, then there is some number n where each A_i is in x_n and each B_j is in y_n. It would follow that $\langle x_n, y_n \rangle$ is not a $\vdash$-pair. So, we have our proof. $\qquad\square$

Now we can prove the theorem we originally wanted.

COROLLARY 5.19 (PRIME THEORIES EXCLUDING FORMULAE)
If $T \nvdash A$, then there is a prime theory $T' \supseteq T$ such that $A \notin T'$.

PROOF $\langle T, \{A\} \rangle$ is a $\vdash$-pair, so there is a full $\vdash$-pair $\langle T', S' \rangle$ extending $\langle T, A \rangle$, so T' is the desired prime theory. Since $A \in S'$, $A \notin T'$. $\qquad\square$

This result will become useful in Chapter 11, when it will be used repeatedly in the construction of models for logics with distribution.

COROLLARY 5.20 (NORMAL PRIME THEORIES EXCLUDING FORMULAE)
If $0 \nvdash A$, then there is a t-normal prime theory T such that $A \notin T$.

PROOF $\langle \{t\}, \{A\} \rangle$ is a $\vdash$-pair, so it is extended by a full $\vdash$-pair $\langle T, S \rangle$, and as $t \in T$, T is t-normal. $\qquad\square$

5.3 Metavaluations

The pair extension technique is a powerful method for proving the existence of prime theories. It is not too good, however, at establishing that a given theory is prime. In this section, we will use another technique which will show us that some theories (in particular, the class of theorems of a wide range of logics) are prime.

DEFINITION 5.21 (METAVALUING THEORIES)
Given set T of formulae the *metavaluation* $M(T)$ of T is a set of formulae defined as follows:

 ⋄ If A is an atomic formula, or t, $\top$ or $\bot$, $A \in M(T)$ iff $A \in T$.
 ⋄ $A \wedge B \in M(T)$ iff $A \in M(T)$ and $B \in M(T)$.
 ⋄ $A \vee B \in M(T)$ iff $A \in M(T)$ or $B \in M(T)$.
 ⋄ $\sim A \in M(T)$ iff $A \notin M(T)$ and $\sim A \in T$.
 ⋄ $\neg A \in M(T)$ iff $A \notin M(T)$ and $\neg A \in T$.

   ◇ $A \rightarrow B \in M(T)$ iff if $A \in M(T)$ then $B \in M(T)$ and $A \rightarrow B \in T$.
   ◇ $B \leftarrow A \in M(T)$ iff if $A \in M(T)$ then $B \in M(T)$ and $B \leftarrow A \in T$.
   ◇ $A \circ B \in M(T)$ iff $A \in M(T)$ and $B \in M(T)$ and $A \circ B \in T$.
   ◇ $\Box A \in M(T)$ iff $A \in M(T)$ and $\Box A \in T$.
   ◇ $\Diamond A \in M(T)$ iff $A \in M(T)$ and $\Diamond A \in T$.

In general, T and $M(T)$ differ. For example, if $A \vee B \in T$, it need not follow that $A \vee B \in M(T)$, as we might have neither $A \in M(T)$ nor $B \in M(T)$. If T is a theory however, we can immediately say something about the connection between T and $M(T)$.

LEMMA 5.22 (METAVALUING A THEORY)
If T is a theory, then $M(T) \subseteq T$.

PROOF   This is a simple induction on the construction of formulae. If A is atomic or $t, \top, \bot$, then $A \in T$ if and only if $A \in M(T)$. If A is a conjunction $B \wedge C$, then if $A \in M(T)$, $B, C \in M(T)$ and by hypothesis, $B, C \in T$, and hence $A = B \wedge C \in T$. Similarly, if A is a disjunction $B \vee C$, either B or C is in T, giving $B \vee C \in T$ (since T is a theory) as desired. Finally, if A is constructed by means of another connective, we have the result by the definition of $M(T)$.   □

Note that all we needed for this proof was that T be closed under $A, B \Rightarrow A \wedge B$, $A \Rightarrow A \vee B$ and $B \Rightarrow A \vee B$. No more complex constraint on T was necessary.

    Furthermore, $M(T)$ has some useful properties. It is *prime*, it is *closed under adjunction*, it is *detached* and it is $\sim$-*consistent*. It is quite well behaved in many ways. However, it is not, in general, a theory.

    To find circumstances in which $M(T)$ is a theory, we need a finer analysis of the formulae A which appear in $M(T)$. For some formulae A, the fact that $A \in M(T)$ follows immediately from the fact that $A \in T$ by virtue of the structure of A.

DEFINITION 5.23 (FORMULAE SURVIVING METAVALUATION)
A formula A *survives metavaluation* in a class $\mathcal{T}$ of theories if for all $T \in \mathcal{T}$, if $A \in T$ then $A \in M(T)$.

We need not only to consider formulae but also to consider rules.

DEFINITION 5.24 (RULES SURVIVING METAVALUATION)
A set X of formulae is *closed under the rule* $A_1, \ldots, A_n \Rightarrow B$ if and only if $A_1, \ldots, A_n \in X$ only if $B \in X$. A rule *survives metavaluation* in a class $\mathcal{T}$ of theories if for all $T \in \mathcal{T}$, if T is closed under $A_1, \ldots, A_n \Rightarrow B$ then so is $M(T)$.

Given this definition, we will show that many of the Hilbert axioms of the previous chapter and all of the Hilbert rules of that chapter survive metavaluation in the class of detached theories. In other words, if A is an axiom, then if T is detached and $A \in T$, then $A \in M(T)$. Similarly, if T is detached, and it is closed under $A_1, \ldots, A_n \Rightarrow B$, then $M(T)$ is also closed under that rule.

LEMMA 5.25 (RULES SURVIVE METAVALUATION)
All Hilbert rules for the connectives $\rightarrow, \leftarrow, \circ, t, \Box, \Diamond, \sim, \neg$ *defined in Chapter 4 survive metavaluation in the class of all detached theories.*

PROOF We will examine a representative sample of the rules and leave the rest to the exercises. The proof is tedious, not difficult.

Consider the rule $A, B \Rightarrow A \wedge B$. No matter what T is, $M(T)$ is closed under this rule by the definition of the operator M. Similarly, $M(T)$ must be closed under the rule *modus ponens*.

Consider $A \rightarrow B, C \rightarrow D \Rightarrow (B \rightarrow C) \rightarrow (A \rightarrow D)$. Suppose that $A \rightarrow B \in M(T)$ and $C \rightarrow D \in M(T)$. We wish to show that $(B \rightarrow C) \rightarrow (A \rightarrow D) \in M(T)$. To do this, we need first that $(B \rightarrow C) \rightarrow (A \rightarrow D) \in T$; but this is simple. We have $A \rightarrow B, C \rightarrow D \in T$, and so we have $(B \rightarrow C) \rightarrow (A \rightarrow D) \in T$, as T is closed under the rule. We also need to show that if $B \rightarrow C \in M(T)$ then $A \rightarrow D \in M(T)$. Now to do this, assume that $B \rightarrow C \in M(T)$. Then we have $B \rightarrow C \in T$, and so, $A \rightarrow D \in T$, as $(B \rightarrow C) \rightarrow (A \rightarrow D) \in T$ and T is detached. We also need to show that if $A \in M(T)$ then $D \in M(T)$. But if $A \in M(T)$, then $A \rightarrow B \in M(T)$ gives us $B \in M(T)$, and $B \rightarrow C \in M(T)$ gives $C \in M(T)$, and $C \rightarrow D \in M(T)$ gives $D \in M(T)$, as desired. This completes our proof that $(B \rightarrow C) \rightarrow (A \rightarrow D) \in M(T)$.

Consider the rule $A \circ B \rightarrow C \Rightarrow B \rightarrow (A \rightarrow C)$. Suppose $A \circ B \rightarrow C \in M(T)$; we want $B \rightarrow (A \rightarrow C) \in M(T)$. Well, $B \rightarrow (A \rightarrow C) \in T$, as $A \circ B \rightarrow C \in T$ and T is closed under this rule. Now suppose $B \in M(T)$, to try to show that $A \rightarrow C \in M(T)$. Well, if $B \in M(T)$, then we have $B \in T$ (as $M(T) \subseteq T$), but $B \in T$ means $A \rightarrow A \circ B \in T$, since $B \vdash A \rightarrow A \circ B$, as is simple to check. So, $A \rightarrow C \in T$, as $A \circ B \rightarrow C \in T$ and T is detached. But we also have that if $A \in M(T)$ then $B \in M(T)$ and $A \circ B \in T$ gives $A \circ B \in M(T)$, and $A \circ B \rightarrow C \in M(T)$ gives $C \in M(T)$, as desired.

Consider the rule $A \rightarrow (C \leftarrow B) \Rightarrow A \circ B \rightarrow C$. Suppose $A \rightarrow (C \leftarrow B) \in M(T)$, to show that $A \circ B \rightarrow C \in M(T)$. First, it is clear that $A \circ B \rightarrow C \in T$. Second, suppose that $A \circ B \in M(T)$. Then $A \in M(T)$ gives $C \leftarrow B \in M(T)$, which with $B \in M(T)$ gives $C \in M(T)$ as desired.

Consider the rule $A \rightarrow \sim B \Rightarrow B \rightarrow \neg A$. Suppose $A \rightarrow \sim B \in M(T)$. We wish to show that $B \rightarrow \neg A \in M(T)$. That $B \rightarrow \neg A \in T$ is clear. Now suppose that $B \in M(T)$, in order to show that $\neg A \in M(T)$. If $B \in M(T)$, then it is not the case that $\sim B \in M(T)$. This means that $A \notin M(T)$, since $A \rightarrow \sim B \in M(T)$. We also know that $\neg A \in T$, since $B \in M(T)$ gives $B \in T$, and $B \rightarrow \neg A \in T$

(and T is detached). So, $\neg A \in M(T)$ as desired. This argument works just as well if $\sim = \neg$, so the reasoning also holds for a simple negation.

Consider the rule $A \to \Box B \;\Rightarrow\; \Diamond A \to B$. Suppose that $A \to \Box B \in M(T)$, to show that $\Diamond A \to B \in M(T)$. Clearly, $\Diamond A \to B \in T$. Now if $\Diamond A \in M(T)$, then $A \in M(T)$, and hence $\Box B \in M(T)$. But this gives $B \in M(T)$, as desired.

Consider the rule $A \to B \;\Rightarrow\; \Diamond A \to \Diamond B$. Suppose $A \to B \in M(T)$. Then $A \to B \in T$ and hence $\Diamond A \to \Diamond B \in T$. Therefore we want to show that if $\Diamond A \in M(T)$ then $\Diamond B \in M(T)$. If $\Diamond A \in M(T)$, then $A \in M(T)$ and $\Diamond A \in T$. Since T is detached, we have $\Diamond B \in T$, and since $A \to B \in M(T)$ we have $B \in M(T)$, giving us $\Diamond B \in M(T)$ as desired.   □

LEMMA 5.26 (MOST AXIOMS SURVIVE METAVALUATION)
All Hilbert axioms — except for double negation elimination and strong excluded middle — defined in Chapter 4 survive metavaluation in the class of all detached theories.

PROOF   Again, a representative sample is enough to give the flavour of the proof. Let us show that $(A \to B) \wedge (A \to C) \to (A \to B \wedge C) \in M(T)$ if it is also in T. Suppose that $(A \to B) \wedge (A \to C) \in M(T)$ to show that $A \to B \wedge C \in M(T)$. Under these circumstances, $A \to B \wedge C \in T$. Now if $A \in M(T)$ then by $A \to B \in M(T)$, we have $B \in M(T)$; and by $A \to C \in M(T)$, we have $C \in M(T)$. But this means that $B \wedge C \in M(T)$, as desired.

Suppose $A \wedge (B \vee C) \to (A \wedge B) \vee (A \wedge C) \in T$. Then to show $A \wedge (B \vee C) \to (A \wedge B) \vee (A \wedge C) \in M(T)$, suppose $A \wedge (B \vee C) \in M(T)$. It follows that $A \in M(T)$ and either $B \in M(T)$ or $C \in M(T)$, so either $A \wedge B \in M(T)$ or $A \wedge C \in M(T)$. It follows that $(A \wedge B) \vee (A \wedge C) \in M(T)$.

Suppose $A \to \sim\sim A \in T$, to show that it is also in $M(T)$. Suppose that $A \in M(T)$ but that $\sim\sim A \notin M(T)$. Then either $\sim A \in M(T)$ or $\sim\sim A \notin T$. The first case is ruled out, since $A \in M(T)$. The second case is ruled out as $A \in T$ and T is detached. Therefore $\sim\sim A \in M(T)$.

Suppose $A \wedge \sim A \to B \in T$, to show that it is also in $M(T)$. For this it is sufficient to show that $A \wedge \sim A \notin M(T)$, but this is immediate from the definition of the negation clause in the definition of M.   □

We will soon see how double negation elimination and strong excluded middle fail to be preserved under metavaluation. Before this, however, we need to consider how to deal with structural rules. To do this, we need to examine the behaviour of punctuation marks (or their corresponding connectives) and theoremhood. For this we need to recall the definition of a confusion from Definition 4.26 and extend it slightly to deal with modal operations.

DEFINITION 5.27 (MODAL CONFUSION)
A *modal confusion* of the propositions in the set Σ is defined inductively as follows.

    ◇ t, $\top$ and any element of Σ are confusions of Σ.

    ◇ If C_1 and C_2 are confusions of Σ, so are $C_1 \circ C_2$, $C_1 \wedge C_2$ and $\Diamond C_1$.

Lemma 4.27 tells us that if Σ is a set of theorems, then any confusion of Σ is also a theorem. We can extend it slightly as follows.

LEMMA 5.28 (CLOSURE OF THEOREMS UNDER MODAL CONFUSION)
If Σ is a set of theorems then any modal *confusion of Σ is a theorem, provided that Kr is valid.*

PROOF Induction on the construction of the confusion, with Kr giving us $t \vdash \Diamond t$ to ensure that if $t \vdash A$ then $t \vdash \Diamond t \vdash \Diamond A$ too. $\square$

LEMMA 5.29 (STRUCTURAL RULES SURVIVE METAVALUATION)
An axiom of the form $A \rightarrow A'$ corresponding to the structural rule $X \Leftarrow X'$ survives metavaluation in a detached theory T containing $A \rightarrow A'$ (provided that Kr holds, if either X or X' contains •).

PROOF We wish to show that $A \rightarrow A' \in M(T)$, given that $A \rightarrow A' \in T$. Therefore we need to show that if $A \in M(T)$ then $A' \in M(T)$ too. A is a confusion of propositions $B_1, \ldots, B_n$ and A' is also such a confusion, with the proviso that it need not contain each of $B_1, \ldots, B_n$. Since $A \in M(T)$ we have each $B_i \in M(T)$ by definition of $M(T)$, and thus each $B_i \in T$, which gives $A' \in T$ as desired, as T is closed under the connectives constructing the confusion. We also have $A' \in M(T)$, as is simple to check. $\square$

The requirement that Kr hold for the closure of T under possibility is necessary in some cases involving $\Diamond$ but not all. For example, the axiom $\Diamond A \circ \Diamond B \rightarrow \Diamond B \vdash \Diamond A$ is preserved by metavaluations independently of the requirement, as you can check. The requirement is necessary in cases such as $\Diamond(A \circ B) \vdash \Diamond A \circ B$. In this case, if $\Diamond(A \circ B) \in M(T)$ we have $\Diamond(A \circ B) \in T$ and $A \circ B \in M(T)$, giving $A \circ B \in T$ and $A, B \in M(T)$. To get $\Diamond A \circ B \in M(T)$ it is necessary to have $\Diamond A \in M(T)$, and for this it seems necessary to use the rule $t \vdash \Diamond t$, to ensure that $\Diamond A \in T$.

THEOREM 5.30 (MANY LOGICS ARE PRIME)
If T is the set of theorems of a logic axiomatised by any of the Hilbert axioms and rules of Chapter 4, other than double negation elimination or strong excluded middle, and in which Kr holds, if $\Diamond$ or $\square$ is present, then T is a prime theory.

PROOF   It suffices to prove that $T = M(T)$ for $M(T)$ is prime. Lemma 5.22 ensures that $M(T) \subseteq T$. Lemmas 5.26 and 5.29 show us that the Hilbert axioms of T are in $M(T)$. (Lemma 5.29 applies since by Lemma 5.28, T is closed under modal confusions.) By Lemma 5.25, $M(T)$ is closed under the Hilbert rules of T. It follows that $T = M(T)$, as desired.   □

The remaining axioms are double negation elimination and strong excluded middle. In the way metavaluations are structured, neither of these formulae need to survive metavaluation in the class of detached theories. Consider double negation elimination. If $\sim\neg A \to A \in T$ and $\sim\neg A \in M(T)$, then we know that $\neg A \notin T$ and $\sim\neg A \in T$. It follows that $A \in T$ (since T is detached), but that is about it. Nothing seems to follow from the claim that $\neg A \notin T$. The only hope seems to be that if T is $\neg$-complete, then $A \in T$, but even this does not bring $A \in M(T)$. Whether $A \in M(T)$ or not depends on the structure of A. A similar case holds for strong excluded middle. To show that these survive metavaluation, even in the class of all complete detached theories, we need a new approach.

LEMMA 5.31 (NEGATION AND $M(T)$)
If T is detached, $\sim$-complete and closed under the rules $A \Rightarrow \sim\sim A$, $A \wedge \sim B \Rightarrow \sim(A \to B)$ (if $\to$ is present) $A \wedge \sim B \Rightarrow \sim(B \leftarrow A)$ (if $\leftarrow$ is present) $\sim A \Rightarrow \sim(A \circ B)$ and $\sim B \Rightarrow \sim(A \circ B)$ (if $\circ$ is present) $\sim A \Rightarrow \sim\Box A$ (if $\Box$ is present) and $\sim A \Rightarrow \sim\Diamond A$ (if $\Diamond$ is present) then $A \notin M(T)$ only if $\sim A \in T$.

PROOF   An induction on the complexity of A.
  ◇ The atomic case holds as T is complete. If A is atomic and $A \notin M(T)$ then $A \notin T$ and hence $\sim A \in T$.
  ◇ If $A \wedge B \notin M(T)$ then $A \notin M(T)$ or $B \notin M(T)$, so $\sim A \notin T$ (and hence $\sim(A \wedge B) \in T$) or $\sim B \notin T$ (and hence $\sim(A \wedge B) \in T$).
  ◇ If $A \vee B \notin M(T)$ then $A \notin M(T)$ and $B \notin M(T)$, giving $\sim A, \sim B \in T$ and so, $\sim(A \vee B) \in T$.
  ◇ If $A \to B \notin M(T)$ then either $A \to B \notin T$ — in which case $\sim(A \to B) \in T$ — or $A \in M(T)$ and $B \notin M(T)$. Then $A \wedge \sim B \in T$, and since T is closed under $A \wedge \sim B \Rightarrow \sim(A \to B)$, $\sim(A \to B) \in T$.
  ◇ The case for $\leftarrow$ is identical to that for $\to$.
  ◇ If $A \circ B \notin M(T)$ then either $A \circ B \notin T$ — giving $\sim(A \circ B) \in T$ — or either $A \notin M(T)$ or $B \notin M(T)$. In the first case, $\sim A \in T$, and by the closure under $\sim A \Rightarrow \sim(A \circ B)$, $\sim(A \circ B) \in T$. The same holds for B.
  ◇ If $\sim A \notin M(T)$ then either $A \in M(T)$ — and by closure under $A \Rightarrow \sim\sim A$, $\sim\sim A \in T$ — or $\sim A \notin T$, and by completeness, $\sim\sim A \in T$.
  ◇ If $\neg A \notin M(T)$ then either $A \in M(T)$ — and since $A \vdash \sim\neg A$, $\sim\neg A \in T$ —

or $\neg A \notin T$, and by $\sim$-completeness, $\sim\neg A \in T$.

⋄ If $\Box A \notin M(T)$ then either $A \notin M(T)$ — so $\sim A \in T$, giving $\sim\Box A \in T$ by $\sim A \Rightarrow \sim\Box A$ — or $\Box A \notin T$ giving $\sim\Box A \in T$.

⋄ If $\Diamond A \notin M(T)$ then either $A \notin M(T)$ — so $\sim A \in T$, giving $\sim\Diamond A \in T$ by $\sim A \Rightarrow \sim\Diamond A$ — or $\Diamond A \notin T$ giving $\sim\Diamond A \in T$.   □

COROLLARY 5.32 (NEGATION AXIOMS SURVIVING METAVALUATIONS)
If T is a theory satisfying the conditions of Lemma 5.31 then $\sim\sim A \to A$ and $A \to B \vee \sim B$ survive metavaluation in T.

PROOF If $\sim\sim A \to A \in T$ then to show that it is also in $M(T)$ we need to show that if $\sim\sim A \in M(T)$ then $A \in M(T)$. Since $\sim\sim A \in M(T)$ we have $\sim A \notin M(T)$, and hence by Lemma 5.31, $A \in M(T)$.

If $A \to B \vee \sim B \in T$, then to show that it is also in $M(T)$ it suffices to show that if $A \in M(T)$ then $B \vee \sim B \in M(T)$. But $B \vee \sim B \in M(T)$ always, as either $B \in M(T)$ or $\sim B \in M(T)$.   □

As a result, we have the following important theorem.

THEOREM 5.33 (ADMISSIBILITY OF DISJUNCTIVE SYLLOGISM)
In R and E if $\vdash A$ and $\vdash \sim A \vee B$, then $\vdash B$.

PROOF We first note that in these logics, $\langle \{t\}, \{B\} \rangle$ is a $\vdash$-pair, under the assumption that $\nvdash B$. Then we can extend this to a full $\vdash$-pair $\langle T, S \rangle$. Now T contains all theorems and it is prime. Since $t \vdash A \vee \sim A$ in both R and E, T must be $\sim$-complete. Since in both R and E, $A \wedge (A \to B) \to B$ is a theorem, T is detached.

Now we wish to apply Lemma 5.31. The difficulty is that T need not be closed under the rule $\sim A \Rightarrow \sim(A \circ B)$ or $\sim B \Rightarrow \sim(A \circ B)$. However, the implication and negation conditions are satisfied: since $A \vdash \sim\sim A$, and $A \wedge \sim B \vdash \sim(A \to B)$ in both R and E. So we deal with implication but not fusion. (We can axiomatise the theory without appeal to fusion, by the results of the previous chapter.)

In this case, $M(T)$ is a theory, $M(T)$ is complete and consistent. Since $B \in S$, $B \notin T$, it follows that either $\nvdash A$ or $\nvdash \sim A \vee B$, as desired.   □

This is a very significant result, as in logics like R and E, the disjunctive syllogism is not valid in the form $A, \sim A \vee B \nvdash B$. Why is this not provable? If it were, we would have $A, \sim A \vdash B$ by a simple cut with $\sim A \vdash \sim A \vee B$. In the pursuit of relevance, we have had to reject $A, \sim A \vee B \vdash B$. However, this is not the end of the story. Given a theory T, if disjunctive syllogism is not *admissible* in the theory, then we have the following situation. $A \in T$, $\sim A \vee B \in T$, but $B \notin T$. In this case, either T is inconsistent or it is, in some sense, incomplete. For if T is prime then either $\sim A \in T$ or $B \in T$. If $B \notin T$ then T is inconsistent.

So it is often desirable for a theory to be closed under disjunctive syllo-gism — at least if it is consistent — even though the rule may not be relevantly *valid*. The theorem above ensures that the theorems of the logics R and E are closed under disjunctive syllogism. The technique of this proof is readily extended to more substantive theories, giving more substantive results. For example, Meyer has shown that in some *relevant arithmetics* (theories of addi-tion, multiplication and identity, based on relevant logics together using rele-vant analogues of Peano's axioms) disjunctive syllogism is not admissible, but in other arithmetics, it is. For details, see the next section.

5.4 History

The Pair Extension Theorem was proved by Belnap in the early 1970s. Dunn circulated a write-up of it in about 1975, and cited it in some detail in 1976 [74]. Gabbay gave an independent proof for first-order intuitionistic logic, also in 1976 [90]. This result, and the use of explicit *pairs* of sets of formulae, with equal time for "good guys" and "bad guys," is vital in the frame semantics of substructural logics we will see in Chapter 11.

Meyer pioneered the technique of metavaluations in relevant logic [155, 158]. The technique was also used be Kleene in his study of intuitionistic theo-ries [124, 125], who was in turn inspired by Harrop, who used the technique in the 1950s to prove primeness for intuitionistic logic [107]. Metavaluations pro-vide a notion like Kleene's *realisability* semantics for intuitionistic logic without explicit realisers. More recently, Shapiro's work on intensional arithmetic [244] and Došen's in modal logic [66] provide other examples of metavaluations at work.

Proofs of the admissibility of disjunctive syllogism vary. Meyer pioneered the technique using metavaluations, and Meyer and Dunn have used other techniques [161, 160]. Friedman and Meyer showed that disjunctive syllo-gism fails in a simple first-order relevant arithmetic [87], but that it holds in that arithmetic when you add an infinitary "omega" rule. Meyer and I have used a different style of metavaluation argument to construct a complete "true" relevant arithmetic [166]. This metavaluation argument treats negation with "one punch" clause: $\sim\!A \in M(T)$ if and only if $A \notin M(T)$. In this arithmetic, $0 = 1 \to 0 = 2$ is a theorem, as you can deduce $0 = 2$ from $0 = 1$ by arithmetic means, while $\sim\!(0 = 2 \to 0 = 1)$ is a theorem, as there is no way, by using multiplication, addition and identity, to deduce $0 = 1$ from $0 = 2$.

There has been a great deal of philosophical discussion on the status of disjunctive syllogism [26, 205, 219, 226]. For more, see Chapter 16.

5.5 Exercises

Practice

{5.1} Which of the following claims are true? The intersection of two theories is a theory. The intersection of two prime theories is a prime theory. The intersection of two t-normal theories is t-normal.

{5.2} Show that the union of two theories is not necessarily a theory.

Problems

{5.3} Show that the intersection $\bigcap_i T_i$ of any family of theories T_i ($i \in I$) is also a theory.

{5.4} Which of the properties from Definition 5.6 are preserved by going to intersections? That is, if each of T_i has property Φ, does $\bigcup T_i$?

{5.5} Define the *sum* of two theories S and T to be the theory $S + T = \bigcap\{U : S, T \subseteq U\}$. That is, it is the intersection of all of those theories containing both S and T, so it is the smallest theory containing them both. Similarly, the sum $\sum_i T_i$ of a class of theories T_i ($i \in I$) is the intersection $\bigcap\{S : T_i \subseteq S\}$. Which of the properties from Definition 5.6 are preserved by going to sums?

{5.6} Does $S \cap (T_1 + T_2) = (S \cap T_1) + (S \cap T_2)$ for each theory S, T_1 and T_2?

{5.7} Complete the Pair Extension Lemma in the case where the language is uncountable but still well-ordered.

{5.8} Complete the proof of the Way Down Lemma.

Project

{5.9} Slaney has extended the metavaluation technique to prove the primeness of certain with logics with a strict de Morgan negation [247]. In this technique, you work with not only $M(T)$, the set of *meta truths* of T, but also $N(T)$, the set of *meta non-falsehoods* of T. To start with, $p \in N(T)$ if and only if $\sim p \notin T$. For negation, $\sim A \in M(T)$ if and only if $A \notin N(T)$, and $\sim A \in N(T)$ if and only if $A \notin M(T)$. Define the clauses for other connectives, and show (for some logics with a strict de Morgan negation) that the set of theorems is prime. (HINT: The proof will not apply to R, which is not prime, but it should apply to DBCK, which is.)

Chapter 6

Gentzen Systems

> ... with the most engaging politeness,
> she eliminated poor Ferkin.
>
> — *William Thackeray*, Vanity Fair, *1848*

A *Gentzen system* for a logic is another sort of proof theory, similar to natural deduction, but with a number of important differences. Gentzen systems parallel natural deduction systems by having two rules for each connective.[1] However, instead of rules for introducing and eliminating connectives in the consequent position, we have rules only for introducing connectives. Connectives are never eliminated by the connective rules. To make up for the loss of one half of our rules, we add new rules to *introduce connectives in the antecedent of a consecution*. Each connective (barring special cases) will have two rules, one licensing an introduction of that connective in the consequent of the consecution, and the other licensing its introduction in the antecedent. This gives Gentzen systems powerful properties.

6.1 An Example System

We will start with one system as an example: the Gentzen system for intuitionistic linear logic, ILL. In this case, the consecutions are pairs of structures of formulae in the antecedent, and formulae in the consequent, just as with the natural deduction system for ILL. The structures here are just built up using the semicolon. We have intensional structure but no extensional structure, since the lattice connectives need not satisfy distribution. We make two small modifications. First, we do not need bracketed formulae to deal with the exponential. This modality will be treated differently. Second, we allow consecutions with *empty* consequents. That is, $X \vdash$ is a consecution for any structure X. The empty consequent will represent a *false* proposition f (which will turn out to be equivalent to $\sim t$).

The usual structural rules for linear logic apply, so we have C and B (and hence, B^c and B').

---

[1] With just a couple of exceptions, which we will see later.

First we see the rules for conjunction.

$$\frac{X(A) \vdash C}{X(A \wedge B) \vdash C} \ [\wedge L_1] \qquad \frac{X(B) \vdash C}{X(A \wedge B) \vdash C} \ [\wedge L_2] \qquad \frac{X \vdash A \quad X \vdash B}{X \vdash A \wedge B} \ [\wedge R]$$

The conjunction rules on the left rely on the entailments $A \wedge B \vdash A$ and $A \wedge B \vdash B$. They have the same effect as $(\wedge E)$ in the natural deduction system, given the cut rule. For fusion, we have similar rules.

$$\frac{X(A; B) \vdash C}{X(A \circ B) \vdash C} \ [\circ L] \qquad \frac{X \vdash A \quad Y \vdash B}{X; Y \vdash A \circ B} \ [\circ R]$$

These rules express the connection between fusion and the semicolon. For implication, the rules are:

$$\frac{X \vdash A \quad Y(B) \vdash C}{Y(A \to B; X) \vdash C} \ [\to L] \qquad \frac{X; A \vdash B}{X \vdash A \to B} \ [\to R]$$

The right rule is the same as in natural deduction. The left rule is more complicated, but it makes sense. If I can use B (in Y) to deduce C, and X gives A, then applying $A \to B$ to X also gives B, which I can use (in Y) to still deduce C. For disjunction, we have:

$$\frac{X(A) \vdash C \quad X(B) \vdash C}{X(A \vee B) \vdash C} \ [\vee L] \qquad \frac{X \vdash A}{X \vdash A \vee B} \ [\vee R_1] \qquad \frac{X \vdash B}{X \vdash A \vee B} \ [\vee R_2]$$

which again preserve the right rules from natural deduction. The left rule for disjunction is smoother than the elimination rule $(\vee E)$ from natural deduction, as we have no need to add the extra premise $Y \vdash A \vee B$ to give the conclusion $X(Y) \vdash C$. Here, since we allow antecedent introduction rules (at the cost of antecedent regularity), we can let $Y = A \vee B$ to get a simpler rule.

The negation rules are straightforward and rely on the equivalence of A with $A \to {\sim}t$.

$$\frac{X \vdash A}{X; {\sim}A \vdash} \ [{\sim}L] \qquad \frac{X; A \vdash}{X \vdash {\sim}A} \ [{\sim}R]$$

It is at this point that we use empty consequents. If we needed to use f (or ${\sim}t$) in the consequent position, we would have a connective rule $[{\sim}R]$ which eliminated a formula from top to bottom. This is not desirable, so we use a blank there.[2]

---

[2]   We could use a new punctuation mark to appear only in consequents of structures. On the other hand, you could think of the blank consequent as a punctuation "mark" itself.

At this point, we should note that since we are allowing empty consequents in our consecutions, our rules should be understood in such a way as to allow this. In some of the rules of the system, the consequent is a parameter — in these cases it is written as 'C' — and in these cases 'C' might be a formula or an empty consequent. (Think of 'C' as 'some consequent'.) In all other cases, the consequent must be populated with a formula.

The rules for the propositional constants are as follows:

$$\frac{X(0) \vdash C}{X(t) \vdash C} \ [tL] \qquad 0 \vdash t \ [tR]$$

$$f \vdash \ [fL] \qquad \frac{X \vdash}{X \vdash f} \ [fR]$$

$$X(\bot) \vdash C \ [\bot L] \qquad X \vdash \top \ [\top R]$$

For the exponential, we have *four* rules, which jointly give it the desired properties:

$$\frac{X \vdash C}{X; !A \vdash C} \ [K!] \qquad \frac{X(!A; !A) \vdash C}{X(!A) \vdash C} \ [WI!] \qquad \frac{X(A) \vdash C}{X(!A) \vdash C} \ [L!] \qquad \frac{!X \vdash A}{!X \vdash !A} \ [R!]$$

The rules [K!] and [WI!] give ! formulae the desired structural rules. [K!] ensures that !A entails A for each A, and [R!] ensures that ! has the usual S4-like properties. In this last rule, we use !X as the structure given from X by prefixing every formula in X by !.

Now to prove anything in the Gentzen system we need a rule to get the system off the ground. This is our usual identity rule.

$$A \vdash A \ [\text{Id}]$$

However, now we do not need [Id] in its full generality. We could do with assuming it simply in the form $p \vdash p$ for atomic propositions p, for we can *prove* it for more complex propositions by induction on the complexity of formulae.

THEOREM 6.1 (PROVING IDENTITIES)
In the Gentzen system for intuitionistic linear logic, $A \vdash A$ may be proved from the instances of identity using atomic propositions alone.

PROOF As you might expect, this is proved by induction on the complexity of formulae. The major base case is dealt with, but we still need to show that each of $t \vdash t$, $f \vdash f$, $\top \vdash \top$ and $\bot \vdash \bot$ can be proved. The cases for $\top \vdash \top$ and $\bot \vdash \bot$

are trivial (instances of their appropriate axioms). For t, from $0 \vdash t$ we deduce $t \vdash t$. For f, from $f \vdash$ we deduce $f \vdash f$.

Now suppose A is a complex formula, and for any subformulae B of A, $B \vdash B$ may be proved. We will show that $A \vdash A$ can also be proved, in the cases in which the main formula of A is an implication, an exponential and a disjunction, to leave the rest to Exercise 6.2.

For implication and the exponential, we proceed as follows:

$$\dfrac{\dfrac{B \vdash B \quad C \vdash C}{B \to C; B \vdash C}\ [\to\text{L}]}{B \to C \vdash B \to C}\ [\to\text{R}] \qquad\qquad \dfrac{\dfrac{B \vdash B}{!B \vdash B}\ [!\text{L}]}{!B \vdash !B}\ [!\text{R}]$$

and for disjunction we have this proof:

$$\dfrac{\dfrac{B \vdash B}{B \vdash B \vee C}\ [\vee\text{R}_1] \qquad \dfrac{C \vdash C}{C \vdash B \vee C}\ [\vee\text{R}_2]}{B \vee C \vdash B \vee C}\ [\vee\text{L}] \qquad\qquad \square$$

This completes the proof system. What we have is equivalent to the natural deduction system for ILL, in the sense that $X \vdash A$ is provable using natural deduction if and only if $X^\tau \vdash A$ is provable in the Gentzen system, where we find X^τ from X by replacing the bracketed formulae $[A]$ in X by $!A$. We can prove this equivalence. However, to do so is *much* easier if we can appeal to the Cut rule, which you will recall, is as follows:

$$\dfrac{X \vdash A \quad Y(A) \vdash C}{Y(X) \vdash C}\ [\text{Cut}]$$

Why is it helpful to appeal to the Cut rule? Try showing that if $X \vdash A \to B$ and $Y \vdash A$ are both provable in the Gentzen system, then so is $X; Y \vdash B$. The most we can readily do without Cut is to deduce $X; Y \vdash (A \to B) \circ A$. We can also prove $(A \to B) \circ A \vdash B$ in the Gentzen system without too much difficulty. Cut then gives $X; Y \vdash B$. To get to $X; Y \vdash B$ *directly*, we are restricted to subformulae of the formulae in X, Y and subformulae of B. There is no guarantee that $A \to B$ or A are even among these! So without Cut we cannot simply "borrow" the proofs of $X \vdash A \to B$ and $Y \vdash A$ to use in our proof. We must somehow use the *fact* that there are proofs of $X \vdash A \to B$ and $Y \vdash A$ to construct a proof of $X; Y \vdash B$.

So, to prove that the Gentzen system and the natural deduction systems for ILL coincide, we will use a two-step process. First, we will show that the Gentzen system *with Cut* matches the natural deduction system. Then we will show that the addition of Cut is redundant. Anything provable with Cut may be proved without it. This second fact is Gentzen's significant result about his systems [93]. He showed that in his proof systems for both intuitionistic and classical logic, Cut is redundant. The simple pasting of proofs together from Chapter 2 will not do, as the Gentzen system, with its left-introduction rules, is not antecedent regular. The Cut elimination proof must proceed on a different basis. Before going on to consider the details of the proof, we will show that the Gentzen system (with Cut) and the natural deduction system for ILL coincide.

THEOREM 6.2 (EQUIVALENCE OF SYSTEMS)
$X \vdash A$ is provable in the natural deduction system for ILL if and only if $X^\tau \vdash A$ is provable in the Gentzen system using Cut.

PROOF The proof proceeds by way of an induction on the construction of the proofs in question. We will consider a few cases to give the flavour of the proof, and leave the rest to Exercise 6.3.

For left-to-right, we proceed by induction on the natural deduction proof of $X \vdash A$. For the identity axioms, we appeal to Theorem 6.1, which shows that all identities are provable in the Gentzen system. Now suppose $X \vdash A$ comes by way of some connective or structural rule, given the hypothesis that the premises (appropriately translated by τ) of the rule are provable in the Gentzen system. The translation of the conclusion of the rule follows immediately if the rule was either B or C, or a connective introduction rule, for these are the same in each system.

For the elimination rules, we consider a few cases. We have seen already the case of deducing $X; Y \vdash B$ from $X \vdash A \rightarrow B$ and $Y \vdash B$. We have $X^\tau \vdash A \rightarrow B$ and $Y^\tau \vdash A$ by hypothesis, $X^\tau; Y^\tau \vdash (A \rightarrow B) \circ A$, and by Cut with $(A \rightarrow B) \circ A \vdash B$ we have our result.

For disjunction elimination, if we have $X(A) \vdash C$, $X(B) \vdash C$ and $Y \vdash A \vee B$, to deduce $X(Y) \vdash C$, then in the Gentzen system we have $X(A)^\tau \vdash C$ and $X(B)^\tau \vdash C$, which gives us $X(A \vee B)^\tau \vdash C$, and by cut with $Y^\tau \vdash A \vee B$ we have $X(Y)^\tau = X(Y^\tau)^\tau \vdash C$ as desired.

For the bracketed structural rule $X \Leftarrow X; [A]$, if the premise is $Y(X) \vdash C$ the conclusion is $Y(X; [A]) \vdash C$. Translating into the Gentzen system we have $Y(X)^\tau \vdash C$, which gives us $Y(X); !A \vdash C$, and by repeated uses of C and B we may "shuffle" the instance of $!A$ inside the structure to get $Y(X; [A])^\tau = Y(X; !A) \vdash C$ as desired.

The other rules present no more difficulty in the translation from the natural deduction system to the Gentzen system. For the reverse, suppose we have $X^\tau \vdash A$ in the Gentzen system, to construct a natural deduction proof of $X \vdash A$. Again, axioms are preserved, as are structural rules and connective rules on the right. We will consider the same connectives for the connective left rules.

If I have a Gentzen proof of $Y(A \to B; X)^\tau \vdash C$, from $Y(B)^\tau \vdash C$ and $X^\tau \vdash A$, we can construct the natural deduction proof in this way: $A \to B; X \vdash B$ is provable by ($\to$E) from $A \to B \vdash A \to B$ and $X \vdash A$. We also have $Y(B) \vdash C$, so Cut in the natural deduction system gives us $Y(A \to B; X) \vdash C$.

If I have a Gentzen proof of $X(A \lor B)^\tau \vdash C$ from $X(A)^\tau \vdash C$ and $X(B)^\tau \vdash C$, then from $X(A) \vdash C$, $X(B) \vdash C$ and $A \lor B \vdash A \lor B$ in the natural deduction system, ($\lor$E) gives us $X(A \lor B) \vdash C$ as desired.

Finally, if I have a Gentzen proof of $X; !A = (X; [A])^\tau \vdash C$ from $X^\tau \vdash C$, we appeal to $X \Leftarrow X; [A]$ to give us $X; [A] \vdash C$ from $X \vdash C$. The other rules are similar, so we pronounce the equivalence settled.   □

Now consider what must be done to prove that Cut is redundant. To do this we need a case-by-case analysis of the proofs leading up to the Cut. The simplest case is when the Cut formula (the formula which has been Cut out of the premises and does not appear in the conclusion) is introduced in both premises to the Cut rule. Here is an example.

$$\cfrac{\cfrac{X \vdash A \to B \quad Y \vdash A}{X; Y \vdash (A \to B) \circ A} \; [\circ\text{R}] \quad \cfrac{\cfrac{\cfrac{A \vdash A \quad B \vdash B}{A \to B; A \vdash B} \; [\to\text{L}]}{(A \to B) \circ A \vdash B} \; [\circ\text{L}]}{}}{X, Y \vdash B} \; [\text{Cut}_{(A \to B)\circ A}]$$

This proof can be transformed to one containing Cuts on proper subformulae of $(A \to B) \circ A$, as follows:

$$\cfrac{\cfrac{X \vdash A \to B \quad \cfrac{A \vdash A \quad B \vdash B}{A \to B, A \vdash B} \; [\to\text{L}]}{X, A \vdash B} \; [\text{Cut}_{A \to B}] \quad Y \vdash A}{X, Y \vdash B} \; [\text{Cut}_A]$$

In this way, we can "trade in" Cuts on larger formulae for cuts on subformulae. This is one way in which Cuts are eliminated.

The next case is when the formula has not been introduced, on at least one side of the proof. Here is an example: the Cut formula C is a *parameter* in the disjunction step on the left

$$\cfrac{\cfrac{X(A) \vdash C \quad X(B) \vdash C}{X(A \lor B) \vdash C} \; [\lor\text{L}] \quad Y(C) \vdash D}{Y(X(A \lor B)) \vdash D} \; [\text{Cut}_C]$$

In this case we can "push the Cut upwards" beyond the disjunction rule, as follows

$$\frac{\dfrac{X(B) \vdash C \quad Y(C) \vdash D}{Y(X(B)) \vdash D} \, [\text{Cut}_C] \quad \dfrac{X(A) \vdash C \quad Y(C) \vdash D}{Y(X(A)) \vdash D} \, [\text{Cut}_C]}{Y(X(A \vee B)) \vdash D} \, [\vee L]$$

In this way we have pushed the Cut upwards in the tree, closer to the point at which the C was introduced. We keep doing this until the Cut operates on *axioms*. And these are *trivial*. If the cut formula is introduced by an axiom, the Cut rule has either of these forms:

$$\frac{p \vdash p \quad Y(p) \vdash C}{Y(p) \vdash C} \qquad \frac{X \vdash p \quad p \vdash p}{X \vdash p}$$

In either case, the rule is redundant. The conclusion is itself one of the premises. The *Cut Elimination Proof* involves showing that procedure works in general. Cuts on formulae introduced on both sides of the cut are eliminable in favour of cuts on subformulae. Cuts on parameters may be pushed upwards. Cuts on identities are redundant.

6.2   The Core Ideas

In this section, we will show that Cut is redundant in any consecution systems satisfying some general criteria. So we will prove the theorem, not only for systems such as ILL but for many others. This will include systems with quite different sorts of consecutions — in the section after this one we will see how Gentzen systems can be constructed using consecutions with *structure* in the consequent. So our proof will be quite general, abstracting away the detail to the general behaviour of consecution systems.

DEFINITION 6.3 (CONSECUTIONS)
A *consecution* is made up of formulae, somehow collected together using some kind of structure. This is intentionally general. Examples of consecutions are sequents, which are of the form $X \vdash A$ or $X \vdash Y$, where A is a formula and X and Y are sequences of formulae; or in systems such as display logic, con- secutions are pairs $X \vdash Y$, where X and Y are *structures* made up of formulae using structure operators.

In every consecution, each formula instance is in either *antecedent* or *con- sequent* position, and not both. In traditional sequents $X \vdash Y$, the formulae appearing in X are in antecedent position, and those in Y are in consequent position. But this need not hold in general. In the case of display logic, some formulae on the left of the turnstile may appear in consequent position, and some on the right of the turnstile may appear in antecedent position. This is allowed in our analysis — all we need is that each formula instance appear either in antecedent position or in consequent position, but not in both.

DEFINITION 6.4 (INFERENCES, PREMISES AND CONCLUSIONS, AND RULES)
An *inference* is a pair of a set (possibly empty) of consecutions (the *premises*) and a consecution (the *conclusion*). A *rule* is a set of inferences. (Rules, of course, may be presented schematically.)

DEFINITION 6.5 (ANALYSES, PARAMETERS AND CONGRUENCES)
We need the rules to be *analysed* in a way that gives us a principled method for deciding when formulae (or structures made up of formulae) are "preserved" in a rule, or when formulae (or structures) are "introduced." An *analysis* of the rules of a system provides the notions of *parameter* and *congruence*. An analysis determines, for each inference falling under each rule, which formula or structure instances are parameters and which are not. Intuitively, the parameters are those things which are either held constant from premises to conclusion or are introduced with no regard to their particulars. (So formulae introduced by weakening are usually parameters.) The *congruence* relation on parameters is some equivalence relation on parameters in an inference.

    We will say that formulae instances which are nonparametric in the *conclusion* of an inference are *principal* in that inference.

Now let us define the Cut rule. In linear logic and related systems, the rule has this form:

$$\frac{X(A) \vdash C \quad Y \vdash A}{X(Y) \vdash C}$$

How are we to generalise the Cut rule appropriately? First, we need to consider the instances of formulae to be cut away. Consider two consecutions C and D, and for some formula A, where A appears in consequent position in C and in antecedent position in D. We will indicate this by writing $C\langle A \rangle$ and $D[A]$. We will write the cut rule as follows:

$$\frac{C\langle A \rangle \quad D[A]}{\mathrm{Cut}_A(C\langle A \rangle, D[A])}$$

Given this form of the Cut rule, we will need a *slight* generalisation to allow a cut of a *number* of occurrences in antecedent position, or in consequent position (but not in both). If the A in $D[A]$ is due to a contraction, WI, then to push the cut up above $D[A]$, we should cut on all of the instances in the premises of $D[A]$. So, given a *set* A of occurrences of A in antecedent position in D, we need the notion of an *antecedent multiple Cut*:

$$\frac{C\langle A \rangle \quad D[\mathcal{A}]}{\mathrm{Cut}_{\mathcal{A}}(C\langle A \rangle, D[\mathcal{A}])}$$

and similarly, given a set $\mathcal{A}$ of occurrences of A in consequent position in C (recall, we leave open the possibility of systems with structure in consequent position) we need the *consequent multiple Cut*:

$$\frac{C\langle \mathcal{A} \rangle \quad D[A]}{\mathrm{Cut}_{\mathcal{A}}(C\langle \mathcal{A} \rangle, D[A])}$$

Typically, these generalised, multiple Cuts are given by repeating the Cut rule a number of times. However, to prove the redundancy of Cut, we do not need to know how multiple Cuts and single Cuts are related, except for a few simple conditions.

DEFINITION 6.6 (CUT CONDITIONS)
A consecution system satisfies the *Cut Conditions* if and only if

⋄ $\mathrm{Cut}_{\mathcal{A}}(C\langle A \rangle, D[\mathcal{A}]) = \mathrm{Cut}_A(C\langle A \rangle, D[A])$, where the displayed occurrences $\mathcal{A}$ in $D[\mathcal{A}]$ is the singleton set of the single occurrence of A displayed in $D[A]$.

⋄ $\mathrm{Cut}_{\mathcal{A}}(C\langle \mathcal{A} \rangle, D[A]) = \mathrm{Cut}_A(C\langle A \rangle, D[A])$, where the displayed occurrences $\mathcal{A}$ in $C\langle \mathcal{A} \rangle$ is the singleton set of the single occurrence of A displayed in $C\langle A \rangle$.

⋄ If $C\langle A \rangle$ is an identity axiom, then $\mathrm{Cut}_A(C\langle A \rangle, D[A]) = D[A]$.

⋄ If $D[A]$ is an identity axiom, then $\mathrm{Cut}_A(C\langle A \rangle, D[A]) = C\langle A \rangle$.

Those conditions on Cut will be used in showing that Cut is redundant. These conditions are satisfied by the Gentzen system for ILL. Once we define the *antecedent multiple Cut*:

$$\frac{X \vdash A \quad Y(\mathcal{A}) \vdash C}{Y(\mathcal{X}) \vdash C} \text{ [AMCut]}$$

where $\mathcal{A}$ is a collection of instances of A, in $Y(\mathcal{A})$ and $Y(\mathcal{X}) \vdash C$ is the result of replacing those instances of A by X. For example:

$$\frac{X \vdash A \quad (A;(B;A)); A \vdash C}{(X;(B;A)); X \vdash C}$$

is an instance of [AMCut] in which the selected instances of A in $(A;(B;A));A$ are the first and the third, but *not* the second.

Given this definition of a multiple Cut, it is simple to verify that the Cut conditions are satisfied in the Gentzen system for ILL.

Now we must look at the behaviour of parameters in Gentzen systems, for we want to know how to keep track of parameters while "pushing" a Cut over one.

DEFINITION 6.7 (PARAMETER CONDITIONS)

  ◇ *Shape-alikeness of parameters.* Congruent parameters are occurrences of the same structure.

  ◇ *Position-alikeness of parameters.* Congruent parameters are either all antecedent or all consequent parts of their respective consecutions.

  ◇ *Non-proliferation of parameters.* A congruence class of parameters in an inference contains at most one formula in the conclusion of the inference.

These may be verified by eye, checking the rules. For ILL, congruent parameters in a rule listed in our presentation of the system are either denoted by the same letter (for formulae in the consequent) or they occupy the same place in a structure denoted by the same letter. For example, in the rule

$$\frac{X(A) \vdash C \quad X(B) \vdash C}{X(A \vee B) \vdash C}$$

the displayed instances of C presented here are congruent. Similarly, any substructure of X in $X(A)$ is congruent with its mates in $X(B)$ and $X(A \vee B)$. In this case, it is clear that parameters are shape-alike and position-alike (none jumps over from antecedent to consequent, or vice versa) and they do not proliferate (there is only one occurrence of X, and only one of C in the conclusion). The same is readily checked for *nearly all* of our rules.

The only rules to beware of are the *structural rules*, which may well violate the non-proliferation condition. Consider the mingle rule $X \Leftarrow X;X$. An instance is

$$\frac{X \vdash A}{X;X \vdash A}$$

This fails the non-proliferation condition. The two displayed occurrences of X in the conclusion are congruent with each other. However, this is no great problem in this case, as M can be expressed by the equivalent rule

$$\frac{X \vdash A \quad Y \vdash A}{X;Y \vdash A}$$

which satisfies the non-proliferation condition. Both X and Y are parameters in the conclusion, but they are not congruent with one another, not even in the case in which $X = Y$. Remember: Congruence entails shape-alikeness, but shape-alikeness need not entail congruence.

From parameters, we move to the behaviour of principal formulae.

DEFINITION 6.8 (PRINCIPAL FORMULA CONDITIONS)

⋄ *Single principal constituents.* If there is an inference ending in C in which some formula A is principal, then A is the only principal formula in C, unless C is an axiom.

⋄ *Eliminability of matching principal constituents.* If there are inferences Inf_1 and Inf_2 with conclusions $C\langle A \rangle$ and $D[A]$ in which the presented occurrence of A is principal, then $Cut_A(C\langle A \rangle, D[A])$ is defined, and either is one of the premises of Inf_1 or Inf_2, or it is possible to pass from the premises of Inf_1 and Inf_2 to $Cut_A(C\langle A \rangle, D[A])$ by means of inferences falling under the rules together with inferences falling under the cut rule in which the cut formula is a proper subformula of A.

Both of these conditions hold in the Gentzen system for ILL. The 'single principal constituent' condition may be verified by eye. The eliminability condition must be verified case by case. We will check two and leave the rest to Exercise 6.4. In the case where the principal formula is an implication, we have

$$\cfrac{\cfrac{X; A \vdash B}{X \vdash A \to B} \, [\to R] \qquad \cfrac{Z \vdash A \quad Y(B) \vdash C}{Y(A \to B; Z) \vdash C} \, [\to L]}{Y(X; Z) \vdash C} \, [\text{Cut}_{A \to B}]$$

and we can cut on A and B to get the proof

$$\cfrac{\cfrac{Z \vdash A \quad X; A \vdash B}{X; Z \vdash B} \, [\text{Cut}_A] \qquad Y(B) \vdash C}{Y(X; Z) \vdash B} \, [\text{Cut}_B]$$

which gives us the same conclusion from the same premises. For the exponential, we can reason as follows. Instead of a cut on $!A$ in

$$\cfrac{\cfrac{!X \vdash A}{!X \vdash !A} \, [!R] \qquad \cfrac{Y(A) \vdash B}{Y(!A) \vdash B} \, [!L]}{Y(!X) \vdash B} \, [\text{Cut}_{!A}]$$

we can cut to the chase and Cut on the A

$$\frac{!X \vdash A \quad Y(A) \vdash B}{Y(!X) \vdash B} \ [\text{Cut}_A]$$

which gives the same results. None of the other cases is any more difficult.

Finally, to complete our set of conditions, we need a *regularity condition*, which shows that Cuts (perhaps multiple cuts) can be "pushed over" rules in which the cut formula is a parameter. This proves the most difficult in general, for the following reason. Consider the following cut on $!A$.

$$\frac{X \vdash !A \quad \dfrac{Y(!A; !A) \vdash B}{Y(!A) \vdash B} \ [!\text{WI}]}{Y(X) \vdash B} \ [\text{Cut}_{!A}]$$

To push the Cut over the inference [!WI] we would need the proof

$$\frac{\dfrac{X \vdash !A \quad Y(!A; !A) \vdash B}{Y(X; X) \vdash B} \ [\text{Cut}_{!A}]}{Y(X) \vdash B} \ [??]$$

But now we need to contract the two instances $X; X$ into one. And this cannot be done in general. We can only contract formulae prefixed with an exponential. X may not be that sort of structure. If it is not, the Cut cannot be pushed back.

However, there is a possibility. If we know that $!A$ is principal in $X \vdash !A$, then we know that X must be of the form $!Z$ for some Z. (Check the [!R] rule.) So our policy for pushing back Cuts involving $!A$ should be as follows. Push back the Cuts in the *consequent* position until $!A$ is principal. At this stage, we have a consecution of the form $!Z \vdash !A$, and we can use this to push the Cut back over rules in which $!A$ appears as a parameter in the antecedent.

DEFINITION 6.9 (REGULARITY)
A formula A is *consequent regular* in a consecution system if and only if the following two conditions hold. First, whenever

$$\frac{C_1 \quad \cdots \quad C_n}{C_{n+1}}$$

is an instance of a rule in the consecution system, and if $\mathcal{A}$ is a congruence class of parametric occurrences of A in consequent position on the inference, such that $\mathcal{A}_i$ is the set of occurrences of A in C_i, then for any $D[A]$, we can pass from each consecution

$$\mathrm{Cut}_A(C_1\langle \mathcal{A}_1\rangle, D[A]) \quad \cdots \quad \mathrm{Cut}_A(C\langle \mathcal{A}_n\rangle, D[A])$$

to the conclusion

$$\mathrm{Cut}_A(C\langle \mathcal{A}_{n+1}\rangle, D[A])$$

by means of any rule in the system, other than Cut.

Second, whenever

$$\frac{D_1 \quad \cdots \quad D_n}{D_{n+1}}$$

is an instance of a rule in the consecution system, and if $\mathcal{A}$ is a congruence class of parametric occurrences of A in antecedent position on the inference, such that $\mathcal{A}_i$ is the set of occurrences of A in D_i, then for any $C\langle A\rangle$, *which is the conclusion of an inference in which the highlighted occurrence of A is principal,* then we can pass from the premises

$$\mathrm{Cut}_A(C\langle A\rangle, D_1[\mathcal{A}_1]) \quad \cdots \quad \mathrm{Cut}_A(C\langle A\rangle, D_n[\mathcal{A}_n])$$

to the conclusion

$$\mathrm{Cut}_A(C\langle A\rangle, D_{n+1}[\mathcal{A}_{n+1}])$$

by means of any rule in the system, other than Cut.

Dually, a formula A is *antecedent regular* in a consecution system if and only if the following two conditions hold. First, whenever

$$\frac{D_1 \quad \cdots \quad D_n}{D_{n+1}}$$

is an instance of a rule in the consecution system, and if $\mathcal{A}$ is a congruence class of parametric occurrences of A in antecedent position on the inference, such that $\mathcal{A}_i$ is the set of occurrences of A in D_i, then for any $C\langle A\rangle$, we can pass from the premises

$$\mathrm{Cut}_A(C\langle A\rangle, D_1[\mathcal{A}_1]) \quad \cdots \quad \mathrm{Cut}_A(C\langle A\rangle, D_n[\mathcal{A}_n])$$

to the conclusion

$$\mathrm{Cut}_A(C\langle A\rangle, D_{n+1}[\mathcal{A}_{n+1}])$$

by means of any rule in the system, other than Cut.

Second, whenever

$$\frac{C_1 \quad \cdots \quad C_n}{C_{n+1}}$$

is an instance of a rule in the consecution system, and if $\mathcal{A}$ is a congruence class of parametric occurrences of A in consequent position on the inference, such that $\mathcal{A}_i$ is the set of occurrences of A in C_i, then for any $D[A]$, *which is the conclusion of an inference in which the highlighted occurrence of A is principal*, then we can pass from each consecution

$$\mathrm{Cut}_A(C_1\langle\mathcal{A}_1\rangle, D[A]) \quad \cdots \quad \mathrm{Cut}_A(C\langle\mathcal{A}_n\rangle, D[A])$$

to the conclusion

$$\mathrm{Cut}_A(C\langle\mathcal{A}_{n+1}\rangle, D[A])$$

by means of any rule in the system, other than Cut.

Now we have our final condition.

DEFINITION 6.10 (REGULARITY CONDITION)
  ⋄ *Regularity.* Every formula is either antecedent or consequent regular.

Most connectives are both antecedent and consequent regular. Checking regularity in ILL is not too difficult. First, we need to check that in a rule if A occurs as a parameter in the *antecedent* then we can cut each premise and the conclusion of the rule with $X \vdash A$. This amounts to replacing each parametric instance of A in the rule by X. This is possible in each rule, except for [!WI]. In that case, if we replace $!A$ by X, we get a step which may not be provable. In this case, we show that $!A$ is *consequent regular*, for it may be replaced anywhere in the consequent, but only in the antecedent by consecutions in which $!A$ is principal — in other words, in the antecedent $!A$ may be replaced by $!X$, but not necessarily by any more general structure. That is the effect of a Cut of a rule with $X \vdash A$. For the dual requirement, we need to consider what happens when we apply a Cut to a parametric C in consequent position. Suppose C is a parameter in some rule, such as [∨L]. We have

$$\frac{X(A) \vdash C \quad X(B) \vdash C}{X(A \vee B) \vdash C}$$

Now suppose we use C as the Cut formula with another consecution, say $Y(C) \vdash D$, where $\mathcal{C}$ is some collection of instances of C in $Y(C)$. The result is

$$\frac{Y(\mathcal{X}(A)) \vdash C \quad Y(\mathcal{X}(B)) \vdash C}{Y(\mathcal{X}(A \vee B)) \vdash C}$$

where $Y(\mathcal{X}(A))$ is the result of replacing each instance of C in $Y(\mathcal{C})$ by $X(A)$, and similarly for $Y(\mathcal{X}(B))$ and $Y(\mathcal{X}(A \vee B))$. Can we get to the conclusion of this "rule" from the premises by way of the rules? Yes we can, by means of n instances of [∨L], where n is the number of instances of C in $\mathcal{C}$. The same holds for each of the other rules in our system. Therefore, each non-exponential formula is both antecedent and consequent regular, and $!A$ is consequent regular. So our system satisfies the regularity condition.

6.3 The Proof

This section is devoted to proving the following theorem:

THEOREM 6.11
In any consecution satisfying the parameter, principal and regularity conditions, if $C\langle A\rangle$ and $D[A]$ are provable then $\mathrm{Cut}_A(C\langle A\rangle, D[A])$ is also provable.

The proof is simple in its general plan, but the detail is rather complex. We will prove a number of lemmas.

LEMMA 6.12 (ANTECEDENT STAGE)
Suppose A is antecedent regular, then the following two conditions hold.

Part 1: For all consecutions C and D, if $D[A]$ is derivable (A1a) and if for all $D'[A]$ in which the presented A is principal, $\mathrm{Cut}_A(C\langle A\rangle, D'[A])$ is derivable (A1b) then $\mathrm{Cut}_A(C\langle A\rangle, D[A])$ is also provable.

Part 2: For all consecutions C and D, if $C\langle A\rangle$ is derivable (A2a) and if for all $C'\langle A\rangle$ in which A is principal, $\mathrm{Cut}_A(C'\langle A\rangle, D[A])$ is derivable (A2b) and if in addition, $D[A]$ is the conclusion of some inference in which A is principal (A2c), then $\mathrm{Cut}_A(C\langle A\rangle, D[A])$ is provable.

The consequent stage is dual to the antecedent stage.

LEMMA 6.13 (CONSEQUENT STAGE)
Suppose that A is consequent regular, then the following two conditions hold.

Part 1: For all consecutions C and D, if $C\langle A\rangle$ is derivable (B1a) and if for all $C'\langle A\rangle$ in which the presented A is principal, $\mathrm{Cut}_A(C'\langle A\rangle, D[A])$ is derivable (B1b) then $\mathrm{Cut}_A(C\langle A\rangle, D[A])$ is also provable.

Part 2: For all consecutions C and D, if $D[A]$ is derivable (B2a) and if for all $D'[A]$ in which A is principal, $\mathrm{Cut}_A(C\langle A\rangle, D'[A])$ is derivable (B2b) and if in addition, $C\langle A\rangle$ is the conclusion of some inference in which A is principal (B2c), then $\mathrm{Cut}_A(C\langle A\rangle, D[A])$ is provable.

LEMMA 6.14 (PRINCIPAL STAGE)
If there are derivations of $C\langle A\rangle$ and $D[A]$ in which the presented instances of A are both principal, and if for all subformulae B of A and for all consecutions C' and D' then $\mathrm{Cut}_B(C'\langle B\rangle, D'[B])$ is derivable, then $\mathrm{Cut}_A(C\langle A\rangle, D[A])$ is derivable.

The proof of the cut elimination theorem follows from the three lemmas above.

PROOF This is performed by induction on the complexity of A. There are two cases to perform, depending on the antecedent or consequent regularity of A. (By the regularity condition, A is either antecedent or consequent regular.) Suppose A is antecedent regular. Suppose that $C\langle A\rangle$ and $D[A]$ are derivable, to show that $\mathrm{Cut}_A(C\langle A\rangle, D[A])$ is derivable. Suppose that $D'[A]$ is derivable and the presented A is principal in the conclusion of that derivation. Suppose also that $C'\langle A\rangle$ is derivable and the presented A is principal in the conclusion of that derivation. It follows by the principal stage that $\mathrm{Cut}_A(C'\langle A\rangle, D'[A])$, using the induction condition that Cut holds for subformulae of A. It follows then that $\mathrm{Cut}_A(C\langle A\rangle, D'[A])$ is provable, by Part 2 of the Antecedent Stage, and then by Part 1 of the antecedent stage, $\mathrm{Cut}_A(C\langle A\rangle, D[A])$ is derivable as desired.

The case for A being consequent regular is dual, appealing to the Consequent Stage instead of the Antecedent Stage.   □

Therefore to complete the proof we need to prove the Antecedent, Consequent and Principal Stage Lemmas. The Principal Stage is simple:

PROOF Follows immediately from the *eliminability of matching principal constituents* condition.   □

The Antecedent and Consequent stages are completely dual. We will prove the antecedent stage lemma.

PROOF We suppose that A is antecedent regular and we let π be some derivation of $D[A]$ (A1a). If A is nonparametric in the conclusion of this derivation, it is principal, and condition (A1b) gives us our result. So suppose A is parametric. We define a set $\mathcal{A}$ of instances of A in π as follows: include the presented instance in $D[A]$, and for all instances in $\mathcal{A}$ include any members of a congruence class (with respect to an inference in π) which already has a member in $\mathcal{A}$. $\mathcal{A}$ is the set of *parametric ancestors* of the presented A in $D[A]$. By the *shape-alikeness of parameters*, $\mathcal{A}$ is a set of instances of the formula A, by the *position-alikeness of parameters* each A is in antecedent position, and by *nonproliferation of parameters* the presented A in $D[A]$ is the only instance in $D[A]$.

For each consecution D_i in π, let $\mathcal{A}_i$ be the elements of $\mathcal{A}$ in D_i. Let $D'_i = \mathrm{Cut}_{\mathcal{A}_i}(C\langle A\rangle, D_i[\mathcal{A}_i])$. We wish to show that each D'_i is provable, as D' is $\mathrm{Cut}_A(C\langle A\rangle, D[A])$ (as the set of instances in $\mathcal{A}$ in $D[A]$ is simply the displayed A by non-proliferation).

We show that D_i' is provable, under the induction hypothesis that the primes of its premises (if there are any) are also provable. Suppose the inference leading to D_i is

$$\frac{E_1 \quad \cdots \quad E_n}{D_i}$$

(call it *Inf* for reference) and by induction, suppose that each E_j' is derivable. Let D_i'' be $\text{Cut}_{\mathcal{A} \bullet}(C\langle A\rangle, D_i[\mathcal{A}^*])$, where $\mathcal{A}^*$ is the set of instances of A in D_i which in addition to being in $\mathcal{A}$ are parametric in *Inf*. Antecedent regularity of A ensures that D_i'' is demonstrable. This is nearly our result for Part 1, unless some instance A is not parametric in D_i in *Inf*. In that case, by the single principal constituent condition, either D_i is an identity axiom, in which case (by the Cut condition) $\text{Cut}_A(C\langle A\rangle, D_i[A]) = C\langle A\rangle$, which is provable, or the principal A is the single instance of A in the congruence class, and in which case $D_i' = \text{Cut}_{\mathcal{A}_i}(C\langle A\rangle, D_i[\mathcal{A}_i]) = \text{Cut}_A(C\langle A\rangle, D_i[A])$ which is provable by (A1b). This completes Part 1.

For Part 2, let π be some derivation of $C\langle A\rangle$ (A2a). If A is nonparametric in the conclusion of this derivation, it is principal, and condition (A2b) gives us our result. So suppose A is parametric. We define a set $\mathcal{A}$ of instances of A in π as follows: include the presented instance in $C\langle A\rangle$, and for all instances in $\mathcal{A}$ include any members of a congruence class (with respect to an inference in π) which already has a member in $\mathcal{A}$. By the *shape-alikeness of parameters*, $\mathcal{A}$ is a set of instances of the formula A, by the *position-alikeness of parameters* each A is in consequent position, and by *non-proliferation of parameters* the presented A in $C\langle A\rangle$ is the only instance in $C\langle A\rangle$.

For each consecution C_i in π, let $\mathcal{A}_i$ be the elements of $\mathcal{A}$ in C_i. Let $C_i' = \text{Cut}_{\mathcal{A}_i}(C\langle \mathcal{A}_i\rangle, D[A])$, where in addition we know that $D[A]$ is a conclusion of an inference in which A is principal (A2c). We wish to show that each C_i' is provable, as C' is $\text{Cut}_A(C\langle A\rangle, D[A])$ (as the set of instances in $\mathcal{A}$ in $C\langle A\rangle$ is simply the displayed A by non-proliferation).

We show that C_i' is provable, under the induction hypothesis that the primes of its premises (if it has any) are also provable. Suppose the inference leading to C_i is

$$\frac{E_1 \quad \cdots \quad E_n}{C_i}$$

(call it *Inf* for reference) and by induction, suppose that each E_j' is derivable. Let C_i'' be $\text{Cut}_{\mathcal{A} \bullet}(C_i\langle \mathcal{A}^*\rangle, D[A])$, where $\mathcal{A}^*$ is the set of instances of A in C_i which in addition to being in $\mathcal{A}$ are parametric in *Inf*. Antecedent regularity of A ensures that C_i'' is demonstrable (as $D[A]$ is the conclusion of some inference in which the presented A is principal). This is nearly our result for Part 2, unless some instance A is not parametric in C_i in *Inf*. In that case, by the single principal constituent condition, either C_i is an identity axiom, in which case (by the Cut condition again) $\mathrm{Cut}_A(C_i\langle A\rangle, D[A]) = D[A]$, which is provable, or the principal A is the single instance of A in the congruence class, and in which case $C_i' = \mathrm{Cut}_{A_i}(C_i\langle A_i\rangle, D[A]) = \mathrm{Cut}_A(C_i\langle A\rangle, D[A])$, which is provable by (A2b). This completes Part 2, and hence, the proof of the Lemma. $\square$

6.4 Examples

We can vary our system for ILL a great deal while keeping its nice properties. First, the structural rules can be varied to your heart's content, provided that we have the non-proliferation condition. We will not explicitly consider any differences here. Instead, we will look at different connective rules. The most obvious absence is the lack of positive modal connectives. We can add them with the simple rules

$$\frac{X(A) \vdash C}{X(\bullet\Box A) \vdash C}\,[\Box\mathrm{L}] \qquad \frac{\bullet X \vdash A}{X \vdash \Box A}\,[\Box\mathrm{R}] \qquad \frac{X(\bullet A) \vdash C}{X(\Diamond A) \vdash C}\,[\Diamond\mathrm{L}] \qquad \frac{X \vdash A}{\bullet X \vdash \Diamond A}\,[\Diamond\mathrm{R}]$$

These can be shown to do the same job as the rules in the natural deduction system (Exercise 6.5). The Identity Theorem also extends to the modal case.

$$\frac{\dfrac{A \vdash A}{\bullet\Box A \vdash A}\,[\Box\mathrm{L}]}{\Box A \vdash \Box A}\,[\Box\mathrm{R}] \qquad \frac{\dfrac{A \vdash A}{\bullet A \vdash \Diamond A}\,[\Diamond\mathrm{R}]}{\Diamond A \vdash \Diamond A}\,[\Diamond\mathrm{L}]$$

So does the eliminability of matching principal constituents.

$$\frac{\dfrac{\bullet X \vdash A}{X \vdash \Box A} \quad \dfrac{Y(A) \vdash C}{Y(\bullet\Box A) \vdash C}}{Y(\bullet X) \vdash C}\,[\mathrm{Cut}_{\Box A}] \qquad \text{becomes} \qquad \frac{\bullet X \vdash A \quad Y(A) \vdash C}{Y(\bullet X) \vdash C}\,[\mathrm{Cut}_A]$$

The other conditions (Cut, Regularity, Principal and Parameter) are preserved. Modal structure does nothing above and beyond the intensional structure.

Gentzen systems can be *structure–structure*. We can make the system for ILL symmetric, by allowing structure in the consequent just as we allow structure in the antecedent. Now instead of allowing empty antecedent and consequent structures, we use a punctuation constant 0 satisfying Left and Right Push and Pop rules. This is the Gentzen system for CLL. In this system, we allow the structural rules C and B. Here are the rules:

$$A \vdash A \qquad \frac{X \vdash Y(A) \quad X'(A) \vdash Y'}{X'(X) \vdash Y(Y')}\,[\mathrm{Cut}]$$

$$\frac{X \vdash A; Y}{X; \sim A \vdash Y} \; [\sim L] \qquad \frac{X; A \vdash Y}{X \vdash \sim A; Y} \; [\sim R]$$

$$\frac{X(A) \vdash Y}{X(A \wedge B) \vdash Y} \; [\wedge L_1] \qquad \frac{X(B) \vdash Y}{X(A \wedge B) \vdash Y} \; [\wedge L_2] \qquad \frac{X \vdash Y(A) \quad X \vdash Y(B)}{X \vdash Y(A \wedge B)} \; [\wedge R]$$

$$\frac{X(A, B) \vdash Y}{X(A \circ B) \vdash Y} \; [\circ L] \qquad \frac{X \vdash Y; A \quad X' \vdash B; Y'}{X; X' \vdash (Y; A \circ B); Y'} \; [\circ R]$$

$$\frac{X(A) \vdash Y \quad X(B) \vdash Y}{X(A \vee B) \vdash Y} \; [\vee L] \qquad \frac{X \vdash Y(A)}{X \vdash Y(A \vee B)} \; [\vee R_1] \qquad \frac{X \vdash Y(B)}{X \vdash Y(A \vee B)} \; [\vee R_2]$$

$$\frac{X; A \vdash Y \quad B; X' \vdash Y'}{(X; A + B); X' \vdash Y; Y'} \; [+L] \qquad \frac{X \vdash Y(A; B)}{X \vdash Y(A + B)} \; [+R]$$

$$\frac{X \vdash Y(A) \quad X'(B) \vdash Y'}{X'(X; A \to B) \vdash Y(Y')} \; [\to L] \qquad \frac{X; A \vdash B; Y}{X \vdash A \to B; Y} \; [\to R]$$

$$\frac{X(0) \vdash Y}{X(t) \vdash Y} \; [tL] \qquad 0 \vdash t \; [tR]$$

$$f \vdash 0 \; [fL] \qquad \frac{X \vdash Y(0)}{X \vdash Y(f)} \; [fR]$$

$$X(\perp) \vdash Y \qquad X \vdash Y(\top)$$

$$\frac{X \vdash Y}{X; !A \vdash Y} \; [K!] \qquad \frac{X(A) \vdash Y}{X(!A) \vdash Y} \; [L!] \qquad \frac{!X \vdash A; ?Y}{!X \vdash !A; ?Y} \; [R!] \qquad \frac{X(!A; !A) \vdash Y}{X(!A) \vdash Y} \; [WI!]$$

$$\frac{X \vdash Y}{X \vdash ?A; Y} \; [K?] \qquad \frac{X \vdash Y(A)}{X \vdash Y(?A)} \; [R?] \qquad \frac{!X; A \vdash ?Y}{!X; ?A \vdash ?Y} \; [L?] \qquad \frac{X \vdash Y(?A; ?A)}{X \vdash Y(?A)} \; [W?]$$

It is not too hard to show that these systems satisfy each of the required conditions for Cut elimination. We will not pause to demonstrate this. Instead, we will note that we have a symmetric treatment of the logic. We have an explicit treatment of *fission* '+' in parallel with fusion. This duality is so deep that you can do away with half of the connectives and one side of the consecution to use a single-sided Gentzen system. See Exercise 6.6.

For negations, we need to rethink the nature of Gentzen systems even further. Note that to introduce the negation in $X \vdash \sim A$, keeping the subformula property, we need to use X and A. The A in the premise ought to be in *antecedent* position, as its negation appears in consequent position. If $A \vdash A'$ then $\sim A' \vdash \sim A$. The "polarity" is reversed by negation. One way to place A in antecedent position is to combine it with the X, using two-place punctuation marks. This is how negation is defined in the Gentzen systems for linear logic. This is appropriate when negation is defined in terms of intensional structure — if $(\sim I; \neg E)$ and similar rules are present — but it is less appropriate where such connections are absent.

One way to define negation in the absence of any connections with two-place structure is to admit a different kind of one-place structure. We let $\sharp$ and $\flat$ be two different one-place punctuation marks, connected together by the following rule.

$$\frac{X \vdash \sharp Y}{Y \vdash \flat X}$$

The position-alikeness of parameters means that in this rule, both of X and Y are in antecedent position. However, $\sharp Y$ and $\flat X$ are in consequent position. This punctuation mark makes us define structure in a new way. If X is an *antecedent structure*, then $\sharp X$ and $\flat X$ are *consequent structure*. We can exploit this form of structure to give the following rules for negation.

$$\frac{X \vdash A}{\sim A \vdash \sharp X} \ [\sim L] \qquad \frac{X \vdash \sharp A}{X \vdash \sim A} \ [\sim R] \qquad \frac{X \vdash A}{\neg A \vdash \flat X} \ [\neg L] \qquad \frac{X \vdash \flat A}{X \vdash \neg A} \ [\neg R]$$

Once we have these rules, $\sim$ and $\neg$ are connected in the appropriate way. For example, we have the following proofs

$$
\cfrac{
\cfrac{
\cfrac{
\cfrac{A \vdash A}{\sim A \vdash \sharp A} \ [\sim L]
}{\sim A \wedge \sim B \vdash \sharp A} \ [\wedge L]
}{A \vdash \flat(\sim A \wedge \sim B)}
\qquad
\cfrac{
\cfrac{
\cfrac{B \vdash B}{\sim B \vdash \sharp B} \ [\sim L]
}{\sim A \wedge \sim B \vdash \sharp B} \ [\wedge L]
}{B \vdash \flat(\sim A \wedge \sim B)}
}{
\cfrac{
\cfrac{A \vee B \vdash \flat(\sim A \wedge \sim B)}{\sim A \wedge \sim B \vdash \sharp(A \vee B)}
}{\sim A \wedge \sim B \vdash \sim(A \vee B)} \ [\sim R]
} \ [\vee L]
$$

We identify $\sharp$ and $\flat$ to get the identity of $\neg$ and $\sim$. To get double negation elimination, we ought to allow these negative structures to appear in antecedent position as well as consequent position. Consecutions in this system (with just $\sim$ and $\neg$ as structure) have a useful property, called the *display property*. If A appears in antecedent position in a consecution, this consecution is equivalent to one of the form $A \vdash Z$, in which A is the displayed antecedent. Similarly, if A appears in consequent position, the consecution is equivalent to one of the form $Y \vdash A$. For this reason, the connective rules can take a simple form in which the formula introduced is the entire antecedent or the entire consequent. Similarly, the Cut rule can take the simple form

$$\frac{X \vdash A \quad A \vdash Y}{X \vdash Y}$$

as we can require that the cut formula in each premise be displayed. Belnap has pioneered this kind of consecution calculus in his papers on *display logic*.

6.5 History

In this presentation I have leaned heavily on the work of Curry's *Foundations of Mathematical Logic* [54] and Belnap's Display Logic [23, 24].

Gentzen's own systems for intuitionistic and classical propositional logics (and predicate logics) are clearly explained in his own papers [93]. Gentzen systems found their way into substructural logics from an early date. Lambek's work on the syntactic calculus was clearly inspired by Gentzen's methods [133, 134]. In relevant logics, it took the work of Dunn [72] and Mints [172] to show how Gentzen systems for positive relevant logics could be formulated. The crucial insight here was the presence of two different kinds of premise combination, as we have already seen. These have been extended in a number of ways to model negation. I have used Belnap's display logic to give proof-theories for logics with split negation [214, 218]. Another possible direction is Brady's work, which adds "signs" to formulae to model a de Morgan negation [39]. Girard's Gentzen systems for linear logic model negation neatly by the ever-present duality in these systems [96]. The Gentzen system for classical linear logic can be simplified to such an extent that only one side of the turnstile is necessary. See Exercise 6.6.

Gentzen systems have been used to provide a *decision procedure* for the consequence relation in many substructural logics, as the subformula property of the system often allows for a proof search procedure. We will see some examples of this in Chapter 14.

6.6 Exercises

Practice

{6.1} Construct Gentzen proofs (without Cut) for the consecutions in Exercises 2.1, 2.4, 2.5 and 2.6.

{6.2} Complete the proof of the remaining cases of the Identity Theorem on page 107.

Problems

{6.3} Complete the proof (on page 109) of the remaining cases of the equivalence of the Gentzen system for ILL (with Cut) with the natural deduction system.

{6.4} Show that eliminability of principal constituents holds in the Gentzen system for ILL.

{6.5} Show that the Gentzen rules for $\square$ and $\Diamond$ are equivalent to the natural deduction rules, extending Theorem 6.2 to apply to modal propositions.

Projects

{6.6} You can exploit the duality present in LL to produce a consecution system with consecutions of the form $X \vdash$ (or equally generally, $\vdash X$). We redefine formulae in such a way that $\sim$ binds only atomic propositions. $\sim(A \circ B) = \sim A + \sim B$, $\sim(A \wedge B) = \sim A \vee \sim B$, $\sim\sim A = A$, and so on. Then we define the Gentzen system in the light of this. Instead of $p \vdash p$ as the identity axiom, we have $p; \sim p \vdash$. For each other connective we take the appropriate left-hand rule, and we allow *duality* to take care of the right-hand rule. So, the fusion and fission rules are

$$\frac{X(A; B) \vdash}{X(A \circ B) \vdash} \qquad \frac{X; A \vdash \quad Y; B \vdash}{(X; A + B); Y \vdash}$$

Then identity is provable, in the sense that $A \circ B, \sim(A \circ B) \vdash$, or equivalently, $A \circ B; \sim A + \sim B \vdash$, as follows:

$$\frac{\dfrac{A; \sim A \vdash \quad B; \sim B \vdash}{(A; B); \sim A + \sim B \vdash}}{A \circ B; \sim A + \sim B \vdash}$$

(suppressing a few structural rules.) Define the whole system, including an appropriate Cut rule. Show that Cut is redundant in the system, and that it is equivalent to the two-sided Gentzen system for LL.

Chapter 7

Formulae as Types, Proofs as Terms

A closer analysis of proofs than what we have managed so far will be aided by giving proofs *names*. After all, if proofs are first-class entities, we will be better-off if we can distinguish different proofs. We will start with a homely example. We will start with the implication and conjunction fragment of intuitionistic logic: $J[\rightarrow, \wedge]$. The language for describing proofs is given by the λ-calculus with pairing. A *term* of this calculus is built up from variables $x, y, \ldots$ using the *constructors* $\langle -, - \rangle$, $\mathsf{fst}\,(-)$, $\mathsf{snd}\,(-)$, $\lambda x.M$ and application (which we write as juxtaposition). A *judgement* is a pair $M{:}A$ of a term M and a formula A. Then in proofs in this system we keep tabs on what is going on by building terms up to represent the ongoing proof. We start with the identity rule $x{:}A \vdash x{:}A$. Then for conjunction, we reason as follows:

$$\frac{\Gamma \vdash M{:}A \quad \Gamma \vdash N{:}B}{\Gamma \vdash \langle M, N \rangle{:}A \wedge B} \qquad \frac{\Gamma \vdash M{:}A \wedge B}{\Gamma \vdash \mathsf{fst}\,(M){:}A} \qquad \frac{\Gamma \vdash M{:}A \wedge B}{\Gamma \vdash \mathsf{snd}\,(M){:}B}$$

If M is the proof of A from Γ, and N is the proof of B from Γ, then the pair $\langle M, N \rangle$ is the proof of $A \wedge B$ from Γ. Similarly, if M is a proof of $A \wedge B$ (from Γ) then $\mathsf{fst}\,(M)$ (the "first part" of M) is the proof of A from Γ. Similarly, $\mathsf{snd}\,(M)$ is the proof of B from Γ. For implication, we have these rules:

$$\frac{\Gamma \vdash M{:}A \rightarrow B \quad \Delta \vdash N{:}A}{\Gamma, \Delta \vdash (MN){:}B} \qquad \frac{\Gamma, x{:}A \vdash M{:}B}{\Gamma \vdash \lambda x.M{:}A \rightarrow B}$$

If M is a proof of $A \rightarrow B$, and N is a proof of A, then you get a proof of B by *applying* M to N. So, this proof is (MN). Similarly, if M is a proof of B from $\Gamma, x{:}A$, then a proof of $A \rightarrow B$ is a function from proofs of A to the proof of B.

It is of type $\lambda x.M$. We put these together to get names for more complex proofs

$$\frac{\dfrac{x{:}A \to B \vdash x{:}A \to B \quad y{:}A \vdash y{:}A}{\dfrac{x{:}A \to B, y{:}A \vdash (xy){:}B}{\dfrac{y{:}A \vdash \lambda x.(xy){:}(A \to B) \to B}{0 \vdash \lambda y.\lambda x.(xy){:}A \to ((A \to B) \to B)}}}$$

The term $\lambda y.\lambda x.(xy)$ encodes the shape of the proof. The first step was an application of one assumption on another (the term (xy)). The second was the abstraction of the first assumption (λx), and the last step was the abstraction of the second assumption (λy). The term encodes the proof. There are a number of important features of these terms.

◇ Terms encoding proofs with no premises are *closed*. They have no free variables.

◇ More generally, if $\Gamma \vdash M{:}A$ is provable and x is free in M then x appears free in Γ too.

◇ Proofs encode connective steps, not structural rules. For example, the rule CI or C was used in the proof of $A \to ((A \to B) \to B)$. It is not encoded in the term explicitly. Its presence can be seen implicitly by noting that the variables x and y are bound in the opposite order to their appearance.

◇ For the application of structural rules, we require that no variables be *merged*. For example, if we have $X; X \Leftarrow X$ in our original proof theory, the rule $\Gamma; \Gamma \Leftarrow \Gamma$ is the corresponding term version. In this case, we want the variables in corresponding positions in each instance of Γ to be identical.

Now, once we have a term system, we have *contracting rules*, which give us the behaviour of *proof reduction*.

$$
\begin{array}{rcl}
\mathsf{fst}\,\langle M, N \rangle & \rightsquigarrow & M \\
\mathsf{snd}\,\langle M, N \rangle & \rightsquigarrow & N \\
(\lambda x.M)N & \rightsquigarrow & M[x := N]
\end{array}
$$

These correspond to cutting the detours out of proofs. For example, consider the reduction

$$\frac{\dfrac{\Gamma \vdash M{:}A \quad \Gamma \vdash N{:}B}{\Gamma \vdash \langle M, N \rangle{:}A \wedge B}}{\Gamma \vdash \mathsf{fst}\,\langle M, N \rangle{:}A} \quad \rightsquigarrow \quad \Gamma \vdash M{:}A$$

Or a slightly more complex case:

$$\frac{\dfrac{\Gamma, x{:}A \vdash M{:}B}{\Gamma \vdash \lambda x.M{:}A \to B \quad \Delta \vdash N{:}A}}{\Gamma, \Delta \vdash (\lambda x.M)N{:}B} \quad \leadsto \quad \Gamma, \Delta \vdash M[x := N]{:}B$$

The term $M[x := N]$ indicates that the assumption(s) marked x in M are replaced by N. This matches the assumption(s) A marked x in $\Gamma, x{:}A$ which are replaced by the Δ in the transformation.

7.1 Defining Terms and Decorating Proofs

We will adapt this simple scheme to our case — to the behaviour of intensional connectives such as fusion and implication, and possibility and necessity.

DEFINITION 7.1 (TERMS AND TYPES)
Every proposition is a type. Given a class of types, we define the class of terms (and the free variables in a term) recursively as follows:

⋄ For every type A there are variables x^A, y^A, ... of type A. The variable x^A is free in x^A, and no other variable is free in x^A. A free variable corresponds to the identity proof.

$$x{:}A \vdash x{:}A$$

⋄ If M has type A and N has type B then $\langle M, N \rangle$ is a term of type $A \wedge B$. The variables free in $\langle M, N \rangle$ are those free in M together with those free in N. Pairing corresponds to conjunction introduction.

$$\frac{\Gamma \vdash M{:}A \quad \Gamma \vdash N{:}B}{\Gamma \vdash \langle M, N \rangle {:}A \wedge B} \text{ (pairing)}$$

⋄ If M has type $A \wedge B$, then $\mathsf{fst}\,(M)$ is a term of type A and $\mathsf{snd}\,(M)$ is a term of type B. The variables free in M remain free in both $\mathsf{fst}\,(M)$ and $\mathsf{snd}\,(M)$. The projection operators fst and snd correspond to conjunction elimination.

$$\frac{\Gamma \vdash M{:}A \wedge B}{\Gamma \vdash \mathsf{fst}\,(M){:}A} \qquad \frac{\Gamma \vdash M{:}A \wedge B}{\Gamma \vdash \mathsf{snd}\,(M){:}B} \text{ (projection)}$$

⋄ If M is a term of type A then $\mathsf{inl}^B(M)$ is a term of type $A \vee B$ and $\mathsf{inr}^B(M)$ is a term of type $B \vee A$. The variables free in M remain free in both $\mathsf{inl}^B(M)$

and inr $^B(M)$. The injection constructors correspond to disjunction introduction.

$$\frac{\Gamma \vdash M{:}A}{\Gamma \vdash \mathsf{inl}\,(M){:}A \vee B} \qquad \frac{\Gamma \vdash M{:}A}{\Gamma \vdash \mathsf{inr}\,(M){:}B \vee A} \text{ (injection)}$$

◇ If L is a term of type $A \vee B$ and M and N are both terms of type C, then
the term let L be x^A in M or y^B in N is also of type C. The free variables
in let L be x^A in M or y^B in N are those in L, M and N, *except for* the
free instances of x^A in M and of y^B in N, which are now *bound*. This is
more difficult to understand than the other constructors. In this term L is
"standing for" whatever it is that gives us $A \vee B$. What is that? Well, if we
have A, it is x in M, and if we have B, it is y in N. Hence, we let L stand
for x in M or y in N.

$$\frac{\Gamma \vdash L{:}A \vee B \quad \Delta(x{:}A) \vdash M{:}C \quad \Delta(y{:}B) \vdash N{:}C}{\Delta(\Gamma) \vdash \text{let } L \text{ be } x \text{ in } M \text{ or } y \text{ in } N{:}C} \text{ (cases)}$$

There is an important proviso in this deduction. In $\Delta(x{:}A)$ the indicated
instance $x{:}A$ must be the only instance of x in the structure. If there are
more, they must be contracted into one instance, or they must be re-lettered
so that there is no clash of variables.

◇ $\star$ is a term of type $\top$.

$$\Gamma \vdash \star{:}\top$$

The star is a simple term that is the proof introducing $\top$ in the consequent.

◇ If M is a term of type $\bot$ then let M be † is a term of type C. No variables
are bound by this construction.

$$\frac{\Gamma \vdash M{:}\bot}{\Delta(\Gamma) \vdash \text{let } M \text{ be } \dagger{:}C}$$

This is also not easy to understand. The bottom type $\bot$ is perhaps best
understood as a zero-place disjunction, and hence the constructor is analogous.

◇ For application and abstraction, it will be simplest to use different constructors for left and for right implication. If M is a term of type $A \rightarrow B$ and N
is a term of type A, then $M^{\backprime}N$ is a term of type B. The free variables in
$M^{\backprime}N$ are those free in M and in N.

$$\frac{\Gamma \vdash M{:}A \rightarrow B \quad \Delta \vdash N{:}A}{\Gamma; \Delta \vdash M^{\backprime}N{:}B} \text{ ($\rightarrow$ app)}$$

◇ If M is a term of type B then $\lambda^{\rangle} x^A M$ is a term of type $A \to B$. The free variables of $\lambda^{\rangle} x^A M$ are those in M, except for x^A, which is now *bound*.

$$\frac{\Gamma; x{:}A \vdash M{:}B}{\Gamma \vdash \lambda^{\rangle} x M{:}A \to B} \; (\to \text{abst})$$

In this rule we require that x not be free in Γ. Again, any other instances of x in Γ must have been contracted with the displayed $x{:}A$ by the time we get to this inference.

◇ If M is a term of type A and N is a term of type $B \leftarrow A$, then $M^{\langle} N$ is a term of type B. The free variables in $M^{\langle} N$ are those free in M and in N.

$$\frac{\Gamma \vdash M{:}A \quad \Delta \vdash N{:}B \leftarrow A}{\Gamma; \Delta \vdash M^{\langle} N{:}B} \; (\leftarrow \text{app})$$

◇ If M is a term of type B then $\lambda^{\langle} x^A M$ is a term of type $B \leftarrow A$. The free variables of $\lambda^{\langle} x^A M$ are those in M, except for x^A, which is now *bound*.

$$\frac{x{:}A; \Gamma \vdash M{:}B}{\Gamma \vdash \lambda^{\langle} x M{:}B \leftarrow A} \; (\leftarrow \text{abst})$$

The same goes for the displayed $x{:}A$ here — it must be the only x in the antecedent of the premise.

◇ $*$ is a term of type t. If N is a term of type t, and M is a term of type C, then let N be $*$ in M is a term of type C. The free variables in let N be $*$ in M are those free in N or in M.

$$0 \vdash *{:}t \qquad \frac{\Delta \vdash N{:}t \quad \Gamma(0) \vdash M{:}C}{\Gamma(\Delta) \vdash \text{let } N \text{ be } * \text{ in } M{:}C}$$

Here the let constructor is similar to the let constructor of disjunction. We use N to take the place of $*$ in the term M.

◇ If M has type A and N has type B then $M \circ N$ is a term of type $A \circ B$. The free variables of $M \circ N$ are those of M and those of N.

$$\frac{\Gamma \vdash M{:}A \quad \Delta \vdash N{:}B}{\Gamma; \Delta \vdash M \circ N{:}A \circ B}$$

◇ If M is has type $A \circ B$ and N has type C then let M be $x^A \circ y^A$ in N is a term of type C. The free variables of let M be $x^A \circ y^A$ in N are those of

M and of N, except for the instances of x^A and y^A in N, which are now *bound*.

$$\frac{\Gamma \vdash M{:}A \circ B \quad \Delta(x{:}A; y{:}B) \vdash N{:}C}{\Delta(\Gamma) \vdash \text{let } M \text{ be } x \circ y \text{ in } N{:}C}$$

Here the let constructor is similar to the other let constructors we have seen. Note that these constructors are used in the rules which use a fixed formula in the consequent. All of the work occurs in the antecedent structure.

◇ If M is a term of type A then up M is a term of type $\Box A$, and if M is a term of type $\Box A$, then down M is a term of type A.

$$\frac{\bullet\Gamma \vdash M{:}A}{\Gamma \vdash \text{up } M{:}\Box A} \qquad \frac{\Gamma \vdash M{:}\Box A}{\bullet\Gamma \vdash \text{down } M{:}A}$$

up and down bind no variables. The behaviour of these terms parallels the behaviour of λ and application in which there is a fixed antecedent formula.

◇ If M is a term of type A, then $\bullet M$ is a term of type $\Diamond A$.

$$\frac{\Gamma \vdash M{:}A}{\bullet\Gamma \vdash \bullet M{:}\Diamond A}$$

◇ If M has type $\Diamond A$ and N has type C then let M be $\bullet x$ in N is a term of type C. The free variables in let M be $\bullet x^A$ in N are those in M and N, except for occurrences of x^A in N, which are *bound*.

$$\frac{\Gamma \vdash M{:}\Diamond A \quad \Delta(\bullet x{:}A) \vdash N{:}C}{\Delta(\Gamma) \vdash \text{let } M \text{ be } \bullet x \text{ in } N{:}C}$$

Possibility here acts like a one-place version of fusion.

Given a term M of type A, and a term N of type B, then $M[x^B := N]$ is given by replacing the free instances of x^B in M by N. A term is *closed* if and only if it has no free variables.

DEFINITION 7.2 (PROOF DECORATION)
A *decorated proof* in a natural deduction system is a chain of proof steps in the *term* proof theory given above, combined with structural rules. A structural rule in a term proof theory is given by replacing formulae by judgements in standard structural rules.

THEOREM 7.3 (PROOFS CAN BE DECORATED)
$X \vdash A$ *is provable in* $\mathfrak{S}$ *if and only if there is a decorated proof* $\Gamma \vdash M{:}A$ *in the corresponding term system, where* Γ *is found by assigning variables to the propositions in* X.

PROOF   For the proof from right to left, if we have a term proof of $\Gamma \vdash M{:}A$, erase the terms to get a proof of $X \vdash A$.

For left to right we proceed by an induction on the complexity of the proof of $X \vdash A$. Clearly the identity axiom and any zero-premise connective rules are provable in the term system. We have $x{:}A \vdash x{:}A$, $\Gamma \vdash \star{:}\top$ and $0 \vdash \ast{:}t$.

Our assumption for the induction step is that the premises of $X \vdash A$ can be proved in the term system, and that furthermore, it can be proved in such a way that no variables in the antecedent of the consecution occur more than once. We call this a *liberal distribution of variables*.

Now suppose $X \vdash A$ comes from another consecution $X' \vdash A$ by way of a structural rule. By hypothesis, there is a proof $\Gamma' \vdash M{:}A$ in the term system. We wish to show that there is a proof of $\Gamma \vdash M{:}A$ too, where Γ corresponds to X. The hypothesis tells us that no variable occurs twice in Γ'. Now consider the structural rule. If any merging of propositions is involved (in the case of W, WI and related rules), we must relabel the variables in Γ' to identify the variables attached to merged propositions, and also relabel the corresponding variables in M. This transformation preserves the property of being a proof, as nothing is assumed about the identity of free variables in any of our rules. If the conclusion of the structural rule introduces *new* formulae (in the case of K and similar rules) we add new variables. The result is a term proof of $\Gamma \vdash M{:}A$, which still has a liberal distribution of variables in Γ.

Now suppose $X \vdash A$ comes from the consecutions $Y \vdash B$ and $Z \vdash C$. (The case for one premise is simpler, and left to the reader.) By the induction hypothesis, we can assume that there are term proofs $\Sigma \vdash M{:}B$ and $\Delta \vdash N{:}C$. Furthermore, we can assume, for the moment, that no variables appear free in both consecutions. If the proof step binds no variables (in the case of pairing, projection, injection, application and so on) then we move to the appropriate conclusion of type $M@N$, where $@$ is the connective involved. The only difficulty is when the rule requires that the antecedents of two different premises be identical — as in the case of pairing. In this case, we rename the variables in one premise to match the other. This process involves transforming the proof of that premise ($\Delta \vdash N{:}C$) to be the proof of $\Delta' \vdash N'{:}C$, so that the free variables used in Δ' match those in Σ.

If the term constructor binds a variable, we must just check the provision that the displayed variable in the proof is the only one bound. But this is given by the condition that the premises involve a liberal distribution of variables. This completes the proof.   □

Here are some examples of decorated proofs. First, here is a proof of $x{:}(A \rightarrow B) \wedge (A \rightarrow C); y{:}A \vdash (\text{fst } x)'y{:}B$.

$$\frac{\dfrac{x{:}(A \rightarrow B) \wedge (A \rightarrow C) \vdash x{:}(A \rightarrow B) \wedge (A \rightarrow C)}{y{:}A \vdash y{:}A \qquad x{:}(A \rightarrow B) \wedge (A \rightarrow C) \vdash \text{fst } x{:}A \rightarrow B}}{x{:}(A \rightarrow B) \wedge (A \rightarrow C); y{:}A \vdash (\text{fst } x)'y{:}B}$$

We will call this proof Π_1. A similar proof (Π_2) can be found of $x{:}(A \rightarrow B) \wedge (A \rightarrow C); y{:}A \vdash (\text{snd } x)'y{:}C$. Then we can use these proofs to construct the following proof of $0 \vdash \lambda'x\lambda'y\langle(\text{fst } x)'y, (\text{snd } x)'y\rangle{:}(A \rightarrow B) \wedge (A \rightarrow C) \rightarrow (A \rightarrow B \wedge C)$.

$$\frac{\dfrac{\Pi_1 \qquad\qquad \Pi_2}{x{:}(A \rightarrow B) \wedge (A \rightarrow C); y{:}A \vdash \langle(\text{fst } x)'y, (\text{snd } x)'y\rangle{:}B \wedge C}}{\dfrac{x{:}(A \rightarrow B) \wedge (A \rightarrow C) \vdash \lambda'y\langle(\text{fst } x)'y, (\text{snd } x)'y\rangle{:}A \rightarrow B \wedge C}{0 \vdash \lambda'x\lambda'y\langle(\text{fst } x)'y, (\text{snd } x)'y\rangle{:}(A \rightarrow B) \wedge (A \rightarrow C) \rightarrow (A \rightarrow B \wedge C)}}$$

Note that this proof used no structural rules at all. We did not have to merge variables or introduce new ones. The next proof uses a structural rule, WI.

$$\frac{\dfrac{\dfrac{x{:}(A \rightarrow B) \wedge A \vdash x{:}(A \rightarrow B) \wedge A}{x{:}(A \rightarrow B) \wedge A \vdash \text{fst } x{:}A \rightarrow B} \quad \dfrac{x{:}(A \rightarrow B) \wedge A \vdash x{:}(A \rightarrow B) \wedge A}{x{:}(A \rightarrow B) \wedge A \vdash \text{snd } x{:}A}}{\dfrac{x{:}(A \rightarrow B) \wedge A; x{:}(A \rightarrow B) \wedge A \vdash (\text{fst } x)'(\text{snd } x){:}B}{x{:}(A \rightarrow B) \wedge A \vdash (\text{fst } x)'(\text{snd } x){:}B} \text{[WI]}}}{0 \vdash \lambda'x((\text{fst } x)'(\text{snd } x)){:}(A \rightarrow B) \wedge A \rightarrow B}$$

In this proof, the WI move applies as we use the same variable (here x) to apply to both instances of $(A \rightarrow B) \wedge A$. Had the branches of the proof used different variables, say x and y, then after the y step we would have had two free variables in the term decorating B — perhaps we would have had $(\text{fst } x)'(\text{snd } y)$ — with only one variable in the antecedent. This will not do, as we need an assumption for every free variable in the term. Free variables represent undischarged assumptions. So, WI and similar moves require shared variables.

The next theorem shows how Cut behaves in term systems. The proof is a simple induction on the complexity of N.

THEOREM 7.4 (SUBSTITUTION THEOREM)

If $\Delta \vdash M{:}A$ and $\Gamma(x{:}A) \vdash N{:}B$ are provable in some system, and Δ and $\Gamma(x{:}A)$ have no variables in common, then $\Gamma(\Delta) \vdash N[x := M]{:}B$ is also provable in that system. $\square$

So Cut, for proofs, corresponds exactly to substitution of proofs.

The next nice result of term systems is the Decomposition Theorem. It is a ready consequence of the nature of terms. Given a term M, we can "read off" the last step of the proof, and then get the terms of the proofs which conclude with the premises of that last step. Then continue.

THEOREM 7.5 (TERM DECOMPOSITION)
If M decorates two proofs, then these proofs share the same order of application of connective rules.   □

As an example, we can tell that the term $\lambda^{\flat} x((\mathsf{fst}\, x)^{\flat}(\mathsf{snd}\, x))$ is a proof of a proposition of the form $(A \to B) \wedge A \to B$. The similar term $\lambda^{\flat} x((\mathsf{snd}\, x)^{\flat}(\mathsf{fst}\, x))$ is a proof of $A \wedge (A \to B) \to B$, for here we have applied the *second* part of our assumption to the *first* part, instead of the other way around.

In this system, the one term can represent a proof in more than one logic. For example, $\lambda^{\flat} x((\mathsf{fst}\, x)^{\flat}(\mathsf{snd}\, x))$ is a proof of $(A \to B) \wedge A \to B$ in any logic with the rule WI. The proofs do not, however, give any explicit information about which structural rules have been used. You can see in this term that implication introduction and elimination have both been used, as has conjunction elimination. It requires more work to see that WI has been used.

However, in some cases we can see from a term what structural rules have been used in its proof. It is simplest to see for terms with simple structure. We will restrict our attention to proofs involving implication alone — so the only constructors are $\lambda^{\flat}$ and $^{\flat}$. Consider the logic R[→]. In any proof in R[→] we allow reordering and contraction of premises, but we do not allow irrelevant premises to be added to the proof. For example, we do not allow this simple proof.

$$\frac{\displaystyle \frac{x{:}A \vdash x{:}A}{x{:}A; y{:}B \vdash x{:}A}\, [\mathsf{K}]}{\displaystyle \frac{x{:}A \vdash \lambda^{\flat} y\, x{:}B \to A}{0 \vdash \lambda^{\flat} x \lambda^{\flat} y\, x{:}A \to (B \to A)}}$$

In this proof an irrelevant premise has been added — here, B. This addition is witnessed by the fact that the variable y is bound by a $\lambda^{\flat}$, despite the fact that it does not appear in the term bound! In R[→], this is not allowed. We have the following theorem, which characterises proofs not only in R[→] but also in BCK[→] and LL[→].

THEOREM 7.6 (CHARACTERISATION OF IMPLICATION TERMS)
Suppose M is a term, and we have a proof $\Gamma \vdash M{:}A$. Then M is a proof in R[→] if and only if each $\lambda^{\flat}$ binds at least one variable, and every variable in Γ is free in

M. It is a proof in BCK[→] *if and only if each* $\lambda^{\prime}$ *binds at most one variable, and every variable in* Γ *is free at most once in* M. *It is a proof in* LL[→] *if and only if each* $\lambda^{\prime}$ *binds exactly one variable, and every variable in* Γ *is free exactly once in* M.

PROOF   The proof from right to left is by induction on the construction of M. If M is a variable, we are done, as there are no abstractions, and the variable appears exactly once in the antecedent. If the result holds for $\Sigma \vdash M{:}A \rightarrow B$ and $\Delta N{:}A$, then the desired binding behaviour is still exhibited by $M^{\prime}N{:}B$, provided that Σ and Γ share no variables. Now consider structural rules. B and C disturb no variables, so these rules preserve the hypotheses. In BCK we allow K, which introduces new variables, but does nothing else, so we still have variables in Γ appearing no more than once in N. In R we allow W, which requires relabelling of variables to allow merges. However, W introduces no new variables, so no variables appear in Γ which are not in N.

Now suppose that we have a proof of $\Gamma; x{:}A \vdash M{:}B$. In BCK and LL, we know that x appears no more than once in $M{:}B$, so in $\lambda^{\prime}xM$ at most one x is bound. In R and LL, we know that x appears at least once in $M{:}B$, so in $\lambda^{\prime}xM$ at least one x is bound, and this completes the proof from right to left.

From left to right, we extract a proof from the term. This is a straightforward re-reading of the definition of a term. If the LL condition is satisfied then B and C will suffice for the proof. If the BCK condition is satisfied, then B, C and K will suffice (you need K to introduce irrelevant premises) and if the R condition is satisfied, then B, C and W will do (you need W to allow the duplication of premises).   □

This condition gives a intuitive justification for the connection between R and relevance. The λ-terms with no vacuous abstraction seem to pin down the class of abstract functions which somehow *depend* on their arguments. Similarly, the *linear* λ-terms — those in which no premise is bound twice, or vacuously bound — seem to be the terms in which resource use is best respected. In these terms nothing is used twice, and nothing is not used. It remains to be seen, however, if this intuitive justification can be extended to a genuine theory of the behaviour of functions and resource use on the one hand, and whether this intuitive account extends to other connectives and constructions. It seems difficult. For example, in *any* of our substructural logics you can prove $(A \rightarrow B) \wedge (A \rightarrow C) \rightarrow (A \rightarrow B \wedge C)$ with the proof we have seen a few pages ago. Its term — $\lambda^{\prime}x\lambda^{\prime}y\langle(\mathsf{fst}\,x)^{\prime}y, (\mathsf{snd}\,x)^{\prime}y\rangle$ — involves the double binding of x and of y. However, we did not use *any* structural rule in its proof. Can a story be told to explain this?

7.2 Introducing Normalisation

The process of *normalisation* is a technique for transforming proofs by eliminating useless "detours." Consider what happens when you introduce a connective and then eliminate it in the next step.

$$\frac{\dfrac{\Gamma; x{:}A \vdash M{:}B}{\Gamma \vdash \lambda^{\backprime} x\, M{:}A \to B \quad \Delta \vdash N{:}A}}{\Gamma; \Delta \vdash (\lambda x\, M)^{\backprime} N{:}B}$$

This detour can be cut out, resulting in a shorter proof from the same premises.

$$\Gamma; \Delta \vdash M[x := N]{:}B$$

This works for other connectives too. For example, if we have a fusion introduction and then elimination

$$\frac{\dfrac{\Gamma \vdash M{:}A \quad \Delta \vdash N{:}B}{\Gamma; \Delta \vdash M \circ N{:}A \circ B \quad \Sigma(x{:}A; y{:}B) \vdash L{:}C}}{\Sigma(\Gamma; \Delta) \vdash \text{let } M \circ N \text{ be } x \circ y \text{ in } L{:}C}$$

we may as well "cut out the middleman."

$$\Sigma(\Gamma; \Delta) \vdash L[x := M, y := N]$$

In this, we *simultaneously* substitute M for the free xs and N for the free ys in L.

This behaviour happens with *every* pair of introduction and elimination rules. It motivates a definition:

DEFINITION 7.7 (INTRODUCTION/ELIMINATION CONTRACTION)
The introduction/elimination *contraction rules* for each connective are as follows:

$$
\begin{aligned}
\text{fst } \langle M, N \rangle &\rightsquigarrow M \\
\text{snd } \langle M, N \rangle &\rightsquigarrow N \\
(\lambda^{\backprime} x M)^{\backprime} N &\rightsquigarrow M[x := N] \\
M(\lambda^{\backprime} x N)^{\backprime} &\rightsquigarrow N[x := M] \\
\text{down up } N &\rightsquigarrow N \\
\text{let } \bullet N \text{ be } \bullet x \text{ in } M &\rightsquigarrow M[x := N] \\
\text{let } * \text{ be } * \text{ in } M &\rightsquigarrow M
\end{aligned}
$$

$$\text{let } M \circ N \text{ be } x \circ y \text{ in } L \quad \rightsquigarrow \quad L[x := M, y := N]$$
$$\text{let inl}\,(M) \text{ be } x \text{ in } N \text{ or } y \text{ in } L \quad \rightsquigarrow \quad L[x := M]$$
$$\text{let inr}\,(M) \text{ be } x \text{ in } N \text{ or } y \text{ in } L \quad \rightsquigarrow \quad L[y := M]$$

It is a simple matter of checking to verify that for each M and M' where $M \rightsquigarrow M'$, M and M' have the same type.

However, these contractions are not the only redundancies which can be eliminated from proofs. 'let ...' terms require special treatment, for the type of the conclusion in these terms is the type of one of the premises.[1] In this case, we can, say, introduce a connective into C, use this as an "innocent bystander" in a let step, and *then* discard that connective. Here is an example, where we use a conjunction as a bystander in a fusion move, only to eliminate it.

$$\frac{\dfrac{\Delta \vdash M{:}A \circ B \qquad \Sigma(x{:}A; y{:}B) \vdash N{:}C \wedge D}{\Sigma(\Delta) \vdash \text{let } M \text{ be } x \circ y \text{ in } N{:}C \wedge D}}{\Sigma(\Delta) \vdash \text{fst}\,(\text{let } M \text{ be } x \circ y \text{ in } N){:}C}$$

This can be modified by eliminating the conjunction *before* the fusion step. In this way, the conjunction elimination is brought earlier, and hopefully, closer to any corresponding conjunction introduction, with which it might contract. So, we swap the order of the rules to get

$$\frac{\Delta \vdash M{:}A \circ B \qquad \dfrac{\Sigma(x{:}A; y{:}B) \vdash N{:}C \wedge D}{\Sigma(x{:}A; y{:}B) \vdash \text{fst}\,(N){:}C \wedge D}}{\Sigma(\Delta) \vdash \text{let } M \text{ be } x \circ y \text{ in fst}\,(N){:}C}$$

This does not shorten the proof, but it does help us to find more contractions to the proof, as it helps to bring together more introduction/elimination pairs.

This behaviour is available in general, but we must be careful. We might be tempted to say that any let step can be commuted with any elimination step. However, this is not quite right, as let steps themselves are elimination steps. If we allow let steps to commute over each other, then, for example, the proof

$$\frac{\Gamma \vdash M{:}A \circ B \qquad \dfrac{\Sigma \vdash N{:}t \quad \Delta(x{:}A; y{:}B)(0) \vdash L{:}C}{\Delta(x{:}A; y{:}B)(\Sigma) \vdash \text{let } N \text{ be } * \text{ in } L{:}C}}{\Delta(\Gamma)(\Sigma) \vdash \text{let } M \text{ be } x \circ y \text{ in } (\text{let } N \text{ be } * \text{ in } L){:}C}$$

---

[1]   Except for the term for $\bot$, which is a special case, in which the appropriate premise is absent. This is another point at which it is helpful to think of $\bot$ as a zero-place disjunction, so the $\bot$ rule acts similarly to the disjunction rule.

which eliminates t and then fusion, will "simplify" to

$$\frac{\Sigma \vdash N{:}t \quad \dfrac{\Gamma \vdash M{:}A \circ B \quad \Delta(x{:}A; y{:}B)(0) \vdash L{:}C}{\Delta(\Gamma)(0) \vdash \text{let } M \text{ be } x \circ y \text{ in } L{:}C}}{\Delta(\Gamma)(\Sigma) \vdash \text{let } N \text{ be } * \text{ in } (\text{let } M \text{ be } x \circ y \text{ in } L){:}C}$$

which can then "simplify" back to the earlier proof! This is not desirable, as we want the process of contraction and simplification to be a one-way process. So we must be careful. We will single out some terms as those appropriate to commute with let steps. These are the *proper* elimination constructors.

DEFINITION 7.8 (PROPER ELIMINATION CONSTRUCTORS)
The *proper elimination constructors* are the elimination constructors which are not let constructors. In particular, they are fst, snd, ⟩, ⟨ and down.

Now we can define the *commuting conversions* for proper elimination terms and let steps.

DEFINITION 7.9 (COMMUTING CONVERSIONS)
Any proper elimination constructor applied to a let term *commutes* with the let term. So, we push proper elimination terms inside let terms, as follows:

$$\Phi(\text{let } \cdots \text{ in } M) \rightsquigarrow \text{let } \cdots \text{ in } \Phi(M)$$

Here are some examples:

$$\text{fst}(\text{let } M \text{ be } x \text{ in } N \text{ or } y \text{ in } L) \quad \rightsquigarrow \quad \text{let } M \text{ be } x \text{ in fst}(N) \text{ or } y \text{ in fst}(L)$$
$$(\text{let } M \text{ be } x \circ y \text{ in } N)^{\rangle}L \quad \rightsquigarrow \quad \text{let } M \text{ be } x \circ y \text{ in } N^{\rangle}L$$
$$M^{\langle}(\text{let } K \text{ be } \dagger) \quad \rightsquigarrow \quad \text{let } K \text{ be } \dagger$$

This completes our suite of ways to simplify proofs. Now we can patch them together.

DEFINITION 7.10 (CONTRACTING, CONVERTING AND REDUCING)
If $M \rightsquigarrow M'$, we say that M is a *redex* and M' is the *contractum* of M. If L is a term with some redex as a subterm, then L is said to *convert* to L', the result of replacing that redex with its contractum. We write this '$L \longrightarrow L'$.' Finally, if we have a sequence of conversions

$$L_1 \longrightarrow L_2 \longrightarrow \cdots \longrightarrow L_{n-1} \longrightarrow L_n$$

we say that L_1 *reduces* to L_n, and we write this as '$L_1 \twoheadrightarrow L_n$.'

An inspection of the rules for contracting redexes shows that during reduction, the type of a term is unchanged.

THEOREM 7.11 (PRESERVATION OF PROOFS UNDER REDUCTION)
If $M{:}A$ and $M \twoheadrightarrow M'$ then $M'{:}A$ too.   □

Not only that, but we have a stronger result.

THEOREM 7.12 (INVARIANCE OF PROOFS UNDER REDUCTION)
If $L \twoheadrightarrow L'$ and L is a proof of A in a system $\mathfrak{S}$, then L' is also a proof of A in $\mathfrak{S}$.

PROOF If a redex is a proof in some system, then so is its contractum. Note that no structural rules are needed when snipping out the irrelevant parts in terms to be contracted.   □

DEFINITION 7.13 (NORMAL TERMS AND NORMALISING TERMS)
If there is no M' where $M \longrightarrow M'$, we say that M is *normal*. A term is *normalising* if it can be reduced to a normal term. A term is *strongly normalising* if all reduction strategies end in a normal term.

Normal terms are desirable in a number of ways. Normal proofs contain no redundancies. In fact, as we will see later, normal proofs have the subformula property. In fact, we will see that they correspond rather tightly to cut-free proofs in Gentzen systems.

Getting normal terms and normal proofs is not necessarily a simple matter. There is a slight modification of the λ-calculus in which not all terms are normalising. Consider the class of *untyped* λ-terms. These are defined with no regard to typing.

◇ Any variable is an untyped λ-term.

◇ If M and N are untyped λ-terms, so is (MN).

◇ If M is an untyped λ-term and x is a variable, then $\lambda x M$ is an untyped λ-term.

The same reduction rules apply. In particular, $(\lambda x M)N \twoheadrightarrow M[x := N]$.

The term $\Omega = (\lambda x(xx))(\lambda x(xx))$ is not normalising. The only reduction which applies gives us $(xx)[x := (\lambda x(xx))] = (\lambda x(xx))(\lambda x(xx))$, so we have an infinite sequence. It does not stop, so there is no normal term to which it reduces.

Some (untyped) λ-terms do normalise but do not strongly normalise. Consider $KI\Omega$, where $K = \lambda x \lambda y\, x$, and where $I = \lambda x\, x$. Then we have

$$(KI)\Omega \longrightarrow (KI)\Omega \longrightarrow (KI)\Omega \longrightarrow \cdots$$

by applying $\Omega \rightsquigarrow \Omega$ at each step. However, we can apply the general contraction $(KM)N \rightsquigarrow M$ to get

$$(KI)\Omega \longrightarrow I$$

and I is normal. So, in the class of all terms (including untyped terms) the choice of normalisation sequence matters. We will show that in the class of typed terms, the choice of reduction does not matter in the same way. We will show that all terms will reduce to a normal term, and that a term does not reduce to more than one normal term.

THEOREM 7.14 (CHURCH–ROSSER THEOREM)
If $M \twoheadrightarrow N_1$ and $M \twoheadrightarrow N_2$ then there is some L where $N_1 \twoheadrightarrow L$ and $N_2 \twoheadrightarrow L$.

This theorem is presented in many places, and I will only sketch its proof here. (See Barendregt's recent survey article for an example of this proof [11].) We proceed by proving this lemma:

LEMMA 7.15 (SLICE LEMMA)
If $M \longrightarrow N_1$ and $M \twoheadrightarrow N_2$ then there is some L where $N_1 \twoheadrightarrow L$ and $N_2 \twoheadrightarrow L$.

Then the Church–Rosser theorem is a simple corollary of the Slice Lemma, by induction on the length of the reduction from $M \twoheadrightarrow N_1$. To prove the Slice Lemma, we keep a track of the reduction from M to N_2 and we apply that reduction to N_1 to get L. To facilitate keeping records of reductions, we define expanded set of terms, the *terms with underlining, $\underline{Terms}$*.

DEFINITION 7.16 (UNDERLINED TERMS)
Any term is in the class of $\underline{Terms}$, and additionally, if M is a redex, then $\underline{M}$ is a $\underline{Term}$ of the same type, and with the same free variables. The class $\underline{Terms}$ is closed under the same formation rules as the original class of terms. And the relation of reduction ($\twoheadrightarrow$) can be defined in this expanded class of terms in the same way as in the class of regular terms. Any underlined redexes contract to their contractum and they lose their underlining. Any other redexes also contract to their contractum.

Furthermore, there are two functions defined on the class of underlined terms. *Forget* : $\underline{Terms} \rightarrow Terms$ forgets the underlining, and *Reduce* : $\underline{Terms} \rightarrow Terms$ reduces all of the underlined redexes, from the inside to the outside.

Given this definition, we can prove the Slice Lemma.

PROOF SKETCH If $M \longrightarrow N_1$, let $M' \in \underline{Terms}$ be the term M with the relevant redex in M underlined. So, $Forget(M') = M$ and $Reduce(M') = N_1$.

FACT: There is a term $N_2' \in \underline{Terms}$ where $M' \twoheadrightarrow N_2'$ and $Forget(N_2') = N_2$. This term is found by following the reduction path from M to N_2 and keeping the underlining as appropriate, following the same path from M' to find N_2'.

FACT: Since $Forget(N_2') = N_2$, $N_2 \longrightarrow Retract(N_2')$. (This follows from the definition of underlined terms.) Now, call the term $Retract(N_2')$, N_3.

FACT: $N_1 \longrightarrow N_3$. This holds, as $Retract(M') = N_1$ and $N_1 \longrightarrow N_2'$, and $Retract(N_2') = N_3$. Therefore, the Slice Lemma holds.

That completes the proof of the Church–Rosser Theorem. Note that it did not use any facts about typing of terms. It holds for untyped terms too. It merely states that no reduction path diverges irrevocably from any other reduction path. It does not say that any reduction path terminates. However, it does tell us that if a reduction path terminates at a normal term N, then any other terminating reduction path must also terminate at that term.

However, all *typable* terms in our system will reduce. There are a number of ways to prove this. A powerful method, devised by Tait [255], proves that all typable terms (in intuitionistic logic) are strongly normalising. We will not go through this proof here (see the History section for more references). Instead, we will explore the connection between normalisation and Cut elimination in Gentzen systems, to prove that every term is normalising.

7.3 Normalisation and Cut Elimination

In this section we will provide two mappings. G maps a natural deduction proof Π to a corresponding Gentzen proof $G(\Pi)$. N maps Gentzen proofs to natural deduction proofs. At the same time, we will associate terms to Gentzen proofs, so that terms are preserved by this mapping. If M is the term of a natural deduction proof Π, it will also be the term of the proof $G(\Pi)$. Similarly, if N is the term of the Gentzen proof Ξ, it will also be the term of the natural deduction proof $N(\Xi)$.

DEFINITION 7.17 (TRANSLATIONS G AND N)
We define the translation $G(\Pi)$ of a natural deduction proof Π, and $N(\Xi)$ of a Gentzen proof Ξ, by induction on the structure of the proof Π and Ξ, in the following way. (We present the proofs in *term* form.) First, each system has identity proofs.

$$G(x{:}A \vdash x{:}A) = x{:}A \vdash x{:}A$$
$$N(x{:}A \vdash x{:}A) = x{:}A \vdash x{:}A$$

Second, each system has structural rules. These are the same in each system.

Now, the implication rules. Given a natural deduction proof Π, ending in an implication introduction, the corresponding Gentzen proof ends in the same step.

$$\cfrac{\cfrac{\Pi}{\Gamma; x{:}A \vdash M{:}B}}{\Gamma \vdash \lambda^{\flat} x M{:}A \to B} \quad \overset{G}{\longrightarrow} \quad \cfrac{\cfrac{G(\Pi)}{\Gamma; x{:}A \vdash M{:}B}}{\Gamma \vdash \lambda^{\flat} x M{:}A \to B}$$

Similarly, given a Gentzen proof ending in an implication right step, the corresponding natural deduction proof ends in the same step.

$$\frac{\displaystyle \frac{\Xi}{\Gamma; x{:}A \vdash M{:}B}}{\Gamma \vdash \lambda^{\flat}xM{:}A \to B} \quad \overset{N}{\longrightarrow} \quad \frac{\displaystyle \frac{N(\Xi)}{\Gamma; x{:}A \vdash M{:}B}}{\Gamma \vdash \lambda^{\flat}xM{:}A \to B}$$

A more difficult transformation happens with implication elimination. Suppose we have the following proof in a natural deduction system.

$$\frac{\displaystyle \frac{\Pi_1}{\Gamma \vdash M{:}A \to B} \qquad \frac{\Pi_2}{\Delta \vdash N{:}A}}{\Gamma; \Delta \vdash M^{\flat}N{:}B}$$

We transform it into the following Gentzen proof, using the Cut rule.

$$\frac{\displaystyle \frac{G(\Pi_1)}{\Gamma \vdash M{:}A \to B} \qquad \frac{\displaystyle \frac{G(\Pi_2)}{\Delta \vdash N{:}A \quad x{:}B \vdash x{:}B}}{x{:}A \to B; \Delta \vdash x^{\flat}N{:}B}}{\Gamma; \Delta \vdash M^{\flat}N{:}B} \text{ [Cut]}$$

Similarly, in the other direction, given a Gentzen proof ending in an implication left step, we provide a natural deduction proof with the same conclusion, using Cut. The Gentzen proof is this:

$$\frac{\displaystyle \frac{\Xi_1}{\Delta(y{:}B) \vdash N{:}C} \qquad \frac{\Xi_2}{\Gamma \vdash M{:}A}}{\Delta(x{:}A \to B; \Gamma) \vdash N[y := x^{\flat}M]{:}C}$$

And it becomes this natural deduction proof:

$$\frac{\displaystyle \frac{N(\Xi_1)}{\Delta(y{:}B) \vdash N{:}C} \qquad \frac{\displaystyle x{:}A \to B \vdash x{:}A \to B \quad \frac{N(\Xi_2)}{\Gamma \vdash M{:}A}}{x{:}A \to B; \Gamma \vdash x^{\flat}M{:}B}}{\Delta(x{:}A \to B; \Gamma) \vdash N[y := x^{\flat}M]{:}C} \text{ [Cut]}$$

The same sort of moves hold for converse implication. For $\leftarrow$ introduction (or $\leftarrow$ right) the rules are the same in each system. For $\leftarrow$ elimination, and $\leftarrow$ left, we have the following transformations. The natural deduction proof

$$\frac{\dfrac{\Pi_2}{\Delta \vdash N{:}A} \qquad \dfrac{\Pi_1}{\Gamma \vdash M{:}B \leftarrow A}}{\Delta;\Gamma \vdash N^{\langle}M{:}B}$$

becomes this Gentzen proof:

$$\frac{\dfrac{G(\Pi_1)}{\Gamma \vdash M{:}B \leftarrow A} \qquad \dfrac{\dfrac{G(\Pi_2)}{\Delta \vdash N{:}A} \qquad x{:}B \vdash x{:}B}{\Delta;x{:}B \leftarrow A \vdash N^{\langle}x{:}B}}{\Delta;\Gamma \vdash M^{\langle}N{:}B} \text{[Cut]}$$

and this Gentzen proof:

$$\frac{\dfrac{\Xi_1}{\Delta(y{:}B) \vdash N{:}C} \qquad \dfrac{\Xi_2}{\Gamma \vdash M{:}A}}{\Delta(\Gamma;x{:}B \leftarrow A) \vdash N[y := M^{\langle}x]{:}C}$$

is transformed into this natural deduction proof:

$$\frac{\dfrac{N(\Xi_1)}{\Delta(y{:}B) \vdash N{:}C} \qquad \dfrac{x{:}B \leftarrow A \vdash x{:}B \leftarrow A \qquad \dfrac{N(\Xi_2)}{\Gamma \vdash M{:}A}}{\Gamma;x{:}B \leftarrow A \vdash M^{\langle}x{:}B}}{\Delta(\Gamma;x{:}B \leftarrow A) \vdash N[y := M^{\langle}x]{:}C} \text{[Cut]}$$

Now for fusion. Again the introduction rule in the natural deduction system corresponds to the right rule in the Gentzen system. For the elimination rule in the natural deduction system, we transform the natural deduction proof

$$\frac{\dfrac{\Pi_1}{\Delta(x{:}A; y{:}B) \vdash N{:}C} \qquad \dfrac{\Pi_1}{\Gamma \vdash M{:}A \circ B}}{\Delta(\Gamma) \vdash \text{let } M \text{ be } x \circ y \text{ in } N{:}C}$$

into the following Gentzen proof:

$$\frac{\dfrac{\dfrac{G(\Pi_1)}{\Delta(x{:}A; y{:}B) \vdash N{:}C}}{\Delta(z{:}A \circ B) \vdash \text{let } z \text{ be } x \circ y \text{ in } N{:}C} \qquad \dfrac{G(\Pi_2)}{\Gamma \vdash M{:}A \circ B}}{\Delta(\Gamma) \vdash \text{let } M \text{ be } x \circ y \text{ in } N{:}C} \text{[Cut]}$$

Conversely, the Gentzen proof

$$\frac{\dfrac{\Xi}{\Delta(x{:}A;y{:}B) \vdash N{:}C}}{\Delta(z{:}A \circ B) \vdash \text{let } z \text{ be } x \circ y \text{ in } N{:}C}$$

is mapped onto the corresponding natural deduction proof:

$$\frac{\dfrac{N(\Xi)}{\Delta(x{:}A;y{:}B) \vdash N{:}C} \qquad z{:}A \circ B \vdash z{:}A \circ B}{\Delta(z{:}A \circ B) \vdash \text{let } z \text{ be } x \circ y \text{ in } N{:}C}$$

For conjunction, we map the elimination rule in the natural deduction system

$$\frac{\dfrac{\Pi}{\Gamma \vdash M{:}A \wedge B}}{\Gamma \vdash \text{fst } M{:}A}$$

to the proof in the Gentzen system using Cut.

$$\frac{\dfrac{G(\Pi)}{\Gamma \vdash M{:}A \wedge B} \qquad \dfrac{x{:}A \vdash x{:}A}{y{:}A \wedge B \vdash \text{fst } y{:}A}}{\Gamma \vdash \text{fst } M{:}A} \text{[Cut]}$$

And the Gentzen proof

$$\frac{\dfrac{\Xi}{\Gamma(x{:}A) \vdash M{:}C}}{\Gamma(y{:}A \wedge B) \vdash M[x := \text{fst } y]{:}C}$$

becomes this natural deduction step:

$$\frac{\dfrac{N(\Xi)}{\Gamma(x{:}A) \vdash M{:}C} \qquad \dfrac{y{:}A \wedge B \vdash y{:}A \wedge B}{y{:}A \wedge B \vdash \text{fst } y{:}A}}{\Gamma(y{:}A \wedge B) \vdash M[x := \text{fst } y]{:}C} \text{[Cut]}$$

and similarly for the rules involving snd. Now for disjunction. The natural deduction elimination rule

$$\frac{\Gamma \vdash L{:}A \vee B \qquad \dfrac{\Pi_1}{\Delta(x{:}A) \vdash M{:}C} \qquad \dfrac{\Pi_2}{\Delta(y{:}B) \vdash N{:}C}}{\Delta(\Gamma) \vdash \text{let } L \text{ be } x \text{ in } M \text{ or } y \text{ in } N{:}C}$$

becomes the Gentzen rule

$$\dfrac{\Gamma \vdash L{:}A \vee B \quad \dfrac{G(\Pi_1) \quad\quad G(\Pi_2)}{\Delta(x{:}A) \vdash M{:}C \quad \Delta(y{:}B) \vdash N{:}C}}{\Delta(\Gamma) \vdash \text{let } L \text{ be } x \text{ in } M \text{ or } y \text{ in } N{:}C} \,[\text{Cut}]$$

and the Gentzen step

$$\dfrac{\dfrac{\Xi_1}{\Delta(x{:}A) \vdash M{:}C} \quad \dfrac{\Xi_2}{\Delta(y{:}B) \vdash N{:}C}}{\Delta(z{:}A \vee B) \vdash \text{let } z \text{ be } x \text{ in } M \text{ or } y \text{ in } N{:}C}$$

becomes the proof in the natural deduction system

$$\dfrac{z{:}A \vee B \vdash z{:}A \vee B \quad \dfrac{N(\Xi_1)}{\Delta(x{:}A) \vdash M{:}C} \quad \dfrac{N(\Xi_2)}{\Delta(y{:}B) \vdash N{:}C}}{\Delta(z{:}A \vee B) \vdash \text{let } z \text{ be } x \text{ in } M \text{ or } y \text{ in } N{:}C}$$

No changes are necessary for $\top$, for it has no elimination or left rules. For $\bot$ we map as follows:

$$\dfrac{\dfrac{\Pi}{\Gamma \vdash M{:}\bot}}{\Delta(\Gamma) \vdash \text{let } M \text{ be } \dagger{:}C}$$

becomes

$$\dfrac{\dfrac{G(\Pi)}{\Gamma \vdash M{:}\bot} \quad \Delta(z{:}\bot) \vdash \text{let } z \text{ be } \dagger{:}C}{\Delta(\Gamma) \vdash \text{let } M \text{ be } \dagger{:}C} \,[\text{Cut}]$$

and conversely,

$$\Delta(z{:}\bot) \vdash \text{let } z \text{ be } \dagger{:}C \quad \xrightarrow{\;N\;} \quad \dfrac{z{:}\bot \vdash z{:}\bot}{\Delta(z{:}\bot) \vdash \text{let } z \text{ be } \dagger{:}C}$$

Now for t, the natural deduction proof

$$\dfrac{\dfrac{\Pi_1}{\Delta \vdash N{:}t} \quad \dfrac{\Pi_2}{\Gamma(0) \vdash M{:}C}}{\Gamma(\Delta) \vdash \text{let } N \text{ be } * \text{ in } M{:}C}$$

becomes the Gentzen proof

$$
\cfrac{
  \cfrac{
    \cfrac{G(\Pi_2)}{\Gamma(0) \vdash M{:}C}
  }{\Gamma(z{:}t) \vdash \text{let } z \text{ be } * \text{ in } M{:}C}
  \qquad
  \cfrac{G(\Pi_1)}{\Delta \vdash N{:}t}
}{\Gamma(\Delta) \vdash \text{let } N \text{ be } * \text{ in } M{:}C} \ [\text{Cut}]
$$

Conversely, the Gentzen proof

$$
\cfrac{
  \cfrac{\Xi}{\Gamma(0) \vdash M{:}C}
}{\Gamma(z{:}t) \vdash \text{let } z \text{ be } * \text{ in } M{:}C}
$$

becomes the natural deduction proof

$$
\cfrac{
  \cfrac{N(\Xi)}{\Gamma(0) \vdash M{:}C} \qquad z{:}t \vdash z{:}t
}{\Gamma(z{:}t) \vdash \text{let } z \text{ be } * \text{ in } M{:}C}
$$

Now for $\Box$, the natural deduction proof

$$
\cfrac{
  \cfrac{\Pi}{\Gamma \vdash M{:}\Box A}
}{\bullet\Gamma \vdash \text{down } M{:}A}
$$

becomes

$$
\cfrac{
  \cfrac{G(\Pi)}{\Gamma \vdash M{:}\Box A}
  \qquad
  \cfrac{x{:}A \vdash x{:}A}{\bullet(y{:}\Box A) \vdash \text{down } y{:}A}
}{\bullet\Gamma \vdash \text{down } M{:}A} \ [\text{Cut}]
$$

and in reverse,

$$
\cfrac{
  \cfrac{\Xi}{\Gamma(x{:}A) \vdash M{:}C}
}{\Gamma(\bullet(y{:}\Box A)) \vdash M[x := \text{down } y]{:}C}
$$

becomes

$$
\cfrac{
  \cfrac{y{:}\Box A \vdash y{:}\Box A}{\bullet(y{:}\Box A) \vdash \text{down } y{:}A}
  \qquad
  \cfrac{N(\Xi)}{\Gamma(x{:}A) \vdash M{:}C}
}{\Gamma(\bullet(y{:}\Box A)) \vdash M[x := \text{down } y]{:}C} \ [\text{Cut}]
$$

Finally, the rules for $\diamondsuit$. The natural deduction step

$$\frac{\begin{array}{c}\Pi_1 \\ \hline \Gamma \vdash M{:}\diamondsuit A\end{array} \qquad \begin{array}{c}\Pi_2 \\ \hline \Delta(\bullet(x{:}A)) \vdash N{:}C\end{array}}{\Delta(\Gamma) \vdash \text{let } M \text{ be } \bullet x \text{ in } N{:}C}$$

becomes in the Gentzen system

$$\frac{\begin{array}{c}G(\Pi_1) \\ \hline \Gamma \vdash M{:}\diamondsuit A\end{array} \qquad \dfrac{\begin{array}{c}G(\Pi_2) \\ \hline \Delta(\bullet(x{:}A)) \vdash N{:}C\end{array}}{\Delta(z{:}\diamondsuit A) \vdash \text{let } z \text{ be } \bullet x \text{ in } N}}{\Delta(\Gamma) \vdash \text{let } M \text{ be } \bullet x \text{ in } N{:}C} \text{ [Cut]}$$

and the Gentzen step

$$\frac{\begin{array}{c}\Xi \\ \hline \Delta(\bullet(x{:}A)) \vdash N{:}C\end{array}}{\Delta(z{:}\diamondsuit A) \vdash \text{let } z \text{ be } \bullet x \text{ in } N}$$

becomes this natural deduction step:

$$\frac{\begin{array}{c}N(\Xi) \\ \hline \Delta(\bullet(x{:}A)) \vdash N{:}C\end{array} \qquad z{:}\diamondsuit A \vdash z{:}\diamondsuit A}{\Delta(z{:}\diamondsuit A) \vdash \text{let } z \text{ be } \bullet x \text{ in } N}$$

This completes the definition of the transformation G of a natural deduction system into a Gentzen system and the converse translation N from the Gentzen system into the natural deduction system.

Note the behaviour of the term system for the Gentzen calculus. We have some interesting properties. First, the antecedents are still populated only with variables. We use *substitution* to deal with the rules which introduce new connectives on the left.

Given this definition, the following theorem can be proved by an induction on the construction of the term M.

THEOREM 7.18 (TERMS OF CUT-FREE PROOFS ARE NORMAL)
If Ξ is a Cut-free Gentzen proof of $\Gamma \vdash M{:}C$, then M is normal.

PROOF   If Ξ is an axiom, then the result clearly holds, as each variable is normal. For any rule modifying terms, it is sufficient to show that no redexes are introduced into the term of the conclusion. Note that the outer constructs of all redexes (fst, snd, $\lambda^\flat x$, $\lambda^\natural x$, down, and so on) are introduced only to apply to *variables*, so no reductions can apply at any stage. This completes the proof. $\square$

Note that had the proof Ξ contained a cut, then this would no longer apply, as the examples in the proof of the next theorem shows.

THEOREM 7.19 (CUT ELIMINATION IS NORMALISATION)
If Ξ, a proof of $\Gamma \vdash M{:}C$, is reducible by applications of cut elimination to a proof of $\Gamma \vdash M'{:}C$, then $M \twoheadrightarrow M'$.

PROOF   Checking this is a tedious business of inspecting the cases of cut reduction. There is nothing interesting in it, so we will examine a couple of cases. Suppose $\to$ has been introduced in both left and right, only to be cut away, in the following proof:

$$\dfrac{\dfrac{\Gamma; x{:}A \vdash M{:}B}{\Gamma \vdash \lambda^\flat x M {:} A \to B} \qquad \dfrac{\Delta(y{:}B) \vdash N{:}C \quad \Sigma \vdash L{:}A}{\Delta(z{:}A \to B; \Sigma) \vdash N[y := z^\flat L]{:}C}}{\Delta(\Gamma; \Sigma) \vdash N[y := zL^\flat][z := \lambda^\flat x M]{:}C} \text{[Cut]}$$

The concluding term is $N[y := z^\flat L][z := \lambda^\flat x M]$, which (as z is not free in N) is the term $N[y := (\lambda^\flat x M)L^\flat]$, which either *is* N (if N contains no free y) or contains a number or redexes $(\lambda^\flat x M)^\flat L$, which each contract to $M[x := L]$, so the entire term reduces to $N[y := M[x := L]]$. This is the conclusion of the proof eliminating the cut on $A \to B$, as follows:

$$\dfrac{\dfrac{\Gamma; x{:}A \vdash M{:}B \quad \Sigma \vdash L{:}A}{\Gamma; \Sigma \vdash M[x := L]{:}B} \text{[Cut]} \qquad \Delta(y{:}B) \vdash N{:}C}{\Delta(\Gamma; \Sigma) \vdash N[y := M[x := L]]{:}C} \text{[Cut]}$$

So this step in the cut elimination proof corresponds to a reduction we have seen. Cuts may introduce non-normal terms, as we create a redex when we substitute a complex term into a variable place.   □

We have the following corollary:

COROLLARY 7.20 (NORMALISATION FOR PROOFS)
If Π is a proof of $\Gamma \vdash M{:}C$, then there is a normal M' such that $M \twoheadrightarrow M'$, and $\Gamma \vdash M'{:}C$.

PROOF   Consider the Gentzen proof $G(\Pi)$. It also has the term M. We can eliminate cut from $G(\Pi)$, resulting in the proof Ξ with term M', such that $M \twoheadrightarrow M'$. It follows that the proof $N(\Xi)$ is a normal proof of $\Gamma \vdash M'{:}C$.   □

COROLLARY 7.21 (NORMAL PROOFS HAVE THE SUBFORMULA PROPERTY)
If Π is a normal proof of $X \vdash A$, then the formulae appearing in Π are subformulae of those appearing in X and in A.

7.4 History

The best explanation of the Curry–Howard isomorphism between intuitionistic logic and the types of terms in the λ-calculus is found in Howard's original paper [117]. Church's original calculus, the λI-calculus, was actually a model for the implicational fragment of R and not intuitionistic logic, as Church's calculus did not allow the binding of variables which were not free in the term in question [44]. Prawitz's little monograph *Natural Deduction* [196] introduced the idea of normalisation. A helpful account of more recent work in types and logic is found in Girard, Lafont and Taylor's *Proofs and Types* [99], and Girard's monograph *Proof Theory and Logical Complexity* [97].

Our account of the types of *modal terms* (using up and down) is new in this chapter — it is the straightforward extension of existing techniques to the modal case.

Tennant has an idiosyncratic approach to normalisation in logics, arguing for a "relevant logic" which differs from our substructural logics by allowing the validity of $A, {\sim}A \vee B \vdash B$ and ${\sim}A \vdash {\sim}A \vee B$, while rejecting $A, {\sim}A \vdash B$ [258, 259]. Tennant's system rejects the unrestricted transitivity of proofs: the 'Cut' which would allow $A, {\sim}A \vdash B$ from the proofs of $A, {\sim}A \vee B \vdash B$ and ${\sim}A \vdash {\sim}A \vee B$ is not admissible. Tennant uses normalisation to motivate this system.

We have not looked at term systems or normalisation for Girard's linear logic and its exponentials. Work in this area has not yet reached stability. The work of Benton, Bierman, Hyland and de Paiva [32, 33, 34] shows the difficulty present in the area. Our approach is most similar to that of Wadler [277, 279], who uses terms to represent connective rules but not structural rules. Wadler's rules for the exponential are simple (we use our convention for 'let' instead of his 'case' term).

$$\frac{[\Gamma] \vdash M\!:\!A}{[\Gamma] \vdash {!}M\!:\!{!}A} \qquad \frac{\Gamma \vdash M\!:\!{!}A \quad \Delta([x\!:\!A]) \vdash N\!:\!B}{\Delta(\Gamma) \vdash \text{let } M \text{ be } {!}x \text{ in } N\!:\!B}$$

with the corresponding reduction rule

$$\text{let } {!}M \text{ be } {!}x \text{ in } N \rightsquigarrow N[x := M]$$

And as with other let terms, we allow commuting conversions to pass through this let term. The proofs in this chapter all go through for Wadler's system.

Wadler and colleagues show that this kind of term system has connections with functional programming and models of computation [146, 275, 276].

7.5 *Exercises*

Practice

{7.1} Which of the following terms are well typed, and for those which are, what are their types? $\mathsf{fst}\, x^{A \wedge B}$; $\mathsf{inl}\,^A x^A$; $\langle M^\rangle N, N^\rangle M \rangle$; let x^A be $\dagger^c$; let N^t be $*$ in M^c.

{7.2} Reduce the following terms to normal form:

$$\mathsf{fst}\,\langle M, \lambda^\rangle x M^\langle N \rangle \quad \mathsf{down}\,(N^\langle(\lambda^\langle x\,\mathsf{up}\,M)) \quad \mathsf{fst}\,(\mathsf{let}\,\mathsf{down}\,(\mathsf{let}\,M\,\mathsf{be}\,*\,\mathsf{in}\,(\mathsf{up}\,L))\,\mathsf{be}\,\dagger)$$

Problems

{7.3} Extend the Term Characterisation Theorem (Theorem 7.6) to deal with the logic $\mathrm{BB}^c[\rightarrow, \leftarrow]$. Show that terms encoding proofs in this logic are those in which the *order* is respected in some way.

{7.4} Extend the Term Characterisation Theorem to deal with more connectives, in the logics LL, R and BCK.

Projects

{7.5} Prove strong normalisation for our systems [68, 223, 261].

{7.6} Provide term rules for negation; prove them to be normalising.

Part II

Propositional Structures

Chapter 8

Defining Propositional Structures

> *Structures are of various kinds,*
> *as Frames, which have their parts connected by pins or mortises;*
> *and Arches, in which the parts are connected only by contact.*
>
> — *William Whewell*, Mechanical Engineering, *1841*

So far, we have focused on *syntax* in studying logical systems. We have defined different formal languages and in each language we have defined different types of proof in that language. In doing this, we have given meanings to connectives by way of the rules in which they feature. The starkest example of this is given in natural deduction systems. The introduction and elimination rules for a connective can be thought to give some account of the *meaning* of that connective. So these largely *syntactic* procedures have a *semantic* purpose.

However, the method of defining and analysing proofs directly is one of many ways to analyse the meaning of connectives and the behaviour of logical consequence. We could instead interpret a language by mapping it into another structure. We explain the meanings of connectives by interpreting them as functions on the structure in question. In mathematical and philosophical logic, this approach is called *model theory*.[1] In the tradition of computer science, this approach is called a *denotational semantics* in contrast to an axiomatic or operational semantics.[2] We will devote this second part of the book to interpreting our logics and languages in this way. Before giving rigorous definitions we will see some examples.

Some propositions are true and others are not true. We can interpret a language in the structure $\{t, f\}$ of *truth values* by setting the interpretation $[\![A]\!]$ of A to be t if A is true, and f otherwise. This interpretation is helpful in the study of logical consequence because of the way it interacts with the traditional propositional connectives. A conjunction is true if and only if both of the conjuncts are true. A disjunction is true if and only if one of the conjuncts is true. A negation

---

[1] For a good text on the mathematics of models of classical first-order logic, Bell and Slomson's *Models and Ultraproducts* [19] is a classic. For the philosophers' perspective, the work of Alfred Tarski on models and truth [257] has an enduring significance.

[2] John Mitchell provides a helpful discussion of the distinction between different sorts of semantics of programming languages in Section 1.3 of his *Foundations for Programming Languages* [175].

is true if and only if the negand is not true.[3] It follows that $[\![A \wedge B]\!]$, $[\![A \vee B]\!]$ are functions of $[\![A]\!]$ and $[\![B]\!]$, in the sense that once the values $[\![A]\!]$ and $[\![B]\!]$ are fixed, the values $[\![A \wedge B]\!]$, $[\![A \vee B]\!]$ are also fixed. The behaviour of the operations of conjunction, disjunction and negation on the set $\{t, f\}$ of truth values goes some way towards telling us the meanings of those connectives. More than that, it gives us an account of the behaviour of logical consequence, as the set of truth values has a natural *order*. We can order the set by saying that $f < t$, in the sense that t is "more true" than f. An argument is $\{t, f\}$-valid if no matter how you interpret the propositions in the argument, the conclusion is never any less true than the premises. Or in this case, you never can interpret the premises as true and the conclusion as false. This is the traditional truth-table conception of validity.

The simple set $\{t, f\}$ of truth values is not the only domain in which a language can be interpreted. For example, we might think that not all propositions or sentences in the language are truth-valued. We might interpret the language in the structure $\{t, n, f\}$, where the true claims are interpreted as t, the false ones as f, and the non-truth-valued sentences are interpreted as n. This path leads one to *many valued logics*.[4]

However, one need not interpret the domain of values as *truth values*. For one very early example of an alternative sort of domain in which sentences can be interpreted, consider the later philosophy of language of Frege. For the Frege of the *Grundgesetze* [86] declarative sentences had a *reference* (*Bedeutung*) and also a *sense* (*Sinn*). We can interpret sentences by mapping them onto a domain of senses (however these are to be conceived) and by interpreting the connectives as functions on senses. This is another denotational semantics for declarative sentences.

For a modern interpretation of Frege's ideas, one could consider a sense of a claim to be the set of possible worlds in which it is true. Now for each sentence you have its interpretation as some set of possible worlds.[5] The connectives are then interpreted as operations on these sets of worlds — and some connectives, like conjunction, disjunction and negation, turn out to be the relatively simple set-theoretic operations of intersection, union and complementation.

---

[3]   This last claim is disputed. Intuitionists (according to whom $A \vee \sim A$ might fail) and dialetheists (according to whom $A \wedge \sim A$ might *not* fail) both think that negation is not truth-functional in the way claimed by this condition [114, 198]. The details of this disagreement need not concern us at this point — the important aspect of this illustration is the idea of truth-functionality, whether or not negation is truth-functional. More discussion of this point will appear in Chapter 16, in which we discuss a particular interpretation of different notions of consequence.

[4]   Dunn and Epstein's edited collection [81] and Urquhart's survey article [268] are good overviews of work in the area.

[5]   For an account of how this approach might be philosophically enlightening, see Robert Stalnaker's *Inquiry* [252], David Lewis' *On the Plurality of Worlds* [137] and a discussion in Chapter 16.

Different applications of logics will bring different sorts of models and domains of semantic values. In the Lambek calculus for syntactic types, the formulae can be mapped onto sets of syntactic strings. In this interpretation, a sentence will be modelled by the set of strings (in the analysed language) which have the type denoted by the sentence.

These last two examples — of possible worlds and of syntactic strings — have similar structures. Formulae are interpreted as *sets* of objects of one kind or other. These are especially interesting models, which we will discuss in detail in the third part of the book. For now, however, we will focus on the general idea of interpreting languages and logics in structures.

With this rough sketch of the land ahead, let us move to some rigorous definitions of the sorts of structures we will consider.

8.1 Definitions

We will start with the core of any propositional structure, the relation of entailment on that structure.

DEFINITION 8.1 (ORDERS)
A *partial order* on a set P is a binary relation $\leqslant$ on P which is

  ◇ REFLEXIVE $a \leqslant a$ for each $a \in P$

  ◇ TRANSITIVE $a \leqslant b$ and $b \leqslant c$ then $a \leqslant c$

  ◇ ANTI-SYMMETRIC if $a \leqslant b$ and $b \leqslant a$ then $a = b$

The *converse* of a partial order $\leqslant$ is the relation $\geqslant$, defined by setting $a \geqslant b$ if and only if $b \leqslant a$. A *strict order* on a set is a relation $<$ which is

  ◇ IRREFLEXIVE $a < a$ for no $a \in P$

  ◇ TRANSITIVE $a < b$ and $b < c$ then $a < c$

  ◇ ASYMMETRIC $a < b$ and $b < a$ for no a and b

The *converse* of a strict order $<$ is the relation $>$, defined by setting $a > b$ if and only if $b < a$. An order R (either partial or strict) is *total* if for each a and b, either aRb or bRa or $a = b$. (If R is a partial order, then this condition is equivalent to aRb or bRa.)

LEMMA 8.2 (ORDER FACTS)
Orders have the following properties.

1. *The converse of a partial order is also a partial order.*

2. *The converse of a strict order is also a strict order.*

3. *Given a partial order $\leqslant$, the relation $<$ given by setting $a < b$ if and only if $a \leqslant b$ and $a \neq b$ is a strict order. This order is simply called the* strict order corresponding to $\leqslant$.

4. *Given a strict order* $<$, *the relation* $\leqslant$ *given by setting* $a \leqslant b$ *if and only if* $a < b$ *or* $a = b$ *is a partial order. This order is simply called the* partial order corresponding to $\leqslant$.

5. $\leqslant$ *is the partial order corresponding to* $<$ *if and only if* $<$ *is the strict order corresponding to* $\leqslant$.

6. *If* $\leqslant$ *is total, so is the strict order corresponding to* $\leqslant$. *If* $<$ *is total, so is the partial order corresponding to* $<$.   □

In our propositional structures, the partial order is the relation of *entailment* between propositions. The requirement that this be a partial order is what distinguishes propositional structures from the syntactic representations of a formal (or informal) language. If a entails b and b entails a, then a and b are *the same*, as far as propositional structures are concerned. There may be structural features different in how they are represented — a might be a conjunction and b might be a disjunction, for example — but if they have the same *inferential force* they are the same. Purely syntactic differences, which have no bearing on the semantics of the expressions, have no place in structures. There is no sense to say that an element in a propositional structure "is a conjunction," as every proposition a is *the same proposition* as the conjunction of a with itself.

EXAMPLE 8.3 (NUMBERS)
The set $\omega = \{0, 1, 2, \ldots\}$ of natural numbers is ordered by the obvious $\leqslant$ relation, which is a total order. The corresponding strict order $<$ is also known.

There are many less well-known orders on the natural numbers. For one example which we will use later, let '$n \mid m$' mean 'n *divides* m *evenly*.' Then $\mid$ is a partial order on ω. The formal definition is as follows: n divides m if and only if for some $l \in \omega$, $l \times n = m$. So, any number divides itself (divides is reflexive); if n divides m and m divides l then n divides l (divides is transitive). Finally, if n divides m and m divides n then $m = n$ (divides is anti-symmetric). So we have a partial order. The order is not total — neither $2 \mid 3$ nor $3 \mid 2$, for example.

EXAMPLE 8.4 (SETS)
Any set of sets is ordered by the subset relation $\subseteq$. This relation is a partial order, but it is not, in general, total. For example, neither of $\{1, 2\}$ and $\{2, 3\}$ is a subset of each other. The set $\mathcal{P}(X)$ of all subsets of the set X, called the *power set of* X, is an important example of a partially ordered set. These partially ordered sets will feature in what follows.

EXAMPLE 8.5 (HASSE DIAGRAMS)
One convenient way to represent partially ordered sets is by way of a *Hasse diagram*. Such a diagram represents the objects in the order by dots, and the

partial order on the structure by lines. The ordering relation $\leqslant$ is read *upwards*: a point a is below b in the order if and only if there is an upward path from a to b in the diagram.

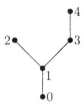

Figure 8.1: A Hasse Diagram

In this partial order, there are five elements, and we have $0 \leqslant 1 \leqslant 3 \leqslant 4$ and $1 \leqslant 2$. The elements 2 and 3 are *incomparable*, as we have $2 \nleqslant 3$ and $3 \nleqslant 4$. Similarly, 2 and 4 are incomparable, as even though 4 appears above 2 on the page, there is no path from 2 to 4 heading upwards. We will regularly use Hasse diagrams to present partial orders in this chapter.

Once we have an order on a set, we can populate the set with *operations* to model connectives in a language, and we have something we can use to study logics.

DEFINITION 8.6 (OPERATIONS AND PROPOSITIONAL STRUCTURES)
An *operation* o on a set P is an n-placed function $o : P^n \to P$ for some $n = 0, 1, 2, \ldots$ A *propositional structure* is a structure $\langle P, \leqslant, C \rangle$ where P is some non-empty set, $\leqslant$ is a partial order on the set P, and C is a set of operations on the set P.

This is an *extremely* general definition. Partially ordered sets with operations are very easy to find, and it is correspondingly very hard to prove interesting theorems about all of them. In the next few pages, we will introduce the sorts of operation which appear in the propositional structures we will study. These will mirror the connectives we have seen in our study of the proof theory of substructural logics. In fact, in many cases we will use the same symbol for the function in a propositional structure as the corresponding connective in a formal language. This will not be a problem, as the context will make clear what we mean in each instance. A rough and ready guide: elements of propositional structures will generally be written with small letters a, b, c or x, y and z. Formulae in our languages are capital letters A, B, C and so on.

Our first stop will be some operations which are tied intimately to the behaviour of the underlying partial order on the propositional structure.

DEFINITION 8.7 (LATTICE OPERATIONS)
A *semilattice* is a partial order with *greatest lower bounds*. That is, for any pair of objects a and b there is an element $a \wedge b$ such that for all c

$$c \leqslant a \text{ and } c \leqslant b \text{ if and only if } c \leqslant a \wedge b$$

The operation $\wedge$ on a semilattice is also called a *meet* operation. We will say that a meet operation on a semilattice *matches extensional conjunction* in a formal language.

A *lattice* is a semilattice with *least upper bounds*. That is, for every pair of objects a and b there is an element $a \vee b$ such that for all c

$$a \leqslant c \text{ and } b \leqslant c \text{ if and only if } a \vee b \leqslant c$$

The operation $\vee$ on a lattice is also called a *join* operation. The join on a lattice *matches extensional disjunction.*

An element $\top$ is a *top* element of an ordering if and only if $a \leqslant \top$ for every a. It is the *bottom* element of an ordering if and only if $\bot \leqslant a$ for every a.

A top element *matches the true constant* $\top$ and a bottom element is *fit for the false constant* $\bot$.

In this definition, we use the symbols '$\wedge$,' '$\vee$,' '$\top$' and '$\bot$' both for operators in a propositional structure and for connectives in a formal language.

EXAMPLE 8.8 (POWER SETS ARE LATTICES)
The power set $\mathcal{P}(X)$ of any set X is a lattice, with the meet of two sets a and b being their intersection $a \cap b$, and their join being their union $a \cup b$. You can verify that for all sets a, b and c

$$c \subseteq a \text{ and } c \subseteq b \text{ if and only if } c \subseteq a \cap b$$
$$a \subseteq c \text{ and } b \subseteq c \text{ if and only if } a \cup b \subseteq c$$

So a power set is a lattice since if $a, b \in \mathcal{P}(X)$, then $a \cap b, a \cup b \in \mathcal{P}(X)$ too.

A power set also has top and bottom elements. X is a top element and the empty set $\emptyset$ is a bottom element.

In this example, we use the already existing notation of intersection '$\cap$' and union '$\cup$' for the lattice operations, instead of the usual '$\wedge$' and '$\vee$.' We will do this in cases where the operation in question has a notation which reminds us of its construction. When the operation has no "enlightening" notation of its own, we use the standard operator names.

EXAMPLE 8.9 (TOTAL ORDERS)
A totally ordered set is always a lattice. For any elements a and b, their *maximum* $\max(a, b)$ is defined to be the greater of the two, and their *minimum* is

the lesser of the two. In a totally ordered set, this definition makes sense in all cases, for a and b are always comparable in the order. Whenever $\min(a,b)$ is defined, $\min(a,b)$ is the meet of a and b, and similarly, whenever $\max(a,b)$ is defined, it is the join of a and b. So totally ordered sets are lattices.

However, total orders need not have top or bottom elements. For example, ω with the standard ordering, has a bottom element 0, but no top element. The set $\mathbb{Z}$ of integers (both negative and positive numbers) ordered in the usual way, has neither a top nor a bottom element, yet it is a totally ordered set.

EXAMPLE 8.10 (HASSE DIAGRAMS FOR LATTICES)
When you have a Hasse diagram for a partially ordered set, it is not too difficult to see whether it is a lattice or not. For example, the partially ordered set in Figure 8.1 is a semilattice but not a lattice. Any two elements a and b have a greatest lower bound. If a and b are comparable, then $a \wedge b$ is the lower of the two. If a and b are not comparable, then one is 2 and the other is either 3 or 4, and $2 \wedge b = 1$ when b is either 3 or 4, as 1 is the greatest element under both 2 and 3 or under 2 and 4.

The element 0 is clearly a bottom element. However, there is no top element, as there is no point in the order which is above both 2 and 3, or above both 2 and 4. For this reason too, the semilattice is not a lattice, as 2 and 3 have no upper bound at all, let alone a least upper bound.

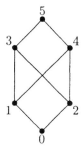
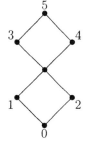

Figure 8.2: A Non-Lattice   Figure 8.3: A Lattice

This is one way in which a partial order can fail to be a lattice — due to the non-existence of upper or lower bounds for suitable pairs. However, you can have partial orders which have upper and lower bounds for all pairs of objects, but no meets or joins. Consider the partial order in Figure 8.2. This order has upper and lower bounds for each pair of objects, as 5 is a top element, and 0 is a bottom element. However, there is no least upper bound for 1 and 2, as 3 and

4 are both upper bounds, but there is no *smallest* upper bound. Similarly 3 and 4 have lower bounds in either of 1 or 2, but neither of these is a *greatest* lower bound.

To repair this, and to make the structure a lattice you need to add at least one new object to be $1 \vee 2$ and to be $3 \wedge 4$. Once that addition is made the new structure is a lattice, as every pair in the structure has least upper and greatest lower bounds. The result is shown in Figure 8.3.

LEMMA 8.11 (UNIQUENESS OF LATTICE OPERATORS)
Any two meet operations on a lattice are identical functions. Similarly, any two join operations, any two top elements or any two bottom elements are the same.

In this lemma we use the notion of identity of functions. If f and g give the same values on each input, we say they are identical functions.

PROOF This is due to the fact that a propositional structure is partially ordered. If $\wedge$ and $\wedge'$ are both meet operations, then $a \wedge b \leqslant a \wedge' b$ since $\wedge'$ is a meet operation and we have $a \wedge b \leqslant a$ and $a \wedge b \leqslant b$, since $\wedge$ is a meet operation. But the reasoning can be reversed to show that $a \wedge' b \leqslant a \wedge b$ too. So $a \wedge b = a \wedge' b$ for all a and b, so $\wedge$ and $\wedge'$ are identical functions. The reasoning for $\vee$, $\top$ and $\bot$ is similar. □

LEMMA 8.12 (LATTICE FACTS)
In any lattice $\langle P, \leqslant \rangle$ the following theses hold for every $a, b, c \in P$.

1. $a \wedge a = a;\ a \vee a = a$
2. $a \wedge b = b \wedge a;\ a \vee b = b \vee a$
3. $a \wedge (b \wedge c) = (a \wedge b) \wedge c;\ a \vee (b \vee c) = (a \vee b) \vee c$
4. $a \wedge (a \vee b) = a;\ a \vee (a \wedge b) = a$

LEMMA 8.13 (TOP AND BOTTOM FACTS)
In any lattice $\langle P, \leqslant \rangle$ with top and bottom, the following theses hold for every a.

1. $a \wedge \top = a;\ a \vee \bot = a$
2. $a \wedge \bot = \bot;\ a \vee \top = \top$

DEFINITION 8.14 (DISTRIBUTIVE LATTICES)
A lattice is *distributive* if it satisfies the distributive law for each a, b and c.

$$a \wedge (b \vee c) = (a \wedge b) \vee (a \wedge c)$$

EXAMPLE 8.15 (POWER SETS ARE DISTRIBUTIVE)
It is not too difficult to show that $x \in a \cap (b \cup c)$ if and only if $x \in (a \cap b) \cup (a \cap c)$. So $a \cap (b \cup c) = (a \cap b) \cup (a \cap c)$ for each set a, b and c, and power set lattices are distributive.

Similarly, total orders are always distributive. Verifying this is a simple exercise of analysing cases of the relative order of a, b and c. Checking the details is left as an exercise at the end of this chapter.

EXAMPLE 8.16 (NON-DISTRIBUTIVE LATTICES)
Despite there being many distributive lattices, not all lattices are distributive. The simplest examples, in Figures 8.4 and 8.5, have five elements.

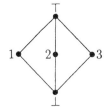

Figure 8.4: The Lattice M_5 Figure 8.5: The Lattice N_5

M_5 fails to be distributive as $3 \wedge (1 \vee 2) = 3 \wedge \top = 3$ and $(3 \wedge 1) \vee (3 \wedge 2) = \bot \vee \bot = \bot$. In N_5, $3 \wedge (1 \vee 2) = 3 \wedge \top = 3$ and $(3 \wedge 1) \vee (3 \wedge 2) = \top \vee 2 = 2$.

Note that in both of these cases we have $(a \wedge b) \vee (a \wedge c) \leqslant a \wedge (b \vee c)$. This half of the distributive law holds in all lattices. We have $a \wedge b \leqslant a \wedge (b \vee c)$ and $a \wedge c \leqslant a \wedge (b \vee c)$, and hence, $(a \wedge b) \vee (a \wedge c) \leqslant a \wedge (b \vee c)$.

DEFINITION 8.17 (COMPLETE SEMILATTICES AND LATTICES)
A semilattice $\langle P, \leqslant \rangle$ is *meet complete* if and only if each subset $X \subseteq P$ has a greatest lower bound $\bigwedge X$. That is, there is an object $\bigwedge X$ such that

$$\bigwedge X \leqslant b \text{ if and only if } a \leqslant b \text{ for each } a \in X$$

A lattice $\langle P, \leqslant \rangle$ is *join complete* if and only if each subset $X \subseteq P$ has a least upper bound $\bigvee X$. That is, there is an object $\bigvee X$ such that

$$a \leqslant \bigvee X \text{ if and only if } a \leqslant b \text{ for each } b \in X$$

A lattice is *complete* if it is both join and meet complete.

EXAMPLE 8.18 (POWER SETS ARE COMPLETE)
The power set lattice $\mathcal{P}(X)$ is a complete lattice, as both the union and the intersection of any set of subsets of X are subsets of X.

A complete lattice must have top and bottom elements, as $\bigwedge P = \bot$ and $\bigvee P = \top$. Note too that according to the definition, for a lattice to be complete, $\bigvee \emptyset$ and $\bigwedge \emptyset$ must be defined, as $\emptyset$ is a subset of the set P of propositions. The natural way to read the definitions tells us that $\bigwedge \emptyset = \top$ and $\bigvee \emptyset = \bot$.

EXAMPLE 8.19 (COMPLETING ω)
The partially ordered set ω of numbers is meet complete but not join complete. Any set of natural numbers has a least element, which is the meet of that set. However, there are sets of numbers without a join — any infinite set of numbers will do. For example, the set $\{0, 2, 4, \ldots\}$ has no join in ω. (If it had a join, which number would it be? You could always pick one bigger.) So ω is not complete.

However, we can add an extra element to "complete" ω. The new set ω' has a "top" element $\infty > n$ for each $n \in \omega$. Now any finite subset of ω' has a join (its greatest element) and any infinite set has ∞ as its join. This new structure is a complete lattice.

DEFINITION 8.20 (COMPLETE DISTRIBUTIVITY)
A lattice $\langle P, \leqslant \rangle$ is *completely distributive* if for each $X \subseteq P$ and each $a \in P$

$$a \wedge \bigvee X = \bigvee \{a \wedge x : x \in X\}$$

Any completely distributive lattice is distributive (take $X = \{b, c\}$ for any b and c). However, the converse is not the case. There are complete distributive lattices which are not completely distributive.

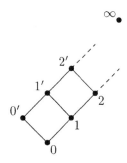

Figure 8.6: A Failure of Complete Distributivity

EXAMPLE 8.21 (DISTRIBUTIVE BUT NOT COMPLETELY DISTRIBUTIVE)
The lattice in Figure 8.6 is an infinite lattice on the set $\{0, 0', 1, 1', 2, 2' \ldots, \infty\}$. The order relation $\leqslant$ is defined as the usual relation on $\omega = \{0, 1, 2, \ldots\}$, while requiring that both $n \leqslant m'$ and $n' \leqslant m'$ if and only if $n \leqslant m$, and $n' \leqslant m$ if and only if $n < m$. Finally, $x \leqslant \infty$ for each x.

This is a complete lattice, and it is not too tedious to verify that it is distributive. However, it fails to be completely distributive, as $0' \wedge \bigvee \omega = 0' \wedge \infty = 0'$, while $\bigvee \{0' \wedge n : n \in \omega\} = \bigvee \{0\} = 0$.

Note again that we do have one direction of the equality. In any complete lattice we have

$$\bigvee \{a \wedge x : x \in X\} \leqslant a \wedge \bigvee X$$

The lattice operators model the extensional connectives in our languages. To model other sorts of connective, we will need other techniques. We will move to operations which cannot simply be "read off" the partial order of a propositional structure.

DEFINITION 8.22 (GROUPOID OPERATORS)
A *groupoid* is a collection of objects together with a binary operation on those objects. A *semigroup* is a groupoid in which the operation is associative: that is, for each a, b and c, $a \cdot (b \cdot c) = (a \cdot b) \cdot c$, where $\cdot$ is the groupoid operation. An *ordered groupoid* is a groupoid with an ordering which *respects* the groupoid operation. That is, if $a \leqslant a'$ and $b \leqslant b'$ then $a \cdot b \leqslant a' \cdot b'$. We will say that a groupoid operation in an ordered groupoid *matches fusion*.

DEFINITION 8.23 (IDENTITIES)
A *left identity* for a groupoid operation is an element e such that $a = e \cdot a$ for each a. The element e is a *right identity* if and only if $a \cdot e = a$ for each a. The element e is an *identity* if and only if it is both a left identity and a right identity for the groupoid operation. A *monoid* is a semigroup with an identity. An identity *matches* t.

LEMMA 8.24 (IDENTITIES OF IDENTITIES)
Any left identity is identical to any right identity.

PROOF   If e_1 is a left identity and e_2 is a right identity, $e_1 = e_1 \cdot e_2 = e_2$.   □

However, it is possible for a groupoid (even a semigroup) to have more than one left identity, or more than one right identity.

DEFINITION 8.25 (RESIDUATION)

A *right-residuated groupoid* is an ordered groupoid, with an operation $\rightarrow$ such that $a \cdot b \leqslant c$ if and only if $a \leqslant b \rightarrow c$. The operation $\rightarrow$ on a right-residuated groupoid *matches a right conditional*. A *left-residuated groupoid* is an ordered groupoid, with an operation $\leftarrow$ such that $a \cdot b \leqslant c$ if and only if $b \leqslant c \leftarrow a$. The operation $\leftarrow$ on a left-residuated groupoid *matches a left conditional*. A *bi-residuated groupoid* is both left- and right-residuated.

DEFINITION 8.26 (POSITIVE MODAL OPERATORS)

A pair of unary operations $\Box$ and $\diamondsuit$ is a *positive pair* on an ordered set if and only if $\diamondsuit a \leqslant b$ if and only if $a \leqslant \Box b$. $\Box$ and $\diamondsuit$ match a pair of a necessity and possibility operators.

LEMMA 8.27 (POSITIVE MODAL CONDITIONS)

If $\Box$ and $\diamondsuit$ are a positive pair, then we have

1. *If $a \leqslant b$ then $\Box a \leqslant \Box b$ and $\diamondsuit a \leqslant \diamondsuit b$.*

2. $\Box a \wedge \Box b \leqslant \Box(a \wedge b)$; $\diamondsuit(a \vee b) \leqslant \diamondsuit a \vee \diamondsuit b$.

3. $\top \leqslant \Box\top$; $\diamondsuit\bot \leqslant \bot$.

4. $\bigwedge \Box X \leqslant \Box \bigwedge X$; $\diamondsuit \bigvee X \leqslant \bigvee \diamondsuit X$.

PROOF   The proofs are similar to those in the natural deduction systems of Chapter 3. We will go through one from each pair.

1. Suppose $a \leqslant b$. $\Box a \leqslant \Box a$, so $\diamondsuit\Box a \leqslant a$. This gives $\diamondsuit\Box a \leqslant b$ and hence $\Box a \leqslant \Box b$.

2. $\diamondsuit a \leqslant \diamondsuit a \vee \diamondsuit b$, and hence $a \leqslant \Box(\diamondsuit a \vee \diamondsuit b)$. Similarly, $b \leqslant \Box(\diamondsuit a \vee \diamondsuit b)$, and these give $a \vee b \leqslant \Box(\diamondsuit a \vee \diamondsuit b)$, which then gives $\diamondsuit(a \vee b) \leqslant \diamondsuit a \vee \diamondsuit b$ as desired.

3. $\diamondsuit\top \leqslant \top$, so $\top \leqslant \Box\top$.

4. $\bigwedge \Box X \leqslant \Box x$ for each $x \in X$, so $\diamondsuit \bigwedge \Box X \leqslant x$ for each $x \in X$. Therefore $\diamondsuit \bigwedge \Box X \leqslant \bigwedge X$, giving $\bigwedge \Box X \leqslant \Box \bigwedge X$.   □

DEFINITION 8.28 (NEGATIVE MODAL OPERATORS)

A pair of unary operations $\sim$ and $\neg$ is an *n-type negative pair* on an ordered set if and only if $a \leqslant \sim b$ if and only if $b \leqslant \neg a$. A pair of unary operations $\frown$ and $\smile$ is a *p-type negative pair* on an ordered set if and only if $\frown a \leqslant b$ if and only if $\smile b \leqslant a$.

If $\sim, \neg$ is an n-type negative pair, then $\sim$ and $\neg$ behave just as you would expect, knowing the proof theory of split negations. We have the following results:

LEMMA 8.29 (N-TYPE NEGATIVE PAIR FACTS)

If $\sim$ and $\neg$ are an n-type negative pair on some propositional structure, then the following inequalities hold (in the presence of the connectives required).

1. *If $a \leqslant b$ then $\sim b \leqslant \sim a$, and $\neg b \leqslant \neg a$.*

2. $\top \leqslant \sim\bot$; $\top \leqslant \neg\bot$.

3. $\sim a \wedge \sim b \leqslant \sim(a \vee b)$; $\neg a \wedge \neg b \leqslant \neg(a \vee b)$.

4. $\bigwedge \sim \bigwedge X \leqslant \sim \bigvee X$; $\bigwedge \neg X \leqslant \neg \bigvee X$. *(where $\sim X = \{\sim x : x \in X\}$ and similarly for $\neg X$).*

PROOF   As with the positive modalities, the proofs are a straightforward reworking of the proof theory.

1. If $a \leqslant b$ then since $\sim b \leqslant \sim b$ we have $b \leqslant \neg\sim b$, and so, $a \leqslant \neg\sim b$, giving $\sim b \leqslant \sim a$. Similarly, $\neg b \leqslant \neg a$, swapping $\sim$ and $\neg$ in this proof.

2. Since $\bot \leqslant \neg\top$, we have $\top \leqslant \sim\bot$.

3. $\neg a \wedge \neg b \leqslant \neg a$, so $a \leqslant \sim(\neg a \wedge \neg b)$, and similarly $b \leqslant \sim(\neg a \wedge \neg b)$ so $a \vee b \leqslant \neg(\neg a \wedge \neg b)$, giving $\neg a \wedge \neg b \leqslant \neg(a \vee b)$ as desired. Swap $\neg$ and $\sim$ to give the other result.

4. This result is the infinitary analogue of the previous one.   □

P-type negative pairs are new connectives which we have not considered in our proof theories. With p-type negative pairs you get the exactly *dual* behaviour to n-type negative pairs, in the following way:

LEMMA 8.30 (P-TYPE NEGATIVE PAIR FACTS)

If $\frown$ and $\smile$ are a p-type negative pair on some propositional structure, then the following inequalities hold (in the presence of the connectives required).

1. *If $a \leqslant b$ then $\frown b \leqslant \frown a$, and $\smile b \leqslant \smile a$.*

2. $\frown\top \leqslant \bot$; $\smile\top \leqslant \bot$.

3. $\frown(a \wedge b) \leqslant \frown a \vee \frown b$; $\smile(a \wedge b) \leqslant \smile a \vee \smile b$.

4. $\frown \bigwedge X \leqslant \bigvee \frown X; \; \smile \bigwedge X \leqslant \bigvee \smile X;$ (where $\frown X = \{\frown x : x \in X\}$ and similarly for $\smile X$).

PROOF These cases are not paralleled in our natural deduction system, so I will go through the detail.

1. If $a \leqslant b$ then since $\frown a \leqslant \frown a$ we have $\smile \frown a \leqslant a$, and thus $\smile \frown a \leqslant b$ and hence $\frown b \leqslant \frown b$. Interchanging $\frown$ and $\smile$ gives us $\smile b \leqslant \smile b$.

2. Clearly $\smile \bot \leqslant \top$, and so, $\frown \top \leqslant \bot$ by the p-type condition. The same proof, interchanging $\frown$ and $\smile$, gives us the second fact.

3. Lattice facts give $\frown a \leqslant \frown a \vee \frown b$, which by the p-type condition gives $\smile (\frown a \vee \frown b) \leqslant a$. Similarly, we have $\smile (\frown a \vee \frown b) \leqslant b$, so we get $\smile (\frown a \vee \frown b) \leqslant a \wedge b$ and the p-type fact again gives $\frown (a \wedge b) \leqslant \frown a \vee \frown b$ as desired. The same proof, interchanging $\frown$ and $\smile$, gives us the second fact.

4. The infinitary conditions are the same. Lattice facts give $\frown x \leqslant \bigvee \frown X$, whenever $x \in X$. It follows that $\smile \bigvee \frown x \leqslant x$ for each $x \in X$, so $\smile \bigvee \frown x \leqslant \bigwedge X$ and hence $\frown \bigwedge X \leqslant \bigvee \frown X$ as desired. The same proof, interchanging $\frown$ and $\smile$, completes our result.

(Note that the fourth condition is sufficient for our second and third results, in complete lattices, as setting X to be the empty set gives us our second result (recall, $\bigwedge \emptyset = \top$ and $\bigvee \emptyset = \bot$) and setting X to be $\{a, b\}$ gives us our third. □

DEFINITION 8.31 (P-TYPE NEGATION)
We will say that $\frown$ is a p-type negation if it satisfies the conditions of the lemma above.

P-type pairs can be constructed in much the same way as n-type pairs.

THEOREM 8.32 (P-TYPE PAIRING)
If $\frown$ is a p-type negation in a complete lattice, then the operator $\smile$ defined by setting

$$\smile b = \bigwedge_{\frown a \leqslant b} a$$

makes $\langle \frown, \smile \rangle$ a p-type pair.

PROOF If $\frown c \leqslant b$ then clearly $\smile b \leqslant c$ as $\smile b = \bigwedge_{\frown a \leqslant b} a \leqslant c$ (since $\frown c \leqslant b$, c is in the range of the variable a). Conversely, if $\smile b = \bigwedge_{\frown a \leqslant b} a \leqslant c$ then $\frown c \leqslant \frown \bigwedge_{\frown a \leqslant b} a$ but $\frown \bigwedge_{\frown a \leqslant b} a \leqslant \bigvee_{\frown a \leqslant b} \frown a \leqslant b$ as desired.   □

We will not consider p-type negations much in what follows, until Chapter 11, when we will see how they naturally arise in the frames for our logics.

Now we have enough machinery to explain how propositional structures model logics.

DEFINITION 8.33 (STRUCTURES FIT FOR A LANGUAGE)

A propositional structure $\langle P, \leqslant, C \rangle$ *fits the language* L if and only if for each connective in L there is an operator $o \in C$ matching that connective.

That is one part of fitness. Another requirement is that the structure be fit for the *logic* in question. If our logic includes the structural rule C, then a propositional structure fit for the logic must mirror this by requiring that for all x, y, z, we have $(x \cdot y) \cdot z \leqslant (x \cdot z) \cdot y$.

DEFINITION 8.34 (TRANSLATION OF STRUCTURAL RULES)

The *translation* of the structural rule $X \Leftarrow Y$ is the universal closure of the condition $[\![Y]\!] \leqslant [\![X]\!]$, where we have defined $[\![\cdot]\!]$ as follows

$$
\begin{aligned}
[\![A]\!] &= x_A \\
[\![X;Y]\!] &= [\![X]\!] \cdot [\![Y]\!] \\
[\![X,Y]\!] &= [\![X]\!] \wedge [\![Y]\!] \\
[\![\bullet X]\!] &= \ominus[\![X]\!]
\end{aligned}
$$

where for each formula A appearing in the statement of the rule, we have associated the variable x_A.

For example, the instance $A; (B; C) \Leftarrow (A; B); C$ of the structural rule B becomes $(x_A \cdot x_B) \cdot x_C \leqslant x_A \cdot (x_B \cdot x_C)$, or relabelling variables for clarity, we have $(x \cdot y) \cdot z \leqslant x \cdot (y \cdot z)$.

The negation conditions need separate treatment, as they are not structural rules. However, they are straightforward re-readings of the rules in algebraic form.

DEFINITION 8.35 (TRANSLATION OF NEGATION CONDITIONS)

⋄ For a simple negation we require just that $\sim\, =\, \neg$.

⋄ For DNE we have $\sim\neg a \leqslant a$ and $\neg\sim a \leqslant a$.

⋄ For ECQ, $a \wedge \neg a \leqslant \bot$.

⋄ For strong excluded middle, $\top \leqslant a \vee \sim a$.

⋄ For $(\neg E; \sim I)$, if $x \cdot y \leqslant \neg z$ then $x \cdot z \leqslant \sim y$.

⋄ For $(\sim I; \neg E)$, if $x \cdot y \leqslant \sim z$ then $x \cdot z \leqslant \neg y$.

Now we can state what it is for a structure to fit a logic.

DEFINITION 8.36 (STRUCTURES FIT FOR A LOGIC)
Given the system $\mathfrak{S}$, the structure $\mathcal{P}$ is fit for $\mathfrak{S}$ if it is fit for the language of $\mathfrak{S}$, and in addition, the translations of the rules of $\mathfrak{S}$ are satisfied in $\mathcal{P}$.

Once we have propositional structures, we can interpret a language in that structure.

DEFINITION 8.37 (INTERPRETATIONS IN STRUCTURES)
The *interpretation* of a language (and structures) in a *propositional structure* is a map $[\![\,]\!]$ from the atomic propositions in the language into the structure P. It is extended to map the whole language by following these clauses

$$
\begin{aligned}
[\![\top]\!] &= \top \\
[\![\bot]\!] &= \bot \\
[\![t]\!] &= e \\
[\![\sim\!A]\!] &= \sim[\![A]\!] \\
[\![\neg A]\!] &= \neg[\![A]\!] \\
[\![\Box A]\!] &= \Box[\![A]\!] \\
[\![\Diamond A]\!] &= \Diamond[\![A]\!] \\
[\![A \wedge B]\!] &= [\![A]\!] \wedge [\![B]\!] \\
[\![A \vee B]\!] &= [\![A]\!] \vee [\![B]\!] \\
[\![A \circ B]\!] &= [\![A]\!] \cdot [\![B]\!] \\
[\![A \rightarrow B]\!] &= [\![A]\!] \rightarrow [\![B]\!] \\
[\![A \leftarrow B]\!] &= [\![A]\!] \leftarrow [\![B]\!]
\end{aligned}
$$

The interpretation of a structure X is defined similarly:

$$
\begin{aligned}
[\![X;Y]\!] &= [\![X]\!] \cdot [\![Y]\!] \\
[\![X,Y]\!] &= [\![X]\!] \wedge [\![Y]\!] \\
[\![\bullet X]\!] &= \Diamond[\![X]\!]
\end{aligned}
$$

We then interpret the consecution $X \vdash A$ as the claim

$$
[\![X]\!] \leqslant [\![A]\!]
$$

We say that $X \vdash A$ is *valid in* $\mathcal{P}$, written $X \vdash_{\mathcal{P}} A$ if and only if $[\![X]\!] \leqslant [\![A]\!]$ for *all* interpretations $[\![\,]\!]$ into $\mathcal{P}$.

We will show that $X \vdash A$ in $\mathfrak{S}$ if and only if for each $\mathcal{P}$ fit for $\mathfrak{S}$, $X \vdash_{\mathcal{P}} A$. Before this, however, we will look at some important propositional structures.

8.2 Example Structures

In this section, we will look at a large number of example propositional structures. Then after seeing the many different ways in which the structures of our logics can be modelled, we will move on in later sections to examine what we can *prove* using propositional structures.

EXAMPLE 8.38 (TRUTH VALUES)
As we have already seen, the truth values {t, f} form a propositional structure. We represent the structure graphically by a Hasse diagram. The other operators in a propositional structure may be expressed by a table.

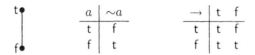

Figure 8.7: The Lattice TV of Truth Values

The diagram encodes the ordering and extensional conjunction and disjunction. The negation and implication tables are read as follows: for negation, the negation of t is f, and that of f is t. For implication, the table is read from row to column. That is, t → f is f, as f is in the t row and the f column.

Truth tables (with just these operations) are fit for quite a large language. Not only are ∧ and ∨ lattice meet and join, but ∧ is also fit for fusion, as it is an ordered semigroup operation. And the implication operation → is both a left and a right residual for ∧, as $a \wedge b \leqslant c$ if and only if $a \leqslant b \rightarrow c$ if and only if $b \leqslant a \rightarrow c$ for each a, b and c, as is tediously verified.

EXAMPLE 8.39 (BN₄)
Truth tables are fit for a large language, and for very many of the logics which interest us. However, we know that not all classical theorems are provable in each of our logics. Other propositional structures draw distinctions left undrawn in truth tables. One example is the structure BN₄, given by the diagram and tables in Figure 8.8

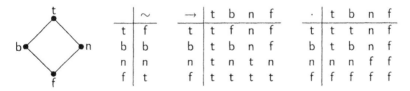

Figure 8.8: BN₄

These tables are not chosen arbitrarily. If you think of the values t, b, n, f as the *sets* of truth values {T}, {T, F}, {} and {F} then the negation of a set of values is simply the set of the negations of values in that set. Implication is similarly defined. The value T is in the set $X \rightarrow Y$ just when if $T \in X$ then $T \in Y$ and if $F \in Y$ then $F \in X$. F is in $X \rightarrow Y$ if and only if $T \in X$ and

$F \in Y$. This gives the implication table. The fusion table is given by setting $X \cdot Y$ to be $\sim(X \rightarrow \sim Y)$.

Fusion is commutative and associative, with an identity b. Negation is definable in terms of implication by setting $\sim X$ to be $X \rightarrow$ b. So in this algebra, the false constant f is modelled by b, as is the true constant t. Fusion is residuated by $\rightarrow$, and the lattice is distributive. It follows that this structure is fit for the logic DMALL.

WI is not satisfied, as n $\not\leqslant$ n · n. The K rule also fails for fusion. We do not have t · b $\leqslant$ b, and hence we do not have b $\leqslant$ t $\rightarrow$ b. So BN$_4$ is a model invalidating $A \vdash B \rightarrow A$, a crucial property of relevant logics.

The connective $\sim$ is a de Morgan negation, $\sim\sim x = x$ and $x \rightarrow \sim y = y \rightarrow \sim x$.

This lattice is also helpful in proving a simple property of logics like DMALL and others. Suppose $A \vdash B$ holds in DMALL, and that A and B are made up of propositional atoms together with $\wedge$, $\vee$ and $\sim$. Then we can show that A and B must share at least one atom. If not, take an interpretation $[\![\,]\!]$ for which $[\![p]\!] =$ b for each p appearing in A, and $[\![p]\!] =$ n for each p appearing in B. As A and B do not share any atomic propositions, this is possible. Then note that $[\![A]\!] =$ b and $[\![B]\!] =$ n, so $[\![A]\!] \not\leqslant [\![B]\!]$. It follows that $A \not\vdash B$ in C (by the soundness theorem, which we prove in the next section).

EXAMPLE 8.40 (ŁUKASIEWICZ MODELS)
Łukasiewicz's three-valued logic is a well-known multiple-valued logic. The propositional structure, given in Figure 8.9, is quite simple.

$\sim$	
1	0
$\frac{1}{2}$	$\frac{1}{2}$
0	1

$\rightarrow$	1	$\frac{1}{2}$	0
1	1	$\frac{1}{2}$	0
$\frac{1}{2}$	1	1	$\frac{1}{2}$
0	1	1	1

·	1	$\frac{1}{2}$	0
1	1	$\frac{1}{2}$	0
$\frac{1}{2}$	$\frac{1}{2}$	0	0
0	0	0	0

Figure 8.9: Łukasiewicz's Three-Valued Logic Ł$_3$

Łukasiewicz interpreted the values as follows: 1 is truth, 0 is falsity, and $\frac{1}{2}$ is *possibility*. Ł$_3$ is the t, n, f fragment of BN$_4$. It follows from what we have already seen that contraction and related principles fail in Ł$_3$. The matrix Ł$_3$ generalises to more values. The $n + 1$-valued logic Ł$_{n+1}$. is the propositional structure on the set

$$\{0, \frac{1}{n}, \frac{2}{n}, \dots, \frac{n-1}{n}, 1\}$$

with the standard ordering, and with the operators defined by setting

$$\sim p = 1 - p \qquad p \to q = \min(1, 1 - (p - q)) \qquad p \cdot q = \max(0, 1 - p - q)$$

You can think of $p \to q$ as the proposition which is false to the extent that p is truer than q. Fusion is commutative and associative, and satisfies K, as $p \cdot q \leqslant p$. However, $p \not\leqslant p \cdot p$, so it does not satisfy WI. For example, $\frac{1}{2} \cdot \frac{1}{2} = 0$. The fusion $p \cdot q$ is the proposition which is false to the degrees that both p and q (added) are false. The order is total, so the lattice operators are distributive.

We can extend our attention to the models $Ł_\mathbb{Q}$ of rational numbers between 0 and 1, or the model $Ł_\mathbb{R}$ on all real numbers between 0 and 1. In these cases, $p \to^n q$ never collapses into $p \to^m q$ for any $m, n \in \omega$, where we define $\to^1 = \to$, and $p \to^{n+1} q = p \to (p \to^n q)$. In any $Ł_n$, $p \to^n q = p \to^{n+1} q$. Similarly, $p^n \neq p^{n+1}$, where we set $p^1 = p$ and $p^{n+1} = p \cdot p^n$.

EXAMPLE 8.41 (SUGIHARA MODELS: RM_n)
Instead of leaving b out of BN_4 to get Łukasiewicz's logics, we can restrict our attention to the t, b, f fragment of BN_4. This gives us the structure known as RM_3. This is generalisable to RM_{2n+1} for any n as follows by setting the domain of propositions to be the numbers

$$\{-n, -(n-1), \ldots, -1, 0, 1, \ldots, n-1, n\}$$

where we set $\sim a$ to be $-a$, and $\to$ and fusion are defined as follows:

$$a \to b = \begin{cases} -a \vee b & \text{if } a \leqslant b \\ -a \wedge b & \text{if } a > b \end{cases} \qquad a \cdot b = \begin{cases} a \wedge b & \text{if } a \leqslant -b \\ a \vee b & \text{if } a > -b \end{cases}$$

Fusion is commutative (verify by eye) and associative (verify by checking case by case), with identity 0. Note that $a \cdot a = a$, so the logic satisfies both W and M — this is a model for RM. Negation is de Morgan, but strong excluded middle and ECQ both fail. For example, $\sim 1 = -1$, so $1 \wedge \sim 1 = -1$ and $1 \vee \sim 1 = 1$.

This model can also be extended by not stopping at $-n$ or n but by including all of $\mathbb{Z}$, the positive and negative integers. This infinite model captures exactly the logic RM in the language $\wedge, \vee, \to, \circ, \sim, t$. The infinite model has no members fit for either $\top$ or $\bot$, but they can be added as ∞ and $-\infty$ without disturbing the logic of the model.

EXAMPLE 8.42 (THE INTEGERS)
The integers feature in the RM algebra above. The choice of the interpretation of implication in that model is only one of many different ways you could go in

this structure. Another is to consider addition as a model of fusion. Addition respects the order in the right way, so it is also fit for fusion in this structure. The residual for addition is obvious: it is subtraction. $X \to Y$ is $Y - X$. This structure is unlike the RM algebra in a number of ways. First, W fails, as $a \nleq a + a$ whenever a is negative. Second, M fails (and so, K and K' do too) as $a + a \nleq a$ whenever a is positive. However, C and B are satisfied in this structure, so we have a structure fit for linear logic. In particular, since the structure is totally ordered, we have the distribution of conjunction over disjunction, so we have a model for distributive linear logic.

More interestingly, $(x \to y) \to y = x$ for each x and y. This does not hold in TV or in any other non-trivial structure with $\top$. If $\top$ were present, then $(a \to \top) \to \top = a$ but $\top \leqslant b \to \top$ for each b (including $a \to \top$) so $\top \leqslant a$.

It is possible to define the negation $\sim a$ as $a \to 0 = -a$. However, other choices are possible. Taking b an arbitrary proposition, we can define $\sim_b a$ as $a \to b$, and the condition $(x \to y) \to y = x$ states, in effect, that $\sim_b \sim_b a = a$. Double negation introduction and elimination holds for *any* negation $\sim_b$ we choose.

This model is a way to invalidate simple consecutions in distributive linear logic. For example, can we prove $A \to (B \to C) \vdash (A \to B) \to (A \to C)$? If this holds in our structure we must have $(z - y) - x \leqslant (z - x) - (y - x)$, but this simplifies to $z \leqslant (z - x) + 2x = z + x$ (add $x + y$ to both sides). And when $x \geqslant 0$ we have $z \leqslant z + x$, but if $x < 0$ this fails. So we have a model invalidating the consecution. Similar manipulations can be used to invalidate other consecutions. However, some consecutions invalid in distributive linear logic do hold in the integers. We have seen that $(A \to B) \to B \vdash A$ already. Another case is $t \vdash (A \to B) \vee (B \to A)$. So the integers do not give an exact fit for distributive linear logic.

(Others have been aware that simple "counting" mechanisms can provide a useful filter for issues of validity in substructural logics [31, 129, 223, 191].)

The logic of this structure is known as *abelian logic*. It was introduced by Meyer and Slaney, who show that it is the logic of ordered abelian groups [153]. There are many more interesting features of this logic, but space prevents my considering them.

EXAMPLE 8.43 (ω UNDER DIVISION)
Using number systems as structures gives us rich mathematical tradition upon which we can build. However, the structures we have seen so far are totally ordered. That is, for any propositions x and y either $x \leqslant y$ or $y \leqslant x$. This is not necessarily desirable — it leads to the truth of $(A \to B) \vee (B \to A)$. Now some "natural" orderings of numbers are total orders, but others are not.

For example, take the positive integers, ordered by *divisibility*. This is a partial ordering — indeed, a lattice ordering — in which join is the lowest common multiple and meet is the greatest common divisor. Fusion, then, has a natural model in multiplication, which obviously respects the order.

This lattice is distributive. This is simple to see when you consider the representation of positive integers as products of primes. Take three positive integers a, b and c. To prove the distribution rule we need to show that

$$\gcd(a, \mathrm{lcm}(b, c)) \mid \mathrm{lcm}(\gcd(a, b), \gcd(b, c))$$

Enumerate the primes as p_1, $p_2,\ldots$, and choose n such that the largest prime divisor of any of a, b or c is p_n. Then represent a as the product $\prod_i p_i^{a_i}$, b as $\prod_i p_i^{b_i}$, and c as $\prod_i p_i^{c_i}$, where a_i is the number of times p_i divides a, and so on. Once so represented, $\mathrm{lcm}(b, c)$ is $\prod_i p_i^{\max(b_i, c_i)}$, $\gcd(a, b)$ is $\prod_i p_i^{\min(a_i, b_i)}$, so

$$
\begin{aligned}
\gcd(a, \mathrm{lcm}(b, c)) &= \prod_i p_i^{\min(a_i, (\max(b_i, c_i)))} \\
&= \prod_i p_i^{\max(\min(a_i, b_i), \min(a_i, c_i))} \\
&= \mathrm{lcm}(\gcd(a, b), \gcd(a, c))
\end{aligned}
$$

giving us the divisibility we require. So, the lattice is distributive, and with fusion modelled as multiplication, 1 is the identity of fusion and we have a distributive lattice-ordered commutative monoid with a unit. Furthermore, the monoid is square-increasing (as $a \mid a^2$), so it models the structural rules of $R[\wedge, \vee, \circ, t]$.

How can you model a conditional which is a residual for fusion? To do this we require the residual condition:

$$xy \mid z \text{ if and only if } x \mid y \to z$$

This works well when y divides z. If y divides z, then we can set $y \to z$ to be z/y. Then for any x you choose, $xy \mid z$ if and only if $x \mid z/y$. However, if y does not divide z, we do not have anything to choose, as 1 is the bottom of the order.

What can we do? The answer is to add another element to the ordering. It will be the lowest element in the ordering, so we will call it 0 (for reasons which will become more obvious later). We can by fiat determine that $0 \mid x$ for every x in the structure, and that $x \mid 0$ only when $x = 0$. Conjunction and disjunction are as before, with the addition that $0 \wedge x = 0$ and $0 \vee x = x$ for each x. The rule for implication is then as follows:

$$
x \to y = \begin{cases} y/x & \text{if } x \mid y, \\ 0 & \text{otherwise.} \end{cases}
$$

Given 0 we need to extend the interpretation of fusion. But this is simple

$$0x = x0 = 0$$

for every x. So defined, the operation is still order-preserving, commutative, square-increasing and with 1 as the identity. This structure is a model for $R[\wedge, \vee, \circ, t, \rightarrow]$. To model the whole of R we need to model a de Morgan negation. That requires an order-inverting involution on the structure. To do this, we need to introduce many more elements in the structure, as no order-inverting involution can be found on what we have here before us: consider the infinite ascending chain

$$0 \mid 1 \mid 2 \mid 4 \mid \cdots \mid 2^n \mid \cdots$$

To negate each element in the series you must get an infinite descending chain. Why? Because we need an involution: $x \mid y$ if and only if $-y \mid -x$, and in particular, if $-x = -y$, then we must have $x = y$. Each element in the inverted chain must be distinct. Alas, there are no such chains in our structure, as every number has only finitely many divisors. So, we need to add more elements to do the job. As our notation has suggested, we will add the negative integers and ∞. The order is as follows:

$$0 \mid x \mid -y \mid \infty$$

for every positive x and y, and

$$-x \mid -y \text{ if and only if } y \mid x$$

So you should read '$\mid$' as divides only when it holds between positive integers. Otherwise, it is defined in these clauses. The infinite ascending chain is then mapped onto the infinite descending chain *above it* as follows:

$$0 \mid 1 \mid 2 \mid 4 \mid \cdots \mid 2^n \mid \cdots \mid -2^n \mid \cdots \mid -4 \mid -2 \mid -1 \mid \infty$$

The resulting order is still a distributive lattice order, and conjunction and disjunction are obviously definable as greatest lower bound and least upper bound, respectively. Implication between all pairs of elements is defined as follows:

  ◇ If x is negative and y is positive, $x \rightarrow y = 0$.
  ◇ If x is positive and y is negative, then $x \rightarrow y = (-x)y$
  ◇ If x and y are both negative, then $x \rightarrow y = -y \rightarrow -x$

Fusion is then defined by setting $xy = -(x \rightarrow -y)$, and it is simple to show that this is commutative, square-increasing and with 1 as the identity.

This lattice is not complete. The ascending chain $0 \mid 1 \mid 2 \mid \cdots \mid 2^n \mid \cdots$ has an upper bound (any negative number will do) but no least upper bound.

This structure was first constructed by Meyer [154]. There is more work which could be done with this structure. Consult Exercises 8.8 to 8.10 for some possibilities.

EXAMPLE 8.44 (BOOLEAN ALGEBRAS)
Truth tables are one of many algebras fit for classical propositional logic. A Boolean algebra is a distributive lattice with a negation $-$ such that $a = --a$ and $a \vee -a$ is a maximum element. There is a finite Boolean algebra of size 2^n for each $n > 0$. We have seen the two-valued Boolean algebra already. The four- and eight-element Boolean algebras are simple.

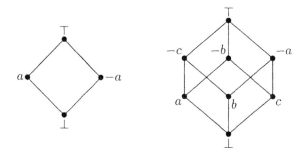

Figure 8.10: Four- and Eight-Element Boolean Algebras

The implication $\rightarrow$ on a Boolean algebra is defined by setting $x \rightarrow y = -x \vee y$. This connective residuates $\wedge$.

Each finite Boolean algebra of size 2^n is isomorphic to the Boolean algebra of subsets of an n-element set.[6] This Boolean algebra has operators of set union and intersection, and complement, and the entailment relation is the subsethood relation.

The power set of *any* set is a Boolean algebra under union, intersection and complement. However, not all Boolean algebras are isomorphic to a power set algebra. For example, given some infinite set, the set of all finite and co-finite subsets of that set is closed under intersection, union and complement. (A set Y is a co-finite subset of X if and only if $Y \backslash X$ is finite.) The union of two finite sets is co-finite. The union of any set with a co-finite set is co-finite. The intersection of two co-finite sets is co-finite, and the intersection of any set with a finite set is finite. The complement of a co-finite set is finite and the complement of any finite set is co-finite. So, the family of finite and co-finite sets is a Boolean algebra.

---

[6] 'Isomorphic' means 'same shape'. For a more rigorous definition of isomorphism, see Definition 9.8 on page 192.

This algebra is not isomorphic to a power set Boolean algebra. Take the example of the finite and co-finite algebra on a countable set. There are countably many finite and co-finite subsets of that set.[7] However, there is no countable power set. The power sets of finite sets are finite, and the power sets of infinite sets are uncountable.

THEOREM 8.45 (UNIQUENESS OF BOOLEAN NEGATION)
In any distributive lattice with $\top$ and $\bot$, if $a \vee b = a \vee c = \top$ and $a \wedge b = a \wedge c = \bot$, then $b = c$.

PROOF   Suppose $a \vee b = a \vee c = \top$ and $a \wedge b = a \wedge c = \bot$. Then since $c \wedge b \leqslant c$, we have $(a \wedge b) \vee (c \wedge b) \leqslant c$ as $a \wedge b = \bot$. By distributivity of the lattice, $(a \vee c) \wedge b \leqslant c$. However, $a \vee c = \top$, so $\top \wedge b \leqslant c$, i.e. $b \leqslant c$. By symmetry of reasoning, $c \leqslant b$, and $b = c$.   □

There has been a great deal of work on the structure of Boolean algebras, much of which is relevant to research in substructural logics. Jónsson and Tarski's "Boolean Algebras with Operators" [122, 123] and Stone's representation theory [253, 254] in particular will be generalised to the non-Boolean setting of substructural logics in Chapters 11 and 12.

EXAMPLE 8.46 (HEYTING LATTICES)
Not all distributive lattices are Boolean algebras. For example, any totally ordered lattice is distributive, but none other than TV (or the trivial one-element algebra) is Boolean. However, on any completely distributive lattice you can define an operation $\supset$ which is a residual for $\wedge$. The operation can be defined as follows. Set $x \supset y$ to be the meet of all of the elements z such that $x \wedge z \leqslant y$. Formally, $x \supset y = \bigvee \{z : x \wedge z \leqslant y\}$. We have $z \wedge x \leqslant y$ if and only if $z \leqslant x \supset y$, since if $z \wedge x \leqslant y$ then $z \leqslant \bigvee \{z' : x \wedge z' \leqslant y\} = x \supset y$. Conversely, if $z \leqslant x \supset y$, i.e. $z \leqslant \bigvee \{z' : x \wedge z' \leqslant y\}$, then $x \wedge z \leqslant x \wedge \bigvee \{z' : x \wedge z' \leqslant y\} = \bigvee \{x \wedge z' : x \wedge z' \leqslant y\} \leqslant y$. This last line of deduction requires the complete distributivity of the lattices. A distributive lattice with a residual of conjunction and a bottom element is called a *Heyting lattice*. A Heyting lattice is a model for intuitionistic logic.

The simplest lattice in which this construction differs from the Boolean algebra construction is the three-element lattice we have already seen as Ł$_3$.

The table for $\supset$ differs slightly from that for $\rightarrow$ in Ł$_3$. We have $n \supset f = f$ but $n \rightarrow f = n$. At all other points the operators are the same.

There are other ways to construct Heyting lattices. For example, given a topological space, the set of open sets in that space forms a Heyting lattice. The intersection of two open sets is open, the union of two open sets is open. The

---

[7]   In Exercise 8.13 you are asked to find an enumeration of this set.

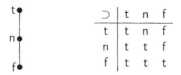

Figure 8.11: The Three-Element Heyting Lattice H_3

complement of an open set is the largest open set disjoint from it — that is, the interior of its complement. Similarly, the residual $X \supset Y$ is the interior of $-X \vee Y$. This is unlike the power set Boolean algebra construction in a number of ways. First, in many topological spaces, the Heyting lattice is not complete. Consider the standard space on the real line. The point set $\{0\}$ is not open, but it is the intersection of the set of open sets of the form $(-\frac{1}{n}, \frac{1}{n})$. Similarly, this space is not atomic. Any open set will have an open proper subset.

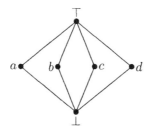

Figure 8.12: A Lattice with two Ortho-Negations

EXAMPLE 8.47 (ORTHO-NEGATIONS)
Ortho-negations generalise away from Boolean algebras by relaxing the distributivity condition on the lattice. The assumption of distributivity in Theorem 8.45 is essential — you can have distinct ortho-negation operators on the one lattice. Take the lattice in Figure 8.12. We can define $\sim a = b$ and $\sim c = d$. This determines one ortho-negation (the values for $\sim\top$ and $\sim\bot$ are determined). Another distinct ortho-negation is given by setting $-a = c$ and $-b = d$.

There are many natural lattices with ortho-negations. One simple lattice is the lattice of subspaces of a vector space. Given any family of subspaces, their intersection is also a subspace. Their union is not necessarily a subspace, but there is a subspace generated by the union of those spaces. Finally, given a subspace, the set of points *orthogonal* to that subspace is itself a subspace, and this is a suitable ortho-negation for the space. Hence we have the name, *ortho*-negation.

EXAMPLE 8.48 (ALGEBRAS OF RELATIONS)
Relation algebras are a generalisation of Boolean algebras of propositions. The idea is simple. Consider the Boolean algebra of subsets of a set as an algebra of *properties*. (It is common to identify properties with their *extensions* — the set of objects with that property.) The Boolean algebra of subsets of some set is like this. A simple generalisation, originally due to de Morgan [178] and Peirce [190] and later developed, for example, by Schröder [237], was to consider algebras of binary relations instead of merely properties. A *concrete relation algebra* is the set of all subsets of some set $D \times D$ of pairs of elements from a set D under not only the Boolean operations of intersection, union and complementation but also under new operations which use the relational structure essentially.

For any two relations R and S there is their composition $R \cdot S$, defined by setting $x(R \cdot S)y$ if and only if $(\exists z \in D)(xRz \wedge zRy)$. This operation distributes over disjunction and furthermore, $\bot \cdot R = R \cdot \bot = \bot$, where $\bot$ is the empty relation, so it is fit for fusion. Fusion has a left and right identity, 1, the identity relation on D. Furthermore, for any relation R we have its converse, given by setting $x\check{R}y$ if and only if yRx. Note that $(R \cdot S)\check{} = \check{S} \cdot \check{R}$.

We can define left and right residuals for composition directly by the residuation conditions, or we can note that they are definable in terms of the Boolean connectives, fusion and converse. $R \rightarrow S = -(-S \cdot \check{R})$ and $S \leftarrow R = -(\check{R} \cdot -S)$.

It is possible to modify the behaviour of these algebras by considering restricted classes of relations. For example, we could look at algebras of reflexive relations. These are odd, in that $1 \leqslant R$ for each R, so the bottom element of the algebra is also the identity for fusion. These algebras are closed under some of the operations at issue, but not all. The Boolean complement of a reflexive relation is not reflexive, but the conjunction or disjunction of two reflexive relations is.

Another possibility is to consider, for example, equivalence relations. When is the composition of two equivalence relations an equivalence relation? It turns out that $R \cdot S$ is also commutative when $R \cdot S = S \cdot R$. And if this obtains, then their composition is the least upper bound of the two relations (in the set of equivalence relations). Therefore, a class of commuting equivalence relations forms a lattice, in which fusion is least upper bound. And it is not too hard to show that this lattice generally fails to be distributive, but it is *modular*. It satisfies the modular law

$$a \wedge (b \vee (a \wedge c)) \leqslant (a \wedge b) \vee (a \wedge c)$$

but not the more general distributive law. Exercise 8.20 asks you to construct a proof theory for the logic of commuting equivalence relations.

EXAMPLE 8.49 (COMBINATOR ALGEBRAS)
Dunn and Meyer have studied combinator algebras with a view to substructural logics [82]. A *weak combinator algebra* is a partially ordered set with one two-place function of composition (which we interpret as fusion) satisfying the standard ordering requirement. It has one or more *combinators* on the set, from among s, k, i, w, c, b and so on, satisfying the following inequalities:

$$
\begin{aligned}
\mathrm{i}x &\leqslant x \\
\mathrm{k}xy &\leqslant x \\
\mathrm{c}xyz &\leqslant xzy \\
\mathrm{w}xy &\leqslant xyy \\
\mathrm{b}xyz &\leqslant x(yz) \\
\mathrm{s}xyz &\leqslant (xz)(yz)
\end{aligned}
$$

We assume association to the left — $\mathrm{k}xy$ is $(\mathrm{k}x)y$. What is $\mathrm{k}x$? It is a function which always returns x.

The relation $\leqslant$ is one of reducibility. We say that $\mathrm{i}x$ *reduces* to x. So, for example, $\mathrm{w}\mathrm{i}x$ reduces to $\mathrm{i}xx$ which in turn reduces to xx. Note the connection between the action of the combinators and the behaviour of similarly named structural rules.

This is *almost* the definition of a weak combinator algebra from [57], except that for us, if x reduces to y and y reduces to x, then x and y are identical. For the weak combinator algebras of Curry's second volume [57], this is not the case.

Suppose composition has a left residual $\rightarrow$. Then in the *absence* of structural rules, we can use combinators to code up rules. They are like 'licenses that must be displayed on the windshield of an inference.' Here are some examples: $\mathrm{k} \leqslant a \rightarrow (b \rightarrow a)$, $\mathrm{w} \leqslant (a \rightarrow (a \rightarrow b)) \rightarrow (a \rightarrow b)$, $\mathrm{skk} \leqslant a \rightarrow a$ (as $(\mathrm{k}a)(\mathrm{k}a) \leqslant a$, so $\mathrm{skk}a \leqslant (\mathrm{k}a)(\mathrm{k}a)$ gives $\mathrm{skk}a \leqslant a$, giving $\mathrm{skk} \leqslant a \rightarrow a$.

There are a number of helpful introductions to work on combinators [55, 56, 57, 116] which ought to be mined for further examples and results.

8.3 Soundness and Completeness

Soundness and completeness theorems are a major part of any semantic study of systems of logic. Properly speaking, soundness and completeness are properties of *proof systems*. A proof system is *sound* for a semantic system if any consecution provable in the proof system is valid in the semantics. The proof system is sound if it makes no mistakes, from the perspective of the semantics.

A proof system is complete if everything valid in the semantics is provable in the proof theory. So it is complete if it covers all the ground.

THEOREM 8.50 (SOUNDNESS IN STRUCTURES)
If $X \vdash A$ is provable in the system $\mathfrak{S}$ then it is valid in every propositional structure fit for $\mathfrak{S}$.

PROOF Take a propositional structure $\mathcal{P}$ fit for $\mathfrak{S}$ and an arbitrary interpretation $[\![\cdot]\!]$. We will show that $[\![X]\!] \leqslant [\![A]\!]$.

The proof proceeds by induction on the length of the proof of $X \vdash A$. We show that all axioms of $\mathfrak{S}$ hold in $\mathcal{P}$, and that if the premises of a rule of $\mathfrak{S}$ hold in $\mathcal{P}$, so does the conclusion.

Let us consider a few cases and leave the rest to Exercise 8.15. For the axiom $A \vdash A$ we are assured that $[\![A]\!] \leqslant [\![A]\!]$, and this holds in any propositional structure.

Consider the implication rules. The premise of $(\to I)$ is $X; A \vdash B$. If $[\![X; A]\!] \leqslant [\![B]\!]$ then $[\![X]\!] \cdot [\![A]\!] \leqslant [\![B]\!]$ giving us $[\![X]\!] \leqslant [\![A]\!] \to [\![B]\!] = [\![A \to B]\!]$, so the conclusion, $X \vdash A \to B$, holds too.

The premises of $(\to E)$ are $X \vdash A \to B$ and $Y \vdash A$. If they hold, we have $[\![X]\!] \leqslant [\![A \to B]\!]$ and $[\![Y]\!] \leqslant [\![A]\!]$. By monotonicity of fusion, we have $[\![X]\!] \cdot [\![Y]\!] \leqslant [\![A \to B]\!] \cdot [\![A]\!]$. But $[\![A \to B]\!] \cdot [\![A]\!] = ([\![A]\!] \to [\![B]\!]) \cdot [\![A]\!] \leqslant [\![B]\!]$. So $[\![X; Y]\!] = [\![X]\!] \cdot [\![Y]\!] \leqslant [\![B]\!]$, so the conclusion of the rule, $X; Y \vdash B$, holds too.

Let us also do the disjunction rules. Since $a \leqslant a \vee b$ and $b \leqslant a \vee b$, the introduction rules are straightforward. The elimination rule is less straightforward. The premises are $X \vdash A \vee B$, $Y(A) \vdash C$ and $Y(B) \vdash C$. So we have $[\![X]\!] \leqslant [\![A \vee B]\!]$, and $[\![Y(A)]\!] \leqslant [\![C]\!]$ and $[\![Y(B)]\!] \leqslant [\![C]\!]$. To show that $[\![Y(X)]\!] \leqslant [\![C]\!]$, we need two facts.

FACT 1: If $[\![Y]\!] \leqslant [\![Z]\!]$ then $[\![X(Y)]\!] \leqslant [\![X(Z)]\!]$.

FACT 2: I$[\![X(A \vee B)]\!] = [\![X(A)]\!] \vee [\![X(B)]\!]$.

Both are proved by a simple induction on the construction of X. For Fact 1, we use the monotonicity of fusion and of possibility. If $a \leqslant b$ then $c \cdot a \leqslant c \cdot b$, and $\Diamond a \leqslant \Diamond b$. For Fact 2, we use the distribution of fusion and of possibility over disjunction. We have $c \cdot (a \vee b) = (c \cdot a) \vee (c \cdot b)$, and $\Diamond(a \vee b) = \Diamond a \vee \Diamond b$.

Having these facts at hand, we proceed to show that the conclusion of the disjunction rule holds. $[\![X]\!] \leqslant [\![A \vee B]\!]$, so Fact 1 gives $[\![Y(X)]\!] \leqslant [\![Y(A \vee B)]\!]$, and Fact 2 shows that this entails $[\![Y(A)]\!] \vee [\![Y(B)]\!]$. Both disjuncts entail $[\![C]\!]$, so we have our result.

The other connective rules use similar techniques and are left to the exercises.

For the structural rules, if we have $Y \Leftarrow X$ then if $Z(X) \vdash A$, we have $[\![Z(X)]\!] \leqslant [\![A]\!]$, and since $[\![Y]\!] \leqslant [\![X]\!]$, we have $[\![Z(Y)]\!] \leqslant [\![Z(X)]\!][\![A]\!]$, as desired.

$\square$

The converse is only marginally more difficult to prove.

DEFINITION 8.51 (THE LINDENBAUM ALGEBRA OF $\mathfrak{G}$)

The Lindenbaum Algebra $\mathcal{P}_{\mathfrak{G}}$ of a system $\mathfrak{G}$ is defined as follows:

⋄ The elements are the sets $[A] = \{B : A \dashv\vdash B\}$ of equivalence classes of provably equivalent formulae.

⋄ The ordering $\leqslant$ is defined by setting $[A] \leqslant [B]$ if and only if $A \vdash B$.

⋄ The two-place operator o is defined by setting $[A] o [B] = [A o B]$, the one-place operator o, by $o[A] = [oA]$ and the constant o by $o = [o]$.

Before proceeding we must ensure that the Lindenbaum algebra is in fact well defined. We must ensure that our choice of representatives of equivalence classes does not prejudice things. Consider the definition of $\leqslant$. If $[A] = [A']$, what if $A \vdash B$ but $A' \not\vdash B$? Is $[A] \leqslant [B]$ in this case or not? It turns out that the choice of A or A' as a representative for the class $[A] = [A']$ is immaterial, since if $[A] = [A']$ then $A \dashv\vdash A'$, and if $A \vdash B$ then by Cut, $A' \vdash B$ too.

Furthermore, if $[A] = [A']$ and $[B] = [B']$ then $A o B \dashv\vdash A' o B'$, so the choice of representatives makes no difference in the definition of binary operators either. The same holds for one-place operators. If $[A] = [A']$ then $oA \dashv\vdash oA'$. So, the Lindenbaum algebra is well defined. It is not only well defined but we also have the following result:

LEMMA 8.52 ($\mathcal{P}_{\mathfrak{G}}$ IS FIT FOR $\mathfrak{G}$)

Given a system $\mathfrak{G}$, the Lindenbaum algebra $\mathcal{P}_{\mathfrak{G}}$ is fit for $\mathfrak{G}$.

PROOF We need to verify that $\leqslant$ is a partial order, that the operators are fit for their respective connectives, and that the structural (and negation) rules are satisfied.

That $\leqslant$ is a partial order follows from $A \vdash A$ and the cut rule.

That the operators are fit for their respective connectives follows from the definition of the rules for each operator. For example, $\cdot$ is an ordered groupoid operation, since if $[A] \leqslant [A']$ and $[B] \leqslant [B']$, then $A \vdash A'$ and $B \vdash B'$, and hence $A o B \vdash A' o B'$, giving $[A] \cdot [B] \leqslant [A'] \cdot [B']$ as desired. The other conditions are just as trivial to verify.

The structural rules are satisfied by the Lindenbaum algebra. If $X \Leftarrow Y$ is a structural rule, then $[\![Y]\!] \leqslant [\![X]\!]$ holds in the algebra straightforwardly. $\square$

THEOREM 8.53 (COMPLETENESS IN STRUCTURES)
If $X \vdash_{\mathcal{P}} A$ for each $\mathcal{P}$ fit for $\mathfrak{S}$ then $X \vdash A$ in $\mathfrak{S}$.

PROOF If $X \vdash_{\mathcal{P}} A$ for each $\mathcal{P}$ fit for $\mathfrak{S}$ then $X \vdash_{\mathcal{P}_{\mathfrak{S}}} A$. It follows that in any interpretation $[\![\cdot]\!]$ into $\mathcal{P}_{\mathfrak{S}}$, $[\![X]\!] \leqslant [\![A]\!]$. Consider the interpretation given by setting $[\![p]\!] = [p]$. By definition of the Lindenbaum algebra, $[\![A]\!] = [A]$ for each A. It follows that $[X] \leqslant [A]$ and hence that $X \vdash A$, as desired. □

We finish this chapter with one simple corollary of this result, which goes some way to exhibiting the power of algebraic methods: the *relevance property* for $R[\wedge, \vee, \rightarrow, \circ, \sim]$ and its subsystems.

THEOREM 8.54 (THE RELEVANCE PROPERTY FOR R)
If $A \vdash B$ is provable in $R[\wedge, \vee, \rightarrow, \circ, \sim]$ (or in any subsystem) then A and B share a propositional variable.

This result goes a little way towards justifying the claim for the account of consequence in R as being *relevant*. There is no way that A can entail B (in R) without A and B sharing some kind of *content*.

PROOF Consider the eight-element propositional structure with the following order and fusion table:

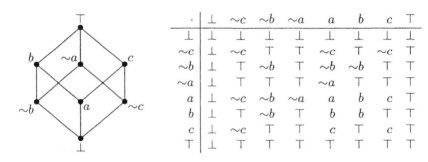

·	⊥	~c	~b	~a	a	b	c	T
⊥	⊥	⊥	⊥	⊥	⊥	⊥	⊥	⊥
~c	⊥	~c	T	T	~c	T	~c	T
~b	⊥	T	~b	T	~b	~b	T	T
~a	⊥	T	T	T	~a	T	T	T
a	⊥	~c	~b	~a	a	b	c	T
b	⊥	T	~b	T	b	b	T	T
c	⊥	~c	T	T	c	T	c	T
T	⊥	T	T	T	T	T	T	T

This is an R structure. Fusion is commutative (the table is symmetric about the diagonal), and associative (this must be checked manually, or with the aid of a computer). We have $x \leqslant x \cdot x$, so WI holds, and therefore so does W given associativity of fusion. The element a is an identity for fusion.

Negation is defined by the names of the elements and the fact that $\sim$ is a de Morgan negation. It is not hard to verify that $\sim$ is indeed a strong de Morgan negation. As a result, $x \rightarrow y = \sim(x \circ \sim y)$, so we have our values for implication.

Now, suppose we have two propositions A and B, in the language $\wedge$, $\vee$, $\sim$, $\circ$ and $\rightarrow$, such that there is no atom shared between A and B. Construct an evaluation $[\![\cdot]\!]$, such that $[\![p]\!]$ is either b or $\sim b$ for any atom p in A, and it is either c or $\sim c$ for any atom p in B.

By induction, we can verify that the value $[\![A]\!]$ is one of b and $\sim b$, and similarly, the value $[\![B]\!]$ is one of c or $\sim c$. Therefore, $[\![A]\!] \not\leq [\![B]\!]$, and since this is a model of R, we have $A \not\vdash B$ in R, and hence, $A \not\vdash B$ in any sublogic of R. □

Note that this theorem would not hold in the presence of any of the constants t, $\top$ or $\bot$. The validity of $t \vdash A \vee \sim A$, $p \vdash \top$ and $\bot \vdash p$ give the lie to that.

Before heading off into a short discussion of the history of propositional structures, we should mention a little of what is necessary for Lindenbaum algebras to work as models for our logics. The major constraint for something like a Lindenbaum algebra to work is that substitutivity of equivalents holds. We need that if $A \dashv\vdash B$ then $C(A) \dashv\vdash C(B)$ for any propositional context C. There are logical systems for which this does not hold. For example, the C_n systems of da Costa fail this requirement [50, 51]. These systems are modelled by a simple two-valued scheme, in which we use a function from sentences to the truth values $\{t, f\}$. The semantics for conjunction is the usual one — a conjunction receives value t if and only if both conjuncts have the value t — but negation is treated non-standardly. The value of $\sim A$ need not be a function of the value of A, so we call such functions *semi-valuations*. In the system C_1, we require just that if A has value f, then $\sim A$ has value t, and that $\sim\sim A$ receives the same value as A. Therefore, we cannot have $\sim A$ and A both f, but they may be both t. This is a rather simple logic, but substitutivity of equivalents fails. On any semi-valuation, A and $A \wedge A$ receive the same value, so $A \dashv\vdash A \wedge A$ in this logic, but $\sim A$ and $\sim(A \wedge A)$ may differ. We cannot extract the behaviour of this logic from its Lindenbaum algebra in the usual way. Different techniques must be used.

Substructural logics are, however, amenable to the treatment of algebras, and they are a fruitful tool in the study of these logics, as the next chapter will show.

8.4 History

The algebraic study of logics has attained great heights in the work of Polish logicians. Helena Rasiowa's *An Algebraic Approach to Non-classical Logics* [204] is a compendium of interesting results in the field. The use of algebra in relevant logics found form in Dunn's doctoral dissertation [70] and in the work of Meyer and Routley [167]. Study of general work in lattice theory [38, 52, 58] and universal algebra [104] repays careful reading for the student of substructural logics.

There has been a long tradition of using finite algebras (also called 'matrices' for obvious reasons) to prove syntactic results about logics, such as the relevance property for R. Section 22 of *Entailment* Volume 1 [6] contains a good discussion of results of this sort.

Tarski [256] helped bring relation algebras back to prominence in modern logic, and there is much contemporary research in the area, particularly in Hungary [8].

Slaney's software package MaGIC, Matrix Generator for Implication Connectives, available at http://arp.anu.edu.au/~jks/magic.html, has made the generation of finite model structures much easier than it was in the pre-computational era [251].

Quantales (a notion due to Mulvey [181] — essentially lattice-ordered semi-groups, with arbitrary meets but only finite joins) are algebraic structures which appear in both pure mathematics and theoretical computer science. They are discussed a little in Vickers' *Topology via Logic* [274], which is a useful source book of other algebraic constructions and their use in modelling processes and observation.

More recently still, Dunn has introduced the notion of a *gaggle*, which generalises the account of propositional structures given here by picking out properties of distribution common to the family of fusion and implication, the modal family, and split negations [76, 77, 78]. This chapter and the next (as well as much of the rest of this book) has been inspired by Dunn's research.

8.5   *Exercises*

Practice

{8.1} Consider the propositional structure on the four-element set $\{-2, -1, 1, 2\}$ ordered in the usual way, with the fusion table

·	-2	-1	1	2
-2	-2	-2	-2	-2
-1	-2	-1	-1	2
1	-2	-1	1	2
2	-2	2	2	2

Find the values of $2 \wedge -1$, $1 \vee -2$ and $-1 \cdot (2 \wedge 1)$ in this structure.

{8.2} What structural rules are satisfied in this structure?

{8.3} Give the table for the connective $\rightarrow$, which residuates fusion in this structure.

Problems

{8.4} Show that total orders are distributive lattices.

{8.5} Show that in any lattice $(a \wedge b) \vee (a \wedge c) \leqslant a \wedge (b \vee c)$ holds for all a, b and c.

{8.6} Show that any non-distributive lattice has a sublattice of either M_5 or N_5.

{8.7} Show that if $\supset$ is a residual for $\wedge$, then $\wedge$ distributes over $\vee$.

{8.8} Consider the divisibility structure for R, Example 8.43, introduced on page 174. Show that this structure has is no residual for extensional conjunction, despite the fact that the structure is distributive. Diagnose this phenomenon. How could you extend the model so that extensional conjunction *is* residuated?

{8.9} The divisibility structure is infinite. Show that by restricting your attention to the factors of a given number, you can construct finite models with a similar behaviour. Now that the model is finite, you have a residual for extensional conjunction. Explain the behaviour of this connective in "arithmetic" terms.

{8.10} Is it possible to define the divisibility structure in such a way as to put the negative numbers *below* the positive ones? It seems like a natural place for them to be. Can you make the construction like this and keep it an R model?

{8.11} A logic is *characterised* by a propositional structure if and only if every consecution $X \vdash A$ is valid if and only if $[\![X]\!] \leqslant [\![A]\!]$ for any interpretation into that structure. Clearly, every logic with a Lindenbaum algebra is characterised by that algebra. Show that Łukasiewicz's infinite-valued logic and all of its sublogics are not characterised by any finite structure, by showing that $p^n \vdash p^{n+m}$ fails in Ł$_R$ for each n and m, but that in any finite Ł$_R$ model, some of these must be valid.

{8.12} Show that RM *and all of its sublogics* are not characterised by any finite structure.

{8.13} Enumerate the set of finite and co-finite subsets of ω.

{8.14} Show that if $\frown$ is a p-type negation then so is $\frown\Box$, where $\Box$ is a necessity operator.

{8.15} Complete the proof of the soundness theorem, Theorem 8.50.

{8.16} Show that the Lindenbaum algebra of any logic with infinitely many atomic propositions, but with connectives of only finite arity, is never complete.

{8.17} An atom in an ordered set with a bottom element $\bot$ is a point a such that $\bot < a$, and for any b, if $b < a$ then $b = \bot$. A lattice is *atomic* if every element is the join of some set of atoms. Show that the Lindenbaum algebra of any logic with a lattice conjunction is not atomic.

{8.18} A *Gelfand quantale* is a lattice with arbitrary joins, with an associative fusion operator, left and right conditionals, and a new operator * (not to be confused with the Kleene star) such that $a^{**} = a$, $(a \cdot b)^* = b^* \cdot a^*$, and $\bigvee a_i^* = (\bigvee a_i)^*$ [5]. Show that in any Gelfand quantale, $b \leftarrow a = (a^* \rightarrow b^*)^*$. Show that * is both necessity-like and possibility-like.

{8.19} Maksimova has shown that the technique of Theorem 8.54 proves something stronger [145]. We know not only that if $A \vdash B$ in R$[\wedge, \vee, \sim, \circ, \rightarrow]$ then A and B share a variable, but that they share a variable in the *same position*, where we define position as follows: p is in positive position in itself. Atomic propositions are either in *positive* or *negative* position in a formula. If p is in some position in A it is in the *same position* in $A \wedge B$, $A \vee B$, $A \circ B$ and $B \rightarrow A$, and it is in the *opposite position* in $\sim A$ and $A \rightarrow B$. Prove Maksimova's theorem by a more judicious choice of $[\![\cdot]\!]$ into the model used in the proof of Theorem 8.54.

Project

{8.20} Construct a proof theory for the logic of commuting equivalence relations in a relation algebra, mentioned in Example 8.48. (Consider the work of Finberg, Mainetti and Rota [83] as a possible starting point.)

Chapter 9

Manipulating Propositional Structures

> *The exquisite manipulation of the master*
> *gives to each atom of the multitude*
> *its own character and expression.*
>
> — *John Ruskin*, Modern Painters, *1843*

In the previous chapter, we defined propositional structures and we showed that they are suitable models for a wide range of our logics. In this chapter, we will examine a number of *algebraic* techniques for manipulating and constructing propositional structures. These techniques help us to clarify the nature of substructural logics. In particular, the main results of this chapter will be *conservative extension results*. Suppose we have a logic L over some language $\mathcal{L}$, and we are interested in extending the language $\mathcal{L}$ to form a new language $\mathcal{L}'$ by adding some *new* connectives. We add new rules to L, giving us a new logic L' on the new language. Now we have a question to answer: is this a good extension? One way the extension can be *good* is as follows:

DEFINITION 9.1 (CONSERVATIVE EXTENSION)
The logic L' on the language $\mathcal{L}'$ is a *conservative extension* of the logic L on the language $\mathcal{L}$ if and only if

⋄ L' extends L: if something is provable in L it is also provable in L', and

⋄ L' is conservative over L: if something is provable in L' and it features none of the new vocabulary in $\mathcal{L}'$, then it was already provable in L.

If L' conservatively extends L then we know that the rules governing the additions to the language truly govern that addition, and do not tell us anything new about our original vocabulary. As one example, we will show that substructural logics on the languages $[\to, \leftarrow, \circ]$ are conservatively extended, in general, by the distributive lattice connectives: $[\wedge, \vee, \top, \bot]$.

Not all extensions are conservative, however. The implication/conjunction fragment of intuitionistic logic, $J[\wedge, \supset]$, is not conservatively extended with Boolean negation. Without Boolean negation you cannot prove Peirce's law $(p \supset q) \supset p \vdash p$, but with Boolean negation you can.

Why not? Consider the three-element Heyting lattice of Figure 8.11 on page 179. In this algebra, $(n \supset f) \supset n = f \supset n = t \not\leq n$, so Peirce's law

189

fails in intuitionistic logic. It succeeds in Boolean algebras as $p \supset q = {\sim}p \vee q$, so $(a \supset b) \supset a = {\sim}({\sim}a \vee b) \vee a = (a \wedge {\sim}b) \vee a = a$.

9.1 Algebra Facts

In this section, we will collect together basic definitions from algebra that apply to the study of propositional structures.

DEFINITION 9.2 (HOMOMORPHISMS)
A function $f : \mathcal{P} \to \mathcal{Q}$ between two propositional structures of the same signature is a *homomorphism* if and only if it is both

⋄ *Order-preserving:*

$$\text{For each } x, y \in \mathcal{P}, \text{ if } x \leqslant y \text{ then } f(x) \leqslant f(y), \text{ and}$$

⋄ *Operator-preserving:* for each operator $o \in Op$

$$\text{For each } x_1, \ldots, x_n \in \mathcal{P}, f(o(x_1, \ldots, x_n)) = o(f(x_1), \ldots, f(x_n)).$$

So a homomorphism between structures is a structure-preserving mapping. All of the relevant features of the structure are preserved. We will consider a few simple homomorphisms between BN_4, RM_3 and the two- and four-element Boolean algebras.

EXAMPLE 9.3 (TV TO RM_3)
Consider the two-element Boolean algebra TV on $\{t, f\}$ and RM_3 on $\{t, b, f\}$, and the maps f and g from TV to RM_3 defined by setting

$$f(t) = t \quad f(f) = f \qquad g(t) = t \quad g(f) = b$$

Both of these maps are order-preserving: If $x \leqslant y$ then $f(x) \leqslant f(y)$ and $g(x) \leqslant g(y)$. Both preserve conjunction and disjunction: $f(x \wedge y) = f(x) \wedge f(y)$, $g(x \wedge y) = g(x) \wedge g(y)$, $f(x \vee y) = f(x) \vee f(y)$ and $g(x \vee y) = g(x) \vee g(y)$. Both preserve $\top$, as $f(\top) = \top$, and $g(\top) = \top$. However, g is not $\perp$ preserving. The bottom element $\perp$ in both structures is f, and g maps f to b.

Furthermore, f preserves negation, while g does not. ${\sim}f(x) = f({\sim}x)$ for each x, while ${\sim}g(f) = b \neq t = g(t) = g({\sim}f)$.

It follows that g is not a homomorphism from TV to RM_3, while f is. However, g is a homomorphism from $TV[\wedge, \vee, \top]$ to $RM_3[\wedge, \vee, \top]$. Whether or not a function is a homomorphism is sensitive to the choice of operators which must be preserved.

EXAMPLE 9.4 (BN$_4$ AND RM$_3$)

There are *no* homomorphisms from BN$_4$ to RM$_3$, as there are no maps which will preserve both negation and conjunction and $\perp$. If there were such a map f, consider $f(n)$ and $f(b)$. However, $n = {\sim}n$, so ${\sim}f(n) = f({\sim}n) = f(n)$; and $b = {\sim}b$, so similarly, ${\sim}f(b) = f(b)$. So, whatever $f(n)$ and $f(b)$ are, they have to be propositions x such that ${\sim}x = x$. Only b does this job in RM$_3$. So $f(n) = f(b) = b$.

However, we need $f(n) \wedge f(b) = f(n \wedge b) = f(f) = f(\perp) = \perp$, and this means that the choice of $f(n) = f(b) = b$ is not allowed, as b is not $\perp$. Therefore, no f will preserve each of negation and conjunction and $\perp$, from BN$_4$ to RM$_3$.

All is not lost, however. It is not too hard to show that the f from BN$_4$ to RM$_3$ given by setting $f(x) = b$ preserves all structure other than $\top$ and $\perp$. To prove this it is sufficient to show that b is a fixed point for all operations o other than $\top$ and $\perp$: that is, $o(b, \ldots, b) = b$ for each o other than $\top$ and $\perp$. Then f must be order- and structure-preserving.

Maps in the other direction are easier to find. The map $g : \text{RM}_3 \to \text{BN}_4$ given by setting $g(x) = x$ preserves all structure, and the map h given by setting $h(t) = t$, $h(f) = f$ and $h(b) = n$ preserves order and $[\wedge, \vee, \top, \perp, {\sim}]$, but not implication or fusion.

LEMMA 9.5 (ORDER-PRESERVATION FOR FREE)

If a map f preserves either $\vee$ or $\wedge$, it preserves order too.

PROOF Note that $a \leqslant b$ if and only if $a \vee b = b$. So, if $a \leqslant b$ then $a \vee b = b$ so $f(a \vee b) = f(b)$ and hence $f(a) \vee f(b) = f(b)$, giving us $f(a) \leqslant f(b)$ as desired. The equivalence of $a \leqslant b$ and $a \wedge b = a$ can be used to the same effect. □

This fact can help to cut down the amount of checking needed to verify that a map is a homomorphism. Now we can consider some special sorts of homomorphism.

DEFINITION 9.6 (ONE-TO-ONE AND ONTO HOMOMORPHISMS)

A homomorphism $f : \mathcal{P} \to \mathcal{Q}$ is *one-to-one* if and only if whenever $f(x) = f(y)$ then $x = y$. f is *onto* if and only if whenever $y \in \mathcal{Q}$, then there is some $x \in \mathcal{P}$ where $f(x) = y$.

DEFINITION 9.7 (EMBEDDINGS)

A homomorphism $f : \mathcal{P} \to \mathcal{Q}$ is an *order embedding* if and only if $f(x) \leqslant f(y)$ only if $x \leqslant y$.

If f is an order embedding, it must be one-to-one. If $f(x) = f(y)$ then $f(x) \leqslant f(y)$ and hence $x \leqslant y$. Similarly, $f(y) \leqslant f(x)$ and so, $y \leqslant x$. So $x = y$. However, the converse does not hold. There are one-to-one maps which are not order embeddings. (Finding one is left to Exercise 9.1.)

DEFINITION 9.8 (ISOMORPHISMS)
An *isomorphism* $f : \mathcal{P} \to \mathcal{Q}$ is a homomorphism such that the inverse map $f^{-1} :$ $\mathcal{Q} \to \mathcal{P}$ — given by setting $f^{-1}(y) = x$ where $f(x) = y$ — is a homomorphism. Two structures are *isomorphic* if and only if there is an isomorphism from one to the other.

LEMMA 9.9 (ISOMORPHISM CONDITIONS)
A homomorphism $f : \mathcal{P} \to \mathcal{Q}$ is an onto order embedding if and only if it is an isomorphism.

PROOF   If f is an onto order embedding we first need to show that f^{-1} is well defined. Since f is onto, for every y there is at least one $x \in \mathcal{P}$ where $f(x) = y$. Since f is an order embedding, it is one-to-one, so there is no more than one x where $f(x) = y$. It follows that the definition of f^{-1} gives us a function, and furthermore, that $f(f^{-1}(y)) = y$ and $f^{-1}(f(x)) = x$ for each $y \in \mathcal{Q}$ and $x \in \mathcal{P}$ respectively.

Now f^{-1} is order-preserving since if $f^{-1}(y) \not\leqslant f^{-1}(y')$ we have $f(f^{-1}(y)) \not\leqslant$ $f(f^{-1}(y'))$ (as f is an order embedding), giving us $y \not\leqslant y'$. Contraposing this, we have $y \leqslant y'$ only if $f^{-1}(y) \leqslant f^{-1}(y')$ as desired.

Finally, for this part, f^{-1} preserves operators. For any n place operator o, $f^{-1}(o(y_1, \ldots, y_n)) \neq o(f^{-1}(y_1), \ldots, f^{-1}(y_n))$ then since f is one-to-one, we have

$$f(f^{-1}(o(y_1, \ldots, y_n))) \neq f(o(f^{-1}(y_1), \ldots, f^{-1}(y_n))$$

and since f is a homomorphism, it follows that

$$f(f^{-1}(o(y_1, \ldots, y_n))) \neq o(f(f^{-1}(y_1)), \ldots, f(f^{-1}(y_n)))$$

But we have $f(f^{-1}(y)) = y$ for all y, we get

$$o(y_1, \ldots, y_n) \neq o(y_1, \ldots, y_n)$$

which is a contradiction. Therefore, f^{-1} must preserve operators, so f is an isomorphism.

Conversely, if f is an isomorphism, then we will show that it is an onto order embedding. First, if $y \in \mathcal{Q}$, we have $f(f^{-1}(y)) = y$, and hence f is onto. Second, if $f(x) \leqslant f(y)$, then $f^{-1}(f(x)) \leqslant f^{-1}(f(y))$, giving us $x \leqslant y$, and hence, that f is an order embedding.   □

DEFINITION 9.10 (SUBSTRUCTURES)
$\mathcal{Q}$ is a *substructure* of $\mathcal{P}$ if and only if $Q \subseteq P$, and Q is closed under all of the operations of $\mathcal{P}$. In other words, if o is some operator, and $x_1, \ldots, x_n \in Q$, then $o(x_1, \ldots, x_n) \in Q$.

EXAMPLE 9.11 (SUBSTRUCTURES OF BN₄)

It is easy to see that RM_3 is a substructure of BN_4, as the set $\{t, b, f\}$ is closed under all operators on BN_4. The structures $Ł_3$ and TV are substructures of BN_4 provided that you ignore the constant t, which in BN_4 is b.

Each homomorphism f into some structure Q defines a substructure of Q.

DEFINITION 9.12 (HOMOMORPHIC IMAGES)

For any homomorphism $f : P \rightarrow Q$, the *homomorphic image of P in Q defined by f* is the set $R \subseteq Q$ of all $y \in Q$ where for some $x \in P$, $f(x) = y$. The operations defined on R are restrictions of those on Q.

LEMMA 9.13 (HOMOMORPHIC IMAGES ARE SUBSTRUCTURES)

R is a homomorphic image of some P in Q if and only if it is a substructure of Q.

PROOF   If R is a homomorphic image of P in Q (by f) then clearly $R \subseteq Q$. If $y_1, \ldots y_n \in R$, then for each i, there is an $x_i \in P$ where $y_i = f(x_i)$. Then it follows that $o(y_1, \ldots, y_n) = o(f(x_1), \ldots, f(x_n)) = f(o(x_1, \ldots, x_n)) \in R$ as desired.

Conversely, if R is a substructure of Q, then the identity map $i(x) = x$ from R to itself is a homomorphism, and the image of R in Q defined by i is R itself. □

DEFINITION 9.14 (PRODUCTS)

Given any two propositional structures P and Q with the same signature, their *product $P \times Q$* is given as follows.

◇ Its domain is the set of all pairs $\langle x, y \rangle$, where $x \in P$, $y \in Q$.

◇ $\langle x, y \rangle \leqslant \langle x', y' \rangle$ if and only if $x \leqslant x'$ and $y \leqslant y'$.

◇ $o(\langle x_1, y_1 \rangle, \ldots, \langle x_n, y_n \rangle) = \langle o(x_1, \ldots, x_n), o(y_1, \ldots, y_n) \rangle$

$P \times Q$ is a propositional structure with the same signature as P and Q, and which satisfies any structural rules satisfied by *both* P and Q.

DEFINITION 9.15 (VARIETIES AND QUASIVARIETIES)

A class $\mathfrak{V}$ of algebraic structures is a *variety* if and only if it is the class of all algebraic structures satisfying some class of equations. The class $\mathfrak{V}$ is a *quasivariety* if and only if it is the class of all algebraic structures satisfying some class of equations and rules.

The class of propositional structures for a logic is almost always at the least a quasivariety.

THEOREM 9.16 (BIRKHOFF'S HSP THEOREM)

$\mathfrak{V}$ is a variety if and only if it is closed under homomorphic images, substructures and products [38, 104].

It turns out, then, that the class of propositional structures fit for a logic is (almost always) a variety.

DEFINITION 9.17 (FREE STRUCTURES)
Given a quasivariety $\mathfrak{V}$ of propositional structures, a *free propositional structure* on the set X is a propositional structure $\mathcal{P}_{\mathfrak{V},X}$ such that for any propositional structure Q in $\mathfrak{V}$, and for any function $f : X \rightarrow Q$, f can be extended to a unique homomorphism $f^* : \mathcal{P}_{\mathfrak{V},X} \rightarrow Q$.

The idea is that $\mathcal{P}_{\mathfrak{V},X}$ is the completely general propositional structure generated by the objects in X. There are no extra logical relationships at all between the objects in X beyond what is dictated by the variety $\mathfrak{V}$, since we can map different objects in X into any other objects in any structure we like, and still extend this into a homomorphism. On the other hand, a map of X into Q extends to only one homomorphism, because the behaviour of every other object in $\mathcal{P}_{\mathfrak{V},X}$ is dictated by the behaviour of X. You can think of the objects in the free structure as *generated* by the objects in X.

We are justified in calling $\mathcal{P}_{\mathfrak{V},X}$ *the* free propositional structure on X because of the following result.

THEOREM 9.18 (ISOMORPHISM OF FREE STRUCTURES)
If X and Y are of the same cardinality, $\mathcal{P}_{\mathfrak{V},X}$ and $\mathcal{P}_{\mathfrak{V},Y}$ are isomorphic.   □

A presentation of the proof would take us too far afield. Consult Chapter 4 of Grätzer's *Universal Algebra* [104], among many places where the proof is presented.

It turns out that the Lindenbaum algebra in a logic is the free propositional structure on the set of atomic propositions in the variety of all algebras of that logic. This shows us that for an X of any size, there is a free propositional structure on X. At this point we are doing *universal algebra*. There are many interesting results here, but we have no time to consider them. Consult Grätzer's canonical text [104] for much more on these techniques.

9.2 Filters, Ideals and Ideal Structures

For another, useful kind of construction of propositional structures, we need a few more definitions. We will look at different sorts of *sets* of objects in propositional structures. The first kind are *filters*, which are to propositional structures what theories are to logics.

DEFINITION 9.19 (FILTERS)
A *filter* in a propositional structure is a set of objects in that structure which is

⋄ *Closed under* ⩽. That is, if $a \leqslant b$ and $a \in F$ then $b \in F$.
⋄ *Closed under* ∧, if ∧ is present in the structure. That is, if $a, b \in F$ then $a \wedge b \in F$.
⋄ *Contains* ⊤, if ⊤ is in the structure.

An ideal is a filter turned upside-down.

DEFINITION 9.20 (IDEALS)
An *ideal* in a propositional structure is a set of objects in that structure which is

⋄ *Closed under* ⩾. That is, if $a \geqslant b$ and $a \in I$ then $b \in I$.
⋄ *Closed under* ∨, if ∨ is present in the structure. That is, if $a, b \in I$ then $a \vee b \in I$.
⋄ *Contains* ⊥, if ⊥ is in the structure.

Ideals are more important than filters in this chapter — filters (and theories) will assume centre stage in Chapters 11 and 12. Ideals are important here as the set of all ideals of a propositional structure $\mathcal{P}$, which we will call $\mathrm{Ideal}(\mathcal{P})$, inherits much of the structure of $\mathcal{P}$.

DEFINITION 9.21 (IDEAL STRUCTURE)
The *ideal structure* $\mathrm{Ideal}(\mathcal{P})$ of a propositional structure $\mathcal{P}$ is the set of all ideals of $\mathcal{P}$, ordered by ⊆.

Each propositional structure has at least as many ideals as it has elements. In particular, each element defines a unique ideal.

DEFINITION 9.22 (PRINCIPAL IDEALS)
For any $x \in \mathcal{P}$, the ideal $\downarrow x = \{y : y \leqslant x\}$ from $\mathrm{Ideal}(\mathcal{P})$ is said to be a *principal ideal*.

It is simple to verify that $\downarrow x$ is in fact an ideal. It is automatically closed downwards. If ∨ is present in $\mathcal{P}$ then if $y_1 \leqslant x$ and $y_2 \leqslant x$ then clearly $y_1 \vee y_2 \leqslant x$. Finally, if ⊥ is present, then since $\bot \leqslant x$ for every x, $\bot \in \downarrow x$ too.

LEMMA 9.23 (↓ IS AN ORDER EMBEDDING)
The map $\downarrow : \mathcal{P} \to \mathrm{Ideal}(\mathcal{P})$ *is an order embedding.*

PROOF   Suppose $\downarrow x \subseteq \downarrow y$. Since $x \in \downarrow x$ we have $x \in \downarrow y$, and hence $x \leqslant y$ as desired.   □

So, the order in $\mathcal{P}$ is embedded into the order in $\mathrm{Ideal}(\mathcal{P})$ by way of principal ideals. $\downarrow$ does more than that, however, and $\mathrm{Ideal}(\mathcal{P})$ is more than a partially ordered set.

LEMMA 9.24 ($\mathrm{Ideal}(\mathcal{P})$ IS A COMPLETE LATTICE)
For any propositional structure $\mathcal{P}$, its ideal structure $\mathrm{Ideal}(\mathcal{P})$ is a complete lattice ordered by $\subseteq$.

PROOF Given any set X of ideals of $\mathcal{P}$, the intersection $\bigcap X$ is also an ideal of $\mathcal{P}$, the greatest lower bound of the ideals in X. Clearly, $\bigcap X$ is closed downwards, as each $I \in X$ is so closed. If $\perp$ is present, then $\perp \in I$ for each $I \in X$, so $\perp \in \bigcap X$. Finally, if $\vee$ is present, then if $x, y \in \bigcap X$ then $x, y \in I$ for each $I \in X$, then $x \vee y \in I$ for each $I \in X$, so $x \vee y \in \bigcap X$ as desired.

For disjunction, given any set X of ideals of $\mathcal{P}$, $\bigcap\{J : I \subseteq J \text{ each } I \in X\}$ is the least upper bound of X. □

So the conjunction of a set of ideals is just their intersection. The disjunction of a set of ideals is their union, if disjunction is not present in the original structure. If disjunction is present in the original structure, then the disjunction $\bigvee X$ is defined as follows

$$\bigvee X = \{z : z \leqslant x_1 \vee \cdots \vee x_n \text{ for some } x_i \in I_i \in X\}$$

This set is clearly an ideal (it is closed downwards, contains $\perp$ and is closed under disjunction) and it contains each $I \in X$. It is also included in any ideal containing each $I \in X$, so $\bigvee X$ is indeed this set. From now on we will use $\bigvee$ and $\bigwedge$ for arbitrary disjunctions and conjunctions in the ideal structure.

LEMMA 9.25 ($\downarrow$ PRESERVES ALL LATTICE OPERATORS)
The map $\downarrow$ preserves all lattice operators present in $\mathcal{P}$.

PROOF Consider $\downarrow\perp$. This is clearly the bottom element of $\mathrm{Ideal}(\mathcal{P})$, as $\perp$ is present in every ideal (if present in $\mathcal{P}$). Consider $\downarrow\top$. Since $x \leqslant \top$ for all x, it follows that $\downarrow\top = P$, which is the top element of $\mathrm{Ideal}(\mathcal{P})$.

Consider $\downarrow(x \wedge y) = \{z : z \leqslant x \wedge y\}$. This is equal to $\{z : z \leqslant x\} \cap \{z : z \leqslant y\} = \downarrow x \cap \downarrow y$, which is the least upper bound of $\downarrow x$ and $\downarrow y$ in $\mathrm{Ideal}(\mathcal{P})$.

Finally, consider $\downarrow(x \vee y) = \{z : z \leqslant x \vee y\}$. This is *not* necessarily equal to $\downarrow x \cup \downarrow y$, but this union is not necessarily an ideal. However, consider *any* ideal I containing both $\downarrow x$ and $\downarrow y$. It contains x and y and hence it contains $x \vee y$ (as disjunction is present in $\mathcal{P}$). It follows that it contains every element of $\downarrow(x \vee y)$. However, $\downarrow(x \vee y)$ itself is an ideal which has both $\downarrow x$ and $\downarrow y$ as subsets, so it follows that $\downarrow(x \vee y)$ is least upper bound of $\downarrow x$ and $\downarrow y$, as desired. □

THEOREM 9.26 (WHEN Ideal($\mathcal{P}$) IS COMPLETELY DISTRIBUTIVE)
If $\mathcal{P}$ contains no counterexample to (finite) distribution, then Ideal($\mathcal{P}$) *is completely distributive.*

That is, if $\mathcal{P}$ is a distributive lattice, then Ideal($\mathcal{P}$) is completely distributive. On the other hand, if disjunction is absent from $\mathcal{P}$, then Ideal($\mathcal{P}$) is still a completely distributive lattice.

PROOF If disjunction is absent from $\mathcal{P}$, then Ideal($\mathcal{P}$) is closed under intersection and union and this is clearly a completely distributive lattice.

If disjunction is present in $\mathcal{P}$, consider $I \wedge \bigwedge_i J_i$, which is

$$I \cap \{z : z \leqslant x_1 \vee \cdots \vee x_n \text{ where } x_j \text{ is in some } J_i\}$$

If $z \in I \wedge \bigwedge_i J_i$ then $z \in I$ and $z \in \bigwedge_i J_i$, and hence $z \leqslant x_1 \vee \cdots \vee x_n$, where each x_j is in some J_i. By finite distributivity, $z \wedge (x_1 \vee \cdots \vee x_n) = (z \wedge x_1) \vee \cdots \vee (z \wedge x_n)$. We have each $z \wedge x_j \in I \wedge J_i$ (for some i), so $(z \wedge x_1) \vee \cdots \vee (z \wedge x_n) \in \bigwedge_i (I \wedge J_i)$. However, $z \wedge x_j = z$ for each j, $z \in \bigwedge_i (I \wedge J_i)$ as desired. □

So we have an order embedding $\downarrow$ from an arbitrary ordered set $\mathcal{P}$ into a complete lattice Ideal($\mathcal{P}$). Furthermore, the complete lattice is completely distributive unless $\mathcal{P}$ contains a failure to finite distribution.

In the rest of this section, we will show how the ideal structure can be equipped with the other propositional operators from $\mathcal{P}$. Then in the next section we will use the ideal structure to prove a number of conservative extension theorems.

We will start with fusion. We can "lift" the operation $\cdot$ on $\mathcal{P}$ up to Ideal($\mathcal{P}$) by setting

$$I \cdot' J = \{z : \exists x \in I, y \in J(z \leqslant x \cdot y)\}$$

The set $I \cdot' J$ is an ideal if I and J are, as is easy to check. (We refrain from writing the prime in $\cdot'$ as the context will make clear whether $\cdot$ is an operator on $\mathcal{P}$ or Ideal($\mathcal{P}$).)

⋄ If $z \in I \cdot J$ and $w \leqslant z$ then $w \in I \cdot J$ by construction.
⋄ Clearly $\bot \in I \cdot J$ if $\bot$ is present in $\mathcal{P}$, as $\bot \leqslant \bot \cdot \bot$, and $\bot \in I, J$.
⋄ If $z, w \in I \cdot J$ then $z \leqslant x \cdot y$ and $w \leqslant x' \cdot y'$, where $x, x' \in I$ and $y, y' \in J$. We wish to show that $z \vee w \in I \cdot J$, if disjunction is present in $\mathcal{P}$. Proceed as follows: $z \vee w \leqslant (x \cdot y) \vee (x' \cdot y')$, but elementary fusion facts show us that $(x \cdot y) \vee (x' \cdot y') \leqslant (x \vee x') \cdot (y \vee y')$. But $x \vee x' \in I$ and $y \vee y' \in J$, so we have $z \vee w \in I \cdot J$ as desired.

Not only that, but the embedding map $\downarrow$ respects fusions, as $\downarrow x \cdot y = \downarrow x \cdot \downarrow y$.

Finally, it is straightforward to verify that $\cdot$ is indeed fit for fusion on the ideal lattice, as we have $\bigvee_i (I_i \cdot J) = (\bigvee_i I_i) \cdot J$.

We can also define the other intensional connectives in similar ways:

DEFINITION 9.27 (LIFTED INTENSIONAL OPERATORS)
- $t' = \downarrow t$
- $I \cdot' J = \{z : \exists x \in I, y \in J(z \leqslant x \cdot y)\}$
- $I \to' J = \{z : \forall x \in I, \exists y \in J(z \leqslant x \to y)\}$
- $J \leftarrow' I = \{z : \forall x \in I, \exists y \in J(z \leqslant y \leftarrow x)\}$
- $\diamondsuit' I = \{z : \exists y \in I(z \leqslant \diamondsuit y)\}$
- $\square' I = \{z : \exists y \in I(z \leqslant \square y)\}$
- $\neg' I = \{z : \forall y \in I(z \leqslant \neg y)\}$
- $\sim' I = \{z : \forall y \in I(z \leqslant \sim y)\}$

DEFINITION 9.28 (IDEAL STRUCTURE)
Given any propositional structure $\mathcal{P} = \langle P, \leqslant, Op \rangle$, its *ideal structure* is $Ideal(\mathcal{P})$, ordered under $\subseteq$ and with the operators o' corresponding to those operators o in Op.

LEMMA 9.29 (IDEAL PRESERVATION)
The operations on an ideal structure $Ideal(\mathcal{P})$ *are well defined. If* $I_1, \ldots, I_n$ *are ideals, so is* $o'(I_1, \ldots, I_n)$.

PROOF   This proof is a simple verification of cases. We have seen the proof in the case where o is fusion. We will work through the case for implication and leave the rest to Exercise 9.10.

- If $z \in I \to J$ and $w \leqslant z$ then $w \in I \to J$ by construction.
- Clearly $\bot \in I \to J$ if $\bot$ is present in $\mathcal{P}$, as $\bot \leqslant x \to \bot$, for whatever $x \in I$ you like, and $\bot \in J$.
- If $z, w \in I \to J$ then for all $x \in I$ there is a $y \in J$, where $z \leqslant x \to y$, and similarly, for all $x' \in I$ there is a $y' \in J$, where $w \leqslant x' \to y'$. We wish to show that for all $x \in I$ there is a y'', where $z \vee w \leqslant x \to y''$. We have some $y \in J$, where $z \leqslant x \to y$ and similarly, a y', where $w \leqslant x \to y'$. So $z \vee w \leqslant (x \to y) \vee (x \to y')$. However, $(x \to y) \vee (x \to y') \leqslant (x \to y \vee y')$ by simple lattice properties, so we have $z \vee w \leqslant x \to y \vee y'$ and since $y \vee y' \in J$, we have $z \vee w \in I \to J$ as desired.   □

LEMMA 9.30 (OPERATOR PRESERVATION)
The operations on an ideal structure $Ideal(\mathcal{P})$ *are almost always fit for their corresponding connectives. In particular:*

- $\cdot$, $\diamondsuit$, $\sim$ *and* $\neg$ *and* $\top$ *on* $Ideal(\mathcal{P})$ *are fit for their corresponding connectives, provided that they are fit for the connective in* $\mathcal{P}$.

◇ $\rightarrow$, $\leftarrow$, $\square$, on $\mathrm{Ideal}(\mathcal{P})$ *are fit for their corresponding connectives, provided that they are fit for the connective in $\mathcal{P}$, and provided that their parent is present in $\mathcal{P}$.*

This lemma uses the notion of the parent of an operator. Recall that the intensional connectives $\leftarrow, \cdot, \rightarrow$ form a family in which $\cdot$ is the parent, as it mimics directly the structure used to model each connective. Similarly, $\square$ and $\Diamond$ are a family in which $\Diamond$ is the parent.

PROOF There are many cases to run through here. We will do some, to show how it is done. Suppose $\cdot$ and $\rightarrow$ are both present in $\mathcal{P}$. Suppose $I \subseteq J \rightarrow K$. We wish to show that $I \cdot J \subseteq K$. Take $z \in I \cdot J$, so $z \leqslant x \cdot y$, where $x \in I \subseteq J \rightarrow K$ and $y \in J$. Since $x \in J \rightarrow K$, it follows that for any $y' \in J$ there is a $w \in K$ where $x \leqslant y' \rightarrow w$. Choose y for y'. There is some $w \in K$, where $x \leqslant y \rightarrow w$. But this means that $z \leqslant x \cdot y \leqslant (y \rightarrow w) \cdot y \leqslant w \in K$, giving $z \in K$ as desired.

Conversely, suppose $I \cdot J \subseteq K$. We want $I \subseteq J \rightarrow K$. Let $z \in I$. To show that $z \in J \rightarrow K$, let $x \in J$. We want some $y \in K$, where $z \leqslant x \rightarrow y$. Well, $z \in I$ and $x \in J$ gives $z \cdot x \in I \cdot J \subseteq K$. It follows that $z \leqslant x \rightarrow z \cdot x$, and we are done.

Suppose now that $\cdot$ is present by itself, without implication. For the distribution laws there are two cases, concerning the presence of disjunction or its absence. Suppose first that disjunction on the ideal structure is just union. Then if $z \in (\bigvee_i J_i) \cdot I$, for some x and y, $z \leqslant y \cdot x$, where $y \in \bigvee_i J_i$ and $x \in I$. Thus there is some J_i, where $y \in J_i$. Then $y \cdot x \in J_i \cdot I$ and hence $z \leqslant y \cdot x \in (\bigvee_i J_i \cdot I)$ as desired. And if $z \in (\bigvee_i J_i \cdot I)$ then $z \in J_i \cdot I$ for some J_i, giving $z \leqslant y \cdot x$, where $y \in J_i$ and $x \in I$. Then clearly $z \in (\bigvee_i J_i) \cdot I$.

If disjunction is not just union but the more complex construction given above, the reasoning is trickier. If $z \in (\bigvee_i J_i) \cdot I$ we have for some $x \in I$ and $y \in \bigvee_i J_i$, $z \leqslant y \cdot x$. This means that for some J_1 to J_n, for each i, $y \leqslant y_1 \vee \cdots \vee y_n$. Then $z \leqslant (y_1 \vee \cdots \vee y_n) \cdot x = (y_1 \cdot x) \vee \cdots \vee (y_n \cdot x) \in (\bigvee_i J_i \cdot I)$ as desired. The converse argument is straightforward. This gives us the infinitary distribution laws we require, and this gives fusion the desired distribution properties.

We will also consider the case for negation. Suppose that $\sim$ and $\neg$ are both present. Suppose that $I \subseteq \sim J$. To show that $J \subseteq \neg I$, take $x \in J$ to show that $x \in \neg I$. Suppose that $y \in I$. We wish to show that $x \leqslant \neg y$. But if $y \in I$ then $y \in \sim J$, and hence $y \leqslant \sim x$ (as $x \in J$). It follows that $x \leqslant \neg y$ as desired.

Now suppose that $\sim$ is present alone, to show that $\bigwedge_i \sim I_i = \sim \bigvee I_i$. First suppose that $z \in \bigwedge_i \sim I_i$. It follows that $z \in \sim I_i$ for each i. We wish to show that $z \in \sim \bigvee I_i$. So for each $y \in \bigvee I_i$ we want $z \leqslant \sim y$. If disjunction is merely union, then we have $y \in I_i$ for some i. But $z \in \sim I_i$ shows that $z \leqslant \sim y$ as desired. If disjunction is not merely union, then $y \leqslant y_1 \vee \cdots \vee y_n$ for y_j chosen from some I_i. Now we have $\sim(y_1 \vee \cdots \vee y_n) \leqslant \sim y$. We wish to show that $z \leqslant \sim(y_1 \vee \cdots \vee y_n)$. Now $z \leqslant \sim y_i$ for each i, so $z \leqslant \sim y_1 \wedge \cdots \wedge y_n = \sim(y_1 \vee \cdots \vee y_n)$ as desired.

Conversely, suppose that $z \in \sim\bigvee_i I_i$. We wish to show that $z \in \bigwedge_i \sim I_i$. If $y \in I_i$ then $I \in \bigvee_i I_i$, so $z \leqslant \sim y$, so $z \in \sim I_i$ for each i, as desired.

The cases for the other connectives are similar and are left as exercises. □

Now suppose that implication is present alone, without fusion. To see how implication on ideals *need not* match implication, consider the following: to show that $\bigwedge_i (I \rightarrow J_i) = I \rightarrow \bigwedge_i J_i$. First suppose that $z \in \bigwedge_i (I \rightarrow J_i)$ to show that $z \in I \rightarrow \bigwedge_i J_i$. To that end, suppose that $x \in I$ to find some $y \in \bigwedge_i J_i$, where $z \leqslant x \rightarrow y$. We know that $z \in I \rightarrow J_i$ for each i, so for any $x \in I$ there is a $y_i \in J_i$ where $z \leqslant x \rightarrow y_i$. It does not seem possible in general to show that for some choice of x, there is some y in *all of the* J_i where $z \leqslant x \rightarrow y_i$.

The same phenomenon occurs when you attempt to show that $\bigwedge_i \Box I_i = \Box \bigwedge_i I_i$. We may have x in each $\Box I_i$ as $x \leqslant \Box y_i$ for some $y_i \in I_i$. However, there may be no $y \in \bigwedge I_i$ where $x \leqslant \Box y$. A simple counterexample can show how this might happen. Take the propositional structure to be $\mathbb{Z}$, ordered in the usual way. Let $\wedge$ be the only propositional connective in question, and let $\Box x = 5$ for each x. (There is nothing special about the choice of 5 in this example, as you will see.) We clearly have $\Box(x \wedge y) = \Box x \wedge \Box y$ for each x and y, and if $x \leqslant y$ then clearly $\Box x \leqslant \Box y$. So $\Box$ satisfies all you need for a necessity on a $\wedge$-semilattice. Now, let $I_i = \{n : n \leqslant -i\}$ for each $i = 0, 1, \ldots$ So $I_0 = \{\ldots, -3, -2, -1, 0\}$, $I_1 = \{\ldots, -4, -3, -2, -1\}$, $I_2 = \{\ldots, -5, -4, -3, -2\}$ and so on. $\Box I_i$ is $\downarrow 5 = \{5, 4, 3, 2, 1, 0, -1, \ldots\}$ for each i, so $\bigwedge_i \Box I_i = \downarrow 5$. However, $\bigwedge_i I_i$ is the empty set, and by the definition of $\Box$ on ideals, so is $\Box \bigwedge_i I_i$.

This case, together with the case of implication, shows that these connectives are not always preserved when mapped into the ideal structure. Better can be said for our structural rules.

LEMMA 9.31 (PRESERVATION OF STRUCTURAL RULES)
If a propositional structure $\mathcal{P}$ satisfies some structural rule, then so does its ideal structure $\mathcal{P}^I$.

PROOF We have already seen that each structural rule amounts to the truth of a general statement of the form

$$O_1(x_1, \ldots, x_n) \leqslant O_2(x_1, \ldots, x_n)$$

Where O_1 and O_2 are complex operations given by composing possibility operators, fusions and conjunctions. For the ideal structure, $O_1(I_1, \ldots, I_n) \leqslant O_2(I_1, \ldots, I_n)$ obtains just when

$$\{z : (\exists x_i \in I_i)(z \leqslant O_1(x_1, \ldots, x_n))\} \subseteq \{z : (\exists x_i \in I_i)(z \leqslant O_2(x_1, \ldots, x_n))\}$$

where 'O_1' and 'O_2' now refer to the corresponding operators in $\mathcal{P}$. Since the rule holds in $\mathcal{P}$, if $z \leqslant O_1(x_1, \ldots, x_n)$ we have $z \leqslant O_2(x_1, \ldots, x_n)$ too, giving us the structural rule in our ideal structure, as desired. □

LEMMA 9.32 (DEFINING RESIDUALS)
In any complete structure without left or right residuals, the functions

$$J \leftarrow I = \bigvee_{K \cdot I \leqslant J} K \qquad I \rightarrow J = \bigvee_{I \cdot K \leqslant J} K$$

of I and J are the right and left residuals of $\cdot$, respectively.

PROOF These are defined to satisfy the residuation conditions. For left residuation, note that if $K \cdot I \leqslant J$ then $K \leqslant J \leftarrow I$ by definition. Conversely, note that $(J \leftarrow I) \cdot I = (\bigvee_{K \cdot I \leqslant J} K) \cdot I = \bigvee_{K \cdot I \leqslant J} K \cdot I \leqslant J$. So, if $K \leqslant J \leftarrow I$ then $K \cdot I \leqslant J$ as desired. □

In the same way, we have the following result:

LEMMA 9.33 (DEFINING □ FROM ◇)
In any complete structure without □, the function $\Box I = \bigvee_{\Diamond J \leqslant I} J$ of I is the matching □ for ◇. □

THEOREM 9.34 (CONSERVATIVE EXTENSION)
A logic without any of disjunction, standard or converse implication is conservatively extended by adding (distributing) disjunction and each implication.

PROOF Consider something not provable in the original vocabulary in the original logic. There is some propositional structure that witnesses that fact. This structure can be embedded in a power structure in which disjunction and the residuals are defined. This is witness to the fact that the consecution is not provable in the extended logic either. □

One kind of conservative extension untouched by this method is that of extending some logic containing an operator by that operator's parent. This cannot be done by the techniques of this chapter, but must wait for Chapter 11.

9.3 Negation

Another problem not yet dealt with is the extension of a positive logic with negation. For some kinds of negation this is trivial — take a propositional letter p, and define $\sim_p A$ to be $A \rightarrow p$. The "negation" $\sim_p$ will satisfy many of the requirements for a negation. However, most often, double negation elimination is not among them. In most substructural logics, $(A \rightarrow p) \rightarrow p \vdash A$ fails. (As it ought: if $p = \top$, then $\top \vdash (A \rightarrow \top) \rightarrow \top$ would give $\top \vdash A$, which is repugnant, given that A is arbitrary.) So, defining negation in terms of a pre-existing intensional structure will not easily give us a de Morgan negation.

   In this section, we will use algebraic techniques to show that certain propositional structures can be embedded in larger structures on which a de Morgan negation can be defined. We dualise Meyer's construction in the case of R [156].

LEMMA 9.35 (EMBEDDING WITH A STRICT DE MORGAN NEGATION)
Any MALL$^+$ propositional structure can be embedded into a MALL propositional structure. If the original structure is distributive, so is the new structure. Similarly, if the original structure satisfies K, so does the new structure.

PROOF We take a MALL structure on the set P and complete it (if necessary) to ensure that it has a top element $\top$. and take another set Q disjoint from P and of the same cardinality as P. Let $-$ be a bijection from P to Q and back such that for any $x \in P \cup Q$, $--x = x$. Now we extend the other operations on $P \cup Q$. Let $a, b \in P$ and $x, y \in P \cup Q$.

$$a \wedge' b = a \wedge b \qquad a \wedge' -b = -b \qquad -a \wedge' b = -a \qquad -a \wedge -b = -(a \vee b)$$

$$a \vee' b = a \vee b \qquad a \vee' -b = a \qquad -a \vee' b = b \qquad -a \vee -b = -(a \wedge b)$$

$$a \cdot' b = a \cdot b \qquad a \cdot' -b = -(a \to b) \qquad -a \cdot' b = -(b \to a) \qquad -a \cdot' -b = \bot$$

$$x \to' y = -(x \cdot' -y)$$

It is tedious to check that the required postulates are satisfied. If the original structure was distributive, then so is the new structure. Similarly, if the original structure satisfies K, so does the new structure, as the top element is still the identity for fusion.

Fusion is clearly commutative. The fusion identity from P is still the identity here, since $t \to x = x$.

It is tedious to check that fusion is associative if it was associative in the original structure. Consider $x \cdot (y \cdot z)$. If $x, y, z \in P$, then associativity follows from that in P. Now suppose $x \in Q$. If $y \cdot z \in Q$ then $x \cdot (y \cdot z) = \bot$. $y \cdot z \in Q$ if and only if at least one of y and z is in Q. If $y \in Q$ then $x \cdot y = \bot$ and then if $z \in Q$, $\bot \cdot z = \bot$, and if $z \in P$ then $\bot \cdot z = -(z \to \top)$. However, $z \to \top = \top$, so $\bot \cdot z = \bot$ as desired. So if $x \in Q$ and $y \cdot z \in Q$ then $x \cdot (y \cdot z) = \bot = (x \cdot y) \cdot z$. Suppose, conversely, that $x \in Q$ and $y \cdot z \in P$. $y \cdot z \in P$ only when $y, z \in P$. In this case, $x \cdot y = -(y \to -x)$ and $(x \cdot y) \cdot z = -(z \to (y \to x))$. And similarly, $x \cdot (y \cdot z) = -((y \cdot z) \to x)$. In our context, $z \to (y \to x) = (y \cdot z) \to x$, so $x \cdot (y \cdot z) = (x \cdot y) \cdot z$. So we have dealt with the case $x \in Q$. Suppose now that $x \in P$, and at least one of $y, z \in Q$. In that case, $x \cdot (y \cdot z) = -(x \to -(y \cdot z))$. Suppose that y, z are both in Q. In that case, $y \cdot z = \bot$ and $x \cdot (y \cdot z) = x \cdot \bot = -(x \to \top) = \bot$. However, $x \cdot y$ in that case is in Q, as is z, so $(x \cdot y) \cdot z = \bot$. Suppose now that $y \in Q$ but $z \in P$. In that case, $y \cdot z = -(z \to -y)$ and $x \cdot (y \cdot z) = -(x \to (z \to -y))$. However, $(x \cdot y) \cdot z = -(x \to -y) \cdot z = -(z \to (x \to -y))$, but clearly this is identical to $-(x \to (z \to -y)) = x \cdot (y \cdot z)$. Our final case is $y \in P$ and $z \in Q$ (with $x \in P$). In that case, $x \cdot (y \cdot z) = x \cdot -(y \to -z) = -(x \to (y \to -z))$. But $(x \cdot y) \cdot z = -(x \cdot y \to -z) = -(x \to (y \to -z)) = x \cdot (y \cdot z)$, as desired.

Similarly, a case-by-case analysis shows that $x \cdot y \leqslant z$ if and only if $x \leqslant y \rightarrow z$. First, consider the case where $x, y \in Q$. Then $x \cdot y = \bot$ and $x \cdot y \leqslant z$. Then $y \rightarrow z = \top$ when $z \in P$ and we have $x \leqslant y \rightarrow z$. When $z \in Q$ then $y \rightarrow z = -(y \cdot -z) = --(-z \rightarrow -y) = -z \rightarrow -y \in P$, so we also have $x \leqslant y \rightarrow z$.

Suppose now that $z \in P$. Then if $x, y \in P$ too, $x \cdot y \leqslant z$ if and only if $x \leqslant y \rightarrow z$ by residuation on P. If one of $x, y \in Q$ then $x \cdot y \in Q$ and $x \cdot y \leqslant z$ follows immediately. Now consider $y \rightarrow z$. If $y \in P$ then $y \rightarrow z \in P$ and $x \leqslant y \rightarrow z$ as desired. If $x \in P$, then $y \in Q$ gives $y \rightarrow z = -(y \cdot -z) = \top$ as $y, -z \in Q$. Therefore, $x \leqslant y \rightarrow z$ as desired.

That deals with the case of $z \in P$. Now consider $z \in Q$. In this case $x \cdot y \not\leqslant z$ when $x \cdot y \in P$. We have $x \cdot y \in P$ if and only if $x, y \in P$, and in that case $y \rightarrow z \notin P$, so $x \not\leqslant y \rightarrow z$.

Suppose now that one of $x, y \in Q$. Deal first with $x \in Q$. Then $x \cdot y = -(y \rightarrow -x)$, and $x \cdot y \leqslant z$ iff $-(y \rightarrow -x) \leqslant z$ iff $-z \leqslant y \rightarrow -x$. Now $x \leqslant y \rightarrow z$ iff $x \leqslant -(y \cdot -z)$ iff $y \cdot -z \leqslant -x$, which holds iff $-z \leqslant y \rightarrow -x$, which is equivalent to $x \cdot y \leqslant z$ as desired. Suppose finally that $y \in Q$ and $x \in P$. Then $x \cdot y \leqslant z$ iff $-(x \rightarrow -y) \leqslant z$ iff $-z \leqslant x \rightarrow -y$. Now $x \leqslant y \rightarrow z$ iff $x \leqslant -(y \cdot -z)$ iff $y \cdot -z \leqslant -x$, which holds iff $-z \leqslant y \rightarrow -x = x \rightarrow -y$ as desired. $\square$

THEOREM 9.36 (CONSERVATIVE EXTENSION BY NEGATION)
Positive intuitionistic linear logic, C, BCK and CK are conservatively extended by a strict de Morgan negation.

It is also possible to show that positive R, E and other logics in their vicinity are similarly conservatively extended. The main difference is that the new propositions are placed *above* the old structure instead of below it, in order to validate $A \vee \sim A$. However, the proofs in these cases are more difficult, as more work must be done to ensure that $\top$ and $\bot$ work as needed. Consult Meyer's original proof [156] for details.

There is one substructural logic for which a conservative extension by negation fails: RM. Recall that RM is given by extending R with the mingle rule $X \Leftarrow X; X$, or equivalently, $A \circ A \rightarrow A$ (or $A \rightarrow (A \rightarrow A)$, if you want to eliminate fusion). We will show that the positive logic RM0, defined by adding mingle to positive R, is not conservatively extended by a de Morgan negation.

FACT: In RM0, $t \vdash (A \rightarrow B) \vee (B \rightarrow A)$ fails. This is is a corollary of the fact that $\top \vdash (A \rightarrow B) \vee (B \rightarrow A)$ fails in intuitionistic logic, which is a logic containing all of the RM0 theorems. In particular, the propositional structure on $\{\perp, a, b, c, \top\}$, with implication table and order

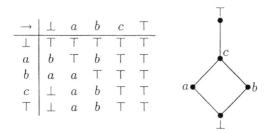

$\to$	$\perp$	a	b	c	$\top$
$\perp$	$\top$	$\top$	$\top$	$\top$	$\top$
a	b	$\top$	b	$\top$	$\top$
b	a	a	$\top$	$\top$	$\top$
c	$\perp$	a	b	$\top$	$\top$
$\top$	$\perp$	a	b	$\top$	$\top$

In this structure, $\top \not\vdash (a \to b) \vee (b \to a) = b \vee a = c$. So this consecution fails in J and hence in RM0. However, it is provable in RM0 with a strong de Morgan negation — i.e. in RM.

To do this, we first show that if we set $A + B$ to be $\sim A \to B$, then $A \dashv\vdash A + A$ in RM, since $A \dashv\vdash A \circ A$. (For this, we use the equivalence $A \circ A \dashv\vdash \sim(A \to \sim A)$, so $\sim A \dashv\vdash \sim(\sim A \to A)$, and hence $\sim A \dashv\vdash \sim A + \sim A$. But every proposition is equivalent to a negation — its double negation — so $A \dashv\vdash A+A$.) Furthermore, $A + B \vdash A \vee B$, since $A \to B \vdash \sim A \vee B$ in R.

Now, second, $A \to B$ is equivalent to $A + \sim B$, and furthermore, $(A + B) + C$ is equivalent to $A + (B + C)$. Neither of these rely on special RM facts. Now we proceed as follows. $t \vdash (A \to A) \wedge (B \to B)$. So $t \vdash (A + \sim A) \wedge (B + \sim B)$, and by the idempotence of fission, $t \vdash ((A + \sim A) \wedge (B + \sim B)) + ((A + \sim A) \wedge (B + \sim B))$. Therefore (since $+$ is monotonic) $t \vdash (A + \sim A) + (B + \sim B)$, and reassociating, we have $t \vdash (A + \sim B) + (B + \sim A)$, giving $t \vdash (A + \sim B) \vee (B + \sim A)$, which finally yields $t \vdash (A \to B) \vee (B \to A)$.

This shows that RM0 is not conservatively extended by a strong de Morgan negation.

9.4 Normal Modalities

We will round off this chapter with two sections on positive modalities. This section will present one more conservative extension given by complete propositional structures. The results in this section are presented in greater detail in my paper "Modalities in Substructural Logics" [210]. We will consider how to add □-style operators to our logics, which satisfy not only traditional modal axioms and rules but also rules that connect the modal part of the language with the behaviour of fusion and implication.

DEFINITION 9.37 (S4 NECESSITIES AND NECESSITIVES)
A □ in a propositional structure is an S4 necessity if and only if it satisfies the structural rules 4, T, mMP and Kr. It is an S5 necessity if and only if it also satisfies $A \vdash \Box \sim \Box \sim A$.

A necessitive in a propositional structure is an element x where $x = \Box y$ for some y.

S4 necessities satisfy the obvious rules. We will state them algebraically:

$$\Box x \leqslant \Box\Box x \ [4] \quad \Box x \leqslant x \ [\text{T}] \quad \Box(x \to y) \leqslant \Box x \to \Box y \ [\text{mMP}] \quad t \leqslant \Box t \ [\text{Kr}]$$

We already have the following conditions, from the usual properties of modal operators:

$$\Box x \wedge \Box y = \Box(x \wedge y) \qquad \Box\top = \top$$

LEMMA 9.38 (CLOSURE PROPERTIES OF NECESSITIVES)
If $\Box$ is an S4 necessity, then the necessitives of $\Box$ include $\bot$, $\top$ and t, and are closed under fusion, conjunction and disjunction.

PROOF   The necessitives of an S4 necessity are closed under $\wedge$ as $\Box x \wedge \Box y = \Box(x \wedge y)$. The necessitives include t, as $\Box t = t$ (by Kr and T), $\top$ as $\Box\top = \top$ and $\bot$ as $\Box\bot = \bot$ (by T). For disjunction we can argue as follows. If $x = \Box a$ and $y = \Box b$, then a simple verification will show that $x \vee y = \Box(x \vee y)$. First, $\Box(x \vee y) \leqslant x \vee y$ by T. Second, $x = \Box a \leqslant \Box\Box a = \Box x$ by 4 and $x \leqslant x \vee y$ gives $\Box x \leqslant \Box(x \vee y)$ so $x \leqslant \Box(x \vee y)$. Similarly, $y \leqslant \Box(x \vee y)$ so $x \vee y \leqslant \Box(x \vee y)$, giving us $x \vee y = \Box(x \vee y)$ as desired.

For fusion we reason similarly. We wish to show that $x \cdot y = \Box(x \cdot y)$. First, $\Box(x \cdot y) \leqslant x \cdot y$. But $x \leqslant y \to x \cdot y$ gives us $\Box x \leqslant \Box(y \to x \cdot y)$, so by mMP you get $\Box x \leqslant \Box y \to \Box(x \cdot y)$ so $\Box x \cdot \Box y \leqslant \Box(x \cdot y)$. However, $\Box x = x$ and $\Box y = y$, so we have $x \cdot y \leqslant \Box(x \cdot y)$ and our result.   □

So, given an S4 necessity, the necessitives are nicely structured. The necessitives form a lattice, including $\top$ and $\bot$ and closed under $\cdot$. Such a set deserves a name.

DEFINITION 9.39 (OPEN ELEMENTS)
A set $\mathcal{O}$ of elements in $\mathcal{P}$ is a *set of open elements* (a 'set of opens' for short) if and only if $\mathcal{O}$ is a sub-semilattice of $\mathcal{P}$, including $\top$ and $\bot$ and closed under $\cdot$.

Such a set is called the set of "opens" because it is very much like a set of open sets in a topological space [120]. This set of opens is all you need to construct the necessity operator. Given a set of opens in a complete propositional structure, we can define an S4 necessity as follows:

LEMMA 9.40 ($\Box$ RECOVERY)
If $\mathcal{O}$ is a set of opens in a completely distributive propositional structure, then the operator $\Box$, given by setting

$$\Box_\mathcal{O} x = \bigvee \{y : y \leqslant x \text{ and } y \in \mathcal{O}\}$$

is an S4 necessity.

PROOF This is a straightforward verification of the conditions for an S4 necessity. We will consider a few and leave the rest to the reader. (We will write '$\Box$' for '$\Box_{\mathcal{O}}$.')

$\Box x \wedge \Box y = \bigvee\{z : z \leqslant x$ and $z \in \mathcal{O}\} \wedge \bigvee\{z : z \leqslant y$ and $z \in \mathcal{O}\}$. By complete distributivity, this is equal to $\bigvee\{z : z \leqslant x, z \leqslant y$ and $z \in \mathcal{O}\}$, which in turn (by lattice properties) is $\bigvee\{z : z \leqslant x \wedge y$ and $z \in \mathcal{O}\} = \Box(x \wedge y)$ as desired.

As $\bot \in \mathcal{O}$, $\Box\bot = \bigvee\{z : z \leqslant \bot$ and $z \in \mathcal{O}\} = \bot$ as desired. As $\top \in \mathcal{O}$, $\Box\top = \bigvee\{z : z \leqslant \top$ and $z \in \mathcal{O}\} = \top$.

As $\mathcal{O}$ is closed under disjunction, $\Box x \in \mathcal{O}$ for each x, so $\Box\Box x = \Box x$ by definition. The other verifications are similar and are left to the reader. □

So we can construct a modal operator $\Box$, given a set of opens in a propositional structure. Choosing $\mathcal{O}$ wisely can mean that extra structural rules for $\Box_{\mathcal{O}}$ are satisfied, in particular the structural rules such as mW, mK and others, which constrain necessitives in ways that the whole propositional structure may not be. The conditions in Table 9.1 show rules which might govern necessitives.

Label	Condition	
mWI	$x \leqslant x \cdot x$	for $x \in \mathcal{O}$
mK	$x \cdot y \leqslant x$	for $x, y \in \mathcal{O}$
mM	$x \cdot x \leqslant x$	for $x \in \mathcal{O}$

Table 9.1: Conditions on Opens

LEMMA 9.41 (THE SET $\{\bot, t, \top\}$)
The set $\mathcal{O} = \{\bot, t, \top\}$ satisfies the rules in Table 9.1.
PROOF It is sufficient to produce a fusion table for $\mathcal{O}$.

$\cdot$	$\bot$	t	$\top$
$\bot$	$\bot$	$\bot$	$\bot$
t	$\bot$	t	$\top$
$\top$	$\bot$	?	$\top$

Only the value of $\top \cdot t$ is not determined by the rules for fusion and t. It is straightforward to check that the rules mWI, mK and mM hold on $\mathcal{O}$. □

The conservative extension result follows immediately from this lemma.

THEOREM 9.42 (CONSERVATIVE EXTENSION BY S4 NECESSITY)
Any logic with a propositional structure semantics including $\top$, $\bot$ and t is conservatively extended by an S4 necessity satisfying the rules mWI, mK and mM.

9.5 The Kleene Star in Structures

The intended interpretation of the Kleene star in a logic is infinitary iteration. In a propositional structure, we would like a^* to be the proposition $t \lor a \lor a^2 \lor a^3 \lor \cdots$ or more succinctly, $\bigvee_n a^n$. This, however, is not always the case. There are propositional structures in which there is an operator satisfying the rules of the star but which is *not* equivalent to $\bigvee_n a^n$. We present one simple example. Consider the structure on the set

$$\{\bot, 0, 1, 2, \ldots, \omega, \top\}$$

This set is ordered by the standard numerical order, with $\bot$ and $\top$ as least and greatest elements, respectively. This is a totally ordered set, so we can define $\land$ and $\lor$, which satisfy distributive lattice postulates. What is more, the lattice is complete. Every set has a least upper and a greatest lower bound. For fusion we use addition. $\top$ takes any "overflow" values, and $\bot \cdot x = \bot = x \cdot \bot$ for all x. In other words, we have the following table (in which n, m are arbitrarily chosen numbers from $\{1, 2, \ldots, \}$)

$\cdot$	$\bot$	0	m	ω	$\top$
$\bot$	$\bot$	$\bot$	$\bot$	$\bot$	$\bot$
0	$\bot$	0	m	ω	$\top$
n	$\bot$	n	$n+m$	$\top$	$\top$
ω	$\bot$	ω	$\top$	$\top$	$\top$
$\top$	$\bot$	$\top$	$\top$	$\top$	$\top$

Fusion is associative and commutative. Furthermore, contraction is valid, as $a \leqslant a^2$ holds for all a. The identity for fusion is 0. Fusion respects the order in the required way: if $a \leqslant a'$ and $b \leqslant b'$ then $a \cdot b \leqslant a' \cdot b'$. So we have a model for distributive lattice logic with fusion, which satisfies B, C and W.

Does this structure have a model for the Kleene star? Clearly $\bot^* = \bot$ and $0^* = 0$ will do. What about 1^*. The obvious choice might be to take ω, as $1 \cdot 1 = 2$, $1 \cdot 1 \cdot 1 = 3$ and so on. The infinite disjunction of these is the disjunction of $\{1, 2, 3, \ldots\}$, which is ω. However, this will not do, for the following reason: consider the rule $(*M)$. In our lattice this is interpreted as follows. If $x \leqslant 1^*$ and $y \leqslant 1^*$, then $x \cdot y \leqslant 1^*$. Therefore, if $\omega \leqslant 1^*$ we must have $\omega \cdot \omega \leqslant 1^*$. In other words, $\top \leqslant a^*$. We must have $1^* = \top$. The choice of ω will not do, as it is not a fixed point for fusion. Any choice of x^*, for whatever x you choose, must satisfy the identity $x^* \cdot x^* = x^*$. The rule $(*M)$ ensures that $x^* \cdot x^* \leqslant x^*$, and $t \leqslant x^*$ ensures that $x^* \leqslant t \cdot x^* \leqslant x^* \cdot x^*$. So any x^* must be a fixed point for fusion. The only fixed points for fusion in our model are $\bot$, 0 and $\top$. This ensures that our table for the Kleene star looks as follows:

x	$\perp$	0	m	ω	$\top$
x^*	$\perp$	0	$\top$	$\top$	$\top$

And it is not too difficult to show that the set defined in this way satisfies all of the rules for the Kleene star. We may describe this as follows. The logic of the Kleene star has *non-normal models*.

DEFINITION 9.43 (NORMAL STRUCTURES FOR THE KLEENE STAR)
A propositional structure with a * is *normal* if and only if for each a, $a^* = \bigvee a^n$.

However, the story does not end there. This propositional structure has other failings, which become clear when we examine the relationship between fusion and the order. This structure is complete, but fusion does not distribute over infinite joins. Consider

$$\bigvee (1 \cdot 1^n) = \bigvee 1^{n+1} = \omega$$

However,

$$1 \cdot \bigvee 1^n = 1 \cdot \omega = \top$$

Therefore, while we have a complete propositional structure, with fusion, the fusion operation does not *completely distribute*. This means that implication cannot be defined on this structure. There is a simple example explaining why. Were implication to be defined, we would have a value for $1 \to \omega$. What would it be? We ought to have $x \leqslant 1 \to \omega$ if and only if $x \cdot 1 \leqslant \omega$. Therefore, $n \leqslant 1 \to \omega$ for each number $n < \omega$, and hence, $\omega \leqslant 1 \to \omega$, since $\omega = \bigwedge \{1, 2, 3, \ldots\}$. However, if $\omega \leqslant 1 \to \omega$ we would have $\top = \omega \cdot 1 \leqslant \omega$, which is impossible. Therefore, implication cannot be defined on this structure. We end this section with a theorem which we name after Vaughan Pratt, who first noticed the connection between implication and normality of models for the Kleene star:

THEOREM 9.44 (PRATT NORMALITY THEOREM)
Any complete propositional structures for the Kleene star containing a residual for fusion is normal.

PROOF If $\to$ residuates $\cdot$, then $\cdot$ distributes over infinite joins where they exist. In any complete propositional structure, infinite joins do exist. It remains to show that $a^* = \bigwedge a^n$ under these conditions. Since $a^n \leqslant a^*$ for each n, we need to prove just that $a^* \leqslant \bigwedge a^n$. For this, we reason as follows: by distribution of fusion over disjunction, $(\bigwedge a^n) \cdot (\bigwedge a^n) = \bigwedge_{n,m} a^n \cdot a^n = \bigwedge_{n,m} a^{n+m} = \bigwedge_n a^n$ (by renumbering the sum appropriately). However, $a \leqslant \bigwedge a^n$ and $a^* \leqslant a^*$. So by $(*E)$ we have $a^* \leqslant \bigwedge a^n$ as desired. $\square$

9.6 History

Ideals come from the study of rings, from algebra. Ideals in rings are used to construct objects out of ring objects, satisfying some extra conditions. For an introduction to ring theory and other elements of modern algebra, Mac Lane and Birkhoff's *Algebra* is a classic [142].

Normality and the existence of non-normal models of the Kleene star comes from Conway's little book *Regular Algebra and Finite Machines* [47].

Došen has a paper examining the behaviour of modal operators in substructural logics and the way in which they facilitate translations from one logic into another [65].

Dunn's thesis pioneered the algebraic study of relevant logics [70]. Meyer and Routley used these techniques to give algebraic analyses of a large sweep of substructural logics [167], and Meyer, especially, used algebraic methods to great effect in proving significant results about relevant logics [154, 156, 157].

9.7 Exercises

Practice

{9.1} Show that a one-to-one and onto homomorphism from one partial order to another need not be an order embedding. (HINT: construct a one-to-one and onto homomorphism from the partial order of BN_4 to the four-element linear order.)

{9.2} Prove that there is no isomorphism between BN_4 and the four-element linear order.)

{9.3} Show that Peirce's law $((p \supset q) \supset p \vdash p)$ holds in every Boolean algebra. (HINT: Show that in a Boolean algebra, $p \supset q$ is equivalent to $\sim p \vee q$. Show that Peirce's law fails in the three-element Heyting lattice H_3, given in Figure 8.11 on page 179.)

{9.4} Consider the propositional structure defined on page 204. Find all split negations on that structure. Verify that none of them are strong de Morgan negations with respect to the implication defined on the structure. Do any negations satisfy the consecution $A \rightarrow \sim B \vdash B \rightarrow \sim A$?

{9.5} Find all necessity and possibility operators defined on the same structure.

Problems

{9.6} Show that if f is an isomorphism, so is f^{-1}.

{9.7} Verify that any structural rule satisfied by $\mathcal{P}$ and by $\mathcal{Q}$ is also satisfied by $\mathcal{P} \times \mathcal{Q}$, by any homomorphic image of $\mathcal{P}$ and by any substructure of $\mathcal{P}$.

{9.8} Verify that for any subset X of P, the domain of a propositional structure $\mathcal{P}$, that there is a smallest substructure $\mathcal{P}[X]$ of $\mathcal{P}$ containing X.

{9.9} Verify that the class of all substructures of $\mathcal{P}$ form a complete lattice under inclusion.

{9.10} Complete the proof of the Ideal Preservation Lemma, given on page 198.

{9.11} Use the map $\downarrow$ to show that if $\mathcal{P}$ is a non-distributive lattice, so is Ideal($\mathcal{P}$).

{9.12} The lattice of ideals of a distributive but not completely distributive lattice is completely distributive. The lattice in Figure 8.6 on page 164 is distributive but not completely distributive. Examine the structure of its lattice of ideals and show that it is indeed completely distributive. Explain how the definition of ideals could be changed to ensure that the ideals of a distributive but not completely distributive lattice themselves form a distributive but not completely distributive lattice.

{9.13} Complete the proof of Lemma 9.30 on page 198.

{9.14} Show that abelian logic, defined on page 174, cannot be given a natural deduction proof theory extending our basic logic with structural rules. (HINT: Consider the characteristic propositional structure $\mathbb{Z}$ for Abelian Logic. Show that it verifies $(A \rightarrow B) \rightarrow B \vdash A$. Show that this means that any Abelian logic propositional structure cannot contain $\top$ and $\bot$. Now consider the ideal structure of $\mathbb{Z}$ and apply Lemma 9.31.)

{9.15} Show that any logic is conservatively extended by what is called a *single alternative* necessity, that is, a necessity operator $\Box$ satisfying the extra conditions $\Box(A \vee B) \vdash \Box A \vee \Box B$ and $\Box \bot \vdash \bot$.

{9.16} Having completed the previous exercise, find which substructural logics can be conservatively extended by a single alternative necessity satisfying the extra rule $A \wedge \Box A \vdash \bot$.

{9.17} This result is taken from Niefield and Rosenthal's "Constructing Locales from Quantales" [185]. A *closure operator* C is a one-place operator on a propositional structure, satisfying $a \leqslant Ca$, $CCa \leqslant Ca$ and $Ca \cdot Ca \leqslant C(a \cdot b)$. The *closed elements* of a propositional structure with a closure operator C are the elements $b = Ca$ for some a. Given a propositional structure with a closure operator C, define $\cdot_C$ on the set of closed elements by setting $a \cdot_C b = C(a \cdot b)$. Show that this is a genuine fusion operator in the new structure of closed elements. What features does this new structure inherit from its parent? If a and b are closed, are $a \rightarrow b$ and $b \leftarrow a$?

This process goes in reverse. Given a propositional structure $\mathcal{P}$ with arbitrary joins, and an onto map $f : \mathcal{P} \rightarrow \mathcal{Q}$, show that f determines a closure operator C_f given by setting $C_f a = \bigwedge \{b : fb = fa\}$.

Projects

{9.18} Modify the embedding of a positive structure into one with a strong de Morgan negation (in Lemma 9.35) in such a way that the $\top$ and $\bot$ from the original positive structure remain the $\top$ and $\bot$ in the new structure.

{9.19} Extend the negation conservative extension result (Theorem 9.35) to include logics with other positive modal operators.

Chapter 10

Categories

The slogan is
"Adjoint functors arise everywhere."
— Saunders Mac Lane, Categories for the Working Mathematician [140], 1971

In propositional structures, we abstract away from the particulars of the languages in which our propositions are expressed to focus on the propositions themselves, ordered under entailment and operated on by conjunction, disjunction, implications, fusion, negations and so on. So in propositional structures, propositions are first-class citizens, and *proofs* between propositions fade into the background. They are merely registered by the presence or absence of the entailment relation. If there is a proof from A to B, then $[\![A]\!] \leqslant [\![B]\!]$. The differences between proofs from A to B are not registered in the algebraic semantics. Proofs are not first-class citizens.

Models do not have to be like this. We may enrich our algebraic modelling to consider not only propositions as objects but also proofs as "arrows" between objects. If we have one proof from A to B, we might indicate this as '$f : A \longrightarrow B$,' where f is the proof. We might have another proof $g : B \longrightarrow C$, and then we could *compose* them to construct another proof $gf : A \longrightarrow C$, which runs though f first and then g second.[1]

Logicians did not have to go to the trouble of inventing structures like this. It turns out that mathematical objects with just these properties have been widely studied for many decades. In this chapter we will run through some of the basic elements of *category theory* to give just a hint of how it is useful in the study of substructural logics. I cannot help but keep the exposition short and swift — but there will be many signposts on the way to more leisurely expositions that can treat the topic in more depth.

10.1 Categories in a Nutshell

Categories are deeply important mathematical structures. Category theory is a helpful language for describing constructions which appear in disparate parts

---

[1]   Can you see why we write this as 'gf' and not 'fg'? The parallel is with function application. If we think of f and g as functions, then $gf(x) = g(f(x))$ is an appropriate way to write the application of g to the result of f.

of mathematics. This means that category theory is, by its nature, very abstract. This also means that category theory is rich in examples. Category theory progresses in a dialectic between abstraction and concreteness, and this chapter is no different.

Before we continue, let me mention a couple of texts, as we cannot help but skirt lightly over this broad topic. Mac Lane's *Categories for the Working Mathematician* is a very good introduction to the area [140], very readable, even by those who are not working mathematicians. Barr and Wells' *Category Theory for Computing Science* is also clear, from a perspective of the theory of computation [14].

DEFINITION 10.1 (CATEGORIES AND FUNCTORS)
A *category* C consists of three things:

- A class of *objects*. (We name these using capital letters.)
- A class of *arrows*. (We name these with lower case letters.) Each arrow f has a *domain* $\text{dom}(f)$ and a *codomain* $\text{cod}(f)$, which are objects of the category. We write '$f : A \longrightarrow B$' to indicate that f is an arrow with domain A and codomain B.
- A notion of *composition* of arrows, such that for any arrows f and g where $\text{dom}(f) = \text{cod}(g)$, the arrow fg has domain $\text{dom}(g)$ and codomain $\text{cod}(f)$. Composition is *associative*, in that $f(gh) = (fg)h$, where the compositions are defined. Finally, for each object A there is an *identity arrow* $\text{id}_A : A \longrightarrow A$ such that $\text{id}_A f = f$ and $g\text{id}_A = g$ whenever these composites are defined.

For any categories C and D, a *functor* $F : C \longrightarrow D$ is a structure preserving mapping from C to D. That is, there are two functions F from objects of C to objects of D, and from arrows of C to arrows of D, satisfying the following conditions:

- If $f : A \longrightarrow B$ is an arrow of C then $F(f) : F(A) \longrightarrow F(B)$ is an arrow of D.
- $F(fg) = F(f)F(g)$ whenever fg is defined.
- $F(\text{id}_A) = \text{id}_{F(A)}$ for every A in A.

A category is *small* if the class of its objects is a set. It is said to be *large* otherwise.

Here are some categories.

EXAMPLE 10.2 (POSET CATEGORIES)
Any partially ordered set $\langle P, \leqslant \rangle$ is also a category, where you have exactly one arrow $\langle a, b \rangle$ between a and b just when $a \leqslant b$. So $\langle a, a \rangle$ is a's identity arrow,

and the composition of $\langle a, b \rangle$ and $\langle b, c \rangle$ is $\langle a, c \rangle$. A functor between two partially ordered sets (considered as categories) is an order-preserving mapping. So $\Box$, on a propositional structure, is a functor from that structure to itself (when considered as a category), for if $a \leqslant b$ then $\Box a \leqslant \Box b$. So is $\lambda x.(x \wedge a)$, the functor which sends an object b to $b \wedge a$. Similarly, $\lambda x.(a \vee x)$, $\lambda x.(a \circ x)$ and $\lambda x.(a \to x)$ are functors as they are all order-preserving.

We will call partially ordered sets, when seen as categories, *poset categories*.

Large categories are populated with many more objects. Here are some examples.

EXAMPLE 10.3 (CONCRETE CATEGORIES)
Given any kind of mathematical structure, such as lattices, groups, topological spaces and almost anything else, you have a category of those objects. The category of lattices contains all lattices as objects, and the arrows are lattice homomorphisms — preserving the lattice connectives. The composition of two lattice homomorphisms is itself a lattice homomorphism, and the identity map from a lattice to itself is also a lattice homomorphism. We will call this category **Lat**. The category of all distributive lattices is **DLat**. **PStruct**$[\circ, \to, \wedge]$ is the category of all propositional structures with fusion, implication and conjunction, with arrows all functions preserving these operations. Similarly, **Grp** is the category of all groups with group homomorphisms, **Top** is the category of all topological spaces and continuous functions, and **Set** is the category of all sets and arbitrary functions between sets. We will call categories of this form *concrete categories*.

For any concrete category, the *forgetful functor* $F : C \longrightarrow$ **Set** maps any algebraic structure to its underlying set, and maps any structure preserving mapping to its underlying set function. So, if L is a lattice, $F(L)$ is its underlying set. If $f : L \longrightarrow M$, then $F(f)$ maps the underlying set of L to the underlying set of M. It is simple to verify that F is indeed a functor.

DEFINITION 10.4 (OPPOSITE CATEGORIES)
Given a category C, its *opposite* C^{op} is the category with the same objects as C, but with arrows "inverted". That is, for each $f : A \longrightarrow B$ in C, there is a $f^{op} : B \longrightarrow A$ in C^{op}. Composition is defined by setting $(fg)^{op} = g^{op}f^{op}$, and $id_A^{op} = id_A$. (Exercise 10.1: Show that function composition in the opposite category is associative.)

A functor $F : C \longrightarrow D^{op}$ is sometimes called a *contravariant* functor $F : C \longrightarrow D$. If $f : A \longrightarrow B$ in C, then $F(f) : F(B) \longrightarrow F(A)$ in D. The functor reverses arrows.

EXAMPLE 10.5 (OPPOSITES OF POSET CATEGORIES)
The opposite of a poset category is the poset inverted. A contravariant functor from one poset to another is an order-inverting map. In particular, if $\sim$ is a negative operator on a propositional structure $\mathcal{P}$, it is a contravariant functor on $\mathcal{P}$.

DEFINITION 10.6 (ISOMORPHISM OF OBJECTS)
Two objects A and B in a category are *isomorphic* if and only if there are arrows $f : A \longrightarrow B$ and $g : B \longrightarrow A$, where $gf = \mathrm{id}_A$ and $fg = \mathrm{id}_B$.

Objects in categories are isomorphic just when anything you can do with one you can do just as well with the other. Any arrow $h : A \longrightarrow C$ can be replaced by the arrow $hg : B \longrightarrow C$ without any loss of information. Any arrow $h' : C \longrightarrow A$ can be replaced by an arrow $fh' : C \longrightarrow B$, and so on.

   Clearly, in a category which is simply a partial order, an object is isomorphic only to itself. In richer categories, more isomorphisms are possible.

DEFINITION 10.7 (Hom SETS AND Hom CLASSES)
Given two objects A and B in a category C, $\mathrm{Hom}_C(A, B)$ is the class of all arrows $f : A \longrightarrow B$. A category in which $\mathrm{Hom}_C(A, B)$ is a *set* for each A, B is said to be *locally small*.

All the categories we will consider in this chapter will be locally small. For example, in any concrete category, since the objects A and B are sets, the class of functions from A to B is bounded above (in size) by $|B|^{|A|}$.[2]

   We have already seen functors, which are the arrows in the category of categories. We need to consider one more level of complexity by introducing mappings between functors.[3]

DEFINITION 10.8 (NATURAL TRANSFORMATIONS)
A *natural transformation* $\alpha : F \longrightarrow G$ between two functors $F, G : C \longrightarrow D$ is a function from objects of C to arrows of D such that

   $\diamond$ $\alpha_A \in \mathrm{Hom}_D(F(A), G(A))$ for all A in C.
   $\diamond$ For all $f : A \longrightarrow B$ in C, $\alpha_B F(f) = G(f)\alpha_A : F(A) \longrightarrow G(B)$.

The definition of a natural transformation is not particularly perspicuous as it stands. It becomes clearer when expressed in a diagram. In the diagram in

---

[2]   Provided that functions in these categories are *extensional*. That is, if $f, g : A \longrightarrow B$ then when $f(x) = g(x)$ for each $x \in A$, we have $f = g$. In this case, there are $|B|$-many choices of output for each of $|A|$-many objects.
[3]   Category theory began when Mac Lane and Eilenberg defined the notion of a natural transformation. For that, they needed to define functors, and for functors, they needed to define categories. See *Categories for the Working Mathematician* for more on this subject [140].

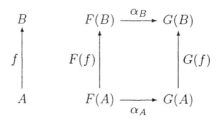

Figure 10.1: A Natural Transformation

Figure 10.1, the leftmost arrow, $f : A \longrightarrow B$ is in C. The arrows on the right are all in D. We say that the diagram *commutes*, as the result of composing arrows to get from $F(A)$ to $G(B)$ by *either* route is the same. In other words, $\alpha_B F(f) = G(f)\alpha_A$, as our definition says. It is clear that the arrows α_A and α_B are mapping the functor F to the functor G, as we had hoped.

EXAMPLE 10.9 (NATURAL TRANSFORMATIONS IN POSETS)
If C and D are poset categories, then $F, G : C \longrightarrow D$ are order-preserving mappings. Consider a natural transformation $\alpha : F \longrightarrow G$. In this case, $\alpha_A \in \mathrm{Hom}_D(F(A), G(A))$ simply means that $F(A) \leqslant G(A)$, as there is only one arrow from $F(A)$ to $G(A)$, if at all. Since α_A must be chosen from this Hom set, we must have $F(A) \leqslant G(A)$. It follows then that there is a natural transformation $\alpha : F \longrightarrow G$ only when $F \leqslant G$ when you compare them pointwise. That is, $F(A) \leqslant G(A)$ for each $A \in C$.

EXAMPLE 10.10 (NATURAL TRANSFORMATIONS IN CONCRETE CATEGORIES)
Any lattice L defines a functor $- \times L : \mathbf{Lat} \longrightarrow \mathbf{Lat}$, which takes a lattice to its product with L and maps lattice homomorphisms $f : M \longrightarrow N$ to $\langle f, \mathrm{id}_L \rangle : M \times L \longrightarrow N \times L$. Any lattice homomorphism $g : L_1 \longrightarrow L_2$ induces a natural transformation $\alpha(g) : - \times L_1 \longrightarrow - \times L_2$ by setting $\alpha(g)_M$ to be $\langle \mathrm{id}_M, g \rangle : M \times L_1 \longrightarrow M \times L_2$.

That is enough from category theory for us to begin examining how categories can model logics.

10.2 Extensional Connectives

We will use categories to model logics. Objects in categories will be interpreted as propositions, and arrows will be interpreted as proofs. Because arrows have one source and one target, we will be modelling consecutions of the form '$A \vdash$

B', instead of the more general '$X \vdash B$'. This is no loss of generality, as we may convert the structure X into a single formula.[4] We have already seen that for any object A in a category, id_A is an arrow from A to itself, so this can do to model the proof from A to itself by the identity axiom. Similarly, if $f : A \longrightarrow B$ and $g : B \longrightarrow C$, then $gf : A \longrightarrow C$ gives us the transitivity of proof. That deals with the connective-free properties of proofs in our logics — what we need now are the properties which deal with logical connectives.

Conjunction is simplest to start with. We know that $A \vdash B$ and $A \vdash C$ if and only if $A \vdash B \wedge C$. So we want a construction $*$ in a category such that if $f : A \longrightarrow B$ and $g : A \longrightarrow C$ then there is some arrow h (preferably constructed out of f and g in some way) such that $h : A \longrightarrow B * C$. Similarly, if $h : A \longrightarrow B * C$ we would like to be able to construct arrows $A \longrightarrow C$ and $A \longrightarrow B$. This sort of construction is known in category theory.

DEFINITION 10.11 (PRODUCTS IN CATEGORIES)
An object $A \times B$, together with arrows $\pi_l : A \times B \longrightarrow A$ and $\pi_r : A \times B \longrightarrow B$, is said to be a *product* of A and B if and only if whenever $f : C \longrightarrow A$ and $g : C \longrightarrow B$ there is a unique arrow $\langle f, g \rangle : C \longrightarrow A \times B$ such that the diagram below commutes.

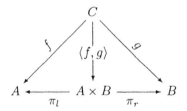

The maps π_l and π_r are the *projection maps* of the product $A \times B$. This construction models conjunction nicely. For example, $\pi_l : A \times B \longrightarrow A$ is the obvious proof which detaches the left conjunct from a conjunction. This then gives us our rules for conjunction.

$$\frac{f : A \longrightarrow B \quad g : A \longrightarrow C}{\langle f, g \rangle : A \longrightarrow B \times C} \qquad \frac{f : A \longrightarrow B \times C}{\pi_l f : A \longrightarrow B} \qquad \frac{f : A \longrightarrow B \times C}{\pi_r f : A \longrightarrow C}$$

EXAMPLE 10.12 (PRODUCTS IN POSET CATEGORIES)
Clearly the product of A and B in a partial order is the greatest lower bound of A and B. The projections π_l and π_r ensure that $A \times B \leqslant A$ and $A \times B \leqslant B$. The other condition ensures that if $C \leqslant A$ and $C \leqslant B$ then $C \leqslant A \times B$ as well.

---

[4] You do not *have* to do this. We could define *multicategories* in the way that Lambek and others have [135]. However, it is unclear whether any conceptual gain is given thereby, and the cost of moving away from standard category theory is significant.

EXAMPLE 10.13 (PRODUCTS IN CONCRETE CATEGORIES)
The product object $A \times B$ is typically constructed as a set of ordered pairs from A and B, which inherits its structure from that of A and B. For example, in the category **Lat** we can set $A \times B = \{\langle a, b \rangle : a \in A \text{ and } b \in B\}$ and define the lattice connectives "pointwise" by setting $\langle a, b \rangle \wedge \langle a', b' \rangle = \langle a \wedge a', b \wedge b' \rangle$ and $\langle a, b \rangle \vee \langle a', b' \rangle = \langle a \vee a', b \vee b' \rangle$. The projection functions work as expected: $\pi_l \langle a, b \rangle = a$ and $\pi_r \langle a, b \rangle = b$.

Our final example of a category with products is an important one. It stands to term assignment in the way that the Lindenbaum algebra stands to proof theory.

EXAMPLE 10.14 (TERM CATEGORIES)
Given a proof system with terms, the *term category* is defined as follows. The objects are the types of the proof system. The arrows are equivalence classes of *pairs*, the first component of which is a variable and the second a term with at most that variable free. So, if M has type B and then $\langle x_A, M \rangle$ is a representative of an arrow in the term category, the equivalence relation $\equiv$ identifies pairs with the same logical content. In particular, we demand that if $M \twoheadrightarrow M'$, then $(x_A, M) \equiv (x_A, M')$. Furthermore, if (y_A, M') results from a change of free or bound variables in (x_A, M) (simultaneously in both x_A and M), then this too is equivalent to (x_A, M). However, equivalent pairs will always have the same type characteristics. If (x, M) is equivalent to (y, M') then x and y have the same type, as do M and M'. In the rest of this chapter, we will write '$((x, M))$' for the equivalence class of all terms equivalent to (x, M).

If x has type A and M has type B, then $((x, M))$ is an arrow in the term category, from A to B. We compose these arrows in the natural way. If $((x, M)) : A \longrightarrow B$ and $((y, N)) : B \longrightarrow C$, then $((x, N[y := M])) : A \longrightarrow C$. It is not hard to check that this composition is associative (provided that equivalence and substitution interact appropriately). Furthermore, $((x_A, x_A)) : A \longrightarrow A$ is the identity arrow at A, as you can check.

Now, if the system of terms is equipped with constructors such as pairing $\langle -, - \rangle$ and fst and snd, then our term category is well on its way to having products. The natural choice is for $A \wedge B$ to be the product of A and B, and for $\pi_l : A \wedge B \longrightarrow B$ to be defined as $((x_{A \wedge B}, \text{fst } x_{A \wedge B}))$, and for π_r similarly to be $((x_{A \wedge B}, \text{snd } x_{A \wedge B}))$. This does the projections nicely. If $((y, M)) : C \longrightarrow A$ and $((y, N)) : C \longrightarrow B$, then the natural choice for the product map $C \longrightarrow A \wedge B$ is to pair the terms. $((y, \langle M, N \rangle)) : C \longrightarrow A \wedge B$ is our desired arrow.

This ensures that the diagram commutes. To see this, consider the composition of $((y_C, \langle M, N \rangle))$ (where $\langle M, N \rangle$ has type $A \wedge B$) with the projection $((x_{A \wedge B}, \text{fst } x))$. This is the equivalence class $((y_C, \text{fst } \langle M, N \rangle))$, and since fst $\langle M, N \rangle \longrightarrow M$ this class is equal to $((y_C, M))$, as we desired. The composition of pairing of arrows with left projection gives the left component of the pair. Similarly, the composition with right projection gives the right component.

However, this is only one part of the definition of products. We need not only that the diagram commutes but also that the pair $((y_C, \langle M, N \rangle))$ is the *only* arrow making the diagram commute. In other words, we have to show that if the arrow $((y_C, L))$ also makes the diagram commute, then $(y_C, L) \equiv (y_C, \langle M, N \rangle)$. (We can choose the same variable y_C in the representatives of the two classes, by simple relettering. This preserves equivalence.) For the diagram to commute, we need $(y_C, \text{fst } L) \equiv (y_C, M)$ and $(y_C, \text{snd } L) \equiv (y_C, N)$. For the identity, we need $(y_C, L) \equiv (y_C, \langle M, N \rangle)$. Substituting equivalents into M and N, we need $(y_C, L) \equiv (y_C, \langle \text{fst } L, \text{snd } L \rangle)$.

Why would this be? If $\equiv$ is generated by renaming variables and by reduction, then there is no need for L to be equivalent to $\langle \text{fst } L, \text{snd } L \rangle$. The reduction rules show us that fst $\langle M, N \rangle$ reduces to M, and that snd $\langle M, N \rangle$ reduces to N. In other words, *components of pairs* are what you would expect. Reduction defined for proofs does not tell us anything about *pairing components*. To provide a model of products in a category, we need to add this as an equivalence of terms. We need that to specify the following new equivalence on terms:

$$(y_C, L) \equiv (y_C, \langle \text{fst } L, \text{snd } L \rangle)$$

for each L of type $A \wedge B$. This corresponds to a reduction, which cuts out a detour consisting of a conjunction elimination and then a conjunction introduction. In this way, categories identify more proofs (more terms) than reduction in natural deduction systems.

Note that the definition of products says that an object is *a* product of A and B, not *the* product. Categories may have very many products of the one pair of objects. If we wished to be perverse, we could well define the product of A and B in the term category to be $B \wedge A$ (this is a different formula than $A \wedge B$, recall), with left projection snd and right projection fst. This would still satisfy the definition of a product. Many other definitions of products are also possible. However, we have the following theorem.

THEOREM 10.15 (ISOMORPHISM OF PRODUCTS)
Any two products of A and B are isomorphic.
PROOF   Suppose $A \times B$, with π_l and π_r as projections and $\langle -, - \rangle$ as the pair-constructor, and $A * B$ with p_l and p_r as projections and $(-, -)$ as the pair-constructor, are both products of A and B. Since $A \times B$ is a product of A and B, and since we have $p_l : A * B \longrightarrow A$ and $p_r : A * B \longrightarrow B$, it follows that $\langle p_l, p_r \rangle$ is the unique map from $A * B$ to $A \times B$. In just the same way, (π_l, π_r) is

the unique map from $A \times B$ to $A * B$. It is enough to show that $(\pi_l, \pi_r)\langle p_l, p_r \rangle$ and $\langle p_l, p_r \rangle (\pi_l, \pi_r)$ are identity arrows. □

If a category has products, then it is also possible to construct product arrows in the following way.

LEMMA 10.16 (PRODUCT ARROWS)
If a category has products, and if $f : A \longrightarrow B$ and $g : C \longrightarrow D$, then there is an arrow $f \times g : A \times C \longrightarrow B \times D$ such that

$$
\begin{array}{ccccc}
A & \xleftarrow{\;\pi_l\;} & A \times C & \xrightarrow{\;\pi_r\;} & C \\
\downarrow{\scriptstyle f} & & \downarrow{\scriptstyle f \times g} & & \downarrow{\scriptstyle g} \\
B & \xleftarrow[\pi_l]{} & B \times G & \xrightarrow[\pi_r]{} & D
\end{array}
$$

commutes.

PROOF Let $f \times g = \langle f\pi_l, g\pi_r \rangle$. This has the required properties. (See Exercise 10.2.) □

It is not too difficult to construct maps from $A \times A$ to A and back, showing that the two propositions $A \times A$ and A are *equivalent* in the sense that they co-entail one another. However, they are not necessarily *isomorphic*.

$$\pi_l : A \times A \longrightarrow A \qquad \langle \mathrm{id}_A, \mathrm{id}_A \rangle : A \longrightarrow A \times A$$

By definition, $\pi_l \langle \mathrm{id}_A, \mathrm{id}_A \rangle = \mathrm{id}_A$. However, $\langle \mathrm{id}_A, \mathrm{id}_A \rangle \pi_l : A \times A \longrightarrow A \times A$ need not be the identity arrow $\mathrm{id}_{A \times A}$. Indeed, in concrete categories, such as the category of sets, $\langle \mathrm{id}_A, \mathrm{id}_A \rangle \pi_l \neq \mathrm{id}_{A \times A}$ nearly always.

For disjunction, there is a dual construction which is given by reversing all the arrows in the definition of a product.

DEFINITION 10.17 (SUMS IN CATEGORIES)
An object $A + B$, together with arrows $\iota_l : A \longrightarrow A + B$ and $\iota_r : B \longrightarrow A + B$ is said to be a *sum* of A and B if and only if whenever $f : A \longrightarrow C$ and $g : B \longrightarrow C$ there is a unique arrow $[f, g] : A + B \longrightarrow C$ such that the diagram below commutes.

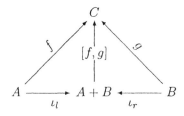

The maps ι_l and ι_r are the *injection* arrows of the sum $A+B$. (Note that a sum of A and B in C is a product of A and B in C^{op}. Sums give us our interpretation for disjunction.

$$\frac{f : B \longrightarrow A \quad g : C \longrightarrow A}{[f,g] : B + C \longrightarrow A} \qquad \frac{f : A \longrightarrow B}{\iota_l f : A \longrightarrow B+C} \qquad \frac{f : A \longrightarrow C}{\iota_r f : A \longrightarrow B+C}$$

To complete the lattice connectives we have special objects in certain categories. Sums in partial order categories are least upper bounds, as you would expect. More interesting is the behaviour of sums in concrete categories.

EXAMPLE 10.18 (SUMS IN CONCRETE CATEGORIES)
Sums in these standard categories are more varied than products. In *Set* and in *Poset* the sum of two objects is their disjoint union. Any maps from A to C and from B to C can be filtered through their disjoint union in a standard way. We inject A and B into $A + B$, and then map the two components of the disjoint union in the one map. A standard union would not do. Consider the map $+2 : \{0,1\} \longrightarrow \{2,3,4\}$ and the map $+1 : \{1,2\} \longrightarrow \{2,3,4\}$. I cannot filter these maps through the union $\{0,1,2\}$, as the object 1 gets mapped in two different ways. If I use the disjoint union $\{0^a, 1^a, 1^b, 2^b\}$, I can filter the maps through this set. I send the a-objects with $+2$, and the b-objects with $+1$.

EXAMPLE 10.19 (SUMS IN TERM CATEGORIES)
As you may expect, in the term category, we may define the sum of A and B as $A \vee B$. The injection arrows are

$$((x_A, \mathsf{inl}\,_B x_A)) : A \longrightarrow A \vee B \qquad ((x_B, \mathsf{inr}\,_A x_B)) : B \longrightarrow A \vee B$$

and given arrows $((y_A, M)) : A \longrightarrow C$ and $((z_B, N)) : B \longrightarrow C$, the arrow $[((y_A, M)), ((z_B, N))] : A \vee B \longrightarrow C$ can be defined as

$$((x_{A \vee B}, \mathsf{let}\ x\ \mathsf{be}\ y\ \mathsf{in}\ M\ \mathsf{or}\ z\ \mathsf{in}\ N)) : A \vee B \longrightarrow C$$

The diagram commutes, by the reduction rules we have defined for let terms, inl and inr. We have

$$((x_A, \mathsf{let}\ (\mathsf{inl}\ L)\ \mathsf{be}\ y\ \mathsf{in}\ M\ \mathsf{or}\ z\ \mathsf{in}\ N)) \equiv ((x_A, N[y := L]))$$

For the uniqueness of the arrow we need a new equivalence among terms. We need

$$((x_{A \vee B}, L)) \equiv ((x_{A \vee B}, \mathsf{let}\ x\ \mathsf{be}\ y\ \mathsf{in}\ L[x := \mathsf{inl}\ y]\ \mathsf{or}\ z\ \mathsf{in}\ L[x := \mathsf{inr}\ z]))$$

which is not demonstrable in our reduction system but again corresponds to the cutting out of an elimination and then an introduction. Once we allow this identification of proofs, we have a term model for sums.

Just as with products, any two sums of an object are isomorphic. (The proof of this fact is left to Exercise 10.3.)

DEFINITION 10.20 (CARTESIAN CATEGORIES)
A category is *cartesian* if every pair of objects has both sums and products.

In any cartesian category, for any objects A, B and C, there is an arrow

$$d_{A,B,C} : (A + B) \times (A + C) \longrightarrow A \times (B + C)$$

(find the arrow: Exercise 10.4). A category is said to be *distributive* if this arrow is an isomorphism. This is the generalisation of the case of distributive lattices, over and above lattices.

DEFINITION 10.21 (INITIAL AND TERMINAL OBJECTS)
An object **0** in a category is an *initial object* if and only if for every object A, there is exactly one arrow

$$\langle\rangle : \mathbf{0} \longrightarrow A$$

An object **1** in a category is a *terminal object* if and only if for every object A, there is exactly one arrow

$$[] : A \longrightarrow \mathbf{1}$$

Clearly, any two initial objects are isomorphic, and any two terminal objects are isomorphic.

We use the notations '$\langle\rangle$' and '$[]$' as initial objects can be thought of as empty products and terminal objects as empty sums.

EXAMPLE 10.22 (INITIAL AND TERMINAL OBJECTS IN CATEGORIES)
In poset categories, **0** is $\perp$ and **1** is $\top$. The situation becomes more interesting in concrete categories. In the category of lattices, **1** is a one-point lattice, as there is exactly one homomorphism from each lattice to a one-point lattice. **0** is the empty lattice, as the empty map is the only map from **0** to each lattice. In the category $\mathbf{Lat}[\top, \perp]$ of bounded lattices with maps preserving $\top$ and $\perp$, **1** is again the single-element lattice, in which $\top = \perp$, **0** is now the *two*-element lattice $\{\top, \perp\}$, as the map from $\{\top, \perp\}$ to any lattice at all is completely determined. Finally, in the category $\mathbf{Lat}[\top]$ of lattices with top elements (and $\top$-preserving mappings), the one-element lattice $\{\top\}$ is *both* initial *and* terminal.

This last example shows that categories and propositional structures can differ greatly. The only posets in which $\top = \perp$ are trivial. A category can have rich structure, while allowing **1** = **0**. In this case, there are arrows between every pair of objects. It does not follow that all objects are *isomorphic*. The category can still make many distinctions between objects and between arrows, despite the fact that when interpreted as a logic, the category is "trivial" in the sense that all propositions entail all others.

EXAMPLE 10.23 (INITIAL AND TERMINAL OBJECTS IN TERM CATEGORIES)
In term categories, we have $\top$ as a terminal object and $\bot$ as an initial object.
$((x_A, \star)) : A \longrightarrow \top$, and $((x_\bot, \text{let } x \text{ be } \dagger_A)) : \bot \longrightarrow A$ are the required arrows
for each A. However, yet again, uniqueness is not satisfied. We need to pos-
tulate extra equivalences to ensure that these are genuine initial and terminal
objects in the term category:

$$((x_A, M)) \equiv ((x_A, \star)) \qquad \text{if } M \text{ has type } \top$$
$$((x_\bot, M)) \equiv ((x_\bot, \text{let } x \text{ be } \dagger_A)) \qquad \text{if } M \text{ has type } A$$

These equivalences are rather heavy-handed. However, they are necessary to
make sure that the term category has genuine initial and terminal objects in the
category-theoretic sense.

Lastly, we have intuitionistic implication to consider. We wish to go from $f : A \times B \longrightarrow C$ to some arrow from A to $[B \Rightarrow C]$, and in reverse. These constructions
are also known in category theory.

DEFINITION 10.24 (FUNCTION OBJECTS IN CATEGORIES)
An object $[A \Rightarrow B]$, together with an arrow $\text{ev} : [A \Rightarrow B] \times A \longrightarrow B$, is said to
be a *function object* from A to B if and only if whenever $f : C \times A \longrightarrow B$ there
is a unique arrow $\lambda f : C \longrightarrow [A \Rightarrow B]$ such that the diagram below commutes.

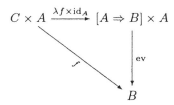

In the category theoretic literature, $[A \Rightarrow B]$ is often written 'B^A' but we write
it with the arrow (following Barr and Wells [14]) to make the connection with
implication clear.

DEFINITION 10.25 (CARTESIAN CLOSED CATEGORIES)
A category is *cartesian closed* if it is cartesian and, in addition, has function
objects.

EXAMPLE 10.26 (FUNCTION OBJECTS IN PARTIAL ORDER CATEGORIES)
In partial order categories, function objects are simply residuals for conjunction:
that is, intuitionistic implication.

EXAMPLE 10.27 (FUNCTION OBJECTS IN CONCRETE CATEGORIES)
$[A \Rightarrow B]$ is usually constructed as the set of all homomorphisms from A to B, equipped with some sort of structure inherited from A and B. For example, in *Lat* we can give a lattice structure to $[A \Rightarrow B]$ as follows: $(f \wedge g)(x) = f(x) \wedge g(x)$, and $(f \vee g)(x) = f(x) \vee g(x)$. The evaluation functor ev : $[A \Rightarrow B] \times A \longrightarrow B$ maps pairs $\langle f, x \rangle$ to $f(x)$. This is a lattice homomorphism.

EXAMPLE 10.28 (FUNCTION OBJECTS IN TERM CATEGORIES)
It should come as no surprise that in the term category, we define the function object from A to B as $A \supset B$. It is intuitionistic implication, where that exists. The evaluation arrow from $(A \supset B) \wedge A$ to B is $((x_{(A \supset B) \wedge A}, (\text{fst } x)(\text{snd } x)))$. It takes an object and applies its first component to its second component. Given an arrow $((x_{C \wedge A}, M)) : C \wedge A \longrightarrow B$, we define $\lambda((x_{C \wedge A}, M)) : C \longrightarrow A \supset B$ by setting it to be $((y_C, \lambda z_A M[x := \langle y_C, z_A \rangle]))$. We verify that the diagram so defined commutes:

$$
\begin{aligned}
&\mathsf{ev}_{(A \supset B) \wedge A}(\lambda((x_{C \wedge A}, M)) \times \mathsf{id}_A) \\
&\equiv \quad \mathsf{ev}((x, \langle (\lambda z_A M[x := \langle y_C, z_A \rangle]) \pi_l, \mathsf{id}_A \pi_r \rangle)) \\
&\equiv \quad \mathsf{ev}((x, \langle (\lambda z M[x := \langle \mathsf{fst}\, x, z \rangle]), \mathsf{snd}\, x \rangle)) \\
&\equiv \quad ((x, \mathsf{fst}\, \langle (\lambda z M[x := \langle \mathsf{fst}\, x, z \rangle]), \mathsf{snd}\, x \rangle \mathsf{snd}\, \langle (\lambda z M[x := \langle \mathsf{fst}\, x, z \rangle]), \mathsf{snd}\, x \rangle)) \\
&\equiv \quad ((x, (\lambda z M[x := \langle \mathsf{fst}\, x, z \rangle]) \mathsf{snd}\, x)) \\
&\equiv \quad ((x, M[x := \langle \mathsf{fst}\, x, \mathsf{snd}\, x \rangle])) \\
&\equiv \quad ((x_{C \wedge A}, M))
\end{aligned}
$$

as desired, because we have $\langle \mathsf{fst}\, x, \mathsf{snd}\, x \rangle \equiv x$. For uniqueness, we need that if $((x, N)) : C \longrightarrow A \supset B$, where $\mathsf{ev}(((x_C, N)) \times \mathsf{id}_A) \equiv ((y_{C \wedge A}, M))$, then $((x_C, N)) \equiv \lambda((y_{C \wedge A}, M))$. For this, the equivalence

$$((x_C, N)) \equiv \lambda\big(\mathsf{ev}(((x_C, N)) \times \mathsf{id}_A)\big)$$

suffices.

We have the following modellings of the implication rules:

$$
\frac{f : A \times B \longrightarrow C}{\lambda f : A \longrightarrow [B \Rightarrow C]}
\qquad
\frac{g : A \longrightarrow [B \to C]}{\mathsf{ev}(g \times \mathsf{id}) : A \times B \longrightarrow C}
$$

This mapping is an isomorphism between $\mathrm{Hom}(A \times B, C)$ to $\mathrm{Hom}(A, [B \Rightarrow C])$. This is an example of a very general concept: an *adjunction*. We will consider this in the next section.

10.3 Intensional Connectives

To model the other connectives of our logics in categories, we need to examine one new category-theoretic concept: the concept of *adjunction*. Let us start with an example.

EXAMPLE 10.29 (FREE AND FORGETFUL FUNCTORS)
Consider the categories *Set* and *RStruct*, of sets and of R propositional structures respectively. Let the functor $F : RStruct \longrightarrow Set$ be the forgetful functor, which sends an R structure to its underlying set, and an R homomorphism to its underlying set function. Let $L : Set \longrightarrow RStruct$ send the set X to the free R structure generated by X. That is, it constructs the Lindenbaum algebra, with atomic propositions taken from X. Any set function $f : X \longrightarrow Y$ extends to the R homomorphism $L(f) : L(X) \longrightarrow L(Y)$, sending atomic propositions in $L(X)$ to their f-values in $L(Y)$.

These functors are related in the following way. Whenever we have a propositional structure P and a set X, any set function $g : X \longrightarrow F(P)$ extends *uniquely* to a corresponding R homomorphism $g^R : R(X) \longrightarrow P$. Furthermore, any function $f : R(X) \longrightarrow P$ can be restricted to the function $f|_X : X \longrightarrow F(P)$, such that $f = (f|_X)^R$. In other words, we have a bijection

$$\phi_{X,P} : \mathrm{Hom}_{Set}(X, F(P)) \cong \mathrm{Hom}_{RStruct}(L(X), P)$$

and furthermore, this bijection is *natural* in both X and P, in the category theoretic sense. That is

$$
\begin{array}{ccc}
X & \mathrm{Hom}_{Set}(X, F(P)) \xrightarrow{\phi_{X,P}} \mathrm{Hom}_{RStruct}(L(X), P) \\
\Big\uparrow{\scriptstyle f} & \Big\downarrow{\scriptstyle f^*} \qquad\qquad\qquad \Big\downarrow{\scriptstyle (Lf)^*} \\
X' & \mathrm{Hom}_{Set}(X', F(P)) \xrightarrow[\phi_{X',P}]{} \mathrm{Hom}_{RStruct}(L(X'), P)
\end{array}
$$

(where if $f : X' \longrightarrow X$ then $f^* : \mathrm{Hom}(X, Y) \longrightarrow \mathrm{Hom}(X', Y)$ is defined in the following way: $f^*(g) = gf$) and

$$
\begin{array}{ccc}
P & \mathrm{Hom}_{Set}(X, F(P)) \xrightarrow{\phi_{X,P}} \mathrm{Hom}_{RStruct}(L(X), P) \\
\Big\downarrow{\scriptstyle g} & \Big\downarrow{\scriptstyle (Fg)^*} \qquad\qquad\qquad \Big\downarrow{\scriptstyle g^*} \\
P' & \mathrm{Hom}_{Set}(X, F(P')) \xrightarrow[\phi_{X,P'}]{} \mathrm{Hom}_{RStruct}(L(X), P')
\end{array}
$$

commute. The commutation of both of these diagrams follows immediately by the definitions of F and L, and by the bijection ϕ between arrows.

This behaviour occurs *everywhere* in mathematics. Many pairs of functors are related in a similar way. It warrants a definition.

DEFINITION 10.30 (ADJOINT PAIRS)
If $F : C \longrightarrow D$ and $G : D \longrightarrow D$, and there is a bijection $\phi : \mathrm{Hom}_C(X, F(Y)) \cong \mathrm{Hom}_D(G(X), Y)$, natural in both X and Y, then we say that $\langle F, G, \phi \rangle$ is an *adjunction*. F is the *left adjoint* and G is the *right adjoint*. We write the presence of the adjunction as '$F \dashv G$.'

We have already seen adjoint pairs.

EXAMPLE 10.31 (ADJUNCTION BETWEEN PRODUCT AND IMPLICATION)
We have seen that we can think of products as functors. In particular, $- \times B$ is a functor $C \longrightarrow C$. Similarly, $[B \Rightarrow -]$ is a functor $C \longrightarrow C$. These functors form an adjunction. If $f : A \times B \longrightarrow C$, then $\lambda f : A \longrightarrow [B \Rightarrow C]$. Conversely, if $g : A \longrightarrow [B \rightarrow C]$, then $\mathrm{ev}(g \times \mathrm{id}_B) : A \times B \longrightarrow C$. This is a bijection $\mathrm{Hom}(A \times B, C) \cong \mathrm{Hom}(A, [B \Rightarrow C])$. Therefore, the connection between products and implication can be expressed rather neatly:

$$- \times B \dashv [B \Rightarrow -]$$

Given this connection, it is obvious how other one-place intensional connectives ought to be modelled in categories. Positive operators $\square$ and $\Diamond$ are both functors $C \longrightarrow C$. These form an adjoint pair $\Diamond \dashv \square$. There is a bijection $\phi : \mathrm{Hom}(\Diamond A, B) \cong \mathrm{Hom}(A, \square B)$, between arrows $f : \Diamond A \longrightarrow B$ and arrows $\phi f : A \longrightarrow \square B$.

EXAMPLE 10.32 (MODALITIES IN THE TERM CATEGORY)
In the term category, we can define the bijection between arrows as follows. If $((x_{\Diamond A}, M)) : \Diamond A \longrightarrow B$ then $((y_A, \mathrm{up}\, M[x := \bullet y])) : A \longrightarrow \square B$. And conversely, if $((y_A, N)) : A \longrightarrow \square B$ then we have $((x_{\Diamond A}, \mathrm{down}\,(\mathrm{let}\; x \;\mathrm{be}\; \bullet y \;\mathrm{in}\; N))) : \Diamond A \longrightarrow B$. For this to be an adjunction, we need the translation to be an isomorphism, and for this we need two reduction rules: one we already have, down up $N \leadsto N$, and one which we do not, up down $N \leadsto N$.

Negative operators are only marginally more difficult. Negation is not a functor $C \longrightarrow C$, as it is *order inverting*. If $f : A \longrightarrow B$, then we have $\sim f : \sim B \longrightarrow \sim A$. So, instead, negation is modelled by a contravariant functor, that is, a normal functor to the opposite category: $C \longrightarrow C^{op}$. Here, the rules from $A \vdash \sim B$ to $B \vdash \neg A$ motivate an adjunction: $\mathrm{Hom}_C(A, \sim B) \cong \mathrm{Hom}_{C^{op}}(\neg A, B)$. We do not have a term category here, as we have not defined term systems for logics with split negations.

Finally, for fusion and implication, fusion is a bifunctor $\circ : C \times C \longrightarrow C$. This means not only that for each pair of objects A and B there is a corresponding object $A \circ B$ but also that when there are arrows $f : A \longrightarrow B$ and $g : C \longrightarrow D$ then there is an arrow $f \circ g : A \circ C \longrightarrow B \circ D$. If we have implication connectives, their properties are given by adjointness.

$$\phi_{\text{left}} : \text{Hom}_C(A \circ B, C) \cong \text{Hom}_C(B, C \rightarrow A)$$
$$\phi_{\text{right}} : \text{Hom}_C(A \circ B, C) \cong \text{Hom}_C(A, B \rightarrow C)$$

This is enough to define the basic logic of fusion and implication in substructural logics. Correspondence with the term category is not any more difficult than what we have seen before, so we will not pause to examine that connection. Instead, we must say a little about structural rules.

In propositional structures, structural rules correspond to entailments between particular fusions of propositions. For example, in the presence of CI we have $a \cdot b \leqslant b \cdot a$. In a category, the corresponding requirement would be for there to be an arrow

$$\gamma_{A,B} : A \circ B \longrightarrow B \circ A$$

for each A and B in the category. It turns out to be advantageous to require that γ be *natural* in both A and B. That is, if $f : A \longrightarrow A'$ and if $g : B \longrightarrow B'$ then the following diagram commutes

$$
\begin{array}{ccc}
A \circ B & \xrightarrow{f \circ g} & A' \circ B' \\
\downarrow{\gamma_{A,B}} & & \downarrow{\gamma_{B',A'}} \\
B \circ A & \xrightarrow{g \circ f} & B' \circ A'
\end{array}
$$

In many applications, it is also advantageous to assume that $\gamma_{A,B}$ is an isomorphism: that $\gamma_{B,A}\gamma_{A,B} = \text{id}_{A \circ B}$. Similar properties can hold given association. In the presence of B and B^c we have an arrow

$$\alpha_{A,B,C} : A \circ (B \circ C) \longrightarrow (A \circ B) \circ C$$

which is natural in A, B and C (draw the appropriate diagram yourself) and satisfies the following *pentagonal condition*.

$$A \circ (B \circ (C \circ D)) \xrightarrow{\alpha_{A,B,C \circ D}} (A \circ B) \circ (C \circ D) \xrightarrow{\alpha_{A \circ B,C,D}} ((A \circ B) \circ C) \circ D$$

$$\text{id}_A \circ \alpha_{B,C,D} \downarrow \qquad\qquad\qquad\qquad\qquad\qquad \downarrow \alpha_{A,B,C} \circ \text{id}_D$$

$$A \circ ((B \circ C) \circ D) \xrightarrow[\alpha_{A,B \circ C,D}]{\qquad\qquad\qquad\qquad\qquad\qquad\qquad} (A \circ (B \circ C)) \circ D$$

and if γ is present, then the following *interaction condition*

$$A \circ (B \circ C) \xrightarrow{\alpha_{A,B,C}} A \circ (B \circ C) \xrightarrow{\gamma_{A \circ B,C}} C \circ (A \circ B)$$

$$\text{id}_A \circ \gamma_{B,C} \downarrow \qquad\qquad\qquad\qquad\qquad\qquad \downarrow \alpha_{C,A,B}$$

$$A \circ (C \circ D) \xrightarrow[\alpha_{A,C,B}]{\qquad} (A \circ C) \circ B \xrightarrow[\gamma_{A,C} \circ \text{id}_B]{\qquad} (C \circ A) \circ B$$

Monoidal categories are those with a fusion operation together with association arrows $\alpha_{A,B,C}$ and an identity for fusion. A monoidal category is *symmetric* when it also has commutation arrows $\gamma_{A,B}$. The *coherence* problem for these categories is to determine which diagrams involving these arrows commute. Mints and Lambek have used logical techniques to solve the coherence problem for symmetric monoidal categories, and monoidal categories [141, 135, 174]. We will not present these proofs here. Instead, we will look at a particular category which exhibits these structures.

10.4   Coherence Spaces

Coherence spaces provide a concrete model for the connectives of linear logic. In particular, they provided the first model which gave Girard an insight into the nature of the exponentials [96]. We will round this chapter off by presenting an account of coherence spaces.

DEFINITION 10.33 (COHERENCE SPACES)
A *coherence space* is a set $\mathcal{A}$ of sets, satisfying the following two conditions.

  ⋄ If $a \in \mathcal{A}$ and $b \subseteq a$ then $b \in \mathcal{A}$, and
  ⋄ If for each $x, y \in a$, $\{x, y\} \in \mathcal{A}$, then $a \in \mathcal{A}$.

We say a *coheres* with b (in $\mathcal{A}$) if $\{x, y\} \in \mathcal{A}$. We write this: '$x \frown y \pmod{\mathcal{A}}$.'

A coherence space is determined by its coherence relation $x \frown y$ (mod $\mathcal{A}$) on the set $|\mathcal{A}|$ of objects x, where $\{x\} \in \mathcal{A}$. If $\mathcal{A}$ and $\mathcal{B}$ have the same coherence relation, then if $x \in \mathcal{A}$, we can show that $a \in \mathcal{B}$. If $a \in \mathcal{A}$ then every $\{x, y\} \subseteq \mathcal{A}$ is in $\mathcal{A}$. Then $x \frown y$, and hence $\{x, y\} \in \mathcal{B}$, for each $\{x, y\} \subseteq a$ is in $\mathcal{B}$, and hence $a \in \mathcal{B}$.

So coherence spaces can be depicted simply as undirected graphs. The coherence relation is reflexive and symmetric, but not, in general, transitive.

In this space, the coherent sets are

$$\emptyset \quad \{0\} \quad \{1\} \quad \{2\} \quad \{3\} \quad \{4\} \quad \{0, 1\} \quad \{0, 2\} \quad \{1, 2\}$$
$$\{1, 3\} \quad \{2, 3\} \quad \{3, 4\} \quad \{0, 1, 2\} \quad \{1, 2, 3\}$$

DEFINITION 10.34 (COHERENCE RELATIONS)
Given a coherence space $\mathcal{A}$, we set

⋄ $x \frown y$ (mod $\mathcal{A}$) iff $x \frown y$ (mod $\mathcal{A}$) and $x \neq y$.
⋄ $x \smile y$ (mod $\mathcal{A}$) iff $\{x, y\} \notin \mathcal{A}$, i.e., if it is not the case that $x \frown y$ (mod $\mathcal{A}$).
⋄ Finally, $x \asymp y$ (mod $\mathcal{A}$) iff it is not the case that $x \frown y$ (mod $\mathcal{A}$), i.e., $x = y$ or $\{x, y\} \notin \mathcal{A}$.

Given a coherence space $\mathcal{A}$, the coherence space $\sim\!\mathcal{A}$ is defined by setting $x \frown y$ (mod $\sim\!\mathcal{A}$) if and only if $x \asymp y$ (mod $\mathcal{A}$). Note that $\sim\!\sim\!\mathcal{A} = \mathcal{A}$.

EXAMPLE 10.35 (SMALL COHERENCE SPACES)
Sgl $= \{\emptyset, \{*\}\}$, the one-point coherence space. Emp $= \{\emptyset\}$, the empty coherence space. Note that $\sim$Sgl $=$ Sgl and $\sim$Emp $=$ Emp.

We will (slowly) make the class of all coherence spaces into a category. However, it will take some time to form the available arrows in the category. However, we will start to consider products and sums in the category, nevertheless.

DEFINITION 10.36 (PRODUCT AND SUM COHERENCE SPACES)
Given coherence spaces A and B, the coherence spaces $A \wedge B$ and $A \vee B$ are
defined on the disjoint union of the points x of the graph of A and y of the
graph of B, as follows:

$$(0, x) \frown (0, x') \pmod{A \wedge B} \quad \text{iff } x \frown x' \pmod{A}$$
$$(1, y) \frown (1, y') \pmod{A \wedge B} \quad \text{iff } y \frown y' \pmod{B}$$
$$(0, x) \frown (1, y) \pmod{A \wedge B} \quad \text{always}$$

$$(0, x) \frown (0, x') \pmod{A \vee B} \quad \text{iff } x \frown x' \pmod{A}$$
$$(1, y) \frown (1, y') \pmod{A \vee B} \quad \text{iff } y \frown y' \pmod{B}$$
$$(0, x) \frown (1, y) \pmod{A \vee B} \quad \text{never}$$

Note that here $\sim(A \wedge B) = \sim A \vee \sim B$, and $\sim(A \vee B) = \sim A \wedge \sim B$. Furthermore,
$A \wedge \mathsf{Emp} = \mathsf{Emp} \wedge A = A = A \vee \mathsf{Emp} = \mathsf{Emp} \vee A$. We will see, later, that Emp
is both initial and terminal in the category of coherence spaces.

To do this, we need to examine the appropriate arrows in the category of
coherence spaces.

DEFINITION 10.37 (CONTINUOUS FUNCTIONS)
$F : A \longrightarrow B$ is *continuous* if and only if

$\diamond$ If $a \subseteq b$ then $F(a) \subseteq F(b)$.

$\diamond$ If $S \subseteq A$ is *directed* (that is, if $a, b \in S$, then $a \cup b \in S$ too) then $F(\bigcup S) = \bigcup \{F(a) : a \in S\}$.

Note that if F is continuous, then $F(a)$ is determined by the value of F at the finite subsets a' of a. In other words, $F(a) = \bigcup \{F(a') : a' \subseteq a$ where a' is finite$\}$.

LEMMA 10.38 (MINIMAL REPRESENTATIVES)
*If $F : A \longrightarrow B$ is continuous, and if $a \in A$ and $y \in F(a)$, then there is a minimal
finite $a' \in A$ where $y \in F(a')$.*

PROOF If $y \in F(a)$ then $y \in F(a^*)$ for some finite a^*. Pick some *smallest* subset
a' of a^* with this property. (This is possible, as a^* is finite.)   □

We want to construct a coherence space representing $F : A \longrightarrow B$. We start by
defining the trace of a function.

$$\mathrm{Trace}(F) = \{(a, y) \in A_{\mathsf{fin}} \times |B| : y \in F(a) \text{ and } a \text{ is minimal}\}$$

Note that $\mathrm{Trace}(F) \subseteq A_{\mathsf{fin}} \times |B|$ has the following properties.

$\diamond$ If $(a, y), (a, y') \in \mathrm{Trace}(F)$ then $y \frown y' \pmod{B}$.

$\diamond$ If $a' \subseteq a$, $(a, y), (a', y) \in \mathrm{Trace}(F)$, then $a = a'$.

Conversely, if $\mathcal{F}$ is any set with these two properties, then define $F_{\mathcal{F}}$ by setting

$$F_{\mathcal{F}}(a) = \{y \in |\mathcal{B}| : \exists a' \subseteq a \text{ where } (a', y) \in \mathcal{F}\}$$

So we can represent continuous functions by their traces. In fact, if F is continuous, then $F = F_{\text{Trace}(F)}$. Can we define a coherence relation on traces? Consider the special case where there are *two* minimal representatives, that is, $(a, y), (a', y) \in \text{Trace}(F)$. Under what circumstances are they coherent? Unfortunately, we need more information in order to define a coherence relation — we need a relationship between a and a'. We can show that in a particular class of continuous functions, there is always a *unique* minimal a.

DEFINITION 10.39 (STABLE FUNCTIONS)
$F : \mathcal{A} \longrightarrow \mathcal{B}$ is *stable* if it is continuous, and in addition, whenever $a, a', a \cup a' \in \mathcal{A}$, then $F(a \cap a') = F(a) \cap F(a')$.

With stable functions, we can choose a unique minimal representative a.

LEMMA 10.40 (UNIQUE MINIMAL REPRESENTATIVES)
$F : \mathcal{A} \longrightarrow \mathcal{B}$ *is stable if and only if for each* $a \in \mathcal{A}$, *where* $y \in F(a)$, *there is a unique minimal* $a' \in \mathcal{A}_{fin}$ *such that* $y \in F(a')$.

PROOF　For left to right, it is straightforward to check that $a' = \bigcap\{a^* \in \mathcal{A} : a^* \subseteq a, \text{ where } y \in F(a^*)\}$ is the required a'. For right to left, monotonicity tells us that $F(a \cap a') \subseteq F(a)$ and $F(a \cap a') \subseteq F(a')$, so $F(a \cap a') \subseteq F(a) \cap F(a')$. Conversely, if $a, a', a \cup a' \in \mathcal{A}$, then if $y \in F(a)$ and $y \in F(a')$, then y is in $F(a'')$ for a unique minimal a''. Therefore $a'' \subseteq a$ and $a'' \subseteq a'$, so $a'' \subseteq a \cap a'$, and hence $y \in F(a'') \subseteq F(a \cap a')$, as desired.　□

The next result is simple to verify.

LEMMA 10.41 (CHARACTERISING STABLE FUNCTIONS)
If F is stable, then whenever $(a, y), (a', y') \in \text{Trace}(F)$

　◇ *If* $a \cup a' \in \mathcal{A}$ *then* $y \bigcirc y' \pmod{\mathcal{B}}$.
　◇ *If* $a \cup a' \in \mathcal{A}$ *then* $y = y' \pmod{\mathcal{B}}$.

Conversely, if the set $\mathcal{F}$ satisfies these conditions, then $F_{\mathcal{F}}$ is stable.　□

Given this, we can define $\mathcal{A} \supset \mathcal{B}$. $|\mathcal{A} \supset \mathcal{B}| = \mathcal{A}_{fin} \times |\mathcal{B}|$ as follows: $(a, y) \bigcirc (a', y')$ $\pmod{\mathcal{A} \supset \mathcal{B}}$ if and only if

　◇ If $a \cup a' \in \mathcal{A}$ then $y \bigcirc y' \pmod{\mathcal{B}}$.
　◇ If $a \cup a' \in \mathcal{A}$ then $y = y' \pmod{\mathcal{B}}$.

That is, $\mathcal{A} \supset \mathcal{B} = \{\text{Trace}(F) \mid F : \mathcal{A} \longrightarrow \mathcal{B} \text{ is stable}\}$.

THEOREM 10.42 (CARTESIAN CLOSURE)
The category of coherent spaces and stable functions between them is cartesian closed.

PROOF Straightforward hacking. The interesting case is for implication and conjunction. We want a bijection $\mathrm{Hom}(A \wedge B, C) \cong \mathrm{Hom}(B, A \supset C)$. If $c \in (A \wedge B)_{\mathrm{fin}}$ then $c = (\{0\} \times a) \cup (\{1\} \times b)$, where a and b are finite. We then map (c, z) to $(a, (b, z))$. This provides the required bijection. □

This construction is *obviously* a two-stage process. It *begs* to be decomposed. We should define a coherence space $!A$ on the set of finite coherent sets of A_{fin} as follows:

$$a \frown a' \ (\mathrm{mod} \ !A) \text{ iff } a \cup a' \in A$$

and define linear implication $A \to B$ by setting $(x, y) \frown (x', y') \ (\mathrm{mod} \ A \to B)$ if and only if

⋄ If $x \frown x' \ (\mathrm{mod} \ A)$ then $y \frown y' \ (\mathrm{mod} \ B)$.

⋄ If $x \frown x' \ (\mathrm{mod} \ A)$ and $y = y'$ then $x = x'$.

Note that $A \to B$ is (isomorphic to) $\sim B \to \sim A$. Furthermore, $\mathrm{Sgl} \to A$ is (isomorphic to) A and $A \to \mathrm{Sgl}$ is (isomorphic to) $\sim A$. The operation $\supset$ stands to stable functions as $\to$ stands to a new kind of function: the *linear* functions.

DEFINITION 10.43 (LINEAR MAPS)
F is a *linear* map if and only if whenever $A \subseteq A$ is linked (that is, if $a, b \in A$ then $a \cup b \in A$) then $F(\bigcup A) = \bigcup \{ F(a) : a \in A \}$.

If F is linear then F is stable (this is straightforward) and in addition, if $x \in F(a)$ then the minimal b where $x \in F(b)$ is a *singleton*. It follows that the trace of F can be simplified. The *linear trace* of a linear map F is defined as follows:

$$\mathrm{Trlin}(F) = \{ (x, y) : y \in F(\{x\}) \}$$

Therefore, $A \to B = \{ \mathrm{Trlin}(F) \mid F : A \longrightarrow B \text{ is linear} \}$.

Given $\to$, we can see that it is connected by an adjunction to a natural fusion operation. We can define $A \circ B$ as follows: $|A \circ B| = |A| \times |B|$, and $(x, y) \frown (x', y')$ if and only if $x \frown x' \ (\mathrm{mod} \ A)$ and $y \frown y' \ (\mathrm{mod} \ B)$.

DEFINITION 10.44 (ADJUNCTION BETWEEN FUSION AND IMPLICATION)
In the category of coherence spaces with linear maps, we have the adjunction

$$\mathrm{Hom}(A \circ B, C) \cong \mathrm{Hom}(A, B \to C)$$

for all A, B and C.

PROOF If $F : A \circ B \longrightarrow C$, then the linear trace of F is a set of triples $((x, y), z)$. We define $G : A \longrightarrow B \to C$ as the function with the linear trace of all corresponding triples $(x, (y, z))$, and conversely. □

The category of coherence spaces with *linear maps* is cartesian (the standard constructions of $A \wedge B$ and $A \vee B$ still work) but it is no longer cartesian closed. The map coherence space $A \supset B$ is still a coherence space in the new category, but there is now no longer an isomorphism between $\text{Hom}(A \wedge B, C) \cong \text{Hom}(A, B \supset C)$, as this category has fewer arrows. A linear map from $A \wedge B$ to C does not necessarily correspond to a linear map from A to $B \supset C$.

10.5   History

A good introduction to the use of categories in logic can be found in Lambek and Scott's *Introduction to Categories and Higher Order Logic* [136]. Other connections between category theory and logic are found in the literature on topos theory [13, 18, 121, 143]. It is not yet known whether any connections can be made between that work and substructural logics.

I have followed Davoren's clear exposition of coherence spaces in her "A Lazy Logician's Guide to Linear Logic" [59]. Other accounts can be found in Girard, Lafont and Taylor's *Proofs and Types* [99], which provides a good explanation of how coherence spaces relate to traditional domain theory, and in Troelstra's *Lectures on Linear Logic* [261].

10.6   Exercises

Practice

{10.1} Show that function composition in the opposite category is associative.

Problems

{10.2} Show that the definition of product arrows in Lemma 10.16 has the desired properties.

{10.3} Show that any two sums of the one pair of objects are isomorphic.

{10.4} Construct the arrow $d_{A,B,C} : (A + B) \times (A + C) \longrightarrow A \times (B + C)$, which exists in any category with sums and products.

{10.5} Show that $0 + A$ and $1 \times A$ are both isomorphic to A.

Project

{10.6} Complete the analogy: As a propositional structure is to its ideal structure, a propositional category is to its . . .

Part III

Frames

Chapter 11

Frames I: Logics with Distribution

> *Yea, every year or so Anderson & Belnap turned out a new logic,*
> *and they did call it* E, *or* R, *or* $E_{\overline{I}}$ *or* P−W,
> *and they beheld each such logic, and they were called relevant.*
> *And these logics were looked upon with favor by many,*
> *for they captureth the intuitions,*
> *but by many they were scorned,*
> *in that they hadeth no semantics.*

— *Richard Routley and Robert K. Meyer,* The Semantics of Entailment [229], 1973

Substructural logics are rich and complex: they allow us to draw many distinctions which are collapsed in classical logic. This richness necessitates some degree of complexity in semantics. The simple two-valued semantics of classical logic will not do. We have already seen one way to enrich two-valued semantics — you can inflate the number of values for a sentence to take. The algebras of Part II provide us with semantic values for sentences with enough richness to model all sorts of behaviour manifest in substructural systems. But this multiplicity of semantic values is not the only way to model substructural logics. It is also possible to keep the simple two-valued scheme — sentences are either true or they fail to be true — and to enrich the scheme instead by providing more *places* at which sentences are evaluated.

This idea is not new. Its richest tradition is found in the possible worlds semantics for modal logic. The idea is that propositions are evaluated not merely once as true or false but rather they are evaluated at many different *possible worlds*. The value of a complex proposition, like $\Box A$, at a world will depend on the value of the proposition A at other worlds.

Possible worlds semantics has been a boon for modal logic. Our understanding of possibility and necessity and their logical relationships have been immeasurably improved by formal accounts involving possible worlds and accessibility relations [29, 40, 43, 90, 118, 119, 243]. The same is true for substructural logics. Similar semantic structures give us a similar understanding of substructural systems. As we shall see, it is misleading to call these structures *possible worlds* semantics. We shall call them *frames*, and they are the focus of our study in this part of the book.

11.1   Examples

Before launching into a formal definition of a frame for a substructural logic, we will consider a number of examples to motivate the definitions of the next section. The examples hark back to the motivating considerations of Section 2.1.

EXAMPLE 11.1 (LANGUAGE FRAMES)
Consider a language made up of strings of some alphabet. We can interpret the propositions of a logic as classifying the strings into syntactic categories. We will write $x \Vdash A$ to mean 'string x is of type A.' Then we can use the by now standard connectives and interpret them as follows.

  ◇ $x \Vdash A \rightarrow B$ iff for each y where $y \Vdash A$, $xy \Vdash B$.
  ◇ $x \Vdash B \leftarrow A$ iff for each y where $y \Vdash A$, $yx \Vdash B$.
  ◇ $x \Vdash A \circ B$ iff for some y and z where $x = yz$, $y \Vdash A$ and $z \Vdash B$.

This gives us the intended meanings of the connectives. $A \circ B$ is the type of concatenations of A-type strings with B-type strings. $A \rightarrow B$-type strings are those which when concatenated with A-type strings give B-type strings, and so on. The structure of strings together with the concatenation function on them is a frame. We evaluate propositions at points (here, at different strings) and the value of a proposition at some string depends on its value at others. Or, using a more appropriate language, the *type* a string takes might depend on the types other strings take. In the case of implicational types, this is the case. In the case of extensional types, like conjunction, it need not be the case. We may evaluate conjunction in the following way

  ◇ $x \Vdash A \wedge B$ iff $x \Vdash A$ and $x \Vdash B$

So a string is of type $A \wedge B$ if and only if it is of type A and of type B. This is a *local* condition, as it depends only on the types of the original string x.

There are many other kinds of model which evaluate propositions at points. One important one for us is the frame semantics for intuitionistic logic.

EXAMPLE 11.2 (INFORMATION STATES AND INTUITIONISTIC LOGIC)
Consider a research project with different stages of development. At each stage, a certain amount of information is known or verified. The project could be developed in different ways, but in each possible course of investigation, more and more information is gathered. (We assume, for the moment, that no information is lost or forgotten, and that no information previously accepted is later rejected.) So we might have a collection of states of inquiry, ordered by the relation $\sqsubseteq$ of *development*. We will assume that this relation is reflexive and transitive.

We will use 'Ⅰ⊦' again, this time to express the relationship holding between a state and the propositions known at that state. A sensible criterion for Ⅰ⊦ to satisfy is the *heredity* condition

⋄ If $x \Vdash p$ and $x \sqsubseteq y$ then $y \Vdash p$.

So, if x is established at stage p, then x is established at later stages. Clauses for the evaluation of formulae involving $\wedge, \vee, \sim, \top$ at stages of development are straightforward:

⋄ $x \Vdash A \wedge B$ if and only if $x \Vdash A$ and $x \Vdash B$.

⋄ $x \Vdash A \vee B$ if and only if $x \Vdash A$ or $x \Vdash B$.

⋄ $x \Vdash \bot$ never.

⋄ $x \Vdash \top$ always.

The clauses for $\wedge, \top$ and $\bot$ are relatively uncontroversial. That for $\vee$ is more difficult to justify, for it seems that we could well have established a disjunction in our investigations without yet having established which of the disjuncts holds. However, we will bear with this difficulty for the moment. In the next chapter, we will see a class of models in which the disjunction clause differs.

None of these clauses involves a 'point shift,' so there is nothing so far in the semantics which uses the ordering of the points. This is left to the clause for implication.

⋄ $x \Vdash A \supset B$ if and only if for each $y \sqsupseteq x$, if $y \Vdash A$ then $y \Vdash B$.

So we have verified $A \supset B$ at a stage of our inquiry if and only if at any future stage of inquiry, if we have verified A we have also verified B. Once $A \supset B$ is verified, then any future discovery of A brings with it the discovery of B.

Given this account of the evaluations of different kinds of formulae, we have a way to interpret *any* formula built up from the atomic propositions using $\wedge, \vee, \top, \bot$ and $\supset$. The values of the complex formulae depend only on the values of the atomic formulae. Furthermore, it can be shown that not only are atomic formulae preserved up the order but also that *all* propositions satisfy the heredity condition.

⋄ For all A, if $x \Vdash A$ and $x \sqsubseteq y$ then $y \Vdash A$.

This can be shown by an induction on the construction of A. We will prove it in a more general setting in Lemma 11.10.

The ordering and the heredity condition is an important part of the semantics of intuitionistic logic, and it will be an important part of the semantics of substructural logics in this chapter.

Once we use the relation $\sqsubseteq$ of development or inclusion, we should be careful to distinguish it from the relation $\leqslant$ of entailment. In fact, they are natural "duals" to each other. If $x \sqsubseteq y$, then x carries *less* information than y. The point y

supports *more* formulae than x (or at any rate, no less). In propositional structures, if $a \leqslant b$, then a entails more propositions than b, for anything entailed by b is also entailed by a. The inconsistent proposition $\perp$, if there is one, is at the *bottom* of the entailment ordering. In frames, $\perp$ is not a point (points are in a different category), but points near the top of the inclusion ordering support more and more propositions. The relation $\sqsubseteq$ is similar to that of the ordering of domain theory [1, 105, 240, 241] (see Example 11.15 below). If $x \sqsubseteq y$, then x is "less defined" than y. If $a \leqslant b$, then a is true "less often" than b.

We will consider just one more example before we get on with the definitions of our models.

EXAMPLE 11.3 (COMPATIBILITY FRAMES)
A negation on intuitionistic frames is given by setting $\sim A$ to be $A \supset \perp$. But there are more kinds of negation than intuitionistic negation. We can extend frames with $\sqsubseteq$ to include a binary relation C of *compatibility* between points. We say that xCy holds when there is nothing that x rejects that y accepts. Given this interpretation, a clause for negation is plausible:

$\diamond$ $x \Vdash \sim A$ if and only if for each y where xCy, $y \nVdash A$.

The point x rejects A (or accepts $\sim A$) just when there is no point compatible with x which accepts A. If xCy and $y \Vdash A$, then x cannot reject A (as x is compatible with y). Conversely, if every point compatible with x does not accept A, then x seems to have ruled A out.

This evaluation for negation is exactly what we need for a substructural negation. If C is not symmetric, (that is, if we can have xCy but not yCx) then a different negation can be defined using the converse of C.

$\diamond$ $x \Vdash \neg A$ if and only if for each y where yCx, $y \nVdash A$.

This makes $\langle \sim, \neg \rangle$ a split pair. If C is symmetric, then $\sim$ and $\neg$ collapse into the one connective, a simple negation.

For all this to work in the presence of $\sqsubseteq$, we must have one proviso — that C interacts properly with $\sqsubseteq$. We must have the following conditions[1]

$\diamond$ If $x' \sqsubseteq x$ then if xCy then $x'Cy$.

$\diamond$ If $y' \sqsubseteq y$ then if xCy then xCy'.

The first condition guarantees that if $x' \Vdash \sim A$ and $x' \sqsubseteq x$ then $x \Vdash \sim A$ too. For if this holds, then suppose that xCy. We wish to show that $y \nVdash A$, to ensure that $x \Vdash \sim A$. Since $x' \sqsubseteq x$ we have $x'Cy$, and given $x' \Vdash \sim A$ we have $y \nVdash A$ as desired. The second condition ensures that $\neg$ is also preserved up the order.

These conditions are not *ad hoc* restrictions. They make sense given the interpretation of C as compatibility and $\sqsubseteq$ as inclusion or development. If xCy

---

[1] Or something much like them: see Definition 11.5 for a possible weakening of the conditions on compatibility and other relations.

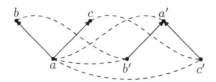

Figure 11.1: A Compatibility Frame

and $x' \sqsubseteq x$, then there can be no clash between x' and y, as x' is included in x. The same holds if $y' \sqsubseteq y$. Figure 11.1 is a particular example of this sort of frame. In this frame, the partial order is depicted by the solid arrows, and the compatibility relation is presented by the dashed lines. Compatibility in this frame is symmetric, so no arrows are necessary on these lines. The frame splits in to two components, the left component — a, b and c — and the right component — a', b' and c'. For each point in the left component, its primed partner is the $\sqsubseteq$-least point with which it is compatible. The same goes from right to left. You can check that the compatibility relation, as defined, satisfies the conditions for a compatibility relation. The point a is compatible with a', and also with the points included in a', namely b' and c'. The point b' is compatible with b, and also the point included in b, namely a. The same goes for the other points in the frame.

Now consider how negation works. Suppose $b \Vdash p$, and no other point in the frame supports p. Then $a \Vdash {\sim}p$, for no point compatible with a (i.e. a') supports p. Furthermore, $b \Vdash {\sim}p$, for nothing compatible with b supports p. So $b \Vdash p \wedge {\sim}p$. Dually to this, $b' \nVdash p$ by hypothesis, and since $b \Vdash p$ and $b'Cb$, we have $b' \nVdash {\sim}p$, so it follows that $b' \nVdash p \vee {\sim}p$.

That should be enough in the way of examples to motivate the definitions.

11.2 Definitions

Now we will introduce frames in their generality. The definitions in this section will generalise the examples we have seen.

DEFINITION 11.4 (POINT SETS AND PROPOSITIONS)
A *point set* $\mathcal{P} = \langle P, \sqsubseteq \rangle$ is a set P together with a partial order $\sqsubseteq$ on P. The set $\mathrm{Prop}(\mathcal{P})$ of *propositions* on $\mathcal{P}$ is the set of all subsets X of P which are *closed upwards*: that is, if $x \in X$ and $x \sqsubseteq x'$ then $x' \in X$. (We will often write $x \in \mathcal{P}$, instead of $x \in P$, where P is the set underlying $\mathcal{P}$.)

We have seen that not all frames need to make use of an inclusion relation $\sqsubseteq$. However, all our frames will be based on point sets as we have defined. This is no loss of generality, as the partial order $\sqsubseteq$ on a point set may well be the identity relation. In this case, we call the point set $\mathcal{P}$ *flat*. In flat point sets, the set $\mathrm{Prop}(\mathcal{P})$ is the power set of the underlying set P.

Now we will define the relations on point sets which will be used in the evaluation of the intensional connectives.

DEFINITION 11.5 (ACCESSIBILITY RELATIONS)
  ⋄ A binary relation S is a *positive two-place accessibility relation* on the point set $\mathcal{P}$ if and only if for any $x, y \in \mathcal{P}$ where xSy, if $x' \sqsubseteq x$ then there is a $y' \sqsupseteq y$, where $x'Sy'$. Similarly, if xSy and $y \sqsubseteq y'$ then there is some $x' \sqsubseteq x$, where $x'Sy'$.
  ⋄ A binary relation S is a *plump positive two-place accessibility relation* on the point set $\mathcal{P}$ if and only if for any $x, y, x', y' \in \mathcal{P}$, where xSy, $x' \sqsubseteq x$ and $y \sqsubseteq y'$ it follows that $x'Sy'$.
  ⋄ A binary relation C is a *negative two-place accessibility relation* on the point set $\mathcal{P}$ if and only if for any $x, y \in \mathcal{P}$, where if xCy and $x' \sqsubseteq x$ there is a $y' \sqsubseteq y$, where $x'Cy'$, and similarly, if yCx and $x' \sqsubseteq x$ then there is a $y' \sqsubseteq y$, where $y'Cx'$.
  ⋄ A binary relation C is a *plump negative two-place accessibility relation* on the point set $\mathcal{P}$ if and only if for any $x, y, x', y' \in \mathcal{P}$ where xCy, $x' \sqsubseteq x$ and $y' \sqsubseteq y$ it follows that $x'Cy'$.
  ⋄ A ternary relation R is a *three-place accessibility relation* if and only if whenever $Rxyz$ and $z \sqsubseteq z'$ then there are $y' \sqsupseteq y$ and $x' \sqsupseteq x$, where $Rx'y'z'$. Similarly, if $x' \sqsubseteq x$ then there are $y' \sqsubseteq y$ and $z' \sqsupseteq z$, where $Rx'y'z'$, and if $y' \sqsubseteq y$ then there are $x' \sqsubseteq x$ and $z' \sqsupseteq z$, where $Rx'y'z'$.
  ⋄ A ternary relation R is a *plump three-place accessibility relation* on the point set $\mathcal{P}$ if and only if for any $x, y, x', y', z, z' \in \mathcal{P}$, where $Rxyz$, $x' \sqsubseteq x$, $y' \sqsubseteq y$ and $z \sqsubseteq z'$ then $Rx'y'z'$.
In general, we say Q is an *accessibility relation* if and only if it is one of the above kinds of relation.

Clearly if Q is a plump accessibility relation, it satisfies the corresponding conditions for an accessibility relation. Furthermore, given an accessibility relation, we can find a plump relative in a a simple way.

DEFINITION 11.6 (PLUMP COUSINS OF ACCESSIBILITY RELATIONS)
Given an accessibility relation Q, its *plump cousin* Q^p is defined as follows:
  ⋄ If S is positive, then xS^py if and only if for some $x' \sqsupseteq x$ and $y' \sqsubseteq y$, $x'Sy'$.
  ⋄ If C is negative, then xC^py if and only if for some $x' \sqsupseteq x$ and $y' \sqsupseteq y$, $x'Cy'$.
  ⋄ If R is three-place, then R^pxyz if and only if for some $x' \sqsupseteq x$, $y' \sqsupseteq y$ and $z' \sqsubseteq z$, $Rx'y'z'$.

It is straightforwardly shown that if Q^p so defined is plump. The "plump" conditions are motivated in most applications of frames (see Example 11.3). However, they are not formally required for an interpretation of substructural logics. The more lax conditions are all that are necessary to prove hereditariness, and in some situations they seem better suited to the task at hand. (See, for example, Section 11.6.)

It may be helpful to have a way to "read" the accessibility relations, as this will aid in remembering the interaction between these relations and the inclusion relation $\sqsubseteq$. We have already seen the case with the compatibility relation C. If x is compatible with y, then if x' is included in x and y' in y, then surely x' is compatible with y'. That much is relatively straightforward.

The cases are similar with S and R. S is the traditional relation of *modal accessibility*. If xSy holds, then everything necessary in x holds in y. So if $x' \sqsubseteq x$ then everything necessary in x' is also necessary in x, and hence, holds in y, and also in any y' where y is included in y'.

For R, $Rxyz$ can be read as follows: if $A \rightarrow B$ is true in x and A is true in y, then B must be true in z. In other words, z contains everything you get from applying the rules in x to the information in y. So, if $x' \sqsubseteq x$ and $y' \sqsubseteq y$ then applying the rules in x' to the information in y' will give you no more information, so whatever results must be true in z, and hence in any z' including z, as we would hope.

Note that if R is a three-place accessibility relation on some point set $\mathcal{P}$, then if $x \in \mathcal{P}$, the relations S_1 and S_2, set by fixing yS_1z if and only if $Rxyz$ and yS_2z if and only if $Ryxz$, are positive two-place accessibility relations, and the relation C, set by fixing yCz if and only if $Ryzx$, is a negative two-place accessibility relation. (These connections may remind you of how necessity, possibility and negation operators may be defined in terms of implication and fusion.)

Note too that if the point set $\mathcal{P}$ is flat, then *any* binary relation is a two-place accessibility relation on $\mathcal{P}$ (both positive and negative) and *any* ternary relation is a three-place accessibility relation on $\mathcal{P}$. The restrictions only take affect when we need a containment relation $\sqsubseteq$.

The only other intensional machinery in our logics (apart from non-normal modal operators, which will come later) is the truth constant t. For this we will need a new definition.

DEFINITION 11.7 (TRUTH SETS FOR A TERNARY RELATION R)
If R is a three-place accessibility relation on a point set $\mathcal{P}$ then for any subset $T \in \text{Prop}(\mathcal{P})$,

  ⋄ T is a *left truth set* for R if and only if for each $x, y \in \mathcal{P}$, $x \sqsubseteq y$ if and only if for some $z \in T$, $Rzxy$.

◇ T is a *right truth set* for R if and only if for each $x, y \in \mathcal{P}$, $x \sqsubseteq y$ if and only if for some $z \in T$, $Rxzy$.

The motivation of this definition is simple: if t is a left identity for fusion, then it will be true at a left truth set of R. Similarly if t is a right identity for fusion. We will see later that this makes sense as a definition.

Now that we have a point set and some accessibility relations (and truth sets) on that set, we have a frame.

DEFINITION 11.8 (FRAME)
A frame $\mathcal{F}$ is a point set $\mathcal{P}$ together with any number of accessibility relations and truth sets on $\mathcal{P}$.

Given a frame we will talk interchangeably of the set $\mathrm{Prop}(\mathcal{P})$ of propositions on its point set and the set $\mathrm{Prop}(\mathcal{F})$ of propositions in the frame. Similarly, we will sometimes write '$x \in \mathcal{F}$' as a shorthand for '$x \in \mathcal{P}$, where $\mathcal{P}$ is the point set of $\mathcal{F}$.'

To evaluate formulae from some language in a frame, we need a mapping associating the intensional connectives in the language with accessibility relations in the frame. For every $\square$ or $\Diamond$ we have a corresponding positive two-place accessibility relation S, for every $\sim$ or $\neg$ a corresponding negative two-place accessibility relation C, and for every $\rightarrow$, $\circ$ or $\leftarrow$ a corresponding three-place accessibility relation R. Furthermore, connectives from the one family are paired with the *same* accessibility relation.

In what follows, I will suppose that some such mapping has been provided. In fact, in practice, we will simply assume that there is at most one connective of each type — keeping track of any more needlessly complicates matters. The generalisation to more connectives makes the results in the following chapters no harder to prove but merely harder to state.

DEFINITION 11.9 (EVALUATIONS ON FRAMES)
A relation $\Vdash$ between points of a frame $\mathcal{F}$ and formulae is said to be an *evaluation* if and only if for each the connectives in the language, the condition from the following list holds.

◇ $\{x \in \mathcal{F} : x \Vdash p\} \in \mathrm{Prop}(\mathcal{F})$.

◇ $x \Vdash \top$ for all $x \in \mathcal{F}$.

◇ $x \Vdash \bot$ for no $x \in \mathcal{F}$.

◇ $x \Vdash A \wedge B$ iff $x \Vdash A$ and $x \Vdash B$, for each $x \in \mathcal{F}$.

◇ $x \Vdash A \vee B$ iff $x \Vdash A$ or $x \Vdash B$, for each $x \in \mathcal{F}$.

◇ $x \Vdash A \supset B$ iff for each $y \in \mathcal{F}$, where $x \sqsubseteq y$, if $y \Vdash A$ then $y \Vdash B$.

◇ $x \Vdash t$ iff $x \in T$, for each $x \in \mathcal{F}$.

⋄ $x \Vdash \Box A$ iff for each $y \in \mathcal{F}$, where xSy, $y \Vdash A$.

⋄ $x \Vdash \Diamond A$ iff for some $y \in \mathcal{F}$, where ySx, $y \Vdash A$.

⋄ $x \Vdash {\sim} A$ iff for each $y \in \mathcal{F}$, where xCy, $y \nVdash A$.

⋄ $x \Vdash \neg A$ iff for each $y \in \mathcal{F}$, where yCx, $y \nVdash A$.

⋄ $x \Vdash A \to B$ iff for each $y, z \in \mathcal{F}$, where $Rxyz$, if $y \Vdash A$ then $z \Vdash B$.

⋄ $x \Vdash A \circ B$ iff for some $y, z \in \mathcal{F}$, where $Ryzx$, $y \Vdash A$ and $z \Vdash B$.

⋄ $x \Vdash B \leftarrow A$ iff for each $y, z \in \mathcal{F}$, where $Ryxz$, if $y \Vdash A$ then $z \Vdash B$.

The value $[\![A]\!]$ of a formula A is the set $\{x \in \mathcal{F} : x \Vdash A\}$ of points at which A is true.

It is useful to extend the scope of an evaluation to also relate points to *structures*.

⋄ $x \Vdash 0$ if and only if $x \in T$.

⋄ $x \Vdash X, Y$ if and only if $x \Vdash X$ and $x \Vdash Y$.

⋄ $x \Vdash X; Y$ if and only if for some y, z, where $Ryzx$, $y \Vdash X$ and $z \Vdash Y$.

⋄ $x \Vdash \bullet X$ if and only if for some y, where ySx, $y \Vdash X$.

A *model* $\mathfrak{M}$ is a frame together with an evaluation on that frame.

The evaluation conditions for a connective determine the logical properties of that connective. These conditions also determine, to some extent, how frames can be interpreted. For example, the conditions for $\wedge, \vee, \top, \bot$ ensure that points in frames are "informationally complete" and non-trivial. That is, no point can support no information (as $x \Vdash \top$ always) or support *everything* (as $x \nVdash \bot$). They are closed under conjunction, and more restrictively, in some sense, under disjunction. That is, all disjunctive information is witnessed. If $x \Vdash A \vee B$ then $x \Vdash A$ or $x \Vdash B$. This rules out points being interpreted as *arbitrary* bodies of information or theories, for surely a theory can admit a disjunction without admitting either disjunct.

The intensional clauses are more wide-ranging. For an intensional connective, the value of a complex proposition at a point is determined by the value of its components at other points. We have already seen the example of negation discussed previously. For necessity and possibility we see relatively standard behaviour: $\Box A$ is true *here* if and only if A is true in all points accessible by S. The difference comes with the behaviour of $\Diamond$. $\Diamond A$ is true here if and only if A is true in some world, not necessarily accessible by S, but accessible by the *converse* of S. So, if $\Box A$ is true here if and only if A is true at all of the points I can see, then $\Diamond A$ is true here if and only if A is true at some world which can *see me*. This gives us the required connections between $\Box$ and $\Diamond$, as we will see soon. We will explore how to model a more standard "possibility" — one for which $\Diamond A$ is true here if and only if I can see an A point — in Section 11.6.

For fusion and implication the justification is similar. $A \rightarrow B$ is true here if and only if for any point at which A is true, B is true wherever the result of applying what is true here to what is true there is true. That is a mouthful, but it is one way of reading the ternary relation R: $Rxyz$ if and only if the result of applying x to y is true in z.

The following lemma ensures that *all* propositions in a model satisfy the heredity condition.

LEMMA 11.10 (PROPOSITIONS IN FRAMES)
In any model $\mathfrak{M}$ the value of any formula A is a proposition in the (point set of the) frame.

PROOF A simple induction on the complexity of A, using the requirements on accessibility relations and truth sets. Clearly $[\![A]\!] \in \text{Prop}(\mathcal{P})$ whenever A is atomic. Suppose the result holds for propositions less complex than A. If A is a conjunction, then $[\![A]\!] = [\![B \wedge C]\!] = [\![B]\!] \cap [\![C]\!]$, and Prop is clearly closed under intersections. Similarly, if A is a disjunction, then $[\![A]\!] = [\![B \vee C]\!] = [\![B]\!] \cup [\![C]\!]$, and Prop is closed under unions.

Consider the intensional connectives. Suppose $A = \Box B$. If $x \Vdash \Box B$ and $x \sqsubseteq x'$ then if $x'Sy$, then we have xSy and hence $y \Vdash B$. Thus $x' \Vdash \Box B$ too, and $[\![\Box B]\!]$ is a proposition. Similarly, if $x \Vdash \Diamond B$ and $x \sqsubseteq x'$ then since ySx for some y where $y \Vdash B$, we also have ySx' and hence $x' \Vdash \Diamond B$ too.

Suppose $A = B \rightarrow C$. If $x \Vdash B \rightarrow C$ and $x \sqsubseteq x'$ then if $Rx'yz$, we have $Rxyz$, so if $y \Vdash B$ then $z \Vdash C$ as desired. The cases for negation, the intuitionistic conditional, right-to-left implication and fusion are similar, and are left to Exercise 11.8.   □

Given a model we have a way to evaluate propositions on points in a frame. Models motivate the following definitions.

DEFINITION 11.11 (ENTAILMENT ON MODELS AND FRAMES)
  ◇ *X entails A in the model $\mathfrak{M}$*, written '$X \vdash_{\mathfrak{M}} A$,' iff for every point x, if $x \Vdash X$ then $x \Vdash A$.
  ◇ *X entails A in the frame $\mathcal{F}$*, written '$X \vdash_{\mathcal{F}} A$,' iff for every model $\mathfrak{M}$ based on $\mathcal{F}$, $X \vdash_{\mathfrak{M}} A$.
  ◇ *X entails A in the class $\mathfrak{F}$ of frames*, written '$X \vdash_{\mathfrak{F}} A$,' iff $X \vdash_{\mathcal{F}} A$ for each $\mathcal{F} \in \mathfrak{F}$.

These frames are good for many substructural logics, but not all. The conjunction and disjunction clause make sure that $A \wedge (B \vee C) \vdash_{\mathcal{F}} (A \wedge B) \vee (A \wedge C)$ for any frame $\mathcal{F}$. To model substructural logics without distribution, we need to wait for the next chapter. We will end this section by looking at a few more examples of frames, which knit together the definitions we have seen so far.

EXAMPLE 11.12 (LANGUAGE FRAMES WITH IDENTITY)
A language frame has the set of strings on some alphabet as its point set. A *language frame with identity* includes the *empty string* ϵ. The ternary relation R is given by setting $Rxyz$ if and only if $xy = z$. This is an acceptable accessibility relation as the point set is flat.

Since $\epsilon x = x\epsilon = x$ for each x, it follows that $\{\epsilon\}$ is both a left and a right truth set. We can use this to interpret t. Note that in linguistic frames with identity, we have $A \vdash_{\mathcal{F}} A \circ (B \to B)$ as if $x \Vdash A$ then $x = x\epsilon$, and $\epsilon = B \to B$. $A \vdash_{\mathcal{F}} A \circ (B \to B)$ does not hold in language frames without identity. Take a language frame including the letter a. Take an interpretation such that $a \Vdash A$. Since $a \neq bc$ for any strings b and c, $a \nVdash A \circ (B \to B)$.

This example shows that the structure of the frame and its accessibility relation affects the logical properties of the evaluation. This influence is *global* because of the behaviour of the rules for implication and fusion. Adding points to a frame will alter the behaviour of the old points, as the implication and fusion clauses (and the necessity or possibility clauses) quantify over all accessible points.

EXAMPLE 11.13 (TWO-DIMENSIONAL FRAMES)
Given a set D, we can define a frame on the set $D \times D$ of pairs of D elements, by defining the ternary relation R on $D \times D$, setting $R\langle a, b \rangle \langle c, d \rangle \langle e, f \rangle$ if and only if $b = c$, $e = a$ and $b = f$. In other words, $\langle a, b \rangle$ composes with $\langle b, c \rangle$ to result in $\langle a, c \rangle$, and no other relations hold between pairs. So, the evaluation conditions on these two-dimensional frames reduce as follows:

$\diamond$ $\langle a, b \rangle \Vdash A \circ B$ if and only if for some $c \in D$, $\langle a, c \rangle \Vdash A$ and $\langle c, b \rangle \Vdash B$.

$\diamond$ $\langle a, b \rangle \Vdash A \to B$ if and only if for each $c \in D$ if $\langle b, c \rangle \Vdash A$ then $\langle a, c \rangle \Vdash B$.

$\diamond$ $\langle a, b \rangle \Vdash B \leftarrow A$ if and only if for each $c \in D$ if $\langle c, a \rangle \Vdash A$ then $\langle c, b \rangle \Vdash B$.

In this frame, the ternary R reduces to a *partial* function on pairs. This function is associative but not symmetric, where defined. The point set is flat — there is no natural notion of inclusion to be imposed. This frame has a truth set, but in this case it is not a singleton $\{\epsilon\}$ but the set $\{\langle a, a \rangle : a \in D\}$. This is both a left and a right truth set, as you can check.

These models are studied by van Benthem, Došen and Orłowska [31, 63, 189] in the context of substructural logics, and they have blossomed into their own industry, under the suggestive name 'arrow logics' [151]. In these logics, we think of the points $\langle a, b \rangle$ as transitions, or arrows, from a to b.

These are important frames for they are closely related to language frames in a number of respects — the relation R is functional: if $Rxyz$ and $Rxyz'$ then $z = z'$. However, in this case the relation is *partial*. For some x, y there is no z such that $Rxyz$.

EXAMPLE 11.14 (ACTION FRAMES)
There are at least two different ways to define frames to model actions. In both
cases, we will let the points in the frames be action types, such as giving away
$10, buying a book, inviting a friend over for dinner and so on. Action types can
be combined serially. If x and y are actions, there may well be the action xy,
of doing x and then y. Now, we could allow the frame to be *flat* and set $Rxyz$
if and only if $xy = z$. Then associativity of composition gives us if $Rxyz$ and
$Rzwv$ then there is a u where $Ryzu$ and $Rxuv$. And conversely. However, this
is only a *partial* accessibility relation, for there is no reason to think that every
pair of action must be able to be combined. Why should there be an action of
giving away all my money and then buying dinner for my friends?

A possible refinement of this approach is to allow action types to be ordered
by inclusion. For example, buying a book $\sqsubseteq$ buying *Entailment* Volume 2, in the
sense that buying a book follows from buying *Entailment* Volume 2 in particular.
Now we can set $Rxyz$ to hold when $xy \sqsubseteq z$. Clearly, inclusion respects compo-
sition. If $x \sqsubseteq x'$ and $y \sqsubseteq y'$ then $xy \sqsubseteq x'y'$. (If x' is a special case of x and y'
is a special case of y then $x'y'$ is a special case of xy.) Then R so defined is a
plump accessibility relation.

EXAMPLE 11.15 (DOMAIN SPACES)
Take a domain theoretic model of the untyped λ-calculus [1, 105, 240, 241].
Scott's construction involves a topological space D such that D is isomorphic
to the space $[D \rightarrow D]$ of continuous functions from D to itself. We do not
need to examine the details of the construction, but some properties of D are
important. Since every element of D is paired with a function in $[D \rightarrow D]$, we
can think of the objects equally well as functions. Therefore, there is a two-
place operation of application on the domain. Consider $x(y)$ — the application
of (the function paired with) x to y. Scott's model D is equipped with a notion
of *approximation* $\sqsubseteq$ such that $x \sqsubseteq y$. If $x \sqsubseteq y$, then x is an approximation of y,
or equivalently, y is a precisification of x. Approximation is a partial order, so
the domain together with approximation forms a point set. Approximation on
the domain interacts with function application by way of the conditions that if
$x \sqsubseteq x'$ and $y \sqsubseteq y'$ then $x(y) \sqsubseteq x'(y')$. (If x approximates x' and y approximates
y' then $x(y)$ approximates $x'(y')$.)

We can assign types to functions in this model by "reading" the model as a
frame for a logic. If we set $Rxyz$ to be $x(y) \sqsubseteq z$, then R is an accessibility relation on the domain, as you can check. Consider now the clauses for evaluating
an implication:

$\diamond$ $x \Vdash A \rightarrow B$ if and only if for each y, z, where $x(y) \sqsubseteq z$, if $y \Vdash A$ then $z \Vdash B$.

Given that the evaluation is hereditary, this simplifies to

◇ $x \Vdash A \to B$ if and only if for each y, where $y \Vdash A$, $x(y) \Vdash B$.

In other words, x is of type $A \to B$ if and only if whenever given an input of type x, the output is of type B. This gives us an intuitively plausible notion of function typing. For example, $\lambda x.(x+1)$ will have type $Even \to Odd$ and $Odd \to Even$. The function $\lambda x.\lambda y.(2x+y)$ has type $N \to (Odd \to Odd)$ (whatever number x is, if y is odd, so is $2x+y$) but it does not have type $Odd \to (N \to Odd)$ (if y is even, the output will be even, not odd). This is an example demonstrating the failure of the permutation-related rule: $A \to (B \to C) \vdash B \to (A \to B)$.

Furthermore, we can use other connectives to expand the type analysis of terms. Conjunction clearly makes sense in this interpretation: $x \Vdash A \wedge B$ if and only if $x \Vdash A$ and $x \Vdash B$. In this way, we have models not only for typing functions with $\to$ but also with intersection. These are models for the Torino type system $\lambda \cap$ [12, 49, 115, 273].

There is also a natural left truth set in our model. The identity function $e = \lambda x.x$ is such that $ex = x$ for every x. Therefore, the set $\{y : e \sqsubseteq y\}$ is a truth set. It naturally models the truth constant t. This is a left truth constant and not a right truth constant.

This example is an important one for motivating *very* weak substructural logics, for it is one of the few natural cases in which the associativity of fusion is manifestly *unwarranted*. Action composition is obviously associative, as is string composition and many other forms of composition. Function application is definitely not associative. There is no reason, in general, to think that $f(g(x)) = (fg)x$.

This connection between functions (and the λ-calculus) and substructural logics is the second we have seen. It is important to see how they differ. For the system of type assignment and proof decoration of Chapter 7, the guiding idea was for λ-terms to code up proofs. In this case, we are using logical machinery to provide a type analysis of functions, with no particular regard for the decoration of proofs. The difference can be illustrated by the way that the treatment of conjunction differs. For proof decoration, it is important that a proof of $A \wedge B$ can be decomposed into a proof of A and a proof of B. So, if M is of type A and N is of type B, take the *pair* $\langle M, N \rangle$ to be of type $A \wedge B$. Considering functions as points in a frame to be typed by terms we use a different analysis. In this case, we say that if M is both of type A and of type B, then it is also of type $A \wedge B$. Now the unique decomposition of proofs is gone. There is nothing in the *term* M which witnesses to the origin of the conjunction $A \wedge B$.

Similarly, in a proof decoration system, the logically valid formulae are those provable with no undischarged assumptions: their proofs are coded by terms with no free variables. Different systems have different allowable terms. In R, we allow multiple variables to be bound by the one λ abstraction, but we do not allow vacuous abstraction. In LL (without exponentials) we allow neither. In the domain spaces under consideration here, the logically valid consecutions are not those with closed terms but are rather the types of the *identity* function. For here, $\lambda x.x$ has type $A \wedge B \to B$, and if $\lambda x.x \Vdash A \to B$ then anything of type A is also of type B, so $\lambda x.x \Vdash (C \to A) \to (C \to B)$ as any C-to-A function is automatically a C-to-B function. If union types are allowed, then $\lambda x.x \Vdash A \wedge (B \vee C) \to (A \wedge B) \vee (A \wedge C)$. The logic of this style of type assignment system is at least the positive fragment of DBSub, the basic substructural logic with distribution.[2]

This is enough examination of example frames. We will now turn to the task of pairing frames with logics. Which frames model which logics?

11.3   Soundness and Completeness

We need to know how varying our accessibility relations on a frame $\mathcal{F}$ varies the consequence $\vdash_{\mathcal{F}}$ of that frame.

EXAMPLE 11.16 (WHEN $A \vdash_{\mathcal{F}} (A \to B) \to B$, AND WHEN $A \circ B \vdash_{\mathcal{F}} B \circ A$)
Take an arbitrary frame $\mathcal{F}$, with an evaluation $\Vdash$. Suppose $x \in \mathcal{F}$ and $x \Vdash A$. We want to see if $x \Vdash (A \to B) \to B$. Take a y, where $y \Vdash A \to B$ and $Rxyz$. We want to see when $z \Vdash B$. For that, we would like to apply the $A \to B$ at y to the A at x. $Rxyz$ is not enough to do this, but $Ryxz$ is. So, if the frame also has $Ryxz$, we are done, and $z \Vdash B$. So, if a frame satisfies the general condition $Rxyz \to Ryxz$, then we will have $A \vdash_{\mathcal{F}} (A \to B) \to B$.
  The consecution $A \circ B \vdash_{\mathcal{F}} B \circ A$ will also be satisfied under these conditions. If $x \Vdash A \circ B$ then there are y, z where $Ryzx$, $y \Vdash A$ and $z \Vdash B$. By the condition on the frame, we have then $Rzyx$, which then gives $x \Vdash B \circ A$ as well. This consecution too is given by the condition which allows us to swap the first two positions in R.

DEFINITION 11.17 (CONDITIONS FOR STRUCTURAL RULES)
The *corresponding condition* for the structural rule $X \Leftarrow Y$ is defined as follows. We assume the constituents of X and Y are from among $A_1, \ldots, A_n$, and that our first-order language contains variables $x, x_1, \ldots, x_n$ and y and z.

---

[2]   Venneri [273] also considers the types of closed terms under intersection typing. This is a strange logic in which the $\to$ theorems are those of intuitionistic logic, but in which conjunction introduction is restricted. Thus, $A \to (B \to A)$ and $A \to ((A \to B) \to B)$ are theorems, as $\lambda x.\lambda y.x$ has the first type, and $\lambda x.\lambda y.yx$ has the second, but the conjunction $(A \to (B \to A)) \wedge (A \to ((A \to B) \to B))$ is not a theorem, as there is no closed term with both types. For *our* models, the "logic" is the type of the identity object, not the type of all closed terms, and this is obviously closed under conjunction.

The variable x stands apart as the main variable, each x_i is related to A_i, and $y, z \ldots$ are used as bound variables.

$$
\begin{aligned}
SR(A_i) &= x_i \sqsubseteq x \\
SR(\top) &= \text{true} \\
SR(0) &= Tx \\
SR(X, Y) &= SR(X) \wedge SR(Y) \\
SR(X; Y) &= \exists y \exists z (Ryzx \wedge SR(X)[x := y] \wedge SR(Y)[x := z]) \\
SR(\bullet X) &= \exists y (ySx \wedge SR(X)[x := y])
\end{aligned}
$$

Then for the translation of the structural rule $X \Leftarrow Y$ is

$$
\forall x, x_1, \ldots, x_n (SR(Y) \to SR(X))
$$

EXAMPLE 11.18 (STANDARD CONDITIONS FOR STANDARD RULES)
Consider the structural rule CI, $X; Y \Leftarrow Y; X$. Its corresponding condition, according to our definitions, is $\forall x, x_1, x_2 (SR(X; Y) \to SR(Y; X))$, which is equivalent to

$$
\forall x, x_1, x_2 (\exists y \exists z (Ryzx \wedge x_1 \sqsubseteq y \wedge x_2 \sqsubseteq z) \to \exists y \exists z (Ryzx \wedge x_2 \sqsubseteq y \wedge x_1 \sqsubseteq z))
$$

This is not a particularly perspicuous condition, but it simplifies under the assumption that R is plump. By the interaction between R and $\sqsubseteq$, we have $Ryzx \wedge x_1 \sqsubseteq y \wedge x_2 \sqsubseteq z$ if and only if Rx_1x_2x. Therefore, our condition simplifies to

$$
\forall x, x_1, x_2 (Rx_1x_2x \to Rx_2x_1x)
$$

which we have already seen as corresponding to $A \vdash (A \to B) \to B$.

Consider another example, the structural rule B: $X; (Y; Z) \Leftarrow (X; Y); Z$. The condition $SR(X; (Y; Z))$ is

$$
\exists y \exists z (Ryzx \wedge \exists u \exists v (Ruvy \wedge x_1 \sqsubseteq u \wedge x_2 \sqsubseteq v) \wedge x_3 \sqsubseteq z)
$$

which simplifies (again, when R is plump) to $\exists y (Ryx_3x \wedge Rx_1x_2y)$. Similarly, $SR((X; Y); Z)$ simplifies to $\exists z (Rx_1zx \wedge Rx_2x_3z)$. This motivates a definition of new terms:

$$
\begin{aligned}
R(xy)zw &= \exists u (Rxyu \wedge Ruzw) \\
Rx(yz)w &= \exists u (Ryzu \wedge Rxuw)
\end{aligned}
$$

Then $SR(X; (Y; Z)) \to SR((X; Y); Z)$ is equivalent to the simple condition on frames:

$$\forall x_1, x_2, x_3, x \big(R x_1 (x_2 x_3) x \to R(x_1 x_2) x_3 x\big)$$

which corresponds, by eye, to the original structural rule. Other structural rules may be analysed in a similar way. Some results are in Table 11.1.

Label	Rule	Condition
B	$X; (Y; Z) \Leftarrow (X; Y); Z$	$R(xy)xw \to Rx(yz)w$
B′	$X; (Y; Z) \Leftarrow (Y; X); Z$	$R(yx)zw \to Rx(yz)w$
B^c	$(X; Y); Z \Leftarrow X; (Y; Z)$	$Rx(yz)w \to R(xy)zw$
C	$(X; Y); Z \Leftarrow (X; Z); Y$	$R(xz)yw \to R(xy)zw$
CI	$X; Y \Leftarrow Y; X$	$Rxyz \to Ryxz$
W	$(X; Y); Y \Leftarrow X; Y$	$Rxyz \to R(xy)yz$
WI	$X; X \Leftarrow X$	$Rxxx$
M	$X \Leftarrow X; X$	$Rxxy \to x \sqsubseteq y$
K	$X \Leftarrow X; Y$	$Rxyz \to x \sqsubseteq z$
K′	$X \Leftarrow Y; X$	$Ryxz \to x \sqsubseteq z$
T	$\bullet X \Leftarrow X$	xSx
4	$\bullet X \Leftarrow \bullet\bullet X$	$xSy \wedge ySz \to xSz$
Kr	$0 \Leftarrow \bullet 0$	$Tx \wedge xSy \to Ty$
mMP	$\bullet X; \bullet Y \Leftarrow \bullet(X; Y)$	$Rzw(Sx) \to R(zS)(wS)x$
mWI	$\bullet X; \bullet X \Leftarrow \bullet X$	$xSy \to R(xS)(xS)y$
mK	$X \Leftarrow X; \bullet Y$	$Rx(Sy)z \to x \sqsubseteq z$
m2t	$\bullet X \Leftarrow X; 0$	$Rx(T)z \to xSz$
t2m	$X; 0 \Leftarrow \bullet X$	$xSz \to Rx(T)z$
m2T	$\bullet X \Leftarrow X; Y$	$Rxyz \to xSz$
T2m	$X; \top \Leftarrow \bullet X$	$xSz \to \exists y(Rxyz)$

Table 11.1: Conditions for Structural Rules, given Plump Relations

In that table, we use some other devices for writing compound relations:

$$R(xS)yz = \exists w(xSw \wedge Rwyz) \quad R(Sx)yz = \exists w(wSx \wedge Rwyz)$$
$$Rx(yS)z = \exists w(ySw \wedge Rxwz) \quad Rx(Sy)z = \exists w(wSy \wedge Rxwz)$$
$$Rxy(Sz) = \exists w(wSz \wedge Rxyw) \quad Rxy(zS) = \exists w(zSw \wedge Rxyw)$$
$$R(T)yz = \exists w(Tw \wedge Rwyz) \quad Rx(T)z = \exists w(Tw \wedge Rxwz)$$

Therefore, T is a left truth set if and only if for each x and y, $R(T)xy$ if and only if $x \sqsubseteq y$. Similarly, it is a right truth set if and only if $Rx(T)y$ just when $x \sqsubseteq y$.

DEFINITION 11.19 (FRAMES FIT FOR A SYSTEM)
Given a system $\mathfrak{S}$, a *frame is fit for* $\mathfrak{S}$ if and only if every condition corresponding to each structural rule holds in the frame.

This section will be devoted to showing that a consecution is provable in a system if and only if it holds in every frame fit for that system — for any natural deduction system extended by structural rules. In the next section, we will extend the result to cover extensions for negation.

The equivalence result splits, as always, into two parts: *soundness* and *completeness*. In this case, the soundness result is the simpler of the two.

THEOREM 11.20 (SOUNDNESS OF FRAMES)
If $\mathcal{F}$ is fit for $\mathfrak{S}$, and if $X \vdash A$ is provable in $\mathfrak{S}$, then $X \vdash_{\mathcal{F}} A$.

To prove this we need to show that, given a frame fit for $\mathfrak{S}$, all axioms hold in the frame, and that if the premises of a rule hold in the frame, so does the conclusion. The structural rules require special treatment, so we will work through a lemma which deals with them before getting to the proof of the main theorem.

LEMMA 11.21 (STRUCTURAL RULES AND THEIR TRANSLATION)
In any model $\mathfrak{M}$, and any structure X, with atomic constituents $A_1, \ldots, A_n$, we have $x \Vdash X$ if and only if there are points $x_1, \ldots, x_n$ such that $x_i \Vdash A_i$ for each i, and $SR(X)$.

PROOF This is an induction on the complexity of X. If X is a formula, then $x \Vdash A_i$ if and only if for some x_i, where $x_i \Vdash A_i$ and $x_i \sqsubseteq x$, simply by choosing x_i to be x. If X is $\top$, then $x \Vdash \top$ always. If X is t, then $x \Vdash t$ if and only if $x \in T$. This deals with the base cases.

Suppose that the result holds for substructures of X. If X is $Y;Z$, then $x \Vdash X$ if and only if there are y, z, where $y \Vdash Y$, $z \Vdash Z$ and $Ryzx$. But by hypothesis, $y \Vdash Y$ if and only if $SR(Y)[x := y]$ and $z \Vdash Z$ if and only if $SR(Z)[x := z]$, so $x \Vdash X$ if and only if there are y, z where $Ryzx$, $SR(Y)[x := y]$ and $SR(Z)[x := z]$, which is exactly $SR(X)$.

The case for the comma is simpler: If X is Y, Z then $x \Vdash X$ if and only if $x \Vdash Y$ and $x \Vdash Z$, if and only if (by hypothesis) $SR(Y)$ and $SR(Z)$ which is exactly $SR(X)$, as desired. This completes the proof. $\qquad \square$

To prove the soundness of our logics with respect to their frames, it will help to have the following result.

LEMMA 11.22 (PRESERVATION OF STRUCTURE)
In any model $\mathfrak{M}$, if $X \vdash_{\mathfrak{M}} A$, then if $x \Vdash Y(X)$ then $X \Vdash Y(A)$.

PROOF A simple induction on the structure of Y. If $Y(X)$ does not involve X, the result holds vacuously. If $Y(X)$ is X then $Y(A)$ is A, and the result is immediate. For the first induction step, suppose $x \Vdash Z_1(X); Z_2(X)$. Then there are y, z where $Ryzx$ and $y \Vdash Z_1(X)$ and $z \Vdash Z_2(X)$. Then by induction, $y \Vdash Z_1(A)$ and $z \Vdash Z_2(A)$. Therefore $x \Vdash Z_1(A); Z_2(A)$ as desired. The case for the comma and for • are just as simple. □

Now we can proceed with the proof of the soundness theorem.

PROOF We will prove that if $X \vdash A$ holds in $\mathfrak{S}$, then $X \vdash_{\mathcal{F}} A$, by induction on the length of the proof of $X \vdash A$.

First of all, $A \vdash_{\mathcal{F}} A$ holds in any frame since if $x \Vdash A$ then $x \Vdash A$. The structural rules are dealt with by Lemma 11.21. Suppose $X \vdash_{\mathcal{F}} A$ and $X \Leftarrow Y$ is a structural rule. We wish to show that $Y \vdash_{\mathcal{F}} A$. The condition $SR(Y) \to SR(X)$ is satisfied by our frame, by hypothesis. Suppose $x \Vdash Y$. It follows that $SR(Y)$ holds, and by the frame condition, $SR(X)$ holds too. But the lemma again gives $x \Vdash X$, which then gives $x \Vdash A$ by $X \vdash_{\mathcal{F}} A$, as desired.

Now consider the connective rules. We will work through a couple, and the rest are left for Exercise 11.11. Consider the $\to$ rules. For $(\to E)$, suppose that $X \vdash_{\mathcal{F}} A \to B$ and $Y \vdash_{\mathcal{F}} A$. We wish to show that $X; Y \vdash_{\mathcal{F}} B$. To that end, suppose $x \Vdash X; Y$. Then there are y, z where $Ryzx$, $y \Vdash X$ and $z \Vdash Y$. Since $X \vdash_{\mathcal{F}} A \to B$, it follows that $y \Vdash A \to B$, and since $Y \vdash_{\mathcal{F}} A$, it follows that $z \Vdash A$. Then $Ryzx$ gives $x \Vdash B$ as desired.

For $(\to I)$, suppose that $X; A \vdash_{\mathcal{F}} B$. We wish to show that $X \vdash_{\mathcal{F}} A \to B$. So, suppose $x \Vdash X$. Then to show that $X \vdash_{\mathcal{F}} A \to B$, take $x \Vdash X$, and check to see whether $x \Vdash A \to B$. For this, assume that $Rxyz$ and $y \Vdash A$. It follows that $z \Vdash X; A$ and hence $z \Vdash B$ as desired.

Consider now the fusion rules. For $(\circ I)$, suppose that $X \vdash_{\mathcal{F}} A$ and $Y \vdash_{\mathcal{F}} B$. If $x \Vdash X; Y$ then there are y, z where $Ryzx$, $y \Vdash X$ and $z \Vdash Y$. Therefore $y \Vdash A$ and $z \Vdash B$, giving $x \Vdash A \circ B$. Therefore $X; Y \vdash_{\mathcal{F}} A \circ B$, as desired.

For $(\circ E)$, suppose that $X \vdash_{\mathcal{F}} A \circ B$ and $Y(A; B) \vdash_{\mathcal{F}} C$. We wish to show that $Y(X) \vdash_{\mathcal{F}} C$. Suppose, therefore, that $x \Vdash Y(X)$. It follows, by Lemma 11.22, that $x \Vdash Y(A \circ B)$, but $x \Vdash Y(A \circ B)$ if and only if $x \Vdash Y(A; B)$ (the clauses for $A; B$ and $A \circ B$ are identical) and hence $x \Vdash C$ as desired.

The extensional rules are simple: if $X \vdash_{\mathcal{F}} A$ and $X \vdash_{\mathcal{F}} B$ then clearly $X \vdash_{\mathcal{F}} A \wedge B$, and conversely. Similarly, if $X \vdash_{\mathcal{F}} A$ then $X \vdash_{\mathcal{F}} A \vee B$, and likewise if $X \vdash_{\mathcal{F}} B$. Trivially, $X \vdash_{\mathcal{F}} \top$ for any X at all. And if $X \vdash_{\mathcal{F}} \bot$, it follows that for no x at all in $\mathcal{F}$ does $x \Vdash X$, and an induction on the structure of Y will show that neither will $x \Vdash Y(X)$, so $Y(X) \vdash_{\mathcal{F}} A$.

The rules for t, $\leftarrow$, $\Box$ and $\diamond$ contain no innovations and are left for Exercise 11.11. □

Frames and natural deduction systems have similar properties. In natural deduction systems, each family of connectives is defined in terms of a particular punctuation mark, and extra structural rules involving the punctuation marks govern the distinctive behaviour of the logical system. In frames, each family of connectives is defined in terms of an accessibility relation, and extra properties satisfied by that relation govern the distinctive behaviour of the logical system. The soundness proof was tedious but straightforward. The completeness proof is more difficult. Here, we need to show that if $X \not\vdash A$ in some system, then there is a model, fit for that system, in which $X \not\Vdash_{\mathfrak{M}} A$. This is not a straightforward verification, as we need to construct the model in which the consecution fails. Here, we need some techniques for building models. Thankfully, most of the raw materials are ready to hand.

Consider the case of completeness for propositional structures, from Chapter 8. In that case, we constructed a propositional structure — the Lindenbaum algebra — out of the language of the logic. Propositions in the structure were equivalence classes of provably equivalent formulae. The same sort of construction will be used here — except now we need to construct points in a frame. For this, individual formulae will not do the trick. To see what will, consider what is needed of points in a model: a point is closed under consequence. That is, if $x \Vdash A$ and $A \vdash B$, then $x \Vdash B$ too. Points are closed under conjunction too. If $x \Vdash A$ and $x \Vdash B$, then $x \Vdash A \wedge B$. Furthermore, points are prime. If $x \Vdash A \vee B$ then $x \Vdash A$ or $x \Vdash B$. (In addition, points are non-trivial: $x \Vdash \top$ and $x \not\Vdash \bot$.) So the set of formulae supported by a point in a model must be a *prime theory*. It is *these* we will use to construct our frame.

DEFINITION 11.23 (THE CANONICAL POINT SET)
Given a logic its *canonical point set* is the set of all non-trivial prime theories in that logic, ordered by the subset relation $\subseteq$.

Next, we define the accessibility relations on the frame. For that, we must consider what we need the accessibility relations to *do*. For example, consider C. If $x \Vdash {\sim}A$ and $y \Vdash A$ then we ought not to have xCy. We will let C hold between x and y *unless* it is explicitly ruled out by whatever is in x and y. Alas, we can define C in terms of $\sim$, or we can define it in terms of $\neg$, if both are present. For the moment, we will allow definitions in terms of any connective, as follows:

DEFINITION 11.24 (THE CANONICAL ACCESSIBILITY RELATIONS)
Given a canonical point set, the *canonical accessibility relations* are defined on
that set as follows:

$$
\begin{aligned}
T_t x &\quad \text{iff} \quad t \in x \\
x S_\Box y &\quad \text{iff} \quad \text{for each } \Box A \in x,\ A \in y \\
x S_\Diamond y &\quad \text{iff} \quad \text{for each } A \in x,\ \Diamond A \in y \\
x C_\sim y &\quad \text{iff} \quad \text{for each } {\sim} A \in x,\ A \notin y \\
x C_\neg y &\quad \text{iff} \quad \text{for each } \neg A \in y,\ A \notin x \\
R_\to xyz &\quad \text{iff} \quad \text{for each } A \to B \in x \text{ and } A \in y,\ B \in z \\
R_\leftarrow xyz &\quad \text{iff} \quad \text{for each } A \in x \text{ and } B \leftarrow A \in y,\ B \in z \\
R_\circ xyz &\quad \text{iff} \quad \text{for each } A \in x \text{ and } B \in y,\ A \circ B \in z
\end{aligned}
$$

This multiplicity of accessibility relations quickly disappears, as the following
lemma tells us.

LEMMA 11.25 (EQUIVALENCE OF ACCESSIBILITY RELATIONS)
*If $\Box$ and $\Diamond$ are both present in L, then $S_\Box$ and $S_\Diamond$ are equivalent. If $\sim$ and $\neg$
are both present in L, then $C_\sim$ and $C_\neg$ are equivalent. If any two of $\to$, $\leftarrow$ and
$\circ$ are present in L, then the corresponding relations between $R_\to$, $R_\leftarrow$ and $R_\circ$ are
equivalent.*

PROOF   We will work through a few cases here and leave the rest to Exer-
cise 11.12. Suppose that $x S_\Box y$. We wish to show that $x S_\Diamond y$. Suppose that
$A \in x$. Then as $A \vdash \Box \Diamond A$, $\Box \Diamond A \in x$ too (as x is a theory). So since $x S_\Box y$,
$\Diamond A \in y$ as desired. Conversely, suppose that $x S_\Diamond y$. We wish to show that
$x S_\Box y$. Suppose that $\Box A \in x$. We wish to show that $A \in y$. Since $x S_\Diamond y$ we have
$\Diamond \Box A \in y$. However, $\Diamond \Box A \vdash A$, so since y is a theory, $A \in y$ as desired.

   Suppose that $R_\to xyz$. We wish to show that $R_\leftarrow xyz$. To that end, suppose
that $A \in x$ and $B \leftarrow A \in y$. We can prove $A \vdash (B \leftarrow A) \to B$, which gives
us $(B \leftarrow A) \to B \in x$ (see Exercise 2.5) and $R_\to xyz$ with $B \leftarrow A \in y$ gives
us $B \in x$ as desired. Conversely, if $R_\leftarrow xyz$, to show that $R_\to xyz$, suppose that
$A \to B \in x$ and $A \in y$. From $A \vdash B \leftarrow (A \to B)$ we get $B \leftarrow (A \to B) \in y$ and
$R_\leftarrow xyz$ with $A \to B \in x$ we get $B \in z$ as desired.

   The other cases ($\sim/\neg$, $\to/\circ$ and $\leftarrow/\circ$) are no more difficult and are left to
Exercise 11.12.   □

From now, then we suppose that on the canonical point set for L we have the accessibility relations S, C and R, as appropriate, defined by whatever intensional
connectives appear in L.

DEFINITION 11.26 (THE CANONICAL FRAME AND MODEL)
The *canonical frame* $\mathcal{F}_L$ for the logic L is given by adding the canonical accessibility relations for L to the canonical point set. The *canonical model* for L is
given by adding the relation $\Vdash$ as follows:

$$x \Vdash A \text{ iff } A \in x$$

The crucial lemma involves showing that this is a sensible relation. That is, the membership relation in the canonical model satisfies the conditions for an evaluation.

LEMMA 11.27 (THE CANONICAL MODEL IS A MODEL)
Given a pair extension acceptable logic L, the 'canonical model' is indeed a model fit for the logic L.

This involves showing that the frame conditions are satisfied by the canonical frame, that the connective rules are satisfied, and the structural rules of the logic in question hold. To prove this lemma we proceed step by step with simpler results. The first shows that the accessibility relations on the canonical model are, indeed, accessibility relations:

LEMMA 11.28 (CANONICAL ACCESSIBILITY RELATIONS)
The relations R, C and S on the canonical model are plump accessibility relations.

PROOF   Suppose $\to$ is present, and R is defined in terms of $\to$. Suppose too that $Rxyz$ and $x' \subseteq x$, $y' \subseteq y$ and $z \subseteq z'$. Then if $A \to B \in x'$ and $A \in y'$, then $A \to B \in x$ and $A \in y$, giving $B \in z$ and hence $B \in z'$ as desired. Therefore $Rx'y'z'$. If $\to$ is absent, and R is defined in terms of $\circ$, then suppose $Rxyz$ and $x' \subseteq x$, $y' \subseteq y$ and $z \subseteq z'$. Then if $A \in x'$ and $B \in y'$ then $A \in x$ and $B \in y$, giving $A \circ B \in z$, and hence $A \circ B \in z'$ as desired.

The other cases, for $\leftarrow$, and for C and S, are just as straightforward and are left to Exercise 11.13.   □

Next we need to show that the accessibility relations interact in the right way with their respective connectives.

LEMMA 11.29 (WITNESS LEMMA)
Whenever x, y, and z are prime theories in some pair extension acceptable logic, then

   ⋄ *If $\Box A \notin x$ then for some y such that xSy, $A \notin y$.*
   ⋄ *If $\Diamond A \in x$ then for some y such that ySx, $A \in y$.*
   ⋄ *If ${\sim}A \notin x$ then for some y such that xCy, $A \in y$.*
   ⋄ *If $\neg A \notin x$ then for some y such that yCx, $A \in y$.*
   ⋄ *If $A \to B \notin x$ then for some y and z such that $Rxyz$, $A \in y$ and $B \notin z$.*
   ⋄ *If $B \leftarrow A \notin x$ then for some y and z such that $Ryxz$, $A \in y$ and $B \notin z$.*
   ⋄ *If $A \circ B \in x$ then for some y and z such that $Ryzx$, $A \in y$ and $B \in z$.*

PROOF   The proof in each case is a simple application of the Pair Extension Theorem (on page 94). We will do the cases for $\Diamond$, $\neg$ and $\rightarrow$. The rest are similar and are left to Exercise 11.14.

Suppose that $\Diamond A \in x$. We wish to find a y where ySx and $A \in y$. Consider the pair $\langle \{A\}, \{B : \Diamond B \not\in x\} \rangle$. This is indeed a pair. If $A \vdash \bigvee B_i$ for some B_i where $\Diamond B_i \not\in x$, then as x is prime, $\bigvee \Diamond B_i \not\in x$, and hence $\Diamond \bigvee B_i \not\in x$ by the distribution of $\Diamond$ over disjunction. However, $A \vdash \bigvee B_i$ gives us $\Diamond A \vdash \Diamond \bigvee B_i$ and $\Diamond A \in x$ gives $\Diamond \bigvee B_i$, conflicting with what we have seen. Thus $\langle \{A\}, \{B : \Diamond B \not\in x\} \rangle$ is a pair and hence can be extended to a full pair $\langle y, z \rangle$. Now $A \in y$ and y is a prime theory. We know too that ySx, since if $B \in y$ then $\Diamond B \in x$, since we cannot have $\Diamond B \not\in x$, as in that case we would have $B \in z$, and we know that z and y do not overlap. Thus ySz as desired.

Suppose that $\sim A \not\in x$. We wish to find a y where xCy and $A \in y$. Consider the pair $\langle \{A\}, \{B : \sim B \in x\} \rangle$. This is indeed a pair. If $A \vdash \bigvee B_i$ for some B_i where $\sim B_i \in x$, then as x is a theory $\bigwedge \sim B_i \in x$, and hence $\sim \bigvee B_i \in x$ too. However, $A \vdash \bigvee B_i$ gives us $\sim \bigvee B_i \vdash \sim A$, and hence $\sim A \in x$, contradicting what we already know. So $\langle \{A\}, \{B : \sim B \in x\} \rangle$ extends to a full pair $\langle y, z \rangle$, giving us a prime theory y. We have $A \in y$ by construction, and xCy as if $\sim A \in x$ then $A \in z$ and hence $A \not\in y$.

Suppose that $A \rightarrow B \not\in x$. We wish to find y and z where $Rxyz$, $A \in y$ and $B \not\in z$. Consider $\langle \{B' : A \rightarrow B' \in x\}, \{B\} \rangle$. This is a pair, since if $\bigwedge B_i' \vdash B$, then since $A \rightarrow B_i' \in x$ for each B_i', $A \rightarrow \bigwedge B_i' \in x$ too. Therefore, if $\bigwedge B_i' \vdash B$ we would have $A \rightarrow B \in x$, contrary to our assumption. Therefore we have a pair, and it can be extended to a full pair $\langle z, v \rangle$, in which z is prime. In particular, $B \not\in z$, since $B \in v$.

Now consider $\langle \{A\}, \{C : \exists D \not\in z, C \rightarrow D \in x\} \rangle$. This is a pair, since if $A \vdash \bigvee C_i$ then since for each i there is a $D_i \not\in z$, where $C_i \rightarrow D_i \in x$, it follows that $\bigwedge (C_i \rightarrow D_i) \in x$, giving $\bigvee C_i \rightarrow \bigwedge D_i \in x$. Therefore, if $A \vdash \bigvee C_i$ we have $A \rightarrow \bigwedge D_i \in x$. But this means that $\bigwedge D_i \in z$, and hence $D_i \in z$ for some z (as z is prime), contrary to our assumption that every $D_i \not\in z$. Therefore we have a pair, and this can be extended to a full pair $\langle y, w \rangle$. Again, y is a prime theory.

Now we can check that $Rxyz$. Take an arbitrary $C \rightarrow D \in x$, where $C \in y$. Then if $D \not\in z$, we have $C \in w$ (by the construction of the full pair $\langle y, w \rangle$) contradicting $C \in y$. Therefore $D \in z$ as desired. $\square$

This result will be enough to show that the connective rules are satisfied, as the next lemma shows.

LEMMA 11.30 (CONNECTIVES IN THE CANONICAL MODEL)
In the canonical model in a pair extension acceptable logic, for any non-trivial prime theory x we have

$\diamond \top \in x$.

⋄ $\bot \notin x$.
⋄ $A \wedge B \in x$ if and only if $A \in x$ and $B \in x$.
⋄ $A \vee B \in x$ if and only if $A \in x$ or $B \in x$.
⋄ $t \in x$ if and only if $x \in T$.
⋄ $\Box A \in x$ if and only if for each y where xSy, $A \in y$.
⋄ $\Diamond A \in x$ if and only if for some y where ySx, $A \in y$.
⋄ $\sim A \in x$ if and only if for some y where xCy, $A \notin y$.
⋄ $\neg A \in x$ if and only if for some y where yCx, $A \notin y$.
⋄ $A \to B \in x$ if and only if for each y and z where $Rxyz$, if $A \in y$ then $B \in z$.
⋄ $B \leftarrow A \in x$ if and only if for each y and z where $Ryxz$, if $A \in y$ then $B \in z$.
⋄ $A \circ B \in x$ if and only if for some y and z where $Ryzx$, $A \in y$ and $B \in z$.

PROOF   The first four conditions are given, since each x is a non-trivial prime theory. The fifth is given by the definition of T. Consider the $\Box$ condition. If $\Box A \in x$ then by the definition of $S_\Box$, if xSy then $A \in y$. Conversely, if $\Box A \notin x$ then the witness lemma assures us that there a prime y where xRy and $A \notin y$. The other cases are just as simple.   □

To deal with the structural rules, we want some way of combining theories that mimics the combination of structure.

DEFINITION 11.31 (COMBINING THEORIES)
Given theories y and z, we define the theories (y, z), $(y; z)$ and $\bullet y$ as follows.

⋄ $(y, z) = \{C : \exists A \in y, \exists B \in z(A, B \vdash C)\}$
⋄ $(y; z) = \{C : \exists A \in y, \exists B \in z(A; B \vdash C)\}$
⋄ $\bullet y = \{C : \exists A \in y(\bullet A \vdash C)\}$

If X is a structure with atomic constituents $A_1, \ldots, A_n$, and if $x_1, \ldots, x_n$ are theories, define $X(x_1, \ldots, x_n)$, the theory corresponding to X, as follows:

$$
\begin{aligned}
A_i(x_1, \ldots, x_n) &= x_i \\
\top(x_1, \ldots, x_n) &= \{A : \top \vdash A\} \\
0(x_1, \ldots, x_n) &= \{A : 0 \vdash A\} \\
(Y, Z)(x_1, \ldots, x_n) &= Y(x_1, \ldots, x_n), Z(x_1, \ldots, x_n) \\
(Y; Z)(x_1, \ldots, x_n) &= Y(x_1, \ldots, x_n); Z(x_1, \ldots, x_n) \\
\bullet Y(x_1, \ldots, x_n) &= \bullet\big(Y(x_1, \ldots, x_n)\big)
\end{aligned}
$$

In this definition, we get $X(x_1, \ldots, x_n)$ from X by replacing the formula A_i by x_i, 0 by $\{A : t \vdash A\}$, $\top$ by $\{A : \top \vdash A\}$, and then by using comma, semicolon and $\bullet$ as operations on theories instead of as punctuation marks in structures.

Once we have such operations on theories, we can see how they interact with structural rules.

LEMMA 11.32 (SQUEEZE LEMMA)

If L is a pair extension acceptable logic, and if x is a non-trivial prime L-theory, and if y, z are L-theories, then

- *If $(y, z) \subseteq x$ then there are non-trivial prime theories $y' \supseteq y$ and $z' \supseteq z$, where $y', z' \subseteq x$.*
- *If $(y; z) \subseteq x$ then there are non-trivial prime theories $y' \supseteq y$ and $z' \supseteq z$, where $y'; z' \subseteq x$.*
- *If $\bullet y \subseteq x$ then there is a non-trivial prime theory $y' \supseteq y$, where $\bullet y' \subseteq x$.*

PROOF   Each case is a corollary of the Pair Extension Theorem.

- Suppose that $(y, z) \subseteq x$. Then $\langle z, \{B : (\exists A \in y, C \not\in x)(A, B \vdash C)\}\rangle$ is a pair. If not, there is a $B' \in z$ where $B' \vdash \bigwedge B_i$, where $A_i, B_i \vdash C_i$ for each i, $A_i \in y$, $C_i \not\in x$. (We need not consider $\bigvee B'_j$ in the antecedent, as z is a theory.) Then it follows that $\bigwedge A_i, \bigvee B_i \vdash \bigvee C_i$ by simple manipulations. Now $\bigvee C_i \not\in x$, as x is prime. Similarly, $\bigwedge A_i \in y$ as y is a theory. So, if $\bigvee B_i \in z$, this contradicts $(y, z) \subseteq x$. Therefore we have a pair, which can be extended to a full pair $\langle z', w' \rangle$. Here z' is prime, and $(y, z') \subseteq x$ since if $A \in y$ and $A, B \vdash C$ with $C \not\in x$ then $B \in w'$ and hence $B \not\in z'$. Now consider $\langle y, \{A : (\exists B \in z', C \not\in x)(A, B \vdash C)\}\rangle$. This, too, is a pair (the reasoning is analogous to the case we have already seen), which can thus be extended to a full pair $\langle y', v' \rangle$, for which y' is prime and $(y', z') \subseteq x$, as required.
- Suppose $(y; z) \subseteq x$. Replace the comma by the semicolon in the proof above.
- Suppose $\bullet y \subseteq x$. Then $\langle y, \{B : (\exists C \not\in x)(\bullet B \vdash C)\}\rangle$ is a pair, since if it is not, $B' \in z$, where $B' \vdash \bigwedge B_i$, where $\bullet B_i \vdash C_i$ for each i, $C_i \not\in x$. It would follow that $\bullet \bigvee B_i \vdash \bigvee C_i$ by simple manipulations. Now $\bigvee C_i \not\in x$, as x is prime. So, if $\bigwedge B_i \in z$, this contradicts $\bullet y \subseteq x$. Therefore we have a pair, which can be extended to a full pair $\langle y', w' \rangle$, with y' prime and $\bullet y' \subseteq x$ as desired.   □

LEMMA 11.33 (STRUCTURAL RULE CONDITIONS)

If $x_1, \ldots, x_n$ and x are points in the canonical model, then $SR(X)$ holds in the canonical model if and only if $X(x_1, \ldots, x_n) \subseteq x$.

PROOF   An induction on the construction of X. The hypothesis holds if X is any of $0, \top$ or A_i. Consider the case for the comma. $SR(Y, Z)$ if and only if $SR(Y)$ and $SR(Z)$ if and only if $Y(x_1, \ldots, x_n) \subseteq x$ and $Z(x_1, \ldots, x_n) \subseteq x$ if and only if $(Y, Z)(x_1, \ldots, x_n) \subseteq x$ as desired.

Similarly, $SR(Y; Z)$ if and only if for some prime theories y, z, where $Ryzx$, $SR(Y)[x := y]$ and $SR(Z)[x := z]$. That is equivalent to there being prime theories y and z, where $Ryzx$, $Y(x_1, \ldots, x_n) \subseteq y$ and $Z(x_1, \ldots, x_n) \subseteq z$.

Now, if this holds, then $(Y; Z)(x_1, \ldots, x_n) \subseteq y; z \subseteq x$ as desired. Conversely, if $(Y; Z)(x_1, \ldots, x_n) \subseteq x$, by the squeeze lemma, there are prime y' and z', where $Y(x_1, \ldots, x_n) \subseteq y'$ and $Z(x_1, \ldots, x_n) \subseteq z'$ where $(y'; z') \subseteq x$. But this is equivalent to $Ry'z'x$, so we have the equivalence.

The case for $\bullet$ is similar and is left to Exercise 11.15. $\qquad\square$

This next lemma is a simple verification by induction on the structure of X. We state it without proof.

LEMMA 11.34 (MEMBERS OF $X(x_1, \ldots, x_n)$)
$A \in X(x_1, \ldots, x_n)$ if and only if for some $B_i \in x_i$, $X(B_1, \ldots, B_n) \vdash A$, where $X(B_1, \ldots, B_n)$ is given from X by replacing each formula A_i by B_i. $\qquad\square$

Now we can see how structural rules behave in the canonical model.

LEMMA 11.35 (RULE PRESERVATION)
If $X \Leftarrow Y$ is a structural rule, then in the canonical model, $X(x_1, \ldots, x_n) \subseteq Y(x_1, \ldots, x_n)$ for all theories $x_1, \ldots, x_n$.

PROOF Suppose $X \leftarrow Y$ holds. Then if $A \in X(x_1, \ldots, x_n)$ we have for some $B_i \in x_i$, $X(B_1, \ldots, B_n) \vdash A$. Therefore, by the structural rule we get $Y(B_1, \ldots, B_n) \vdash A$, and hence, $A \in Y(x_1, \ldots, x_n)$ as desired. $\qquad\square$

This corollary shows us when the conditions corresponding to a structural rule hold in the canonical frame.

COROLLARY 11.36 (STRUCTURAL RULES IN THE CANONICAL FRAME)
The conditions corresponding to the structural rules holding in $\mathfrak{S}$ hold in the canonical frame for $\mathfrak{S}$.

PROOF Suppose $X \leftarrow Y$ holds. Then if $SR(Y)$ we have $Y(x_1, \ldots, x_n) \subseteq x$ and hence, by Lemma 11.35, $X(x_1, \ldots, x_n) \subseteq x$, giving $SR(X)$ as desired. $\qquad\square$

Now we can finish the proof of the completeness theorem.

THEOREM 11.37 (COMPLETENESS OF FRAMES)
If $X \vdash_{\mathcal{F}} A$ for each frame $\mathcal{F}$ fit for $\mathfrak{S}, s$ then $X \vdash A$ is provable in $\mathfrak{S}$, then

PROOF We prove the converse and show that if $X \nvdash A$ then there is some frame in which X holds and A does not. We choose the canonical frame. We must show that the accessibility relations are indeed accessibility relations. That has been given by Lemma 11.28. We need to check that the canonical relation $\Vdash$ satisfies the required conditions. That has been delivered by Lemma 11.30. Finally, we need to show that the structural rules hold, but that has been completed in Corollary 11.36. $\qquad\square$

The soundness and completeness theorems together show us that certain classes of frames (classes satisfying structural rule conditions) fit exactly our substructural logics. This is a powerful result, as techniques for manipulating frames will help us to prove more things about our logics. In Section 11.7, we will extend our conservative extension results to deal with a wide range of connectives. In Section 13.3, we will show that certain substructural logics may be conservatively extended by Boolean negation. Furthermore, for many applications of substructural logics, a particular frame forms the *intended interpretation* of the logic. For example, a class of strings under composition is a frame, and the relation ⊩ between points in the frame and propositions simply *is* the notion of string typing to be modelled by the logic. So a soundness and completeness result shows that the natural deduction system captures validity in the intended domain. In Chapter 16, we will consider whether frame semantics can give an intended model for when we use a substructural logic to model consequence between propositions in general. Before we can do this, however, we need to extend our work to deal with negation, which is not covered by our techniques so far.

11.4 Negation

Our negation conditions are not expressed as structural rules, so we need to deal with these on a case-by-case basis.

Rule	Condition
$\sim\,=\,\neg$	$xCy \to yCx$
$\sim\top \vdash \bot$	$\forall x \exists y (xCy)$
$A \wedge \sim A \vdash \bot$	xCx
$\top \vdash A \vee \sim A$	$xCy \to y \sqsubseteq x$
$\sim(A \wedge B) \vdash \sim A \vee \sim B$	$xCy_1 \wedge xCy_2 \to (\exists z)((y_1 \sqsubseteq z) \wedge (y_2 \sqsubseteq z) \wedge xCz)$
$\sim\sim A \vdash A$	$\forall x \exists y (xCy \wedge \forall z (yCz \to z \sqsubseteq x))$
$\sim I; \neg E$	$\exists x (Ryzx \wedge xCw) \to \exists v (Rywv \wedge zCv)$
$\neg I; \sim E$	$\exists v (Rywv \wedge zCv) \to \exists x (Ryzx \wedge xCw)$

Table 11.2: Conditions for Negation

THEOREM 11.38 (SOUNDNESS FOR THE NEGATION CONDITIONS)
If a frame satisfies a condition in Table 11.2, then the corresponding consecution is valid in that frame.

The proof of this theorem is a straightforward verification.

PROOF   Suppose that $xCy \rightarrow yCx$ for each x and y. Then take an arbitrary point x in the frame. If $x \Vdash {\sim}A$ then for any y where xCy, $y \not\Vdash A$. It follows that for any y where yCx, that $y \not\Vdash A$, so $y \Vdash \neg A$ too. The converse also holds, so ${\sim}A$ is equivalent to $\neg A$, as desired.

Suppose that $\forall x \exists y(xCy)$ in $\mathcal{F}$. Then it follows that $x \not\Vdash {\sim}\top$, as there is a y where xCy, and we have $y \not\Vdash \bot$. Therefore ${\sim}\top \vdash_{\mathcal{F}} \bot$ holds, as desired.

Suppose that xCx for each $x \in \mathcal{F}$. Then if $x \Vdash A$, since xCx we have $x \not\Vdash {\sim}A$, and hence, $A \wedge {\sim}A \vdash_{\mathcal{F}} \bot$ as desired.

Suppose that $xCy \rightarrow y \sqsubseteq x$ for each $x, y \in \mathcal{F}$. Then if $x \not\Vdash A$, if xCy then $y \sqsubseteq x$, so $y \not\Vdash A$, and hence $x \Vdash {\sim}A$. Therefore, for any x, $x \Vdash A \vee {\sim}A$, and thus, $\top \vdash_{\mathcal{F}} A \vee {\sim}A$, as desired.

Suppose that $xCy_1 \wedge xCy_2 \rightarrow (\exists z)((y_1 \sqsubseteq z) \wedge (y_2 \sqsubseteq z) \wedge xCz)$ for each $x, y_1, y_n \in \mathcal{F}$. Take $x \Vdash {\sim}(A \wedge B)$. Now we ask whether $x \Vdash {\sim}A \vee {\sim}B$. To prove this we need to show that there are no y_1 and y_2 where xCy_1 and xCy_2, $y_1 \Vdash A$ and $y_2 \Vdash B$. Are there any such? If there are, then there is a z where xCz, $y_1 \sqsubseteq z$ and $y_2 \sqsubseteq z$. This gives $z \Vdash A \wedge B$, which contradicts $x \Vdash {\sim}(A \wedge B)$. Therefore, there are no such y_1 and y_2, and we have $x \Vdash {\sim}A \vee {\sim}B$ as desired.

Suppose that $\forall x \exists y(xCy \wedge \forall z(yCz \rightarrow z \sqsubseteq x))$ in $\mathcal{F}$. Suppose that $x \Vdash {\sim}{\sim}A$. To show that $x \Vdash A$, we reason as follows: there is a y such that xCy, and for any z, $yCz \rightarrow z \sqsubseteq x$. Now, since $x \Vdash {\sim}{\sim}A$ we have $y \not\Vdash {\sim}A$, so there is a z where yCz, and $z \Vdash A$. Since $z \sqsubseteq x$, we have $x \Vdash A$ as we wished.

Suppose that $(\exists x)(Ryzx \wedge xCw)$ gives $(\exists v)(Rywv \wedge zCv)$. Suppose that $A; B \vdash_{\mathcal{F}} \neg C$. We wish to show that $A; C \vdash_{\mathcal{F}} {\sim}B$. If $x \Vdash A; C$ then there are y, z where $y \Vdash A$, $z \Vdash C$ and $Ryzx$. We wish to show that $x \Vdash {\sim}B$. So, we want to know that if xCw then $w \not\Vdash B$. The frame condition tells us that there is a v where $Rywv$ and zCv. So, $z \Vdash C$ ensures that $v \not\Vdash \neg C$, and so, since $A; B \vdash \neg C$, we have $v \not\Vdash A; B$. So since $y \Vdash A$ and $Rywv$, we have $w \not\Vdash B$ as desired.

The rule $(\neg I; {\sim}E)$ is dual to the rule $({\sim}I; \neg E)$ and its verification is dual to that given above. This completes the proof. $\square$

The conditions, then, guarantee that the corresponding consecution holds in the frame. For the reverse, we show that the canonical frame for a logic including a consecution in the table also satisfies the condition corresponding to it.

THEOREM 11.39 (COMPLETENESS FOR THE NEGATION CONDITIONS)
The canonical frame for a logic including a consecution in Table 11.2 satisfies the condition corresponding to that consecution.

PROOF   Suppose that in some logic ${\sim}$ and $\neg$ are identified, and suppose that xCy in the canonical frame. To show that yCx, take ${\sim}A \in y$. If $x \in A$ then ${\sim}{\sim}A \in x$ (as $A \vdash {\sim}{\sim}A$) we have ${\sim}A \notin y$, contradicting what we assumed. Therefore $x \notin A$, and yCx as desired.

Suppose that in our logic $\sim\top \vdash \bot$ holds. Take a non-trivial prime theory x. We want a prime theory y such that xCy. Consider $\langle\{\top\}, \{A : \sim A \in x\}\rangle$. This is a pair, since if $\top \vdash \bigvee A_i$ for some choice of A_i where $\sim A_i \in x$, then $\sim\bigvee A_i \vdash \sim\top$. But $\sim\bigvee A_i \dashv\vdash \bigwedge\sim A_i \in x$, and $\sim\top \vdash \bot$. This would give $\bot \in x$, which is not possible, as x is non-trivial. Therefore $\langle\{\top\}, \{A : \sim A \in x\}\rangle$ is a pair, which can be extended to a full pair $\langle y, z\rangle$, with y prime, and for which xCy. (Since if $\sim A \in x$ then $A \in z$ and hence $A \notin y$.)

Suppose that in our logic we have $A \wedge \sim A \vdash \bot$. Take a non-trivial prime theory x. If $\sim A \in x$ then $A \notin x$ since $A \wedge \sim A \vdash \bot$. Therefore xCx as desired.

Suppose that in our logic we have $\top \vdash A \vee \sim A$. Then in any non-trivial prime theory x, $A \vee \sim A \in x$, so either $A \in x$ or $\sim A \in x$. Therefore, if xCy, and $A \in y$, then $\sim A \notin x$, and hence $A \in x$. Since A is arbitrarily chosen, $y \subseteq x$ as desired.

Suppose that $\sim(A \wedge B) \vdash \sim A \vee \sim B$, and that xCy_1 and xCy_2. We want a prime theory z where $y_1 \subseteq z$, $y_2 \subseteq z$ and xCz. Consider $\langle y_1 \cup y_2, \{A : \sim A \in x\}\rangle$. This is a pair, since if $B \wedge C \vdash \bigvee A_i$, where $B \in y_1$ and $C \in y_2$, and where $\sim A_i \in x$, then since $\sim \bigvee A_i \dashv\vdash \bigwedge\sim A_i$, we have $\bigwedge\sim A_i \vdash \sim(B \wedge C)$. But then $\bigwedge\sim A_i \vdash \sim B \vee \sim C$, giving $\sim B \vee \sim C \in x$ (as $\bigwedge\sim A_i \in x$). Since x is prime, $\sim B \in x$ (contradicting xCy_1) or $\sim C \in x$ (contradicting xCy_2). Therefore we have a pair, which can be extended to $\langle z, w\rangle$, giving us our prime z, for which it is easily verified that xCz.

Suppose that $\sim\sim A \vdash A$, and that x is a prime theory. We wish to show that for some y, xCy and for all z where yCz we have $z \sqsubseteq x$. To verify this, first note that if $\sim\sim A \vdash A$ then $\sim(A \wedge B) \vdash \sim A \vee \sim B$. Since $\sim A \vdash \sim A \vee \sim B$ gives $\sim(\sim A \vee \sim B) \vdash \sim\sim A$ and hence $\sim(\sim A \vee \sim B) \vdash A$. Similarly, $\sim(\sim A \vee \sim B) \vdash B$ giving $\sim(\sim A \vee \sim B) \vdash A \wedge B$ and hence $\sim(A \wedge B) \vdash \sim\sim(\sim A \vee \sim B)$, which gives $\sim(A \wedge B) \vdash \sim A \vee \sim B$ as desired.

Now to construct the desired y, consider the set $x^* = \{A : \sim A \notin x\}$. We will show that this is the desired prime theory. First, xCx^*, by definition. Second, if x^*Cz then whenever $\sim A \in x^*$, $A \notin z$. Now suppose that $B \in z$. First, x^*Cz gives $\sim B \notin x^*$, and thus, $\sim\sim B \in x$ by definition of x^*. Therefore $B \in x$ as desired.

Then we need to show that x^* is a prime theory. It is clearly closed under entailment — if $A \vdash B$ then $\sim B \vdash \sim A$. For conjunction, if $A, B \in x^*$ then $\sim A, \sim B \notin x$, so the primeness of x ensures that $\sim A \vee \sim B \in x$, so we have $\sim(A \wedge B) \notin x$, giving $A \wedge B \in x^*$. For primeness, if $A \vee B \in x^*$ then $\sim(A \vee B) \notin x$, and hence $\sim A \wedge \sim B \notin x$, so since x is a theory, at least one of $\sim A$ and $\sim B$ is not in x, giving one of A and B in x^*. Similarly, for not-triviality, if $\bot \in x^*$ then $\sim\bot \notin x$, which would mean that $\top \notin x$, which is not the case, so $\bot \notin x^*$. And since $\sim\bot \vdash \top$ we have $\sim\top \vdash \sim\sim\bot \vdash \bot$, so $\sim\top \notin x$, giving $\top \in x^*$, which completes our demonstration that x^* is a prime theory.

Now for $(\sim I; \neg E)$, we wish to show that if $Ryzw$ and xCw then there is a prime theory v where $Rywv$ and zCv. To do this, we consider whether $zC(y; w)$. Suppose that $\neg A \in yw$. Is $A \notin z$? Well, since $\neg A \in yw$ there are $B \in y$ and $C \in w$, where $B; C \vdash \neg A$, and by $(\sim I; \neg E)$ it follows that $B; A \vdash \sim C$. So $C \in w$ and xCw ensures that $\neg C \notin x$, so $B; A \notin x$, giving $A \notin z$ as desired, as $Ryzx$ and $B \in y$. Therefore, $zC(y; w)$. Now use the Pair Extension Lemma to find a prime v where $(y; w) \subseteq v$ and zCv. (How? $\langle (y; w), \{B : \sim B \in z\}\rangle$ is a pair.) It follows that $Rywv$, and we have our condition.

The condition $(\neg I; \sim E)$ is dual, and proved similarly.   □

That deals with our negation conditions. We know that all of the logics defined by structural rules, or negation rules (or a mix of both) are modelled by frame semantics.

11.5   *Correspondence*

Soundness and completeness together provide us with quite an understanding of how frames work. However, another kind of relationship can hold between consecutions and conditions on frames.

DEFINITION 11.40 (FRAME CORRESPONDENCE)
The condition C on frames *corresponds to* the consecution $X \vdash A$ just when $X \vdash_{\mathcal{F}} A$ if and only if $\mathcal{F}$ satisfies C.

Consider the consecution $p \vdash \sim\sim p$. If I have a frame on the set $\{a, b\}$, where aCb but $\sim(bCa)$, then I can construct an evaluation on the frame which will make $p \vdash \sim\sim p$ fail. Take $a \Vdash p$, and $b \nVdash p$. Since b is not compatible with any point at which A is true (in particular, it is not compatible with a) we have $b \Vdash \sim A$. Therefore since b is compatible with a, $a \nVdash \sim\sim A$. Therefore $A \vdash \sim\sim A$ fails.

It is easy to spot how this counterexample to double negation elimination works. It is made possible by the failure of the symmetry of C. In fact, in *any* frame which is not symmetric, we can construct a failure of double negation elimination in a similar way. Consider a frame $\mathcal{F}$ in which aCb and $\sim(bCa)$. Now define $\Vdash$ by setting $x \Vdash p$ if and only if $a \sqsubseteq x$. So we have made p true at x and true at as few other places as possible. Now consider b. Does $b \Vdash \sim p$? Consider all y such that bCy. If bCy then we could not have $y \Vdash p$, since that would mean that $a \sqsubseteq y$, which would give bCa, which we know we do not have. Therefore, $y \nVdash p$, for any y where bCy, and hence, $b \Vdash \sim p$. Therefore, since aCb, $a \nVdash \sim\sim p$. Therefore, $p \nVdash_{\mathcal{F}} \sim\sim p$.

This reasoning works no matter what else is going on in the frame $\mathcal{F}$. Therefore, we have the following *correspondence* theorem.

THEOREM 11.41 (DNE CORRESPONDS TO SYMMETRY)
If C is plump, then C is symmetric in $\mathcal{F}$ if and only if $p \vdash_{\mathcal{F}} \sim\sim p$.

By the soundness theorem we have the left-to-right direction, and the reasoning we have just given provides justification for the right-to-left direction.

This sort of "correspondence" result is well known in modal logics. For an overview of results in correspondence theory, consult van Benthem's survey article [30].

We must underline that correspondence results are not the same as soundness and completeness results. We may have a correspondence result without a completeness result if the canonical model for the logic fails to satisfy the correspondence condition. In this case, the model (with its privileged evaluation relation) will validate the theses of the logic, but the canonical frame underlying the model will not. In the other direction, it is possible to have conditions for which a logic is sound and complete. For example, S4 is sound and complete for *finite tree models* of modal logic, but the condition of being a finite tree does not correspond to the logic S4, for there are S4 frames which are not finite trees.

It is quite straightforward to expand our catalogue of correspondence results to the other negation conditions.

THEOREM 11.42 (NEGATION CORRESPONDENCE RESULTS)
Each consecution in Table 11.2 corresponds to its matching frame condition (in plump frames).

PROOF This is a simple verification of cases. We will show how it is done for $(\sim I; \neg E)$. We have already seen that if $\mathcal{F}$ satisfies the condition $\exists x (Ryzx \wedge xCw) \rightarrow \exists v(Rywv \wedge zCv)$ then the rule $(\sim I; \neg E)$ holds in the frame. (That is the soundness result.) For the converse, suppose the condition fails. That is, we have points x, y, z, w where $Ryzx$ and xCw but there is no v where $Rywv$ and zCv. We will construct an evaluation in which $p; q \vdash \neg r$ holds but $p; r \vdash \sim q$ fails. We need some point x where $x \Vdash p; r$ (so, some y and z where $Ryzx$, $y \Vdash p$ and $z \Vdash r$) but in which $x \nVdash \sim q$. So, we set $[\![p]\!] = \{y' : y \sqsubseteq y'\}$, $[\![q]\!] = \{w' : w \sqsubseteq w'\}$ and $[\![r]\!] = \{z' : z \sqsubseteq z'\}$. We have $x \nVdash \sim q$, since xCw and $w \Vdash q$. To show that $p; q \vdash \neg r$, suppose that $u \Vdash p; q$ then there are y', w' where $Ry'w'u$. Since R is plump, it follows that $Rywu$. Now suppose that sCu. Can we have $s \Vdash r$? If we do, then $z \sqsubseteq s$, and hence zCu, which does not holds by our condition on the frame (there is no point v where $Rywv$ and zCv, so u cannot be such a point). This ensures that $u \nVdash \neg r$, so we have $p; q \nvdash_{\mathcal{F}} \neg r$ as desired. □

So much holds for our negation conditions. We will end this section by showing that correspondence results also hold for our structural rules.

For now, in a statement $Y \Leftarrow X$ of a structural rule, we will assume that the formulae occurring in Y and X are atomic propositions $p_1, \ldots, p_n$, or $\top$. This is no restriction, for the rules are closed under substitution for formulae.

THEOREM 11.43 (CORRESPONDENCE FOR STRUCTURAL RULES)
For any structural rule $Y \Leftarrow X$, we have $X \vdash_{\mathcal{F}} Y$ (i.e. for each x, if $x \Vdash X$ then $x \Vdash Y$) if and only if the frame $\mathcal{F}$ satisfies the condition $SR(X) \to SR(Y)$.

To prove this we need one more lemma in the style of those proved for the completeness theorem.

LEMMA 11.44 (SR CORRESPONDENCE)
Given a structure X with constituents from among $p_1, \ldots, p_n$, and a model $\mathfrak{M}$ with points $x_1, \ldots x_n$, such that $[\![p_i]\!] = \{y : x_i \sqsubseteq y\}$, then $x \Vdash X$ if and only if $SR(X)$ holds in $\mathfrak{M}$.

This is a simple induction on the complexity of X.

PROOF Suppose that X is p_i. Then $x \Vdash p_i$ if and only if $x_i \sqsubseteq x$, by the definition of $[\![p_i]\!]$, but $x_i \sqsubseteq x$ is the definition of $SR(p_i)$. If X is 0, then $x \Vdash X$ if and only if Tx, which is $SR(0)$. If X is $\top$, then $x \Vdash X$ always, and this is $SR(\top)$.

Suppose that $X = Y; Z$ and the hypothesis holds for Y and Z. Then $x \Vdash Y; Z$ if and only if for some y and z where $Ryzx$, $SR(Y)[x := y]$ and $SR(Z)[x := z]$. This is the definition of $SR(Y; Z)$.

Similar reasoning verifies the cases for Y, Z and $\bullet Z$. This completes the proof. □

Now we have the correspondence result.

PROOF One half of the correspondence is established by soundness, as always. For the other half, assume that $\mathcal{F}$ does not satisfy $SR(X) \to SR(Y)$. Let the atomic propositions in X and Y come from $p_1, \ldots, p_n$. Since the condition fails, there are points $x, x_1, \ldots, x_n$ in $\mathcal{F}$ such that $SR(X)$ holds and $SR(Y)$ fails. Define $[\![\cdot]\!]$ by setting $[\![p_i]\!] = \{y : x_i \sqsubseteq y\}$. By Lemma 11.44, since $SR(X)$ holds, $x \Vdash X$. By the same lemma, since $SR(Y)$ fails, $x \nVdash Y$. Therefore $X \vdash_{\mathcal{F}} Y$ fails, as desired. □

11.6 New Conditions and New Logics

Frames give us natural ways to do things that we cannot do simply with other approaches to our logics. One is to define an operator $\Diamond$ which is dual with $\Box$ in the following way. We can set

$$x \Vdash \Diamond A \text{ iff for some } y, \text{ where } xSy, \ y \Vdash A.$$

Note that $\Diamond$ differs from $\diamondsuit$ in the direction of the accessibility relation. In classical logic, we can define $\Diamond$ in terms of $\Box$ simply: $\Diamond$ is $\sim\Box\sim$. But in our logics, $\sim\Box\sim$ is nothing like $\Diamond$: its evaluation clause will involve the compatibility relation C as well as S. This will only work to define $\Diamond$ when $\sim$ is Boolean negation. Once we define $\Diamond$ with the above clause, it is straightforward to show that the following conditions are satisfied in any model (and hence frame, or class of frames).

$$\Box(A \vee B) \vdash \Box A \vee \Diamond B \qquad \Box A \wedge \Diamond B \vdash \Diamond(A \wedge B)$$

We will call these the *Dunn conditions*, as Dunn was the first to explain their significance in the study of modal logics without Boolean negation.[3]

THEOREM 11.45 (SOUNDNESS OF THE DUNN CONDITIONS)
In any frame $\mathcal{F}$ in which $S_\Box = \check{S}_\Diamond$, we have

$$\Box(A \vee B) \vdash_{\mathcal{F}} \Box A \vee \Diamond B \qquad \Box A \wedge \Diamond B \vdash_{\mathcal{F}} \Diamond(A \wedge B)$$

PROOF   If $x \Vdash \Box(A \vee B)$ then to show that $x \Vdash \Box A \vee \Diamond B$, suppose that $x \not\Vdash \Box A$. Then there is some y where $xS_\Box y$, where $y \not\Vdash A$. However, $x \Vdash \Box(A \vee B)$ gives $y \Vdash B$. Therefore, since $S_\Box \subseteq \check{S}_\Diamond$ there is some y where $yS_\Diamond x$ and $y \Vdash B$, giving $x \Vdash \Diamond B$ as desired.

The other condition is given by $\check{S}_\Diamond \subseteq S_\Box$ in a similar way. $\Box$

What is less obvious is that the logic of $\Box$ and $\Diamond$ tied together with those clauses is sound and complete with respect to the class of frames in which $S_\Box = \check{S}_\Diamond$.

For this, we need to abandon our plump accessibility relations, as the next lemma shows. For the statement of this lemma we need one definition.

DEFINITION 11.46 (COMPONENTS IN POINT SETS)
A $\sqsubseteq$-*component* in a point set $\mathcal{P}$ is a non-empty subset $X \subseteq \mathcal{P}$ such that, first, if $x \in X$ and $x \sqsubseteq y$ or $y \sqsubseteq x$ then $y \in X$, and second, X has no proper subset with this property.

So, an $\sqsubseteq$-component is a set X such that any two points in X are connected by some path which goes up and down the relation $\sqsubseteq$, and *any* point so accessible from X is in X.

LEMMA 11.47 (TRIVIALITY OF PLUMP RELATIONS)
If S and $\check{S}$ are both plump positive two-place accessibility relations, then if xSy and x' is in the same $\sqsubseteq$-component as x and y' is in the same $\sqsubseteq$-component as y, then $x'Sy'$. As a result, in any frame so defined, $\top \vdash_{\mathcal{F}} \Box A \vee (\Box A \supset \bot)$, where $\supset$ is intuitionistic implication.

---

3   Dunn called these the $\Box$–$\Diamond$ interaction rules [79].

PROOF Since S is plump and positive, if xSy, $x' \sqsubseteq x$ and $y \sqsubseteq y'$ then $x'Sy'$. Similarly, since $\check{S}$ is plump and positive, if xSy and $x \sqsubseteq x'$ and $y' \sqsubseteq y$, then $x'Sy'$. So, if x' is in the same $\sqsubseteq$-component as x, and y' is in the same $\sqsubseteq$-component as y, then there is some zig-zag $\sqsubseteq$-path between x and x', another between and y and y'. C is preserved across such a path.

Therefore, for any point x in such a frame $\mathcal{F}$, if $x \Vdash \Box A$, then $x' \Vdash \Box A$ for each x' in the same $\sqsubseteq$-component as x. Therefore, if $x \nVdash \Box A$, $x' \nVdash \Box A$ for each $x' \sqsupseteq x$, and it follows that $x' \Vdash \Box A \supset \bot$, as desired. $\qquad\square$

This proves that plump relations S such that $\check{S}$ is also plump, are not enough to model the many possible logics of $\Box$ and $\Diamond$. Here is an example of such a logic.

EXAMPLE 11.48 (POSSIBILITY IN LINEAR $\sqsubseteq$-FRAMES)
Take the class of linear $\sqsubseteq$-frames, in which $x \Vdash \Diamond A$ if and only if for some $y \sqsupseteq x$, $y \Vdash A$. (Linearity is necessary to ensure that $\Diamond$ formulae satisfy the heredity condition.) This is a possibility relation. Furthermore, its corresponding necessity is the vacuous modality, since we have

$$A \vee B \vdash A \vee \Diamond B \qquad A \wedge \Diamond B \vdash \Diamond(A \wedge B)$$

which are the Dunn conditions when $\Box$ is the *vacuous* operator. However, in these models we do *not* have $\vdash A \vee (A \supset \bot)$.

To model this logic, at least, we need to move away from plump frames. This means we need to move away from our standard canonical model construction, since $S_\Box$ and $S_\Diamond$, as defined in the canonical model, are plump. To prove completeness we need to do something else. Here, we define xSy in the canonical model structure if and only if $xS_\Box y$ and $yS_\Diamond x$. In other words, xSy if and only if whenever $\Box A \in x$, $A \in y$, and *furthermore*, if $A \in y$, $\Diamond A \in x$.

LEMMA 11.49 (S IS A POSITIVE TWO-PLACE ACCESSIBILITY RELATION)
If $x'Sy'$ then if $x \subseteq x'$ there is a $y \subseteq y'$ where xSy, and similarly, if $y \subseteq y'$ then there is an $x \subseteq x'$ where xSy.

PROOF Suppose that $x'Sy'$, and $x \subseteq x'$. We want some $y \subseteq y'$ where xSy. Consider $\langle \Box^{-1}x, \overline{y'} \cup \Diamond^{-1}\overline{x} \rangle$ (where $\overline{x}$ is the set of formulae *not* in x, $\Box^{-1}x = \{A : \Box A \in x\}$, and $\Diamond^{-1}x = \{A : \Diamond A \in x\}$). This is a pair. Suppose that $\bigwedge A_i \vdash B \vee \bigvee B_j$, where $A_i \in \Box^{-1}x$ (so each $\Box A_i \in x$ for each i), $B \in \overline{y'}$ (so $B \notin y'$) and $B_j \in \Diamond^{-1}\overline{x}$ (so $\Diamond B_j \notin x$ for each x). Therefore $\Box \bigwedge A_i \vdash \Box(B \vee \bigvee B_j)$. But $\Box(B \vee \bigvee B_j) \vdash \Box B \vee \Diamond \bigvee B_j \vdash \Box B \vee \bigvee \Diamond B_j$. However, $\Box \bigwedge A_i \in x$ and neither $\Box B$ nor $\Diamond B_j \in x$ for any j. So we have a pair, and it is extended by a full pair $\langle y, z \rangle$. Then y is prime, and xSy, since if $\Box A \in x$, $A \in y$, and if $A \in y$ then

$\Diamond A \in x$ (by the converse: if $\Diamond A \notin x$, then $A \in z$ and hence $A \notin y$). Finally, $y \subseteq y'$, as $z \supseteq \overline{y'}$.

Similarly, if $x'Sy'$ and $y \subseteq y'$, then we construct x where xSy. Consider $\langle \Diamond y, \overline{x'} \cup \Box \overline{y} \rangle$. This is a pair, since if $A_i \in y$ and $B \notin x$ and $B_j \notin y$, we cannot have $\bigwedge \Diamond A_i \vdash B \vee \bigvee \Box B_j$. Since whenever $A_i \in y$, $\Diamond A_i \in x$, so $\bigwedge \Diamond A_i \in x$. However, $B \notin x$ (as $B \notin x' \supseteq x$) and $\Box B_j \notin x$ (since xSy, and $B_j \notin y$). So, we have a pair, which is extended by the full pair $\langle x, w \rangle$, in which x is prime, $x \subseteq x'$ and xSy. Since if $\Box A \in x$, then $A \in y$ (if $A \notin y$ then $\Box A \in w$, so $\Box A \notin x$) and if $A \in x$ then $\Diamond A \in y$. □

LEMMA 11.50 (COUNTEREXAMPLES WITH S)
Whenever x is a prime theory, then if $\Box A \notin x$, there is some prime theory y where xSy and $A \notin y$. Similarly, if $\Diamond A \in x$, then there is some prime theory y where xSy and $A \in y$.

PROOF   Suppose that $\Diamond A \in x$. We want some y where xSy and $A \in y$. Consider $\langle \Box^{-1}x \cup \{A\}, \Diamond^{-1}\overline{x} \rangle$. This is a pair, since if $A \wedge A_1 \wedge \cdots \wedge A_n \vdash B_1 \vee \cdots \vee B_m$ where each $A_i \in \Box^{-1}x$ and $B_j \in \Diamond^{-1}\overline{x}$ then we have $\Diamond A \in x$, $\Box A_i \in x$ and $\Diamond B_j \notin x$. By properties of necessity and the fact that x is a theory, we have $\Diamond A \wedge \Box(A_1 \wedge \cdots \wedge A_n) \in x$. By the second Dunn condition we have $\Diamond(A \wedge A_1 \wedge \cdots \wedge A_n) \in x$. By monotonicity of $\Diamond$, we have $\Diamond(B_1 \vee \cdots \vee B_m) \in x$, giving $\Diamond B_1 \vee \cdots \vee \Diamond B_m \in x$. This contradicts the fact that each $\Diamond B_i \notin x$, given the primeness of x.

So, our pair is extended by a prime pair $\langle y, w \rangle$. We have xSy, since if $\Box A \in x$, $A \in y$, and if $A \in x$ then $\Diamond A \in y$ too.

For the second condition, we reason similarly. If $\Box A \notin x$ then consider $\langle \Box^{-1}x, \Diamond^{-1}\overline{x} \cup \{A\} \rangle$. This is a pair (for similar reasons, using the other Dunn condition) and its full extension $\langle y, w \rangle$ gives us a prime y such that xSy and $A \notin y$. □

There is a similar phenomenon with negation. We can define negation connectives with "possibility-like" properties, giving them existentially quantified causes.

$$x \Vdash \frown A \text{ iff for some } y \text{ where } xCy, y \not\Vdash A$$
$$x \Vdash \smile A \text{ iff for some } y \text{ where } yCx, y \not\Vdash A$$

In this case, it is simple to verify the following connections between our new negations and our other negation connectives.

$$\sim\!\!A \wedge \neg B \vdash \frown(A \vee B) \quad \sim\!\!(A \wedge B) \vdash \sim\!\!A \vee \neg B$$
$$\neg A \wedge \smile B \vdash \smile(A \vee B) \quad \neg(A \wedge B) \vdash \neg A \vee \smile B$$

We will leave it to the exercises to prove the soundness and completeness of these conditions.

11.7 Conservative Extensions from Frames

Now we will show that many more conservative extensions are possible.

LEMMA 11.51 (ADDING FAMILY)
Given a model for some language Lang, *we can extend the evaluation* ⊩ *to model the language* Lang', *which adds to* Lang *the whole family for every intensional or modal connective.*

PROOF Consider the case for □ and ◇. If we have □, we can define ◇ on this model by using the □ accessibility relation, and similarly, if we have ◇ we can define □ on this model by using the ◇ accessibility relation.   □

So, given a frame for → we can add ∘ and ←. For ∼ we can add ¬, for □ we can add ◇, and so on.

   This will give us a much stronger conservative extension result than is possible using the ideal structure of Section 9.2. That construction would not give us the conservative extension of → by ∘, or of □ by ◇. Now we have that result.

THEOREM 11.52 (CONSERVATIVE EXTENSION BY FAMILY)
Any logic L *which is sound and complete for a class of frames is conservatively extended by a logic which adds the mates of any connectives in* L.

PROOF Suppose that $X \vdash A$ fails in some model on some frame. Extend the model to also evaluate the mates of the connectives in L, in the manner of Lemma 11.51. Then $X \vdash A$ can be invalidated in this extended model. This model is a model of the extended logic as it validates the family conditions.   □

So frames give us powerful results when it comes to proving theorems about our logics. Frames also give us very concrete models for our logics. In the next chapter, we will see how to use frames to model logics without distribution.

11.8 History

The frame semantics for modal logics has a long and involved history. The original papers of Kripke no doubt popularised the possible worlds semantics [126, 128], but the ideas had many antecedents in many different fields.[4] Early antecedents of the frame semantics for substructural logics can be found in Jónsson and Tarski's work on the representation of Boolean algebras with operators [122, 123]. This work presents what amounts to a soundness and completeness result for frames of substructural logics (with Boolean negation), though it takes a certain amount of hindsight to see it as such. The papers are written very much from the perspective of algebra and representation theory.

---

[4] Copeland's essay on "Prior's Life and Legacy" [48] explains Arthur Prior's involvement, among many others in the history of possible worlds semantics.

Urquhart [262, 263, 264, 265], in a series of papers, explored what is now known as an *operational* semantics for relevant implication. In this semantics, the accessibility relation is an operation: $Rxyz$ if and only if $z = x \sqcup y$, where $\sqcup$ has the properties of a semilattice join operator. This is good for the semantics of $\rightarrow$ and $\wedge$ in relevant logics, but it does not do well for disjunction. The points in the semantics are theories, not necessarily *prime* theories. If x and y are theories, so is $x \sqcup y$ — '$(x; y)$' in our notation. However, if x and y are prime, there is no assurance that $(x; y)$ is a prime theory. We might have $p \rightarrow q \vee r \in x$ and $p \in y$, giving $q \vee r \in (x; y)$, without any guidance as to which of q or r ought to go in $(x; y)$. To deal with this problem, we need either a different clause for disjunction, and to keep the operational account of implication, or a different account of implication. Routley and Meyer [227, 228, 229] chose the latter route, and Fine [84, 85] chose the former. For Routley and Meyer, using a ternary relation for implication means that we can use prime theories, and hence use the standard clause for disjunction in the semantics. For Fine, implication can be modelled using the operational semantics, and a non-standard clause for disjunction is used. An extensive study of the properties of ternary frames is given in Routley, Meyer, Brady and Plumwood's *Relevant Logics and their Rivals* [231]. Gabbay [89] also gave a ternary relational semantics for implication, independently of the tradition of Routley and Meyer.

According to Cresswell [119, page 50] the term 'frame' was first used in print by Segerberg [242].

Frames can be viewed from an algebraic point of view — with an eye on the definitions of Chapter 8. The class $\mathrm{Prop}(\mathcal{F})$ of propositions of the frame is a completely distributive lattice under intersection and union, and it is equipped with the appropriate operators, defined by the clauses in the evaluation conditions. For example, the implication clause gives us

$$\alpha \rightarrow \beta = \{x : (\forall y, z \in \mathcal{F})(Rxyz \rightarrow (y \in \alpha \rightarrow z \in \beta))\}$$

Similarly, $\sim\alpha = \{x : (\forall y \in \mathcal{F})(xCy \rightarrow y \notin \alpha)\}$, and so on. We will call the resulting propositional structure '$\mathrm{Alg}(\mathcal{F})$' the *algebra* of the frame $\mathcal{F}$. Furthermore, any interpretation $\Vdash$ on a frame gives you an evaluation $v_{\Vdash}$ given by setting $v_{\Vdash}(A)$ to be $[\![A]\!]$. The connections with algebra run even deeper. Our canonical model is constructed out of prime theories in a language. A similar construction can work with the *prime filters* of a propositional structure. Dunn's work on gaggles [76, 77, 78] generalises the results here to operators with arbitrary arity. An n-ary operator is modelled with an $n + 1$-place relation.

Duality theory is the study of the relationship between algebras and their representations in terms of frames. There is an important strand of recent work in the semantics of substructural logic exploring duality theory in this context [108, 109, 111, 236, 271].

Dunn is also responsible for the results modelling possibility and necessity in the absence of Boolean negation [79]. Meyer and Mares have important work on the particular case of adding an S4-type necessity for R [149], and they have shown that disjunctive syllogism is admissible in this case, using the frame semantics to prove it. (Traditional proofs for the admissibility of gamma break down in the presence of the Dunn conditions for possibility and necessity.) Meyer and Mares have also studied the extensions of these logics with Boolean negation [148, 162].

I have used the frame semantics for negations to show how logics such as intuitionistic logic can be conservatively extended with other negations [217].

Study of the frame conditions corresponding to rules brings forward questions of canonicity and correspondence. When is the canonical frame for a logic itself a model of the logic? This is not always the case in modal logics, and also, not always the case in substructural logics. There has been some work in attempting to pin down the class of substructural logics for which canonicity holds [94, 129].

Not all logics have connectives which are amenable to the treatment of accessiblity relations. We will see this when we consider ! from linear logic. Another case is the counterfactual conditional. These are more aptly modelled by *neighbourhood frames*. There has been a little work considering how neighbourhood frames can be used in a substructural setting [3, 88, 147].

11.9 Exercises

Practice

{11.1} Consider the partially ordered set $\{a, b, c, d\}$ presented here

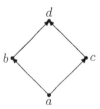

Define the relation X on this set by fixing aXb, aXc and aXd. Is it an accessibility relation? If so, is it positive or is it negative?

{11.2} Define an accessibility relation R on the set $\{1, 2, 3, \ldots\}$ of positive integers, ordered by divisibility, by setting $Rxyz$ if and only if $xy \mid z$. Is R a plump three-place accessibility relation?

{11.3} In this frame, let p_n be true at all m where $n \mid m$. At what points is $p_n \wedge p_m$ true? Where is $p_n \to p_m$ true? How about $p_n \circ p_m$?

{11.4} Does the frame of the previous two exercises have a truth set? What structural rules are satisfied in this frame?

{11.5} Construct a frame in which $A \wedge (A \to B) \vdash B$ fails.

{11.6} Construct a frame with a non-plump R on which $A \vdash (A \to B) \to B$ holds, but in which there are points x, y, z where $Rxyz$ but *not* $Ryxz$.

{11.7} Construct a frame with *two different* de Morgan negations.

Problems

{11.8} Complete the proof of Lemma 11.10 by showing that $[\![B \leftarrow A]\!]$ and $[\![A \circ B]\!]$ are always propositions on a frame.

{11.9} Consider frames defined in terms of domains. If the domain contains only *strict* functions, then the totally undefined object $\bot$ (written in bold here to distinguish it from the false constant $\bot$) which approximates *everything*: $\bot \sqsubseteq x$ for each x. In this domain, $x\bot \sqsubseteq y$ for each y. So for each x, z there is a y where $Rxyz$. It follows that $A \vdash B \circ \top$, which makes $\circ$ look very much *unlike* conjunction! Explore the logic of domains containing strict functions. What other odd properties does it have?

{11.10} Construct a simple function of type $A \to B$ which is not also of type $(C \to A) \to (C \to B)$, proving that B fails for function application.

{11.11} Complete the proof, on page 252, of the soundness theorem by supplying the analyses for the connective rules missed out there.

{11.12} Complete the proof of Lemma 11.25 by showing that $C_\sim$ and $C_\neg$ are equivalent, and that any pair of $R_\to$, $R_\circ$ and $R_\leftarrow$ are equivalent.

{11.13} Complete the proof of Lemma 11.28 by showing that no matter how you define the canonical accessibility relations, they are, indeed, accessibility relations.

{11.14} Complete the proof of Lemma 11.29 by showing that witnesses exist for $\Box$, $\sim$, $\leftarrow$ and $\circ$ formulae in the canonical model.

{11.15} Complete the proof of Lemma 11.33 by dealing with the inductive step for $\bullet$.

{11.16} Suppose that $\Box$ is a necessity and $\sim$ is a negation. Under what conditions is $\sim\Box\sim$ a possibility operator? What is its accessibility relation? Under what conditions is $\sim\Box\sim$ equivalent to $\Diamond$? When is it equivalent to $\Diamond$? (Where $\Diamond$ and $\Box$ are related by the Dunn conditions.)

{11.17} Something for first-order equivalents. Take a first-order language with predicates P_i for each atomic formula p_i. Fix a variable x, and let $\alpha[z := y]$ be the result of substituting y for all free occurrences of z in α. The *standard translation* ST of a substructural formula is a first-order formula defined as follows:

$$
\begin{aligned}
ST(p_i) &= P_i x \\
ST(\top) &= \text{true} \\
ST(\bot) &= \text{false} \\
ST(A \wedge B) &= ST(A) \wedge ST(B)
\end{aligned}
$$

$$
\begin{aligned}
ST(A \vee B) &= ST(A) \vee ST(B) \\
ST(t) &= Tx \\
ST(A \to B) &= \forall y \forall z (Rxyz \to (ST(A)[x := y] \to ST(B)[x := z])) \\
ST(B \leftarrow A) &= \forall y \forall z (Ryxz \to (ST(A)[x := y] \to ST(B)[x := z])) \\
ST(A \circ B) &= \exists y \exists z (Ryzx \wedge ST(A)[x := y] \wedge ST(B)[x := z])
\end{aligned}
$$

where y and z are fresh variables in each instance. Extend the definition to model positive and negative modal operators, and show that $\mathfrak{M}, x \Vdash A$ if and only if $\mathfrak{M} \models \alpha[x]$, where $\models$ is simple first-order satisfaction.

{11.18} Show that the logic of p-type negations is sound and complete for the frame conditions given on page 268.

{11.19} Mitchell's *IE models*, defined below, are models of linear logic with distribution of $\wedge$ over $\vee$ [176]. In these models, points are *pairs* $\langle m, n \rangle$ whose elements are taken from a commutative monoid R of *resources*. As R is a commutative monoid, there is an operation $+$ on R, such that $m + n = n + m$, with an identity 0, such that $m + 0 = m = 0 + m$. We evaluate propositions at points as follows: $\langle m, n \rangle \Vdash A \circ B$ if and only if for some n_1, n_2 where $n = n_1 + n_2$, $\langle m + n_1, n_2 \rangle \Vdash A$ and $\langle m + n_2, n_1 \rangle \Vdash B$. $\langle m, n \rangle \Vdash {\sim} A$ if and only if $\langle n, m \rangle \not\Vdash A$. $\langle m, n \rangle \Vdash A \to B$ if and only if for each m_1, m_2 where $m = m_1 + m_2$, if $\langle n + m_2, m_1 \rangle \Vdash A$ then $\langle m_2, n + m_1 \rangle \Vdash B$. Conjunction, disjunction, $\top$ and $\bot$ are defined in the usual way. What are the relations R and C on this frame? How ought you to interpret t? Show that in this frame $!A$, defined as $t \wedge A$, satisfies the conditions for the ! modality. Find a consecution valid in this frame which is not valid in LL with distribution. Find a consecution not using exponentials valid in this frame, and that cannot be proved in LL with distribution.

Projects

{11.20} Continuing on from Exercise 11.17, characterise the first-order formulae which are equivalent to formulae of the form $ST(A)$ for some formula A.

{11.21} Continuing on from Exercise 11.19, find a sound and complete axiomatisation from the logic of Mitchell's IE models.

{11.22} Consider Meyer and Mares' proof of the admissibility of γ for R4 [148]. Characterise a larger class of logics for which it holds. Find some logics for which it does not.

Chapter 12

Frames II: Logics Rejecting Distribution

Closure occurs
when the concluding portion of a poem
creates in the reader
a sense of appropriate cessation.
— Barbara Herrnstein Smith, Poetic Closure, *1968*

12.1 How to Reject Distribution

Substructural logics with extensional conjunction and disjunction need not satisfy the distributive law. However, the distributive law follows inexorably from three conditions in the frame semantics for our logics.

1. $A \vdash_{\mathfrak{M}} B$ if and only if for each x, if $x \Vdash A$ then $x \Vdash B$.
2. $x \Vdash A \wedge B$ if and only if $x \Vdash A$ and $x \Vdash B$.
3. $x \Vdash A \vee B$ if and only if $x \Vdash A$ or $x \Vdash B$.

Given these three conditions, it follows that $A \wedge (B \vee C) \vdash_{\mathfrak{M}} (A \wedge B) \vee (A \wedge C)$.[1] To live without distribution, we need to modify one of our three conditions. Which should it be?

In answering this question, you need to consider how the completeness result for a frame semantics is demonstrated. In the previous chapter, we proved completeness by considering the canonical frame, made up of prime theories. In the class of prime theories, the conditions (1), (2) and (3) are respected. $A \vdash B$ if and only if in every prime theory x, if $A \in x$ then $B \in x$. Similarly, $A \wedge B \in x$ iff $A \in x$ and $B \in x$, and $A \vee B \in x$ iff $A \in x$ or $B \in x$. If prime theories respect all three conditions, the natural weakening is to consider the class of theories. In this case, (1) and (2) are respected, but (3) fails. We can have a theory including $A \vee B$ without the theory containing A or containing B. A natural way to construct models for logics without distribution is to consider models in which condition (3) fails. It is clear that we need it to fail in the left-to-right direction: that is, we require points x at which $x \Vdash A \vee B$ while $x \not\Vdash A$

---

[1]   Belnap's "Life in the Undistributed Middle" [25] makes this point rather forcefully and examines the case for living without distribution.

and $x \not\Vdash B$. The right-to-left direction is assured by condition (1), as we have $A \vdash A \vee B$ and $B \vdash A \vee B$. Before we consider formal definitions of our frames for non-distributive logic, we will cast about to see how the issue of semantics for disjunction has been treated in the past.

EXAMPLE 12.1 (BETH FRAMES)

The oldest account of a frame semantics with a non-standard clause for disjunction seems to be Beth's semantics for intuitionistic logic. Recall the "informational interpretation" of frames for intuitionistic logic. Points are stages of research ordered by inclusion. We have $x \Vdash A$ just when at x, A has been established. Beth's interpretation for disjunction relaxes the condition to say that it might be possible to have $x \Vdash A \vee B$ without having either $x \Vdash A$ or $x \Vdash B$, provided that from x, you will either demonstrate A or demonstrate B *eventually*. I can know now that $A \vee B$ if I know now that either A or B will be demonstrated at some time in the future. To formalise this, we need two notions. (For Beth's work on these frames, see his original papers [35, 36], and also Chapter 15 of his book *The Foundations of Mathematics* [37].)

DEFINITION 12.2 (CHAINS AND BARS)

Given a point set $\mathcal{P}$, a subset α of $\mathcal{P}$ is totally ordered iff for each $x, y \in \alpha$, either $x \sqsubseteq y$ or $y \sqsubseteq x$. α is a *chain* in $\mathcal{P}$ just when it is a maximal totally ordered subset of $\mathcal{P}$. That is, α is totally ordered, and there is no $y \in \mathcal{P}$ such that $y \notin \alpha$ and $\alpha \cup \{y\}$ is totally ordered too. A subset $B \subseteq \mathcal{P}$ *bars* a point x iff every chain α through x intersects B.

Beth's rule for disjunction is simple:

$\diamond$ $x \Vdash A \vee B$ if and only if $[\![A]\!] \cup [\![B]\!]$ bars x

In other words, for any possible course of research through x (that is, on any chain through x) either A or B will be verified.

Nearly all else remains the same in the semantics for the intuitionistic connectives, except for one thing. We restrict the propositions to be closed under barring. That is, if $[\![A]\!]$ bars x for some x, we must have $x \in [\![A]\!]$ too. After all, if I am assured that A will be found out at some stage of my research (no matter how my research goes) then I am assured that A now. It is sufficient to know that $[\![p]\!]$ is closed under barring for atomic propositions p, as this property is inherited by all of the complex propositions.

This is a simply understood semantics for a formal logic with a non-standard evaluation of disjunction. However, it is not too much help with the failure of distribution, as distribution is still valid in these models. (What should we expect? It is meant to be a semantics for intuitionistic logic, after all.) Before going to another example, let us see how distribution succeeds in this model.

If $x \Vdash A \wedge (B \vee C)$ then $x \Vdash A$ and $x \Vdash B \vee C$. Therefore every chain through x is barred by $[\![B]\!] \cup [\![C]\!]$. To show that $x \Vdash (A \wedge B) \vee (A \wedge C)$ we will show that x is barred by $[\![A \wedge B]\!] \cup [\![A \wedge C]\!]$. Take any chain through x. There is some point y on this chain where $y \Vdash B$ or $y \Vdash C$. Now either $x \sqsubseteq y$ or $y \sqsubseteq x$ (chains are totally ordered), so let z be the *later* of x and y. Since $x \sqsubseteq z$, we have $z \Vdash A$. Since $y \sqsubseteq z$ we have $z \Vdash B$ or $z \Vdash C$. So, we have $z \Vdash A \wedge B$ or $z \Vdash A \wedge C$, and as a result, the chain passes through $[\![A \wedge B]\!] \cup [\![A \wedge C]\!]$ as desired. So, we must look for another way to modify the clause for disjunction in order to reject distribution.

The first prominent example of a frame with a non-standard evaluation of disjunction, for which distribution fails, was given by Robert Goldblatt, who explicitly considered frames for a logic without distribution.

EXAMPLE 12.3 (GOLDBLATT FRAMES)
Consider *orthologic*: the logic of an ortho-negation with lattice connectives. Here a frame will most likely appeal to a two-place compatibility relation C to deal with negation. The compatibility relation will probably be reflexive (so $A \wedge \sim A \vdash \bot$) and symmetric (so $A \vdash \sim\sim A$). The question remains as to how to deal with disjunction. Goldblatt [100] solved that problem by considering a simple compatibility frame $\langle P, C \rangle$, where P is a set of points (unordered by any inclusion relation) and C is a symmetric, reflexive compatibility relation on P. Conjunction and negation are modelled exactly as you would expect.

⋄ $x \Vdash A \wedge B$ iff $x \Vdash A$ and $x \Vdash B$

⋄ $x \Vdash \sim A$ iff for each y where xCy, $y \nVdash A$

However, as it stands, this semantics does not validate $\sim\sim A \vdash A$. To add an extra condition on C to validate double negation elimination would result in C being the identity relation (see the results in Section 11.4) and the logic would collapse into classical propositional logic. Goldblatt's insight was to instead restrict the evaluation of propositions on the frame to those propositions for which $\sim\sim A \vdash A$ is valid.

Given a set $\alpha \subseteq P$, let $\alpha^\sim = \{y : \forall x(x \in \alpha \rightarrow \sim yCx)\}$, or equivalently, $\{y : \forall x(yCx \rightarrow x \notin \alpha)\}$. Therefore, for any evaluation, $[\![A]\!]^\sim = [\![\sim A]\!]$. A set $\alpha \subseteq P$ is said to be *C-closed* if and only if $\alpha = \alpha^{\sim\sim}$. The C-closed sets will model our propositions. If C is symmetric (as it is, here) then $\alpha \subseteq \alpha^{\sim\sim}$, since $x \in \alpha^{\sim\sim}$ if and only if for each y where xCy there is a z where yCz and $z \in \alpha$. If $x \in \alpha$, then choosing x for z will do here, to show that $x \in \alpha^{\sim\sim}$.

It is enlightening to see why whenever α_i is a family of C-closed sets, that their intersection $\bigcap_i \alpha_i$ is also C-closed. α_i is C-closed iff

$$\forall y(xCy \rightarrow \exists z(yCz \wedge z \in \alpha_i)) \rightarrow x \in \alpha_i$$

So, suppose that $\forall y(xCy \rightarrow \exists z(yCz \wedge z \in \bigcap_i \alpha_i))$. It follows that $x \in \alpha_i$ for each i, and therefore that $x \in \bigcap_i \alpha_i$ as desired. Therefore $\bigcap_i \alpha_i$ is C-closed, as we had wished.

As with Beth frames, a disjunction is true not only at the points at which either disjunct is true but also at the closure of that set of points. Here, however, it is C-closure at work.

$\diamond$ $x \Vdash A \vee B$ iff $x \in (\llbracket A \rrbracket \cup \llbracket B \rrbracket)^{\sim\sim}$

This semantics gives us the failure of distribution well enough. However, it relies on the presence of negation. It would be good to be able to model the failure of distribution in logics in which there is no negation — or at the very least, logics in which $\sim\sim A$ is not equivalent to A. The double negation closure operation is not general enough for our purposes.

EXAMPLE 12.4 (DEDEKIND–MACNEILLE FRAMES)
There is a way to define a different closure operation on frames which needs no connection to negation. Define '$y \sqsubseteq \alpha$' to mean $y \sqsubseteq x$ for each $x \in \alpha$. Then the closure $\Gamma\alpha$ of a set α of points can be given as follows:

$$\Gamma\alpha = \{z : \forall y(y \sqsubseteq \alpha \rightarrow y \sqsubseteq z)\}$$

So, if whenever y comes before everything in α it also comes before z, then z is in the closure of α. To see how this works, consider the closure operation on the class of all theories of some logic. If α is a set of theories, then suppose $y \sqsubseteq \alpha$ — that is, $y \sqsubseteq x$ for each $x \in \alpha$. This is equivalent to saying that $y \sqsubseteq \bigcap\alpha$: y is no bigger than the intersection of the set of the theories in α, which is itself a theory. So, if $y \sqsubseteq z$, then we must have $\bigcap\alpha \sqsubseteq z$ too. This is the idea that the Dedekind–MacNeille closure operator models. If $x \in \Gamma\alpha$, then anything true in all of α must also be true in x. So in these frames, to model disjunction we require $x \Vdash A \vee B$ if and only if $x \in \Gamma(\llbracket A \rrbracket \cup \llbracket B \rrbracket)$.

The name for this closure operation refers to MacNeille, who generalised Dedekind's construction of the real numbers from rational numbers in terms of "cuts" to construct an embedding of an arbitrary ordered set into the set of closed subsets of that set [144]. The closure operation Γ can be seen as the composition of two simpler operations. Define α^l and α^u, the *lower* and *upper* sets of α, as follows:

$$\alpha^l = \{x : (\forall a \in \alpha)(x \sqsubseteq a)\} \qquad \alpha^u = \{x : (\forall a \in \alpha)(a \sqsubseteq x)\}$$

The lower set of α is the set of all of its lower bounds, and its upper set is the set of its upper bounds. Then $\Gamma\alpha = \alpha^{lu}$, the upper set of the lower set of α.

It is not too difficult to show that any set generated by a single point x, $\uparrow x = \{y : x \sqsubseteq y\}$, is closed under Γ. $(\uparrow x)^l = \{y : y \sqsubseteq x\}$, and hence, $(\uparrow x)^{lu} = \{y : x \sqsubseteq y\} = \uparrow x$.

12.2 Definitions

Armed with these examples, we can see a general pattern occurring. Propositions on frames are still (interpreted by) sets of points, but we restrict our attention to sets of points which are closed in some particular way. The required properties of closure operators are as follows:

DEFINITION 12.5 (CLOSURE OPERATORS)
Γ is a *closure operator* on the set P if it is a function from the power set of P to itself, satisfying the following conditions:

1. Γ is INCREASING: $\alpha \subseteq \Gamma\alpha$

2. Γ is IDEMPOTENT: $\Gamma\Gamma\alpha = \Gamma\alpha$

3. Γ is MONOTONE: If $\alpha \subseteq \beta$ then $\Gamma\alpha \subseteq \Gamma\beta$

A set $\alpha \subseteq P$ is said to be *closed* if $\alpha = \Gamma\alpha$. A set P equipped with a closure operator is called a *closure set*, and we will write $x \in \mathcal{P}$ for $x \in P$, as we did with point sets.

It is not too difficult to show that the closure operators of our three examples each satisfy the conditions of this definition. The verification is left to Exercise 12.1.

It is perhaps a *little* misleading to call Γ a *closure operator*. Closure operators are widely present in topological spaces. The closure of a set in a topological space is found by adding the "boundary" to the set (this is merely a suggestive explanation — there are formal definitions for these concepts). The same sort of thing happens here in our cases, so to an extent, 'closure' fits well. However, in topological spaces, closure operators satisfy more postulates than those in Definition 12.5. In any topological space, the union of two closed sets is also closed. This is manifestly out of place here. If the union of two closed sets was itself closed, then we could not invalidate distribution. The least upper bound of two closed sets would be their union, and distribution would be satisfied. Furthermore, while the intersection of a family of closed sets is still closed (as we will see in the next lemma) we do not have $\Gamma\bigcap_i \alpha_i = \bigcap_i \Gamma\alpha_i$. The closure of an intersection need not equal the intersection of the closure.

So, our closure operators are more general than topological closure operators. However, the usage 'closure' is established in the lattice theory literature (it is used by Davey and Priestley [58], for example) so with the proviso that not all closures are *topological* closures we continue with the usage.

LEMMA 12.6 (CLOSURE FACTS)
For any closure operator Γ, the following conditions hold:

1. *If $\alpha = \Gamma\beta$ for some β, then $\alpha = \Gamma\alpha$.*

2. *If α_i is closed for each i, so is $\bigcap_i \alpha_i$.*

3. *The class of closed subsets in a closure set forms a complete lattice with intersection as greatest lower bound and the closure of the union as least upper bound.*

4. *There are closure sets in which $\emptyset$ is not a closed set.*

5. *There are closure sets in which $\Gamma(\alpha \cup \beta) \neq \Gamma\alpha \cup \Gamma\beta$.*

6. *There are closure sets in which $\Gamma(\alpha \cap \beta) \neq \Gamma\alpha \cap \Gamma\beta$.*

PROOF We take these facts in turn.

1. If $\alpha = \Gamma\beta$ then $\alpha = \Gamma\beta = \Gamma\Gamma\beta = \Gamma\alpha$.

2. Since $\bigcap \alpha_i \subseteq \alpha_i$, by monotonicity, and since each α_i is closed, we have $\Gamma \bigcap \alpha_i \subseteq \alpha_i$ for each i. Therefore $\Gamma \bigcap \alpha_i \subseteq \bigcap \alpha_i$. Conversely, $\bigcap \alpha_i \subseteq \Gamma \bigcap \alpha_i$ as Γ is increasing.

3. The intersection of any class of closed sets is closed, by the previous item. So the class of closed subsets in a closure set forms a complete semilattice, ordered by $\subseteq$ and with $\bigcap$ as greatest lower bound. For the least upper bounds, $\bigvee \mathcal{A}$ is the smallest closed set containing each $\alpha \in \mathcal{A}$. Clearly, $\Gamma(\bigcup \mathcal{A})$ is that smallest closed set, so $\bigvee$ is the closure of the union as desired.

4. Consider the Dedekind–MacNeille closure operator Γ on some ordered set with a greatest element ∞. Consider $\Gamma\emptyset = \{z : \forall y(y \sqsubseteq \emptyset \rightarrow y \sqsubseteq z)\}$. Since $y \sqsubseteq \infty$ for any y at all, we have $\infty \in \Gamma\emptyset$. It follows that $\emptyset$ is not closed.

5. Take an ordered set with a least element 0 and two elements a and b above 0 but incomparable with each other. Consider the Dedekind–MacNeille closure operator on this set. $\{a\}$ and $\{b\}$ are closed, but $\{a, b\}$ is not closed, as its closure is $\{0, a, b\}$.

6. Take an ordered set with a least element 0, and now with *four* elements a, b, c and d above 0 but incomparable with each other, and consider again the Dedekind–MacNeille closure operator on this set. Now $\Gamma\{a, b\} = \{0, a, b, c, d\} = \Gamma\{c, d\}$. Therefore $\Gamma\{a, b\} \cap \Gamma\{c, d\} = \{0, a, b, c, d\}$. However, $\{a, b\} \cap \{c, d\} = \emptyset$, and $\Gamma\emptyset = \emptyset$. $\square$

Given a closure set $\mathcal{P}$, we can model the lattice connectives. We use the notation '$\Vdash$' and '$\llbracket \; \rrbracket$' as before for a relation between $\mathcal{P}$ and formulae, and a function from formulae to closed subsets of $\mathcal{P}$, respectively.

Definition 12.7 (Modelling Lattice Connectives)
A relation ⊩ between points in $\mathcal{P}$ and formulae *respects lattice connectives* if and only if the following conditions are satisfied:

⋄ $\Gamma[\![p]\!] = [\![p]\!]$.

⋄ $x \Vdash \top$ always.

⋄ $x \Vdash \bot$ iff $x \in \Gamma\emptyset$.

⋄ $x \Vdash A \wedge B$ iff $x \Vdash A$ and $x \Vdash B$.

⋄ $x \Vdash A \vee B$ iff $x \in \Gamma([\![A]\!] \cup [\![B]\!])$.

This definition always assigns closed sets to formulae, as the following theorem explains.

Theorem 12.8 (Closure of Lattice Connectives)
Given any closure set $\mathcal{P}$ and any model on $\mathcal{P}$, $[\![A]\!]$ is closed for any formula A consisting purely of lattice connectives.

Proof We know that $[\![\top]\!]$ and $[\![\bot]\!]$ are closed, as is $[\![p]\!]$ for each atomic p. By induction on the construction of propositions, if $[\![A]\!]$ and $[\![B]\!]$ are closed, then $[\![A \wedge B]\!] = [\![A]\!] \cap [\![B]\!]$ must be closed as intersections of closed sets are closed, and $[\![A \vee B]\!] = \Gamma([\![A]\!] \cup [\![B]\!])$ is defined to be closed. □

You may have noticed that we are doing without the heredity condition on points and evaluations. At least, we do not explicitly mention ⊑ in our conditions on evaluations. This is not without reason. All we need for ⊑ is already given to us by Γ. We can see how this works by attending to Dedekind–MacNeille frames:

Lemma 12.9 (⊑ in Dedekind–MacNeille Frames)
Given a Dedekind–MacNeille closure operator Γ, the inclusion $x \sqsubseteq y$ holds if and only if $\Gamma\{x\} \supseteq \Gamma\{y\}$.

Proof Suppose that $x \sqsubseteq y$ and $z \in \Gamma\{y\} = \{v : \forall w(w \sqsubseteq y \rightarrow w \sqsubseteq v)\}$. Clearly, if $\forall w(w \sqsubseteq y \rightarrow w \sqsubseteq z)$ then $\forall w(w \sqsubseteq x \rightarrow w \sqsubseteq z)$ and hence $z \in \Gamma\{x\}$ as desired. Conversely, if $\Gamma\{x\} \supseteq \Gamma\{y\}$, then $y \in \Gamma\{x\}$ and hence $\forall w(w \sqsubseteq x \rightarrow w \sqsubseteq y)$ and so $x \sqsubseteq x \rightarrow x \sqsubseteq y$, giving $x \sqsubseteq y$ as desired. □

This motivates a definition of inclusion on the points in an arbitrary closure set:

Definition 12.10 (Inclusion on Closure Sets)
Given a closure set $\mathcal{P}$, define the relation of *inclusion* $\sqsubseteq_\Gamma$ on the points of $\mathcal{P}$ by setting

$$x \sqsubseteq_\Gamma y \text{ if and only if } \Gamma\{x\} \supseteq \Gamma\{y\}$$

Once we have inclusion defined in this way, we can show that it acts roughly as we would expect inclusion to act.

LEMMA 12.11 (INCLUSION FACTS)
On any closure set $\mathcal{P}$ the inclusion relation $\sqsubseteq_\Gamma$ has the following properties.

1. *$\sqsubseteq_\Gamma$ is transitive and reflexive, but not necessarily antisymmetric.*

2. *$x \sqsubseteq_\Gamma y$ if and only if in every model on $\mathcal{P}$, for every formula A, if $x \Vdash A$ then $y \Vdash A$.*

PROOF

1. $\sqsubseteq_\Gamma$ inherits its transitivity and reflexivity from that of $\supseteq$. It is not necessarily antisymmetric because $\Gamma\{x\}$ might equal $\Gamma\{y\}$ even though x and y are distinct. Take the trivial closure set on some two-element set $\{x, y\}$ in which the only closed sets are $\emptyset$ and the whole set. There the closures of both $\{x\}$ and of $\{y\}$ are $\{x, y\}$, so $x \sqsubseteq_\Gamma y$ and $y \sqsubseteq_\Gamma x$, but $x \neq y$.

2. If $x \sqsubseteq_\Gamma y$ then if $x \Vdash A$ we have $x \in [\![A]\!]$. We must have $y \in [\![A]\!]$ too as $y \in \Gamma\{y\} \subseteq \Gamma\{x\} \subseteq [\![A]\!]$. Conversely, if $x \not\sqsubseteq_\Gamma y$, then $\Gamma\{x\} \not\supseteq \Gamma\{y\}$ and hence $y \notin \Gamma\{x\}$. (If y were in $\Gamma\{x\}$ then $\Gamma\{x\} \cap \Gamma\{y\}$ would be a smaller closed set containing $\{y\}$ which is impossible.) So take some evaluation $\Vdash$ which sets $z \Vdash p$ if and only if $z \in \Gamma\{x\}$. We have $x \Vdash p$ but $y \not\Vdash p$, as desired. $\square$

So our closure sets bring with themselves a notion of heredity which mimics our familiar notion quite closely, except for the failure of antisymmetry. However, Exercise 12.6 shows how every closure set can be replaced by one which differs in no essential respects, except for the fact that $\sqsubseteq_\Gamma$ in the new set is antisymmetric.

Once we have defined a closure set which models the lattice connectives, we need then to add some machinery to our sets in order to model the intensional connectives. For this, we need to impose some conditions to ensure that the interpretation of formulae using intensional connectives are also closed sets of points. For this, we need the following conditions.

DEFINITION 12.12 (ACCESSIBILITY RELATIONS)
R, C and S are accessibility relations on a closure set when the following conditions are satisfied

$\diamond$ $\Gamma\alpha \circ \Gamma\beta \subseteq \Gamma(\alpha \circ \beta)$

$\diamond$ $\Diamond\Gamma\alpha \subseteq \Gamma\Diamond\alpha$

$\diamond$ $\Gamma{\sim}\alpha \subseteq {\sim}\Gamma\alpha$

for all sets α and β of points in the closure set.

We choose these definitions because they give us the following results. First, Γ "floats to the top" of structure combinations.

LEMMA 12.13 (CLOSURE FLOATING)
If R and S are accessibility relations on a closure set, then for any α and β we have

$\diamond$ $\Gamma(\Gamma\alpha \circ \Gamma\beta) = \Gamma(\alpha \circ \beta)$

$\diamond$ $\Gamma\Diamond\Gamma\alpha = \Gamma\Diamond\alpha$

for any α and β.

PROOF By assumption $\Gamma\alpha \circ \Gamma\beta \subseteq \Gamma(\alpha \circ \beta)$, so by monotonicity and idempotence, $\Gamma(\Gamma\alpha \circ \Gamma\beta) \subseteq \Gamma(\alpha \circ \beta)$. Conversely, since $\alpha \circ \beta \subseteq \Gamma\alpha \circ \Gamma\beta$ (as $\circ$ is order-preserving) we have $\Gamma(\alpha \circ \beta) \subseteq \Gamma(\Gamma\alpha \circ \Gamma\beta)$, so we have the identity desired. The case for $\Diamond$ is similar. □

On any closure frame, we can have operations $\circ$, $\to$, $\leftarrow$ and so on, defined on sets of points, in terms of the accessibility relations, just as in the case with distributive frames in the previous chapter. Here we need to make sure we know when the results of these operations are closed, given that the inputs are.

LEMMA 12.14 (INTENSIONAL COMBINATIONS OF CLOSED SETS)
In any closure set with accessibility relations, if α and β are closed, so are $\Box\alpha$, $\alpha \to \beta$, $\beta \leftarrow \alpha$, $\sim\alpha$ and $\neg\alpha$.

PROOF Consider the case for $\Box$. When α is closed, $\Box\alpha \subseteq \Gamma\Box\alpha$ by the monotonicity of Γ. Conversely, by the behaviour of $\Diamond$ and Γ we have $\Diamond\Gamma\Box\alpha \subseteq \Gamma\Diamond\Box\alpha$. However, $\Diamond\Box\alpha \subseteq \alpha$ by the definition of $\Diamond$ on sets. Therefore, $\Diamond\Gamma\Box\alpha \subseteq \alpha$ and hence $\Gamma\Box\alpha \subseteq \Box\alpha$. Therefore, $\Box\alpha = \Gamma\Box\alpha$ when α is closed.

Consider the case for $\to$. Note that $\Gamma\alpha \circ \Gamma(\alpha \to \beta) \subseteq \Gamma(\alpha \circ (\alpha \to \beta)) \subseteq \Gamma\beta$. Therefore, $\alpha \to \beta \subseteq \Gamma(\alpha \to \beta) \subseteq \Gamma\alpha \to \Gamma\beta = \alpha \to \beta$. Therefore, $\alpha \to \beta$ is closed. The case for $\leftarrow$ is similar.

For $\sim$, since $\sim\alpha \subseteq \Gamma\sim\alpha$ by monotonicity, we wish to show that $\Gamma\sim\alpha \subseteq \sim\alpha$ when α is closed. This is given to us by our assumption: $\Gamma\sim\alpha \subseteq \sim\Gamma\alpha = \sim\alpha$, since α is closed.

For $\neg$, $\neg\alpha \subseteq \Gamma\neg\alpha$ by monotonicity. For the converse, since $\alpha \subseteq \sim\neg\alpha$ we have $\Gamma\alpha \subseteq \Gamma\sim\neg\alpha \subseteq \sim\Gamma\neg\alpha$ (the first step by monotonicity, the second by the interaction between $\sim$ and Γ). But $\alpha \subseteq \sim\Gamma\neg\alpha$ gives $\Gamma\neg\alpha \subseteq \neg\alpha$ as desired. □

This lemma means that the connectives $\Box$, $\to$, $\leftarrow$, $\sim$ and $\neg$ can be modelled by their usual conditions on closure sets. These connectives have *universal* quantifiers in their modelling conditions they distribute over *conjunction*. The remaining intensional connectives, $\Diamond$ and $\circ$, call on *existential* quantifiers in their modelling conditions, and they distribute over *disjunction*. It is no surprise, then, that the clauses for these connectives must explicitly appeal to a closure operator, just as disjunction does. The proposition $A \circ B$ will be true not merely at $[\![A]\!] \circ [\![B]\!]$ but also at $\Gamma([\![A]\!] \circ [\![B]\!])$. Similarly, $\Diamond A$ will be true not merely at

$\Diamond \llbracket A \rrbracket$ but also at $\Gamma \Diamond A$. So we have the following evaluation clauses for our connectives.

◇ $\{x \in \mathcal{F} : x \Vdash p\} \in \text{Prop}(\mathcal{F})$.

◇ $x \Vdash \top$ for all $x \in \mathcal{F}$.

◇ $x \Vdash \bot$ iff $x \in \Gamma \emptyset$.

◇ $x \Vdash A \wedge B$ iff $x \Vdash A$ and $x \Vdash B$.

◇ $x \Vdash A \vee B$ iff $x \in \Gamma(\llbracket A \rrbracket \cup \llbracket B \rrbracket)$.

◇ $x \Vdash t$ iff $x \in \Gamma T$.

◇ $x \Vdash \Box A$ iff for each $y \in \mathcal{F}$ where xSy, $y \Vdash A$.

◇ $x \Vdash \Diamond A$ iff $x \in \Gamma \Diamond \llbracket A \rrbracket$.

◇ $x \Vdash \sim A$ iff for each $y \in \mathcal{F}$ where xCy, $y \nVdash A$.

◇ $x \Vdash \neg A$ iff for each $y \in \mathcal{F}$ where yCx, $y \nVdash A$.

◇ $x \Vdash A \to B$ iff for each $y, z \in \mathcal{F}$ where $Rxyz$, if $y \Vdash A$ then $z \Vdash B$.

◇ $x \Vdash A \circ B$ iff $x \in \Gamma(\llbracket A \rrbracket \circ \llbracket B \rrbracket)$.

◇ $x \Vdash B \leftarrow A$ iff for each $y, z \in \mathcal{F}$ where $Ryxz$, if $y \Vdash A$ then $z \Vdash B$.

DEFINITION 12.15 (CLOSURE FRAMES, AND FRAMES FIT FOR $\mathfrak{S}$)
A closure set equipped with a number of accessibility relations is said to be a *closure frame*.

Given a system $\mathfrak{S}$, a *frame is fit for* $\mathfrak{S}$ iff every condition corresponding to each structural rule holds in the frame. Furthermore, if $\mathfrak{S}$ contains extensional combination, the frame must be distributive.

This definition expands the definition of the previous chapter.

EXAMPLE 12.16 (STANDARD FRAMES ARE CLOSURE FRAMES)
If $\mathcal{F}$ is a standard frame, then it is not too difficult to show that it is a closure frame, in which $\Gamma \alpha = \{x : \exists y \in \alpha$ where $y \sqsubseteq x\}$. Here the closed sets are the closed upwards sets. We need just to show that the accessibility relations on $\mathcal{F}$ satisfy the conditions for accessibility relations on a closure frame, and that the evaluation conditions which appeal to Γ may as well not. For the first, we need $\Gamma \alpha \circ \Gamma \beta \subseteq \Gamma(\alpha \circ \beta)$ (if R is present) and similarly for $\Diamond$ and S, and $\sim$ and C. If $x \in \Gamma \alpha \circ \Gamma \beta$, there are y, z where $Ryzx$, $y \in \Gamma \alpha$ and $z \in \Gamma \beta$. It follows that there are $y' \in \alpha$ where $y' \sqsubseteq y$ and $z' \in \beta$ where $z' \sqsubseteq z$. We then have $Ry'z'x$, and hence $x \in \alpha \circ \beta$ and therefore, $x \in \Gamma(\alpha \circ \beta)$ as desired for $\Diamond$ and $\sim$ are similar.

To show that the evaluation conditions for fusion, disjunction and possibility need not appeal to the closure operator, we simply need to note that in standard frames, whenever α and β are closed, then so are $\alpha \circ \beta$, $\alpha \cup \beta$ and $\Diamond \alpha$. But that we have already proved.

To show that closure frames model logics, we need to show that the intensional connectives act in the appropriate ways. As the following lemma shows, they do.

LEMMA 12.17 (RESIDUATION ON CLOSURE FRAMES)
For any closed sets α, β and γ in a closure frame,

1. $\Gamma(\alpha \circ \beta) \subseteq \gamma$ *iff* $\alpha \subseteq \beta \to \gamma$ *iff* $\beta \subseteq \gamma \leftarrow \alpha$
2. $\Gamma\Diamond\alpha \subseteq \beta$ *iff* $\alpha \subseteq \Box\beta$
3. $\alpha \subseteq {\sim}\beta$ *iff* $\beta \subseteq \neg\alpha$.

Closure frames are concrete models of substructural logics. They generalise away from the distributive frames of the last chapter by allowing a notion of closure stronger than that given by heredity and the ordering $\sqsubseteq$. The propositions on a closure frame form a complete lattice under the subset ordering, as before. Lattice connectives are modelled by their set theoretic analogues, albeit with the intervention of Γ in the case of $\vee$ and $\bot$. The intensional connectives are also modelled by set theoretic representatives, given by accessibility relations. Again, this is just as the case with distributive frames, except for the parents in each family of connectives, which require a closure operation. In the next section, we will prove that these models fit substructural logics exactly.

12.3 Soundness and Completeness

In this section we will show that closure frames do model substructural logics. First, we will deal with soundness.

THEOREM 12.18 (SOUNDNESS FOR CLOSURE FRAMES)
If $X \vdash A$ in $\mathfrak{S}$, then $X \vdash_{\mathcal{F}} A$ in all frames $\mathcal{F}$ fit for $\mathfrak{S}$.

PROOF The verification is exactly as before. By Lemma 12.17 the connective rules are satisfied, as the residuation conditions hold.

We need to deal only with the additional rules. First, with structural rules. For a structural rule $X \Leftarrow Y$ we require that the frame satisfy the condition $SR(X) \to SR(Y)$. Then we need to verify that if $x \Vdash X$ then $x \Vdash Y$. (Where we read '$x_i \sqsubseteq x$' as '$x_i \sqsubseteq \Gamma\{x_i\}$', which ensures that if $x_i \Vdash A$ then $x \Vdash A$ too.) The verification is as before, with one modification. We need to deal with the closure operator Γ, which interrupts in the evaluation of structure. Suppose $x \Vdash X$. Then in our model, X is interpreted as a modal confusion of closed sets, with closure operators liberally distributed throughout the confusion. Consider an example. If $X = A; (\bullet B, C)$, then $[\![X]\!] = \Gamma[\![A]\!] \circ \Gamma(\Gamma\Diamond[\![B]\!] \cap [\![C]\!])$. By Lemma 12.13 this is the set $\Gamma([\![A]\!] \circ (\Diamond[\![B]\!] \cap [\![C]\!]))$, since we can "float" the Γ to the top of the expression. Therefore $[\![X]\!] = \Gamma X^*$, where X^* is a modal confusion which does not appeal to Γ. Now, since $SR(X) \to SR(Y)$, we have $X^* \subseteq Y^*$ (where Y^* is the modal confusion of closed sets, corresponding to Y) by the reasoning in the distributive case. Therefore $\Gamma X^* \subseteq \Gamma Y^*$, by the monotonicity of Γ, and since $x \Vdash X$, we have $x \Vdash Y$ as desired.

Now we need to deal with negation. The only differences here are with rules which appeal to the closure operator. Rules which do not, like $\sim\, =\, \neg$ and ECQ, go through as before.

For $\sim(A \wedge B) \vdash \sim A \vee \sim B$, note that if $x \Vdash \sim(A \wedge B)$ then by the reasoning in the distributive case, if $x \Vdash \sim(A \wedge B)$ then $x \Vdash \sim A$ or $x \Vdash \sim B$. It follows that $x \Vdash \sim A \vee \sim B$. The closure condition will give us *more* points at which $\sim A \vee \sim B$ is true, not fewer, so there is no problem here.

Similarly, for $\top \vdash A \vee \sim A$, note that for any x we will have $x \Vdash A$ or $x \Vdash \sim A$, as before. Therefore, for any x, $x \Vdash A \vee \sim A$ as desired. $\qquad \Box$

That shows that closure frames are models of each of our logics. To show that they fit snugly, we need to show that anything unprovable is invalid in a closure frame. For this, we produce the canonical closure frame.

There are a number of ways to define a canonical closure frame. Perhaps the most obvious one is to generalise the canonical frames for distributive logics to consider the set of *all* theories of the logic instead of just the prime theories. This is entirely acceptable, and it leads to a simple completeness proof. We will not pursue this line of attack here. We will do with *fewer* points, by taking them to be *formulae*.

DEFINITION 12.19 (THE CANONICAL CLOSURE FRAME)
The points in a canonical closure frame for $\mathfrak{S}$ are the formulae. We will define $A \Vdash p$ to be $A \vdash p$. Therefore, $[\![p]\!]$ is $\{A : A \vdash p\}$. We then aim to show that $[\![B]\!] = \{A : A \vdash B\}$ for each formula B.

Formulae are ordered by $\vdash$. We will write '$A \vdash B$', where appropriate, as '$B \sqsubseteq A$' to keep to the notation of frames. The closure operation Γ is the Dedekind–MacNeille closure operation defined by $\sqsubseteq$. That is, $A \in \Gamma\alpha$ if and only if for each B, if $B \sqsubseteq \alpha$ then $B \sqsubseteq A$, or equivalently, for each B where $C \vdash B$ for each $C \in \alpha$, then $A \vdash B$ also.

Finally, $RABC$ if and only if $C \vdash A \circ B$, ASB if and only if $B \vdash \Diamond A$, and ACB if and only if $A \nvdash \sim B$.

We must show that this is, indeed, a closure frame.

THEOREM 12.20 (THE CANONICAL FRAME IS A CLOSURE FRAME)
For any system $\mathfrak{S}$, the canonical closure frame for $\mathfrak{S}$ is a closure frame. Furthermore, it is a frame fit for $\mathfrak{S}$. In other words:

$\diamond$ Γ *is a closure operator.*

⋄ R, S and C, so defined, are accessibility relations.
⋄ The conditions corresponding to the structural rules of $\mathfrak{S}$ hold in the frame.
⋄ For each p, $[\![p]\!] = \{A : A \vdash p\}$ is closed.
⋄ For each A and B, $A \Vdash B$ if and only if $A \vdash B$.

Before going through the proof, it will be helpful to see how this frame works. In the canonical frame, the closed sets are *co-theories*. That is, they are the natural duals of theories. If $A \in \Gamma\alpha$ and $A' \vdash A$ then $A' \in \Gamma\alpha$ too. Furthermore, if $A, B \in \Gamma\alpha$ then $A \vee B \in \Gamma\alpha$. This makes this Dedekind–MacNeille structure look a lot like the ideal structure from Chapter 9. However, the closure operation here is more miserly. Not all co-theories (or ideals) are closed. For example, consider the smallest co-theory containing $\alpha = \{p_0, p_2, p_4, \dots\}$. It is not too difficult to show that in many logics (anything included in classical logic, at least) p_1 is not in this co-theory. (Why? Look for falsity preservation. You can make each of $\alpha = \{p_0, p_2, p_4, \dots\}$ false and p_1 true in some assignment.) Now consider $\Gamma\alpha$. If $p_{2n} \vdash A$ for each A, then we can choose some $2n$ such that p_{2n} does not appear in A. Therefore if $p_{2n} \vdash A$ for each $2n$, then $B \vdash A$ for each B whatsoever, so $p_1 \in \Gamma\alpha$. So, the closure of α can outstrip the co-theory generated by α.

PROOF   We deal with the cases one by one.

⋄ Γ is a closure operator, as it is a Dedekind–MacNeille operator.
⋄ Is R an accessibility relation? We want to show that $\Gamma\alpha \circ \Gamma\beta \subseteq \Gamma(\alpha \circ \beta)$. Now $\alpha \circ \beta = \{C : \exists A \in \alpha, B \in \beta(C \vdash A \circ B)\}$. Therefore, $(\alpha \circ \beta)^l = \{D : C \vdash D$ for each $C \in \alpha \circ \beta\} = \{D : A \circ B \vdash D$ for each $A \in \alpha$ and $B \in \beta\}$. Therefore, $\Gamma(\alpha \circ \beta) = (\alpha \circ \beta)^{lu} = \{C : \forall D((A \circ B \vdash D$ for each $A \in \alpha$ and $B \in \beta) \to C \vdash D)\}$. Now suppose that $A \in \Gamma\alpha$ and $B \in \Gamma\beta$, to show that $A \circ B \in \Gamma(\alpha \circ \beta)$. We need to show that for each D where $A_\alpha \circ B_\beta \vdash D$ for each $A_\alpha \in \alpha$, $B_\beta \in \beta$, then $A \circ B \vdash D$. We reason as follows. If $A_\alpha \circ B_\beta \vdash B$ for each $A_\alpha \in \alpha$ and $B_\beta \in \beta$, then $A_\alpha \vdash B_\beta \to D$ for each $A_\alpha \in \alpha$, so $A \vdash B_\beta \to D$, as $A \in \Gamma\alpha$. Therefore, $B_\beta \vdash D \leftarrow A$ for each $B_\beta \in \beta$, so $B \vdash D \leftarrow A$ and hence $A \circ B \vdash D$ as desired.
The case for $\Diamond\Gamma\alpha \subseteq \Gamma\Diamond\alpha$ is similar.

The case for negation is made as follows. We wish to show that $\Gamma{\sim}\alpha \subseteq {\sim}\Gamma\alpha$. Let $B \in \Gamma{\sim}\alpha$. To show that $B \in \neg\Gamma\alpha$, we want to show that for each $C \in \Gamma\alpha$, $B \vdash {\sim}C$. Now $B \in \Gamma{\sim}\alpha$ ensures that for each F where $(\forall E \in {\sim}\alpha \Rightarrow E \vdash F)$ gives $B \vdash F$. To show that $B \vdash {\sim}C$, we want to show that $\forall E \in {\sim}\alpha$, $E \vdash {\sim}C$ whenever $C \in \Gamma\alpha$. That is, we know that

$$\forall D(\forall A_\alpha \in \alpha \text{ and } A_\alpha \vdash D \Rightarrow C \vdash D)$$

Now $E \in \sim\alpha$ if and only if for each $A_\alpha \in \alpha$, $E \vdash \sim A_\alpha$. So we want $\forall E((\forall A_\alpha \in \alpha$ and $E \vdash \sim A_\alpha) \Rightarrow E \vdash \sim C)$, or equivalently, $\forall E((\forall A_\alpha \in \alpha$ and $E \vdash \sim A_\alpha) \Rightarrow C \vdash \neg E)$. But we have this, substituting $\neg E$ for D in the displayed condition. This completes the demonstration.

⋄ For structural rules, we have an easy induction to show that $SR(X)$ holds of A if and only if $A \vdash F(X)$, where $F(X)$ is the formula version of the structure X. So $SR(X) \to SR(Y)$ holds if and only if $A \vdash F(X) \Rightarrow A \vdash F(Y)$, for each A, if and only if $F(X) \vdash F(Y)$, or equivalently, $Y \Leftarrow X$ holds.

⋄ Since $[\![p]\!] = \{A : A \vdash p\} = {\uparrow}p$, the atomic propositions are closed.

⋄ We can show that $A \Vdash B$ if and only if $A \vdash B$ by induction on B. We do the two most difficult cases. First, $A \Vdash B \circ C$ if and only if $A \in \Gamma([\![B]\!] \circ [\![C]\!])$. By hypothesis, $[\![B]\!] = \{B' : B' \vdash B\}$ and $[\![C]\!] = \{C' : C' \vdash C\}$, so $[\![B]\!] \circ [\![C]\!] = \{D : D \vdash B \circ C\}$ and $[\![B]\!] \circ [\![C]\!]$ is closed, so $A \in \Gamma([\![B]\!] \circ [\![C]\!])$ iff $A \in [\![B]\!] \circ [\![C]\!]$ iff $A \vdash B \circ C$ as desired.

Similarly, $A \vdash B \lor C$ iff $A \in \Gamma([\![B]\!] \cup [\![C]\!])$. Now this holds iff $\forall D$ where $B \vdash D$ or $C \vdash D$, $A \vdash D$ too (by the induction hypothesis). That is, equivalent to $A \vdash B \lor C$, as we desired.

This completes the proof. □

Instead of going on to consider particular negation axioms or rules, we will examine a particularly important class of closure frames — Girard's *phase spaces*.

12.4   Phase Spaces

In this section, we will look at phase spaces for linear logic as an example of a closure frame. A *phase space* is a quadruple $\langle P, \cdot, 1, \mathbf{0} \rangle$ in which $\langle P, \cdot, 1 \rangle$ is a commutative monoid, and in which $\mathbf{0}$ is a distinguished subset of P. The elements of P are *phases*, and $\mathbf{0}$ is the set of *orthogonal phases* of P.[2] In a phase space, the binary operator $\cdot$ is used for the ternary relation for implication. Here, $Rxyz$ if and only if $x \cdot y = z$. For any subset $G \subseteq P$, the *dual* $G^\sim$ of G is defined as follows:

$$G^\sim = \{x \in P : \text{ for all } y \in G(x \cdot y \in \mathbf{0})\}$$

In other words, $G^\sim$ is the set of all objects which send each element of G (by the monoid operation) to $\mathbf{0}$. For any set G of phases, $G^{\sim\sim}$ is the *closure* of G. It is not too hard to verify that this is indeed a closure operation, by showing the following:

1. $G \subseteq G^{\sim\sim}$.

---

[2]   In the linear logic literature, '$\perp$' is used instead of '$\mathbf{0}$' for the set of orthogonal phases. We use $\perp$ for the bottom element of a lattice, so we will use $\mathbf{0}$ for the set of orthogonal phases.

2. $G^{\sim\sim\sim} = G^\sim$.

3. If $G \subseteq H$ then $H^\sim \subseteq G^\sim$.

4. $G = G^{\sim\sim}$ iff $G = H^\sim$ for some $H \subseteq P$.

The closed sets are called *facts*. The set of facts can be equipped with a natural monoid operation, $(G \cdot H)^{\sim\sim}$, where $G \cdot H$ is defined in the obvious way as $\{x \cdot y : x \in G \text{ and } y \in H\}$. This operation is residuated by the operation $\rightarrow$ defined by setting $G \rightarrow H = \{x : \forall y \in G(xy \in H)\}$, which can be shown to equal $(GH^\sim)^\sim$.

For negation, we define xCy to hold if and only if $x \cdot y \notin \mathbf{0}$. C is symmetric, given the commutativity composition, and the negation of a fact G is $G^\sim$. The negation of a fact is itself a fact. (We could have verified this using the conditions of the previous section: $\Gamma\sim G \leqslant \sim\Gamma G$ as $G^{\sim\sim\sim} \leqslant G^{\sim\sim\sim}$.)

It follows that this is a model for linear logic without exponentials. R satisfies the conditions for C and B, as composition is associative and commutative. The set $\mathbf{1} = \{1\}^{\sim\sim}$ is the identity (both left and right) for fusion.

Phase spaces are a particular kind of closure frame. They are special in a number of ways. Not only is the closure operation defined by negation, and not only are the structural rules B and C satisfied, but the accessibility relation R underlying the frame is *functional*. Nevertheless, phase spaces are still a faithful model for MALL. We have the following theorem.

THEOREM 12.21 (SOUNDNESS AND COMPLETENESS IN PHASE SPACES)
$X \vdash A$ is provable in MALL if and only if $X \vdash A$ holds in all phase spaces.

PROOF If $X \vdash A$ is provable in MALL then it must hold in all phase spaces because phase spaces are closure frames satisfying B and C. To prove the converse, it suffices to show that the canonical MALL closure frame, defined in the previous section, is a phase space. For that, we need to verify that R, C and Γ on the closure frame satisfy the conditions for a phase space. Unfortunately, as we have defined it, this is not *quite* the case. We need to make some small modifications.

In the canonical closure space, the points are formulae, and the accessibility relation R is set as $RABC$ iff $A \vdash B \circ C$. We tinker with R ever so slightly, and set $RABC$ iff $A = B \circ C$. Then for $\mathbf{0}$, we have $\{A : 0 \vdash \sim A\}$. The *false* elements are the set of all formulae whose negations are provable, as you would expect. This is the correct choice, as $G^\sim = \{A : \forall B \in G(B \vdash \sim A)\}$, and so, $G^{\sim\sim} = \{A : \forall B \in G^\sim(B \vdash \sim A)\} = \{A : \forall B(\forall C \in G \text{ where } C \vdash \sim B)B \vdash \sim A\}$, and this, when you replace B by $\sim B$ you get the Dedekind–MacNeille closure, ΓG, from the canonical closure space. The other definitions of accessibility relations in the canonical model structure go over from before, and we have the completeness result. □

The definition of a phase space gives us a nice result. It motivates an embedding of the whole logic MALL into its fragment MALL$[\to, \wedge, t]$. You choose f to be some arbitrary proposition, a translation as follows (where we set $\sim A = A \to f$).

$$
\begin{array}{rcl}
p^t & = & \sim\sim p \\
(A \wedge B)^t & = & \sim\sim(A^t \wedge B^t) \\
(A \vee B)^t & = & \sim(\sim A^t \wedge \sim B^t) \\
(A \circ B)^t & = & \sim(A^t \to \sim B^t) \\
(A \to B)^t & = & A^t \to B^t \\
t^t & = & \sim\sim t
\end{array}
$$

THEOREM 12.22 (ALL OF MALL, USING JUST $\to$, $\wedge$ AND t)
$A \vdash B$ holds in MALL *if and only if* $A^t \vdash B^t$ in MALL$[\to, \wedge, t]$.

PROOF First, if $A^t \vdash B^t$ is provable in MALL$[\to, \wedge, t]$, then $A^t \vdash B^t$ is provable in MALL, and in particular, it is provable when we choose $\sim t$ for f. In this case, A^t is equivalent to A in MALL, and therefore, $A \vdash B$ is provable in MALL.

Conversely, if $A^t \vdash B^t$ does not hold in MALL$[\to, \wedge, t]$, then in the canonical model (constructed simply out of *theories*, not prime theories, in the absence of disjunction) we have a counterexample to $A^t \vdash B^t$. Construct a phase space out of this model. The phases are the theories in the canonical model. The monoid operation is theory fusion, and the set $\mathbf{0}$ is $\{x : f \in x\}$. It is straightforward to check that any set of the form $[\![\sim\sim A]\!]$ in the original canonical model is a fact in the phase space we are constructing. Construct an interpretation of the language of MALL by setting $[\![A]\!]$ in the phase space to be $[\![A^t]\!]$ in the canonical model. As the definition of the translation ^{t} mimics the evaluation clauses in a phase space, this is an acceptable phase space evaluation, and it is one which invalidates $A \vdash B$, so this consecution fails in MALL. □

Note that this construction works in logics other than MALL. For example, it will work to embed the whole of R without distribution into R$[\to, \wedge, t]$, for if the original model satisfies W, so will the phase model for R without distribution.

We will end this section by sketching how to cope with non-normal modal operators, such as ! and ? of linear logic. The difficulty with operators like these is the way the distribution properties of normal operators fail. We do not have $!A \wedge !B \vdash !(A \wedge B)$. So, we cannot use standard accessibility relations. However, something is possible.

DEFINITION 12.23 (TOPOLINEAR SPACES)
A *topolinear space* is a phase space equipped with a set $\mathfrak{F}$ of facts satisfying the following conditions:

⋄ If $X \subseteq \mathfrak{F}$ then $\bigcap X \in \mathfrak{F}$.

⋄ If $F, G \in \mathfrak{F}$ then $F + G \in \mathfrak{F}$.
⋄ If $F \in \mathfrak{F}$ then $F + F = F$.
⋄ $\bigcap \mathfrak{F} = \mathbf{0}$.

G is a *closed fact* iff $G \in \mathfrak{F}$, and G is a *open fact* iff $G^{\sim} \in \mathfrak{F}$.

Now, given any fact G, the *consideration* of G, $?G$, is

$$?G = \bigcap \{F : G \subseteq F \text{ and } F \in \mathfrak{F}\}$$

It is simply the smallest element of $\mathfrak{F}$ containing G. Its dual, the *affirmation* of G, $!G$ is

$$!G = (\bigcup \{H : H \subseteq G \text{ and } H^{\sim} \in \mathfrak{F}\})^{\sim\sim}$$

These are duals, as you can readily check.

LEMMA 12.24 (DUALITY OF ! AND ?)
For any fact G, $!(G^{\sim}) = (?G)^{\sim}$, and dually, $?(G^{\sim}) = (!G)^{\sim}$.   □

This definition gives us a semantics for the exponentials. The semantics does as we would expect: by construction $G \subseteq ?G$, for any fact G, so by duality, $!G \subseteq G$. Furthermore, $?G$ is itself a closed fact, so $?G = ??G$, and dually, $!G = !!G$. Similarly, all of the closed facts are fixed points for fission, $?G + ?G = ?G$, and by duality, $!G \circ !G = !G$. Finally, $\mathbf{0} \subseteq ?G$ by construction, so by duality $!G \subseteq t$, and by the behaviour of t, $G \circ t = t$ gives $F \circ !G \subseteq F$.

Each of these simple verifications shows that the construction of ! and ? satisfies the rules for the exponentials in linear logic. This gives us the first part of the following theorem.

THEOREM 12.25 (SOUNDNESS AND COMPLETENESS IN TOPOLINEAR SPACES)
$X \vdash A$ is provable in LL if and only if $X \vdash A$ holds in all topolinear spaces.

PROOF As we have seen, the rules for the exponentials hold in topolinear spaces. For the converse, we must verify that the canonical topolinear space satisfies the conditions required for a topolinear space. So how should we construct the canonical topolinear space?

We will use the canonical phase space we have seen to construct a set of closed facts. Obviously, each $\{A : ?B \vdash A\}$ ought to be a closed fact for any choice of B. This cannot be the whole thing, as the intersection of a class of closed facts is not necessarily a set of the form $\{A : ?B \vdash A\}$. So we add these intersections. For any class of formulae B_i, we will let $\bigcap_i \{A : ?B_i \vdash A\}$ be a closed fact. Once we do this, it is straightforward to check that $?[\![A]\!] = \bigcap \{F : [\![A]\!] \subseteq F \text{ and } F \in \mathfrak{F}\}$ for any formula A in the canonical model structure. The duality of ? and !, together with the duality of their defining conditions, ensures that the result for ! holds too.

We need to check then that the class $\mathfrak{F}$ of closed facts so defined satisfies the four conditions of a set of closed facts. The first condition holds because we have defined the intersection of a class of closed facts to be closed. For the second condition, suppose that $F, G \in \mathfrak{F}$. So $F = \bigcap_i \{A : ?B_i \vdash A\}$ and $G = \bigcap_j \{A : ?C_j \vdash A\}$ for some choice of the formulae B_i and C_j. But then $F + G = \bigcap_{\langle i,j \rangle} \{A : ?B_i + ?C_j \vdash A\}$, but $?B_i + ?C_j$ is equivalent to $?(B_i \vee C_j)$ (this is dual to the equivalence of $!A \circ !B$ and $!(A \wedge B)$) so the set $F + G$ is indeed a closed fact. Similarly, $F + F = F$, since $?B_i + ?Bi$ is equivalent to $?B_i$.

Finally, since $?B_i \vdash {\sim}t$ for each ${\sim}t$, if $F \in \mathfrak{F}$ then $\mathbf{0} \subseteq F$. However, $\mathbf{0} = \{A : {\sim}t \vdash A\} = \{A : ?{\sim}t \vdash A\}$, which is a closed fact, so $\mathbf{0} \in \mathfrak{F}$, giving us $\mathbf{0} = \bigcap \mathfrak{F}$ as desired.   □

So this kind of closure operation works well to model the exponentials in phase spaces.

12.5   *History*

The idea of a general notion of frames, of which Kripke and Beth frames are special cases, has been presented by Dragalin [68]. I was drawn to the idea of Dedekind–MacNeille closure by Hartonas [109]; and the idea is also in Troelstra's account of linear logic [261]. A helpful discussion of the notion can be found in Grätzer's *General Lattice Theory* [103].

Došen's "Rudimentary Kripke Models for Intuitionistic Propositional Calculus" is another generalisation of Kripke frames, in particular for intuitionistic logic [67].

Sambin and others have used the notion of a "pretopology" (in our language, a set with a closure operator) not only as a model of substructural logics but also as a constructive generalisation of a topological space [110, 233, 234, 235]. Došen [60, 62], Ono and Komori [187], and Ono [188] have also given semantics like these.

In this chapter, the approach has been to see these semantics as a generalisation of the frame semantics for logics with distribution. This is a little idiosyncratic, as in all of the accounts in the literature, the emphasis is on *operational* semantics. Once we have a non-traditional evaluation of disjunction, we are free to use a two-place function instead of a three-place relation to model implication. This obscures the connections between frames for logics with distribution and the models for those without. I have tried to make clear the connections between the two.

We have not examined Allwein and Dunn's modelling of linear logic, as their model uses two different evaluations of propositions — one to keep track of where a proposition is true and another to keep track of where it is false [4]. This is also a model of a substructural logics, but it is out of our ken in this chapter.

Bell gives a philosophical analysis of Goldblatt's semantics for ortho logic, in which C is interpreted as *proximity* [17]. It is as yet unknown whether a similar analysis can be given to motivate the treatment of disjunction in non-distributive substructural logics.

12.6 Exercises

Practice

{12.1} Show that the closure operators of Dedekind–MacNeille frames, Beth frames and compatibility frames each satisfy the conditions of Definition 12.5.

{12.2} Show that the function ^{ul}, which maps a set α to α^{ul}, is also a closure operator on a point set.

Problems

{12.3} Given a point set $\mathcal{P}$, for what subsets α of $\mathcal{P}$ does $\alpha^{lu} = \alpha^{ul}$?

{12.4} *Quantum logic* extends orthologic with the rule $A \wedge (\sim A \vee (A \wedge B)) \vdash B$. In this exercise, we will provide a frame semantics for quantum logic. To do this, we need to modify Goldblatt's closure operator. Given an orthoframe $\langle P, C \rangle$, and given subsets $\alpha, \beta \subseteq P$ we will say that α is C-closed in β iff for all $x \in \beta$, if $x \notin \alpha$ then there is a $y \in \beta$ where $\forall z(z \in \alpha \rightarrow \sim yCz)$ and xCy. (So $\alpha = \alpha^{\sim\sim}$ iff α is C-closed in P.) Show that in any orthomodel $\mathfrak{M}$, $[\![A]\!]$ is C-closed in $[\![B]\!]$ iff $B \wedge (\sim B \vee A) \vdash_{\mathfrak{M}} A$. Let a *quantum frame* be a defined to be an orthoframe $\langle P, C \rangle$ together with a non-empty family $\mathfrak{C}$ of C-closed subsets of α such that

⋄ $\mathfrak{C}$ is closed under intersection.
⋄ If $\alpha \in \mathfrak{C}$ then $\{x : \forall z(z \in \alpha \rightarrow \sim xCz)\} \in \mathfrak{C}$ too.
⋄ If $\alpha, \beta \in \mathfrak{C}$ then $\alpha \subseteq \beta$ only if α is C-closed in β.

An *interpretation* in a quantum frame is a map $[\![\cdot]\!]$ from atomic propositions to the elements of $\mathfrak{C}$, extended in the usual way. Show that $A \vdash B$ is valid in quantum logic if and only if in every interpretation in quantum frames, $[\![A]\!] \subseteq [\![B]\!]$. (The proof is due to Goldblatt [101].)

{12.5} Continuing on from the last question, show that this approach is as good as you can do. That is, show that there is no condition on C that you can add to restrict orthoframes to model exactly quantum logic. (This is also due to Goldblatt [101].)

{12.6} Given a closure frame, define a relation $\equiv$ between points on the frame, setting $x \equiv y$ if and only if $\Gamma\{x\} = \Gamma\{y\}$. Construct an appropriate closure operator on the set of $\equiv$-equivalence classes of the original frame. Show that $\sqsubseteq_\Gamma$ in this new frame is antisymmetric. Then show that for any interpretation $[\![\cdot]\!]$ on the original frame, there is an interpretation on the "slimmer" frame which invalidates exactly the same formulae as its "fatter" ancestor.

{12.7} Consider the embedding of MALL into positive MALL[$\rightarrow$, $\wedge$] (Theorem 12.22). Prove it directly, without using phase spaces.

{12.8} This exercise and the next examine a different canonical model construction, due to Okada [186]. Construct the *Okada phase space* as follows. Use the Cut-free single-sided consecution calculus from Exercise 6.6. Points are structures, set $X \cdot Y = X; Y$, $\mathbf{0} = \{X : \vdash X\}$, and $[\![p]\!] = \{p\}^\sim = \{X : \vdash X; A\}$. Show that $[\![A]\!] \subseteq \{A\}^\sim$ by induction on A.

{12.9} We can use the semantics of the previous exercise to prove cut elimination. Show that $\vdash A$ with cut $\Rightarrow A$ holds in all phase spaces $\Rightarrow A$ holds in the Okada canonical model $\Rightarrow \vdash A$ is provable without cut.

Project

{12.10} Consider Bell's *proximity* account of the compatibility relation C [17]. Can the account be extended to give a justification of a ternary accessibility relation, and the resulting logic of implication and fusion? Can a similar account be given of the phase spaces of MALL?

Chapter 13

Frame Constructions

> *Simulation is the seeming to be what we are not;*
> *dissimulation, the seeming not to be what we are.*
>
> — *John Wesley*, Works, *1791*

In this chapter, we will examine some techniques for constructing and manipulating frames in order to prove results about substructural logics.

13.1 Directed Bisimulations

Hennessy and Milner have provided us with a valuable tool in the study of frames for substructural logics [113, 171]. They provided an account of what it is for a model M_1 to *simulate* another model, M_2. (In their case, these were models of processes, not necessarily frames for logics.) M_1 *simulates* M_2 if whenever a state of M_1 is paired with a state of M_2, whatever holds of the M_1 state also holds of the M_2 state. We will write the pairing relation as 'Z', so xZy if and only if x (from M_1) is paired with y (from M_2). If we allow Boolean negation to modify the information carried by states, then it is simple to see that if xZy, then the information carried by y is also carried by x. After all, if $y \Vdash A$, then $y \nVdash -A$, and hence $x \nVdash -A$ (as y carries everything carried by x). Therefore, $x \Vdash A$ too. So, in the presence of Boolean negation, simulation becomes a two-way thing. Not only will states in M_2 simulate those in M_1, but states in M_1 will simulate those in M_2. Simulations become *bisimulations*, and these have been widely studied and applied in the semantics for classical modal logics — in which Boolean negation is present.

For application to substructural logics, where Boolean negation is usually absent, *bisimulations* are not the appropriate tool. But neither are simple simulations. For to simulate the substructural model $\mathfrak{M}_1$ by $\mathfrak{M}_2$, we need to know not only what is true in each point in each model (so we need not only to see truth in $\mathfrak{M}_1$ preserved in model $\mathfrak{M}_2$), but for connectives such as negation and implication we also need to see that *untruth* in $\mathfrak{M}_1$ is preserved in $\mathfrak{M}_2$ in an appropriate way. In other words, we need truth in $\mathfrak{M}_2$ to be preserved in $\mathfrak{M}_1$. However, in the absence of Boolean negation, this need not be a one-to-one matter. If y simulates x, then everything true in x is also true in y. We might

have y simulate z, so everything true in y is true in z — or equivalently, everything untrue in z is untrue in y. There is no compulsion for x and z to agree
on everything. More complex relations of simulation apply in the absence of
Boolean negation. We need what are called *directed binary relations*.

DEFINITION 13.1 (DIRECTED BINARY RELATIONS)
A *directed binary relation* Z between two sets M_1 and N_2 is a pair of binary
relations $Z_1 \subseteq M_1 \times M_2$ and $Z_2 \subseteq M_2 \times M_1$.

So, given M_1 and M_2, and a directed binary relation $Z = \langle Z_1, Z_2 \rangle$ on this pair,
if xZ_1y, then $x \in M_1$ and $y \in M_2$. The intended meaning in our applications is
that x is simulated by y. Everything true in x is also true in y. Similarly, if wZ_2z,
then $w \in M_2$ and $y \in M_1$, and in this case too, we read this as 'w is simulated
by y'. You can think of a directed binary relation as a system of one-way bridges
from one side of a river to the other — we can consider when such a system
does the work of simulation we require.

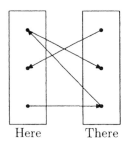

Here   There

Figure 13.1: Bridges from Here to There and Back

In this definition, and in the rest of this section, we will use some shorthand
to cut down on the number of cases to state in any definition or proof. Instead
of saying, for example, 'if $x \Vdash p$ and xZ_1y then $y \in M_2$ and $y \Vdash p$ too, and
similarly if $x \Vdash p$ and xZ_2y then $y \in M_1$ and $y \Vdash p$' we will say that whenever
$\{i, j\} = \{1, 2\}$, then if $x \Vdash p$ and xZ_iy then $y \in M_j$ and $y \Vdash p$. To say that
$\{i, j\} = \{1, 2\}$ is to say that either $i = 1$ and $j = 2$, or that $i = 2$ and $j = 1$.
Think of yourself as on one side of the river, and using 'i' to mean 'here' and 'j'
to mean 'there' — and you do not know which side of the river you are on.

DEFINITION 13.2 (DIRECTED BISIMULATIONS)
A *directed bisimulation* between two models $\mathfrak{M}_1$ and $\mathfrak{M}_2$ (with the same systems
of accessibility relations) is a directed binary relation on their carrier sets such
that whenever $\{i, j\} = \{1, 2\}$

$\diamond$ If xZ_iy and $x \Vdash p$ then $y \Vdash p$.

If the models contain three-place accessibility relations R_1 and R_2, then

$\diamond$ If xZ_iy and R_jywz then there are u, v where R_ixuv, wZ_ju and vZ_iz.

$\diamond$ If xZ_iy and R_jwyz then there are u, v where R_iuxv, wZ_ju and vZ_iz.

$\diamond$ If xZ_iy and R_iuvx then there are w, z where R_jwzy, uZ_iw and vZ_iz.

If the models contain truth sets T_1 and T_2, then

$\diamond$ If xZ_iy and $x \in T_i$ then $y \in T_j$.

If the models contain positive two-place accessibility relations S_1 and S_2, then

$\diamond$ If xZ_iy and yS_jv then there is a u where xS_iu and uZ_iv.

$\diamond$ If xZ_iy and uS_ix then there is a v where vS_jy and uZ_iv.

If the models contain negative two-place accessibility relations C_1 and C_2, then

$\diamond$ If xZ_iy and yC_jv then there is a u where xC_iu and vZ_ju.

$\diamond$ If xZ_iy and vC_jy then there is a u where uC_ix and vZ_ju.

We indicate that there is a directed bisimulation Z between $\mathfrak{M}_i$ and $\mathfrak{M}_j$, at which xZ_iy, by writing '$\mathfrak{M}_i, x \rightrightarrows \mathfrak{M}_j, y$'.

The bisimulation conditions relating Z to the accessibility relations can be written more compactly if we use the conventions for writing composed relations from Chapter 11. The conditions can then be stated as follows. For each $\{i, j\} = \{1, 2\}$ we have

$$
\begin{aligned}
&\text{If } R_iuv(Z_iy) \text{ then } R_j(uZ_i)(vZ_i)y \\
&\text{If } R_j(xZ_i)wz \text{ then } R_ix(wZ_j)(Z_iz) \\
&\text{If } R_jw(xZ_i)z \text{ then } R_i(wZ_j)x(Z_iz) \\
&\qquad\text{If } T_iZ_iy \text{ then } T_jy \\
&\qquad xZ_iS_jv \text{ iff } xS_iZ_iv \\
&\qquad xZ_iC_jv \text{ iff } xC_i\check{Z}_jy
\end{aligned}
$$

Before examining any directed bisimulations, we will show how bisimulations work by proving the major result concerning them. This will motivate the conditions from the definition.

THEOREM 13.3 (PRESERVATION THEOREM)

If $\mathfrak{M}_1$ and $\mathfrak{M}_2$ are models with a directed bisimulation between them, if $\mathfrak{M}_i, x \rightrightarrows \mathfrak{M}_j, y$ (where $\{i, j\} = \{1, 2\}$) and $x \Vdash A$ then $y \Vdash A$ too.

PROOF The proof is a direct induction on the construction of A. The clauses are exactly what you need to give the induction steps for each connective.

⋄ If A is an atom, then if $x \Vdash p$ and xZ_iy then $y \Vdash p$ by construction.

⋄ If A is either $\top$ or $\bot$ then clearly x and y must agree about A.

⋄ If A is t, then if xZ_iy we have $x \in T_i$ and hence $y \in T_j$ as desired.

⋄ If $A = \Box B$, then if xZ_iy and $x \Vdash \Box B$ then to show that $y \Vdash \Box B$, suppose that yS_jv. We wish to show that $v \Vdash B$, as then we have $y \Vdash \Box B$ as desired. By the S condition, we have some u where uZ_jv and xS_iu. Since xS_iu, we have $u \Vdash B$. Since uZ_jv, we have $v \Vdash B$, by the induction hypothesis, as we wished.

⋄ If $A = \Diamond B$, then if xZ_iy and $x \Vdash \Diamond B$, then to show that $y \Vdash \Diamond B$, we want some v where vS_jy and $v \Vdash B$. We know that $x \Vdash \Diamond B$, so there is some u where uS_ix and $u \Vdash B$. Therefore, since uS_ix and xZ_iy, there is a v where uZ_jv and vS_jy. By the induction hypothesis, $u \Vdash B$ gives $v \Vdash B$, as we wished.

⋄ If xZ_iy and $x \Vdash \sim B$, we wish to show that $y \Vdash \sim B$. Suppose that yC_jv, to show that $v \nVdash B$. By the C condition we have a u where xC_iu and vZ_ju. Since xC_iu, $u \nVdash B$, and therefore $v \nVdash B$, giving $y \Vdash \sim A$ as desired.

⋄ The case for $\neg B$ is similar — you just replace C_i and C_j by their converses.

⋄ If $A = B \to C$, then suppose that xZ_iy with $x \Vdash B \to C$. To show that $y \Vdash B \to C$, suppose that R_iywz with $w \Vdash A$. We wish to show that $z \Vdash B$. Since xZ_iy and R_jywz, there are u, v where R_ixuv, wZ_ju and vZ_iz. Since wZ_ju and $w \Vdash B$ we have $u \Vdash B$. Since $x \Vdash B \to C$, we have $v \Vdash C$. Since vZ_iz we have $z \Vdash C$ as desired.

⋄ If $A = C \leftarrow B$, we reason similarly, permuting the first two places of R_i and R_j.

⋄ If $A = B \circ C$, then suppose that xZ_iy and $x \Vdash B \circ C$. To show that $y \Vdash B \circ C$, we reason as follows. Since $x \Vdash B \circ C$, there are u, v where R_iuvx, $u \Vdash B$ and $v \Vdash C$. Since xZ_iy, and R_iuvx, we have w, z where uZ_iw, vZ_iz and R_jwzy. Therefore $w \Vdash B$, $z \Vdash C$, and $y \Vdash B \circ C$ as desired.

This completes the induction, so we have verified that if $x \Vdash A$, and xZ_iy, then $y \Vdash A$ for any A at all.   □

To see how directed bisimulations work, let us look at some particular examples. First, consider the diagram in Figure 13.2. The dashed arrows provide the directed bisimulation between the two models, one on $\{a, b, c, d\}$, the other on $\{a', b', c', d'\}$.

This directed bisimulation shows us some of the distinctive features of this relation between models. First, there are some pairs of points: b and c', and c and b', which support exactly the same propositions. We have $b \Vdash q$, $b \nVdash \sim p$, and $c' \Vdash q$, $c' \nVdash \sim p$, for example. There are also pairs in which one point

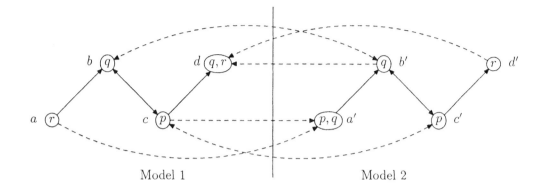

Figure 13.2: A Directed Bisimulation Between Compatibility Models

simulates the other but *not* vice versa. For example, d simulates a' — $a' \Vdash r$ and $d \Vdash r$, but $a \not\Vdash q$ while $d \Vdash q$.

As another example, we will use a directed bisimulation between two models to prove the following theorem.

THEOREM 13.4 (ON $\forall a \exists b Rabb$, $\exists b \forall a Rabb$ AND $\exists a \exists b Rabb$)
There is no consecution valid in all and only those frames in which $\forall a \exists b Rabb$. Similarly, there is no consecution valid on all and only those frames in which $\exists b \forall a Rabb$ or in which $\exists a \exists b Rabb$.

PROOF Take the flat frame $\mathcal{F}_1$ on the set ω of positive integers in which $R_1 xyz$ if and only if $x + y < z$. It is clear that in this frame each of $\exists a \exists b R_1 abb$, $\forall a \exists b R_1 abb$ and $\exists b \forall a R_1 abb$ fails, since $R_1 abb$ if and only if $a + b < b$, which never holds for any $a, b \in \omega$.

We will construct another frame in which $\exists b \forall a R_2 abb$ (and hence $\forall a \exists b R_2 abb$ and $\exists a \exists b R_2 abb$) holds, and in which the same consecutions are valid. The frame $\mathcal{F}_2$ is given by adjoining to $\mathcal{F}_1$ a new object ∞, which interacts with R_2 as follows

$$R_2 xy\infty \text{ for each } x \text{ and } y.$$
$$R_2 \infty xy \text{ if and only if } R_2 x\infty y \text{ if and only if } y = \infty.$$

The rest of the behaviour of R_2 in $\mathcal{F}_2$ is inherited from R_1 in $\mathcal{F}_1$. This completely determines the behaviour of R_2 in $\mathcal{F}_2$. Note that $R_2 a\infty\infty$ for any a in $\mathcal{F}_2$, so each of $\forall a \exists b R_2 abb$, $\exists b \forall a R_2 abb$ and $\exists a \exists b R_2 abb$ holds in $\mathcal{F}_2$.

Now given any model $\mathfrak{M}_1$ on $\mathcal{F}_1$, we will construct a model $\mathfrak{M}_2$ on $\mathcal{F}_2$ and a directed bisimulation between them. We define the bisimilarity as follows

$$xZ_1y \quad \text{iff} \quad x = y \text{ or } y = \infty$$
$$yZ_2x \quad \text{iff} \quad x = y$$

The idea here is that each number in the new model behaves exactly as it does in the original model, and that anything true at *any* number at all is true also at ∞, as ∞ simulates each element of the original model. Of course, nothing in the original frame simulates ∞, as we cannot expect there to be any point in the original model at which that many things are true.

Consistent with this, we fix $\Vdash'$ from $\mathfrak{M}_2$ in terms of $\Vdash$ from $\mathfrak{M}_1$ as follows:

$$x \Vdash' p \quad \text{iff} \quad x \Vdash p$$
$$\infty \Vdash' p \quad \text{iff} \quad x \Vdash p \text{ for some } x \in \omega$$

We will demonstrate that Z so defined is a bisimulation. The clauses for the atomic propositions are satisfied by definition, and we need not consider the clauses for T, C or S, as our frame does not contain them. We need to verify just the three clauses for R.

⋄ Suppose that xZ_1y and R_1uvx. We want w, z where R_2wzy, wZ_2u and zZ_2v. There are two cases here. If $x = y$ then we can take $w = u$ and $z = v$. Similarly, if $y = \infty$, then we can take $w = u$ and $z = v$ as $R_2wz\infty$ holds.

Suppose that xZ_2y and R_1uvx. Then we know that $x = y$ and hence there are w, z where R_2wzy, wZ_1u and zZ_1v, as again, we take $w = u$ and $z = v$.

⋄ Suppose that xZ_1y and R_2ywz. We want there to be u, v where wZ_2u, vZ_1z and R_1xuv. If $x = y$ then we can take $w = u$ and $v = z$ and we are done. If $y = \infty$, then since $R_2\infty wz$ we know that $z = \infty$. Therefore, if we take $u = w$ and $v = x+u+1$, then we are done, since R_1xuv (as $x+u < x+u+1$) and wZ_2u ($u = w$) and vZ_1z (as $(x + u + 1)Z_1\infty$).

Suppose that xZ_2y and R_1ywz. Then we know that $x = y$ and hence R_2xuv, where $u = w$ and $v = z$, giving wZ_1u and vZ_2z as desired.

⋄ Suppose that xZ_1y and R_2wyz. We want there to be u, v where wZ_2u, vZ_1z and R_1uxv. If $x = y$ then we can take $w = u$ and $v = z$ and we are done. If $y = \infty$, then since $R_2w\infty z$ we know that $z = \infty$. Therefore, if we take $u = w$ and $v = u+x+1$, then we are done, since R_1uxv (as $u+x > u+x+1$) and wZ_2u ($u = w$) and vZ_1z (as $(u + x + 1)Z_1\infty$).

Suppose that xZ_2y and R_1wyz. Then we know that $x = y$ and hence R_2uxv, where $u = w$ and $v = z$, giving wZ_1u and vZ_2z as desired.

That completes the verification that Z is a bisimulation. Therefore, if $A \vdash B$ is valid in all and only those frames in which $\exists a \exists b Rabb$ (or $\exists b \forall a Rabb$, or $\forall a \exists b Rabb$) then it is valid on $\mathcal{F}_2$. We will show that it is valid on $\mathcal{F}_1$ too, contradicting the claim that it is valid on exactly those frames in which the condition holds (as none of the conditions holds on $\mathcal{F}_1$). Take any model $\mathfrak{M}_1$ on $\mathcal{F}_1$, and a point x in $\mathcal{F}_1$ in which $x \Vdash A$. We will show that $x \Vdash B$ too. Construct the model $\mathfrak{M}_2$ on $\mathcal{F}_2$ by the definitions above. Therefore we have both $\mathfrak{M}_1, x \rightleftharpoons \mathfrak{M}_2, x$ $\mathfrak{M}_2, x \rightleftharpoons \mathfrak{M}_1, x$, by the reasoning above. By the first, if $x \Vdash A$ (in $\mathfrak{M}_1$) then $x \Vdash' A$ (in $\mathfrak{M}_2$). Now $A \vdash_{\mathcal{F}_2} B$, so $x \Vdash' B$. It follows that $x \Vdash B$ (in $\mathfrak{M}_2$) as desired. Therefore $A \vdash B$ holds in $\mathcal{F}_1$, contradicting the claim that $A \vdash B$ holds in all and only those frames satisfying the given condition. $\square$

We can see how any directed bisimulation with Boolean negation becomes a standard bisimulation. If we wish to preserve Boolean negation, we need to respect the Boolean compatibility relation C such that xC_iy if and only if $x = y$. Then since xZ_iC_jv if and only if $xC_i\check{Z}_jy$ it follows that $xZ_iy = x\check{Z}_jy$, every bridge from $\mathfrak{M}_1$ to $\mathfrak{M}_2$ becomes a two-way street, and we have a standard bisimulation.

Had we required that our models have Boolean negation, then the construction of our theorem would not work, since were we to require that ∞ simulate each $x \in \mathfrak{M}_1$, we would require then that each $x \in \mathfrak{M}_1$ simulate ∞, which we could not manage.

We have seen that standard bisimulations Z are directed bisimulations of the form $\langle Z_1, \check{Z}_1 \rangle$. Another important class of directed bisimulations are the *simulations* $\langle Z_1, \emptyset \rangle$, in which only one-way traffic is allowed. For example, if the language in question does not contain $\rightarrow, \leftarrow, \sim$ and $\neg$, whenever $\langle Z_1, Z_2 \rangle$ is a directed bisimulation, so are $\langle Z_1, \emptyset \rangle$ and $\langle \emptyset, Z_2 \rangle$. All of the conditions for Z_i in this language make no appeal to Z_j. This is because each of the remaining connectives — $\wedge, \vee, \top, \bot, t, \circ, \square, \Diamond$ — is purely *positive*. They introduce no negative occurrences of formulae. (Formally speaking, if $A \vdash B$ and $C(-)$ is a context made up purely of those connectives, then $C(A) \vdash C(B)$, by induction on the construction of C.) Therefore, with these formulae, there is no need to keep track of where propositions fail to be true in order to find out where they are true. All propositions are *monotone*.

The converse of the preservation theorem is a trickier matter. The major hiccup is the fact that we need the restriction to *finite alternative* models. These are models in which for each x, there are only finitely many y where xCy, or yCx, or xSy or ySx, and similarly, there are only finitely many $\langle y, z \rangle$ pairs, where $Rxyz$, $Ryzx$ or $Ryxz$. You will see in the proof below where this assumption is required.

THEOREM 13.5 (DIRECTED BISIMULATION EXISTENCE THEOREM)
If $\mathfrak{M}$ and $\mathfrak{N}$ are finite alternative models with $x \in \mathfrak{M}$ and $y \in \mathfrak{N}$, such that for all formulae A, if $\mathfrak{M}, x \Vdash A$ then $\mathfrak{N}, y \Vdash A$, then there is a directed bisimulation Z between M and N such that xZy.

PROOF   Set xZ_iy if and only if for every formula A if $x \Vdash A$ then $y \Vdash A$. This is
a directed bisimulation. To show this is a tedious case-by-case verification. We
will show one case for R. We will verify that if xZ_iy and R_jywz then there are
u and v where R_ixuv, wZ_ju and vZ_iz.

Suppose that xZ_iy and R_jywz. Let $X = \{\langle u, v\rangle : Rxuv\}$. This is non-empty,
for if it were not, then $x \Vdash \top \vdash \bot$, but we know that $y \nVdash \top \vdash \bot$, and we
have xZ_iy. So, since X is non-empty, and since the model is finite alternative,
$X = \{\langle u_1, v_1\rangle, \ldots, \langle u_n, v_n\rangle\}$ for some finite n. Now suppose that there are no
u and v where R_ixuv, wZ_ju and vZ_iz. Therefore, for each m, at least one of
wZ_ju_m and v_mZ_iz fails. So, for each m, if wZ_ju_m fails, then there is some A_m
where $w \Vdash A_k$ and $u_m \nVdash A_m$ (by the definition of Z_j). In this case, let $B_m = \bot$.
On the other hand, v_mZ_iz might fail, and in this case, there is a B_m where
$v_m \Vdash B_m$ and $z \nVdash B_m$. In this case, let $A_m = \top$.

So, given this definition of each A_m and B_m, we have $w \Vdash A_m$ always,
and $z \nVdash B_m$ always. Therefore, $w \Vdash \bigwedge_m A_m$ and $z \nVdash \bigvee_m B_m$. As a result,
since R_jywz, $y \nVdash \bigwedge_m A_m \to \bigvee_m B_m$. Therefore, $x \nVdash \bigwedge_m A_m \to \bigvee_m B_m$.
But what does this mean? It means that there is some l where $u_l \Vdash \bigwedge_m A_m$
and $v_l \Vdash \bigvee_m B_m$. (As the $\langle u_m, v_m\rangle$ pairs are the only points where Rxu_mv_m.)
However, for each l, either $u_l \nVdash A_l$ or $v_l \Vdash B_l$, by definition. Therefore, we
cannot have $x \nVdash \bigwedge_m A_m \to \bigvee_m B_m$, and our assumption fails. There must be
some u and v where R_ixuv.

The other conditions are similar but appeal to whichever of $\leftarrow$, $\circ$, $\sim$, $\neg$, $\square$
or $\diamondsuit$ are tied to the bisimulation clause. $\square$

We will end this section by using the technique of bisimulations to prove a
number of *transfer theorems*. In these theorems, we will show that if a frame
has some property, then so do other frames constructed from our original frame.

DEFINITION 13.6 (GENERATED SUBFRAMES AND SUBMODELS)
Given a frame $\mathcal{F}$ and a point x in $\mathcal{F}$ then the *subframe of $\mathcal{F}$ generated by x*, written '$GSF(\mathcal{F}, x)$', is based on the smallest subset $X(x)$ containing x and closed
under all accessibility relations of the frame. That is, if yCz and either of y or
z is in $X(x)$, then so is the other. If ySz and either of y or z is in $X(x)$, then
so is the other. And similarly, if $Ryzw$ and one of y, z and w are in $X(x)$, then
so are the other two. The accessibility relations on $GSF(\mathcal{F}, x)$ are those from $\mathcal{F}$
restricted to $X(x)$.

THEOREM 13.7 (GENERATED SUBFRAME PRESERVATION)
If $\mathfrak{M}, x \Vdash A$, and $\mathfrak{M}$ is a model on the frame $\mathcal{F}$, then if we define $\Vdash$ on $GSF(\mathcal{F}, x)$
as the restriction of $\Vdash$ to $GSF(\mathcal{F}, x)$, then $\mathfrak{M}', y \Vdash A$ if and only if $\mathfrak{M}, y \Vdash A$ for
each A, for any $y \in X(x)$.

PROOF   Define a directed bisimulation Z between $\mathfrak{M}$ and $\mathfrak{M}'$ by setting yZ_1z if and only if zZ_2y if and only if $y = z$ and $y \in X(x)$. So the bisimulation maps a point in the generated subframe to its correlate in the original frame, and vice versa, and those points not in the generated subframe are not mapped anywhere.

This relation satisfies the bisimulation conditions. The base case is satisfied by the definition of $\mathfrak{M}'$. The accessibility relation cases are dealt with by the fact that $X(x)$ is closed under each accessibility relation. For example, if yZ_2z and $Rzuv$ (where $Rzuv$ holds in the *large* model) then we have $y = z$, and we know that u and v are in the generated subframe, so $Rzuv$ holds in the generated subframe, so we have $Rzuv$, uZu and vZv. The other conditions are verified similarly.

Therefore, $\mathfrak{M}', y \Vdash A$ if and only if $\mathfrak{M}, y \Vdash A$ for any $y \in X(x)$, since yZy. $\square$

There is a simple corollary of this result.

COROLLARY 13.8 (UNDEFINABILITY OF NON-REFLEXIVITY)
The non-reflexivity of R — $\sim\forall x Rxxx$ is not definable in the language of substructural logics.

PROOF   Take a non-reflexive frame with an isolated reflexive point x. The generated subframe at x is the reflexive one-point (Boolean) frame. $\square$

A similar process is the taking of *disjoint unions*.

DEFINITION 13.9 (DISJOINT UNIONS)
Given a class of models $\mathfrak{M}_i$ ($i \in I$), then their *disjoint union* is a model too, by setting the relations to be the disjoint union of the original relations, and the evaluation similarly.

THEOREM 13.10 (DISJOINT UNION PRESERVATION)
If $\mathfrak{M}_i$ is a model of the logic L_i then the disjoint union of the models $\mathfrak{M}_i$ is a model of $\bigcap_i L_i$.

PROOF   Each $\mathfrak{M}_i$ is a generated submodel of the disjoint union $\mathfrak{M}$. Therefore $X \vdash_{\mathfrak{M}} A$ if and only if $X \vdash_{\mathfrak{M}_i} A$ for each i. It follows that if $X \vdash A$ is provable in each L_i, then $X \vdash A$ holds in $\mathfrak{M}$, as desired. $\square$

This condition gives us another result about the definability of frame conditions.

COROLLARY 13.11 (UNDEFINABILITY OF $\forall x \forall y \exists z Rxyz$)
There is no substructural consecution valid in all and only those frames in which $\forall x \forall y \exists z Rxyz$.

PROOF   Take two frames in which your chosen consecution is valid, and take
their disjoint union. The consecution is valid in the disjoint union, by our theorem. Now select x from the first frame and y from the second. There is no z
such that $Rxyz$ in the disjoint union, as there is no communication between the
two components of the new frame. Therefore no consecution is valid in all and
only those frames in which $\forall x \forall y \exists z Rxyz$. $\Box$

13.2   Reduced Frames

A frame is *reduced* if and only if the truth set T is generated by a single point.
That is, if and only if $T = \{x : 0 \sqsubseteq x\}$ for some 0. In this case, $x \sqsubseteq y$ if and
only if $R0xy$. Many useful frames are reduced. For example, linguistic frames
of the Lambek calculus are reduced if they have identity objects. The null string
ϵ is such that $\epsilon x = x = x\epsilon$ for each x. Similarly, in action frames the null action
generates a truth set.

However, canonical frames for our logics are not typically reduced. In a
canonical frame, the set T is the set of all prime theories x, where $t \in x$. This
is generated by a single set if and only if the set $\{A : t \vdash A\}$ of t-theorems is
prime. This is not always the case. (For example, if we have Boolean negation,
the set of t-theorems is typically not prime, as $p \vee -p$ is a t-theorem, but in any
of our logics neither p nor $-p$ is a theorem.) So, can we model our logics with
reduced frames? The answer is yes, *sometimes*.

DEFINITION 13.12 (REDUCTION-READY LOGICS)
A logic is *reduction-ready* if and only if whenever $A \vdash_H B$ is provable in the
Hilbert system of the logic, so is $A \vee C \vdash_H B \vee C$.

Reduction-ready logics are useful for the following reason.

LEMMA 13.13 (REDUCTION READINESS AND PAIR EXTENSION)
*If a logic is reduction-ready, and its standard consequence relation $\vdash$ is pair ex-
tension acceptable, then its Hilbert consequence relation $\vdash_H$ is also pair extension
acceptable.*

PROOF   Every condition of pair extension acceptability is satisfied by $\vdash_H$, given
that $\vdash$ is pair extension acceptable, except for the disjunction rule: if $A \vdash_H C$
and $B \vdash_H C$ then $A \vee B \vdash_H C$. This is given by the reduction readiness
condition. If $A \vdash_H B$ then $A \vee B \vdash_H B \vee C$. Similarly, if $B \vdash C$ then $B \vee C \vdash_H$
$C \vee C$. So by transitivity, $A \vee B \vdash_H C \vee C$. But we have $C \vee C \vdash_H C$, so
$A \vee B \vdash_H C$ as desired. $\Box$

Not all substructural logics are reduction-ready. One prominent example is E. In E, we have $A \vdash_H t \to A$ (this is the rule of necessitation); however, there are cases where $A \vee C$ is a theorem while $(t \to A) \vee C$ is not. For example, $A \vee {\sim}A$ is a theorem, while $(t \to A) \vee {\sim}A$ is not an E theorem. (Why not? Well, $\Box A \vee {\sim}A$ is not a theorem of any decent modal logic.)

Now we can show that reduction-ready logics are modelled by reduced frames.

THEOREM 13.14 (REDUCTION READINESS AND REDUCED FRAMES)
If a logic is reduction-ready, then it is sound and complete for a class of reduced frames.

PROOF   Soundness is trivial, as we have simply cut down the class of frames.

Completeness is not so trivial. Suppose that $A \vdash B$ fails in our logic. We wish to construct a *reduced* frame in which it fails. As before, we take the pair $\langle \{t\}, \{A \to B\} \rangle$ and expand this to a prime pair, according to the relation $\vdash_H$. Since $\vdash_H$ is pair extension acceptable, it is extended by a full pair. Call the left set of the resulting full pair, Θ. The set Θ is a non-trivial prime theory, but in addition, it is closed under $\vdash_H$. Therefore, if $C \to D, C \in \Theta$ then $D \in \Theta$, and $C \in \Theta$ if and only if $t \to C \in \Theta$, and so on.

To construct the canonical frame, we consider not the set of all non-trivial prime theories but the set of all non-trivial prime Θ-theories. A Θ-theory is a theory with respect to the relation $\vdash_\Theta$. $C \vdash_\Theta D$ if and only if $C \to D \in \Theta$. This is pair extension acceptable, and it extends the consequence relation of our logic. Furthermore, since $A \to B \notin \Theta$, there is some prime Θ-theory containing A but not B.

Now consider T in this frame: we have $x \in T$ if and only if $t \in x$. Suppose that $t \in x$, and suppose that $C \in \Theta$. Since $t \to C \in \Theta$, $t \vdash_\Theta C$, and hence, $C \in x$. Therefore, if $x \in T$, $x \subseteq \Theta$. But the converse holds too. Clearly if $\Theta \subseteq x$, since $t \in \Theta$, $t \in x$ too, and hence $x \in T$. Therefore, $T = \{x : \Theta \subseteq x\}$, and the canonical Θ-frame is reduced.

As Θ is a superset of the set of theorems of the logic, it is trivial to show that the frame satisfies the structural rules of the logic in question. The proof of the case of the canonical frame suffices.   □

This theorem is all well and good, but it does not tell us to which logics the result applies. It is not particularly clear when a logic is reduction-ready. We have a sufficient condition in the next result.

THEOREM 13.15 (SUFFICIENT CONDITION FOR REDUCTION READINESS)
If a logic is such that every non-theorem is invalidated in some prime regular theory, and in addition, it is axiomatisable in such a way that the only rules are adjunction $(A, B \vdash_H A \wedge B)$ and modus ponens $(A, A \to B \vdash_H B)$, then the logic is reduction-ready.

PROOF We show that the disjunctive forms of the rules of adjunction and *modus ponens* are valid. For adjunction, the rule is $A \vee C, B \vee C \vdash (A \wedge B) \vee C$. That follows from distribution. For *modus ponens*, the rule is $A \vee C, (A \rightarrow B) \vee C \vdash_H B \vee C$. Suppose that it is invalid. Then there is a prime regular theory in which we have $A \vee C$ and $A \rightarrow B \vee C$. So, in the theory we have C or we have A and $A \rightarrow B$, so in either case we have $B \vee C$ as desired. $\qquad \square$

As a result, we have the reduction readiness of R, DMALL and Lambek's logics L and LI. So these logics are sound and complete for reduced frames.

13.3 Doing Without Inclusion

Boolean negation on a frame $\mathcal{F}$ is that connective characterised by the following condition

$$x \Vdash -A \text{ if and only if } x \nVdash A.$$

Substructural logics are typically defined without Boolean negation. This gives these logics some of their distinctive properties. However, it is often possible to add Boolean negation without disturbing the behaviour of the logic. This section is dedicated to proving the following result.

THEOREM 13.16 (BOOLEAN NEGATION THEOREM)
If a logic is modelled by a class of frames characterised by frame conditions which do not appeal to the partial order condition $\sqsubseteq$, then that logic is conservatively extended by Boolean negation.

PROOF Suppose that $A \nvdash B$ in the logic in question. Therefore, there is a model $\mathfrak{M}$ in which $A \nvDash_{\mathfrak{M}} B$. We show that this can be extended to a model in which we add evaluation conditions for Boolean negation. The necessity is that we *flatten* the frame. That is, we replace $\sqsubseteq$ by $=$. This new frame is still a frame for the logic, as any frame conditions (not appealing to $\sqsubseteq$) are still satisfied. Given that the frame is flat, we can add an interpretation for Boolean negation. Now $x \Vdash -C$ if and only if $x \nVdash C$ for each C.

This is still a counterexample for $A \Vdash B$ as the evaluation of the non-Boolean connectives is not disturbed. Therefore, we have a counterexample to our consecution in the logic with the addition of Boolean negation. $\qquad \square$

This technique does not work with logics like J or CK, which have frame conditions which make use of the inclusion relation. We will consider CK. If we attempt to use the technique of this proof, the new frames will not satisfy the K condition: $Rxyz \rightarrow y \sqsubseteq z$, or other conditions appealing to $\sqsubseteq$. For we will not necessarily have $Rxyz \rightarrow y = z$. The logic of the new frame will not include all of CK.

However, the technique works for many logics. In particular, for any of the logics extending DBSub with the structural rules B, B^c, B', C, W, T, 4, Kr, mMP, mWI and many others.

COROLLARY 13.17 (CONSERVATIVE EXTENSION WITH BOOLEAN NEGATION)
The logics R, DMALL and the Lambek calculi L and LI are all conservatively extended with Boolean negation. $\qquad\qquad\Box$

Well, this has *almost* been proved. We have not quite dealt with t. If t is a left identity for fusion, the modelling condition for T is that $y \sqsubseteq z$ if and only if there is some $x \in T$ where $Rxyz$, and this condition requires the inclusion relation to state. How can we do away with this? The answer has already been given. If we use *reduced* frames $T = \{x : 0 \sqsubseteq x\}$ for a point 0. We can perform a little surgery on the reduced frame by modifying the behaviour of R on 0. We rejig things so that $R0xy$ if and only if $x = y$, and similarly, if CI holds in the logic, $Rx0y$ if and only if $x = y$. This does not alter the evaluation of any formula at 0, for if in the old model $0 \Vdash A \to B$, then $0 \Vdash A \to B$ in the new model too — and if $0 \nVdash A \to B$ in the old model, then for some x, y where $x \sqsubseteq y$, $x \Vdash A$ and $y \nVdash B$. Then $x \nVdash B$ and in the new model, $0 \nVdash A \to B$. Similarly, if we have $R0xy$ in the old model to give $y \Vdash A \circ B$, then since $x \sqsubseteq y$ we have $R0yy$ and $y \Vdash A \circ B$ still. The "rewiring" of R does not alter the evaluation of any formulae.

Similarly, you can check that the standard structural rules, such as B, B', B^c, C and W, are preserved by this shift. This ensures that each of R, DMALL, L and LI are conservatively extended by Boolean negation.

The philosophical significance of this proof is to be examined in Chapter 16.

13.4 Linguistic Frames

There is another way we might want our frames to look. If we are interested in using the Lambek calculus to model languages, we will be interested in *linguistic frames*.

DEFINITION 13.18 (LINGUISTIC FRAMES)
A *linguistic frame* is a frame in which there is a free semigroup operation $\cdot$, such that $Rxyz$ if and only if $x \cdot y = z$.

We have a simple result on the adequacy of language frames for a fragment of the Lambek calculus, proved first by Buzskowski [41].

THEOREM 13.19 (LAMBEK CALCULUS AND LANGUAGE FRAMES)
The logic $L[\to, \leftarrow, \wedge, \top]$ *is sound and complete for the class of language frames.*

PROOF Soundess is trivial, as the ternary accessibility relation on language frames satisfies B and B^c. Completeness is less trivial. We cannot use the canonical model, as the canonical model is nothing like a language frame. However, we define a model as follows.

Let the points in the model be sequences of formulae in the language $[\rightarrow, \leftarrow, \wedge, \top]$ and we set the accessibility relation as follows:

$$RXYZ \text{ iff } Z = X; Y$$

Assign truth for atomic propositions as follows:

$$X \Vdash p \text{ iff } X \vdash p$$

We will show by induction on B that $X \Vdash B$ if and only if $X \vdash B$.

Clearly, the result holds for atomic B and $B = \top$. If $B = B_1 \wedge B_2$, then $X \Vdash B_1 \wedge B_2$ if and only if $X \Vdash B_1$ and $X \Vdash B_2$, if and only if $X \vdash B_1$ and $X \vdash B_2$, if and only if $X \vdash B_1 \wedge B_2$ as desired. If $B = B_1 \rightarrow B_2$, then $X \Vdash B_1 \rightarrow B_2$ if and only if $X; B_1 \Vdash B_2$, if and only if $X; B_1 \vdash B_2$, if and only if $X \vdash B_1 \rightarrow B_2$ as desired. The result for $\leftarrow$ is dual.

So we have a linguistic model in which $X \Vdash A$ if and only if $X \vdash A$. Therefore, if $A \vdash B$ is not provable in $BB^c[\rightarrow, \leftarrow, \wedge, \top]$, in this model we consider the point A. Clearly $A \Vdash A$, but $A \nVdash B$, so the entailment $A \vdash B$ fails in the model, as desired.   □

This technique does not work for logics containing fusion, as we will be unable to show that $A \circ B \Vdash A \circ B$. The sequence $A \circ B$ is not the concatenation of any two sequences, so we will not have $A \circ B \Vdash C \circ D$ for *any* C or D at all.

13.5 History

Hennessy and Milner's work on bisimulations and simulations has been exceedingly useful in the study of frame semantics of modal logics [31, 113, 171]. The applications to substructural logics are very much in their infancy. The directed bisimulation results of this chapter are due to Kurtonina and de Rijke [129, 130].

For reduced frames, comprehensive studies are available in the work of Slaney [248], and the work of Priest and Sylvan [201], extended by me [211, 215].

Pentus has shown that the language completeness for the Lambek calculus holds for $BB^c[\circ, \rightarrow, \leftarrow]$ [191]. His proof is quite complex and beyond the scope of this book.

13.6 Exercises

{13.1} Show how even with $\sqsubseteq$ we can conservatively extend with BN by judicious use of an S4 modality.

{13.2} Show that the logic of linguistic frames is not $BB^c[\wedge, \vee, \circ, \rightarrow, \leftarrow, \top, \bot]$ but that we also need to have $A \wedge (A \rightarrow \bot) \vdash \bot$ and the inference from $A \vdash B \rightarrow \bot$ to $B \vdash A \rightarrow \bot$. At least.

Part IV

Decidability

Chapter 14

Decision Procedures

The *deducibility problem* for a logic goes like this: we are presented with a consecution $X \vdash A$, and we wish to know whether it is valid or not. Is there an algorithm to determine its validity? A logic is said to be *decidable* if and only if there is an algorithm determining decidability, and it is *undecidable* if there is no such algorithm.

In some logics, there is a simple algorithm. For example, in the two-valued classical propositional logic TV, one algorithm is a truth table test. You check to see whether there are any truth table evaluations for which the antecedent is true and the conclusion false. If there are any, the argument is invalid, otherwise, it is valid. This process can be generalised — if any logic has a finite characteristic algebra, then we have an algorithm for testing its validity. You check! However, many logics are not characterised by a finite algebra.[1] In these cases, we need a more subtle method for determining the validity of arguments. In this chapter, we will examine a few such methods. The first section will focus on methods involving proof theories and the second, on models.

14.1   Proof Search

One method for determining validity is to search for a proof, provided that you have reassurance that you will not have to look *too far*. If there are bounds on the length of the search, then searching for a proof can provide an algorithm for determining validity. (If there is no such bound, then you do not have an algorithm, as you are not assured that the search will end with an answer.) Proof search is quite simple in the case of *non-expansive* logics.

---

[1]   See Exercises 8.11 and 8.12.

DEFINITION 14.1 (COMPLEXITY AND EXPANSIVE RULES)
The complexity of a consecution is the number of instances of connectives or punctuation marks in that consecution. A structural rule is *expansive* if and only if it has some instance in which the complexity of the premise is greater than the complexity of the conclusion.

Note that WI is expansive, as $p; p \vdash q$ is more complex than $p \vdash q$. However, B, B^c, B', C and K are all non-expansive, as an inspection of the rules will verify. If a logic is axiomatised with a Gentzen system with non-expansive rules, then the logic is decidable, as the next theorem shows.

THEOREM 14.2 (NON-EXPANSIVE LOGICS ARE DECIDABLE)
A logic axiomatised with a non-expansive Gentzen calculus is decidable.

This theorem exploits one of the useful properties of Gentzen systems — the elimination of the Cut rule. For the Cut rule is, in many instances, expansive. In the inference from $X \vdash A$ and $A \vdash B$, to $X \vdash B$, we may move from complex premises to a simpler conclusion, in cases where A is complex.

PROOF We will provide an algorithm for determining the validity of the consecution $X \vdash A$. The procedure uses induction on the complexity of $X \vdash A$. At each step, we suppose that the issue of the validity of consecutions less complex than $X \vdash A$ has been decided.
    There are number of important properties of our Gentzen systems.

  ⋄ In any proof of $X \vdash A$, the formulae appearing are subformulae of those in X and A.

  ⋄ In any proof of $X \vdash A$, the complexity of consecutions does not increase from root to leaves.

  ⋄ There are a finite number of consecutions with complexity no greater than $X \vdash A$, composed of subformulae of X and A.

These results are straightforward, given the Gentzen rules.
    Now we give our algorithm. Suppose that $X \vdash A$ has complexity zero. Then a simple check verifies validity. $p_i \vdash p_j$ is valid when and only when $i = j$. $A \vdash \top$ is always valid, as is $\bot \vdash A$ and $0 \vdash t$. No other consecutions of this complexity are valid.
    Now suppose that we have an algorithm for deciding the validity of consecutions of complexity less than n, and suppose that $X \vdash A$ has complexity n. We list all possible premises for $Y \vdash B$, for each consecution $Y \vdash B$ of complexity n, constructed of subformulae of $X \vdash A$. There are finitely many such consecutions. For those premises of complexity less than n, we have an algorithm determining validity. For those consecutions of complexity n, we set aside as valid those which follow from the valid consecutions of lower complexity. We

proceed through the list, setting aside as valid those which have valid premises. As the set of consecutions is finite, this process will eventually stop, with the valid consecutions of complexity n set aside, and those invalid remaining. This tells us which consecutions of complexity n are valid.   □

The result gives us the decidability of logics such as LL, Lambek's logic L, BCK and others axiomatised with non-expansive rules. However, logics with extensional structure are not shown to be decidable in this way, for eWI is expansive. Similarly, the system R[→] is not shown to be decidable, as W is expansive. However, a refinement of this technique, due to Kripke [127], gives us an algorithm for R[→] and nearby logics.

The main strategy of this is to limit applications of the contraction rule so as to prevent a proof search from running on for ever. We need one simple notion before strategy can be achieved.

DEFINITION 14.3 (CONTRACTIONS OF CONSECUTIONS)
The consecution $X' \vdash A$ is a *contraction* of $X \vdash A$ when it can be derived from $X \vdash A$ by repeated applications of the structural rules.

In fact, we will *identify* consecutions which are related by applications of B and C. In effect, the antecedent structure will be treated as a *multiset*.

Kripke's idea is to allow a contraction of the conclusion of a rule only in so far as the same result could not be obtained by first contracting the premises. This means no change for the rule [→R], and that we should modify [→L] as follows:

$$\frac{X \vdash A \quad Y(B) \vdash C}{[Y(A \to B; X)] \vdash C}$$

where $[Y(A \to B; X)] \vdash C$ is any contraction of $Y(A \to B; X) \vdash C$ where

1. $A \to B$ occurs only 0, 1, or 2 times fewer than in $Y(A \to B; X) \vdash C$.

2. Any formula other than $A \to B$ occurs only 0 or 1 time fewer.

We can prove this lemma by induction on the length of the proof:

LEMMA 14.4 (CURRY'S LEMMA)
If a consecution C' is a contraction of a consecution C and C has a derivation of length n, then C' has a derivation of length $\leq n$.   □

This lemma shows that the modification of R[→] leaves the same consecutions derivable (since the lemma says the effect of contraction is retained).

Curry's Lemma also shows that every derivable consecution has an *irredundant* derivation in the following sense: one containing no branch with a consecution C' below a consecution C of which it is a contraction.

We now need to verify that proof search cannot go on indefinitely, given the restriction of our attention to irredundant proofs. For this, we need another notion:

DEFINITION 14.5 (COGNATE CONSECUTIONS)
Two consecutions $X \vdash A$ and $X' \vdash A$ are *cognate* just when exactly the same formulae (not counting multiplicity) occur in X as in X'. Thus, e.g. all of the following are cognate with each other:

$$X;Y \vdash A \quad X;X;Y \vdash A \quad X;Y;Y \vdash A \quad X;X;Y;Y \vdash A$$

We call the class of all consecutions cognate with a given consecution a *cognation class*.

LEMMA 14.6 (KRIPKE'S LEMMA)
Suppose that a sequence of cognate consecutions $C_0, C_1, \ldots,$ is irredundant in the sense that for no C_i, C_j with $i < j$, is C_i a contraction of C_j. Then the sequence is finite.

Recall that Gentzen systems have the subformula property. This means that the number of cognation classes occurring in any derivation (and hence in each branch) is finite. But Kripke's Lemma further shows that only a finite number of members of each cognation class occur in a branch (this is because we have constructed the complete proof search tree to be irredundant). So every branch is finite, so the proof search tree is finite and there is a decision procedure.

Returning now to elaborating Kripke's Lemma itself, before proving it we will explain a helpful way to picture what is going on. Consider a family of consecutions as points in an n-dimensional graph, where there is an axis for each different formula appearing in the antecedent of the consecutions in the cognation class. The A-th co-ordinate of a point is then the number of times A appears in the consecution. This will range from 1 upwards. Now, each C_n in the graph casts a *shadow* over all possible positions of consecutions which would contract to C_n. This is depicted in Figure 14.1. No later consecution can be placed in the shaded areas. The result of Kripke's lemma is that eventually there will be no room to place new consecutions. Try it yourself to see what happens! Here is a formal proof that irredundant sequences terminate.

PROOF Suppose that $\mathfrak{S} = C_i$, $i \in \omega$ is the sequence of cognate consecutions. We will show that if $\mathfrak{S}$ is irredundant, it is finite. We use induction on the number n of distinct formulae occuring in $\mathfrak{S}$. If $n = 1$, then the claim is immediate. Suppose now that the hypothesis holds for all sequences containing n formulae and consider a sequence $\mathfrak{S}$ containing $n + 1$. Pick one formula occuring in $\mathfrak{S}$: call it A. C_k is critical in a sequence if and only if for each $m > k$ the number of

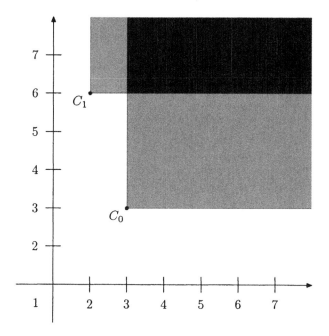

Figure 14.1: Regions and Redundant Sequences

occurrences of A in C_k is less than or equal to the number of occurrences of A in C_m. Let C_i' be the result of deleting all occurrences of A from C_i. We define a new sequence $\mathfrak{S}'$ of consecutions, D_i, $i \in \omega$ as follows. Let C_k be the first consecution critical in the original sequence. $D_0 = C_k'$. Suppose that D_m has been defined and is C_j'. If C_{j+1} exists, find the first critical consecution in the sequence $C_{j+1}, C_{j+2}, \ldots$ call it C_l and let $D_{m+1} = C_l'$. Note that $\mathfrak{S}'$ terminates only if the $\mathfrak{S}$ terminates. Now $\mathfrak{S}'$ is a sequence of cognate consecutions, containing only n distinct formulae. Therefore, if $\mathfrak{S}'$ is irredundant, $\mathfrak{S}'$ terminates. However, since $\mathfrak{S}$ is irredundant, so is $\mathfrak{S}'$. Therefore $\mathfrak{S}'$ terminates, and hence, so does $\mathfrak{S}$. $\square$

This algorithm can be immediately extended to logics with conjunction, disjunction, fusion, t, $\top$ and $\perp$ with the rules

$$\frac{X \vdash A \quad X \vdash B}{X \vdash A \wedge B} \qquad \frac{X(A) \vdash C}{[X(A \wedge B)] \vdash C} \qquad \frac{X(B) \vdash C}{[X(A \wedge B)] \vdash C}$$

$$\frac{X(A) \vdash C \quad X(B) \vdash C}{[X(A \vee B)] \vdash C} \qquad \frac{X \vdash A}{X \vdash A \vee B} \qquad \frac{X \vdash B}{X \vdash A \vee B}$$

$$\frac{X \vdash A \quad Y \vdash B}{[X;Y] \vdash A \circ B} \qquad \frac{X(A,B) \vdash C}{[X(A \circ B)] \vdash C}$$

$$\vdash t \qquad \frac{X \vdash C}{[X;t] \vdash C}$$

$$X \vdash \top \qquad X; \bot \vdash C$$

where in each bracketed antecedent we have allowed appropriate contractions. In each of these cases, the proof of Curry's Lemma holds, and Kripke's Lemma does not rely on the presence of any particular connectives, so the decidability of the extended system follows.

However, in this system, we are unable to prove the distribution of disjunction over conjunction. We do not have an algorithm for the whole of R$^+$. (And we will *not*, due to the result of Urquhart's reported in the next chapter.)

The decidability of the system reported here extends to the system with a strong de Morgan negation. There are a number of ways to do this. One is to extend the proof theory to include structured consequents. Another simpler technique is to use the embedding result from Theorem 12.22. Any algorithm for the logic, including $\rightarrow$ and $\wedge$ and t, becomes an algorithm for the whole logic, without distribution.

14.2 Finite Model Property

Another way to prove that there is an algorithm for determining the consequence relation in a logic is to exploit the model theory of the logic in question. A logic has the *finite model property* if and only if any consecution invalid in the logic can be invalidated in a finite model. If, then, we have an algorithm for producing all of the proofs in our logic, and we have an algorithm for producing all of the finite models, then we can combine these to produce an algorithm for testing the validity of consecutions. The algorithm is not particularly efficient, but it works. It goes as follows. Construct model number 1. Test $X \vdash A$ in this model. If it is invalid in this model, you stop, as you know that $X \vdash A$ is not valid. If not, construct proof number 1. If this is a proof of $X \vdash A$, you are finished as you know that $X \vdash A$ is valid. Now construct model number 2. Test $X \vdash A$ in this model ... Now construct proof number n. Now construct model number n ... If the logic has the finite model property, you know that this procedure must terminate at some stage. We will construct a proof, or construct a countermodel to our consecution. In this section, we will consider one powerful technique for showing when a logic has the finite model property, the technique of *filtrations*.

DEFINITION 14.7 (EQUIVALENT POINTS)
Given a model $\mathfrak{M}$, and a set F of formulae, we say that two points x and y are F-equivalent (written $x \equiv_F y$) if and only if for each $A \in F$, $x \Vdash A$ if and only if $y \Vdash A$.

It is clear that for any F, $\equiv_F$ is an equivalence relation. If F is finite, then $\mathfrak{M}$ can contain at most finitely many $\equiv_F$-equivalence classes. Given a particular set F of formulae, and a particular model $\mathfrak{M}$, we let $\overline{x} = \{y : x \equiv_F y\}$. The set of all equivalence classes $\overline{x}$ is finite if F is finite. The idea of filtrations is to construct a model on the set of these equivalence classes.

We will try, as far as possible, for the evaluation on the points $\overline{x}$ to mirror the evaluation on x, as far as formulae in F go. We set $\overline{x} \Vdash p$ if and only if $x \Vdash p$, whenever $p \in F$. The value of other formulae can be whatever we like. To model the accessiblity relations, we have the following definition.

DEFINITION 14.8 (F-FILTRATIONS)
Given a model $\mathfrak{M}$, another model $\overline{\mathfrak{M}}$ is an *F-filtration* of $\mathfrak{M}$ if and only if the points in $\overline{\mathfrak{M}}$ are the equivalence classes $\overline{x}$, with $x \in \mathfrak{M}$, such that $\overline{x} \Vdash p$ if and only if $x \Vdash p$, whenever $p \in F$, and such that the accessiblity relations S, R and C on $\overline{\mathfrak{M}}$ satisfy the following conditions:

⋄ If xSy then $\overline{x}S\overline{y}$.
⋄ If $\overline{x}S\overline{y}$, $\Box A \in F$, and $x \Vdash \Box A$ then $y \Vdash A$.
⋄ If $\overline{x}S\overline{y}$, $\Diamond A \in F$ and $x \Vdash A$, then $y \Vdash \Diamond A$.
⋄ If $Rxyz$ then $R\overline{x}\overline{y}\overline{z}$.
⋄ If $R\overline{x}\overline{y}\overline{z}$, $A \to B \in F$, $x \Vdash A \to B$ and $y \Vdash A$ then $z \Vdash B$.
⋄ If $Rxyz$, $B \leftarrow A \in F$, $y \Vdash B \leftarrow A$ and $x \Vdash A$ then $z \Vdash B$.
⋄ If $Rxyz$, $A \circ B \in F$, $x \Vdash A$ and $y \Vdash B$ then $z \Vdash A \circ B$.
⋄ If xCy then $\overline{x}C\overline{y}$.
⋄ If $\overline{x}C\overline{y}$, $\sim A \in F$ and $x \Vdash \sim A$ then $y \nVdash A$.
⋄ If $\overline{x}C\overline{y}$, $\neg A \in F$ and $y \Vdash \sim A$ then $x \nVdash A$.

The clauses in these definitions are chosen purely to prove the following lemma:

LEMMA 14.9 (FILTRATION LEMMA)
If $\overline{\mathfrak{M}}$ is a filtration of $\mathfrak{M}$, then for any $x \in \mathfrak{M}$, and for any $A \in F$ we have $\mathfrak{M}, x \Vdash A$ if and only if $\overline{\mathfrak{M}}, \overline{x} \Vdash A$.

PROOF The verification is an induction on the construction of A. It holds for atoms by definition. The induction steps for conjunction and disjunction are immediate. Consider $\Box$ formulae. If $x \Vdash \Box A$ then $\overline{x} \Vdash \Box A$ if and only if whenever $\overline{x}S\overline{y}$ then $\overline{y} \Vdash A$. But since $\Box A \in F$ we have $y \Vdash A$, and by induction, $\overline{y} \Vdash A$. Conversely, if $\overline{x} \Vdash \Box A$ then if xSy we have $\overline{x}S\overline{y}$ and hence $\overline{y} \Vdash A$, giving $y \Vdash A$, which in turn gives $x \Vdash \Box A$ as desired.

Consider implication formulae. If $x \Vdash A \to B$ and $R\overline{xyz}$, we wish to know that if $\overline{y} \Vdash A$ then $\overline{z} \Vdash B$. Well, if $\overline{y} \Vdash A$ then by induction $y \Vdash A$, and so by our hypothesis on R on the filtration frame, $z \Vdash B$, giving $\overline{z} \Vdash B$ by the induction hypothesis. Conversely, if $\overline{x} \Vdash A \to B$ and $Rxyz$, if $y \Vdash A$ then $R\overline{xyz}$ gives $\overline{y} \Vdash A$ and hence $\overline{z} \Vdash B$, giving $z \Vdash B$ and hence $x \Vdash A \to B$ as desired.

The same holds for negation and fusion, and we pronounce the proof completed.   □

Here are some example accessibility relations on a filtration frame.

EXAMPLE 14.10 (FILTRATIONS)
The *smallest filtration*: $\overline{x}S^s\overline{y}$ if and only if $x'Sy'$ for some $x' \equiv_F x$ and $y' \equiv_F y$. $R^s\overline{xyz}$ if and only if $Rx'y'z'$ for some $x' \equiv_F x$, $y' \equiv_F y$ and $z' \equiv_F x$. (And similarly for C.)

The *largest filtration*: $\overline{x}S^l\overline{y}$ if and only if for each $\Box A \in F$, where $x \Vdash \Box A$, $y \Vdash B$ too, and for each $\Diamond A \in F$, if $x \Vdash A$ then $y \Vdash \Diamond A$. (And similarly for R and C.)

The technqiue of filtration gives us an immediate decidability argument for the basic distributive substructural logic DBSub.

THEOREM 14.11 (CONSEQUENCE IN DBSub IS DECIDABLE)
DBSub *is decidable, as it has the finite model property.*

PROOF Suppose that $A \nvdash B$ in DBSub. Therefore there is a model $\mathfrak{M}$ in which $A \nvDash_\mathfrak{M} B$. Now let F be the set of all subformulae of A or of B, and consider the filtration $\overline{\mathfrak{M}}$ in which we define R, S and C to be the *smallest* filtration relations. This is a finite model, and it invalidates $A \vdash B$, since if $x \Vdash A$ and $x \nVdash B$, for some $x \in \mathfrak{M}$, we have $\overline{x} \Vdash A$ and $\overline{x} \nVdash B$. Furthermore, $\mathfrak{M}$ is actually a model for DBSub, as *every* substructural model is a model for DBSub.   □

This technique can be extended to provide decidability of other substructural logics too. For example, given a model in which the structural rule WI holds, we have $Rxxx$ for each x. It follows that $R\overline{xxx}$ will hold in any filtration of this model, so this is a model for DBSub plus WI. Similarly, if CI holds in $\mathfrak{M}$, it will also hold in any filtration of $\mathfrak{M}$. So adding CI does not disturb decidability.

However, not all structural rules fare so well. In particular, B is not preserved by filtrations. Suppose that $\mathfrak{M}$ satisfies B. Consider a filtration $\overline{\mathfrak{M}}$. Does B hold in this frame? If we have $R\overline{xy}v$ and $R\overline{vz}w$, is there some $\overline{u}$ where $R\overline{xu}w$ and $R\overline{yz}\overline{u}$? In the case of the smallest filtration, it does not seem that there has to be. For if $x \equiv x'$, $y \equiv y'$, $v \equiv v'$ and $Rx'y'v'$ (to give $R\overline{xy}v$) and $v \equiv v''$, $z \equiv z'$, $w \equiv w'$ and $Rv''z'w'$ (to give $R\overline{vz}w$) then there is no assurance that $v'' = v'$. It is unknown whether any other technique for defining R on a filtration can preserve associativity axioms such as B and B$'$.

14.3 History

Kripke's original work has been reported in abstract form only [127]. The technique was extended to model E with negation by Belnap and Wallace [27], and their work is discussed in *Entailment* Volume 1 [6]. The algorithm has been implemented by Thistlewaite and McRobbie and Meyer [260] in the theorem prover KRIPKE, available from the *Automated Reasoning Project* at the Australian National University at //arp.anu.edu.au/~jks/kripke.html.

Meyer has noted that Kripke's Lemma is equivalent to a theorem of Dickson about prime numbers: Let $\mathcal{M}$ be a set of natural numbers, all of which are products of the first m primes. Then every $n \in \mathcal{M}$ is of the form $p_1^{n_1} \times p_2^{n_2} \times \cdots \times p_k^{n_k}$, and hence it can be regarded as a sequence of the p_i's in which each p_i is repeated n_i times. Divisibility corresponds to contraction (neglecting the case $n_i = 0$). Dickson's theorem says that if no member of $\mathcal{M}$ has a proper divisor in $\mathcal{M}$, then $\mathcal{M}$ is finite.

McRobbie and Belnap [152] have reformulated the Gentzen system for non-distributive R in an analytic tableau style, and Meyer has extended this to give analytic tableau for linear logic and other systems in the vicinity of R [164].

Curry's Lemma is named after an analogous lemma about classical and intuitionistic Gentzen systems [53]. With K available, Curry proves his lemma with [$\rightarrow$L] stated as:

$$\frac{\Gamma, A \rightarrow B \vdash A \quad \Gamma, A \rightarrow B, B \vdash C}{\Gamma, A \rightarrow B \vdash C}$$

This rule uses the the maximum contraction permitted in our statement of [$\rightarrow$L] above, but this is not a problem since items contracted away can always be returned using K. Giambrone [95], Brady [39] and I [218] have extended the proof search method to deal with extensional structure, thereby proving the decidability of logics without contraction, but with extensional structure.

Meyer and Ono [165] show that R[$\rightarrow$, $\wedge$] and BCK[$\rightarrow$, $\wedge$] have the finite model property, using Kripke's Lemma. Their construction stays close to the techniques from proof theory. Buszkowski extends the result to prove the finite model property for MALL[$\rightarrow$, $\wedge$] [42]. Lafont has gone further to use phase spaces to give the finite model property for MALL [132]. See Exercise 14.3.

It would be a grave omission not to call the reader's attention to a major open problem: it is still unknown whether the implication fragment of T is decidable.

14.4   Exercises

Practice

{14.1} Step through a proof search procedure for proofs of simple consecutions, such as $A \to B; B \to C \vdash A \to C$ in Lambek's logic L, and $A \vdash (A \to B) \to B$ in MALL.

{14.2} Step through a proof search procedure to argue that $A \vdash B \to A$ is not provable in MALL and that $A \vdash (A \to B) \to B$ is not valid in Lambek's logic L.

Problems

{14.3} For the finite model property of MALL, we use the Okada canonical model construction from Exercise 12.8. Define the finitely generated phase space PS[A] to be the Okada phase space generated by all subformulae of A and structures made out of these formulae, and using the logic $\vdash_{\text{MALL}[A]}$ in which proofs are restricted to subformulae of A. Define **0** as before, and show that $[\![B]\!] = \{B\}^\sim$ if B is a subformula of A, and is $\{\sim B\}^{\sim\sim}$ if $\sim B$ occurs in A and B does not.

{14.4} A relation $\equiv$ is a *congruence* on a phase space if and only if whenever $x \equiv x'$ and $y \equiv y'$ then $xy \equiv x'y'$, and if $x \in \mathbf{0}$ and $x \equiv y$ then $y \in \mathbf{0}$. Let $\pi : \mathfrak{M} \to \mathfrak{M}/\!\equiv$ be the quotient map which sends a phase to its $\equiv$-equivalence class. Prove that $\pi(x) \Vdash A$ if and only if $x \Vdash A$ for each $x \in \mathfrak{M}$.

{14.5} Now define $X \preceq Y$ as follows: $X \preceq X; Y, B; C; X \preceq B+C; X, B; X \preceq B*C; X$ and $C; X \preceq B * C; X$ whenever $*$ is one of $\wedge$, $\vee$ or $\circ$. Show that for any B there are finitely many X where $X \preceq B$.

{14.6} Let MALL$\langle A \rangle$ be MALL[A] extended with the axioms $\vdash X$ whenever $X \not\preceq A$. Define $\equiv_A$ on PS$\langle A \rangle$ by setting $X \equiv_A Y$ if and only if $X = Y$ or $X \not\preceq A$ and $Y \not\preceq A$. Show that $\equiv_A$ is a congruence.

{14.7} Show that PS$\langle A \rangle/\equiv_A$ is finite.

{14.8} Show that $\vdash A$ in MALL $\Rightarrow \vdash A$ holds in finite phase spaces $\Rightarrow A$ is satisfied in PS$\langle A \rangle/\equiv_A \Rightarrow A$ is satisfied in Cut-free MALL$\langle A \rangle \Rightarrow \vdash A$ in MALL. (Only the last part here is difficult, and it relies on the behaviour of $\preceq$.)

{14.9} Show that abelian logic is decidable, and that it has the *infinite model property*: no consecution has a counterexample in a finite model.

Projects

{14.10} Show that $T[\to]$ is decidable.

{14.11} Show that $T[\to, \wedge]$ is decidable.

Chapter 15

Undecidability

Things so utterly undetermined,
that they are indeed altogether undecidable.

— *Bishop Joseph Hall*, Episcopacie by Divine Right Asserted, *1640*

In this chapter, we will examine some of the most surprising results in the study of substructural logics. We will show that the Hilbert consequence relation $\vdash_H$ is undecidable in most major substructural logics, and that as a consequence, the standard entailment relation $\vdash$ is undecidable in many major substructural logics. That follows in logics with WI in which $\vdash_H$ is related to $\vdash$ closely enough for an algorithm for $\vdash$ to give an algorithm for $\vdash_H$. This result is important, as these logics provide the simplest examples of propositional logics known to be undecidable.

Proving undecidability is, at least initially, more difficult than proving decidability. To demonstrate decidability, you construct an algorithm. To demonstrate *undecidability* you have to show that no such algorithm can be constructed. To do that, it is not enough to try and then fail! Thankfully, the task for the logician is not that difficult. If there is a problem that someone *else* has verified to be undecidable, we can show that our favourite problem is undecidable by showing that if we have an algorithm for our problem, we can use this algorithm to also solve *their* problem. As they have managed to show that there is no algorithm for their problem, it follows that there cannot be an algorithm for our problem either.

In this chapter, we will see two examples of undecidable problems, and we will reduce them to decision procedures for substructural logics. First, we will show how the *word problem* for semigroups reduces to the problem of demonstrating validity on R, or E or similar logics. The word problem for semigroups is known to be undecidable, therefore the consequence in R and E is also undecidable. Second, we will show that an algorithm for determining consequence in linear logic with exponentials would give us an algorithm for determining the behaviour of certain abstract machines which are known to be undecidable. Again, this shows that linear logic with exponentials is undecidable. To start with, we will examine one of the first undecidability results in substructural

logics — Urquhart's demonstration that KR is undecidable. This will set the
scene for the undecidability proof of R, which follows it.

15.1 KR and Projective Spaces

The logic KR is given by making the negation of R Boolean: we add the axiom
$A \wedge {\sim} A \to B$ to R. It follows then that a KR frame is one satisfying the following
conditions.

◇ $R0ab$ iff $a = b$.

◇ $Raaa$ for each a.

◇ $Rabc$ iff $Rbac$ iff $Racb$ (total permutation).

◇ R^2abcd only if R^2acbd.

The total permutation condition follows from the condition CI together with the
contraposition condition $\exists x(Ryzx \wedge xCw) \to \exists v(Rywv \wedge zCv)$ once we require
C to be Boolean: xCy if and only if $x = y$. The clauses for the connectives on
KR frames are the standard clauses for R, with the modification needed to make
negation Boolean: we have $a \Vdash {\sim}A$ if and only if $a \nVdash A$.

KR frames are related to projective spaces.

DEFINITION 15.1 (PROJECTIVE SPACES)
A *projective space* $\mathcal{P}$ is a set P of points, and a collection L of subsets of P called
lines, such that

◇ Any two distinct points are on exactly one line.

◇ Any two distinct lines intersect in exactly one point.

Given a projective space $\mathcal{P}$, its collinearity relation C is a ternary relation satisfying the condition:

> $Cabc$ iff $a = b = c$, or a, b and c are distinct and they lie on a
> common line.

LEMMA 15.2 (COLLINEARITY CONDITIONS)
*If $\mathcal{P}$ is a projective space, then its collinearity relation C satisfies the following
conditions:*

◇ $Caaa$ for each a.

◇ $Cabc$ iff $Cbac$ iff $Cacb$.

◇ C^2abcd only if C^2acbd.   □

In this lemma, the composition C^2 is defined in the same way as R^2 is defined
in terms of R. This last condition is the only part of the lemma which is hard to
verify, and it is best checked using a diagram.

Note that we could define a projective space to be a set with a collinearity
relation, satisfying these conditions.

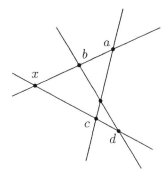

Figure 15.1: Associating Collinearity

DEFINITION 15.3 (THE FRAME OF A SPACE)
If $\mathcal{P}$ is a projective space, the frame $\mathcal{F}(\mathcal{P})$ generated by P is given by adjoining
a new point 0, and adding the condition $C0aa$, $Ca0a$, and $Caa0$.

If $\mathcal{P}$ is a projective space, the frame $\mathcal{F}(\mathcal{P})$ is a KR frame.

DEFINITION 15.4 (SUBSPACES IN PROJECTIVE SPACES)
A *subspace* of a projective space is a subset which is also a projective space under
its inherited collinearity relation. Furthermore, given any two subspaces $\mathcal{X}$ and
$\mathcal{Y}$, the subspace $\mathcal{X} + \mathcal{Y}$ is the set of all points on lines through points in X and
points in Y.

The subspaces of a projective space satisfy certain algebraic conditions.

LEMMA 15.5 (THE ALGEBRA OF SUBSPACES)
*Given a projective space $\mathcal{P}$, the lattice algebra $\langle \mathcal{L}, \cap, + \rangle$ of all subspaces of the
projective space, under intersection and $+$, is a modular lattice. That is, it is a
lattice satisfying the modularity condition $a \geqslant c \Rightarrow (\forall b)\big(a \cap (b + c) \leqslant (a \cap b) + c\big)$.
(Or equivalently: $a \cap (b + (a \cap c)) \leqslant (a \cap b) + (a \cap c)$.)*

In fact, the lattice of subspaces of a projective space satisfies a few more conditions.

DEFINITION 15.6 (GEOMETRIC LATTICES)
A geometric lattice is a lattice in which every element is a join of atoms, and if
a is an atom and X is a set where $a \leqslant \bigvee X$ then there is some finite $Y \subseteq X$,
where $a \leqslant \bigvee Y$. And it is complete.

It is then clear that the lattice of subspaces of a projective space is in fact a
modular geometric lattice. The connection is in fact quite deep. We have the
converse:

THEOREM 15.7 (MODULAR GEOMETRIC LATTICES AND PROJECTIVE SPACES)
Any modular geometric lattice is isomorphic to the lattice of subspaces of some projective space.

PROOF Given a modular geometric lattice, construct a projective space by taking the points to be the atoms and the lines to be the sets of atoms $\{x : x \leqslant a + b\}$. This is a projective space.

Let $\mathcal{L}_P$ be the lattice of its subspaces, and send $\phi : \mathcal{L}_P \to \mathcal{L}$ by setting $\phi(\mathcal{X}) = \bigvee \mathcal{X}$. This is an isomorphism. □

Now in KR frames we have propositions which are analogous to subspaces in projective spaces. First, we need a convention to deal with the point 0. The convention is that 0 should be *in* every "subspace." This is simply dealt with as follows.

DEFINITION 15.8 (POSITIVE IDEMPOTENTS)
A *positive idempotent* in a frame is a proposition X that is *positive* (so $0 \in X$) and *idempotent* (so $X = X \circ X$).

For any sentence A and any KR model $\mathfrak{M}$, the extension of A, $[\![A]\!]$ in $\mathfrak{M}$ is a positive idempotent if and only if $0 \Vdash A \wedge (A \leftrightarrow A \circ A)$. Now to get the undecidability of KR, we need a fact.

THEOREM 15.9 (UNDECIDABILITY FACT)
The word problem for any class of modular lattices which includes the subspace lattice of an infinite dimensional projective space is undecidable. □

The word problem for a class of algebras is the issue of determining the validity of rules involving equations in those algebras. An example word problem for a class of lattices is this:

$$\text{If } x = y \wedge z, z = x \vee (y \wedge w) \text{ then } x \wedge y = v \vee w$$

The question is: does this hold in that class of lattices? A solution to the word problem is an algorithm which will determine a solution to *any* problem of this form it is given. Problems are always of the form

$$\text{If } v_1 = w_1 \cdots v_n = w_n \text{ then } v = w$$

where each v_i and w_j is made up of connectives from the algebra and variables.

A space has dimension n if and only if there is a chain $\mathcal{X}_1 \subset \cdots \subset \mathcal{X}_{n+1}$ of subspaces, no two of which are identical, and no longer chain. A space has infinite dimension if and only if it contains an infinite descending chain of subspaces.

Now we can extract undecidability in KR from this result. Given an infinite dimensional projective space $\mathcal{P}$, the logic of the frame $\mathcal{F}(\mathcal{P})$ is said to be a *strong* logic.

THEOREM 15.10 (UNDECIDABILITY OF KR)
Any logic in between KR and a strong logic is undecidable.
PROOF Take any word problem you like. Say

$$\text{If } v_1 = w_1 \cdots v_n = w_n \text{ then } v = w$$

Then its translation is the KR sentence

$$\left(B \wedge (v_1 = w_1)^t \wedge \cdots \wedge (v_n = w_n)^t\right) \supset (v = w)^t$$

Where $(v_i = w_i)^t$ is $v_i^t \leftrightarrow w_i^t$, and the sentence B is the conjunction of all sentences $p \wedge (p \leftrightarrow p \circ p)$ for each p. If the word problem is valid, then so is the translation. If the word problem is invalid, then there is a counterexample in terms of a projective space out of which we can construct a frame which invalidates the corresponding formula. □

15.2 The KR Result Generalised

Unfortunately, these techniques do not work for systems weaker than KR. The proof that positive idempotents are modular uses essentially the special properties of KR. Not every positive idempotent in R need be modular, but nonetheless, the techniques of the proof can be extended to apply to a much wider range of systems. Urquhart examined the structure of the modular lattice undecidability result, and he showed that you could make do with much less. You do not need to restrict your attention to modular lattices to construct an undecidable word problem. But to do that, you need to examine Lipshitz and Hutchinson's proof more carefully. In the rest of this section, we will sketch the structure of Urquhart's undecidability proof. The techniques are quite involved, so we do not have the space to go into extensive detail. For that, the reader is referred to Urquhart [267].

Lipshitz and Hutchinson proved that the word problem for modular lattices was undecidable by embedding into that problem the already known undecidable word problem for semigroups. It is enough to show that a structure can define a "free associative binary operation", for then you will have the tools for representing arbitrary semigroup problems. (A semigroup is a set with an associative binary operation. An operation is a "free associative" operation if it satisfies those conditions satisfied by any associative operation but no more.) We will sketch how this can be done without resorting to a modular lattice.

We require what Urquhart calls a *0-structure*,[1] and a *modular 4-frame* defined within a 0-structure. A 0-structure is a set equipped with the following structure:

---

[1] This is best read "zero structure."

⋄ A semilattice with respect to $\sqcap$.

⋄ A binary operator $+$ that is associative and commutative.

⋄ $x \leqslant y \Rightarrow x + z \leqslant y + z$.

⋄ $0 + x = x$.

⋄ $y \geqslant 0 \Rightarrow x \sqcap (x + y) = x$.

A 4-frame in a 0-structure is a set $\{a_1, a_2, a_3, a_4\} \cup \{c_{ij} : i \neq j, i, j = 1, \ldots, 4\}$ such that

⋄ The a_i's are *independent*. If $G, H \subseteq \{a_1, \ldots, a_4\}$ then $(\sum G) \sqcap (\sum H) = \sum(G \cap H)$ (where $\sum \emptyset = 0$, and $\sum\{a_1, a_2, a_3\} = a_1 + a_2 + a_3$, and so on)

⋄ If $G \subseteq \{a_1, \ldots, a_4\}$ then $\sum G$ is modular

⋄ $a_i + a_i = a_i$

⋄ $c_{ij} = c_{ji}$

⋄ $a_i + a_j = a_i + c_{ik}$; $c_{ij} \sqcap a_j = 0$, if $i \neq j$

⋄ $(a_i + a_k) \sqcap (c_{ij} + c_{jk}) = c_{ik}$ for distinct i, j, k

Now we are nearly at the point where we can define a semigroup structure. First, for each distinct i, j, we define the set L_{ij} to be $\{x : x + a_j = a_i + a_j$ and $x \sqcap a_j = 0\}$. Then if $b \in L_{ij}$ and $d \in L_{jk}$, where i, j, k are distinct, then we set $b \otimes d = (b + d) \sqcap (a_i + a_k)$, and it follows that $b \otimes d \in L_{ik}$. (This is Exercise 15.2.) Then we can define a semigroup operation '.' on L_{12} by setting

$$x.y = (x \otimes c_{23}) \otimes (c_{31} \otimes y)$$

It is quite an involved operation to show that this is in fact an associative operation, but it can be done. (This is Exercise 15.3.)

And in certain circumstances, the operation is a free associative operation. Given a countably infinite-dimensional vector space $\mathcal{V}$, its lattice of subspaces is a 0-structure, and it is possible to define a modular 4-frame in this lattice of subspaces, such that any countable semigroup is isomorphic to a subsemigroup of L_{12} under the defined associative operation. (Urquhart gives the complete proof of this result [267].)

The rest of the work of the undecidability proof involves showing that this construction can be modelled in a logic. Perhaps surprisingly, it can all be done in a weak logic like TW[$\wedge, \vee, \rightarrow, \top, \bot$]. We can do without negation by picking out a distinguished propositional atom f, and by *defining* $\sim A$ to be $A \rightarrow f$, t to be $\sim f$, and $A : B$ to be $\sim(A \rightarrow \sim B)$. A is a *regular* proposition if and only if $\sim\sim A \leftrightarrow A$ is provable. The regular propositions form a 0-structure, under the assumption of the formula $\Theta = \{R(t, f, \top, \bot), N(t, f, \top, \bot), \sim\top \leftrightarrow \bot\}$, where $R(A)$ is $\sim\sim A \leftrightarrow A$, $N(A)$ is $(t \rightarrow A) \rightarrow A$, and $R(A, B, \ldots)$ is $R(A) \wedge R(B) \wedge \cdots$ and similarly for N. In other words, we can show that the conditions for a 0-

structure hold in the regular propositions, assuming Θ as an extra premise. To interpret the 0-structure conditions we interpret $\sqcap$ by $\wedge$, $+$ by $:$ and 0 by t.

Now we need to model a 4-frame in the 0-structure. This can be done as we get just the modularity we need from another condition which is simple to state. Define $K(A)$ to be $R(A) \wedge (A \wedge {\sim}A \leftrightarrow \perp) \wedge (A \vee {\sim}A \leftrightarrow \top) \wedge (A : {\sim}A \leftrightarrow {\sim}A) \wedge (A \leftrightarrow A : A)$. Then we can show the following:

$$K(A), R(B,C), C \rightarrow A \vdash_H A \wedge (B:C) \leftrightarrow (A \wedge B):C$$

(This is Exercise 15.4.) In other words, if $K(A)$, then A is modular in the class of regular propositions. Then the conditions for a 4-frame are simple to state. We pick out our atomic propositions $A_1, \ldots, A_4$ and $C_{12}, \ldots, C_{34}$, which will do duty for $a_1, \ldots, a_4$ and $c_{12}, \ldots, c_{34}$. Then, for example, one independence axiom is

$$(A_1 : A_2 : A_3) \wedge (A_2 : A_3 : A_4) \leftrightarrow (A_2 : A_3)$$

and one modularity condition is

$$K(A_1 : A_3 : A_4)$$

We will let Π be the conjunction of the statements that express that the propositions A_i and C_{ij} form a 4-frame in the 0-structure of regular propositions. So $\Theta \cup \Pi$ is a finite (but complex) set of propositions. In any algebra in which $\Theta \cup \Pi$ is true, the lattice of regular propositions is a 0-structure, and the denotations of the propositions A_i and C_{ij} form a 4-frame. Finally, when coding up a semigroup problem with variables $x_1, x_2, \ldots, x_m$, we will need formulae in the language which do duty for these variables. Thus we need a condition which picks out the fact that p_i (standing for x_i) is in L_{12}. We define $L(p)$ to be $(p : A_2 \leftrightarrow A_1 : A_2) \wedge (p \wedge A_2 \leftrightarrow t)$. Then the semigroup operation on elements of L_{12} can be defined in terms of $\wedge$ and $:$ and the formulae A_i and C_{ij}. We assume that done, and we will simply take it that there is an operation $\cdot$ on formulae which picks out the algebraic operation on L_{12}. This is enough for us to sketch the undecidability argument.

THEOREM 15.11 (UNDECIDABILITY OF DEDUCIBILITY)
The deducibility problem for any logic between TW$[\wedge, \vee, \rightarrow, \top, \perp]$ *and* KR *is undecidable.*

PROOF Take a semigroup problem which is known to be undecidable. It may be presented in the following way

$$\text{If } v_1 = w_1 \quad \cdots \quad v_n = w_n \text{ then } v = w$$

where each term v_i, w_i is a term in the language of semigroups, constructed out of the variables $x_1, x_2, \ldots, x_m$ for some m. The translation of that problem into the language of TW$[\wedge, \vee, \rightarrow, \top, \bot]$ is the deducibility problem

$$\Theta, \Pi, L(p_1, \ldots, p_m), v_1^t \leftrightarrow w_1^t, \ldots, v_n^t \leftrightarrow w_n^t \vdash_H v^t \leftrightarrow w^t$$

where the translation u^t of each term u is defined recursively by setting x_i^t to be p_i and $(u_1.u_2)^t$ to be $u_1^t \cdot u_2^t$.

Now the undecidability result will be immediate once we show that for any logic between TW and KR the word problem in semigroups is valid if and only if its translation is valid in that logic.

For left to right, if the word problem is valid in the theory of semigroups, its translation must be valid, for given the truth of Θ and Π and $L(p_1, \ldots, p_m)$, the operator $\cdot$ is provably a semigroup operation on the propositions in L_{12} in the algebra of the logic, and the terms v_i and w_i satisfy the semigroup conditions. As a result, we must have v^t and w^t picking out the same propositions, hence we have a proof of $v^t \leftrightarrow w^t$.

Conversely, if the word problem is invalid, then it has an interpretation in the semigroup S defined on L_{12} in the lattice of subspaces of an infinite-dimensional vector space. The lattice of subspaces of this vector space is the 0-structure in our countermodel. However, we need a model for the whole logic — the 0-structure is not such a model, since it just models the regular propositions. How can we construct this? Consider the argument for KR. There, the subspaces were the positive idempotents in the frame. The other propositions in the frame were *arbitrary* subsets of points. Something similar can work here. On the vector space, consider the subsets of points which are closed under multiplication (that is, if $x \in \alpha$, so is kx, where k is taken from the field of the vector space). This is a de Morgan algebra, defining conjunction and disjunction by means of intersection and union as is usual. Negation is modelled by set difference. The fusion $\alpha \circ \beta$ of two sets of points is the set $\{x + y : x \in \alpha \text{ and } y \in \beta\}$. It is not too difficult to show that this is commutative and associative, and square-increasing, when the vector space is in a field of characteristic other than 2, since if $x \in \alpha$ then $x = \frac{1}{2}x + \frac{1}{2}x \in \alpha \circ \alpha$. Then $\alpha \rightarrow \beta$ is simply $-(\alpha \circ -\beta)$. Therefore, this is a propositional structure for KR, and all weaker logics, and the regular propositions in this model are exactly the subspaces of the vector space. It follows that our counterexample in the 0-structure is a counterexample in a model of KR to the translation of the word problem. As a result, the translation is not provable in KR or in any weaker logic.   □

This result applies to systems between TW and KR, and it shows that the deducibility problem is undecidable for any of these systems. In the presence of

the *modus ponens* axiom $A \wedge (A \rightarrow B) \rightarrow B$ (which follows from WI) this immediately yields the undecidability of the *theoremhood* problem, as the deducibility
problem can be rewritten as a single formula.

$$\left(\Theta \wedge \Pi \wedge L(p_1, \ldots, p_m) \wedge (v_1^t \leftrightarrow w_1^t) \wedge \cdots \wedge (v_n^t \leftrightarrow w_n^t)\right) \rightarrow (v^t \leftrightarrow w^t)$$

As a result, the theoremhood problem for logics between T and KR is undecidable.

THEOREM 15.12 (UNDECIDABILITY OF THEOREMHOOD)
Theoremhood in any of R, E and T is undecidable.   □

The restriction to TW is necessary in the theorem. Without the prefixing and
suffixing axioms, you cannot show that the lattice of regular propositions is
closed under the 'fusion-like' connective ':'.

15.3   Undecidability via Machines

Another technique for proving undecidability is to code up the behaviour of
abstract machines. This is important, for there are undecidability results known
for logics without distribution. Our results so far apply only to logics with
distribution of conjunction over disjunction.

DEFINITION 15.13 (AND-BRANCHING TWO-COUNTER MACHINES)
An *and-branching two-counter machine* (or ACM) M has a finite collection of
basic states $q_1, \ldots, q_n$, including distinguished final state q_f. The state q_f has no
outgoing transitions. The machine also includes two *counters*, a and b.

   An *instantaneous description* (or ID) of an ACM is a finite list of triples of the
form $\langle q_i, x, y \rangle$, each representing a state and the values of the counters a and
b, respectively. The instantaneous description describes the general state of the
machine at any moment of time.

The *instructions* for a machine have the following forms:

Instruction		Effect
$q_i + aq_j$	$\ldots, \langle q_i, x, y \rangle, \ldots$ $\mapsto$	$\ldots, \langle q_j, x+1, y \rangle, \ldots$
$q_i + bq_j$	$\ldots, \langle q_i, x, y \rangle, \ldots$ $\mapsto$	$\ldots, \langle q_j, x, y+1 \rangle, \ldots$
$q_i - aq_j$	$\ldots, \langle q_i, x+1, y \rangle, \ldots$ $\mapsto$	$\ldots, \langle q_j, x, y \rangle, \ldots$
$q_i - bq_j$	$\ldots, \langle q_i, x, y+1 \rangle, \ldots$ $\mapsto$	$\ldots, \langle q_j, x, y \rangle, \ldots$
$q_i f q_j q_k$	$\ldots, \langle q_i, x, y \rangle, \ldots$ $\mapsto$	$\ldots, \langle q_j, x, y \rangle, \langle q_k, x, y \rangle, \ldots$

The instructions have the following effects. An *addition instruction* $q_i + aq_j$ has
the effect of taking any part of the ID in state q_i into state q_j and incrementing
the counter a. The same thing happens with $q_i + bq_j$, except that b is incre-
mented. The *subtraction instruction* $q_i - aq_j$ takes a part of the ID in state q_i

into state q_j and decrements a — *if and only if a is non-zero*. Similarly, $q_i - bq_j$ decrements b and shifts to state q_j from q_i. The *forking* instruction $q_i f q_j q_k$ takes a part of the ID in state q_i and duplicates it, transferring one triple to state q_j and the other to q_k.

A *computation* of an ACM is a list of IDs such that each ID in the list (except for the first one, of course) is given by applying some instruction in the ACM to the previous member of the list, and such that if the list has a last member, then no instructions apply to that ID.

An ID S is *accepted* by M if and only if every computation starting with S terminates with an ID consisting solely of triples of the form $\langle q_f, 0, 0 \rangle$.

EXAMPLE 15.14 (A SIMPLE ACM)
Consider the machine with the instructions

$$\delta_1 : q_1 - aq_2 \quad \delta_2 : q_2 - bq_2$$
$$\delta_3 : q_2 + bq_4 \quad \delta_4 : q_3 - bq_f$$
$$\delta_5 : q_4 f q_3 q_2$$

Consider the ID $\langle q_1, 1, 1 \rangle$. Here is a computation starting with this ID:

$$\langle q_1, 1, 1 \rangle \overset{\delta_1}{\mapsto} \langle q_2, 0, 1 \rangle \overset{\delta_2}{\mapsto} \langle q_2, 0, 0 \rangle \overset{\delta_3}{\mapsto} \langle q_4, 0, 1 \rangle \overset{\delta_5}{\mapsto}$$
$$\langle q_3, 0, 1 \rangle, \langle q_2, 0, 1 \rangle \overset{\delta_2}{\mapsto} \langle q_3, 0, 1 \rangle, \langle q_2, 0, 0 \rangle \overset{\delta_4}{\mapsto} \langle q_f, 0, 0 \rangle, \langle q_2, 0, 0 \rangle \overset{\delta_3}{\mapsto}$$
$$\langle q_f, 0, 0 \rangle, \langle q_4, 0, 1 \rangle \overset{\delta_5}{\mapsto} \langle q_f, 0, 0 \rangle, \langle q_3, 0, 1 \rangle, \langle q_2, 0, 1 \rangle \cdots$$

and as you can see, it does not terminate.

Computations in this system are not deterministic. If an ID includes a part of the form $\langle q_2, x, y \rangle$ with a non-zero value for y, we have a choice as to whether to apply δ_2 or δ_3.

Some processes *do* terminate in a final state. Any ID consisting of the triple $\langle q_3, 0, 1 \rangle$ will decrement 0 and go straight to the final state.

Now we state the undecidability result upon which we will rely.

THEOREM 15.15 (ACCEPTANCE OF IDS IS UNDECIDABLE)
There is no algorithm for determining whether a given ACM accepts an ID.   □

We will not prove this. The result is demonstrated by Lincoln, Mitchell, Scedrov and Shankar in their paper [138]. We will rely on this result, showing that if we have an algorithm for determining validity in LL, we can use this to determine acceptance of IDS in ACMS. To do this, we will associate a *theory* with each ACM.

DEFINITION 15.16 (THE THEORY OF A MACHINE)
An ACM M has a *theory* Theory(M), given by collecting together the following consecutions for each instruction

Instruction	Consecution
$q_i + aq_j$	$Q_i \vdash Q_j \circ A$
$q_i + bq_j$	$Q_i \vdash Q_j \circ B$
$q_i - aq_j$	$Q_i; A \vdash Q_j$
$q_i - bq_j$	$Q_i; B \vdash Q_j$
$q_i f q_j q_k$	$Q_i \vdash Q_j \vee Q_k$

where each Q_i, A and B are atomic propositions.

DEFINITION 15.17 (THE THEORY OF A STATE)
Given an instantaneous description S consisting of a finite number of triples of the form $\langle q_i, x, y \rangle$, its *theory* $\theta(S)$ is the set of all consecutions $Q_i; A^x; B^y \vdash Q_f$, where A^x is the list of x instances of A, and similarly, B^y is the list of y instances of B.

Now we will use this theory to simulate the behaviour of the ACM. First, we will show that an accepted ID S corresponds to the proof of each consecution in $\theta(S)$, *given that we allow the consecutions in Theory(M) as axioms.*

THEOREM 15.18 (IF S IS ACCEPTED, THEN $\theta(S)$ IS PROVABLE)
Given an and-branching two-counter machine M, then if M accepts S we can prove each element of $\theta(S)$ in Theory(M).

PROOF   We show by induction on the length of the sequence of transitions from S to the final ID. If there are no transitions, then every element of S is the triple $\langle q_f, 0, 0 \rangle$, and the consecution corresponding to this is $Q_f \vdash Q_f$, which is provable.

Now suppose that the first transition was an addition $q_i + aq_j$, leading from $\langle q_i, x, y \rangle$ to $\langle q_j, x + 1, y \rangle$. By hypothesis, we have a proof of $Q_j; A^{x+1}; B^y \vdash Q_f$, as we have a shorter sequence accepting the triple $\langle q_j, x + 1, y \rangle$. We use this deduction to prove $Q_i; A^x; B^y \vdash Q_f$ as follows:

$$\frac{Q_i \vdash Q_j \circ A \qquad \dfrac{Q_j; A; A^x; B^y \vdash Q_f}{Q_j \circ A; A^x; B^y \vdash Q_f} [\circ \text{L}]}{Q_i; A^x; B^y \vdash Q_f} [\text{Cut}]$$

which uses the axiom $Q_i \vdash Q_j \circ A$, which is present in Theory(M). The case for the other addition instruction is no different, given the presence of CI allowing the commuting of A^x and B^y.

If the first transition was a subtraction $q_i - aq_j$, leading from $\langle q_i, x+1, y \rangle$ to $\langle q_j, x, y \rangle$, by hypothesis, we have a proof of $Q_j; A^x; B^y \vdash Q_f$. This then gives us

$$\frac{Q_i; A \vdash Q_j \quad Q_j \circ A^x; B^y \vdash Q_f}{Q_i; A^{x+1}; B^y \vdash Q_f} \text{ [Cut]}$$

as we wished. The same holds (using Cl) for subtraction of the counter b.

Finally, for a forking instruction $q_i f q_j q_k$, if the first step transforms $\langle q_i, x, y \rangle$ into $\langle q_j, x, y \rangle, \langle q_k, x, y \rangle$, then we have proofs of both $Q_j; A^x; B^y \vdash Q_f$ and $Q_k; A^x; B^y \vdash Q_f$, and $Q_i \vdash Q_j \vee Q_k$ is a member of Theory(M). So, we have the following proof

$$\frac{Q_i \vdash Q_j \vee Q_k \quad \dfrac{Q_j; A^x; B^y \vdash Q_f \quad Q_k; A^x; B^y \vdash Q_f}{Q_j \vee Q_k; A^x; B^y \vdash Q_f} \text{ [$\vee$L]}}{Q_i; A^x; B^y \vdash Q_f} \text{ [Cut]}$$

as we wished. These are the only instructions, so the the proof is completed. $\square$
This gives us one half of the equivalence. Now for the other.

THEOREM 15.19 (IF $\theta(S)$ IS PROVABLE THEN S IS ACCEPTED)
Given an ACM *M, if each element of $\theta(S)$ is provable from* Theory(M), *then M accepts S.*

PROOF Lincoln, Mitchell, Scedrov and Shankar show this by a fine analysis of proofs of the elements of $\theta(S)$. For that style of proof, consult their paper [138]. Instead, we will prove the contrapositive, showing that if S is not accepted by M, then there is no proof of each element of $\theta(S)$ in Theory(M). We will do this by constructing a countermodel from the ACM.

The model will be a propositional structure, in which the elements are sets of multisets of the atoms a, b and each q_i. So $\{abq_1, b\}$ is an element of our propositional structure, as is $\{a, abbq_1q_2q_2, aabb\}$. The fusion of two such elements is defined as follows:

$$\{d_i : i \in I\} \circ \{e_j : j \in J\} = \{d_i e_j : i \in I \text{ and } j \in J\}$$

So, for example, $\{abq_1, b\} \circ \{a, abbq_1q_2q_2, aabb\}$ is the set

$$\{aabq_1, aabbbq_1q_1q_2q_2, aaabbbq_1, ab, abbbq_1q_2q_2, aabbb\}$$

We interpret the *disjunction* as the union of two sets, and the *conjunction* as their intersection. This makes entailment set inclusion. And it is clear, by the very definition of the fusion of two sets, that fusion distributes over disjunction. It is also clear that fusion is commutative, as multiset union is commutative. So, this is a MALL$[\circ, \wedge, \vee]$ structure. (In fact, it is a completely distributive MALL$[\circ, \wedge, \vee]$ structure, but that is not important).

Given an ID as a list of triples, its *corresponding proposition* is the set of triples in the ID written as multisets. So for example, for the ID $\langle q_1, 1, 0 \rangle, \langle q_2, 1, 2 \rangle$ we have the set $\{q_1 a, q_2 abb\}$.

An M-interpretation of the language Q_i, A, B into this structure is one which respects the axioms of Theory(M). That is, it is one in which we have the following conditions on $[\![\cdot]\!]$ corresponding to each instruction in M.

Instruction	Condition
$q_i + a q_j$	$[\![Q_i]\!] \subseteq [\![Q_j]\!] \circ [\![A]\!]$
$q_i + b q_j$	$[\![Q_i]\!] \subseteq [\![Q_j]\!] \circ [\![B]\!]$
$q_i - a q_j$	$[\![Q_i]\!] \circ [\![A]\!] \subseteq [\![Q_j]\!]$
$q_i - b q_j$	$[\![Q_i]\!] \circ [\![B]\!] \subseteq [\![Q_j]\!]$
$q_i f q_j q_k$	$[\![Q_i]\!] \subseteq [\![Q_j]\!] \cup [\![Q_k]\!]$

Given any M interpretation $[\![\cdot]\!]$, the consecutions in Theory(M) hold. So, our problem reduces to finding an M interpretation such that one element of $\theta(S)$ fails. Then the result follows, as we have our countermodel. For the failure of $\theta(S)$, we pick one triple in S such that it is not accepted. (There must be one such.) Suppose it is $\langle q_i, x, y \rangle$. Then the offending consecution in $\theta(S)$ is $Q_i; A^x; B^y \vdash Q_f$. We will find an interpretation such that $[\![Q_i]\!] \circ [\![A]\!]^x \circ [\![B]\!]^y \not\subseteq [\![Q_f]\!]$.

What is the M interpretation? Let $[\![Q_i]\!]$ be the set containing $\{q_i\}$ (the proposition corresponding to the ID $\langle q_i, 0, 0 \rangle$) together with propositions corresponding to *all* IDs which can be found using the instructions in M, starting from $\langle q_i, 0, 0 \rangle$. Let $[\![a]\!] = \{a\}$, and let $[\![b]\!] = \{b\}$. This interpretation satisfies each of the conditions specified above, as you can check. This is a special case of the result that $[\![Q_i]\!] \circ [\![A]\!]^x \circ [\![B]\!]^y$ will include the propositions corresponding to all and only those IDs found in a computation starting with $\langle q_i, x, y \rangle$, which follows directly from the definition of $[\![\cdot]\!]$.

Now consider $\theta(S)$, the consecution $Q_i; A^x; B^y \vdash Q_f$. $[\![Q_i]\!] \circ [\![A]\!]^x \circ [\![B]\!]^y$ consists of the propositions corresponding to all and only those IDs found in a computation starting with $\langle q_i, x, y \rangle$, and it follows that $[\![Q_f]\!] = \{q_f\}$ (as q_f has no outgoing states). However, since you cannot get to $\langle q_f, 0, 0 \rangle$ from $\langle q_i, x, y \rangle$, it follows that $[\![Q_i]\!] \circ [\![A]\!]^x \circ [\![B]\!]^y \not\subseteq [\![Q_f]\!]$, and so, the corresponding consecution cannot be proven. The result follows. □

Putting these results together, we have the corollary we want.

COROLLARY 15.20 (LINEAR LOGIC IS UNDECIDABLE)
There is no algorithm for determining validity of consecutions in either intuitionistic or classical linear logic.

15.4 History

There is a significant and growing literature on the undecidability of substructural logics. Urquhart's original papers repay careful reading [266, 267]. The first explains the undecidability result for KR, and the connections between KR and projective geometry. The second paper is the undecidability proof for R and nearby logics. Urquhart has also adapted techniques from the undecidability proofs of linear logic to give complexity bounds for R$[\to, \wedge]$ [270]. These techniques have been taken up by the Hungarian school of algebraic logicians to prove the undecidability of many algebraic systems [8, 131].

15.5 Exercises

Problems

{15.1} Show that KR is not a conservative extension of the negation-free fragment of R.

{15.2} Show that if $b \in L_{ij}$ and $d \in L_{jk}$, where i, j, k are distinct and we have defined $b \otimes d = (b + d) \sqcap (a_i + a_k)$ in some 4-frame, then it follows that $b \otimes d \in L_{ik}$.

{15.3} Show that the dot, defined by setting $x.y = (x \otimes c_{23}) \otimes (c_{31} \otimes y)$, is an associative operation.

{15.4} Show that $K(A), R(B, C), C \to A \vdash_H A \wedge (B : C) \leftrightarrow (A \wedge B) : C$.

Projects

{15.5} Prove the undecidability of R by a simpler means than Urquhart's.

{15.6} Show that T$[\to, \wedge]$ is undecidable.

{15.7} Show that T$[\to]$ is undecidable

Part V

Coda

Chapter 16

Using Substructural Logic

> There were two rooms attached to the stables.
> One was occupied by a man who was "generally useful."
> — Henry Lawson, Middleton's Peter, 1900

If we wish to examine the philosophical significance of substructural logics, there are a number of possible paths to follow. One obvious path is to look at the philosophical significance of the proof theory of substructural logics. There are many important works which explore the connections between proof theories and theories of meaning.[1] However, I do not want to examine proof theory here. Instead, I wish to examine the frame semantics for substructural logics, to see whether they can be used for any philosophical gain. What is the significance of the point semantics for these logics?

16.1   Internal and External Perspectives

This starting point is not arbitrarily chosen. Frame semantics is philosophically useful in the study and application of modal logics [137, 193, 252]. In this chapter, we will see whether the same holds for substructural logics. The discussion will be structured around the status of Boolean negation in substructural logics. This question should bring to light what distinguishes the substructural technique from the techniques of modal logic. The question is this: can we, or ought we, define a connective, written '$-$' which is evaluated as follows?

$$x \Vdash -A \text{ if and only if } x \nVdash A$$

If we *can* have Boolean negation, then substructural logics are simply a breed of classical modal logic. They may well be an interesting breed of classical modal logic, but they are a subspecies of that larger class. In particular, the negations of substructural logics may be interesting connectives, but the issue arises: which is the *genuine* negation? Surely one satisfying the clause for

---

[1]   A serious study of this would have to examine Prior's important note on inference tickets [202] and the debate it sparked, starting with Belnap's reply [20]. The constructivists' accounts of meaning in Prawitz [196], Martin-Löf [150] and Dummett [69] deserve examination. Then Došen's important article on the status of logical constants as "punctuation marks" bears close examination as it brings the discussion into contact with work on substrucutral logics [61].

Boolean negation has an important claim to being the *real* negation! These worries have been well expressed by Belnap and Dunn.

> ... what was all the fuss about "fallacies of relevance"? What were the complaints lodged against contradictions' implying everything and against the disjunctive syllogism? Boolean negation trivially satisfies these principles; so what can be the interest of de Morgan negation's failing to satisfy them? Will the real negation please stand up?   [7, page 174]

The thesis we will explore is this: Boolean negation is sometimes warranted, and sometimes not. In particular, if you take an "external perspective," on a frame, Boolean negation is warranted. If you take an "internal perspective" it is quite likely that Boolean negation cannot be defined. Before going on to look at a particular understanding of the frames for substructural logic, for which Boolean negation cannot be defined, let me go on to explain and explore the difference between the internal and external perspectives on points in a frame.

The crux of the matter is the notion of "support" between a point and a proposition. Does this relation simply codify information *about* points in a model, or does it somehow give us an account of the information *carried by* points in a model? The former account is an *external* perspective, as we are classifying points "from the outside." The support relation is a way of describing or classifying points. The latter account is an *internal* perspective, as we are classifying points "from the inside." Let me examine different readings of models which are canonical examples of these different perspectives.

First, consider the Lambek calculus, used as an account of the syntactic typing of language. We type parts of language as verbs, nouns, noun phrases and other syntactic categories. If a string is not a noun, we can classify it, if we like, as a "non-noun." In fact, any string is a "non-noun" if and only if it is not a noun. For any syntactic category X, there is also the category *non-X*, which collects together all and only those things which do not have type X. This is Boolean negation in the Lambek calculus. It seems warranted as a constructor of new types.

Of course, there may be reason even in the Lambek calculus to prefer a logical language *without* Boolean negation. For example, the language without Boolean negation might have useful properties (such as decidability) not shared by the language with Boolean negation. However, from the point of view of the interpretation of the syntax in its intended domain, Boolean negation makes sense.

Not all domains of classification like this are so amenable to extension with Boolean negation. For a trivial example, consider the relationship between

knowers and the propositions they know. Let us symbolise 'x knows that A'
as '$x \Vdash A$.' Given this definition, it is possible to declare that from now on we
will read '$x \Vdash -A$' is equivalent to '$x \nVdash A$.' However, this is an abuse of language. If we follow this convention, we are no longer reading all sentences of
the form '$x \Vdash B$' as 'x knows that B', for we are now reading some as 'x does
not know that . . .'. There will most likely not be anything in the class of things
known by x which answers to the call of being $-A$, the Boolean negation of A.
Our edict that $-A$ is defined in that way is at most a shorthand for codifying
information *about* our knowers. It does not actually pick out anything known
by them. If we restrict our attention to the things known by our knowers, there
is no reason to expect that there is *any* proposition B at all such that $x \Vdash B$
iff $x \nVdash A$. Why should we expect that there is? If the relation '$\Vdash$' is to tell
us something about the nature of the objects it relates, the mere postulation
of the conditions of Boolean negation does not ensure that there is anything
answering to those descriptions.

The external perspective on our model structures is one in which the sup-
porting relation $\Vdash$ codifies information about points in the model structure.
This account sees logics of frames (whether traditional modal logics or substructural logics) as a language for describing structures. The best exponents
of such a perspective on logic are what might be called the Amsterdam school
of van Benthem, de Rijke and others [31, 220]. For this approach, modal logic
is a logic for the classification of relational structures. Modal logics are useful
sublogics or refinements of first-order logic. Modal formulae are simplifications
of particular first-order claims about models. The standard translation ST of a
formula is taken very seriously indeed. Intensional formulae are codifications
of what is true *about* points. According to this perspective, Boolean negation
makes a great deal of sense. If $x \nVdash A$ then 'not A' is true of the point.

If '$x \Vdash A$' codifies information carried by the point x, then there may well be
nothing which corresponds to the definition of Boolean negation, just as there
might well be nothing such that you believe *it* if and only if you do not believe
Goldbach's conjecture.[2]

Let us go on to consider a particular, internal, reading of the semantics
of substructural logics, for which a connective answering to the clauses for
Boolean negation will be manifestly unwarranted.

16.2   Points as States

Points are states of the world. These include actual states of the world and
merely possible states of the world. (That is, states the world might have but

---

[2]   Goldbach's conjecture, that any even number greater than 2 is the sum of two primes, is a
famous unsolved problem in number theory.

does not actually have.) They can also be *partial* — they can be states of parts of the world. States that parts of the world actually are, or states that parts of the world could be, but are not. Furthermore, points can be *impossible states*. They can be states that part of the world, or the whole world, *cannot* be.

Any adequate semantics of conditionality seems to *require* some account of alternative states or possibilities. Furthermore, as we have seen, it seems that a semantics which invalidates consecutions such as $A \vdash B \vee \sim B$ and $A \wedge \sim A \vdash B$ ought to appeal to inconsistent and incomplete states.

There is a growing trend in semantics to agree that complete and consistent entities like possible worlds are not enough to give a semantics of entailment, necessity and related notions. Some take it that we need *incomplete* entities, in which for some propositions p, neither p nor its negation $\sim p$ are true. For *situation theorists* [15, 16, 192] these entities are situations. This does not mean that situation theorists reject the law of excluded middle. They can agree that for every proposition p, either p or its negation $\sim p$ is true. They simply reject that every situation decides between p and $\sim p$. The situation of my office at work may carry a lot of information, but it certainly does not in and of itself carry information about the current members of the Brazilian national football team. For that, you have to look elsewhere: you might need to check a different part of the world to determine who they are. Proponents of theories of *truthmakers* [180, 216] similarly hold that some objects make certain claims true and others false. They do not hold that all truthmakers decide all truths equally. The set of truths made true by a particular truthmaker (or the set of truths true in a particular situation) is incomplete.

Similarly, some (but clearly, not as many) have held that there is call not only for incomplete entities in our semantics but also inconsistent ones. For some, this is because they hold that the actual world is inconsistent [198, 197, 230].[3] Others hold that inconsistent entities are important in our semantics, not because the actual world is inconsistent, and not because some possible world is inconsistent, but instead because some important *theories* are inconsistent. Inconsistent bodies of information (like naïve set theory, like the infinitesimal calculus, before Abraham Robinson [221, 222] had his way with it, and like your beliefs or mine) have a certain degree of logical closure, without being consistent [21, 22, 71, 163]. If this is the case, then there may be space in our semantics for different ways that things *cannot* be. Different inconsistent states of affairs, which describe different ways that things cannot happen. If this is the case, then ontologies including inconsistent worlds may well have their place.

---

[3] This is typically because of the paradoxes of self-reference and similar phenomena. As there is no acceptable solution to the liar and like paradoxes, we ought to accept the argument to the paradoxical conclusion as not only valid but sound. The liar is both true and not true.

Before continuing, we need to make clear that when we say "inconsistent state of affairs" we do not mean a state of affairs which has contradictory properties, any more than an inconsistent system of equations has contradictory properties. The inconsistency of a system of equations means that it *cannot be solved*. Similarly, inconsistent states of affairs may exist (in the same sense as any other non-actualised state of affairs might be said to exist). Their inconsistency means simply that they *could not be actualised*. An inconsistent plan (such as one which involves me being in two sufficiently separated places at the one time) cannot be carried out. However, it can be debated, discussed and feature in planning in the same way as consistent plans. The same holds with inconsistent states of affairs. They can feature in theorising and semantics. Their inconsistency simply means that they cannot be made actual.

So what I have in mind is an "intended semantics" for entailment, in which the points are states of affairs, both complete and consistent (these are *world*), incomplete — some of these are possible or actual states of this world, much like the "situations" of Barwise and Perry, and others are incomplete states which are non-actual — and inconsistent (different ways the world cannot be, as well as ways the world can be). These states are related in a number of different ways. First, states can be contracted or expanded, and they are related by inclusion. Given two states x and y, we have $x \sqsubseteq y$ if and only if everything true in x (or determined by x, or whatever) is also true in y. For example, the state of my office in included in the state of the building in which my office is situated, which is in turn included in the state encompassing the whole of Macquarie University.

Second, there is the binary relation of *compatibility*. State x is compatible with state y just when x rules out nothing in y. Granted that states need not always be consistent, there is no reason for xCx to hold universally. Is compatibility symmetric? There are obvious reasons to think so; however, perhaps a case could be made that it is not. I need not assume it here. What we have so far is enough to ensure that $A \wedge {\sim}A \vdash B$ fails (pick a state x where ${\sim}(xCx)$, let A and ${\sim}A$ be true there, and let B fail), and the logic of this semantics is significantly non-classical.

So much is fairly clear. The story of how to use this account as a theory of implication or entailment is less clear. One difficulty is the general logical opacity of the conditional '$\rightarrow$'. A ternary accessibility relation seems suited for modelling *entailment*, for if we read '$A \rightarrow B$' as 'that A entails that B' then there is no doubt that the rule: if $A \vdash B$ and $C \vdash D$ then $B \rightarrow C \vdash A \rightarrow D$, by the transitivity of entailment. However, if we read '$\rightarrow$' as a more homely *conditional*, it seems that the strengthening of the antecedent — $A \vdash B$ therefore $B \rightarrow C \vdash A \rightarrow C$ — ought to fail. After all, if I have a cup of coffee in the morning, my writing goes well. However, if I have a cup of coffee in the morning and I find out someone has deleted all of the files on my computer, my writing *does not* go well. One way to proceed might be to apply to our semantics of points insights from the neighbourhood semantics of counterfactual conditionals [3, 88, 147].

Difficulties with this non-classical position arise once we deal with negation, for once we allow inconsistent and incomplete points, the behaviour of negation in our semantics has changed significantly. In the next sections, I will consider some issues which are raised by this sort of semantic system.

In a state semantics like this, there is no connective '−' on propositions such that $A \wedge -A \vdash B$ and $A \vdash B \vee -B$ come out as valid for all choices of A and B. For if there were, then either the relation $\sqsubseteq$ would collapse into identity or propositions would fail (in general) to be persistent. Of course, we can *define* the locution '$x \Vdash -A$' to be read as saying that $x \nVdash A$. But that does not mean that claims of that form express a relationship between a state and a new kind of proposition. For $-A$ is not a proposition (on pain of failing to be preserved upwards by $\sqsubseteq$). Talk of $-A$ can be said to be meaningful, but when you engage in that kind of talk, you are no longer simply talking of what is supported *by* states — you are also considering other things which are true *of* states.[4]

16.3 Disjunctive Syllogism and Worlds

The argument, *disjunctive syllogism*, $A \vee B, \sim A \vdash B$ has been the cause of much ink being spilled [26, 159, 219, 226] in the relevant logic literature. This is understandable, as the argument is widely agreed to be valid. However, according to many relevant logicians, it is not valid. There seems to be a problem here.[5]

The problem (if it is really a problem) besets our semantics. Take some point x where $x \Vdash A \wedge \sim A$ but $x \nVdash B$. Then $x \Vdash A \vee B$ and $x \Vdash \sim A$. However, $x \nVdash B$, so inconsistent points give us a counterexample to disjunctive syllogism. It is invalid on our semantics.

However, disjunctive syllogism seems *valid*. If the premises of the argument are true, then the conclusion *has* to be true. We use disjunctive syllogism regularly in inferring, and it is not clear that we are doing something wrong when doing so. This tension has caused some to give up on the project of substructural logics. I think this is mistaken, and I think that clarifying the mistake helps us to understand the nature of substructural logics.

---

[4] And you may ask how the proposition $x \nVdash A$ is to be cashed out on our terms. Well, a plausible choice is that $w \Vdash \sim(x \Vdash A)$, where w is the actual world.

[5] Belnap and Dunn write: "... the reaction does not surprise us; the [disjunctive syllogism] was one of the Stoic's "Five Indemonstrables." Still, on the other hand we do take some small solace in the fact that it was the fifth of them — recalling the tradition of notoriety, starting with Euclid's *Elements*, regarding fifth postulates. Also, we suppose that it is better to deny an Indemonstrable than a Demonstrable" [7, page 488].

The problem cannot be fixed by adding disjunctive syllogism as an extra rule to our formal systems, for once you do that, all sorts of irrelevancies come along for the ride. Disjunctive syllogism can be done away with only by rejecting all inconsistent worlds (or allowing only inconsistent worlds at which *everything* is true) and once that is done, $A \wedge \sim A \vdash B$ is valid, and significant relevant distinctives are gone. No, disjunctive syllogism cannot be added to frame semantics in a relevant framework.

Some have tried to remedy the situation by recovering disjunctive syllogism in a weaker sense. Perhaps $A \vee B, \sim A \vdash B$ is not valid as it stands, but it is valid with some extra premises. Let C stand for 'things are consistent.' Perhaps $A \vee B, \sim A, C \vdash B$ is valid. After all, if $A \vee B$ is true, and if $\sim A$ is true, and if the world is consistent, then surely B follows.

The strategy of adding premises does not work. Under the plausible assumption that an inconsistent state of affairs is formed by adjoining something which has not obtained to this world, then since C is true here, it is true too in this larger inconsistent state of affairs. (We have been *adding* information, not taking anything else away.) It follows that we can get no guarantee that C is true only in consistent worlds. If w is consistent, then if $w \sqsubseteq x$, then $x \Vdash C$ too, despite the fact that x need not be consistent. And an inconsistent x is just the sort of point at which disjunctive syllogism finds counterexamples. Adding extra premises does not lead us to the validity of disjunctive syllogism.

However, this strategy contains an important insight. Although on our semantics disjunctive syllogism fails, it is true that in every *world* w, if $A \vee B$ is true at w and if $\sim A$ is true at w, then either A or B is true at w (as worlds are prime), and A is not true at w (as worlds are consistent) so B is true at w. So disjunctive syllogism will not find counterexamples at *worlds* in our models.

Let us define another sort of entailment. We already have '$A \vdash B$' to encode truth preservation across all states: For each x, if $x \Vdash A$ then $x \Vdash B$. Let us read '$A \vdash_W B$' to mean: for all *worlds* w, if $w \Vdash A$ then $w \Vdash B$. What is a world? It is a consistent and complete point. What is a world in our frames for negation? It is a point w where wCw (so w is consistent) and further, if wCx then $x \sqsubseteq w$ (so w is complete).

The argument of the earlier paragraph shows us that we ought not expect $A \vdash_W B$ to be of the form $A, C \vdash B$ for any particular C. However, this does not mean that $\vdash_W$ does not make sense. Why should $\vdash_W$ be expressible in terms of prior notions in the object language and $\vdash$?

Once we admit $\vdash_W$, we will see that it is a classical notion of consequence. It interacts in the expected ways with the classical lattice connectives and negation. In one sense, then, substructural logics are an *extension* of classical logic into new areas. However, this is misleading. The substructural logic R is not an extension of classical logic with some new connectives in the way that, say, a classical modal logic is such an extension. In classical logic and in its extensions, we have the substitutivity of *classical* equivalents. A and $A \wedge (B \vee \sim B)$ are classically equivalent, so they are inter-substitutable in all *classical* contexts. This is true in classical propositional logics and in modal extensions of classical logic. A is true in exactly the same worlds as $A \wedge (B \vee \sim B)$. This is not the case in R. In R the substitutivity of classical equivalents does not hold. In R, we have $A \wedge (B \vee \sim B) \vdash B \vee \sim B$. However we do *not* have $A \vdash B \vee \sim B$.

This is simply explained in terms of worlds and other points in a model for R. A and $A \wedge (B \vee \sim B)$ are true in exactly the same *worlds*, but they are true in different points. There may be points at which A is true but $B \vee \sim B$ fails, as a logical truth need not be true at all points. The classical connectives, when evaluated at a world, appeal only to that world, so they will not be able to distinguish between classical equivalents, such as A and $A \wedge (B \vee \sim B)$. Similarly, a modal connective, which at a world evaluates a formula by looking only at other *worlds*, will not distinguish between classical equivalents. The conditional of R is evaluated by looking at other points, and these need not be worlds. And once this happens, the semantic values of A and $A \wedge (B \vee \sim B)$ may split apart.

So substructural logics, like R, require us to draw more distinctions between propositions than classical logic considers on its own. It follows that according to R, disjunctive syllogism is invalid. There are states of affairs in which $A \vee B$ and $\sim A$ hold, but in which B fails to hold. These are inconsistent states of affairs, it is true. They are states of affairs in which A and $\sim A$ both hold, so they are impossible. However, these impossible states of affairs might be important to consider when we are interested in distinguishing between different claims with different subject matters — a distinction that substructural logics are designed to draw.

Substructural logics invite us to draw these distinctions. However, they do not demand that we do so all the time. If we like, we can squint our eyes, shut out most of the surroundings and consider only possible worlds. Once we do that, we have a wider range of logical consequences as we have a smaller range of counterexamples available in the semantics. When we do this, we recover classical validity. In this way, different forms of evaluating arguments may coexist. Furthermore, they coexist within, and are justified by, the one formal semantics. The one and the same frame can be used to model relevant and classical validity. The way is open to a *logical pluralism*.

16.4 Pluralism about Consequence

This leads us towards a *pluralist* view about logical consequence. In one sense, disjunctive syllogism is valid, as it is impossible for the premises to be true and the conclusion false: in every world in which the premises are true, so is the conclusion. However, in another sense, disjunctive syllogism is invalid: in some states of affairs the premises are true and the conclusion fails. The premises do not automatically bring with them the conclusion. Were A and $\sim A$ to both be true, then $A \lor B$ would be true too, but it would not follow that B.

Is this an unhealthy pluralism? If we use logic as a tool for analysing arguments and as a norm to which arguments ought to comply, then is not having a fixed answer on each issue desirable? Given a particular reasoning situation should a logic not tell us what we ought to deduce? Ought one to reason with all of classical logic, or ought one to eschew disjunctive syllogism and other classical moves?

The problem gets progressively more stark once you realise that we have absolutely no reason to stop at just *two* forms of logical consequence. Why consider just the set of worlds and the set of all points? Why not the set of consistent points? Why not the set of complete points? Why not the set of physically possible worlds? Why not the set of worlds closed under modus ponens for an intensional conditional? There are a whole host of different accounts of logical consequence.

So we need an answer to our question: in a reasoning situation, what *ought* one deduce from premises? What rules can be used? A thoroughly pluralist answer to this will go as follows. What one ought to do depends on what one is trying to achieve. Obligations in inference follow from norms of evaluation. Different logics give you different norms. For classical logic, the norm is the impossibility of inferring falsehood from truth. For relevant logics the norm is tighter. Not only is necessary truth preservation required, but furthermore, the relevance of the premises to the conclusion is required. Other forms of consequence will bring along other norms. Obviously, the classical norm is one important criterion for evaluating arguments. It seems that norms involving relevance are also important. Perhaps other criteria of a broadly logical nature may be developed and studied. If this is the case, then there will be a broad range of different systems of logic which each have their use in evaluating arguments, and which each deserve the name 'consequence' for they pick out a notion of 'following from.' There is no need to expect that we will zero in on one set of norms which must all be satisfied for an argument to be a "good" one and which will pick out a single formal system which would be our *One True Logic*.

16.5 History

There is a great deal of work on paraconsistency which is important to consider [9] The major philosophical proponents have been Australasians: Graham

Priest [198, 199, 200] and Richard Sylvan (formerly 'Routley') [224, 225, 230, 226, 231] have carved out distinctive philosophical positions. Other traditions of reasoning from inconsistency exist. One early one is due to Rescher and Manor [208]. The position argued here bears some family resemblance to the position of Stephen Read, presented in his text *Relevant Logic* [206] and his more introductory *Thinking about Logic* [207]. However, the position argued here is more thoroughly pluralist than any position explicitly argued elsewhere by relevant logicians.

Bibliography

[1] SAMSON ABRAMSKY AND ACHIM JUNG. "Domain Theory". In SAMSON ABRAMSKY, DOV M. GABBAY, AND T. S. E. MAIBAUM, editors, *Handbook of Logic in Computer Science*, Volume 3, pages 1–168. Clarendon Press, Oxford, 1994. ⟨238, 246⟩

[2] WILHELM ACKERMANN. "Begründung Einer Strengen Implikation". *Journal of Symbolic Logic*, 21:113–128, 1956. ⟨2, 42, 87⟩

[3] SEIKI AKAMA. "Relevant Counterfactuals and Paraconsistency". In *Proceedings of the First World Conference on Paraconsistency, Gent, Belgium.*, 1997. ⟨271, 344⟩

[4] GERARD ALLWEIN AND J. MICHAEL DUNN. "A Kripke Semantics for Linear Logic". *Journal of Symbolic Logic*, 58(2):514–545, 1993. ⟨293⟩

[5] GERARD ALLWEIN AND WENDY MACCAULL. "A Kripke Semantics for the Logic of Gelfand Quantales". Unpublished note, Visual Inference Laboratory, Indiana University, 1998. ⟨187⟩

[6] ALAN ROSS ANDERSON AND NUEL D. BELNAP. *Entailment: The Logic of Relevance and Necessity*, Volume 1. Princeton University Press, Princeton, 1975. ⟨2, 9, 10, 32, 41, 42, 87, 185, 321⟩

[7] ALAN ROSS ANDERSON, NUEL D. BELNAP, AND J. MICHAEL DUNN. *Entailment: The Logic of Relevance and Necessity*, Volume 2. Princeton University Press, Princeton, 1992. ⟨2, 42, 340, 344, 350⟩

[8] HAJNAL ANDRÉKA, STEVEN GIVANT, AND ISTVÁN NÉMETI. "Decision Problems for Equational Theories of Relation Algebras". *Memoirs of the American Mathematical Society*, 126(604), 1997. ⟨186, 336⟩

[9] A. I. ARRUDA. "Aspects of the Historical Development of Paraconsistent Logic". In GRAHAM PRIEST, RICHARD SYLVAN, AND JEAN NORMAN, editors, *Paraconsistent Logic: Essays on the Inconsistent*, pages 99–130. Philosophia Verlag, 1989. ⟨347⟩

[10] H. P. BARENDREGT. *The Lambda Calculus: Its Syntax and Semantics*. North Holland, second edition, 1984. ⟨13⟩

[11] H. P. BARENDREGT. "Lambda Calculi with Types". In SAMSON ABRAMSKY, DOV GABBAY, AND T. S. E. MAIBAUM, editors, *Handbook of Logic in Computer Science*, Volume 2, chapter 2, pages 117–309. Oxford University Press, 1992. ⟨141⟩

[12] H. P. BARENDREGT, M. COPPO, AND M. DEZANI-CIANCAGLINI. "A Filter Lambda Model and the Completeness of Type Assignment". *Journal of Symbolic Logic*, 48:931–940, 1983. ⟨247⟩

[13] MICHAEL BARR AND CHARLES WELLS. *Toposes, Triples and Theories*, Volume 278 of *Grundlehren der math. Wiss.* Springer-Verlag, 1985. ⟨232⟩

[14] MICHAEL BARR AND CHARLES WELLS. *Category Theory for Computing Science*. Prentice-Hall, 1990. ⟨*212, 222*⟩

[15] JON BARWISE AND JOHN PERRY. *Situations and Attitudes*. MIT Press, Bradford Books, 1983. ⟨*342*⟩

[16] JON BARWISE AND JOHN PERRY. "Shifting Situations and Shaken Attitudes". *Linguistics and Philosophy*, 8:105–161, 1985. ⟨*342*⟩

[17] J. L. BELL. "A New Approach to Quantum Logic". *British Journal for the Philosophy of Science*, 37:83–99, 1986. ⟨*293, 294*⟩

[18] J. L. BELL. *Toposes and Local Set Theories: An Introduction*. Clarendon Press, Oxford, 1988. ⟨*232*⟩

[19] J. L. BELL AND A. B. SLOMSON. *Models and Ultraproducts: An Introduction*. North Holland, 1969. ⟨*155*⟩

[20] NUEL D. BELNAP. "Tonk, Plonk and Plink". *Analysis*, 22:130–134, 1962. ⟨*339*⟩

[21] NUEL D. BELNAP. "How a Computer Should Think". In G. RYLE, editor, *Contemporary Aspects of Philosophy*. Oriel Press, 1977. ⟨*342*⟩

[22] NUEL D. BELNAP. "A Useful Four-Valued Logic". In J. MICHAEL DUNN AND GEORGE EPSTEIN, editors, *Modern Uses of Multiple-Valued Logics*, pages 8–37. Reidel, Dordrecht, 1977. ⟨*342*⟩

[23] NUEL D. BELNAP. "Display Logic". *Journal of Symbolic Logic*, 11:357–417, 1982. ⟨*125*⟩

[24] NUEL D. BELNAP. "Linear Logic Displayed". *Notre Dame Journal of Formal Logic*, 31:15–25, 1990. ⟨*125*⟩

[25] NUEL D. BELNAP. "Life in the Undistributed Middle". In PETER SCHROEDER-HEISTER AND KOSTA DOŠEN, editors, *Substructural Logics*, pages 31–41. Oxford University Press, 1993. ⟨*46, 275*⟩

[26] NUEL D. BELNAP AND J. MICHAEL DUNN. "Entailment and the Disjunctive Syllogism". In F. FLØISTAD AND G. H. VON WRIGHT, editors, *Philosophy of Language / Philosophical Logic*, pages 337–366. Martinus Nijhoff, The Hague, 1981. Reprinted as Section 80 in *Entailment* Volume 2 [7]. ⟨*102, 344*⟩

[27] N. D. BELNAP JR. AND J. R. WALLACE. "A Decision Procedure for the System $E_{\bar{I}}$ of Entailment With Negation". Technical Report 11, Contract No. SAR/609 (16), Office of Naval Research, New Haven, 1961. Also published as [28]. ⟨*321*⟩

[28] N. D. BELNAP JR. AND J. R. WALLACE. "A Decision Procedure for the System $E_{\bar{I}}$ of Entailment With Negation". *Zeitschrift für Mathematische Logik und Grundlagen der Mathematik*, 11:261–277, 1965. ⟨*350*⟩

[29] JOHAN VAN BENTHEM. *Modal and Classical Logic*. Bibliopolis, 1983. ⟨*235*⟩

[30] JOHAN VAN BENTHEM. "Correspondence Theory". In DOV M. GABBAY AND FRANZ GÜNTHNER, editors, *Handbook of Philosophical Logic*, Volume 2, pages 167–247. Reidel, Dordrecht, 1984. ⟨*264*⟩

[31] JOHAN VAN BENTHEM. *Language in Action: Categories, Lambdas and Dynamic Logic*. North Holland, 1991. ⟨*174, 245, 308, 341*⟩

[32] NICK BENTON, G. M. BIERMAN, J. MARTIN E. HYLAND, AND VALERIA DE PAIVA. "Linear λ-Calculus and Categorical Models Revisited". In E. BÖRGER, editor, *Proceedings of the Sixth Workshop on Computer Science Logic*, Volume 702 of *Lecture Notes in Computer Science*, pages 61–84. Springer-Verlag, 1992. ⟨*150*⟩

[33] NICK BENTON, G. M. BIERMAN, J. MARTIN E. HYLAND, AND VALERIA DE PAIVA. "Term Assignment for Intuitionistic Linear Logic". Technical Report 262, Computer Laboratory, University of Cambridge, August 1992. ⟨*150*⟩

[34] NICK BENTON, G. M. BIERMAN, J. MARTIN E. HYLAND, AND VALERIA DE PAIVA. "A Term Calculus for Intuitionistic Linear Logic". In M. BEZEM AND J. F. GROOTE, editors, *Proceedings of the International Conference on Typed Lambda Calculi and Applications*, Volume 664 of *Lecture Notes in Computer Science*, pages 75–90. Springer-Verlag, 1993. ⟨*150*⟩

[35] EVERT W. BETH. "Semantic Entailment and Formal Derivability". *Koninklijke Nederlandse Akademie van Wentenschappen, Proceedings of the Section of Sciences*, 18:309–342, 1955. ⟨*276*⟩

[36] EVERT W. BETH. "Semantic Construction of Intuitionistic Logic". *Koninklijke Nederlandse Akademie van Wentenschappen, Proceedings of the Section of Sciences*, 19:357–388, 1956. ⟨*276*⟩

[37] EVERT W. BETH. *The Foundations of Mathematics: A Study in the Philosophy of Science*. Harper & Row, Second edition, 1964. ⟨*276*⟩

[38] GARETH BIRKHOFF. *Lattice Theory*. American Mathematical Society Colloquium Publications, Rhode Island, 1973. ⟨*185, 193*⟩

[39] ROSS T. BRADY. "Gentzenization and Decidability of some Contraction-Less Relevant Logics". *Journal of Philosophical Logic*, 20:97–117, 1991. ⟨*125, 321*⟩

[40] ROBERT A. BULL AND KRISTER SEGERBERG. "Basic Modal Logic". In DOV M. GABBAY AND FRANZ GÜNTHNER, editors, *Handbook of Philosophical Logic*, Volume 2, pages 1–88. Reidel, Dordrecht, 1984. ⟨*235*⟩

[41] WOJCIECH BUSZKOWSKI. "Completeness Results for Lambek Syntactic Calculus". *Zeitschrift für Mathematische Logik und Grundlagen der Mathematik*, 32:229–238, 1986. ⟨*307*⟩

[42] WOJCIECH BUSZKOWSKI. "The Finite Model Property for BCI and Related Systems". *Studia Logica*, 57:303–323, 1996. ⟨*321*⟩

[43] BRIAN F. CHELLAS. *Modal Logic: An Introduction*. Cambridge University Press, Cambridge, 1980. ⟨*235*⟩

[44] ALONZO CHURCH. *The Calculi of Lambda-Conversion*. Number 6 in Annals of Mathematical Studies. Princeton University Press, 1941. ⟨*150*⟩

[45] ALONZO CHURCH. "The Weak Positive Implication Calculus". *Journal of Symbolic Logic*, 16:238, 1951. Abstract of "The Weak Theory of Implication" [46]. ⟨*351*⟩

[46] ALONZO CHURCH. "The Weak Theory of Implication". In A. MENNE, A. WILHELMY, AND H. ANGSIL, editors, *Kontroliertes Denken: Untersuchungen zum Logikkalkül und zur Logik der Einzelwissenschaften*, pages 22–37. Kommissions-Verlag Karl Alber, Munich, 1951. Abstracted in "The Weak Positive Implication Calculus" [45]. ⟨*2, 42, 351*⟩

[47] J. H. CONWAY. *Regular Algebra and Finite Machines*. William Clowes and Sons,
      1971. ⟨209⟩

[48] JACK COPELAND. "Prior's Life and Legacy". In JACK COPELAND, editor, *Logic and
      Reality: Essays on the Legacy of Arthur Prior*. Clarendon Press, Oxford, 1996. ⟨269⟩

[49] M. COPPO, M. DEZANI-CIANCAGLINI, AND B. VENNERI. "Functional Characters of
      Solvable Terms". *Zeitschrift für Mathematische Logik und Grundlagen der
      Mathematik*, 27:45–58, 1981. ⟨247⟩

[50] N. C. A. DA COSTA. "On the Theory of Inconsistent Formal Systems". *Notre Dame
      Journal of Formal Logic*, 15:497–510, 1974. ⟨185⟩

[51] N. C. A. DA COSTA AND E. H. ALVES. "A Semantical Analysis of the Calculi C_n".
      Notre Dame Journal of Formal Logic, 18:621–630, 1977. ⟨185⟩

[52] P. CRAWLEY AND R. P. DILWORTH. *Algebraic Theory of Lattices*. Prentice-Hall,
      1973. ⟨185⟩

[53] HASKELL B. CURRY. *A Theory of Formal Deducibility*, Volume 6 of *Notre Dame
      Mathematical Lectures*. Notre Dame University Press, 1950. ⟨321⟩

[54] HASKELL B. CURRY. *Foundations of Mathematical Logic*. Dover, 1977. Originally
      published in 1963. ⟨3, 43, 61, 125⟩

[55] HASKELL B. CURRY. "Some Philosophical Aspects of Combinatory Logic". In
      J. BARWISE, H. J. KEISLER, AND K. KUNEN, editors, *The Kleene Symposium*, pages
      85–101. North Holland, Amsterdam, 1980. ⟨88, 181⟩

[56] HASKELL B. CURRY AND R. FEYS. *Combinatory Logic*, Volume 1. North Holland,
      1958. ⟨26, 88, 181⟩

[57] HASKELL B. CURRY, J. ROGER HINDLEY, AND JONATHAN P. SELDIN. *Combinatory
      Logic*, Volume 2. North Holland, 1972. ⟨88, 181⟩

[58] B. A. DAVEY AND H. A. PRIESTLEY. *Introduction to Lattices and Order*. Cambridge
      University Press, Cambridge, 1990. ⟨185, 279⟩

[59] JENNIFER DAVOREN. "A Lazy Logician's Guide to Linear Logic". Technical Report,
      Department of Mathematics, Monash University, January 1992. ⟨232⟩

[60] KOSTA DOŠEN. "Sequent Systems and Groupoid Models, Part 1". *Studia Logica*,
      47:353–386, 1988. ⟨292⟩

[61] KOSTA DOŠEN. "Logical Constants as Punctuation Marks". *Notre Dame Journal of
      Formal Logic*, 30:362–381, 1989. ⟨339⟩

[62] KOSTA DOŠEN. "Sequent Systems and Groupoid Models, Part 2". *Studia Logica*,
      48:41–65, 1989. ⟨292⟩

[63] KOSTA DOŠEN. "A Brief Survey of Frames for the Lambek Calculus". *Zeitschrift für
      Mathematische Logik und Grundlagen der Mathematik*, 38:179–187, 1992. ⟨245⟩

[64] KOSTA DOŠEN. "The First Axiomatisation of Relevant Logic". *Journal of
      Philosophical Logic*, 21:339–356, 1992. ⟨2, 42⟩

[65] KOSTA DOŠEN. "Modal Translations in Substructural Logics". *Journal of
      Philosophical Logic*, 21:283–336, 1992. ⟨209⟩

[66] KOSTA DOŠEN. "Modal Translations in K and D". In MAARTEN DE RIJKE, editor,
      Diamonds and Defaults, pages 103–127. Riedel, Dordrecht, 1993. ⟨102⟩

[67] KOSTA DOŠEN. "Rudimentary Kripke Models for the Intuitionistic Propositional Calculus". *Annals of Pure and Applied Logic*, 62:21–49, 1993. ⟨292⟩

[68] ALBERT GRIGOREVICH DRAGALIN. *Mathematical Intuitionism: Introduction to Proof Theory*, Volume 67 of *Translations of Mathematical Monographs*. American Mathematical Society, 1987. ⟨151, 292⟩

[69] MICHAEL DUMMETT. *Elements of Intuitionism*. Oxford University Press, Oxford, 1977. ⟨339⟩

[70] J. MICHAEL DUNN. *The Algebra of Intensional Logics*. PhD thesis, University of Pittsburgh, 1966. ⟨185, 209⟩

[71] J. MICHAEL DUNN. "An Intuitive Semantics for First Degree Relevant Implications (abstract)". *Journal of Symbolic Logic*, 36:363–363, 1971. ⟨342⟩

[72] J. MICHAEL DUNN. "A 'Gentzen' System for Positive Relevant Implication". *Journal of Symbolic Logic*, 38:356–357, 1974. (Abstract). ⟨35, 125⟩

[73] J. MICHAEL DUNN. "A Kripke-style semantics for R-mingle using a binary accessibility relation". *Studia Logica*, 35:163–172, 1976. ⟨72⟩

[74] J. MICHAEL DUNN. "A Variation on the Binary Semantics for RM". *Relevance Logic Newsletter*, 1:56–67, 1976. ⟨102⟩

[75] J. MICHAEL DUNN. "Relevance Logic and Entailment". In DOV M. GABBAY AND FRANZ GÜNTHNER, editors, *Handbook of Philosophical Logic*, Volume 3, pages 117–229. Reidel, Dordrecht, 1986. ⟨2⟩

[76] J. MICHAEL DUNN. "Gaggle Theory: An Abstraction of Galois Connections and Residuation with Applications to Negation and Various Logical Operations". In *Logics in AI, Proceedings European Workshop JELIA 1990*, Volume 478 of *Lecture Notes in Computer Science*. Springer-Verlag, 1991. ⟨186, 270⟩

[77] J. MICHAEL DUNN. "Partial-Gaggles Applied to Logics with Restricted Structural Rules". In PETER SCHROEDER-HEISTER AND KOSTA DOŠEN, editors, *Substructural Logics*. Oxford University Press, 1993. ⟨30, 186, 270⟩

[78] J. MICHAEL DUNN. "Star and Perp: Two Treatments of Negation". In JAMES E. TOMBERLIN, editor, *Philosophical Perspectives*, Volume 7, pages 331–357. Ridgeview Publishing Company, Atascadero, California, 1994. ⟨70, 186, 270⟩

[79] J. MICHAEL DUNN. "Positive Modal Logic". *Studia Logica*, 55:301–317, 1995. ⟨69, 266, 271⟩

[80] J. MICHAEL DUNN. "Generalised Ortho Negation". In HEINRICH WANSING, editor, *Negation: A Notion in Focus*, pages 3–26. Walter de Gruyter, Berlin, 1996. ⟨62, 70⟩

[81] J. MICHAEL DUNN AND G. EPSTEIN, editors. *Modern Uses of Multiple-Valued Logic*. Reidel, Dordrecht, 1977. ⟨156⟩

[82] J. MICHAEL DUNN AND ROBERT K. MEYER. "Combinators and Structurally Free Logic". *Logic Journal of the IGPL*, 5:505–357, 1997. ⟨181⟩

[83] DAVID FINBERG, MATTEO MAINETTI, AND GIAN-CARLO ROTA. "The Logic of Commuting Equivalence Relations". In *Logic and Algebra (Pontignan, 1994)*, Volume 180 of *Lecture Notes in Pure and Applied Mathematics*, pages 69–96. Dekker, 1996. ⟨188⟩

[84] KIT FINE. "Models for Entailment". *Journal of Philosophical Logic*, 3:347–372, 1974. ⟨*270*⟩

[85] KIT FINE. "Semantics for Quantified Relevance Logic". *Journal of Philosophical Logic*, 17:27–59, 1988. ⟨*5, 270*⟩

[86] GOTTLOB FREGE. *Grundgesetze der Arithmetik, Begriffsschriftlich abgeleitet*. Verlag Hermann Pohle, Jena, 1893–1903. Parts translated in *Gottlob Frege: Logical Investigations* [92]. ⟨*156*⟩

[87] HARVEY FRIEDMAN AND ROBERT K. MEYER. "Whither Relevant Arithmetic?". *Journal of Symbolic Logic*, 57:824–831, 1992. ⟨*102*⟩

[88] ANDRÉ FUHRMANN AND EDWIN D. MARES. "On S". *Studia Logica*, 53:75–91, 1994. ⟨*271, 344*⟩

[89] D. M. GABBAY. "A General Theory of the Conditional in Terms of a Ternary Operator". *Theoria*, 38:39–50, 1972. ⟨*270*⟩

[90] D. M. GABBAY. *Investigations in Modal and Tense Logics with Applications to Problems in Philosophy and Linguistics*. Reidel, Dordrecht, 1976. ⟨*102, 235*⟩

[91] P. T. GEACH. "On Insolubilia". *Analysis*, 15:71–72, 1955. ⟨*3, 43*⟩

[92] PETER GEACH AND MAX BLACK, editors. *Translations from the Philosophical Writings of Gottlob Frege*. Oxford University Press, 1952. ⟨*354*⟩

[93] GERHARD GENTZEN. *The Collected Papers of Gerhard Gentzen*. North Holland, 1969. Edited by M. E. Szabo. ⟨*41, 109, 125*⟩

[94] SILVIO GHILARDI AND GIANCARLO MELONI. "Constructive Canonicity in Non-Classical Logic". *Annals of Pure and Applied Logic*, 86:1–32, 1997. ⟨*271*⟩

[95] STEVE GIAMBRONE. "TW_+ and RW_+ are Decidable". *Journal of Philosophical Logic*, 14:235–254, 1985. ⟨*321*⟩

[96] JEAN-YVES GIRARD. "Linear Logic". *Theoretical Computer Science*, 50:1–101, 1987. ⟨*3, 5, 44, 70, 125, 227*⟩

[97] JEAN-YVES GIRARD. *Proof Theory and Logical Complexity*. Bibliopolis, Naples, 1987. ⟨*150*⟩

[98] JEAN-YVES GIRARD. "On the Unity of Logic". *Annals of Pure and Applied Logic*, 59:201–217, 1993. ⟨*70*⟩

[99] JEAN-YVES GIRARD, YVES LAFONT, AND PAUL TAYLOR. *Proofs and Types*, Volume 7 of *Cambridge Tracts in Theoretical Computer Science*. Cambridge University Press, 1989. ⟨*1, 150, 232*⟩

[100] ROBERT GOLDBLATT. "Semantic Analysis of Ortholateral". *Journal of Philosophical Logic*, 3:19–35, 1974. Reprinted as Chapter 3 of *Mathematics of Modality* [102]. ⟨*277*⟩

[101] ROBERT GOLDBLATT. "Orthomodularity is not Elementary". *Journal of Symbolic Logic*, 49:401–404, 1984. Reprinted as Chapter 4 of *Mathematics of Modality* [102]. ⟨*293*⟩

[102] ROBERT GOLDBLATT. *Mathematics of Modality*. CSLI Publications, 1993. ⟨*354*⟩

[103] GEORGE GRÄTZER. *General Lattice Theory*. Academic Press, 1978. ⟨*292*⟩

[104] GEORGE GRÄTZER. *Universal Algebra*. Springer-Verlag, second edition, 1979. ⟨185, 193, 194⟩

[105] C. A. GUNTER AND D. S. SCOTT. "Semantic Domains". In J. VAN LEEUWEN, editor, *Handbook of Theoretical Computer Science*, pages 633–674. Elsevier Science Publishers B.V., 1990. ⟨238, 246⟩

[106] CHRIS HANKIN. *Lambda Calculi: A Guide for Computer Scientists*, Volume 3 of *Graduate Texts in Computer Science*. Oxford University Press, 1994. ⟨13⟩

[107] R. HARROP. "On Disjunctions and Existential Statements in Intuitionistic Systems of Logic". *Mathematische Annalen*, 132:347–361, 1956. ⟨102⟩

[108] C. HARTONAS. "Order-Duality, Negation and Lattice Representation". In H. WANSING, editor, *Negation: Notion in Focus*, pages 27–37. De Gruyter Publication, New York–Berlin, 1996. Paper presented at the conference ANALYOMEN 2, Leipzig, 1994, Workshop on Negation. ⟨270⟩

[109] C. HARTONAS. "Duality for Lattice-Ordered Algebras and Normal Algebraizable Logics". *Studia Logica*, 58(3):403–450, 1997. ⟨270, 292⟩

[110] C. HARTONAS. "Pretopology Semantics for Bimodal Intuitionistic Linear Logic". *Journal of the Interest Group in Pure and Applied Logics*, 5(1):65–78, 1997. ⟨292⟩

[111] C. HARTONAS AND J. MICHAEL DUNN. "Stone Duality for Lattices". *Algebra Universalis*, 37:391–401, 1997. ⟨62, 70, 270⟩

[112] ALLEN HAZEN. "Aspects of Russell's Logic in 1906". Letter, dated October 21, 1997. ⟨44⟩

[113] M. HENNESSY AND R. MILNER. "Algebraic Laws for Indeterminism and Concurrency". *Journal of the ACM*, 32:137–162, 1985. ⟨295, 308⟩

[114] AREND HEYTING. *Intuitionism: An Introduction*. North Holland, Amsterdam, 1956. ⟨156⟩

[115] J. R. HINDLEY. "The Simple Semantics for Coppo-Dezani-Sallé Types". In M. DEZANI-CIANCAGLINI AND H. MONTANARI, editors, *International Symposium on Programming*, Volume 137 of *Lecture Notes in Computer Science*, pages 212–226. Springer-Verlag, 1983. ⟨247⟩

[116] J. R. HINDLEY AND J. P. SELDIN. *Introduction to Combinators and λ-Calculus*. Cambridge University Press, 1986. ⟨13, 88, 181⟩

[117] W. A. HOWARD. "The Formulae-as-types Notion of Construction". In J. P. SELDIN AND J. R. HINDLEY, editors, *To H. B. Curry: Essays on Combinatory Logic, Lambda Calculus and Formalism*, pages 479–490. Academic Press, London, 1980. ⟨150⟩

[118] G. HUGHES AND M. CRESSWELL. *An Introduction to Modal Logic*. Methuen, London, 1968. ⟨235⟩

[119] G. HUGHES AND M. CRESSWELL. *A New Introduction to Modal Logic*. Routledge, London, 1996. ⟨235, 270⟩

[120] KLAUS JANICH. *Topology*. Springer-Verlag, 1984. Translation of *Topologie* by Silvio Levy. ⟨205⟩

[121] PETER T. JOHNSTONE. *Topos Theory*. Academic Press, 1977. ⟨232⟩

[122] BJARNI JÓNSSON AND ALFRED TARSKI. "Boolean Algebras with Operators: Part I". *American Journal of Mathematics*, 73:891–939, 1951. ⟨*178, 269*⟩

[123] BJARNI JÓNSSON AND ALFRED TARSKI. "Boolean Algebras with Operators: Part II". *American Journal of Mathematics*, 75:127–162, 1952. ⟨*178, 269*⟩

[124] S. C. KLEENE. "Disjunction and Existence under Implication in Elementary Intuitionistic Formalisms". *Journal of Symbolic Logic*, 27:11–18, 1962. (This paper has an addendum [125]). ⟨*102, 356*⟩

[125] S. C. KLEENE. "An Addendum". *Journal of Symbolic Logic*, 28:154–156, 1963. (Addendum to "Disjunction and Existence under Implication in Elementary Intuitionistic Formalisms" [124]). ⟨*102, 356*⟩

[126] SAUL A. KRIPKE. "A Completeness Theorem in Modal Logic". *Journal of Symbolic Logic*, 24:1–15, 1959. ⟨*269*⟩

[127] SAUL A. KRIPKE. "The Problem of Entailment". *Journal of Symbolic Logic*, 24:324, 1959. Abstract. ⟨*315, 321*⟩

[128] SAUL A. KRIPKE. "Semantical Analysis of Modal Logic I: Normal Modal Propositional Calculi". *Zeitschrift für Mathematische Logik und Grundlagen der Mathematik*, 9:67–96, 1963. ⟨*269*⟩

[129] NATASHA KURTONINA. *Frames and Labels: A Modal Analysis of Categorial Inference*. PhD thesis, Institute for Logic, Language and Computation, University of Utrecht, 1995. ⟨*174, 271, 308*⟩

[130] NATASHA KURTONINA AND MAARTEN DE RIJKE. "Simulating Without Negation". *Journal of Logic and Computation*, 7:501–522, 1997. ⟨*308*⟩

[131] ÁGNES KURUCZ. *Decision Problems in Algebraic Logic*. PhD thesis, Budapest, 1997. Available from http://www.math-inst.hu/pub/algebraic-logic/Contents.html. ⟨*336*⟩

[132] YVES LAFONT. "The Finite Model Property for Various Fragments of Linear Logic". *Journal of Symbolic Logic*, 62:1202–1208, 1997. ⟨*321*⟩

[133] JOACHIM LAMBEK. "The Mathematics of Sentence Structure". *American Mathematical Monthly*, 65:154–170, 1958. ⟨*3, 43, 125*⟩

[134] JOACHIM LAMBEK. "On the Calculus of Syntactic Types". In R. JACOBSEN, editor, *Structure of Language and its Mathematical Aspects*, Proceedings of Symposia in Applied Mathematics, XII. American Mathematical Society, 1961. ⟨*3, 43, 125*⟩

[135] JOACHIM LAMBEK. "Deductive Systems and Categories II". In PETER HILTON, editor, *Category Theory, Homology Theory and their Applications II*, Volume 86 of *Lecture Notes in Mathematics*. Springer-Verlag, 1969. ⟨*216, 227*⟩

[136] JOACHIM LAMBEK AND PHILIP J. SCOTT. *Introduction to Higher Order Categorical Logic*. Cambridge University Press, 1986. ⟨*232*⟩

[137] DAVID K. LEWIS. *On the Plurality of Worlds*. Blackwell, Oxford, 1986. ⟨*156, 339*⟩

[138] P. LINCOLN, J. MITCHELL, A. SCENROV, AND N. SHANKAR. "Decision Problems for Propositional Linear Logic". *Annals of Pure and Applied Logic*, 56:239–311, 1992. ⟨*332, 334*⟩

[139] JAN ŁUKASIEWICZ. "On Determinism". In L. BORKOWSKI, editor, *Selected Works*. North Holland, Amsterdam, 1970. ⟨3⟩

[140] SAUNDERS MAC LANE. *Categories for the Working Mathematician*. Number 5 in Graduate Texts in Mathematics. Springer-Verlag, 1971. ⟨211, 212, 214⟩

[141] SAUNDERS MAC LANE. "Why Commutative Diagrams Coincide with Equivalent Proofs". *Contemporary Mathematics*, 5, 1982. ⟨227⟩

[142] SAUNDERS MAC LANE AND GARRETT BIRKHOFF. *Algebra*. Macmillan, 1967. ⟨209⟩

[143] SAUNDERS MAC LANE AND IEKE MOERDIJK. *Sheaves in Geometry and Logic: A First Introduction to Topos Theory*. Springer-Verlag, 1992. ⟨232⟩

[144] H. M. MACNEILLE. "Partially Ordered Sets". *Transactions of the American Mathematical Society*, 42:416–460, 1937. ⟨278⟩

[145] L. L. MAKSIMOVA. "O modéláh isčisléniá E". *Algébra i Logika, Séminar*, 6:5–20, 1967. (English title: On Models of the System E). ⟨187⟩

[146] JOHN MARAIST, MARTIN ODERSKY, DAVID N. TURNER, AND PHILIP WADLER. "Call-by-name, call-by-value, call-by-need, and the linear lambda calculus". In *11th International Conference on the Mathematical Foundations of Programming Semantics*, New Orleans, Lousiana, March–April 1995. ⟨150⟩

[147] EDWIN D. MARES AND ANDRÉ FUHRMANN. "A Relevant Theory of Conditionals". *Journal of Philosophical Logic*, 24:645–665, 1995. ⟨271, 344⟩

[148] EDWIN D. MARES AND ROBERT K. MEYER. "The Admissibility of γ in R4". *Notre Dame Journal of Formal Logic*, 33:197–206, 1992. ⟨271, 273⟩

[149] EDWIN D. MARES AND ROBERT K. MEYER. "The Semantics of R4". *Journal of Philosophical Logic*, 22:95–110, 1993. ⟨271⟩

[150] PER MARTIN-LÖF. *Notes on Constructive Mathematics*. Almqvist and Wiksell, Stockholm, 1970. ⟨339⟩

[151] MAARTEN MARX, LÁSZLÓ PÓLOS, AND MICHAEL MAUSCH, editors. *Arrow Logic and Multi-Modal Logic*. CSLI Publications, 1996. ⟨245⟩

[152] M. A. MCROBBIE AND N. D. BELNAP JR. "Relevant Analytic Tableaux". *Studia Logica*, 38:187–200, 1979. ⟨321⟩

[153] R. K. MEYER AND J. K. SLANEY. "Abelian Logic from A to Z". In GRAHAM PRIEST, RICHARD SYLVAN, AND JEAN NORMAN, editors, *Paraconsistent Logic: Essays on the Inconsistent*, pages 245–288. Philosophia Verlag, 1989. ⟨174⟩

[154] ROBERT K. MEYER. "R_I—the Bounds of Finitude". *Zeitschrift für Mathematische Logik und Grundlagen der Mathematik*, 16:385–387, 1970. ⟨177, 209⟩

[155] ROBERT K. MEYER. "On Coherence in Modal Logics". *Logique et Analyse*, 14:658–668, 1971. ⟨102⟩

[156] ROBERT K. MEYER. "Conserving Positive Logics". *Notre Dame Journal of Formal Logic*, 14:224–236, 1973. ⟨201, 203, 209⟩

[157] ROBERT K. MEYER. "Intuitionism, Entailment, Negation". In H. LEBLANC, editor, *Truth, Syntax and Modality*, pages 168–198. North Holland, 1973. ⟨209⟩

[158] ROBERT K. MEYER. "Metacompleteness". *Notre Dame Journal of Formal Logic*, 17:501–517, 1976. ⟨102⟩

[159] ROBERT K. MEYER. "Why I am not a Relevantist". Technical Report 1, Logic Group, RSSS, Australian National University, 1978. ⟨344⟩

[160] ROBERT K. MEYER. "⊃E is Admissible in 'True' Relevant Arithmetic". *Journal of Philosophical Logic*, 27:327–351, 1998. ⟨102⟩

[161] ROBERT K. MEYER AND J. MICHAEL DUNN. "*E*, *R* and γ". *Journal of Symbolic Logic*, 34:460–474, 1969. ⟨102⟩

[162] ROBERT K. MEYER AND EDWIN MARES. "Semantics of Entailment 0". In PETER SCHROEDER-HEISTER AND KOSTA DOŠEN, editors, *Substructural Logics*. Oxford University Press, 1993. ⟨271⟩

[163] ROBERT K. MEYER AND ERROL P. MARTIN. "Logic on the Australian Plan". *Journal of Philosophical Logic*, 15:305–332, 1986. ⟨61, 342⟩

[164] ROBERT K. MEYER, MICHAEL A. MCROBBIE, AND NUEL D. BELNAP. "Linear Analytic Tableaux". In *Proceedings of the Fourth Workshop on Theorem Proving with Analytic Tableaux and Related Methods*, Volume 918 of *Lecture Notes in Computer Science*, 1995. ⟨321⟩

[165] ROBERT K. MEYER AND HIROAKIRA ONO. "The Finite Model Property for BCK and BCIW". *Studia Logica*, 53:107–118, 1994. ⟨321⟩

[166] ROBERT K. MEYER AND GREG RESTALL. "'Strenge' Arithmetic". Automated Reasoning Project, Australian National University. Submitted for publication, 1996. ⟨102⟩

[167] ROBERT K. MEYER AND RICHARD ROUTLEY. "Algebraic Analysis of Entailment". *Logique et Analyse*, 15:407–428, 1972. ⟨26, 44, 185, 209⟩

[168] ROBERT K. MEYER AND RICHARD ROUTLEY. "Classical Relevant Logics I". *Studia Logica*, 32:51–66, 1973. ⟨87⟩

[169] ROBERT K. MEYER AND RICHARD ROUTLEY. "Classical Relevant Logics II". *Studia Logica*, 33:183–194, 1973. ⟨87⟩

[170] ROBERT K. MEYER, RICHARD ROUTLEY, AND J. MICHAEL DUNN. "Curry's Paradox". *Analysis*, 39:124–128, 1979. ⟨43⟩

[171] R. MILNER. *Communication and Concurrency*. Prentice-Hall, 1989. ⟨295, 308⟩

[172] G. MINC. "Cut-Elimination Theorem in Relevant Logics". In J. V. MATIJASEVIC AND O. A. SILENKO, editors, *Isslédovaniá po konstructivnoj mathematiké i matematičeskoj logike V*, pages 90–97. Izdatél'stvo "Nauka", 1972. (English translation in "Cut-Elimination Theorem in Relevant Logics" [173]). ⟨35, 125, 358⟩

[173] G. MINC. "Cut-Elimination Theorem in Relevant Logics". *The Journal of Soviet Mathematics*, 6:422–428, 1976. (English translation of the original article [172]). ⟨358⟩

[174] G. MINC. "Closed Categories and the Theory of Proofs". *Zapiski Nauchnykh Seminarov Leningradskogo Otdeleniya Matematischeskogo Instituta im. V. A. Steklova AN SSSR*, 68:83–114, 1977. (Russian, English summary). ⟨227⟩

[175] JOHN C. MITCHELL. *Foundations for Programming Languages*. MIT Press, 1996. ⟨155⟩

[176] WILLIAM P. R. MITCHELL. "The Carcinogenic Example". *Logic Journal of the IGPL*, 5(6):795–810, 1997. ⟨*273*⟩

[177] MICHIEL MOORTGAT. *Categorial Investigations: Logical Aspects of the Lambek Calculus*. Foris, Dordrecht, 1988. ⟨*3*⟩

[178] A. DE MORGAN. "On the Syllogism: IV, and on the Logic of Relations". *Transactions of the Cambridge Philosophical Society*, 10:331–358, 1864. Read before the Cambridge Philosophical Society on April 23, 1860. ⟨*180*⟩

[179] GLYN MORRILL. *Type Logical Grammar: Categorial Logic of Signs*. Kluwer, Dordrecht, 1994. ⟨*3*⟩

[180] KEVIN MULLIGAN, PETER SIMONS, AND BARRY SMITH. "Truth-Makers". *Philosophy and Phenomenological Research*, 44:287–321, 1984. ⟨*342*⟩

[181] C. J. MULVEY. "&". In *Second Topology Conference*, Rendiconti del Circolo Matematico di Palermo, ser.2, supplement no. 12, pages 99–104, 1986. ⟨*186*⟩

[182] D. NELSON. "Constructible Falsity". *Journal of Symbolic Logic*, 14:16–26, 1949. ⟨*72*⟩

[183] K. C. NG. *Relation Algebras with Transitive Closure*. PhD thesis, University of California, Berkeley, 1984. ⟨*55*⟩

[184] K. C. NG AND A. TARSKI. "Relation Algebras with Transitive Closure". *Notices of the American Mathematical Society*, 24:A29–A30, 1977. Abstract. ⟨*55*⟩

[185] SUSAN B. NIEFIELD AND KIMMO I. ROSENTHAL. "Constructing Locales from Quantales". *Mathematical Proceedings of the Cambridge Philosophical Society*, 104:215–234, 1988. ⟨*210*⟩

[186] MITSUHIRO OKADA. "Phase Semantics for Higher Order Completeness, Cut-Elimination and Normalization Proofs". *Electronic Notes in Theoretical Computer Science*, 3:22 pages, 1996.
http://www.elsevier.nl/locate/entcs/volume3.html. ⟨*294*⟩

[187] H. ONO AND Y. KOMORI. "Logic without the Contraction Rule". *Journal of Symbolic Logic*, 50:169–201, 1985. ⟨*292*⟩

[188] HIROAKIRA ONO. "Semantics for Substructural Logics". In PETER SCHROEDER-HEISTER AND KOSTA DOŠEN, editors, *Substructural Logics*, pages 259–291. Oxford University Press, 1993. ⟨*292*⟩

[189] E. ORŁOWSKA. "Relational Interpretation of Modal Logics". *Bulletin of the Section of Logic*, 17:2–14, 1988. ⟨*245*⟩

[190] CHARLES S. PEIRCE. "Description of a notation for the logic of relatives, resulting from an amplification of the conceptions of Boole's calculus of logic". *Memoirs of the American Academy of Science*, 9:317–378, 1870. ⟨*180*⟩

[191] MATI PENTUS. "Models for the Lambek Calculus". *Annals of Pure and Applied Logic*, 75(1–2):179–213, 1995. ⟨*174, 308*⟩

[192] JOHN PERRY. "Possible Worlds and Subject Matter". In STURE ALLÉN, editor, *Possible Worlds in Humanities, Arts and Sciences*, pages 124–137. Walter de Gruyter, Berlin, 1989. ⟨*342*⟩

[193] ALVIN PLANTINGA. *The Nature of Necessity*. Clarendon Press, Oxford, 1975. ⟨*339*⟩

[194] V. R. PRATT. "Dynamic Algebras and the Nature of Induction". In *12th ACM Symposium on the Theory of Computation*, Los Angeles, 1980. ⟨*55, 69*⟩

[195] V. R. PRATT. "Dynamic Algebras as a Well-Behaved Fragment of Relation Algebras". In *Algebraic Logic and Universal Algebra in Computer Science*, number 425 in Lecture Notes in Computer Science. Springer-Verlag, 1990. ⟨*55, 69*⟩

[196] DAG PRAWITZ. *Natural Deduction: A Proof Theoretical Study*. Almqvist and Wiksell, Stockholm, 1965. ⟨*41, 150, 339*⟩

[197] GRAHAM PRIEST. "The Logic of Paradox". *Journal of Philosophical Logic*, 8:219–241, 1979. ⟨*342*⟩

[198] GRAHAM PRIEST. *In Contradiction: A Study of the Transconsistent*. Martinus Nijhoff, The Hague, 1987. ⟨*156, 342, 348*⟩

[199] GRAHAM PRIEST. *Beyond the Limits of Thought*. Cambridge University Press, Cambridge, 1995. ⟨*348*⟩

[200] GRAHAM PRIEST AND RICHARD SYLVAN. "Introduction". In GRAHAM PRIEST, RICHARD SYLVAN, AND JEAN NORMAN, editors, *Paraconsistent Logic: Essays on the Inconsistent*, pages xix–xxi. Philosophia Verlag, 1989. ⟨*348*⟩

[201] GRAHAM PRIEST AND RICHARD SYLVAN. "Simplified Semantics for Basic Relevant Logics". *Journal of Philosophical Logic*, 21:217–232, 1992. ⟨*308*⟩

[202] ARTHUR N. PRIOR. "The Runabout Inference-Ticket". *Analysis*, 21:38–39, 1960. ⟨*339*⟩

[203] W. V. QUINE. "Three Grades of Modal Involvement". In *Proceedings of the XIth International Congress of Philosophy*. North Holland, Amsterdam, 1953. Reprinted in *The Ways of Paradox*, Random House, New York, 1966. ⟨*10*⟩

[204] H. RASIOWA. *An Algebraic Approach to Non-classical Logics*. North Holland, 1974. ⟨*185*⟩

[205] STEPHEN READ. "What is Wrong with Disjunctive Syllogism?". *Analysis*, 41:66–70, 1981. ⟨*102*⟩

[206] STEPHEN READ. *Relevant Logic*. Basil Blackwell, Oxford, 1988. ⟨*2, 348*⟩

[207] STEPHEN READ. *Thinking about Logic*. Oxford University Press, 1995. ⟨*348*⟩

[208] N. RESCHER AND R. MANOR. "On Inference from Inconsistent Premises". *Theory and Decision*, 1:179–217, 1970. ⟨*348*⟩

[209] GREG RESTALL. "Deviant Logic and the Paradoxes of Self Reference". *Philosophical Studies*, 70:279–303, 1993. ⟨*43*⟩

[210] GREG RESTALL. "Modalities in Substructural Logics". *Logique et Analyse*, 141–142:25–38, 1993. ⟨*204*⟩

[211] GREG RESTALL. "Simplified Semantics for Relevant Logics (and some of their rivals)". *Journal of Philosophical Logic*, 22:481–511, 1993. ⟨*308*⟩

[212] GREG RESTALL. *On Logics Without Contraction*. PhD thesis, The University of Queensland, January 1994. ⟨*3*⟩

[213] GREG RESTALL. "A Useful Substructural Logic". *Bulletin of the Interest Group in Pure and Applied Logic*, 2(2):135–146, 1994. ⟨43⟩

[214] GREG RESTALL. "Display Logic and Gaggle Theory". *Reports in Mathematical Logic*, 29:133–146, 1995. ⟨125⟩

[215] GREG RESTALL. "Four Valued Semantics for Relevant Logics (and some of their rivals)". *Journal of Philosophical Logic*, 24:139–160, 1995. ⟨308⟩

[216] GREG RESTALL. "Truthmakers, Entailment and Necessity". *Australasian Journal of Philosophy*, 74:331–340, 1996. ⟨342⟩

[217] GREG RESTALL. "Combining Possibilities and Negations". *Studia Logica*, 59:121–140, 1997. (Special Issue on Combining Logics). ⟨271⟩

[218] GREG RESTALL. "Displaying and Deciding Substructural Logics 1: Logics with contraposition". *Journal of Philosophical Logic*, 27:179–216, 1998. ⟨125, 321⟩

[219] GREG RESTALL. "Negation in Relevant Logics: How I Stopped Worrying and Learned to Love the Routley Star". In DOV GABBAY AND HEINRICH WANSING, editors, *What is Negation?*, Volume 13 of *Applied Logic Series*, pages 53–76. Kluwer Academic Publishers, 1999. ⟨102, 344⟩

[220] MAARTEN DE RIJKE. "What is Modal Logic?". In MAARTEN MARX, LÁSZLÓ PÓLOS, AND MICHAEL MAUSCH, editors, *Arrow Logic and Multi-Modal Logic*. CSLI Publications, 1996. ⟨341⟩

[221] ABRAHAM ROBINSON. *Non-Standard Analysis*. North Holland, 1966. ⟨342⟩

[222] ABRAHAM ROBINSON. *Selected Papers of Abraham Robinson*. Yale University Press, 1979. Three volumes. Edited by H. J. Keisler et al. ⟨342⟩

[223] D. ROORDA. *Resource Logics: Proof-theoretical Investigations*. PhD thesis, Amsterdam, 1991. ⟨151, 174⟩

[224] RICHARD ROUTLEY. "Ultralogic as Universal". *Relevance Logic Newsletter*, 2:51–89, 1977. Reprinted in *Exploring Meinong's Jungle* [225]. ⟨348⟩

[225] RICHARD ROUTLEY. *Exploring Meinong's Jungle and Beyond*. Philosophy Department, RSSS, Australian National University, 1980. Interim Edition, Departmental Monograph number 3. ⟨348, 361⟩

[226] RICHARD ROUTLEY. "Relevantism, Material Detachment, and the Disjunctive Syllogism Argument". *Canadian Journal of Philosophy*, 14:167–188, 1984. ⟨102, 344, 348⟩

[227] RICHARD ROUTLEY AND ROBERT K. MEYER. "Semantics of Entailment — II". *Journal of Philosophical Logic*, 1:53–73, 1972. ⟨270⟩

[228] RICHARD ROUTLEY AND ROBERT K. MEYER. "Semantics of Entailment — III". *Journal of Philosophical Logic*, 1:192–208, 1972. ⟨270⟩

[229] RICHARD ROUTLEY AND ROBERT K. MEYER. "Semantics of Entailment". In HUGUES LEBLANC, editor, *Truth Syntax and Modality*, pages 194–243. North Holland, 1973. Proceedings of the Temple University Conference on Alternative Semantics. ⟨235, 270⟩

[230] RICHARD ROUTLEY AND ROBERT K. MEYER. "Dialectal Logic, Classical Logic and the Consistency of the World". *Studies in Soviet Thought*, 16:1–25, 1976. ⟨348⟩

[231] RICHARD ROUTLEY, VAL PLUMWOOD, ROBERT K. MEYER, AND ROSS T. BRADY. *Relevant Logics and their Rivals*. Ridgeview, 1982. *(2, 270, 348)*

[232] BERTRAND RUSSELL. "The Theory of Implication". *American Journal of Mathematics*, 28:159–202, 1906. *(44)*

[233] GIOVANNI SAMBIN. "Intuitionistic Formal Spaces and their Neighbourhood". In C. BONOTTO, R. FERRO, S. VALENTINI, AND A. ZANARDO, editors, *Logic Colloquium '88*, pages 261–286. North Holland, 1989. *(292)*

[234] GIOVANNI SAMBIN. "The Semantics of Pretopologies". In PETER SCHROEDER-HEISTER AND KOSTA DOŠEN, editors, *Substructural Logics*, pages 293–307. Oxford University Press, 1993. *(292)*

[235] GIOVANNI SAMBIN. "Pretopologies and Completeness Proofs". *Journal of Symbolic Logic*, 60(3):861–878, 1995. *(292)*

[236] GIOVANNI SAMBIN AND V. VACCARO. "Topology and duality in modal logic". *Annals of Pure and Applied Logic*, 37:249–296, 1988. *(270)*

[237] E. SCHRÖDER. *Vorlesungen über die Algebra der Logik (exacte Logik), Volume 3, "Algebra und Logik der Relative"*. Leipzig, 1895. Part I. *(180)*

[238] PETER SCHROEDER-HEISTER AND KOSTA DOŠEN, editors. *Substructural Logics*. Oxford University Press, 1993. *(2)*

[239] DANA SCOTT. "On Engendering an Illusion of Understanding". *Journal of Philosophy*, 68:787–807, 1971. *(10)*

[240] DANA SCOTT. "Models for Various Type-Free Calculi". In PATRICK SUPPES, LEON HENKIN, ATHANASE JOJA, AND GR. C. MOISIL, editors, *Logic, Methodology and Philosophy of Science IV*, pages 157–187. North Holland, Amsterdam, 1973. *(238, 246)*

[241] DANA SCOTT. "Lambda Calculus: Some Models, Some Philosophy". In J. BARWISE, H. J. KEISLER, AND K. KUNEN, editors, *The Kleene Symposium*, pages 223–265. North Holland, Amsterdam, 1980. *(238, 246)*

[242] KRISTER SEGEBERG. *Results in Non-Classical Logic*. Berlingska Boktryckereit, Lund, 1968. *(270)*

[243] KRISTER SEGERBERG. "An Essay in Classical Modal Logic". Filosofiska Studier, Uppsala, 1971. *(235)*

[244] STEWART SHAPIRO. "Epistemic and Intuitionistic Arithmetic". In STEWART SHAPIRO, editor, *Intensional Mathematics*, pages 11–45. North Holland, 1985. *(102)*

[245] MOH SHAW-KWEI. "The Deduction Theorems and Two New Logical Systems". *Methodos*, 2:56–75, 1950. *(2, 42)*

[246] MOH SHAW-KWEI. "Logical Paradoxes for Many-Valued Systems". *Journal of Symbolic Logic*, 19:37–40, 1954. *(43)*

[247] JOHN K. SLANEY. "A Metacompleteness Theorem for Contraction-Free Relevant Logics". *Studia Logica*, 43:159–168, 1983. *(103)*

[248] JOHN K. SLANEY. "Reduced Models for Relevant Logics without WI". *Notre Dame Journal of Formal Logic*, 28:395–407, 1987. *(308)*

[249] JOHN K. SLANEY. "Vagueness Revisited". Technical Report TR-ARP-15/88, Automated Reasoning Project, Australian National University, 1988. ⟨313⟩

[250] JOHN K. SLANEY. "A General Logic". *Australasian Journal of Philosophy*, 68:74–88, 1990. ⟨44⟩

[251] JOHN K. SLANEY. "MaGIC Matrix Generator for Implication Connectives: Release 2.1 Notes and Guide". Technical Report, Automated Reasoning Project, 1995. ftp://arp.anu.edu.au/pub/techreports/1995/TR-ARP-11-95.dvi.gz. ⟨186⟩

[252] ROBERT STALNAKER. *Inquiry*. Bradford Books, MIT Press, 1984. ⟨156, 339⟩

[253] M. H. STONE. "The Theory of Representation for Boolean Algebras". *Transactions of the American Mathematical Society*, 40:37–111, 1936. ⟨178⟩

[254] M. H. STONE. "The Theory of Representations of Distributive Lattices and Brouwerian Logics". *Časopis pro pestování matematiky a fysiky*, 67:1–25, 1936. ⟨178⟩

[255] W. W. TAIT. "Intensional Interpretation of Functionals of Finite Type I". *Journal of Symbolic Logic*, 32:198–212, 1967. ⟨142⟩

[256] ALFRED TARSKI. "On The Calculus of Relations". *Journal of Symbolic Logic*, 6:73–89, 1941. ⟨186⟩

[257] ALFRED TARSKI. *Logic, Semantics, Metamathematics: papers from 1923 to 1938*. Clarendon Press, Oxford, 1956. Translated by J. H. Woodger. ⟨155⟩

[258] NEIL TENNANT. *Autologic*. Edinburgh University Press, 1992. ⟨150⟩

[259] NEIL TENNANT. "The Transmission of Truth and the Transitivity of Deduction". In DOV GABBAY, editor, *What is a Logical System?*, Volume 4 of *Studies in Logic and Computation*, pages 161–177. Oxford University Press, Oxford, 1994. ⟨150⟩

[260] PAUL THISTLEWAITE, MICHAEL MCROBBIE, AND ROBERT K. MEYER. *Automated Theorem Proving in Non-Classical Logics*. Wiley, New York, 1988. ⟨321⟩

[261] ANNE TROELSTRA. *Lectures on Linear Logic*. CSLI Publications, 1992. ⟨3, 151, 232, 292⟩

[262] ALASDAIR URQUHART. "The Completeness of Weak Implication". *Theoria*, 37:274–282, 1972. ⟨270⟩

[263] ALASDAIR URQUHART. "A General Theory of Implication". *Journal of Symbolic Logic*, 37:443, 1972. ⟨270⟩

[264] ALASDAIR URQUHART. "Semantics for Relevant Logics". *Journal of Symbolic Logic*, 37:159–169, 1972. ⟨270⟩

[265] ALASDAIR URQUHART. *The Semantics of Entailment*. PhD thesis, University of Pittsburgh, 1972. ⟨270⟩

[266] ALASDAIR URQUHART. "Decidability and the Finite Model Property". *Journal of Philosophical Logic*, 10:367–370, 1981. ⟨336⟩

[267] ALASDAIR URQUHART. "The Undecidability of Entailment and Relevant Implication". *Journal of Symbolic Logic*, 49:1059–1073, 1984. ⟨327, 328, 336⟩

[268] ALASDAIR URQUHART. "Many-Valued Logics". In DOV M. GABBAY AND FRANZ GÜNTHNER, editors, *Handbook of Philosophical Logic*, Volume 3, pages 71–116. Reidel, Dordrecht, 1986. ⟨156⟩

[269] ALASDAIR URQUHART. "The Complexity of Decision Procedures in Relevance Logic". In J. MICHAEL DUNN AND ANIL GUPTA, editors, *Truth or Consequences*, pages 77–95. Kluwer, 1990. ⟨5⟩

[270] ALASDAIR URQUHART. "Decision Problems for Distributive Lattice-Ordered Semigroups". *Algebra Universalis*, 34:399–418, 1995. ⟨336⟩

[271] ALASDAIR URQUHART. "Duality for Algebras of Relevant Logics". *Studia Logica*, 56:263–276, 1996. ⟨270⟩

[272] ALASDAIR URQUHART. "The Complexity of Decision Procedures in Relevance Logic II". Available from the author, University of Toronto, 1997. ⟨5⟩

[273] BETTI VENNERI. "Intersection Types as Logical Formulae". *Journal of Logic and Computation*, 4:109–124, 1994. ⟨247, 248⟩

[274] STEVEN VICKERS. *Topology via Logic*, Volume 5 of *Cambridge Tracts in Theoretical Computer Science*. Cambridge University Press, 1990. Revised edition. ⟨186⟩

[275] PHILIP WADLER. "Linear Types can Change the World!". In M. BROY AND C. JONES, editors, *Programming Concepts and Methods*, Sea of Galilee, Israel, April 1990. North Holland. IFIP TC 2 Working Conference. ⟨150⟩

[276] PHILIP WADLER. "Is there a Use for Linear Logic?". In *ACM Conference on Partial Evaluation and Semantics-Based Program Manipulation*, New Haven, Connecticut, June 1991. ⟨150⟩

[277] PHILIP WADLER. "There's No Substitute for Linear Logic". In *Workshop on Mathematical Foundations of Programming Semantics*, Oxford, UK, April 1992. (No proceedings published. Available from `http://www.cs.bell-labs.com/who/wadler/topics/linear-logic.html`). ⟨150⟩

[278] PHILIP WADLER. "A Syntax for Linear Logic". In *9th International Conference on the Mathematical Foundations of Programming Semantics*, New Orleans, Lousiana, April 1993. ⟨70⟩

[279] PHILIP WADLER. "A Taste of Linear Logic". In *Mathematical Foundations of Computer Science*, Volume 711 of *Lecture Notes in Computer Science*, Gdansk, Poland, August 1993. Springer-Verlag. ⟨70, 150⟩

[280] HEINRICH WANSING. *The Logic of Information Structures*. Number 681 in Lecture Notes in Artificial Intelligence. Springer-Verlag, 1993. ⟨72⟩

[281] HEINRICH WANSING. "Sequent Calculi for Normal Propositional Modal Logics". *Journal of Logic and Computation*, 4:125–142, 1994. ⟨69⟩

Index

365

Printed in Great Britain
by Amazon